# Interpretations of American History

*Patterns and Perspectives*

Fourth Edition

**Gerald N. Grob &
George Athan Billias**

**Volume I
to 1877**

THE FREE PRESS
*A Division of Macmillan Publishing Co., Inc.*
NEW YORK

Collier Macmillan Publishers
LONDON

The Free Press
A Division of Macmillan Publishing Co., Inc.
866 Third Avenue, New York, N.Y. 10022

Collier Macmillan Canada, Inc.

Library of Congress Catalog Card Number: 81-69222

Printed in the United States of America

printing number
1  2  3  4  5  6  7  8  9  10

Library of Congress Cataloging in Publication Data
Main entry under title:

Interpretations of American history.

Includes bibliographical references and indexes.
Contents: v. 1. To 1877 -- v. 2. Since 1877.
1. United States--History--Addresses, essays,
lectures. 2. United States--Historiography--Addresses,
essays, lectures. I. Grob, Gerald N.
II. Billias, George Athan        . III. Title.
E178.6.I53 1982      973        81-69222
ISBN 0-02-912690-8 (v. 1)       AACR2
ISBN 0-02-912700-9 (v. 2)

This volume is affectionately
and gratefully dedicated to
my brother, my sisters, and
their spouses: Ted and Penny Billias, Emily and Rip Hoomis,
Marie Antonakos

# CONTENTS

# PREFACE TO THE FOURTH EDITION

This two-volume book of essays and readings is based upon our philosophy of teaching American history to advanced students. Simply stated, this philosophy holds to four premises: (1) the approach to history should be analytical, not factual; (2) students should be exposed to the newest viewpoints as well as to traditional interpretations; (3) readers should be provided with a brief historiographical background in order to appreciate more fully the selections assigned for outside readings; and (4) reading assignments should be exciting intellectual adventures rather than dull chores.

The first purpose of this work, then, is to bring together selections that approach American history from an analytical point of view. In most instances these readings represent interpretive pieces that illuminate different problems and periods in America's past. Students will be struck, however, by a single thread that runs through both volumes and ties together the diverse readings. The selections reproduced here underscore one major theme: that the view of American history has been a constantly changing one.

Generally speaking, new interpretations in American history have arisen for two reasons. First, the perspective of American historians of a given generation has been shaped in large measure by the sweep of events in the external world—occurrences outside the scholar's study. Scholars, in short, have tended to reflect either consciously or unconsciously in their works the problems and predilections of the age in which they have written. Each succeeding generation, therefore, seems to have rewritten American history to suit the felt needs of its time. Some selections in this work are indicative of this generational change. We have sometimes sought to show how the age in which the historian was writing often influenced starting assumptions, the gathering of evidence, and the interpretation of events. In recent years, for example, the consciousness of historians has been influenced by distinctive social changes reflecting the forces of racism, sexism, war, violence, and economic and urban problems that have profoundly affected the lives of most Americans.

The second reason for the constantly changing picture of our nation's past has come from internal intellectual changes within the historical profession itself—inside the scholar's study, so to speak. History, like most other academic disciplines, seems to have a built-in tendency toward self-generating change. When scholars sense that they have reached the outer limits in applying the tenets of what has become an accepted interpretation, they do one of two things: introduce major revisions to correct the prevailing point of view, or strike off in new directions. Some articles in this work, therefore, represent the writings of scholars who seek to revise some of the more traditional interpretations; other selections reflect the work of a current generation of historians who apply concepts borrowed from the social and behavioral sciences, or employ quantitative techniques. The decades of the 1960s and 1970s were marked by attempts to create a "new social history," a "new political history," and a "new economic history." These efforts focused primarily, though not exclusively, on the study of group behavior, with the group being defined by a set of variables that often lend themselves to quantification. Other efforts of a nonquantitative nature were either cross-disciplinary in purpose, or resorted to new methodological approaches.

To meet the needs of our third premise, we have written chapter-length introductions for each group of selections. These introductions will enable students to approach the readings with greater ease and understanding by providing a historiographical context for the topic under discussion.

Finally, we have searched the literature for selections that have a lively literary style. It is our firm conviction that the readings represent spirited writing as well as sound scholarship. Much of the exciting work in American history has been done by scholars who possess a real literary flair. Students will discover the pleasures of history when they read in these pages the selections by Perry Miller, Darrett Rutman, Bernard Bailyn, Daniel Boorstin, Gordon Wood, Edward Pessen, Stanley Elkins, Allan Nevins, Eric Foner, Gabriel Kolko, Dexter Perkins, Arthur Link, Arthur M. Schlesinger, Jr., Frederick Jackson Turner, Eugene Genovese, William A. Williams, and John Kenneth Galbraith.

In preparing this work, we have drawn upon the help of several friends. In particular, we should like to thank four of them, Milton M. Klein of the University of Tennessee, and Ronald P. Formisano, Ronald Petrin, and Frank Couvares of Clark University.

G.N.G.
G.A.B.

# 1

# Introduction

"Every true history is contemporary history." Thus wrote Benedetto Croce, the great Italian philosopher and historian, over a half century ago. By his remark Croce meant that history—as distinguished from mere chronicle—was meaningful only to the degree it struck a responsive chord in the minds of contemporaries who saw mirrored in the past the problems and issues of the present.

Croce's remark has special relevance to the writing of American history. Every generation of American scholars has reinterpreted the past in terms of its own age. Why is this so? One compelling reason, no doubt, has been the constant tendency of scholars to reexamine the past in light of the prevailing ideas, assumptions, and problems of their own day. Every age has developed its own climate of opinion—or particular view of the world—which, in turn, has partially conditioned the way it looks upon its own past and present. Thus, each succeeding generation of Americans has rewritten the history of the country in such a way as to suit its own self-image. Although there were other reasons for this continual reinterpretation of American history, the changing climate of opinion more than any other single factor caused historians to recast periodically their view of the past.

Changing interpretations arose also from the changing nature of American historians and their approach to the discipline. The writing of history in America, broadly speaking, has gone through three distinct stages. In the first stage—the era of Puritan historians during the seventeenth century—historical writing was dominated by ministers and political leaders of the Puritan colonies who sought to express the religious justification for their New World settlements. The second stage—the period of the patrician historians—saw the best history being written by members of the patrician class from the early eighteenth century to the late nineteenth century. Patrician historians—often gentlemen of leisure with private incomes—normally had little or no connection with the church or other formal institutions, as had the Puritan historians. They were stirred to write history by a strong sense of social responsibility that characterized the class from which they sprang, and by a personal conviction that each individual had a moral obligation to employ his best talents for the betterment of mankind. Their works, as a general rule, reflected the ideology and preconceptions of their class. Although

1

they were amateur scholars for the most part, many patrician writers succeeded in reaching a high level of literary distinction and accuracy. The third stage—the period of the professional scholars—began during the 1870s and may properly be called "the age of the professional historians." These scholars qualified as professionals on several counts: they were specifically trained for their craft; they supported themselves by full-time careers of teaching, writing, and research at colleges and universities; and they looked to their professional group to set the standards of achievement by which historical studies were evaluated. Their work has been characterized by constant revisionism: They attempted to correct one another, to challenge traditional interpretations, and to approach old historical problems from new points of view.[1]

During each of these three stages of historical writing, the intellectual milieu in America was distinctly different. In the seventeenth century, the best histories were written by Puritan ministers and magistrates who saw history as the working out of God's will. Theirs was a Christian interpretation of history—one in which events were seen as the unfolding of God's intention and design. Borrowing the concept of a Chosen People from the ancient Hebrews, they viewed the colonization of America in Biblical terms. They cast the Puritans in the same role as the Jews in the Old Testament—as a regenerate people who were destined to fulfill God's purpose. New England became for them New Canaan— the place God had set apart for man to achieve a better way of Christian living. Massachusetts, therefore, was more than simply another colony. In the words of John Winthrop, it was to be a "city upon a hill"—a model utopia to demonstrate to the rest of the world that the City of God could be established on earth along the lines set forth in the New Testament.

The major theme of most Puritan historians, whether they were ministers or lay leaders, was the same—to demonstrate God's special concern for His Chosen People in their efforts to build a New Canaan. New England's history served their purposes best because it was here that God's mercy could be seen more clearly than in any other part of the globe. To the Puritans, New England's history was one long record of the revelation of God's providence toward His people. Their disasters as well as their triumphs were seen only in relation to God, and the setbacks they suffered were viewed as evidence of God's wrath and displeasure.

Of all the Puritan histories, William Bradford's *Of Plimouth Plantation* was, perhaps, the preeminent work of art. Written in the 1630s and 1640s while Bradford was governor of the colony, this book recounted

---

[1]John Higham *et al.*, *History* (Englewood Cliffs, N.J., 1965), pp. 3–5.

the tale of the tiny band of Pilgrims who fled first to Holland and then to the New World. No other narrative captured so perfectly the deep feeling of religious faith of New England's early settlers. None illustrated better the Puritan ideal of a plain and simple literary style, or mastered so well the rhythms of Biblical prose. Yet, like most Puritan literature, it was written during the few spare moments that Bradford could find from his more important activities as a governor of a new community in the wilderness.

The patrician historians of the eighteenth century replaced the Puritan historians when the church ceased to be the intellectual center of American life. The Christian theory of history with its emphasis on supernatural causes increasingly gave way to a more secular interpretation based upon the concepts of human progress, reason, and material well-being. Influenced by European Enlightenment thinkers, American historians came to believe that man, by use of his reason, could control his destiny and determine his own material and intellectual progress in the world.

The patrician historians were profoundly influenced also by ideas derived from the writings of Sir Isaac Newton. This seventeenth-century English scientist, by applying a rational, mathematical method, had arrived at certain truths, or "natural laws," concerning the physical universe. Newton's systematization of scientific thought led many men to conclude that the same mathematical-scientific method could be employed to formulate similar natural laws in other fields. In order to develop a theory of history in keeping with Newtonian thought, writers began to postulate certain natural laws in the field of history. Thus, patrician historians abandoned the Christian theory in which God determined the events for a view of the universe in which natural laws were the motivating forces in history.

This shift from a Christian interpretation of history to a more secular approach was reflected in the change of leaders among American historians. Minister-historians were increasingly replaced by members of the patrician class—political leaders, planter-aristocrats, merchants, lawyers, and doctors.[2] In the eighteenth century, for example, America's outstanding historians included Thomas Hutchinson, member of the Massachusetts merchant aristocracy and royal governor of that colony; William Smith of New York, doctor, landowner, and lieutenant governor of that colony; and Robert Beverley and William Byrd of Virginia, who were planter-aristocrats, large landowners, and officeholders. Most of these men possessed a classical education, a fine private library, and the leisure time in which to write. With the growth of

---

[2]Harvey Wish, *The American Historian* (New York, 1960), p. 25.

private wealth and the opening up of new economic opportunities, more members of the upper classes were in a position to take up the writing of history as an avocation.[3]

The reaction against the Christian interpretation of history was particularly evident in the writings of Thomas Jefferson. In his *Notes on the State of Virginia*, first published in 1785, Jefferson stressed reason and natural law instead of divine providence as the basis for historical causation. Jefferson believed also that men were motivated by self-interest, and he employed this concept as one means of analyzing the course of historical events. As he wrote in his history of Virginia, "Mankind soon learn to make interested uses of every right and power which they possess, or may assume."

Jefferson's history showed the impact of yet another major influence—nationalism—which affected historical writing after 1776. As author of the Declaration of Independence, Jefferson felt a fierce, patriotic pride in the free institutions that emerged from the Revolution. He was convinced that America as a democratic nation was destined to pave the way for a new era in world history. A whole new generation of patrician historians sprang up after the Revolution, writing in a similar nationalistic vein—David Ramsay, Mercy Otis Warren, Jeremy Belknap, and Jared Sparks. They likewise contrasted America's free institutions with what they considered to be Europe's corrupt and decadent institutions.

During the first three quarters of the nineteenth century, the writing of history continued to be dominated by patrician historians. The influence of the romantic movement in the arts with its heightened appreciation of the past, emphasis upon pictorial descriptions, and stress upon the role of great men, caused history to be viewed increasingly as a branch of literature. Many outstanding literary figures—Washington Irving, Francis Parkman, Richard Hildreth, William H. Prescott, and John Lothrop Motley—wrote narrative histories about America, other lands, and other times, in a romantic style calculated to appeal to a wide reading public. Such authors were often part of a trans-Atlantic literary culture, for many English historians were writing in the same vein.

America's patrician historians, however, were not always content to provide only a colorful narrative. Writing within a developmental framework, they sought to reveal some of the underlying principles which they believed lay behind the rational evolution of historical events. For the most part, their writings reflected certain assumptions that were common to many historians on both sides of the Atlantic in the

---

[3]Higham, *History*, p. 3.

first half of the nineteenth century—the idea that history was essentially the story of liberty; that man's record revealed a progressive advance toward greater human rights down through the ages; and that peoples of Anglo-Saxon origin had a special destiny to bring democracy to the rest of the world.

Many of these American historians, influenced by the pronounced nationalism of the period, used such broad assumptions within a chauvinistic framework. They felt a responsibility to help establish the national identity of the new United States. Thus, they employed history as a didactic tool to instruct their countrymen along patriotic lines and presented America's story in the best light possible. Running through their writings were three basic themes: the idea of progress—that the story of America was one of continuous progress onward and upward toward greatness; the idea of liberty—that American history, in essence, symbolized the trend toward greater liberty in world history; and the idea of mission—that the United States had a special destiny to serve as a model of a free people to the rest of mankind in leading the way to a more perfect life. The last theme, in effect, was nothing more than a restatement of the idea of mission first set forth by the Puritan historians.

George Bancroft, the most distinguished historian of the mid-nineteenth century, organized his history of the United States around these three themes. After studying in Germany in the 1820s, Bancroft returned to America determined to apply Teutonic ideas of history to the story of his own country. Bancroft believed in the progressive unfolding of all human history toward a future golden age in which all men would eventually achieve complete freedom and liberty. This march of all mankind toward a greater freedom was in accordance with a preordained plan conceived by God. One phase of God's master plan could be seen in the way that a superior Anglo-Saxon people developed a distinctive set of democratic institutions. The United States, according to Bancroft, represented the finest flowering of such democratic institutions. American democracy, then, was the fruition of God's plan, and the American people had a unique mission in history to spread democracy throughout the rest of the world. Such was the central theme of Bancroft's famous twelve-volume work, *History of the United States from the Discovery of the American Continent*, written between 1834 and 1882.

Francis Parkman, a patrician historian from New England, held many views similar to those of Bancroft. Writing about the intercolonial wars in his work, *France and England in North America*, Parkman portrayed the American colonists as democratic Anglo-Saxons of Protestant persuasion whose superior qualities enabled them to conquer authoritarian-minded French Catholics in Canada. But in many other ways the two writers were quite different. Parkman was more representative of the gentlemen-historians of the nineteenth century who, being drawn from the upper classes, usually reflected an aristocratic bias in their writings, advocated a conservative Whig philosophy, and were distrustful of the American masses. Bancroft, on the other hand, eulogized the common man and was a Jacksonian in politics; his history was distinctly democratic in outlook.

By the 1870s two profound changes began to influence the writing of American history. The first was the change in leadership from amateur patricians to professional historians. Until the last quarter of the nineteenth century, American history had been written almost exclusively by men who had received no special training as historians—except, of course, for a few individuals like Bancroft. From this point on, however, the writing of history was dominated by professionally trained scholars educated in the universities of America and Europe. Professionalization in the field was made possible by developments in higher education as graduate schools appeared in increasing numbers in America to train college history teachers. In the last three decades of the century, this trend proceeded at a rapid rate: the Johns Hopkins University, the first institution devoted to graduate study and research, began its activities in 1876; the American Historical Association was founded in 1884; and the *American Historical Review* made its appearance in 1895.

The advent of professional historians brought about a marked transformation in the field. No longer was historical writing to be vested mainly in the hands of amateurs—though it should be emphasized that many patrician historians had been superb stylists, creative scholars, and researchers who made judicious use of original sources. Nor would historians be drawn almost exclusively from the patrician class in the Northeast, particularly from New England. Professional scholars came from all walks of life, represented a much broader range of social interests than the patricians, and hailed from different geographic regions. Finally, instead of being free-lance writers, as many patricians had been, professionals made their living as teachers in colleges and universities.

The second major development affecting the writing of American history was the emergence of a new intellectual milieu that reflected the growing dominance of novel scientific ideas and concepts. Influenced by Darwinian biology and its findings in the natural sciences, historians began to think of history as a science rather than as a branch of literature. Why couldn't the historian deal with the facts of history in much the same way that the scientist did with elements in the laboratory? If there were certain laws of organic development in the scientific field, might there not be certain laws of historical development? What historian, wrote Henry Adams, with "an idea of scientific method can have helped dreaming of the immortality that would be achieved by the man who should successfully apply Darwin's method to the facts of human history?"[4]

The first generation of professional historians—who held sway from about 1870–1910—was best exemplified by two outstanding scholars, Henry Adams and Frederick Jackson Turner. Henry Adams, a descendant of the famous Adams family that contributed American presidents, statesmen, and diplomats, turned to history and literature as his avocation after his hopes for high political office were dashed. In 1870 he was invited to Harvard and became the first teacher to introduce a history seminar at that institution. Adams pioneered in training his students in the meticulous critical methods of German scholarship, and searched for a time for a scientific philosophy of history based on the findings in the field of physics. His nine-volume history of the United States during the administrations of Jefferson and Madison was destined to become one of the classics of American historical literature. Although he left Harvard after a few years, his career symbolized the transformation from patrician to professional historian and the changing intellectual climate from romanticism to a more scientific approach in the writing of American history.

While Henry Adams was attempting to assimilate history and physics, Frederick Jackson Turner—perhaps the most famous and influential representative of the scientific school of historians in the first generation of professional historians—was applying evolutionary modes of thought to explain American history. Born and reared in a frontier community in Wisconsin, Turner attended the University of Wisconsin, received his Ph.D. from the Johns Hopkins University, and then went on to a teaching career first at Wisconsin and later at Harvard. Like Adams, Turner believed that it was possible to make a science out of history; he attempted, therefore, to apply the ideas of Darwinian evolution to the writing of history. Turner emphasized the concept of evolutionary stages of development as successive frontier environments in America wrought changes in the character of the people and their institutions. As one frontier in America succeeded another, each more remote from Europe than its predecessor, a social evolutionary process was at work creating a democratic American individualist. The unique characteristics of the American people—their rugged individualism, egalitarianism, practicality, and materialistic outlook on life—all resulted from the evolutionary process of adapting to successive frontier environments. Turner's famous essay "The Significance of the Frontier in American History," written in 1893, remains a superb statement of one approach that was employed by the scientific school of historians.

---

[4]Henry Adams, "The Tendency of History," *Annual Report of the American Historical Association for the Year 1894* (Washington, D.C., 1895), p. 19.

Between 1910 and 1945, a second generation of professional scholars—the Progressive historians—came to maturity and helped to transform the discipline by introducing new ideas and methodologies. Many of them were influenced by the Progressive movement of the early 1900s—a period when the future of American democracy appeared to be threatened by new economic and social forces arising from the rapid industrialization of American society. Rejecting the views of the older and more conservative patrician historians, the Progressive scholars viewed history as an ideological weapon that might explain the present and perhaps help to control the future. In sympathy with the aims and objectives of the Progressive movement between 1900 and 1920, these scholars continued to write history from a Progressive point of view even after the decline of the Progressive movement following the First World War.

Unlike the New England patrician historians of the nineteenth century, the Progressive scholars tended to hail more from the Midwest and South. These Progressives complained that in the past American history had been presented mainly as an extension of the history of New England. American civilization, they argued, was more than a transplanted English and European civilization that had spread out from New England; it had unique characteristics and a mission all its own. But while the Progressive historians were as nationalistic as the patrician school, their nationalism was different in nature. The patricians had conceived of nationalism as a stabilizing force, preserving order and thus assuring the continued ascendancy of the aristocratic element in American life. The Progressives, on the other hand, considered nationalism a dynamic force. To them the fulfillment of democracy meant a continued and protracted struggle against those individuals, classes, and groups who had barred the way to the achievements of a more democratic society in the past.

In changing the direction of American historical writing, Progressive scholars drew upon the reform tradition that had grown out of the effort to adjust American society to the new demands of an urban-centered and industrialized age. This tradition had originated in the 1890s and reached maturity in the early part of the twentieth century with the Progressive movement. Drawing upon various sources, the adherents of the Progressive movement rejected the idea of a closed system of classical economic thought which assumed that certain natural laws governed human society. Society, these reformers maintained, was open-ended and dynamic; its development was determined not by immutable laws, but by economic and social forces that grew out of the interaction between the individual and his environment.

Reacting against the older emphasis upon logic, abstraction, and deduction, these reformers sought a meaningful explanation of human society that could account for its peculiar development. Instead of focusing upon immutable laws, they began viewing society and individuals as products of an evolutionary developmental process. This process could be understood only by reference to the past. The function of the historian, then, was to explain how the present had come to be, and then to try and set guidelines for future developments. As a result of this approach, history and the other social sciences drew together, seeking to explain the realities of social life by emphasizing the interplay of economic, technological, social, psychological, and political forces.

History, according to its Progressive practitioners, was not an abstract discipline whose truths could only be contemplated. On the contrary, historians had important activist roles to play in the construction of a better world. By explaining the historical roots of contemporary problems, historians could provide the knowledge and understanding necessary to make changes which would bring further progress. Like the Enlightenment *philosophes*, historians could reveal prior mistakes and errors, and thus liberate men from the chains of tyranny and oppression of the past. When fused with the social sciences, history could become a powerful tool for reform. "The present has hitherto been the willing victim of the past," wrote James Harvey Robinson, one of the greatest exponents of Progressive history; but "the time has now come when it should turn on the past and exploit it in the interests of advance."[5]

Clearly, the sympathy of this school lay with change and not with the preservation of the status quo. Committed to the idea of progress, they saw themselves as contributing to a better and more humane world for the future. Consequently, they rejected the apparent moral neutrality and supposed objectivity of the scientific school in favor of a liberal philosophy of reform. In so doing, they rewrote much of American history, greatly widening its scope and changing its emphasis. Instead of focusing on narrow institutional studies of traditional political, diplomatic, and military history, they sought to delineate those determinant forces that underlay human institutions. In their hands American history became a picture of conflict—conflict between polarities of American life: aristocracy versus democracy; economic "haves" versus "have-nots"; politically overprivileged groups versus those underprivileged; and between geographical sections, as the East versus West. In short, the divisions were between those dedicated to democratic and egalitarian ideals and those committed to a static conservatism.

Believers in inevitable progress, the Progressive historians assumed that America was continually moving on an upward path toward an ideal social order. Not only was American society growing in affluence,

---

[5]James Harvey Robinson, "The New History," *The New History: Essays Illustrating the Modern Historical Outlook* (New York, 1912), p. 24.

but in freedom, opportunity, and happiness as well. The primary determinant of progress was the unending conflict between the forces of liberalism and those of conservatism. Thus all periods in American history could be divided into two clear and distinct phases: periods of active reform and periods of conservative reaction. As Arthur M. Schlesinger, Sr., wrote in 1939: "A period of concern for the rights of the few has been followed by one of concern for the wrongs of the many."[6]

Turner, a transitional figure between the scientific and Progressive historians, with Charles A. Beard and Vernon L. Parrington, best presented the Progressive point of view. After his epochal essay on the frontier in 1893—an essay that emphasized unity rather than conflict—Turner's interest turned elsewhere, particularly to the idea of sectional conflict. From the late 1890s until his death in 1932, he elaborated and refined his sectional conflict hypothesis. Turner and his students attempted to understand not only how a section came into being, but also the dynamics of conflict that pitted the East against West, North against South, labor against capital, and the many against the few. Under Turner's guiding hand, American scholars wrote a series of brilliant monographs as well as broad interpretive studies that emphasized the class and sectional divisions in American society. Although a few favored the conservative side, the overwhelming majority of historians made clear their preference for democratic liberalism and progress.

While Turner was developing and elaborating his sectional approach, Charles A. Beard was applying the hypothesis of an overt class conflict to the study of American institutions. His book, *An Economic Interpretation of the Constitution,* written in 1913, was perhaps the most influential historical work of the twentieth century. Beard attempted to demonstrate that the Constitution, far from representing a judicious combination of wisdom and idealism, was actually the product of a small group of propertied individuals who were intent upon establishing a strong central government capable of protecting their interests against the encroachments of the American masses. In a series of books, climaxed by *The Rise of American Civilization* in 1927, Beard argued that American history demonstrated the validity of the class conflict hypothesis between "haves" and "have-nots." Time and again, he showed the paramount role that economic factors played in determining human behavior. Fusing his ardent faith in progress with a qualified economic determinism, Beard made clear that his sympathies lay with the forces of democracy as opposed to those of reaction and privilege.

The culmination of the Progressive interpretation came with the publication of Vernon L. Parrington's *Main Currents in American Thought.*

---

[6]Arthur M. Schlesinger, Sr., "Tides of American Politics," *Yale Review* 29 (December 1939):220.

Using literature as his vehicle, Parrington portrayed American history in clear and unmistakable terms. The two central protagonists of Parrington's work were Jefferson and Hamilton. Jefferson stood for a decentralized agrarian democracy that drew its support from the great masses of people. Hamilton, on the other hand, represented a privileged and aristocratic minority seeking to maintain its dominant position. American history, according to Parrington, had witnessed a continual struggle between the liberal Jeffersonian tradition and the conservative Hamiltonian one. Underlying Parrington's approach was one major assumption that had also governed the thought of Turner and Beard, namely, that ideology was determined by the materialistic forces in history. Like Turner and Beard, Parrington clearly preferred the forces of reform and democracy, but there were times when he was much less certain of their eventual triumph than his two intellectual companions.

The Progressive point of view generally dominated the field of American historical scholarship down to the end of World War II. Class and sectional conflict, Progressive historians implied, was a guarantor of progress. Even during those eras in American history when the forces of reaction triumphed—as in the post–Civil War period—their victory was only temporary; ultimately the forces of progress and good regrouped and thereby gained the initiative once again. Such an approach, of course, led to broad and sweeping interpretive syntheses of American history, for the basic framework or structure was clear and simple, and the faith of historians in the ultimate triumph of good over evil remained unquestioned.

Beginning in the 1930s, however, some American scholars began to question the idea of progress that was implicit in this view. The rise of Nazism in the 1930s and 1940s, and the menace of communism in the 1950s and 1960s, led to a questioning of older assumptions and generalities. How, some asked, could one subscribe to the optimistic tenets of liberalism after the horrors of Auschwitz, Buchenwald, Hiroshima, Nagasaki, and the threat of modern totalitarianism? Indeed, had not American historians, through their own optimistic view of history and their faith in progress, failed to prepare the American people for the challenges and trials that they would face during the middle of the twentieth century? Parrington himself had recognized as early as 1929 that the Progressive faith was under attack by those who did not subscribe to its basic tenets. "Liberals whose hair is growing thin and the lines of whose figures are no longer what they were," he wrote, "are likely to find themselves today in the unhappy predicament of being treated as mourners at their own funerals. When they pluck up heart to assert that they are not yet authentic corpses, but living men with brains in their heads, they are pretty certain to be gently chided and led back to the comfortable armchair that befits senility. Their counsel is smiled at as the chatter of a belated post-Victorian generation that knew not Freud, and if they must go abroad they are bidden take the air in the garden where other old-fashioned plants—mostly of the family *Democratici*—are still preserved."[7]

Following the end of World War II, a third generation of professional historians appeared on the scene to challenge the Progressive point of view. They were sometimes called neoconservatives because they seemed to hark back to the conservative historical position that had prevailed prior to Turner and Beard. Their rise was partly a result of pressures—both external and internal—upon the historical profession in the postwar era.

External pressures resulting from changing political conditions in the world at large brought about a major change in the mood of many Americans. Some neoconservative historians reflected, either consciously or unconsciously, an outlook that prevailed in the United States as the nation assumed the sober responsibility of defending the world against the threat of communism. During the Cold War era, when the country felt its security endangered from abroad, these scholars wanted, perhaps, to present an image to the rest of the world of an America that had been strong and united throughout most of its history. Hence, the neoconservative scholars pictured American history in terms of consensus rather than conflict.

Internal pressures within the profession itself likewise brought changes. Particular points of view expressed in any academic discipline seem to have an inner dynamism of their own. After subscribing to a given interpretation for a time, scholars often sense that they have pushed an idea to its outermost limits and can go no farther without risking major distortion. A reaction inevitably sets in, and revisionists begin working in a different direction. Such was the case of the Progressive interpretation of history. Having written about American history from the standpoint of conflict and discontinuity, scholars now began to approach the same subject from an opposite point of view—that of consensus and continuity.

One way this new group of scholars differed from the Progressives was in their inherent conservatism. Progressive historians had had a deep belief in the idea of progress. Neoconservative historians, on the other hand, often rejected progress as an article of faith. Skeptical of the alleged beneficial results of rapid social change, they stressed instead the thesis of historical continuity.

Given their emphasis on continuity, the neoconservatives were less

---

[7]Vernon L. Parrington, *Main Currents in American Thought*, 3 vols. (New York, 1927–1930), 3:401.

prone to a periodized view of American history. Progressive scholars had seen American history in terms of class or sectional conflicts marked by clearly defined turning points—the Revolution, the Constitution, the Jeffersonian era, the Jacksonian period, the Civil War, and so forth. These periods represented breaks, or discontinuities, from what had gone on before. For the Progressives, American history was divided into two distinct phases that followed one another in a cyclical pattern: periods of reform or revolution when the popular and democratic forces in society gained the upper hand and forced social changes, and periods of reaction and counterrevolution, when vested interests resisted such changes. For the neoconservative scholars, however, the enduring and unifying themes in history were much more significant. To them the continuity of common principles in American culture, the stability and longevity of institutions, and the persistence of certain traits and traditions in the American national character represented the most powerful forces in history.

Consensus, as well as continuity, was a characteristic theme of the neoconservative historians. Unlike the Progressives, who wrote about the past in terms of polarities—class conflicts between rich and poor, sectional divisions between North and South or East and West, and ideological differences between liberals and conservatives—the neoconservatives abandoned the conflict interpretation of history and favored instead one that viewed American society as stable and homogeneous. The cement that bound American society together throughout most of its history was a widespread acceptance of certain principles and beliefs. Americans, despite their differences, had always agreed on the following propositions: the right of all persons in society to own private property; the theory that the power of government should always be limited; the concept that men possessed certain natural rights that could not be taken from them by government; and the idea of some form of natural law.

One of the foremost neoconservative historians writing in the 1950s was Louis Hartz. In his book, *The Liberal Tradition in America*, Hartz took issue with those Progressive historians who had viewed the American Revolution as a radical movement that fundamentally transformed American society. America had come into being after the age of feudalism, Hartz claimed, and this condition had profoundly shaped its development. Lacking a feudal past, the country did not have to contend with the established feudal structure that characterized the *ancien régime* in Europe—a titled aristocracy, national church, national army, and the like. Hence, America was "born free" and did not require a radical social revolution to become a liberal society—it was one already. What emerged in America, according to Hartz, was a unique society characterized by a consensus upon a single tradition of thought—the liberal tradition. The absence of a feudal heritage enabled the liberal-bourgeois ideas embodied in the political principles derived from John Locke to flourish in America almost unchallenged. "The ironic flaw in American liberalism," wrote Hartz, "lies in the fact that we have never had a conservative tradition."[8]

What, then, of the "conservatives" in American history about whom the Progressive scholars had written? When viewed within the context of comparative history, Hartz said, American conservatives had much more in common with their fellow American liberals than with their European counterparts. Many of the presumed differences between so-called American "conservatives" and "liberals" was in the nature of shadowboxing rather than actual fighting, he concluded, because both groups agreed on a common body of liberal political principles. The Federalists, for example, were not aristocrats but whiggish liberals who misunderstood their society; they misread the Jeffersonian Democrats as being "radicals" rather than recognizing them as fellow liberals. What was true of the Federalists and Jeffersonians held for the other political confrontations in American history; if measured in terms of a spectrum of thought that included European ideologies, the American conflicts took place within the confines of a Lockean consensus.

Daniel J. Boorstin, another major neoconservative historian, also offered a grand theory which pictured American history in terms of continuity and consensus. Boorstin, like Hartz, stressed the uniqueness of American society, but he attributed this development to other causes. A neo-Turnerian, Boorstin postulated an environmental explanation of the American national character. To him the frontier experience was the source of America's conservatism.

In two books written in the 1950s—*The Genius of American Politics* and *The Americans: The Colonial Experience*—Boorstin denied the significance of European influences and ideas upon American life. Boorstin's premise was that the Americans were not an "idea-centered" people. From the very beginning Americans had abandoned European political theories, European blueprints for utopian societies, and European concepts of class distinctions. Americans concerned themselves instead with concrete situations and the practical problems experienced by their frontier communities. Thus, they developed little knack for theorizing or any deep interest in theories as such. The "genius of American politics" lay in its emphasis on pragmatic matters—its very distrust of theories that had led to radical political changes and deep divisions within European societies.[9]

---

[8]Louis Hartz, *The Liberal Tradition in America* (New York, 1955), p. 57.

[9]Daniel J. Boorstin, *The Genius of American Politics* (Chicago, 1953) and *The Americans: The Colonial Experience* (New York, 1958). Boorstin further elaborated on his views in two more volumes: *The Americans: The National Experience* (New York, 1965) and *The Americans: The Democratic Experience* (New York, 1973).

The American way of life which evolved during the colonial period, wrote Boorstin, set the pattern for the nation's later development. That pattern placed a premium on solutions to practical problems, adaptations to changing circumstances, and improvisations based upon pragmatic considerations. Lacking a learned class or professional traditions, the colonists were forced to create their own ways of doing things in the areas of education, law, medicine, science, diplomacy, and warfare. During this process the "doer" dominated over the "thinker" and the generalist over the specialist. Over the course of time, this nontheoretical approach developed into a distinctive American life style—one characterized by a naive practicality that enabled Americans to unite in a stable way of life and to become a homogeneous society made up of undifferentiated men sharing the same values.

The "cult of the 'American Consensus,'" as one scholar called it, made the nation's past appear tame and placid; it was no longer a history marked by extreme group conflicts or rigid class distinctions.[10] The heroes in America's past—Jefferson, Lincoln, Wilson, and Franklin D. Roosevelt—became less heroic because there occurred no head-on clash between individuals on the basis of ideology since all Americans shared the same middle-class Lockean values. Conversely, the old villains— Hamilton, Rockefeller, and Carnegie—became less evil and were portrayed as constructive figures who contributed much to their country. The achievements of the business community in particular were glorified. Without the material achievements of American entrepreneurs, according to some scholars, the United States could not have withstood the challenges to democracy during World War I and World War II. The underdogs in American history—the reformers, radicals, and working class—were presented as being less idealistic and more egocentric as neoconservative scholars sought to demonstrate that the ideology of these elements in society was no less narrow and self-centered than that of other elements. The "cult" of the neoconservatives continued into the 1960s—though "cult" was perhaps too strong a term, and implied a unanimity rarely found in the historical profession.

Besides Boorstin and Hartz, other neoconservative scholars published specialized studies which revised the Progressive point of view in virtually every period of American history. The neoconservative trend, marked by a new respect for tradition and a de-emphasis on class conflict, brought many changes in American historiography: the revival of a sympathetic approach to the Puritans; the treatment of the American Revolution as a conservative movement of less significance; the conclusion that the Constitution was a document faithfully reflecting a middle-class consensus; the favorable, if not uncritical, attitude toward

---

[10]John Higham, "The Cult of the 'American Consensus': Homogenizing Our History," *Commentary* 27 (February 1959):93–100.

the founding fathers of the new republic; the diminution of the traditional ideological differences between Hamiltonianism and Jeffersonianism; the consensus interpretation of the Jacksonian era; the enhanced reputation of America's business tycoons; a renewed appreciation of such controversial political leaders as Theodore Roosevelt; the
inclination to play down the more radical aspects of the Progressive and
New Deal periods; the predisposition to support the correctness of
America's recent foreign policy; and the tendency to view American
society as being satisfied, unified, and stable throughout most of the
nation's history. Implicit in the neoconservative approach was a fear of
extremism, a yearning to prove that national unity had almost always
existed, and a longing for the security and way of life America presumably had enjoyed before becoming a superpower and leader of the free
world.

During the decades of the 1960s and 1970s, the assumptions and
conclusions of the neoconservative historians were rudely overturned
by two major developments. First, the mood of the American people
shifted markedly as the seemingly placid decade of the 1950s was succeeded by tumultuous events in America's foreign and domestic affairs.
Second, within the historical profession itself a reaction to the neoconservative point of view led to the rise of many revisionist interpretations.
The result was a pronounced fragmentation in the field of American
historiography.

The prevailing mood among the American people shifted dramatically in the 1960s and 1970s because of a series of shattering events on
the domestic scene. Gone were the complacency, national self-
confidence, optimism, and moral composure that seemed to have
characterized the 1950s. Many historians were stirred by the great social
upheavals that undermined previously held assumptions. A marked
trend toward racial divisions within American society appeared with the
newfound militancy among blacks during the civil rights movement.
The resulting hostility to integration among many whites showed that
American society was hardly as homogeneous as had been previously
believed. At the same time, an increased tendency toward violence during the urban riots in the 1960s indicated that Americans were not always committed to the idea of peaceful compromise. President Kennedy's assassination in 1963 followed by that of Martin Luther King and
Robert Kennedy revealed that the United States was as vulnerable to
political terrorism as other societies. There was also a renewed awareness of poverty with the economic downturn in the 1970s, and some
scholars began voicing doubts about the supposed social mobility within
American society, the virtues of technological change, and the benefits
of economic growth.

The appearance of numerous social-protest movements during those two decades also made many American historians more conscious of the importance of minority groups in the nation's past. Having witnessed protest movements by the blacks, the poor, and the women's liberation movement, some scholars took a greater interest in black history, women's history, and to protest groups like the Populists and IWW. Generally speaking, historians became more sympathetic to the role of the underdog in American history.

Changes in America's foreign affairs during these decades similarly had a profound effect on the writing of history. The Vietnam War, above all, divided the American people. Students participated in large-scale antiwar demonstrations, and college campuses were transformed into centers of political protest and activism. Many intellectuals grew disenchanted with the government's military policy and became increasingly suspicious of the political establishment in general. The Vietnam War also exposed the dangers of what one historian termed the imperial presidency. President Nixon and the Watergate scandal revealed further the threat posed to constitutional government by this concept of the presidency. As some historians grew more critical of America's foreign policy, they began to question the credibility of the government both in the present and past.

During the course of the 1960s and 1970s, scholars were affected also by sweeping intellectual changes within the historical profession itself. Some began by challenging the traditional approach to history—one that assumed the discipline was separate and self-contained. Acting on the premise that the other social sciences—psychology, sociology, anthropology, and political science—could contribute to the study of history, they turned more to an interdisciplinary approach. In doing so, these historians applied concepts, laws, and models from other social sciences in order to understand the conduct of individuals and social groups in the past. This interdisciplinary approach could hardly be called new for it had been employed during the first half of the twentieth century. Still, there was a stronger tendency among scholars to apply social science techniques during these two decades.

A second major development was the use of new methodological approaches to the study of history. Some historians began relying more on quantitative techniques in their efforts to derive scientifically measurable historical data to document their studies. Other scholars turned to a comparative history approach—comparing entire societies or segments of societies—to illuminate the American past. Quantitative and comparative history were but two of a number of methodological approaches which were employed with greater frequency in the 1960s and 1970s.

It was within this general context that there arose a significant challenge to the neoconservative historians in the 1960s from a group of younger radical scholars known as the New Left. Like the older Progressives, these historians sought to fuse historical scholarship with political activism, and might be called "neo-Progressives." Unlike the neoconservatives who emphasized consensus, continuity, and stability, the New Left saw social and economic conflict as the major theme in American history. Of all historians, the individuals identified with the New Left were the most disenchanted with the course of events in recent American history. As a result they presented a radical critique of American society and took a more jaundiced view of the American past.

These scholars reinterpreted American history along more radical lines and insisted that their colleagues pay far greater attention to the lower classes and minority groups of all kinds. Members of the New Left were exceedingly critical in particular, of those neoconservative scholars who tended to celebrate the virtues and achievements of the American people. Because the neoconservatives had excluded conflict in their interpretation, the New Left argued, the American people were unprepared to cope with the social upheavals that occurred in the 1960s. These younger historians declared that the resort to violence by social groups to achieve their goals was a theme that had deep roots in the American past. The New Left historians sought to create a "usable past"—a history that would account for the country's social problems such as racism, militarism, economic exploitation, and imperialism, and would serve as the basis for reforming American society. American history had too often been written from "the top down"—that is, from the point of view of elites and the articulate like Washington, Lincoln, and Franklin D. Roosevelt. History, they argued, should be written "from the bottom up," a perspective which would reflect the concerns of the common people, the inarticulate masses, and nonelites. Viewing history in this way, scholars would discover the radicalism inherent in the American past.

In their treatment of America's foreign policy, for example, the New Left developed a much more critical interpretation than previous historians. America from its beginnings, they argued, had been an aggressive, expansionist, and imperialist nation. It expanded first at the expense of the Indians, and then later at the expense of its weaker neighbors like Mexico. The United States turned subsequently to an overseas imperialist foreign policy based on its need for foreign markets, raw materials, and investment opportunities. This expansionist foreign policy had global ramifications, the New Left claimed. America had played a major role in precipitating two world wars and was primarily responsible for bringing about the Cold War. The Vietnam War, according to the New Left, was simply a logical extension of America's aggressive and expansionist foreign policy.

The New Left view of American history never attained the importance or cohesion of either the Progressive or the neoconservative interpretation. One reason was that few Americans were prepared to accept either the analyses or the solutions proposed by these radical historians. Another was that the American withdrawal from Vietnam and the economic downturn of the 1970s brought a halt to most radical protest movements. Although New Left scholarship failed to develop the potential many had expected of it, some of its insights and concerns were absorbed by nonradical historians seeking to break out of the mold and limitations of the neoconservative approach of the 1950s.

A more significant challenge to both the neoconservatives and the "older Progressive scholars was the "new social history" of the 1960s and 1970s. This group of scholars, in general, were concerned with defining the nature of America's social structure and its changes over time. They were called the "new social historians" to distinguish them from the old social historians who had been occupied primarily with descriptive and narrative history which dealt with the manners and mores of the common people.

The "new social historians" criticized both the neoconservatives and Progressives for their choice of subject matter and use of evidence. These historians claimed that previous scholars had focused too narrowly upon political, diplomatic, and institutional matters. Older scholars, moreover, were interested in describing isolated historical events. The "new social historians" hoped to widen the scope of history by showing that the relationship between social, economic, and political events inevitably involved changes in the social structure.

These scholars claimed also that earlier historians had sometimes made generalizations based on vague and limited evidence. Historical evidence, according to the "new social historians," should be more precise and approached in a more scientific manner. If at all possible, evidence should be expressed in quantifiable terms so that it might be measured to provide a greater degree of precision. It should be subjected also to systematic analysis in order to test broad conceptual hypotheses about human behavior advanced by the other social sciences. Their hope for history was likewise more ambitious than that of their predecessors. They aimed to create a "new social history" that would illuminate America's social structure and explain social change throughout all of American history.

The growing interest of American historians in the "new social history" was the result of several influences. First, French scholars since the 1930s had been moving away from narrow political and institutional studies and raising new questions which employed novel methodologies. The most significant outlet for the work of these European scholars was the *Annales,* a French publication. The aim of this distinguished journal was to break down the traditional disciplinary barriers and to create a new and unified approach to the understanding of the totality of human activity within a given society or geographical region. Under the editorship of two French scholars, Lucien Febvre and Marc Bloch, the *Annales* became the acknowledged leader in creating the new field of social history or historical sociology. Continuing its innovative beginnings after World War II, the *Annales* increasingly served scholars employing quantitative and demographic techniques, or resorting to multidisciplinary approaches. Slowly but surely, the influence of this French scholarship made itself felt in the United States.

A second influence shaping the "new social history" was the proliferation of work in the social and behavioral sciences after World War II on contemporary problems that vitally affected the lives of many Americans. Among these were included the issues of race relations, family problems, patterns of social and geographical mobility, crime, and educational as well as economic opportunities. Inevitably American historians began to examine the historical roots and antecedents of these social problems.

The final influence was the increased use of the computer and new quantitative techniques which permitted these newer scholars to analyze historical evidence from heretofore unusable sources. Before the advent of the computer, scholars found it difficult, if not impossible, to collect and analyze massive amounts of data. Historians, for instance, were now able to make use of the manuscript census schedules which formed the basis for the published federal and state censuses. These census schedules, which provided much information about individuals and households in the past, had remained unused for the most part because of problems encountered in reducing such a mass of discrete bits of information to usable form. Computer technology made it possible to gather and manipulate these data, while new quantitative techniques enabled researchers to analyze the information in more meaningful ways.

Although the "new social historians" were more or less unified in their desire to examine social structure and social change, their approaches to these problems led them in many different directions. The fragmentation characteristic of American history in general during this period was especially true among these scholars. It manifested itself in the appearance of a number of separate groups of historians who focused upon specific problems all of which came under the general heading of the "new social history."

The so-called "new economic historians" were among the first to employ quantitative techniques and computer technology. Their outstanding characteristic was the use of historical data to test hypotheses derived from economic theories. One of their main interests was to describe and explain the patterns of America's economic growth. They hoped also to identify in a more precise manner the forces that had shaped the complex pattern of the economy, the role of entrepreneurs, and the development of different kinds of labor groups and systems.

The "new political historians" represented another fragment group. These scholars were especially influenced by the behavioral approach of the political scientists. Unlike earlier scholars, these newer historians were less concerned with describing presidential elections and political developments in traditional terms. These scholars were interested instead in quantitative analyses of voting behavior, roll-call analyses of legislatures, and shifts in public opinion on political issues. In studying political behavior, they introduced new techniques for the collection and measurement of data, and developed and refined concepts for analyzing the political process. In doing so, they moved political history closer to social history by seeking to portray the social bases of political behavior.

Yet a third group consisted of the "new urban historians" who studied many processes that occurred within a city setting. These scholars examined such diverse topics as the process of urbanization, growth of suburbs, development of neighborhoods, educational systems, and the rise of political bosses and machines. In approaching these topics, these scholars also made use of computer technology and quantitative techniques to analyze new sources such as manuscript census schedules, city directories, and municipal records. At the same time, many of them resorted to multidisciplinary approaches which drew heavily from concepts of the social and behavioral sciences.

These three groups represent only a few of the new departures undertaken by the "new social historians." In their attempts to understand the American social structure and social change over time, still other scholars in this tradition turned to demography—the study of population in terms of statistical analyses of rates of births, deaths, and marriages. Many of these demographic studies focused upon the family and the community as units of analysis, and led to the establishment of two subfields within the "new social history"—family history and community studies. Others examined the experiences of ethnic and racial groups, giving rise to what was sometimes called an ethnocultural approach to American history. Still others turned to a study of the social, economic, and geographical patterns of mobility in order to identify the conditions that led to success or failure within American society.

Concern with social structure and social change led also to a greater interest in previously neglected social groups. In researching the history of welfare and dependency, scholars studied the ways American society had responded to these groups. The means of caring for the poor, the unemployed, the sick and infirm, the insane, and the aged were subjected to close scrutiny. This interest was accompanied by a corresponding concern for the history of crime and delinquency as historians sought to deal with the experiences of the less fortunate and less successful elements in American society.

The fragmentation of American history so obvious in the many manifestations of the "new social history" was marked by the emergence of four approaches to the discipline which continued along more traditional lines. First of all, as mentioned previously, the old Progressive tradition was continued after World War II by the group of historians called "neo-Progressives." These scholars, including the New Left and others, approached the study of American history in ways similar to the older tradition but modified the Progressive interpretation in many ways.

Another development along similar lines was the extension of the work of Perry Miller and other older intellectual historians into the post–World War II era by the so-called "new intellectual historians." Like Miller and others, these more recent scholars placed more emphasis on analyzing rather than describing ideas. Many of these historians reflected a different orientation from the Progressives because they stressed the primacy of ideas as determinants in history.

The two other developments—comparative history and the organizational school of scholars—likewise represented a continuation of the more traditional approaches to history. The comparative historians usually studied the histories of two or more countries in search of similarities or dissimilarities in national experiences. At other times they compared ideas and concepts like *democracy, nationalism,* or *imperialism* to discover to what extent these concepts were the same or different within diverse historical settings. The organizational school of scholars, on the other hand, developed new syntheses to explain American history since the advent of industrialism. They regarded the rise of bureaucratic structures in society and the acceleration in professionalization as the most significant influences shaping American life since the closing of the frontier in the 1890s. These scholars emphasized that the behavior of individuals might be better understood when seen within an organizational context.

What have been the effects of fragmentation within the discipline of history during the 1960s and 1970s? For one thing, it has prevented the rise of any new major synthesis comparable to that of the neoconservative or the older Progressive interpretations. Diversity and disagreement characterized the historical profession as the decade of the 1970s came to a close. Scholars could only agree that America's past was infinitely more varied and complex than earlier generations of historians had imagined. It may well be that the writing of American history in the future—given the diverse social backgrounds and varied interests of its practitioners—may never again attain the degree of unity it sometimes had achieved in the past.

Another effect of fragmentation has been the pronounced trend toward overspecialization. To be sure, greater specialization has resulted in the proliferation of historical works, and led to new methodologies and more sophisticated interpretations. At the same time, however, it has caused some historians to divorce artifically the "new economic history" from traditional political history, and the "new social history" from intellectual history. Overspecialization, moreover, has posed a problem for those scholars seeking to maintain the integrity of the discipline as a whole.

Fragmentation was also evident in the concept of *community* recently employed by some historians. Many current scholars seemed to agree that their neoconservative predecessors had overemphasized national unity and consensus throughout American history. As scholars de-emphasized consensus, it might have been expected that they would return to conflict as a major theme. A number of historians applied instead the concept of community within different contexts in order to understand how certain institutions might have served to bring about greater cohesion and unity in a pluralistic nation. John Higham noted in the mid-1970s that the "exciting advances in contemporary scholarship have more to do with understanding cohesive structures: the New England town, the family, the ethnic subculture, the professional and trade associations, the political machines." Higham went on to warn, however, that the study of these different kinds of communities could lead to an even more fragmented view of America's past. [11]

To sum up, this introduction has postulated two major assumptions regarding the writing of American history: that "every true history is contemporary history" because external pressures of contemporary events have tended to color to some degree the view of scholars writing about the past; and that scholars have been affected also by internal pressures within the historical profession itself which led them to reevaluate and revise their points of view periodically. If these premises were valid in the past, we may be certain that our view of American history is destined to undergo changes in the future.

---

[11]John Higham, "Hanging Together: Divergent Unities in American History," *Journal of American History* 61 (June 1974):5.

# 2

# *The Puritans*

## Bigots or Builders?

Puritanism occupies a crucial position in the mainstream of American thought. The term *Puritanism* is normally used to identify the religious philosophy and intellectual outlook which characterized New England's first settlers. But as the descendants of New Englanders migrated from the Northeast to pioneer in the West, they carried with them traits of the Puritan mind clear across the continent. Many historians, therefore, have postulated a direct connection between Puritanism and the subsequent development of American civilization. Indeed, one colonial scholar has gone so far as to remark, "Without some understanding of Puritanism . . . there is no understanding of America."[1]

Just what that understanding of Puritanism should be, however, is a matter of dispute. To one group of historians, the Puritans were reactionary bigots—people opposed to freedom of thought, religious liberty, and the idea of democratic government. For these historians, Massachusetts represents a perfect case study of the kind of undemocratic colony the Puritans founded. Massachusetts was a theocracy—a state in which the civil government was under the control of the ministers or churches. The colony was dominated by a Puritan oligarchy of ministers and religious-minded lay leaders who worked hand-in-hand to maintain a rigid religious orthodoxy and to keep themselves in political power. Resisting change and repressing all dissenting views, these Puritan oligarchs banished independent-minded persons like Anne Hutchinson and Roger Williams whose radical religious ideas represented a threat to the more orthodox views in the colony. The Puritan clergy in particular were intolerant and narrow in their viewpoint. By rejecting the new ideas of Newtonian science and remaining indifferent to cultural matters, the ministers froze all freedom of thought in Massachusetts; they imposed a "glacial period" on the intellectual life of the colony from the 1630s to the outbreak of the American Revolution.

A second group of historians, however, took a much more sympa-

---

[1] Perry Miller, *The American Puritans* (New York, 1956), p. ix.

thetic view of the Puritans and developments in Massachusetts. To them the Puritans represented the torchbearers of religious liberty and political freedom—brave pioneers who contributed significantly to the formation of American democracy. The strict discipline and control exercised by the Puritan oligarchy in Massachusetts was necessitated by the rigors and demands of a frontier environment. Rather than being hostile to science and indifferent to culture, the Puritan clergy did everything possible to stimulate intellectual activity. In fact, it was largely through the efforts of their ministers that the Puritans founded the first college and public school system in the American colonies. These conflicting interpretations of the Puritans and the question of the influence of Puritanism on American life began with the founding of New England and are with us still.

The image of the Puritans down through American history has been a favorable one for the most part. One need not look far for the reasons behind this pro-Puritan attitude. Until well into the nineteenth century, the writing of American history and literature was dominated by New Englanders who were themselves the descendants of Puritans. The so-called filiopietist school of historians, reflecting both ancestor worship and provincial pride, identified the Puritans as the source of all virtues attributed to the American people—thrift, hard work, moral earnestness, and a sense of social responsibility. The accepted view among these historians was that America's political and religious liberty of the nineteenth century sprang from the seventeenth-century Puritan tradition.

John Gorham Palfrey, a leader of the filiopietist school, took this typical approach in his five-volume *History of New England* (1858–1890). A descendant of early-seventeenth-century New England stock, Harvard graduate, and Unitarian clergyman from Boston, Palfrey deeply admired his ancestors and his work was one long paean of praise in their behalf. "In the colonial history of New England," he wrote, "we follow the strenuous action of intelligent and honest men in building up a free, strong, enlightened, and happy state."[2] John Winthrop emerged as one of Palfrey's heroes, because in his eyes this builder of the Bay Colony had helped to establish the idea of self-government in America. "The influence of his genius and character," said Palfrey, "have been felt through seven generations of a rapidly multiplying people."[3] Biased in favor of the Puritan oligarchy, Palfrey could see few flaws in the Massachusetts clergy and defended the actions of the ministers against such disruptive religious radicals as Anne Hutchinson.

A few New England historians, like Charles Francis Adams and

---

[2] John Gorham Palfrey, *History of New England* (Boston, 1875), 4:x.
[3] *Ibid.* (Boston, 1860), 2:266.

Brooks Adams, managed to shake off their chauvinism in looking back at their forebears. Although the two brothers were members of the famous Adams family, Harvard graduates, and eminent New Englanders, they took a dim view of the interpretations that pictured their Puritan ancestors as the founders of America's religious and political liberty. Both men considered the Puritan clergy in Massachusetts a tyrannical force—one which fostered religious intolerance, political oligarchy, and intellectual apathy. But the Adams brothers represented very much of a minority view among American historians near the turn of the century.

As early as the 1920s there was a marked change in attitude toward New England Puritanism as historians and commentators began to reexamine different aspects of American culture. The shift in emphasis to a large degree arose from the intellectual currents at work during that period. Disillusioned by the bickering that broke out among the Allies at the close of World War I and longing to return to the supposed isolationist ways of the prewar days, America turned her back on Europe and underwent a wave of cultural nationalism. Some writers began to disparage or minimize the influence of Europe upon American society and institutions in the past. They turned instead to a reexamination of the nation's history with the hope of discovering what was unique and indigenous in the American tradition. It was in this spirit that many writers took a second look at Puritanism.

In certain literary circles the reexamination of Puritanism in these terms led to the conclusion that the Puritan heritage was *not* an integral part of America's true tradition. H. L. Mencken, the social satirist, typified many of the alienated intellectuals who took a debunking attitude toward the Puritans in the 1920s. Defining Puritanism as "the haunting fear that someone, somewhere, may be happy," Mencken equated the Puritan heritage of the 1600s with the narrow-minded bigots of his own day who wanted to censor books, to continue Prohibition, and to perpetuate an inhibited way of life. Mencken attacked the Puritan heritage primarily because he believed it had held back the growth of realism in American literature.[4]

In historical circles the burst of cultural nationalism manifested itself in a reaction against the imperial school of colonial historians led by Herbert L. Osgood and Charles M. Andrews. The imperial school of historians viewed the American colonies as a natural outgrowth and extension of British culture. Influenced by the disenchantment with Europe, however, scholars began searching for uniquely American traditions—such as Puritanism—that might have developed differently and apart from our British heritage. Thus, many historians writing about

---

[4]Richard Schlatter, "The Puritan Strain," in *The Reconstruction of American History*, ed. John Higham (New York, 1962), p. 30.

Puritanism in the 1920s did so with the hope of relating the Puritan
heritage to the development of certain peculiar national characteristics of
the American people as a whole.

The rise of intellectual history in the post–World War I period was,
perhaps, an even more important force than cultural nationalism in
directing attention of scholars to the study of Puritanism. Throughout
the nineteenth and early twentieth centuries, historians who wrote
about Puritanism dealt almost exclusively with its political and institutional aspects. Relatively little attention was paid to Puritan ideas and
culture. In the 1920s, however, American historians began to question
whether they could properly assess the function of Puritan governments, churches, and schools without understanding the history of
ideas behind such institutions. Throwing off the old distrust of the study
of ideas that had characterized much of nineteenth-century scholarship,
historians now forged ahead on the assumption that the study of Puritan
thought was crucial to any examination of Puritanism.

One final development during the 1920s which also affected the approach to Puritanism was the influence of the Progressive school of
historians. This school had arisen during the Populist and Progressive
era, and, in many instances, its adherents were strongly committed to
reform endeavors. Viewing the contemporary social problems which
they felt had resulted from the inequities in the distribution of wealth
and power in modern industrialized America, the Progressive historians
tended to read the social conflicts of their own day back into the nation's
past. Hence they began to rewrite American history in terms of
conflict—as a continuous struggle between the forces of liberalism and
conservatism, aristocracy and democracy, and the rich and the poor.
Many of these scholars also adopted an economic interpretation of history which colored their view of movements and men in America's past.
Some of the proponents of the Progressive school who took up the topic
of Puritanism, therefore, were destined to arrive at strikingly different
conclusions than earlier historians.

Influenced by these forces, a triumvirate of scholars—James Truslow
Adams, Vernon L. Parrington, and Thomas J. Wertenbaker—founded
an anti-Puritan school of historians in the 1920s which rejected the findings of the filiopietists. Adopting a more critical attitude, these historians pictured the Puritans as reactionary rather than progressive, authoritarian rather than democratic, bigoted rather than broad-minded,
and pious hypocrites rather than sincere and devoted believers. These
scholars prided themselves on being "realists" and in the debunking era
of the postwar period they found a receptive audience when they attacked the myth that the Puritans had founded American democracy.

James Truslow Adams inaugurated this cult of anti-Puritanism with
his book, *The Founding of New England*, published in 1921. Viewing the

Puritans largely in political terms, Adams came to the conclusion that their leaders were totally undemocratic. In Massachusetts, he observed, the ministers and magistrates worked together to regulate the public lives of the inhabitants in order to bring them into harmony with the expressed will of God, as it was interpreted by these self-appointed rulers. "In such a church-state, no civil question could be considered aside from its possible religious bearings; no religious opinion could be discussed apart from its political implications. It was a system which could be maintained permanently only by the most rigid denial of political free speech and religious toleration."[5]

Puritanism repressed not only the public life of the individual, Adams claimed, but his private behavior as well. With the ministers and magistrates interpreting the will of God, the Puritan was left with no "free spaces in life." No detail of the Puritan's personal conduct was too small to escape a ruling by the oligarchy. "The cut of clothes, the names he bore, the most ordinary social usages, could all be regulated in accordance with the will of God," concluded Adams.[6] As a historian with a libertarian outlook, Adams resented the conformity he felt had been forced upon Massachusetts colonists.

Adams reflected also the economic interpretation of history which influenced the thinking of many historians in the 1920s. He interpreted the Puritan creed as being primarily an economic ideology fashioned by the middle class to rationalize its dominance over the lower classes. In his opinion, the Puritan leaders of Massachusetts had been motivated mainly by economic rather than religious considerations in moving to the New World. Once in America, "they looked with fear, as well as jealousy, upon any possibility of allowing control of policy of law and order, and of legislation concerning person and property, to pass to others."[7] To Adams the ministers, together with many of the lay leaders, formed an elite class that perpetuated an oligarchical form of government in order to protect their socioeconomic interests.

Vernon L. Parrington's stand on the Puritans was similar to that of Adams, but Parrington approached the problem from a different viewpoint. The first volume of his *Main Currents in American Thought,* published in 1927, *The Colonial Mind,* was intellectualized literary history. Viewing literature as a body of ideas, Parrington read the leading authors, intellectuals, and politicians with the hope of writing a general history of American thought. Parrington symbolized the stimulus toward American intellectual history and helped to redefine the meaning of Puritanism in terms of the history of ideas.

---

[5]James T. Adams, *The Founding of New England* (Boston, 1921), p. 143.
[6]*Ibid.,* p. 79.
[7]*Ibid.,* p. 143.

Parrington's interpretation, however, was conditioned by the reformist spirit of the Populist-Progressive era through which he lived. Born in Kansas in 1871, he had grown up in the Populist period of rebellious agrarian radicalism. Although his work was not published until some years later, Parrington began writing in 1913—a peak year in the Progressive movement when reformers were fighting to achieve certain goals of social justice within American society. Observing these social struggles about him, Parrington tended to interpret all of American history in terms of continuous conflict. Broadly speaking, he saw the American past as a clash of ideologies between liberals and conservatives running from the colonial period to his own time.

Liberalism was America's true tradition, Parrington concluded, and Puritanism had contributed little to this heritage. Parrington frankly admitted in his preface to *The Colonial Mind* that his viewpoint was "liberal rather than conservative, Jeffersonian rather than Federalistic." In his opinion the history of American thought in the colonial and early national period could best be seen in the figure of Thomas Jefferson and within the ideological framework of Jeffersonian liberalism. Seeing much of American history as Jeffersonianism versus Hamiltonianism writ large, Parrington proceeded to push this dichotomy backwards into the colonial period. To his satisfaction at least, there emerged a consistent pattern in colonial thought. There was a line of liberalism running from Roger Williams to Benjamin Franklin and down to Jefferson. The line of conservatism could be traced through John Cotton and Jonathan Edwards to Hamilton.

To Parrington, orthodox Puritanism was a reactionary theology. In New England, the "absolutist theology . . . conceived of human nature as inherently evil . . . postulated a divine sovereignty absolute and arbitrary, and projected caste divisions into eternity."[8] A succession of liberal heroes, like Roger Williams and Anne Hutchinson, rose up to oppose such reactionary views. These religious liberals and heretics, Parrington wrote, represented the liberal tradition that America was destined to follow. "In banishing the Antinomians and Separatists and Quakers, the Massachusetts magistrates cast out the spirit of liberalism."[9] For Parrington, then, Puritanism played no part in the native tradition of American liberalism.

Thomas J. Wertenbaker, the third member of the anti-Puritan school, agreed with Parrington that the Massachusetts oligarchy was illiberal and intolerant. "The sermons and published writings of the founders of Massachusetts," Wertenbaker wrote in 1927, "make it clear that they

---

[8]Vernon L. Parrington, *Main Currents in American Thought*, 3 vols. (New York, 1927–1930), 1:iv.

[9]*Ibid.*, 1:15.

never entertained the thought of opening the doors of their new Zion to those who differed from them. So far from being champions of toleration, they opposed it bitterly."[10] Two decades later in his book *The Puritan Oligarchy*, Wertenbaker claimed that the Puritan leaders had held Massachusetts back and that New England failed to make any contribution to the mainstream of American life until the power of the ministers and magistrates was broken. His work strikes a note similar to that of Parrington: "Most of the contributions were made after the fall of the Puritan oligarchy, and the men to whom the chief credit is due were not its supporters, but, on the contrary, those who rebelled against it."[11] To Wertenbaker, then, the Puritans were bigots who blocked the path of progress in the development of a better America.

The anti-Puritan writers of the 1920s were followed in the 1930s by a host of historians at Harvard University who were more sympathetic and understanding in their study of seventeenth-century Puritanism. Three of these scholars—Samuel Eliot Morison, Clifford K. Shipton, and Perry Miller—proceeded to rehabilitate the somewhat battered reputation of the early Puritan leaders. Less imbued with the idea of progress than their predecessors, these historians did not view the Puritan oligarchy as a barrier blocking the irresistible march of events toward a better world in which freedom of thought and the idea of representative government would inevitably triumph. Rather than judging the Puritans in terms of twentieth-century liberalism, the Harvard historians studied these early pioneers in terms of their own age and background.

The work of these three scholars also showed an increasing awareness of the role of ideas in history. All of them devoted more time to reconstructing the circumstances surrounding Puritan thought and culture. Unlike Parrington, they evaluated Puritan ideas on their own merit rather than trying to fit them into a rigidly deterministic framework. One result of their efforts was that the study of the colonial period showed more emphasis upon intellectual history than works written in the 1930s about other eras in American history.

Samuel Eliot Morison, then a professor at Harvard, published in 1930 his *Builders of the Bay Colony*, a book which proved to be the turning point in this fresh appraisal of the Puritans. Writing in a brilliant literary style, Morison transformed the rigidly stereotyped Puritans presented by Adams, Parrington, and Wertenbaker into living, breathing human beings. As he recalled two decades later, his was a lonely voice at the time "crying in the wilderness against the common notion of the grim Puritan . . . the steeple-hatted, long-faced Puritan living in a log cabin

---

[10]Thomas J. Wertenbaker, *The First Americans, 1607–1690* (New York, 1927), pp. 90–91.
[11]Thomas J. Wertenbaker, *The Puritan Oligarchy* (New York, 1947), p. 345.

and planning a witch-hunt or a battue of Quakers as a holiday diver-
sion."[12] Morison humanized many of the major Puritan figures by showing that they were not averse to the simple pleasures of life—sex, strong
drink, and colorful clothes—but that their dedication and unswerving
zeal to serve God provided them with even greater satisfaction.

In a second work, *The Puritan Pronaos*, published in 1936, Morison
emphasized the intellectual content of Puritanism. Morison described
the Puritans as humanists, intellectual heirs of the Renaissance as well as
of the Reformation and medieval Christianity. They preserved in their
culture certain aspects of the Renaissance humanist tradition—especially
the study of classical literature—far better than the non-Puritan settlers
in other English colonies. From the Reformation, the Puritans had
gained such a zeal for education and love of learning that they insisted
upon founding elementary and grammar schools and setting up a university even while they were still clearing the forests in the hostile frontier environment in Massachusetts. Morison noted that the Puritans
were not only vitally interested in schools, printing presses, and li-
braries, but also in contemporary English literature and the latest scientific theories of their day. The Puritan creed, he concluded, was "an
intellectualized form of Christianity that steered a middle course between a passive acceptance of ecclesiastical authority on the one hand
and ignorant emotionalism on the other, [and] stimulated mental activity on the part of those who professed it."[13]

Morison's books helped to establish the changed view of the Puritans
which was basically sympathetic in outlook. To Morison the Puritans'
greatest contribution was their success in transmitting the intellectual
and cultural heritage of western civilization to the New World. While the
struggle with frontier conditions in other colonies led to intellectual
degeneracy and, in some instances to spiritual decay, the Puritans at
great sacrifice managed to transplant those features of civilized life and
learning which have characterized the finer aspects of American civilization. The primitive ideas and beliefs of the Puritans, Morison maintained, represented the first, faint stirrings of the American mind that
emerged in full bloom in the nineteenth and twentieth centuries.

Clifford K. Shipton, the second of the Harvard historians, produced
a series of articles in the 1930s whose general theme was expressed in
the title of one of them—"A Plea for Puritanism." One of the most
militant defenders of the Puritan contribution to American democratic
thought, Shipton was particularly concerned about what he felt was an

---

[12]Samuel Eliot Morison, "Faith of a Historian," *American Historical Review* 56 (January
1951):272.

[13]Samuel Eliot Morison, *The Puritan Pronaos* (New York, 1936), p. 264. This work was
reissued under the title *The Intellectual Life of Colonial New England* (New York, 1956).

unfair portrayal of the Puritan clergy as undemocratic and bigoted leaders. He rejected the thesis of James Truslow Adams, who claimed that
an unpopular clergy had tyrannized Massachusetts in the early years
and had maintained an undemocratic hold over the people by means of
a religious requirement for suffrage exercised under the old Bay Colony
charter. Once the oppressed masses gained the franchise under the new
charter of 1691, Adams had suggested, they had promptly used the
ballot to overthrow the unpopular theocracy made up of clergy-
dominated magistrates. Shipton pointed out, however, that there was
no widespread anticlerical feeling in the Puritan colonies. Moreover,
once the religious requirement for the franchise was removed, there was
no great turnover in political leaders.

Shipton likewise attacked the stereotyped picture of a bigoted clergy
that prohibited freedom of thought and stifled intellectual inquiry. The
clergy were the most learned class in the Puritan colonies, according to
Shipton; they were always open-minded and receptive to new ideas.
"Far from being narrow bigots, the ministers were the leaders in every
field of intellectual advance in New England."[14] They were tolerant in
religious matters, leading their congregations in the changes that
Puritanism was undergoing, and making allowances for the theological
differences with other sects.

Three decades later, in the 1960s, Shipton was still challenging those
historians who claimed Massachusetts was a theocracy. The sources of
both civil and religious authority in the colony, he noted, were located
on the local level. In the political sphere, authority tended to devolve
upon the town governments rather than to remain at the provincial
level. In the area of religion, the churches evolved along congregational
lines, each church developing its own doctrine from a consensus of the
religious views of the congregation or town inhabitants. If political
power rested for the most part in the towns, and if the magistrates had
to look to the local level for approval of their actions, how, asked Shipton, could an oligarchy of Puritan ministers control the government of
Massachusetts as a theocracy? If each church developed its own doctrine
from a consensus of the congregation or inhabitants of individual communities, how could historians speak of the "Puritan orthodoxy" or an
"established church" in describing the religious situation in Massachusetts?[15]

The work of Perry Miller, the third of the Harvard historians, constituted an important landmark in American intellectual history. In the

---

[14]Clifford K. Shipton, "A Plea for Puritanism," *American Historical Review* 40 (April
1935):467.

[15]Clifford K. Shipton, "The Locus of Authority in Colonial Massachusetts," in *Law and
Authority in Colonial America,* ed. George A. Billias (Barre, 1965), pp. 136–148.

1930s Miller published two works, *Orthodoxy in Massachusetts* and *The New England Mind: The Seventeenth Century*, which dissected the principal ideas in Puritan thought. Miller argued that reason had played a major role in Puritan theology; that the Puritans looked upon man as an essentially rational and responsible being despite their belief that he was tainted by original sin. By holding such views, the Puritans were taking part in the great intellectual revolution that was being fought all over Europe—the revolt against scholasticism. "Puritanism," according to Miller, "was one of the major expressions of the Western intellect, [in] that it [had] achieved an organized synthesis of concepts which are fundamental to our culture."[16]

In *Orthodoxy in Massachusetts,* published in 1933, Miller showed the seriousness with which people in the early 1600s took their religious ideas and their willingness to act upon them. He held there was a continuous line of thought stretching from the early stages of Puritanism in old England to the founding of the political, religious, and social institutions of early New England. The founders of the Bay Colony, while still in England, believed in a congregational form of church government, he noted, and had opposed the hierarchical structure of the Church of England. As nonseparating Congregationalists they remained within the fold of the church, however, hoping to persuade others to their point of view. After moving to the New World, they could claim that any church founded in Massachusetts was an integral part of the Church of England—since they still considered themselves nonseparatists. With such a claim to legitimacy they could set up a church and state, define heresy, and maintain religious orthodoxy without fear of British reprisal. The problems the Puritans encountered in putting their ideas of church government into practice in Massachusetts, Miller observed, arose more from their experiences in New England than opposition from old England. Much of what Miller had to say in this work was not new, but he demonstrated as never before that the history of the Bay Colony during its first two decades could be "strung on the thread of an idea."[17]

Six years after the publication of his first work, Miller produced *The New England Mind: The Seventeenth Century,* a more detailed analysis of the ideas of New England Puritanism. Viewing Puritanism as a coherent intellectual system, Miller took up its principal concepts and showed how each was related to the whole and to the Puritan view of man. He described the interlocking system of covenants—the covenant of grace, social covenant, and church covenant—which formed the core of Puritan theology. Miller demonstrated more conclusively than earlier

---

[16]Perry Miller, *The New England Mind: The Seventeenth Century* (New York, 1939), p. viii.
[17]Perry Miller, *Orthodoxy in Massachusetts 1630–1650* (Cambridge, Mass., 1933), p. xii.

scholars that the doctrine of the covenant was the keystone to Puritan thought. He argued that this covenant theology made allowances for man's activity in the process of his own salvation; thus Puritanism, rather than being fatalistic in outlook, was a stimulus to action. Some of these ideas he traced back to their origins in Renaissance humanism, scholasticism, and the writings of the French philosopher Petrus Ramus. Running throughout this work was the major theme that Miller had introduced in his earlier book: the transformation of Puritan thought as New World experiences and the passage of time made an impact upon the ideas the settlers had originally brought over with them.

In the second volume of *The New England Mind*, published in 1953 and subtitled *From Colony to Province*, Miller explored his main theme more fully. The first generation of Puritans, he noted, was imbued with a deep sense of mission and viewed themselves as Europeans participating in a worldwide struggle which pitted Protestantism against all its enemies. During the second and third generations, however, much of this zeal was lost and the Puritans became more provincial as they began grappling with the day-to-day problems in the New World. The original Puritan idea of society broke down, or, at any rate, underwent a profound alteration. Material success within the colony undermined spiritual life; Christian brotherhood and Puritan consensus gave way to personal squabbles; theological conflicts were replaced by political struggles; and secular values triumphed over religious aims. Miller's description of the metamorphosis of the Puritan mind from the arrival of the first settlers in the 1620s to the beginnings of Enlightenment thought in the 1720s thereby became a tale of irony as well as change.

Miller's works succeeded in lifting the study of New England Puritanism out of the narrow framework of national history and placed it within the much broader context of world history. He was able to discover hitherto unsuspected connections between the ideas in America and those in the rest of the world—between New England Puritanism and Renaissance humanism, the Reformation, and scholasticism. In his hands the study of Puritanism became more than a history of the ideas of the New England founders; it became instead a study of an important epoch in the intellectual history of the Western world. The first selection presents Miller's point of view and is drawn from a book of readings he coauthored with Thomas H. Johnson.

Miller's work was continued and expanded by his outstanding student, Edmund S. Morgan, one of America's most distinguished colonial historians. Morgan wrote a number of works on the Puritans which clearly followed the intellectual history tradition established by Miller. One was the biography of John Winthrop entitled *The Puritan Dilemma*, published in 1958. Winthrop's dilemma was that of every Puritan: whether to withdraw from a world he believed immoral in order to maintain the purity of his religious principles; or to struggle to live a righteous life within a world he viewed as being wrong. In *Visible Saints* (1963) Morgan revised Miller by showing that the practice of admitting to church membership persons professing a declaration of religious conversion was first put into effect in Massachusetts Bay by nonseparatist Puritans. Although theologians of English congregationalism had written about limiting church membership to such "visible saints," congregationalism in this form was an American and not an English "invention" as Miller had argued.

After World War II, there was a reappraisal of the work of the three Harvard historians on the grounds that their writings had tended to overintellectualize the Puritans and to place them too much in the European tradition. A new group of historians—the neoconservative school—arose to challenge not only the findings of the Harvard historians but those of historians like Parrington who viewed American intellectual history in somewhat oversimplified terms. The neoconservative scholars were reacting against those Progressive historians, like Parrington, Beard, and Turner, who pictured American history in terms of a continuous conflict or clash of ideologies—as a struggle either of class against class, of section against section, or of a liberal ideology versus a conservative one.

The neoconservative school of historians, on the whole, tended to view the nation's past in terms of a basic consensus among the American people. To reinforce America's national unity—which was threatened by a series of seemingly endless crises during the Cold War years—many neoconservative historians stressed the power of long-established institutions rather than the influence of ideas. Indeed, in some cases, these scholars argued that the Puritans had developed a tradition that was uniquely American rather than European in origin.

The outstanding spokesman of the neoconservative school on the subject of the Puritans was Daniel J. Boorstin, then professor of history at the University of Chicago. In two works published in the 1950s, *The Genius of American Politics* and *The Americans: The Colonial Experience,* Boorstin argued that the Puritans arrived in the New World with their theology already fully developed and therefore felt less of a need to theorize or to indulge in idle speculation on philosophical questions. Once in America, the Puritans were not distracted much by theological questions, because they insisted upon orthodoxy in religious matters and allowed no dissent. Dissenters were driven out of Massachusetts, but the presence of vast reaches of free land in New England made it possible for them to go off and found their own colonies. "A dissension which in England would have created a new sect within Puritanism," wrote Boorstin, "simply produced another colony in New England."[18]

---

[18]Daniel J. Boorstin, *The Americans: The Colonial Experience* (New York, 1958), p. 8.

Boorstin's Puritans were a practical people, more preoccupied in applying their religious beliefs to the communities they were building than in
debating the finer points of theology.

Pragmatism, Boorstin believed, was the outstanding characteristic of
the New England Puritans. Taking their religious beliefs for granted,
they concentrated upon establishing institutions—political, legal, social,
and educational—which would embody their point of view. While these
institutions proved successful in building communities, they led ultimately to the undoing of Puritan philosophy. As Boorstin so aptly put it,
Puritanism moved from "Providence to Pride"—from a belief in divine
providence as a prime mover in history to pride in man as the shaper of
events as he succeeded in mastering America's frontier environment.
Success led increasingly to a nontheoretical approach to problems and a
greater reliance upon man-made institutions rather than religious ideas.
For Boorstin, then, the Puritans were successful because of their practicality, not their philosophy.

Boorstin believed that the Puritan tradition—that of scrapping a
European blueprint for a society based upon the ideas of English
Puritanism and substituting instead a pragmatic approach arising from
American experiences—was symbolic of our entire history as a people.
Such a pragmatic approach, in time, led to the development of an
American way of life characterized by an absence of ideological conflicts,
an emphasis upon practical politics, and a distrust of theories as a solu-
tion to problems. This American life-style was unique and differed
markedly from that of Europe. In New England Puritanism, Boorstin
saw the beginnings of America's pragmatic tradition.

American historians thus seemed to come full circle on the question
of Puritanism. Moving from an uncritical acceptance of the Puritans in
the nineteenth century to an anti-Puritan bias in the 1920s which almost
refused to recognize any role for them in the American tradition, historians now praised the Puritans and restored them to an important place
in our heritage. Neoconservative scholars, however, appeared to admire
the Puritans for different reasons from their predecessors. Having studied the mind of the Puritans, they admired their institutional achievements, sober practicality, moral vigor, and religious dedication. They
appreciated the Puritan belief in religious absolutes that enabled these
settlers to build communities, churches, and colleges in the midst of a
wilderness. At times they even seemed to condone the tendency on the
part of the Puritans to force these absolutes upon dissenters on the
grounds that the individualistic ideas of such men might threaten to
destroy the whole community.

Since the 1950s, two new developments have occurred in the study
of Puritanism. One was the revisionist movement that modified the
approach and findings of the most profound of the Puritan scholars—
Perry Miller. Among Miller's most important interpretations were the

following: the heavy emphasis upon reason and intellectualism within the Puritan creed; the point that the New England Puritans had formulated the covenant theology to free themselves from the strictness of Calvin's teachings; and the idea of a spiritual decline and gradual disintegration of the New England "mind" primarily as the result of the weakening of religious orthodoxy in Massachusetts in the seventeenth century.

Revisionist historians challenged Miller's conclusions on these points. Alan Simpson's work, which compared Puritanism in England and New England, stressed the emotional and experiential side of the religion because Simpson felt that Miller had overintellectualized the Puritans. Norman Pettit's *The Heart Prepared* suggested that the philosophical differences between John Calvin and Puritanism were less great than Miller had presented them. Robert Pope in his *Half-Way Covenant* argued that New England Puritans in the latter part of the seventeenth century did not decline from the religious fervor of the first founders, and resorted to quantitative techniques to support his conclusions. Michael Walzer, a political scientist, has used theories and models of contemporary political behavior to study the attitudes of the radical religious "saints" of seventeenth-century England.[19]

Darrett B. Rutman, like Robert Pope, placed the intellectual history of the Puritans within a different social and economic context than Miller. Miller presented Puritanism from the point of view of the leadership, i.e., the minister in the pulpit. Rutman in *American Puritanism* analyzed religion from the perspective of the followership—the common man seated in the congregation. He argued that Puritanism was best understood in terms of the interaction between the practices of laymen and the ideas of ministers. Puritanism, according to Rutman, was not only a philosophy but a way of life. The second selection in this chapter is from Rutman's work.

Recent historians of New England such as David Hall and Timothy Breen approached the problem of Puritanism in a different way by examining the relationship between Puritanism ideas and the region's social and economic environment. Hall's study of the Puritan ministry, *The Faithful Shepherd*, went beyond Miller. He maintained that the migration from England and community-building in the New World posed new problems for many ministers and forced them to rethink the older teachings they had inherited from English Puritanism. But Hall concluded

---

[19]Alan Simpson, *Puritanism in Old and New England* (Chicago, 1955); Norman Pettit, *The Heart Prepared: Grace and Conversion in Puritan Spiritual Life* (New Haven, 1966); Darrett B. Rutman, *Winthrop's Boston: Portrait of a Puritan Town, 1630–1649* (Chapel Hill, 1965); Robert G. Pope, *The Half-Way Covenant; Church Membership in Puritan New England* (Princeton, 1969); and Michael Walzer, *The Revolution of the Saints: A Study in the Origins of Radical Politics* (Cambridge, 1965).

that the ideas and values derived from England were probably more influential in shaping the New England ministers than the new environment itself. Breen, in his book *The Character of a Good Ruler,* did for political thought what Hall had done for religious thought; he pointed out there was an essential continuity in Puritan thinking about political matters. At the same time, Breen showed that ideas sometimes changed with conditions—even though such changes did not necessarily represent a decline in religious fervor. For these two scholars the transition from the age of faith to the age of reason was not nearly so abrupt as Miller had seemed to imply. Taking all these revisions into account, many scholars still consider Miller's work to be the best modern synthesis we have of Puritanism.[20]

A second major development was the appearance of the "new social historians" who focused their attention upon the communities the Puritans built and upon their communitarian values. These scholars emphasized the need to understand the nature of Puritan institutions and behavior, and they turned away increasingly from Miller's intellectual approach, which stressed theology. They employed instead multidisciplinary methods to demonstrate how Puritan values had shaped the formation of New England communities.

The Puritans, according to many "new social historians," emphasized consensus and conformity and proceeded to erect communities on the basis of these values. Kai T. Erikson, for example, used sociological and psychological theories to analyze Puritan values. In his *Wayward Puritans,* Erikson studied those groups the Puritans defined as deviants and then sought to establish the social norms that constituted the "boundaries" of behavior within Puritan society. Michael Zuckerman, on the other hand, applied the conceptual tools of cultural anthropology. He concluded that a kind of communal consensus created peace, order, and harmony within a number of eighteenth-century Massachusetts towns, and that these communities were "peaceable kingdoms" despite the existence of certain underlying social tensions.[21]

A host of New England community case studies analyzed the impact of Puritanism on the everyday life of early pioneers. Sumner Chilton Powell's *Puritan Village,* for instance, demonstrated that the local English institutions and customs in communities were transformed by the New World setting and modified by the Puritans to produce a new kind of town. What had been transplanted was also transformed. Kenneth

---

[20]David D. Hall, *The Faithful Shepherd: A History of the New England Ministry in the Seventeenth Century* (Chapel Hill, 1972) and Timothy Breen, *The Character of a Good Ruler: Puritan Political Ideas in New England, 1630–1730* (New Haven, 1970).

[21]Kai T. Erikson, *Wayward Puritans: A Study in the Sociology of Deviance* (New York, 1966) and Michael Zuckerman, *Peaceable Kingdoms: New England Towns in the Eighteenth Century* (New York, 1970).

Lockridge's *A New England Town* traced the evolution of local institutions in Dedham, Massachusetts, over a one-hundred-year period. Lockridge concluded that Dedham during its first fifty years had been a "Christian Utopian Closed Corporate Community." In the second fifty years, however, conflicts eroded the prevailing consensus and shattered the Puritan vision of a perfect society. Paul Boyer and Stephen Nissenbaum in their study of witchcraft in seventeenth-century Massachusetts, *Salem Possessed,* investigated the tensions that arose as the result of a growing gap between Puritan ideals and social realities. Major problems developed because of the explosive rate of population growth, decreasing availability of land, economic pressures, and the changing role of the church. All these developments conflicted with accepted Puritan values. The outbreak of witchcraft hysteria in Salem, according to Boyer and Nissenbaum, was caused by this conflict rather than by the Puritan dogmatism and bigotry stressed in the older and more traditional interpretations.[22]

Studies of the colonial family also provided important insights into Puritan values and behavior. Edmund Morgan's old monograph, *Puritan Family,* broke new ground by revealing the influence that Puritan ideas had exerted upon family functions and the personal relationships among family members. John Demos in his book *A Little Commonwealth* used the techniques of demography, social psychology, and archaeology to analyze family life in Plymouth colony during the seventeenth century. Philip Greven in his *Four Generations,* like Demos, concluded that the family was the key institution within the Puritan community. Greven studied changes in the family household and community structure in Andover, Massachusetts, over a long span of time and demonstrated that birth and death rates, marriage customs, the relations between generations, and landholding practices helped to shape the outlines of this Puritan community.[23]

All of these recent trends in writing about Puritans reveal a shift away from intellectual history and Miller's older synthesis. By using a multidisciplinary approach, the "new social historians" have come up with new research strategies to analyze Puritanism. They have been able also to raise probing questions on the subject by resorting to social science techniques. The "new social historians" have moved away from Miller's focus upon Puritan elites—the ministers and the magistrates—and have

[22]Sumner Chilton Powell, *Puritan Village* (Middleton, 1963); Kenneth A. Lockridge, *A New England Town: The First Hundred Years* (New York, 1970); and Paul Boyer and Stephen Nissenbaum, *Salem Possessed: The Social Origins of Witchcraft* (Cambridge, 1974).

[23]Edmund S. Morgan, *Puritan Family: Essays on Religion and Domestic Relations in Seventeenth-Century New England* (Boston, 1944); John Demos, *A Little Commonwealth: Family Life in Plymouth Colony* (New York, 1970); and Philip J. Greven, Jr., *Four Generations: Population, Land, and Family in Colonial Andover, Massachusetts* (Ithaca, 1970).

concentrated more upon ordinary men and women living within communities, congregations, and families. The newfound emphasis upon Puritan communities and communitarian values has in many ways incorporated and redirected questions about consensus and conflict that older interpretations had emphasized. The study of Puritanism, in short, has clearly entered upon a post-Miller era.

In view of the conflicting schools of thought, how is the student of history to arrive at any proper evaluation of the Puritans? To do so, he must first ask the following questions. Were the Puritans primarily religious bigots or community builders? Were the Puritans pious idealists concerned mainly with establishing a Christian way of life, as Miller suggested? Or were they practical pioneers seeking only to erect frontier settlements? Were they the avant-garde of the movement that flowered into the evangelical Pietism of the eighteenth century in America? Or were they part of a reactionary movement that helped to extend the sixteenth century world of Calvin into the seventeenth century? Was Puritanism primarily a theology dedicated to a search for individual salvation? Or was it also a way of life that called for the regeneration of an entire society and thereby inspired the creation of new kinds of communities? Only by coming to grips with such crucial questions can one come to any meaningful conclusion about the place of the Puritan tradition in American history.

# Perry Miller and

# Thomas H. Johnson

PERRY MILLER (1905–1963) was professor of American literature at Harvard University until his death. He was the author of numerous articles and books, including *The New England Mind,* 2 vols. (1939–53), *Errand into the Wilderness* (1956), *Jonathan Edwards* (1949), and *The Life of the Mind in America: From the Revolution to the Civil War* (1965). THOMAS H. JOHNSON (1902– ) taught for many years at the Lawrenceville School in New Jersey as well as at a number of universities. He is the author of *Emily Dickinson: An Interpretive Biography* (1955) and *The Oxford Companion to American History* (1966).

Puritanism may perhaps be described as that point of view, that philosophy of life, that code of values, which was carried to New England by the first settlers in the early seventeenth century. Beginning thus, it has become one of the continuous factors in American life and American thought. Any inventory of the elements that have gone into the making of the "American mind" would have to commence with Puritanism. It is, indeed, only one among many: if we should attempt to enumerate these traditions, we should certainly have to mention such philosophies, such "isms," as the rational liberalism of Jeffersonian democracy, the Hamiltonian conception of conservatism and government, the Southern theory of racial aristocracy, the Transcendentalism of nineteenth-century New England, and what is generally spoken of as frontier individualism. Among these factors Puritanism has been perhaps the most conspicuous, the most sustained, and the most fecund. Its role in American thought has been almost the dominant one, for the descendants of Puritans have carried at least some habits of the Puritan mind into a variety of pursuits, have spread across the country, and in many fields of activity have played a leading part. The force of Puritanism, furthermore, has been accentuated because it was the first of these traditions to be fully articulated, and because it has inspired certain traits which have persisted long after the vanishing of the original creed. Without some understanding of Puritanism, it may safely be said, there is no understanding of America.

Perry Miller and Thomas H. Johnson, eds., *The Puritans* (New York: American Book Company, 1938), pp. 1–19. Reprinted with omissions by permission of the American Book Company.

Yet important as Puritanism has undoubtedly been in shaping the nation, it is more easily described than defined. It figures frequently in controversy of the last decade, very seldom twice with exactly the same connotation. Particularly of recent years has it become a hazardous feat to run down its meaning. In the mood of revolt against the ideals of previous generations which has swept over our period, Puritanism has become a shining target for many sorts of marksmen. Confusion becomes worse confounded if we attempt to correlate modern usages with anything that can be proved pertinent to the original Puritans themselves. To seek no further, it was the habit of proponents for the repeal of the Eighteenth Amendment during the 1920s to dub Prohibitionists "Puritans," and cartoonists made the nation familiar with an image of the Puritan: a gaunt, lank-haired killjoy, wearing a black steeple hat and compounding for sins he was inclined to by damning those to which he had no mind. Yet any acquaintance with the Puritans of the seventeenth century will reveal at once, not only that they did not wear such hats but also that they attired themselves in all the hues of the rainbow, and furthermore that in their daily life they imbibed what seem to us prodigious quantities of alcoholic beverages, with never the slightest inkling that they were doing anything sinful. True, they opposed drinking to excess, and ministers preached lengthy sermons condemning intoxication, but at such pious ceremonies as the ordination of new ministers the bill for rum, wine, and beer consumed by the congregation was often staggering. Increase Mather himself—who in popular imagination is apt to figure along with his son Cotton as the archembodiment of the Puritan—said in one of his sermons:

> Drink is in it self a good creature of God, and to be received with thankfulness, but the abuse of drink is from Satan; the wine is from God, but the Drunkard is from the Devil.

Or again, the Puritan has acquired the reputation of having been blind to all aesthetic enjoyment and starved of beauty; yet the architecture of the Puritan age grows in the esteem of critics and the household objects of Puritan manufacture, pewter and furniture, achieve prohibitive prices by their appeal to discriminating collectors. Examples of such discrepancies between the modern usage of the word and the historical fact could be multiplied indefinitely. It is not the purpose of this volume to engage in controversy, nor does it intend particularly to defend the Puritan against the bewildering variety of critics who on every side today find him an object of scorn or pity. In his life he neither asked nor gave mercy to his foes; he demanded only that conflicts be joined on real and explicit issues. By examining his own words it may become possible to establish, for better or for worse, the meaning of Puritanism as the Puritan himself believed and practiced it.

Just as soon as we endeavor to free ourselves from prevailing conceptions or misconceptions, and to ascertain the historical facts about seventeenth-century New Englanders, we become aware that we face still another difficulty: not only must we extricate ourselves from interpretations that have been read into Puritanism by the twentieth century, but still more from those that have been attached to it by the eighteenth and nineteenth. The Puritan philosophy, brought to New England highly elaborated and codified, remained a fairly rigid orthodoxy during the seventeenth century. In the next age, however, it proved to be anything but static; by the middle of the eighteenth century there had proceeded from it two distinct schools of thought, almost unalterably opposed to each other. Certain elements were carried into the creeds and practices of the evangelical religious revivals, but others were perpetuated by the rationalists and the forerunners of Unitarianism. Consequently our conception of Puritanism is all too apt to be colored by subsequent happenings; we read ideas into the seventeenth century which belong to the eighteenth, and the real nature of Puritanism can hardly be discovered at all, because Puritanism itself became two distinct and contending things to two sorts of men. The most prevalent error arising from this fact has been the identification of Puritanism with evangelicalism in many accounts, though in histories written by Unitarian scholars the original doctrine has been almost as much distorted in the opposite direction.

Among the evangelicals the original doctrines were transformed or twisted into the new versions of Protestantism that spawned in the Great Awakening of the 1740s, in the succeeding revivals along the frontier and through the back country, in the centrifugal speculations of enraptured prophets and rabid sects in the nineteenth century. All these movements retained something of the theology or revived something of the intensity of spirit, but at the same time they threw aside so much of authentic Puritanism that there can be no doubt the founding fathers would vigorously have repudiated such progeny. They would have had no use, for instance, for the camp meeting and the revivalist orgy; "hitting the sawdust trail" would have been an action exceedingly distasteful to the most ardent among them. What we know as "fundamentalism" would have been completely antipathetic to them, for they never for one moment dreamed that the truth of scripture was to be maintained in spite of or against the evidences of reason, science, and learning. The sects that have arisen out of Puritanism have most strikingly betrayed their rebellion against the true spirit of their source by their attack upon the ideal of a learned ministry; Puritans considered religion a very complex, subtle, and highly intellectualized affair, and they trained their experts in theology with all the care we would lavish upon preparing men to be engineers or chemists. For the same reasons, Puritans would object strenuously to almost all recent attempts to "humanize" religion, to smooth over hard doctrines, to introduce sweetness and light at the cost of hardheaded realism and invincible logic. From their point of view, to bring Christ down to earth in such a fashion as is implied in statements we sometimes encounter—that He was the "first humanitarian" or that He would certainly endorse this or that political party—would seem to them frightful blasphemy. Puritanism was not only a religious creed, it was a philosophy and a metaphysic; it was an organization of man's whole life, emotional and intellectual, to a degree which has not been sustained by any denomination stemming from it. Yet because such creeds have sprung from Puritanism, the Puritans are frequently praised or blamed for qualities which never belonged to them or for ideas which originated only among their successors and which they themselves would have disowned.

On the other hand, if the line of development from Puritanism tends in one direction to frontier revivalism and evangelicalism, another line leads as directly to a more philosophical, critical, and even skeptical point of view. Unitarianism is as much the child of Puritanism as Methodism. And if the one accretion has colored or distorted our conception of the original doctrine, the other has done so no less. Descendants of the Puritans who revolted against what they considered the tyranny and cruelty of Puritan theology, who substituted taste and reason for dogma and authority and found the emotional fervor of the evangelicals so much sound and fury, have been prone to idealize their ancestors into their own image. A few decades ago it had become very much the mode to praise the Puritans for virtues which they did not possess and which they would not have considered virtues at all. In the pages of liberal historians, and above all in the speeches of Fourth of July orators, the Puritans have been hymned as the pioneers of religious liberty, though nothing was ever farther from their designs; they have been hailed as the forerunners of democracy, though if they were, it was quite beside their intention; they have been invoked in justification for an economic philosophy of free competition and laissez-faire, though they themselves believed in government regulation of business, the fixing of just prices, and the curtailing of individual profits in the interests of the welfare of the whole.

The moral of these reflections may very well be that it is dangerous to read history backwards, to interpret something that was by what it ultimately became, particularly when it became several things. . . . The Puritans were not a bashful race, they could speak out and did; in their own words they have painted their own portraits, their majestic strength and their dignity, their humanity and solidity, more accurately than any admirer had been able to do; and also they have betrayed the motes and beams in their own eyes more clearly than any enemy has been able to point them out.

Puritanism began as an agitation within the Church of England in the latter half of the sixteenth century. It was a movement for reform of that institution, and at the time no more constituted a distinct sect or denomination than the advocates of an amendment to the Constitution of the United States constitute a separate nation. In the 1530s the Church of England broke with the pope of Rome. By the beginning of Elizabeth's reign it had proceeded a certain distance in this revolt, had become Protestant, had disestablished the monasteries and corrected many abuses. Puritanism was the belief that the reform should be continued, that more abuses remained to be corrected, that practices still survived from the days of popery which should be renounced, that the Church of England should be restored to the "purity" of the first-century church as established by Christ Himself. In the 1560s, when the advocates of purification first acquired the name of Puritans, no one, not even the most radical, knew exactly how far the process was to go or just what the ultimate goal would be; down to the days of Cromwell there was never any agreement on this point, and in the end this failure of unanimity proved the undoing of English Puritanism. Many Puritans desired only that certain ceremonies be abolished or changed. Others wanted ministers to preach more sermons, make up their own prayers on the inspiration of the moment rather than read set forms out of a book. Others went further and proposed a revision of the whole form of ecclesiastical government. But whatever the shade or complexion of their Puritanism, Puritans were those who wanted to continue a movement which was already under way. Their opponents, whom we shall speak of as the Anglicans—though only for the sake of convenience, because there was at that time not the remotest thought on either side of an ultimate separation into distinct churches, and Puritans insisted they were as stoutly loyal to the established institution as any men in England—the Anglicans were those who felt that with the enthronement of Elizabeth and with the "Elizabethan Settlement" of the church, things had gone far enough. They wanted to call a halt, just where they were, and stabilize at that point.

Thus the issue between the two views, though large enough, still involved only a limited number of questions. On everything except matters upon which the Puritans wanted further reformation, there was essential agreement. The Puritans who settled New England were among the more radical—though by no means the most radical that the movement produced—and even before their migration in 1630 had gone to the lengths of formulating a concrete platform of church organization which they wished to see instituted in England in place of the episcopal system. Joining battle on this front gave a sufficiently extended line and provided a vast number of salients to fight over; the gulf between the belief of these Puritans and the majority in the Church of England grew so wide that at last there was no bridging it at all. But notwithstanding the depth of this divergence, the fact still remains that only certain specific questions were raised. If we take a comprehensive survey of the whole body of Puritan thought and belief as it existed in 1630 or 1640, if we make an exhaustive enumeration of ideas held by New England Puritans, we shall find that the vast majority of them were precisely those of their opponents. In other words, Puritanism was a movement toward certain ends within the culture and state of England in the late sixteenth and early seventeenth centuries; it centered about a number of concrete problems and advocated a particular program. Outside of that, it was part and parcel of the times, and its culture was simply the culture of England at that moment. It is necessary to belabor the point, because most accounts of Puritanism, emphasizing the controversial tenets, attribute everything that Puritans said or did to the fact that they were Puritans; their attitudes toward all sorts of things are pounced upon and exhibited as peculiarities of their sect, when as a matter of fact they were normal attitudes for the time. Of course, the Puritans acquired their special quality and their essential individuality from their stand on the points actually at issue, and our final conception of Puritanism must give these concerns all due importance. Yet if first of all we wish to take Puritan culture as a whole, we shall find, let us say, that about 90 percent of the intellectual life, scientific knowledge, morality, manners and customs, notions and prejudices, was that of all Englishmen. The other 10 percent, the relatively small number of ideas upon which there was dispute, made all the difference between the Puritan and his fellow Englishmen, made for him so much difference that he pulled up stakes in England, which he loved, and migrated to a wilderness rather than submit them to apparent defeat. Nevertheless, when we come to trace developments and influences on subsequent American history and thought, we shall find that the starting point of many ideas and practices is as apt to be found among the 90 percent as among the 10. The task of defining Puritanism and giving an account of its culture resolves itself, therefore, into isolating first of all the larger features which were not particularly or necessarily Puritan at all, the elements in the life and society which were products of the time and place, of the background of English life and society rather than of the individual belief or peculiar creed of Puritanism.

Many of the major interests and preoccupations of the New England Puritans belong to this list. They were just as patriotic as Englishmen who remained at home. They hated Spain like poison, and France only a little less. In their eyes, as in those of Anglicans, the most important issue in the Western world was the struggle between Catholicism and Protestantism. They were not unique or extreme in thinking that religion was the primary and all-engrossing business of man, or that all human thought and action should tend to the glory of God. . . .

In its major aspects tbe religious creed of Puritanism was neither peculiar to the Puritans nor different from that of the Anglicans. Both were essentially Protestant; both asserted that men were saved by their faith, not by their deeds. The two sides could agree on the general statement that Christians are bound to believe nothing but what the Gospel teaches, that all traditions of men "contrary to the Word of God" are to be renounced and abhorred. They both believed that the marks of a true church were profession of the creed, use of Christ's sacraments, preaching of the word—Anglican sermons being as long and often as dull as the Puritan—and the union of men in profession and practice under regularly constituted pastors. The Puritans always said that they could subscribe to the doctrinal articles of the Church of England; even at the height of the controversy, even after they had left England rather than put up with what they considered its abominations, they always took care to insist that the Church of England was a "true" church, not Anti-Christ as was the Church of Rome, that it contained many saints, and that men might find salvation within it. Throughout the seventeenth century they read Anglican authors, quoted them in their sermons, and even reprinted some of them in Boston.

The vast substratum of agreement which actually underlay the disagreement between Puritans and Anglicans is explained by the fact that they were both the heirs of the Middle Ages. They still believed that all knowledge was one, that life was unified, that science, economics, political theory, aesthetic standards, rhetoric and art, all were organized in a hierarchical scale of values that tended upward to the end-all and be-all of creation, the glory of God. They both insisted that all human activity be regulated by that purpose. Consequently, even while fighting bitterly against each other, the Puritans and Anglicans stood shoulder to shoulder against what they called "enthusiasm." The leaders of the Puritan movement were trained at the universities, they were men of learning and scholars; no less than the Anglicans did they demand that religion be interpreted by study and logical exposition; they were both resolute against all pretenses to immediate revelation, against all ignorant men who claimed to receive personal instructions from God. They agreed on the essential Christian contention that though God may govern the world, He is not the world itself, and that though He instills His grace into men, He does not deify them or unite them to Himself in one personality. He converses with men only through His revealed word, the Bible. His will is to be studied in the operation of His providence as exhibited in the workings of the natural world, but He delivers no new commands or special revelations to the inward consciousness of men. The larger unanimity of the Puritans and the Anglicans reveals itself whenever either of them was called upon to confront enthusiasm [as seen in] . . . Governor John Winthrop's account of the so-called Antinomian affair, the crisis produced in the little colony by the teachings of Mistress Anne Hutchinson in 1636 and 1637. . . . Beneath the theological jargon in which the opinions of this lady appear we can see the substance of her contention, which was that she was in direct communication with the Godhead, and that she therefore was prepared to follow the promptings of the voice within against all the precepts of the Bible, the churches, reason, or the government of Massachusetts Bay. Winthrop relates how the magistrates and the ministers defended the community against this perversion of the doctrine of regeneration, but the tenor of his condemnation would have been duplicated practically word for word had Anne Hutchinson broached her theories in an Anglican community. The Anglicans fell in completely with the Puritans when both of them were confronted in the 1650s by the Quakers. All New England leaders saw in the Quaker doctrine of an inner light, accessible to all men and giving a perfect communication from God to their inmost spirits, just another form of Anne Hutchinson's blasphemy. John Norton declared that the "light of nature" itself taught us that "madmen acting according to their frantick passions are to be restrained with chaines, when they can not be restrained otherwise. . . ." Enthusiasts, whether Antinomian or Quaker, were proposing doctrines that threatened the unity of life by subduing the reason and the intellect to the passions and the emotions. Whatever their differences, Puritans and Anglicans were struggling to maintain a complete harmony of reason and faith, science and religion, earthly dominion and the government of God. When we immerse ourselves in the actual struggle, the difference between the Puritan and the Anglican may seem to us immense; but when we take the vantage point of subsequent history, and survey religious thought as a whole over the last three centuries, the two come very close together on essentials. Against all forms of chaotic emotionalism, against all oversimplifications of theology, learning, philosophy, and science, against all materialism, positivism or mechanism, both were endeavoring to uphold a symmetrical union of heart and head without impairment of either. By the beginning or middle of the next century their successors, both in England and America, found themselves no longer capable of sustaining this unity, and it has yet to be reachieved today, if achieved again it ever can be. The greatness of the Puritans is not so much that they conquered a wilderness, or that they carried a religion into it, but that they carried a religion which, narrow and starved though it may have been in some respects, deficient in sensuous richness or brilliant color, was nevertheless indissolubly bound up with an ideal of culture and learning. In contrast to all other pioneers, they made no concessions to the forest, but in the midst of frontier conditions, in the very throes of clearing the land and erecting shelters, they maintained schools and a college, a standard of scholarship and of competent writing, a class of men devoted entirely to the life of the mind and of the soul.

Because the conflict between the Puritans and the Churchmen was as much an intellectual and scholarly issue as it was emotional, it was in great part a debate among pundits. This is not to say that passions were not involved; certainly men took sides because of prejudice, interest, irrational conviction, or for any of the motives that may incite the human race to conflict. The disagreement finally was carried from the field of learned controversy to the field of battle. There can be no doubt that many of the people in England, or even in New England, became rabid partisans and yet never acquired the erudition necessary to understand the intricate and subtle arguments of their leaders. A great number, perhaps even a majority, in both camps were probably not intelligent or learned enough to see clearly the reasons for the cause they supported. . . .

The wonder is that by and large the populace did yield their judgments to those who were supposed to know, respected learning and supported it, sat patiently during two- and three-hour sermons while ministers expounded the knottiest and most recondite of metaphysical texts. The testimony of visitors, travelers, and memoirs agrees that during the Puritan age in New England the common man, the farmer and merchant, was amazingly versed in systematic divinity. A gathering of yeomen and "hired help" around the kitchen fire of an evening produced long and unbelievably technical discussions of predestination, infant damnation, and the distinctions between faith and works. In the first half of the seventeenth century the people had not yet questioned the conception of religion as a difficult art in which the authority of the skilled dialectician should prevail over the inclinations of the merely devout. This ideal of subjection to qualified leadership was social as well as intellectual. Very few Englishmen had yet broached the notion that a lackey was as good as a lord, or that any Tom, Dick, or Harry, simply because he was a good, honest man, could understand the Sermon on the Mount as well as a master of arts from Oxford, Cambridge, or Harvard. Professor Morison has shown that the life of the college in New England was saved by the sacrifice of the yeomen farmers, who contributed their pecks of wheat, wrung from a stony soil, taken from their none too opulent stores, to support teaching fellows and to assist poor scholars at Harvard College, in order that they and their children might still sit under a literate ministry "when our present Ministers shall lie in the Dust."

When we say that the majority of the people in the early seventeenth century still acceded to the dictation of the learned in religion and the superior in society, we must also remark that the Puritan leaders were in grave danger of arousing a revolt against themselves by their very own doctrines. Puritans were attacking the sacerdotal and institutional bias which had survived in the Church of England; they were maintaining a theology that brought every man to a direct experience of the spirit and removed intermediaries between himself and the deity. Yet the authority of the infallible church and the power of the bishops had for centuries served to keep the people docile. Consequently when the Puritan leaders endeavored to remove the bishops and to deny that the church should stand between God and man, they ran the hazard of starting something among the people that might get out of hand. Just as the Puritan doctrine that men were saved by the infusion of God's grace could lead to the Antinomianism of Mrs. Hutchinson, and often did warrant the simple in concluding that if they had God's grace in them they needed to pay no heed to what a minister told them, so the Puritan contention that regenerate men were illuminated with divine truth might lead to the belief that true religion did not need the assistance of learning, books, arguments, logical demonstrations, or classical languages. There was always a possibility that Puritanism would raise up a fanatical anti-intellectualism, and against such a threat the Puritan ministers constantly braced themselves. It was no accident that the followers of Mrs. Hutchinson, who believed that men could receive all the necessary instructions from within, also attacked learning and education, and came near to wrecking not only the colony but the college as well....

[T]he New England leaders were face to face with a problem as old as the history of the Christian church. Throughout the Middle Ages there had been such stirrings among the people as those to which Mrs. Hutchinson or the Fifth Monarchy Men gave voice. The great scholastic synthesis always remained incomprehensible to the vulgar, who demanded to be fed again and again with the sort of religious sustenance they craved. The Reformation drew upon these suppressed desires. Common men turned Protestant primarily because Protestantism offered them a religion which more effectively satisfied their spiritual hunger. Yet in Europe theologians and metaphysicians retained the leadership and kept Protestantism from becoming merely an emotional outburst. They supplied it with a theology which, though not so sophisticated as scholastic dogma, was still equipped with a logic and organon of rational demonstration. Though Protestantism can be viewed as a "liberation" of the common man, it was far from being a complete emancipation of the individual. It freed him from many intellectual restraints that had been imposed by the church, but it did not give him full liberty to think anything he pleased; socially it freed him from many exactions, but it did not permit him to abandon his traditional subjection to his social and ecclesiastical superiors. The original settlers of New England carried this Protestantism intact from Europe to America. Except for the small band that was driven into exile with Anne Hutchinson, and one or two other groups of visionaries who also were hustled across the borders into Rhode Island, the rank and file did follow their leaders, meekly and reverently. Captain Johnson probably represents the average layman's loyalty to the clergy. The New England "theocracy" was simply a Protestant version of the European social ideal, and except for its Protestantism was thoroughly medieval in character.

It was only as the seventeenth century came to a close that the imported structure began to show the strain. In Europe social tradition had conspired with the ministers to check enthusiasts in religion and "levellers" in society; in England the authorities, whether Anglican or Puritan, royal or Cromwellian, were able to suppress the assault upon the scholarly and aristocratic ideal. In America the character of the people underwent a change; they moved further into the frontier, they became more absorbed in business and profits than in religion and salvation, their memories of English social stratification grew dim. A preacher before the General Court in 1705 bewailed the effects of the frontier in terms that have been echoed by "Easterners" for two hundred years and more; men were no longer living together, he said, in compact communities, under the tutelage of educated clergymen and under the discipline of an ordered society, but were taking themselves into remote corners "for worldly conveniences." "By that means [they] have seemed to bid defiance, not only to Religion, but to Civility it self: and such places thereby have become Nurseries of Ignorance, Prophaneness and Atheism." In America the frontier conspired with the popular disposition to lessen the prestige of the cultured classes and to enhance the social power of those who wanted their religion in a more simple, downright and "democratic" form, who cared nothing for the refinements and subtleties of historic theology. Not until the decade of the Great Awakening did the popular tendency receive distinct articulation through leaders who openly renounced the older conception, but for half a century or more before 1740 its obstinate persistence can be traced in the condemnations of the ministers.

The Puritan leaders could withstand this rising tide of democracy only by such support as the government would give them—which became increasingly less after the new charter of 1692 took away from the saints all power to select their own governors and divorced the state and church—or else by the sheer force of their personalities. As early as the 1660s and '70s we can see them beginning to shift their attentions from mere exposition of the creed to greater and greater insistence upon committing power only to men of wisdom and knowledge.... By the beginning of the eighteenth century the task of buttressing the classified society, maintaining the rule of the well-trained and the culturally superior both in church and society seems to have become the predominant concern of the clergy. Sermon after sermon reveals that in their eyes the cause of learning and the cause of a hierarchical, differentiated social order were one and the same. . . . Leadership by the learned and dutiful subordination of the unlearned—as long as the original religious creed retained its hold upon the people these exhortations were heeded; in the eighteenth century, as it ceased to arouse their loyalties, they went seeking after gods that were utterly strange to Puritanism. They demanded fervent rather than learned ministers and asserted the equality of all men.

Thus Puritanism appears, from the social and economic point of view, to have been a philosophy of social stratification, placing the command in the hands of the properly qualified and demanding implicit obedience from the uneducated; from the religious point of view it was the dogged assertion of the unity of intellect and spirit in the face of a rising tide of democratic sentiment suspicious of the intellect and intoxicated with the spirit. It was autocratic, hierarchical, and authoritarian. It held that in the intellectual realm holy writ was to be expounded by right reason, that in the social realm the expounders of holy writ were to be the mentors of farmers and merchants. Yet in so far as Puritanism involved such ideals it was simply adapting to its own purposes the ideals of the age. Catholics in Spain and in Spanish America pursued the same objectives, and the Puritans were no more rigorous in their application of an autocratic standard than King Charles himself endeavored to be—and would have been had he not been balked in the attempt.

# Darrett B. Rutman

DARRETT B. RUTMAN (1929–    ) is professor of history at the University of New Hampshire. He has published many articles and books in American colonial history, including *Winthrop's Boston: Portrait of a Puritan Town, 1630–1649* (1965) and *American Puritanism: Faith and Practice* (1970).

## Two Puritans

A day early in May 1628, in the Cornhill ward of London: Robert Keayne, "citizen and merchant tailor of London," settled comfortably into a chair in the home of Matthew Cradock, governor of the New England Company. Carefully Keayne sharpened his quill pen, set an ink bottle beside him, and opened his journal, then waited expectantly for the lecturer to begin. The minister invited to address the company that day was Master John Cotton of Boston, Lincolnshire, and as Cotton rose to speak, Keayne poised his pen to jot down the text: Isaiah, chapter 26, verse 20—in the minister's peculiar translation, "Come my children."

The text, Cotton explained, was clear: God would not have his children lost, even in times of greatest danger. And this was assuredly a "comfort to the Godly." In times of peace God might seem "to neglect his children" for "all things fall alike to all." "Yet in the times of public danger and calamity, God will provide and take care of his." Some might object to this interpretation, pointing out that "affliction often begins at God's house and stays at his sanctuary." True! "God may begin his judgments at the sanctuary," yet he will "take care to provide for his people, his marked ones"; "he will press and depress his love to his hidd[en] children," yet it is not the children he is after but the "many hypocrites, loose Christians" who have entered the sanctuary.

The text, therefore, comforts God's children. It exhorts as well. If you want God's love and protection, "give yourselves more to God. Let his law bear sway in you. Give up yourselves with gladness of heart to obey his command and observe his statutes." "That which terrifies men in evil hours and hinders the light of God's countenance . . . is guiltiness of the conscience, when it has gone astray from God's love and command." Moreover, the text "seems to teach God's children, in all their passions, hates and extremities, not to dishonor the name of God" for "God is never in such a passion, but he can hide and save us, and shall we forget God in our hearts and speak unadvisedly when he never forgets us; shall we deal worse with God than he deals" with us? . . .

What shall the good children do when the Father vents His wrath toward the bad? Heed Isaiah! "Behold, thou shalt see in that day when thou shalt go into an inner chamber to hide thyself." "My children, get you into your houses! Enter into your chamber and shut the door after you! Hide yourselves till wrath be passed over!" Hide in a "private and secret place to search and examine [thy] heart and ways. Look into your hearts and there stilly and privately search thoroughly and see what is in you that might move God to punish you as well as all the world." But what does this mean? "By entering into the chamber is signified mewing and sighing and pouring out our grief for our sins." "By shutting the door after us is meant shutting out our sins and evils." By hiding ourselves "is meant our looking up to Christ Jesus for protection and salvation and preservation—to hide ourselves in Christ by faith."

> Oh get you home [to search] into your own hearts. See what evils they be that hang upon you, and whatsoever you see in family, church or commonwealth. And go into your chambers moved for them. Bewail them and leave them not there. But . . . look to God for mercy. Hide yourselves in the covenant and promises of God, and whatsoever evils come, keep they own souls. Be quiet and all shall be well with you.

Let none delude themselves. God's punishment is "poured out upon the inhabitants of the earth . . . with indignation"; it "is provoked by the indignity and base dealing" of men toward God. "We are," therefore, "worthy" of all that God pours out upon us, "for have not we dealt unworthily with God?" Have we not disdained "his words, ordinances, ministers?"

> Did not we deal unworthily with God when we loathed his food and in our hearts waxed weary of it and turned back to Egypt again? When we look upon sanctification and all ways of holiness as upon base and unworthy things? When a man will not be seen publicly to profess religion? When we think it will not stand with our countenance to speak for religion or profess it? Did we not deal unworthily with God when we are so proud that we despise entering into our chambers and searching into our hearts and shutting out sin? Have we not dealt unworthily with God when we looked upon God's blessings and our great deliverance as unworthy things, and so when we look at all kinds of reformation [in the church] and good laws against popery and profaneness as at unworthy things, and think scorn at the purity of God's ordinances and religion?

What is the lesson in all this? To "the state in general": "Take in good part of God's blessings and look not at his ordinances with a disdainful eye; deal not unworthily with God." To "every man in particular": "Learn to deal well with God. Receive his message, Law, spirit! Obey [and] serve him!"

The lecture ended and Keayne closed his journal. Later, perhaps that night, he would open it again for study, casting up in his own mind whether he was dealing well with the Lord, whether he was properly hid in his chamber with the other children of the Lord. But for now there was business to be attended to. He was, after all, a mercant tailor of the city, and the New England Company, in which he had invested one hundred pounds sterling, was a business venture.

## What Is Puritanism? Several Definitions and an Approach

Robert Keayne, citizen and merchant, and John Cotton, minister, are both considered English Puritans; both would eventually journey to what has been labeled Puritan New England, there to live out their lives. But what is the meaning of this word *Puritan*? What does it denote by way of a concept useful in understanding the life, structure, and course of events in early New England?

The word, if it is to be useful to us, is certainly not to be defined as simple religiosity. A useful definition must stipulate the peculiar quality of the thing denoted by the word defined, and religiosity is not peculiar to any single thing of the seventeenth century. Indeed, religiosity pervades the air of that time. In England, men argued and finally fought their civil war "in the name of God, Amen." Ships sailing from England's ports carried chaplains to pray for the souls of men and the subsiding of God-angried seas. England's expansion overseas was both commanded and justified by God. Thus the English migration to Virginia was that of "a peculiar people, marked and chosen by the finger of God, to possess it, for undoubtedly he is with us." And in English colonies scattered around the Atlantic littoral, prayers were constantly sent heavenward from thousands of throats.

This seventeenth century was an age when all men defined themselves, their society, their activities, and their institutions in terms of God; when the meanest plowboy could feel himself to be, like the sparrow, the immediate object of God's concern; when life itself was considered but a layover on a trip that led to infinity's end. "If it be for his glory," John Winthrop wrote to his wife upon leaving England for New England in 1630, God "will bring us together again." If not, "blessed be our God, that we are assured, we shall meet one day, if not as husband and wife, yet in a better condition." And almost seventy years later Virginian William Fitzhugh would write to his mother: "Before I was ten years old, as I am sure you very well remember, I look'd upon this life here as but going to an Inn, no permanent being[.] By God's [will] I continue the same good thoughts and notions still, therefore am always prepared for my certain dissolution." This is, of course, not to say that religion pervaded life and thought to such an extent that one can approach the century by no other avenue but the religious. To pervade is not necessarily to dominate. There are economic, political, and esthetic themes in the seventeenth century as well as religious, and if religion pervades these other themes, it does not follow that it dominates them. When, for example, a given venture is put forth as one

> Whence glory to the name of God, and countries
>    good shall spring,
> And unto all that further it, a private gain
>    shall bring. . . .

are we to say that the venture is set afoot for purely religious purposes? Religion pervaded seventeenth-century society as an absolute premise, an aspect of life and thought which it was inconceivable to be without, no more and no less.

Puritanism, therefore, is not to be defined simply as religiosity. It must, however, be defined within the context of a pervasive religiosity.

Neither is Puritanism usefully defined as a peculiar and unique set of social, economic, or political attitudes, although to do so is highly fashionable in some quarters. Two related arguments lie behind such a definition. In the first, England, as the sixteenth century turned to the seventeenth, is conceived to have been in the midst of economic transition as a pastoral, semifeudal system slowly gave way to modern industrial capitalism. Puritanism arose with a creed and ethic to rationalize the activities and aspirations of a new "middle class"—a class midway between lord and peasant which was coming to monopolize capital. Therefore, Puritanism is definable by describing a certain set of middle-class attitudes toward society, economics, and political structure. That set of ideas arrived in America via New England to form the basis of a peculiar American ethic. The second argument is a variant of the first. Again, England is conceived to have been in the midst of transition; flux and change evoked feelings of insecurity in some which in turn evoked a desire to perfect and purify the world within the Christian tradition— perfect and purify the church (thus Puritanism is to be defined as a peculiar religious phenomenon), but also society as a whole (Puritanism defined as a peculiar set of social, political, and economic ideas). Both arguments have application far beyond Puritanism. The same flux and change are seen as pervasive throughout western Europe, evoking either the same rationalization for an emerging middle class or the same desire to perfect and purify. On this larger scale the phenomenon is conceived as the Protestant Reformation and Puritanism as the Reformation "writ small."

Puritanism (and the Reformation) must assuredly be conceived within a complex of change and insecurity. And whatever the words are meant to denote must certainly be conceived within a body of social, economic, and political thought, shaping and being shaped by that body of thought. But it hardly seems useful to define such concepts by describing the flux and insecurity within which they are conceived to be operating or the thought which they are conceived to have provoked. Concepts so defined are invariably overburdened by the infusion of causes and effects, so all-embracing and amorphous as to be useless as analytic tools, and in their tendency to subsume the general within conceptual boundaries pretending to be particular, conducive to sterile controversy.

Finally, Puritanism does not seem usefully defined in geographic terms. No English historian has yet had the audacity to suggest that the people of a given area were English Puritans, hence what those people were and what they thought was English Puritanism. Yet American historians concerned with American Puritanism habitually do just this. "Important as Puritanism has undoubtedly been in shaping the nation," one wrote, "it is more easily described than defined." And it "may perhaps best be described as that point of view, that philosophy of life, that code of values which was carried to New England by the first settlers in the early seventeenth century." The writer was Perry Miller, undoubtedly the most erudite American commentator on Puritanism in the twentieth century. The approach is not without its rationalization. Throughout the seventeenth century New England's leaders proclaimed their society to be Puritan and unique. But one can suggest that the definition is inadequate for our purposes. In order to explore the workings of whatever we define as Puritanism in the forming of New England—even in forming this persistent self-identification of New England leaders—we must first separate Puritanism *from* New England.

Certainly the definition of Puritanism by description of New England leads to awkward assumptions. If, for example, Puritanism cannot be explicitly defined, only described as a point of view carried to New England in the early seventeenth century, then one easily assumes that what one finds in early New England is Puritanism. And inasmuch as Puritanism is implicitly unique—else why use such a qualitative word at all?—what one finds in New England is by implication unique. New England is marked by religiosity; religiosity is therefore a mark of Puritanism and is unique to New England. But of course we have already noted that religiosity is pervasive in the century, to be found in New England and old, in old England and Virginia. The data, consequently, do not fit. Or to choose another example: The custom of parents putting their children out to work as servants in other families is found in New England; it is, therefore, a Puritan trait rationalized in Puritan terms—the Puritan felt that children were degenerate until they underwent godly conversion and put them out to other families so that parental love would not vitiate the discipline required toward the degenerate. Yet the custom of putting children out to serve in other families was not peculiar but customary in the traditional England from which Puritanism emerged.

Moreover, American Puritanism, approached in this way, is a single entity—"*that* point of view, *that* philosophy . . . *that* code." The implication is that there was a single "unity" running "in Puritan thought, expression, and manners." Given this, and given the tendency to equate Puritanism and early New England, it follows that one can assume an absolute unity in early New England, that one can talk of the early New Englanders monolithically. In other words, if one finds among one group of New Englanders a given idea, that idea is a Puritan idea, therefore a New England idea, therefore an idea held by all New Englanders. One example suffices: an excellent study of the doctrine of preparation as held by New England ministers which begins, "*Seventeenth-century New Englanders* examined their hearts with an intensity now quite alien to the American mind." The assumption of a monolithic New England is undoubtedly serviceable to historians of the later colonial years who address themselves to the transition from "Puritan to Yankee." One can write trenchantly of the disintegration of Puritan New England, of the "decline of the animating ideal of a whole society." And the stereotype Puritan New England of the early years is a marvelous contrast against which one can display the vibrant Yankeeism of the later. But the close study of the structure of life—a mark of the most recent scholarly excursions into the seventeenth century—is ill-served by a definition of Puritanism in which is inherent the notion of a New England monolith. Data cannot be made to conform. The monolith, as such studies are showing, simply did not exist.

If not in terms of religiosity per se, peculiar and unique social notions, or the people of a particular area, how are we to conceptualize Puritanism in such a way that we can use the concept in understanding the society of early New England and, to an extent, American society as a whole? The scene with which this chapter opened—that of layman Robert Keayne listening to minister John Cotton and jotting down the main points of the sermon for future study—suggests what might be a useful approach. Assuming both men to be Puritans, Puritanism can be conceived as something imparted by ministers such as Cotton to laymen such as Keayne. Our focus is immediately upon ministers as the givers of this gift of Puritanism.

# 3

# British Mercantilism and the American Colonies

## Help or Hindrance?

Historians have often employed British mercantilism as a yardstick by which to measure the fairness of the mother country toward her American colonies. British mercantilist policies, after all, provided the impetus for much of the imperial legislation passed in the seventeenth and eighteenth centuries. The question historians traditionally have asked was this: To what degree did these policies subordinate the interests of the American colonies to those of Britain? Implicit in the first question was a second of far greater importance: Was British mercantilism so unfair and one-sided that it helped bring on the American Revolution?

In answering these questions, historians disagreed widely. Some argued that Britain's mercantilism was a selfish system which deprived American colonists of the fruits of their labors and stifled their economic growth by repressive measures. Others stressed the economic advantages inherent in the mother country's mercantilist system and noted that prior to 1763 American colonists rarely protested against Britain's policies. Still another group of historians concluded that British mercantilism did not have the great impact usually ascribed to it because the colonists evaded or ignored Britain's economic regulations and resorted to smuggling. These opposing points of view, as we shall see, often reflected the political, economic, and social climate of the era in which a given historian was writing.

Before tracing the impact of mercantilism on the American colonies, it is necessary to understand the British background of mercantilist theory and practice. The term *mercantilism* itself did not come into general use until the eighteenth century, and even then was used to bring together a number of disparate ideas that were never clearly defined. Although mercantilism was never the coherent system pictured in most textbooks, some generalizations may be made about this complex concept.

When the first colonies were being settled, one assumption of English mercantilist thinkers was that nation-states should regulate their economic life so as to strengthen themselves for competition with other nation-states. As far back as the fifteenth century, the English government had adopted policies on a nationwide basis regulating the buying and selling of goods in order to encourage trade which was good for England and to discourage that which was bad. England was not alone in accepting the concept of mercantilism; the same economic philosophy was being practiced by all major countries of western Europe. Each nation, however, tended to stress those distinctive features of mercantilism which would produce for it the greatest prosperity and national strength. Spain, for example, stressed the amassing of precious metals, Holland the control of external trade, and France the regulation of internal trade.

England, on the other hand, appeared to emphasize four major aims in her mercantilism: (1) to encourage the growth of a native merchant marine fleet so that England might control the shipping of her own goods; (2) to provide protection for England's manufactures; (3) to protect England's agriculture, especially her grain farmers; and (4) to accumulate as much hard money as possible. The ultimate goal of these mercantilist measures invariably was the same—to make England self-sufficient, rich and strong as a military power.

Beginning in the seventeenth century, these mercantilist principles were expanded to include the idea of colonies. Mercantilist thinkers began emphasizing that no nation could achieve greatness without colonies, and Britain rather belatedly embarked upon her career as a colonizing power. Colonies presumably were to supplement the economy of the mother country in three ways: by supplying the mother country with raw materials, serving as markets for English manufactures, and conducting their trade in such a way as to benefit Britain. In order that various segments of the British Empire might fit within this mercantilist framework, Parliament passed laws which regulated, in part, the economic life of all her colonies.

Parliament's program for the American colonies in this regard during the century between the 1650s and 1750s was called the Old Colonial System. The emphasis in this chapter, for the most part, will be on this program and period. One of the main features of this system was a series of navigation acts designed to channel colonial commerce into paths profitable for the mother country. To assure the dominance of Britain's merchant marine fleet over the lucrative carrying trade between

England and America, Parliament passed the Navigation Act of 1651. This act required all goods traded within the empire to be carried in British or American ships, or in the ships of the country of manufacture. To make certain that the mother country would receive the benefit of valuable raw materials produced in the colonies, the Enumerated Commodities Act of 1660 was passed. This law specified that certain colonial products such as tobacco, sugar, and indigo could be shipped only to England or to other English colonies. The mother country exercised control over colonial imports as well as exports. Under the Staples Act of 1663, Parliament ruled that some goods shipped from Europe to the American colonies had to pass through English ports first. Thus, duties could be placed on European goods before they were shipped to America, thereby protecting British merchants from foreign competition in the colonial market.

A second aim of the Old Colonial System was to make it possible for England to continue to accumulate hard money. The balance of trade between Britain and the American colonies favored the mother country and, whenever possible, she insisted on being paid in specie. Consequently, whatever hard money the colonies obtained in their trade with the West Indies or other parts of the world was drained off to Britain. English merchants refused for the most part to accept colonial paper money in payment for debts, and Parliament backed them by ruling that colonial notes were not legal tender for such transactions. British merchants also made it a general rule never to send bullion or gold or silver coins to America, and eventually Parliament passed a law to that effect. Statutes regulating the flow of hard money, then, were designed to protect the mother country.

Certain American industries were also subjected to regulation under the system to prevent them from competing with Britain. The woolen industry was restricted to some degree by the Woolens Act of 1699, which prohibited the export of wool, yarn, or woolen cloth in foreign or intercolonial trade. In 1732, the Hat Act prohibited the sale of hats abroad or to any other colonies. Under the Iron Act of 1750, steps were taken to prohibit the making of many finished iron products. American attempts at manufacturing were also discouraged to some degree by British laws which made it a crime to lure skilled workers or import textile machinery from England.

Although historians agreed on the essential features of the Old Colonial System, they disagreed about its effects on the American economy. The idea that the navigation acts were so oppressive as to constitute a primary cause of the American Revolution was first given prominence by George Bancroft in his multivolume *History of the United States*. Writing in the late 1830s, Bancroft in his second volume portrayed the acts as a prime example of British selfishness. Colonial trade was confined so strictly by regulations, according to Bancroft, that Americans were allowed to sell to foreign nations only those goods in which England had no interest. When it came to buying goods, the colonies were restricted to so few markets that they could not compete on a fair basis. "The commercial liberties of rising states were shackled by paper chains, and the principles of natural justice subjected to the fears and covetousness of English shopkeepers." Prepared to believe the worst about Britain, Bancroft misunderstood the provisions of the Navigation Act of 1660 and wrote mistakenly that under this law the carrying trade within the British Empire was open only to those merchants residing in England. Such economic exploitation ruined the relations between Britain and her colonies, said Bancroft, and helped to bring about the Revolution. "It converted commerce, which should be the bond of peace, into a source of rankling hostility, and scattered the certain seeds of a civil war. The navigation act contained a pledge of the ultimate independence of America."[1]

Bancroft believed that Britain's restrictions on American manufacturing were equally burdensome. Carelessly reading the laws that prohibited the production of hats, woolens, and finished iron goods under certain circumstances, he jumped to the conclusion that the mother country had stifled *all* manufacturing. "America was forbidden, by act of parliament, not merely to manufacture those articles which might compete with the English in foreign markets," wrote Bancroft, "but even to supply herself, by her own industry, with those articles which her position enabled her to manufacture with success for her own wants."[2] Once again, he was in error. The three industries noted above were the only ones upon which Britain had imposed any major limitations. But right or wrong, Bancroft was convinced that British restrictions of any kind on colonial trade and manufacturing were mischievous, wicked, and hopelessly one-sided.

Bancroft's sharp condemnation of Britain's regulatory measures becomes more understandable when one recalls the economic theories current in the 1830s and 1840s—the decades in which he wrote his volumes on the pre-Revolutionary period. The older concept of mercantilism was giving way by this time to the ideas of laissez-faire capitalism which sought to minimize the role of government in economic affairs. Many of the theories current in the 1830s and 1840s harked back to the teachings of Adam Smith, who had favored free trade and opposed government controls which might affect the laws of supply and demand. Both Britain and the United States were moving in the direction

---

[1]George Bancroft, *History of the United States* (1st ed., Boston, 1837), 2:42–47, 122, 157–158, and 198–199.

[2]*Ibid.*, p.44.

of free trade and more modern laissez-faire practices. Bancroft was injecting the economic doctrines of his day into the past when he criticized the navigation acts and other mercantilist restrictions over the American colonies.

An entire generation of Americans formed their ideas of the British mercantilist system on the basis of Bancroft's writings. Before Bancroft wrote, few textbooks had mentioned the navigation acts in connection with the Revolution. But Bancroft kept insisting that British economic restrictions had caused the break between the colonies and mother country. In his fifth volume, Bancroft stated unequivocally: "American independence, like the great rivers of the country, had many sources; but the head-spring which colored all the stream was the Navigation Act."[3] Most schoolbooks in the 1850s, as a result, listed the acts as one of the chief causes of the American Revolution.

Fifty years after Bancroft had published his first volumes, a new group of scholars—the imperial school of historians—appeared in the 1880s and 1890s to challenge his findings. The imperial school reacted against Bancroft's intensely nationalistic approach which viewed the colonies solely within the narrow context of American history. These scholars proposed to look at the American colonies within a much broader framework—as parts of the British Empire as a whole. Many of the members of the imperial school had a pro-British bias. Hence they looked upon the British policies and actions in the colonial period in a much different light than Bancroft. Two members of the imperial school in particular—George L. Beer and Charles M. Andrews—studied the way in which the British had regulated the economic life of the American colonies in accordance with certain mercantilist ideas.

Beer began his first work, *The Commercial Policy of England toward the American Colonies,* published in 1893, by criticizing Bancroft and other nineteenth-century nationalist historians for writing with an ultrapatriotic point of view. "They start," he wrote, "with the idea that England consciously pursued an egotistic and tyrannical policy. By making the facts conform to this preconception, they have produced books that are notably unjust to England."[4] Freed from such a patriotic bias, Beer said he was able to study his subject in a more objective light. But Beer was to err in the opposite direction; he exhibited a pro-British bias in his writings. Indeed, in his work as a publicist and propagandist during World War I, Beer went so far as to call for a reunion of the English-speaking peoples in Britain and America to help maintain world peace.

---

[3]*Ibid.*, 5:159. This volume appeared in 1852.

[4]George L. Beer, "The Commercial Policy of England toward the American Colonies," *Columbia College Studies in History, Economics and Public Law*, vol. 3, pt. 2 (New York, 1893), pp. 7–8.

Beer was likewise critical of the present-minded approach of Bancroft and other historians who had evaluated Britain's mercantilist policy from the point of view of nineteenth-century ideas of free trade and laissez-faire doctrine. In his own work, Beer examined mercantilism within the context of seventeenth- and eighteenth-century economic ideas. "No institution can be condemned from the historical standpoint," he wrote, "if it is really in advance of that which preceded."[5] Viewing the mercantilist system in this light, Beer concluded that mercantilism represented a marked advance over the economic theory of balance of bargain upon which Britain had been relying.

In his overall evaluation of the British mercantilist system, Beer saw benefits as well as burdens for America. He stressed the constructive side of mercantilism by showing that the navigation acts were actually responsible in large measure for the commercial prosperity of British North America. After all, he noted, colonial goods were guaranteed markets within the British Empire—one of the major trading blocs of the Western world. Moreover, American ships were permitted to participate in Britain's lucrative carrying trade on a favorable basis. Beer discussed certain disadvantages such as restrictions on colonial trade and manufacturing, but he felt that these regulations were a fair exchange for the protection provided to the colonists by the British army and navy, and the monopoly granted to certain American goods on the English market. After comparing the mother country's mercantilist policy with that of other nations, Beer declared that Britain's was "much more liberal."[6] The system as a whole, he concluded, "was thus based on the idea of the mutual reciprocity of the economic interests of the mother country and colony."[7]

Contrary to Bancroft's findings, Beer believed that the economic restrictions imposed by Britain's colonial policy had little to do with the coming of the Revolution. Beer's work dealt primarily with the Old Colonial System and he concluded: "The colonial system, as it was administered before 1763, contributed but slightly in bringing about the revolution of 1776."[8] It was only after 1763, when economic principles were subordinated to political considerations in Britain's colonial policy, Beer declared, that relations between the mother country and colonies deteriorated rapidly.

Beer published three more works between 1907 and 1912 dealing with various aspects of Britain's mercantilist policy. In *The Origins of the*

---

[5]*Ibid.*, p. 8.

[6]*Ibid.*, p. 9.

[7]George L. Beer, *British Colonial Policy, 1754–1765* (New York, 1907), p. 195.

[8]Beer, "Commercial Policy of England toward the American Colonies," p. 157.

*British Colonial System, 1578–1660* and *The Old Colonial System, 1660–1754*, he showed how the British gradually evolved what he considered to be an efficient administrative machinery for running the empire. These two works broadened the investigation of Britain's colonial policy by describing the workings of mercantilism not only in the thirteen American colonies but in Newfoundland and the West Indies as well. Beer's most brilliant book, *British Colonial Policy, 1754–1765,* carried the story forward to the period during and after the French and Indian War. In this work Beer argued that the mother country had to make sacrifices equally as great as those of the colonies in order to maintain a self-sufficient empire. The picture that emerged from Beer's works was that of a well-regulated and reasonable mercantilist system in which the economic benefits and burdens were neatly balanced between the colonies and mother country.

Charles M. Andrews, a second member of the imperial school, took a sympathetic view of Britain's mercantilist policy, similar to that of Beer, when he wrote his four-volume *magnum opus* in the 1930s—*The Colonial Period of American History.* To Andrews the navigation acts did not represent a policy of economic oppression but rather a sincere attempt by Britain to organize the administration of the empire. In his fourth volume, Andrews described in detail the various agencies such as the vice-admiralty courts, the Board of Trade, and customs service which Britain employed to administer colonial trade and commerce. Andrews came to the conclusion that Britain's mercantilist regulations in the main proved ineffectual because the imperial policy of supervision and administration was weak and defective. American colonists, Andrews claimed, were restrained very little in their economic activities by the regulations of British mercantilism.

While the imperial school of historians was proclaiming Britain's mercantilist policies as being eminently fair, another group of American scholars was taking issue with this point of view. The reaction against Bancroft's highly nationalistic interpretation of the colonial period was in full swing by the turn of the twentieth century, and certain scholars, influenced by the Populist and Progressive movements, were digging beneath the surface of events to discover what to them appeared to be the true underlying forces which shaped the course of history. Many became convinced that economic forces were the single most important factor in history, and an economic interpretation of history grew increasingly popular during the first three decades of the century. Charles and Mary Beard wrote their *Rise of American Civilization* in the late 1920s in this vein and were critical of the sympathetic view taken by the imperial school of historians toward the British mercantilist system. "Modern calculators," they wrote, "have gone to some pains to show that on the whole American colonists derived benefits from English policy which greatly outweighed their losses from the restraints laid on them. For the sake of argument the case may be conceded; it is simply irrelevant to the uses of history. The origins of the legislation are clear; and the fact that it restricted American economic enterprise in many respects is indisputable."[9]

But the most rigid application of an economic interpretation of the British mercantilist system came during the Great Depression of the 1930s in the Marxist point of view of Louis M. Hacker. A professor at Columbia University, Hacker set forth his thesis in three works: a sketch of American economic history entitled *The United States: A Graphic History;* an article in the 1937 *Marxist Quarterly;* and a fully documented work, *The Triumph of American Capitalism,* in 1940. In both books Hacker pictured Britain and the American colonies as two rival capitalisms, or competing economic systems. British mercantile capitalism, Hacker wrote, sought constantly to keep the American colonies in a subordinate relationship within the empire. The whole aim of the mercantilist system was to force the colonists to conduct their economic life in such a way as to enrich the English capitalist class. In America two sets of capitalists, merchants in the northern colonies and planters in the South, consistently resisted such efforts. As the colonies grew in wealth, power, and maturity, clashes between the British and American economic systems grew more intense and led ultimately to the break with Britain. "In its fullest historical meaning . . . [the American Revolution] had as its function the release of American merchant and planting capitalism from the fetters of the English Mercantile System," Hacker concluded.[10]

To Hacker British mercantilist policies represented "prison walls" from which there was no escape by American capitalists as long as they remained within the empire. English capitalists deliberately choked off any areas of economic growth in America by passing imperial legislation that denied colonial capitalists opportunities for investments in profitable trade outside the empire, native manufacturing, or speculation in western lands. Few benefits were to be derived by Americans in the British mercantilist system, he wrote, and a clash between the two competing systems became inevitable.

Hacker's books were, in fact, not so much an attack upon British mercantile capitalism in colonial times as a full-scale assault upon the capitalist system itself as a way of life. As the depression deepened in the 1930s, many Americans questioned the effectiveness of laissez-faire

---

[9]Charles and Mary Beard, *The Rise of American Civilization,* 2 vols. (New York, 1927), 1:196.

[10]Louis M. Hacker *et al., The United States: A Graphic History* (New York, 1936), p. 28. Although two other coauthors were listed for this work, Rudolf Modley and George R. Taylor, Hacker himself was solely responsible for the written text. See also *The Triumph of American Capitalism* (New York, 1940).

capitalism. Disillusioned by the economic disintegration that seemed to be taking place in many parts of the Western world, Hacker became a formidable critic of the capitalist system. It seemed to him that capitalism was incapable of providing abundance, work, and security for vast numbers of people. With the economic crises uppermost in his mind, Hacker examined the American past and rewrote the nation's history along bold new lines. Hacker's analysis of the British mercantilist system, then, was set within the framework of a Marxist interpretation of American history. For Hacker freedom from the British merchant capitalists prepared the way for the native industrial capitalists to dominate society in America; the American people merely exchanged one capitalist master for another. Hacker's article from the *Marxist Quarterly* is reprinted as the first selection in this chapter.

Although Beer, Andrews, and Hacker shed new light upon the imperial regulations and possible motives behind the mercantilist system, much research remained to be done on the laws themselves. What were the specific provisions of the navigation acts, for example, and how well had these measures been administered? What was the effect of the navigation laws upon England's economy? To what degree had these laws achieved the purpose for which they had been passed? Such specific questions were raised and answered in the works of Lawrence A. Harper.

Harper's book *The English Navigation Laws: A Seventeenth Century Experiment in Social Engineering*, published in 1939, viewed this legislation primarily from the point of view of English administration and policy. In dealing with the navigation acts of the 1600s, Harper attempted to put these laws in proper historical context by showing that they were the culmination of a three-century-long program to build up England's shipping fleet. By examining the period both before and after the passage of these acts, Harper was able to ascertain that they had a decidedly beneficial effect upon England's economy. The laws, he concluded, had stimulated England's shipbuilding industry, provided employment for England's shipwrights, and enabled England's sailors to receive training in the merchant marine that stood them in good stead when called to serve in the Royal Navy. Some historians had assumed the navigation acts were ineffective in America because the colonists had evaded them, but Harper's study showed that in the 1600s, at least, there was very little smuggling in the trade across the Atlantic. Although Harper's conclusions were based only upon estimates of English shipping (because complete statistics were unavailable), his book remains the most thoroughgoing evaluation of the navigation acts in the seventeenth century.

Harper, as his subtitle indicates, approached the navigation acts as an experiment in the idea of a planned economy. That is, he looked upon the acts as a deliberate attempt by the English government to regulate the economic conduct of the state along predetermined lines by means of social planning. His work appeared at precisely the time that similar efforts were being made in America under the New Deal. Indeed, Harper confessed at the beginning of his book that he was interested in analyzing the process of social engineering "in the hope that it may throw some light upon the problems involved in our present social experiments."[11]

In a penetrating essay written in the same year as his book, Harper turned his attention to the effect of the navigation acts upon the economic life of the American colonies. Harper took exception to the conclusions of Beer that the Old Colonial System was so fair that economic benefits and burdens were neatly balanced between Britain and the American colonies. In his statistical analysis, Harper found that the burdens of the navigation acts outweighed the benefits received and that such legislation had actually retarded the economic growth of the mainland colonies. But, Harper quickly added, this did not mean that British mercantilism was bad or that the navigation acts had caused the Revolution; the American colonies received many advantages from the imperial tie—such as military and naval protection—which he admittedly did not take up in his essay.[12]

Harper discussed the broader question of British mercantilism and the American Revolution in another article published in 1942. In this piece Harper sought to measure in quantitative terms the burdens imposed by British mercantilist policies on various segments of the American economy. So far as commerce across the Atlantic was concerned, he estimated that it cost the Americans between \$2 million and \$7 million each year to trade within the framework laid down in the regulations of the mother country. The picture was less clear, however, when it came to British regulations on American manufacturing. The Woolens Act of 1699 probably had little impact on the woolen industry, and opportunities for exporting woolen goods from one colony to another were limited. The Hat Act of 1732 had restricted the colonial hat industry, but, Harper added, this type of manufacturing played only a minor part in the American economy. As for the Iron Act of 1750, Harper was dubious whether the legislation had had much influence upon the iron industry. In his overall evaluation, Harper concluded that "an analysis of the economic effects of British mercantilism fails to establish its exploitive features as the proximate cause of the Revolution."[13]

---

[11]Lawrence A. Harper, *The English Navigation Laws: A Seventeenth Century Experiment in Social Engineering* (New York, 1939), p. viii.

[12]Lawrence A. Harper, "The Effect of the Navigation Acts on the Thirteen Colonies," in *Era of the American Revolution*, ed. Richard B. Morris (New York, 1939), pp. 3–39.

[13]Lawrence A. Harper, "Mercantilism and the American Revolution," *Canadian Historical Review* 23 (March 1942):12.

The study of history reveals that it is not events as they actually are, but as people think that they are, which often determines the course of history. Although it was true that many historians concluded that the Old Colonial System did not exploit the colonists, it was conceivable that many Americans *thought* the British mercantilist system was taking advantage of them, and upon the basis of supposed economic grievances, embarked upon the Revolution. It was left to Oliver M. Dickerson to investigate just what the American reaction was to one aspect of British mercantilism—the navigation acts.

Dickerson's book *The Navigation Acts and the American Revolution*, published in the 1950s, dealt a severe blow to those who still clung to a strict economic interpretation on the coming of the Revolution and to the acts as one of the important long-range causes for the separation from Britain. The colonists, Dickerson concluded, did not object to the navigation acts as such nor to the mercantilist policies of the Old Colonial System. Searching through much of the contemporary literature— newspapers, pamphlets, broadsides, and writings of leading political figures—Dickerson discovered that the colonists rarely raised the British mercantile system as an issue before 1763. Instead of driving the colonies and mother country apart, Britain's trade and navigation laws, according to Dickerson, provided "the most important cement of empire."[14]

It was only after 1763, Dickerson went on, when the British altered their mercantilist system to raise revenue rather than to control trade within the empire, that the colonists began protesting. In the period after the French and Indian War, the dominant motive of British mercantilism changed from the regulation of trade and commerce to regulation for the sake of revenue and political exploitation. George III and his corrupt faction sought to shift part of the burden of defending British North America to the colonies by levying a series of new taxes and to use the taxing power to create jobs as customs officials in America for their political henchmen. America was exploited by these newly-appointed officials who resorted to "customs racketeering" to victimize wealthy colonial merchants under the technicalities of the law. Within a decade, the loyalty and mutual interest that bound the colonies and mother country together in a "cement of empire" had dissolved. "The hostility was not [due] to the old navigation and trade system," concluded Dickerson, "but to a new policy contrary to that system."[15] Dickerson's book attempted to demonstrate that the colonies were not only prosperous under the old navigation laws, but loyal and satisfied as well.

One of the most ardent defenders of the British mercantilist system

---

[14]Oliver M. Dickerson, *The Navigation Acts and the American Revolution* (Philadelphia, 1951), p. 157.

[15]*Ibid.*, p. xiv.

in the mid-twentieth century was Lawrence H. Gipson, a prolific scholar who continued to uphold the tradition of the imperial school of historians. Unlike Harper and Dickerson, who were openly critical of the change in mercantilist policy after 1763, Gipson took the position that the mother country was perfectly justified in levying taxes to pay part of the costs of administering the empire in America. Gipson viewed the mercantilist system in the broadest possible context and wrote a multivolume work on the British Empire in the period prior to the Revolution which placed the development of the American colonies in a world setting. The wars Britain waged against France in America were not motivated by a lust for empire, Gipson claimed, but rather by an ardent desire to protect her colonies from being conquered by the French. Gipson felt it only fair that the Americans, having been the beneficiaries of Britain's military might from 1754 to 1763, should pay part of the bill for such protection. Gipson also took up the question of oppressive taxation as a cause of the Revolution and concluded that in view of the protection Britain had provided, the taxes imposed upon the American colonists after 1763 were neither excessive nor oppressive.[16]

Gipson's works were as important for their pro-British interpretation as for their presentation of the mercantilist system from an imperial point of view. During the war with France, the Americans were pictured as being shortsighted and selfish by their unwillingness to accept their responsibilities as members of the British Empire. Britain, on the other hand, was presented in very favorable terms. The mother country spent enormous sums of money in defending America, subsidized colonial defense efforts, and sent over large numbers of redcoats to fight the French. Gipson stated in a one-volume work published in the 1950s that the Americans continued their selfish ways once the war was over. With the threat of the French removed from Canada, the Americans felt less of a need for the mother country. They began demanding more autonomy, resisted the payment of taxes, and refused to accede to Parliamentary laws passed to bring greater order and organization to Britain's enlarged empire in North America. According to Gipson, then, the Americans were lacking in that loyalty that might reasonably have been expected of them after they had received the benefits of a mercantilist system that had provided both military protection and profitable commerce.[17]

Thus, the changing view of the mercantilist system had moved from a pro-American position of George Bancroft in the 1850s to a pro-British interpretation by Lawrence Gipson in the 1950s. Gipson's work had

---

[16]Lawrence H. Gipson, *The British Empire before the American Revolution*, 15 vols. (Caldwell, Idaho, and New York, 1936–1970).

[17]Lawrence H. Gipson, *The Coming of the Revolution, 1763–1775* (New York, 1954), pp. xi–xiv, 26–27, and 230–34.

demonstrated one thing: that in the past century American historians had found it possible at long last to break free from the bonds of the narrow, nationalist bias in evaluating the mercantilist system.

In the 1960s and 1970s, two new approaches to the study of imperial relations emerged. One group of scholars might be termed the neoimperialists to distinguish them from the more traditional school. The second group—the self-styled "new economic historians"—revolutionized the study of economic history, employing research strategies that involved quantitative techniques and the use of economic model-building.

These two groups of scholars were less concerned with determining the benefits or burdens of the Old Colonial System than in raising different questions regarding the political and economic life of the British Empire. The neoimperialists focused more upon the informal structures within the political and administrative institutions of the Old Colonial System. The "new economic historians"—who were a fragment group within the "new social history"—on the other hand, concentrated on two other issues. First, they described the workings of the North Atlantic economic community as a whole. Second, they sought to explain America's economic growth within the broad context of the Anglo-American commercial world. The contributions of the two groups illuminated not only some hitherto unknown forces at work within the empire but also introduced new methodologies in doing research on economic developments in the mother country as well as the colonies.

Many of the historians of the traditional imperial school—such as Gipson—were favorably inclined toward Britain and pictured America as being too selfish, self-centered, and shortsighted. The neoimperial historians were less interested in taking sides and concerned more with analyzing the complexities of the relationships between mother country and colony. In writing about British politics they focused more upon the informal structure of authority—the attitudes, goals, and rivalries of the groups and individuals running the machinery of the empire—than upon the formal structure of public institutions, officials, and agencies. When dealing with the perpetual struggle for power within the British bureaucracy, they wrote about the colonial agent-lobbyists, interest groups, and social groupings within Parliament who contributed to the decision-making process on imperial policies. And in discussing ideology, they were more cognizant of the central role that ideas played in precipitating the Revolution—the conspiracy theory held by many British officials that the colonists were determined to throw off their dependence upon the Crown; the conspiracy theory among Americans that the mother country was aiming to deprive them of their rights and liberties under the British constitution; and the colonists' attitudes toward their status as subordinates within the British Empire.

The neoimperialist scholars partly reflected both external and internal pressures upon the historical profession. In the world at large the collapse of the old European empires in Asia and Africa after World War II resulted in a reexamination of the effects of imperialism. With many former colonies emerging into nationhood, some American historians felt there were parallels between the American colonial experience in the seventeenth and eighteenth centuries and the experiences of other colonial peoples who gained their independence in the mid-twentieth century.

Some neoimperial scholars revised an earlier school of historians who had followed the lead of Lewis B. Namier, a distinguished British scholar who had destroyed the old idea of the existence of Whig and Tory parties in England during the reign of George III. Namier substituted instead an atomistic picture of British politics with a fragmented Parliament made up of competing factions and family groupings whose members were concerned solely with securing political offices for themselves, their kin, or local constituents. Thus Parliament's outlook was narrow-minded, factious, and provincial, and its workings were organized around material interests, family connections, and patronage. This situation made it impossible for Parliament to achieve the kind of broad-minded, imperial view required for sound policies of empire. Because of this grasping, circumscribed, and nonideological approach to politics, Namier concluded, Britain could not have produced a viable imperial policy, resolved her quarrel with the colonies, or prevented the loss of her empire.

Certain neoimperial scholars, however, were prone to see the ideology of interest groups at work within the Parliament in the formulation of imperial policy. A leading representative of the neoimperial approach, Michael Kammen, studied the workings of such interest groups in British politics from the mid-1600s to 1800 in his *Empire and Interest,* published in 1970. He claimed that British mercantilism gave rise to a host of interest groups—men bound together by special interests who united their efforts to advance, maintain, and defend those interests. Kammen examined the total environment of each of these groups—the concepts, assumptions, and attitudes as well as the material motivation of its members—and used the history of such interest groups to analyze and explain changes in domestic and imperial politics. Such an approach, among other things, enabled him to place the coming of the American Revolution within the broader context of interest-group politics inside the British Empire.

Thomas C. Barrow, another scholar identified with the neoimperial approach, sought to examine the inner workings of the formal institution he was studying in his *Trade and Empire: The British Customs Service in Colonial America, 1660–1775.* In this work Barrow inquired into the motivation and ideology of the men who ran this part of the imperial machinery. Rather than concentrating only on the operation of the customs service, Barrow analyzed the experiences and reactions of the British bureaucrats in London who were administering that agency. Barrow concluded that these administrators were mainly concerned with the domestic affairs of the mother country and paid only casual attention to American problems. When they did interest themselves in colonial affairs, these men revealed that they were operating on one underlying assumption: that the interests of the mother country were in conflict and inherently incompatible with those of the colonies, and that the Americans—aware of this fact—were looking forward to the day when they would be free from Britain. In contrast to the older school of imperial historians who sometimes suggested that Anglo-American relations prior to 1760 were essentially harmonious, Barrow concluded that the relationship engendered hostility among British administrators; they were haunted continually by the fear of eventual American independence.

The "new economic historians," like the neoimperialists, moved in quite a different direction from the scholars who had preceded them. Prior to the 1960s, American economic historians tended to be primarily descriptive in their writings. They focused largely on studies of individual businessmen, institutional changes, and separate sectors of the economy. Some of the problems they dealt with concerned the nature of economic institutions and the impact of social and political factors upon economic development or stagnation. To support their conclusions, they tended to rely upon traditional literary sources, impressionistic information, and scattered statistical evidence. The new generation of economic historians were skeptical of both the problems posed and the evidence presented by these older scholars. They insisted instead that the study of economic history be analytical rather than descriptive, systematic instead of fragmentary, and that it focus on economic growth rather than on piecemeal economic developments. The study of economic history, they believed, should be firmly grounded in statistical information— hard quantitative data capable of empirical verification. With the help of high-speed computers such data could be interpreted in the light of models derived from contemporary economic theory. Their emphasis on these new research techniques led them to study long-term trends and more sweeping economic developments.

Applying the techniques of quantification and model-building, the "new economic historians" raised once again the question of how severely the navigation acts had affected America's economy. Harper had attempted earlier to quantify the burdens resulting from British regulations which compelled colonial merchants to reroute their trade. Robert Paul Thomas, using more sophisticated quantitative techniques, wrote an article in the 1960s which confirmed Harper's findings. Thomas estimated that between 1763 and 1772 the annual per capita loss to the American colonies from Britain's mercantile system averaged only about twenty-six cents per person, or about 0.5 percent of the estimated per capita income. On this basis, he argued, neither the navigation acts nor the new British imperial regulations applied after 1763 imposed any significant economic burden upon America.[18] Thomas's article is the second selection in this chapter.

Gary M. Walton and James F. Shepherd in their book, *The Economic Rise of Early America*, summarized the findings of several quantitative historians and came to somewhat similar conclusions. The studies they examined concurred that any exploitation resulting from the navigation acts ranged from 1 to 3 percent of the colonial national income—with 1 percent being the most acceptable estimate. Although 1 percent was not trivial—especially because the heaviest burden fell on one region, the upper South—it was by no means intolerable.[19]

The overall result of these recent findings has been to de-emphasize the impact of the navigation acts on the colonial economy. Stuart Bruchey in his book, to be sure, argued that Britain's mercantilist policies probably hindered America's economic growth prior to the Revolution. But he went on to caution that this generalization was by no means conclusive, for the problem required further study. George R. Taylor, in an essay on America's economic growth from its founding in the early 1600s to 1840, produced evidence that suggested the rate of growth from 1710 to 1775 was almost as high as it had been from 1775 to 1840. Besides de-emphasizing the effect of the navigation acts, Taylor's essay demonstrated the virtue of looking at the process of economic development over long periods of time.[20]

Other scholars have examined America's colonial economic growth in a similar light. Shepherd and Walton, in another book, examined the long-range economic development of the colonies within the context of the Anglo-American commercial community. Their conclusion was that though the balance of trade may have been against the colonies, the balance of payments was not. The sale of ships made in America to Britain, purchases by the British army in America, and insurance and freight charges all contributed to make up the deficit. The balance of

---

[18]Robert Paul Thomas, "A Quantitative Approach to the Study of the Effects of British Imperial Policy upon Colonial Welfare: Some Preliminary Findings," *Journal of Economic History* 25 (1965): 615–38.

[19]Gary M. Walton and James F. Shepherd, *The Economic Rise of Early America* (New York, 1979).

[20]Stuart Bruchey, *The Roots of American Economic Growth, 1607–1861* (New York, rev. ed., 1968); and George R. Taylor, "American Economic Growth Before 1840: An Exploratory Essay," *Journal of Economic History* 24 (1964): 427–44.

payments between Britain and America from 1768 to 1772, in fact, was even.[21]

Marc Egnal approached the problem of America's economic growth in the colonial period from a somewhat different perspective. Like most "new economic historians," Egnal turned away from the questions raised by Harper and Hacker; he did not focus his attention either on the navigation acts or upon the structure of the Old Colonial System. Concerned primarily with explaining America's economic growth, Egnal concentrated instead upon certain key determinants during the early colonial period—the dynamics of population increase, the rising prices of products, and the increasing availability of capital within the international Atlantic economy.

Egnal argued that much of the economic development of the colonies was affected by conditions outside of America. It was the fluctuations within the British economy between 1720 and 1775 that helped determine to a large degree the pace at which both the colonial population and the American standard of living grew. The increase in new settlers and per capita income in the colonies was characterized by two long waves of expansion: the years 1720–1745 and 1745–1775—though there were patterns of acceleration and retardation within these long swings. Thus, by noting that colonial economic development was largely dependent upon incoming immigrants (as well as on the rise in population by natural means, of course) and upon the influx of British funds, Egnal succeeded in placing America's economic growth within an international rather than a narrow, nationalistic context.[22]

In reviewing the question of whether or not British mercantilism was a help or hindrance to the American colonies, students must draw a balance sheet of the relative benefits and burdens resulting from the imperial system. Were military and naval protection, the markets for colonial products, and the commercial credit that Britain provided to the colonies absolutely essential to their survival, well-being, and growth? Did the colonists pay too dearly for such benefits by the burdens they had to bear as members of the British Empire? Does the absence of much opposition to the Old Colonial System before 1763 indicate that Ameri-

---

[21]James F. Shepherd and Gary Walton, *Shipping, Maritime Trade and the Economic Development of Colonial America* (Cambridge, England, 1973). Two studies which dealt with America's economic growth after the Revolution but which discussed briefly the situation in the colonial period were Douglass C. North's *The Economic Growth of the United States 1790–1860* (rev. ed. New York, 1966); and Gordon Bjork, "The Weaning of the American Economy: Independence, Market Changes, and Economic Development," *Journal of Economic History* 24 (1964): 541–60.

[22]Marc Egnal, "The Economic Development of the Thirteen Continental Colonies, 1720 to 1775," *William and Mary Quarterly*, 3d ser. 32 (April 1975): 191–222.

cans did not object seriously to the system? Or were the Americans content to leave well enough alone because the system was so ineffective and left them virtually free to do as they pleased? Was the older school of imperial historians correct in assuming that the Americans were selfish and shortsighted because they refused to pay taxes and to accept the other responsibilities required of them as members of the British Empire? Or were the historians of the 1960s and 1970s more accurate in taking a neutral position on this matter when they analyzed the complex imperial relationship from different perspectives and with new research techniques? Were the "new economic historians" on the right track when they insisted upon viewing colonial economic development within the framework of the North Atlantic commercial community rather than in an American framework? In answering such questions, students are apt to come to some conclusions not only about the British mercantilist system but about the causes of the American Revolution itself.

# Louis M. Hacker

LOUIS M. HACKER (1899– ) taught at Columbia University and other American and English universities. Among his many books are *The Triumph of American Capitalism* (1940), *Alexander Hamilton in the American Tradition* (1957), and *The World of Andrew Carnegie: 1865–1901* (1968).

At the outbreak of the American Revolution the great majority of the American population—perhaps nine-tenths of it—was engaged on the land. The owning farmers, whether they were planter lords or modest family farmers, were commercial agriculturists: for either they produced cash crops for sale in a market or they developed subsidiary activities to net them a money return. Self-sufficiency, even on the frontier, is impossible under capitalist organization. Cash is needed everywhere, whether it is to pay taxes or for harvesting the crop or to buy salt, iron, and a squirrel gun. Hence, the colonial farmer either produced a cash crop or he tried to find employment among a number of occupations that did not interfere with his agricultural activities. He either trapped or hunted; or worked in logging operations; or shipped with a fishing fleet. Often he really obtained his cash from land speculation: that is to say, as the result of constantly mounting land values, the farmer was in a position to sell his improved land and buy a cheaper farm in the frontier areas. Thus, the American farmer was a dealer in land from the very dawn of settlement until 1920, a period of three centuries. When land values began to decline after 1921, the basis of American agricultural well-being was shaken to its foundations.

This need to develop a cash crop made for the production of staples everywhere. By the eighteenth century New England was producing and sending to market beef, cattle and hogs, work animals and corn to be used for stall feeding. The Middle Colonies had become the great granary of the English settlements, and on the big farms of New York and Pennsylvania, where tenants and indentured servants were being employed, wheat was being grown, processed into flour and sold in the towns and the faraway West Indies. In the Southern Colonies agriculture

Louis M. Hacker, "The American Revolution: Economic Aspects," *Marxist Quarterly* 1 (January–March 1937): 46–67. Reprinted, with omissions, by permission of Louis M. Hacker.

was the keystone of the whole economic structure: Virginia and Maryland planters grew tobacco for sale in England; interior farmers grew grains and raised cattle to be used in the West Indian trade; the tidewater planters of the Carolinas and Georgia cultivated and harvested rice, indigo and some cotton. These crops were sent to seaports, put on ships and carried to distant places to furnish those funds which were the basis of the commercial enterprise of the day. . . .

The plantation economy sprang up in colonial Virginia and Maryland, notably, for obvious reasons. The cultivation of a staple like tobacco served excellently the purposes of the Mercantilist System: it did not compete with an important English crop and hence might be grown on a grand scale; it produced a colonial return on the basis of which large English exports might be sent to the Southern Colonies; it furnished opportunities for the investment of English capital—short-term funds for the financing of the crops and long-term funds for the hypothecation of plantation properties; and it created an outlet for England's surplus populations. Thus tobacco cultivation was closely bound to English mercantilist policy. . . .

There was no question that the tobacco market kept on expanding: at the end of the seventeenth century Maryland and Virginia were exporting 35 million pounds to the mother country; by 1763 the quantity had trebled. On the other hand, the industry was at the mercy of the imperial system. Tobacco was on the enumerated list and could be sent, therefore, only to England; high sumptuary taxes were placed on it; prices were controlled in London and tended to drop periodically below the cost of production. In addition, capital costs of plantation operation continued to mount, due to the high cost of labor (the price of indentured servants and, more particularly, that of slaves went up while their productivity remained constant), the exhaustion of the soil in the older regions, and the necessity on the part of the planters to buy new lands to which they could be ready to transfer their activities. The other charges against operations—of freight costs, insurance, merchants' commissions and profits, interest on borrowings—hung like millstones about the necks of the encumbered planters.

The plantation system was particularly dependent upon credit. The tobacco grower required credit to assist in the acquisition of the labor force; to market his cash crop; to furnish his equipment; and to finance his purchase of consumers goods. The only source of funds was the English merchant capitalist: and to him the southern planter was compelled to pay high interest rates, mortgage his land and slaves and turn for the supplying of those necessaries without which his home and plantation could not continue. Constantly weighed down by debt, it was small wonder that the planters of colonial America ever sought to expand their activities, by extending their tobacco lands and engaging in the more speculative aspects of land dealing; and that they turned to thoughts of inflation as relief from debt oppression was also to be expected.

Because the wild lands of the frontier areas were so important to the maintenance of the stability of the southern planting economy, southern capitalists were constantly preoccupied with them. The West was not opened up by the hardy frontiersman; it was opened up by the land speculator who preceded even the Daniel Boones into the wilderness. But the English (and also the Scotch) had also learned to regard with more than a curious interest these wild lands of the West: they saw in them profits from the fur trade and from the speculative exploitation of the region by their own capitalist enterprise. It was at this point that English and southern merchant capital came into conflict; and when, as a result of the promulgation of the Proclamation Line of 1763 and the Quebec Act of 1774, the western lands were virtually closed to colonial enterprising, the southern planting economy began to totter. Without the subsidiary activity of land speculation, planters could not continue solvent; there is no cause for wonder, therefore, that the owners of great plantation properties should be among the first to swell the ranks of the colonial revolutionary host in 1775.

Colonial producers and enterprisers engaged in all those other activities that are associated with a newly settled region. The trapping and slaying of the wild animals of the forests early attracted pioneers and promoters; and the prevalence of the beaver, otter, mink, bear, raccoon and fox in the New England and Middle Colonies and of the deer, raccoon, fox and beaver in the Southern Colonies led to the creation of a thriving peltry and hide industry and trade. The English demand for furs and skins was constant, profits were great, and quickly capitalism became interested and sought to monopolize the field. This it was not difficult to do, particularly when the lines of the traffic lengthened as the wild lands kept on receding beyond the tidewater settlements. English merchants and the great southern and northern landlords financed the individual hunters, trappers, and traders, or employed them as their agents, and furnished the truck and firearms which served as the basis for the Indian barter. As the extermination of wildlife went on, the keeping open of an ever-extending frontier zone became one of the necessities of the colonial economy: the struggle over the fur trade had involved England and France in the long series of colonial wars in America; and the desire to continue the fur traffic was one of the reasons for colonial interest in the wild lands beyond the crest of the Appalachians—and, hence, collision with the mother country. . . .

There existed no manufacturing, in the commercial or industrial sense, in colonial America: and in this fact we are to find one of the important keys to the outbreak of the American Revolution. Household manufacturing there was: the colonial farming households, particularly of the more modest sort and where the necessaries of indentured servants and Negro slaves were concerned, supplied many of their own needs. Food was prepared for home consumption: bread was baked, butter was churned, shoulders and hams were salted and smoked, fruits were dried, beer was brewed. Wool, flax, hemp, and, in the South, cotton for clothing and home uses were carded, spun, woven, and sometimes even rudely dyed. Leather was tanned and made into shoes, caps, gloves, and rough workclothes. The woodlot furnished the timber for house and barn, shingles, furniture, carts, implement handles, casks, and staves. Ashes were leached, soap was boiled, candles were molded, and kitchen utensils of wood, horn, and gourd were devised. Sometimes working with his family, sometimes assisted by traveling artisans, the colonial farmer was able to fabricate many crude articles for his daily needs out of those raw materials that he had at hand. Occasionally a surplus of cloth, linen, butter, or honey was taken to the local village and sold or exchanged for the salt, iron, paint, and tools that were essential to the conduct of the household; for self-sufficiency, of course, was never fully attained.

This was not manufacturing in the capitalist sense. The conversion of raw materials into finished goods and their sale in large and distant markets, in modern times, has been under the supervision of two different types of organization. Sometimes found side by side but in the broad and abstract sense existing in a sequential relationship, these have been domestic manufacturing, or the putting-out system, and industrial manufacturing, or the factory system. . . .

Neither of this type of manufacturing organization was to be found in colonial America. Why was this? Colonial America did not want for liquid capital: witness the extraordinary extension of capitalist enterprise, the work of both English and American capitalists, in trade, shipbuilding, land speculation, the financing of the plantation system, and crude iron production. Colonial America had its fair share of wealthy men: as early as 1680, there were said to be at least thirty merchants in Massachusetts alone who were worth between $50,000 and $100,000. Thomas Amory, one of the greatest early colonial merchants, left an estate worth $100,000; Peter Faneuil, who died a generation later, left many times that amount. Every colony could boast of its big merchants, who were, in fact, capitalists; indeed, George Washington, the greatest of these, in the 1770s was calling himself not "planter" but "merchant." It did not want for the means of creating a free labor supply: the engrossing, or monopolization, of the lands in the settled areas had compelled small farmers either to become tenants or to move westward where they squatted on the wild lands held by absentee landlords. The frontier had not been made secure against the Indians because of the fur trade, and the necessity for maintaining tidewater land values; but had the owners of the wild lands so desired it, the pacification of the western areas would have driven the landless into domestic manufacturing or workshops. It did not want for a market: by 1770, concentrated in a relatively small area and excellently served by harbors and rivers, lived a population one-third as great as England's; too, the very rich market for finished goods of the sugar islands easily was capable of exploitation. It did not want for raw materials: for never was a land endowed with richer natural resources. Manufacturing did not appear in colonial America because the very nature of the Mercantilist System prohibited it.

The English Mercantilist System, in its imperial-colonial relations, following the triumph of English merchant capital in the Puritan Revolution, was based on the economic subservience of the colonies. Indeed, every imperial and administrative agency had this end constantly in view: and most significant among these was the Board of Trade. The Board of Trade, in its final form, had been established in 1696, and, among its various instruments for control over the colonies, these three were notable: it had the right to deny charters or patents to English-financed companies seeking to engage in enterprises in the colonies which were inimical to the interests of home merchant capitalists; it had the power to review colonial legislation and recommend to the Privy Council the disallowance of such colonial enactments as ran counter to the welfare of the mother country; and it prepared specific instructions for the deportment of the royal governors in the colonies, in particular indicating where the veto power was to be used to prevent colonial encroachments on the privileges and prerogatives of English citizens.

Ever vigilant, the Board of Trade proceeded against the colonies when they threatened to impinge on the interests of Englishmen: it refused to tolerate colonial interference with the mother country's hold on foreign trade and shipping; it checked colonial attempts to control the traffic in convicts and slaves; it prevented colonies from lowering interest rates, easing the judicial burden on debtors, and seeking to monopolize the Indian trade. Most significant were the stern checks imposed on attempts by the colonial assemblies to encourage native manufacturing and to relieve the oppression of debts by the increase of the money supply of the colonies.

Following in the footsteps of the English themselves, colonials looked to public authority to aid in the development of native industries. In the best mercantilist tradition, therefore, colonial statute books came to be filled with legislation which offered bounties to enterprisers, extended public credit to them, exempted them from taxation, gave them easy access to raw materials, and in their behalf encouraged the location of new towns.

Against such legislation the Board of Trade regularly moved. On important matters, appeal was had to Parliament and general statutes were passed, notably the Woolens Act of 1699, which barred colonial wool, woolen yarn and woolen manufactures from intercolonial and foreign commerce; the Hat Act of 1732, which prevented the exportation of hats out of the separate colonies and restricted colonial hatmakers to two apprentices; and the Iron Act of 1750. In addition, the axe of disallowance descended regularly. As early as 1705 a Pennsylvania law for building up the shoemaking industry was disallowed; in 1706, a New York law designed to develop a sailcloth industry was disallowed; in 1706, 1707 and 1708, laws of Virginia and Maryland, providing for the establishment of new towns, were disallowed on the grounds that such new communities must invariably lead to a desire to found manufacturing industries and that their existence would draw off persons from the countryside where they were engaged in the production of tobacco. Indeed, in 1756, when the Board of Trade recommended disallowance of a Massachusetts law for aiding the production of linen, it could say flatly: "the passing of laws in the plantations for encouraging manufactures, which in any ways interfere with the manufacture of this kingdom, has always been thought improper, and has ever been discouraged."

Also, the royal governors were closely instructed to veto all legislation designed to assist the development of such manufactures as might compete with those of England. This had its effect, so that E. A. Russell, an outstanding American authority upon the subject, has been led to conclude: "Largely as a result of the government's determined attitude in the matter, comparatively few laws for this purpose were enacted in the plantations." In no small measure the general result was heightened by the limitations imposed on English capital seeking investments in the colonies. English balances in the colonies and English new capital were kept away from manufactures; and they might be placed only in land and land operations. The overextension of sugar planting, in the West Indies, and of tobacco planting, in the mainland colonies, undoubtedly was due to this restriction and therefore helped in the shaping of the crisis in the imperial-colonial relations which set in in the 1760s.

Thus, at the very time in England when the domestic system was rapidly being converted into the factory system and great advances were being made in the perfection of machinery exactly because the existence of a growing market was demanding more efficient methods of production, in the colonies methods of production remained at a hopelessly backward level because English and colonial capital could not enter manufacturing. An important outlet for accumulated funds was barred. The colonial capitalist economy, therefore, was narrowly restricted largely to land speculation, the dealing in furs and the carrying trade. When English mercantilism, for the protection of its home merchant capital, began to narrow these spheres then catastrophe threatened. The American Revolution can be understood only in terms of the necessity for colonial merchant capital to escape from the contracting prison walls of the English Mercantilist System.

In an imperial economy the capitalist relationships between mother country and colonies as a rule lead to a colonial unfavorable balance of trade. The colonies buy the goods and services of the mother country and are encouraged to develop those raw materials the home capitalists require. In this they are aided by the investment of the mother country's balances and by new capital. Thus, in the Southern Colonies, tobacco largely was being produced to furnish returns for the English goods and services the plantation lords required; but, because the exchange left England with a favorable balance, by the 1770s its capitalists had more than £4 million invested in southern planting operations. To meet the charges on this debt, southern planters were compelled constantly to expand their agricultural operations and to engage in the subsidiary activities of land speculation and the fur trade.

The Northern Colonies were less fortunately placed. The Northern Colonies directly produced little of those staples necessary to the maintenance of the English economy: the grains, provisions, and work animals of New England, New York, and Pennsylvania could not be permitted to enter England lest they disorganize the home commercial agricultural industry; and the same was true of the New England fishing catches. The Northern Colonies, of course, were a source for lumber, naval stores, furs, whale products and iron, and these England sorely needed to maintain her independence of European supplies. England sought to encourage these industries by bounties and other favored positions; but in vain. Notably unsuccessful was the effort to divert northern colonial capital from shipbuilding and shipping into the production of naval stores by the Bounty Act of 1706.

The Northern Colonies, therefore, produced little for direct export to England to permit them to pay their balances, that is to say, for the increasing quantities of English drygoods, hardware, and house furnishings they were taking. In view of the fact, too, that the Northern Colonies presented slight opportunities for the investment of English capital, it was incumbent upon the merchants of the region to develop returns elsewhere in order to obtain specie and bills of exchange with which to balance payments in England.

Out of this necessity arose the economic significance of the various triangular trading operations (and the subsidiary industries growing out of trade) the northern merchants organized. Northern merchants and shipowners opened up regular markets in Newfoundland and Nova Scotia for their fishing tackle, salt, provisions, and rum; they established an ever-growing commercial intercourse with the wine islands of the

Canaries and Madeira, from which they bought wines direct and to which they sold barrel staves, foodstuffs and live animals; they sold fish to Spain, Portugal and Italy; their ports acted as entrepots for the transshipment of southern staples to England and southern Europe.

The trade with the West Indian sugar islands—as well as the traffic in Negro slaves and the manufacture of rum, which grew out of it—became the cornerstone of the northern colonial capitalist economy. Northern merchants loaded their ships with all those necessaries the sugar planters were unable to produce—work animals for their mills; lumber for houses and outbuildings; staves, heads, and hoops for barrels; flour and salted provisions for their tables; and refuse fish for their slaves—and made regular runs to the British islands of Barbados, the Leeward Islands and Jamaica, and then increasingly to the French, Spanish, Dutch, and Danish islands and settlements dotting the Caribbean. Here they acquired in return specie with which to pay their English balances, indigo, cotton, ginger, allspice, and dyewoods for transshipment to England, and, above all, sugar and molasses for conversion into rum in the distilleries of Massachusetts and Rhode Island. It was rum that served as the basis of the intercourse between the Northern Colonies and the African Coast: rum paid for ivory, gums, beeswax, and gold dust; and rum paid for Negroes who were carried to the sugar islands on that famous Middle Passage to furnish the labor supply without which the sugar plantation economy could not survive.

Such commercial transactions—in addition, of course, to the profits derived from the fisheries, whaling and shipbuilding—furnished the needed sources of return and their conduct the outlets for northern merchant capitalist accumulations. But they were not enough with which to pay all the English bills and to absorb all the mounting funds of the Amorys, Faneuils, Hancocks, and Boylstons of Boston, the Whartons, Willings, and Morrises of Philadelphia, the Livingstons, Lows and Crugers of New York, the Wantons and Lopezes of Newport and the Browns of Providence. In three illegal forms of enterprises—in piracy, smuggling generally, and the illicit sugar and molasses trade with the foreign West Indian islands—northern merchants found opportunities for the necessary expansion.

Piracy—at least up to the end of the seventeenth century, when England was able to exterminate it—played a significant part in maintaining the merchant capital of the Northern Colonies. English and colonial pirates, fitted out in northern ports and backed financially by reputable merchants, preyed on the Spanish fleets of the Caribbean and even boldly fared out into the Red Sea and the Indian Ocean to terrorize ships engaged in the East Indies trade; and with their ships heavily laden with plate, drygoods, and spices, put back into colonial ports where they sold their loot and divided their profits with the merchants who had financed them.

Smuggling contributed its share to the swelling of merchant fortunes. In the first place, there was the illegal direct intercourse between the colonies and European countries in the expanding list of enumerated articles; and, in the second place, sl ps on the homebound voyages from Europe or the West Indies broug..t large supplies of drygoods, silk, cocoa and brandies into the American colonies without having declared these articles at English ports and paid the duties. Most important of all was the trade with the foreign West Indian sugar islands, which was rendered illegal, after 1733, as a result of the imposition by the Molasses Act of prohibitive duties on the importation into the colonies of foreign sugar, molasses and rum.

In this West Indian trade was to be found the strength and the weakness of colonial merchant capital. The English sugar interest was the darling of the Mercantilist System. Sugar, more so even than tobacco, was the great oversea staple of the eighteenth-century world; and not only to it was bound a ramified English commercial industry made up of carriers, commission men, factors, financiers, processors, and distributors: but sugar was converted into molasses and in turn distilled into rum to support the unholy slave traffic and the unsavory Indian trade. The sugar cultivation therefore had the constant solicitude of English imperial officialdom and a sugar bloc, made up of absentee landlords, exerted a powerful influence in Parliament. Indeed, so significant a role did sugar play in the imperial economy that in the 1770s the capital worth of West Indian sugar properties stood at £60 million: of which at least one-half was the stake of home English investors. When it is noted that in the whole of the northern American mainland colonies the English capitalist stake at most was only one-sixth as great, then the reason for the favoring of the sugar colonies as against the northern commercial colonies, after 1763, is revealed in a single illuminating flash.

The feud had long been smoldering. With the third decade of the eighteenth century, northern merchants increasingly had taken to buying their sugar and molasses from the foreign sugar islands. Prices were cheaper by from 25 percent to 40 percent: due largely to the fact that the English planters were engaged in a single-crop exploitative agriculture in the interests of an absentee landlordism, while the French, Spanish, Dutch, and Danish planters were owners-operators who cultivated directly their small holdings and diversified their crops; too, the foreign sugar was not encumbered by imposts and mercantilist marketing restrictions. In the foreign sugar islands, as well, northern ship captains and owrers found it possible to develop new markets for their flour, provisions, lumber, work animals, and fish, thus obtaining another source from which specie and bills of exchange could be derived.

So heavy had this traffic become that the alarmed British sugar interest in Parliament succeeded in having passed the Molasses Act of 1733, which was designed virtually to outlaw the colonial-foreign island trade.

But the act did not have the desired effect because it could not be adequately enforced: the British customs machinery in the colonies was weak and venal and the naval patrols that could be allocated to this duty were inadequate because of England's engagement in foreign wars from 1740 almost continuously for twenty years. . . .

It is not to be wondered that British planters, threatened with bankruptcy, kept up a constant clamor for the enforcement of the laws and the total stoppage of the foreign island trade. Beginning with 1760, imperial England began to tighten the screws with the stricter enforcement of the Acts of Trade and Navigation; from thence on, particularly after France had been compelled to sue for peace in 1763, England embarked on a systematic campaign to wipe out the trade between the Northern Colonies and the foreign West Indies. Northern merchant capital, its most important lifeline cut off, was being strangulated; it is not difficult to see why wealthy merchants of Philadelphia, New York, Boston, Newport, and Providence should be converted into revolutionists. . . .

Such were the objective economic factors which resulted in making the position of the colonies, within the framework of the imperial-colonial relations, intolerable. The period of 1763–1775 was one of crisis, economically and politically: for in that decade it was demonstrated that English and colonial merchant capital both could not operate within a contracting sphere in which clashes of interest were becoming sharper and sharper. From 1760 on, pushed by those various groups whose well-being had been neglected during the years England was engaged in foreign wars, the rulers of the empire labored mightily to repair the rents that had appeared in the Mercantilist System.

The northern "smuggling interest" was hunted down vigorously. The admiralty courts and their procedure were augmented and strengthened; placemen in the customs service who were living in England were ordered to their colonial posts; in 1763 the navy was converted into a patrol fleet with power of search even on the high seas; informers were encouraged; and suits involving the seizure of cargoes and the payment of revenues were taken out of the hands of the local courts.

Utilizing the tax measures of 1764 and later (presumably designed to raise a revenue for the defense of the colonies) as a screen, Parliament imposed limitation after limitation upon the activities of the merchants. The Act of 1764 and the Stamp Act of 1765 called for the payment of duties and taxes in specie, thus further draining the colonies of currency and contracting the credit base. To divert colonial capital into raw materials, the first measure increased the bounties paid for the colonial production of hemp and flax, placed high duties on the colonial importation of foreign indigo, and removed the British import duties on colonial whale fins. To cripple the trade with the foreign West Indies a high duty was placed on refined sugar; while the importation of foreign rum was forbidden altogether and lumber was placed on the enumerated list. To give English manufacturers a firmer grip on their raw materials, hides and skins, pig and bar iron, and potash and pearl ashes were also included among the enumerated articles. To maintain the English monopoly of the colonial-finished goods market the entrance into the colonies of certain kinds of French and Oriental drygoods was taxed for the first time.

In 1764, to weaken further colonial merchant activity, high duties were imposed on wine from the wine islands and wine, fruits and oil from Spain and Portugal brought directly to America (in American ships, as a rule), while such articles brought over from England were to pay only nominal duties. And in 1766, in order to extend the market of English merchants in Europe, Parliament ordered that all remaining nonenumerated articles (largely flour, provisions and fish) bound for European ports north of Cape Finisterre be landed first in England.

It is significant to note that the revenue features of these acts were quickly abandoned: the Stamp Tax was repealed in 1766; and, in 1770, three years after their passage, the Townshend duties on paper, paint, and glass were lifted. Only the slight tax on tea remained: and even this was used as an instrument to bludgeon the aggressive northern merchant class into helplessness.

In order to save the East India Company from collapse, in 1773 that powerful financial organization was given permission to ship in its own vessels and dispose of, through its own merchandising agencies, a surplus stock of 17 million pounds of tea in America: and, in this way, drive out of business those Americans who carried, imported and sold in retail channels British tea (and, indeed, foreign tea, for the British tea under the new dispensation could be sold cheaper even than the smuggled Holland article). The merchants all over America were not slow to read the correct significance of this measure. As the distinguished historian Arthur M. Schlesinger has put it, pamphleteers set out to show "that the present project of the East India Company was the entering wedge for larger and more ambitious undertakings calculated to undermine the colonial mercantile world. Their opinion was based on the fact that, in addition to the article of tea, the East India Company imported into England vast quantities of silks, calico and other fabrics, spices, drugs, and chinaware, all commodities of staple demand; and on their fear that the success of the present venture would result in an extension of the same principle to the sale of the other articles."

The southern landlords did not escape. The Proclamation Line of 1763, for the purpose of setting up temporary governments in the far western lands wrested from France after the Seven Years' War, in effect shut off the whole area beyond the crest of the Appalachians to colonial fur traders and land dealers. By taking control of the region out of the hands of the colonial governors, putting it in charge of imperial agents and ordering the abandonment of the settlements already planted, the British looked forward to the maintenance of a great Indian reservation in which the fur trade—in the interests of British concessionaires— would continue to flourish. A few years later these rigorous regulations were relaxed somewhat: but the designs of English land speculators on the area, the prohibition of free land grants, the ordering of land sales at auctions only and the imposition of high quitrents, hardly improved matters. The planters were lost to the English cause. Their situation, already made perilous by the Currency Act of 1764, was now hopeless.

Thus, merchant capitalists—whether land speculators or traders— were converted from contented and loyal subjects into rebellious enemies of the Crown. Tea was destroyed in Boston harbor, turned back unloaded from New York and Philadelphia, and landed but not sold in Charleston. In 1774 the First Continental Congress, to which came dele- gates from all the colonies, met and wrote the Continental Association, an embargo agreement, which was so successfully enforced that imports from England virtually disappeared in 1775.

The discontents of planters and merchants, in themselves, were not enough to hasten the releasing process. To be successful, assistance was required from the ranks of the more numerous lower-middle-class small farmers, traders, artisans, and mechanics, and the working-class sea- men, fishermen, and laborers. This was not difficult: for the material well-being of the lower classes was tied to the successful enterprising of the upper.

The colonies had enjoyed a period of unprecedented prosperity dur- ing the years of the war with France. The expanding market in the West Indies, the great expenditures of the British quartermasters, the illegal and contraband trade with the enemy forces, all had furnished steady employment for workers on the fleets and in the shipyards and ports and lucrative outlets for the produce of small farmers. But with the end of the war and the passage of the restrictive legislation of 1763 and after, depression had set in to last until 1770. Stringency and bankruptcy everywhere confronted the merchants and big farmers; seamen and laborers were thrown out of work, small tradesmen were compelled to close their shops and small farmers were faced by ruin because of their expanded acreage, a diminished market and heavy fixed charges made particularly onerous as a result of currency contraction. Into the bargain, escape into the frontier zones—always the last refuge of the dispossessed—was shut off as a result of the Proclamation of 1763.

In addition, the colonial petty bourgeoisie groaned under specific class political and economic disabilities. Politically, almost universal disfranchisement, unequal legislative representation for the newer areas and the wide absence of local government placed state power in the hands of a small group of big propertied interests closely identified with the Crown. In colonial America only men of sizable properties could vote and hold office; indeed, before the Revolution, the proportion of potential voters varied from one-sixth to one-fiftieth of the male population in the different colonies. In the economic sphere, the constricting hand of monopoly everywhere was to be found. On the land, the legal institutions of entail and primogeniture checked opportunity for younger sons; engrossing landlords and land speculators (whether they were the Crown, the proprietaries, absentee owners, or the New England "common" land proprietors) prevented the settlement and improvement of small properties; in the South, the tidewater lords would not erect warehouses to encourage tobacco cultivation among the farmers of the up-country; and in New York, inadequate boundary surveys furnished the big manor lords with an easy instrument of oppression over their smaller neighbors. Everywhere, the threat of Indian uprisings, in the interests of the fur trade and the maintenance of land values in the settled regions, filled the days and nights of frontiersmen with dread.

In the towns, small tradesmen and mechanics and artisans were compelled to struggle unequally against the great merchant interests. Peddlers were submitted to close regulation and forced to pay high license fees. It was impossible to maintain city markets for long, because small merchants here tended to compete successfully with the big ones. In New England, a small company of candlers had got the whole whaling industry in its grip and not only choked off the competition of the lesser manufacturers but fixed the prices for the basic raw material. In New York, and undoubtedly in the other urban communities as well, opportunities to obtain the freedom of the city—which meant the right to engage in certain occupations, whether as tradesmen or artisans— were very severely restricted.

Men of little property were weighed down by debts and oppressed by an inadequate currency; they were forced to support, in many of the colonies, an established church; and they were at the mercy of arbitrary executive and judicial authority. On many sides, too, they saw looming larger and larger the threat of a slave economy to the free institutions of small properties and independent craftsmen. These were the persons who constituted the left-wing of the colonial revolutionary host.

Such was the concentration of colonial forces that made possible the challenging of the power of Great Britain; and the American Revolution proceeded inexorably through the preliminary stages of discussion and illegal organization into the revolutionary one of armed resistance.

# Robert P. Thomas

ROBERT P. THOMAS (1938–    ) is professor of economics at the University of Washington. He has edited and written several books with Douglass C. North, including *The Growth of the American Economy to 1860* (1968) and *The Rise of the Western World: A New Economic History* (1973).

Historians have long debated whether the American colonies on balance benefited or were hindered by British imperial regulation. George Bancroft thought the regulations worked a definite hardship on the colonies. George L. Beer believed these regulations nicely balanced and that the colonies shared in the general advantages. Lawrence Harper, in a now classic article, actually attempted to calculate the cost and found that British policies "placed a heavy burden upon the colonies." Oliver Dickerson wrote that "no case can be made... that such laws were economically oppressive," while Curtis P. Nettels, writing at the same time to the same point, stated: "British policy as it affected the colonies after 1763 was restrictive, injurious, negative." It is quite evident that a difference of opinion exists among reputable colonial historians over this important historical issue.

In this paper an effort is made to meet this issue head on. I shall attempt to measure, relative to a hypothetical alternative, the extent of the burdens and benefits stemming from imperial regulation of the foreign commerce of the thirteen colonies. The main instruments of this regulation were the Navigation Acts, and we shall confine our attention to evaluating the effect of these acts upon colonial welfare. Various other imperial regulations such as the revenue acts, enacted after 1764, the modification of naturalization and land regulations, the interference with colonial issues of paper money, and the various regulations discouraging manufactures will not be dealt with in this paper. The assumption is that the direct effects of these regulations upon the economic welfare of the American colonists were insignificant compared to the effects of the Navigation Acts.

Robert P. Thomas, "A Quantitative Approach to the Study of the Effects of British Imperial Policy upon Colonial Welfare: Some Preliminary Findings," *Journal of Economic History* 25 (December 1965): 615–38. Reprinted, with omissions, by permission of the Economic History Association and Robert P. Thomas.

The hypothesis of this paper is that membership in the British Empire, after 1763, did not impose a significant hardship upon the American colonies. To test this hypothesis I shall endeavor to bias the estimates against the hypothesis, thus not attempting to state what actually would have happened but only that it would not have amounted to as much as my estimate. The end result will, therefore, err on the side of overstating the real costs of the Navigation Acts to the thirteen colonies.

The traditional tools of economic theory will guide the preparation of these estimates. Two series of estimates will be prepared where possible: one, an annual average for the period 1763–1772, based upon official values; the other, for the single year 1770. The official trade statistics for the year 1770 have been adjusted to make them more accurate. . . .

All attempts at measurement require a standard to which the object being measured is made relative or compared. In the case of this paper, the colonies either on balance benefited or were burdened by British imperialism, relative to how they would have fared under some alternative political situation. The problem is to pick the most probable alternative situation.

The only reasonable alternative in this case is to calculate the burdens or benefits of British regulation relative to how the colonies would have fared outside the British Empire but still within a mercantilist world. Considered within this political environment there is little doubt that prior to February 1763, when the Treaty of Paris was signed, the American colonies on balance benefited from membership in the British Empire. Before that date, the colonies were threatened on two sides by two superior colonial powers. C. M. Andrews has pointed out that, before 1763, in addition to remaining within the protection of Great Britain, the American colonies had only one other alternative: domination by another European power, probably France or Spain. Clearly, from a colonial point of view, belonging to the British Empire was superior to membership in any other.

The French and Indian War ended the menace of foreign domination through the cession to Great Britain of Canada by the French and of Florida by Spain. Immediately, thereupon, several Englishmen voiced their fears that these spoils of victory, by removing the foreign threat, made inevitable the independence of the American colonies. Even the French foreign minister, Choiseul, lent his voice to this speculation when, soon after the Treaty of Paris, he predicted the eventual coming of the American Revolution. In 1764, Choiseul went so far as to send his agents to America to watch developments. Knollenberg has pointed out that English suspicions of a desire for independence on the part of the colonies do not prove that the suspicions were well founded. They do, however, suggest that an independent America was, by 1763, a distinct possibility; and thereafter the American colonists possessed another alternative to membership in a European empire. This alternative was an independent existence outside the British Empire but still within a mercantilist world.

The alternative situation that I shall employ to calculate the economic effects of the Navigation Acts after 1763 is that of a free and independent thirteen colonies outside the British Empire. This new nation would, therefore, be subject to most of the same restrictions hindering foreign nations attempting to carry on commerce with the eighteenth-century British Empire. . . .

This "unique" commercial economy developed within the British Empire subject to the rules and regulations of the Navigation Acts. The American colonies in a sense grew up with the empire, which, after the successful conclusion of the Seven Years' War in February 1763, was the wealthiest, most populous colonial empire in the world. It included the kingdom of Great Britain and Ireland with the outlying islands of Europe; trading forts on the Gold Coast of Africa; enclaves in India, and some minor islands in Asia; Newfoundland, Hudson Bay, Nova Scotia, Quebec, the thirteen American colonies, East Florida, and West Florida on the continent of North America; the Bahamas, Bermuda, Jamaica, Antigua, Barbados, and the Leeward and Windward groups of minor islands in the West Indies, as well as the settlement of Belize in Central America.

The American colonies by 1763 formed the foundation of Great Britain's Atlantic empire and had become, as a group, England's most important commercial ally. The basis of this commerce was a vigorous colonial export trade. The total exports in 1770 amounted to £3,165,225. Trade with Great Britain and Ireland accounted for 50 percent of colonial exports. The West Indies trade constituted another 30 percent, and commerce with southern Europe and the Wine Islands, another 17 percent. Trade with Africa and South America accounted for most of the residual.

The colonists, of course, used their exports to purchase imports. They were Great Britain's most important customer and Great Britain their most important supplier. The British Isles shipped to the American colonies in 1768 (a year for which a detailed breakdown is available) £2,157,000 worth of goods, or nearly 75 percent of all colonial imports, which totaled £2,890,000. Of this, £421,000 were British reexports from northern Europe. The West Indies, the other important source of imports, accounted for 20.5 percent of the colonial imports; southern Europe and the Wine Islands, 2.9 percent; and Africa, a little less than 2.0 percent.

The thirteen American colonies carried on this foreign commerce subject to the constraints of a series of laws designed to alter the trade of the British Empire in the interests of the mother country. This commercial system can be viewed as being made up of four types of laws: (1) laws regulating the nationality, crews, and ownership of the vessels in which goods could be shipped; (2) statutes regulating the destination to which certain goods could be shipped; (3) laws designed to encourage specific primary industries via an elaborate system of rebates, drawbacks, import and export bounties, and export taxes; (4) direct prohibition of colonial industries and practices that tended to compete with English industries or to harm a prominent sector of the British economy or even, occasionally, the economy of a British colony. These laws, it should be stressed, did not regulate the American colonies alone, but with occasional local modifications applied equally to the entire British Empire.

The laws regulating the nationality of vessels were designed to insure a monopoly of the carrying trade of the empire to ships of the empire. In the seventeenth and eighteenth centuries the freight factor on goods traded internationally probably averaged at least 20 percent, and these laws were designed to insure that this revenue stayed within the empire. The Navigation Acts also insured, to the extent that they were effective, that England would be the entrepôt of the empire and that the distributing trade would be centered in the British Isles.

The commodity clauses of these various regulatory acts controlled the destination to which certain goods could be shipped. These enumerated commodities generally could be shipped only to England. The original list contained tobacco, sugar, indigo, cotton-wool, ginger, fustic, and other dyewoods. Later, naval stores, hemp, rice, molasses, beaver skins, furs, and copper ore were added. The Sugar Act of 1764 added coffee, pimiento, coconuts, whale fins, raw silk, hides and skins, potash and pearl ash to the list. In 1766, the law was amended to prohibit the direct export of any colonial product north of Cape Finisterre.

There were exceptions and compensations to these commodity clauses which benefited the American colonies. Rice, after 1730, could be directly exported south of Cape Finisterre and, after 1764, to South America. Tobacco was given a monopoly in Great Britain, as its local cultivation was prohibited. While the list appears extensive, of the enumerated commodities only tobacco, indigo, copper ore, naval stores, hemp, furs and skins, whale fins, raw silk, and potash and pearl ash were products of the thirteen colonies, and only tobacco, rice, and perhaps indigo and naval stores could be considered major exports of the colonies that later became the United States.

An elaborate series of laws was enacted by the English Parliament to encourage specific industries in the interest of a self-sufficient empire. These included preferential tariffs for certain goods of colonial origin. A distinctive feature of these laws was an elaborate system of rebates and drawbacks to encourage the exports of certain commodities from England and extensive bounties to encourage the production of specific goods for export to Great Britain.

Most enumerated goods benefited from a preferential duty. These goods were thus given a substantial advantage in the markets of the mother country. Goods receiving preferential treatment included cotton-wool, ginger, sugar, molasses, coffee, tobacco, rice, naval stores, pitch, rosin, hemp, masts, whale fins, raw silk, potash and pearl ash, bar and pig iron, and various types of lumber. Certain of these goods also received drawbacks of various amounts upon their reexport from Great Britain. Foreign goods competing in the English market with enumerated colonial commodities were thus subject to a disadvantage from these preferential duties.

A system of bounties was also implemented to encourage the production of specific commodities in the colonies or to allow the British manufacturers to compete with foreign exports in the colonial markets. The production of naval stores, silk, lumber, indigo, and hemp was encouraged in the colonies with bounties. In the mother country the manufacture of linen, gunpowder, silks, and many nonwoolen textiles was encouraged by a bounty to allow these products to compete with similar foreign manufactures in the colonial markets.

Certain of the colonial commodities favored by legislation were given what amounted to a monopoly of the home market of the mother country. The colonial production of tobacco, naval stores, sugar and sugar products was so favored. In the case of tobacco, the major share of total imports was reexported, so the local monopoly proved not a great boon.

In economic terms, the Navigation Acts were designed to insure that the vast bulk of the empire's carrying trade was in ships owned by Englishmen. The design of the commodity clauses was to alter the terms of trade to the disadvantage of the colonists, by making all foreign imports into the colonies, and many colonial exports whose final destination was the Continent, pass through England. The effect was to make colonial imports more expensive and colonial exports less remunerative by increasing the transportation costs of both. Finally, through tariff preferences, bounties, and outright prohibitions, resources were allocated from more efficient uses to less.

I shall approach the problem of assessing the overall effect of the various British regulations of trade by considering their effect on the following aspects of the colonial economy: (1) exports of colonial products; (2) imports into the colonies; (3) colonial foreign commerce; and (4) colonial shipping earnings. An assessment will then be undertaken of compensating benefits arising from membership in the British Empire. Finally, an attempt will be made to strike a balance on the total impact of British imperial policy upon the colonial economy. . . .

The export trade between the colonies and the mother country was subjected to regulations which significantly altered its value and composition over what it would have been if the colonies had been independent. The total adjusted value of exports from the American colonies to Great Britain in 1770 was £1,458,000, of which £1,107,000, or 76 percent, were enumerated goods. Such goods were required to be shipped directly to Great Britain. The largest part, 85.4 percent, of the enumerated goods was subsequently reexported to northern Europe and thus when competing in these markets bore the burden of an artificial, indirect routing through England to the Continent. The costs of this indirect route took the form of an added transhipment, with the consequent port charges and fees, middlemen's commissions, and what import duties were retained upon reexport. The enumerated goods consumed in England benefited from preferential duties relative to goods of foreign production. A few of these enumerated commodities also were favored with import bounties. . . . Our analysis of the effect of the Navigation Acts on colonial exports has included the burden on exports, the benefit of the preferential duties, and the net gain from bounty payments. The sum total of these burdens and benefits is a net burden upon exports of £411,000 for 1770. The average annual burden for the decade 1763–1772 was calculated to be £307,000. . . .

British law required that the colonies purchase their East Indian and European goods in England. The colonies actually purchased three-quarters of their imports from the mother country, of which about 20 percent were goods originally manufactured in Europe or Asia. These imported goods also bore the burden of an indirect route to the colonies, analogous to that borne by tobacco destined to be consumed in Europe. This burden was reflected in higher prices for goods of foreign manufacture in the colonies than otherwise would have been the case.

Our method for calculating the burden borne by colonial imports of foreign manufactures is similar to the method used to calculate the cost of enumeration on colonial goods reexported to Europe. Two commodities, tea and pepper, for which both colonial and Amsterdam prices are available, were selected as our sample. Tea and pepper accounted for about 16 percent of the value of foreign goods imported into the colonies through England. The price that would have obtained in the colonies had they been independent was calculated for these goods exactly as in the case of tobacco. The alternative prices of these commodities, according to our estimates, would have averaged 16 percent lower than they in fact were. Thus, the colonists paid more for their imports of foreign origin than they would have paid had they been independent.

The colonies actually imported foreign goods to the average value of £412,000 for the decade 1763–1772 and of £346,000 for the single year 1770. The burden on the goods, according to our measurement, averaged £66,000 for the decade, or £55,000 for 1770. However, the burden on imports should not be calculated on the basis of foreign goods alone. The burden should also be calculated on goods of English manufacture which were made competitive in the colonial markets by virtue of the artificially increased cost of foreign goods forced to travel an indirect route to the colonies.

The bounty laws benefiting English manufactures which were designed to make English goods competitive with those of foreign manufacture give us a clue to the identity of these English manufactures. If goods of English manufacture required a bounty to compete with similar foreign goods suffering the handicap of an indirect shipment, then the colonists, if independent, would have purchased foreign instead of English goods. Thus, some English goods actually purchased by the colonists would not have been purchased if the colonies had been independent.

Linen was the most important of these goods; the list also included cottons and silks. The colonies thus paid more for most nonwoolen textiles than they would have if they had existed outside the British Empire. The additional monetary loss resulting from the purchase of English rather than foreign goods was calculated to average £73,000 for the decade or £61,000 for 1770 alone. The colonists thus paid a total of £116,000 more in 1770 or £139,000 average for the decade for their imports than they would have if independent. If we assume, for convenience, a price elasticity of demand for imports of one, the colonists would have spent the same amount on imports but they would have received more goods for their money. . . .

The results of this preliminary investigation into the effects of the Navigation Acts upon the foreign commerce of the American colonies [shows] . . . an overall burden for the year 1770 of £532,000, and an average of £451,000 for the decade.

The purpose of the various clauses in the Navigation Acts dealing with shipping was to insure that ships built and manned by Englishmen monopolized this aspect of the foreign commerce of the empire. Colonial vessels, for all intents and purposes, were considered English and shared in the benefits of the monopoly.

Calculation of the resultant colonial benefits was hampered by a lack of available data; therefore, the conclusions should be considered tentative. The estimate was constructed in the following manner: an estimated percentage of the total tonnage entering and clearing colonial ports in 1770 that was colonial-owned was calculated from the American inspector general's ledger. Using an estimated average earnings per ton, it was possible to approximate the shipping earnings deriving from the foreign commerce of the American colonies. The total earnings from shipping the foreign commerce of the thirteen colonies were calculated to be £1,228,000, of which 59.4 percent, or £730,000, was earned by American vessels.

The next question considered was what these earnings would have been had the colonies been independent. Using as a guide what actually did happen between 1789–1792, after the Revolution but before the outbreak of the war in Europe, I found that the colonies' share of the trade carrying their own commerce declined from 59.4 percent to 53.2 percent. On this basis, their shipping earnings in 1770 would have been £653,000 instead of £730,000—a difference of £77,000.

However, as we have seen, had the American colonies been independent their volume of foreign commerce would have been greater. Their ships would have carried a portion of the increased amounts of tobacco, rice, and other exports that would have been shipped, as well as a portion of the larger volume of imports.

My calculations suggest that the volume of shipping required to carry this additional output would have amounted to over 53,000 tons. If American vessels had carried the same percentage of this increased volume as they carried of the total volume in 1789, their earnings in 1770 would have increased to over £742,000—or a little more than they in fact were during the late colonial period. The composition of the trade, however, would have been different.

Thus, it seems fruitless to do more with the effect of the Navigation Acts upon shipping earnings until we know more about shipping rates before and after the Revolution. The best guess, at this time, is that on balance the colonial shipping industry neither gained nor lost from the Navigation Acts. . . .

The main obligation of the mother country to its colonies in a mercantilist world was to provide protection. In this area lies the significant benefit to the colonies from membership in an empire. The empire of course also performed certain administrative functions for the colonies from which they benefited.

Great Britain in the defense of the empire could provide for the protection of the American colonies at very little additional expense to itself. That is to say that the colonies, if independent, would have had to expend more resources in their own defense than did England, just to maintain the same level of protection. Our estimate of the value of military and naval protection provided by the British to the colonists, since it is based in part upon actual British expenditures, is therefore too low.

The value of British military protection was estimated as follows. Great Britain, before 1762, maintained a standing army in America of 3,000 officers and men. After 1762, the size of this troop complement was increased to 7,500 men. These troops were garrisoned throughout the colonies, including the frontiers where they served as a defensive force against the incursions of hostile Indians. Each man stationed in America cost the mother country an average of £29 a year, or annually a total expense of at least £217,500.

The colonists constantly complained about the quality of the "red-coats" as Indian fighters. Furthermore, they believed the larger standing army in the colonies after 1762 was there not primarily to protect them but for other reasons. However, they found after independence that a standing army of at least 5,000 men was required to replace the British. Thus the benefit to the colonies from the British army stationed in America was conservatively worth at least the cost of 5,000 troops, or £145,000.

Another large colonial benefit stemmed from the protection offered colonial shipping by the British navy, which included the Crown's annual tribute to the Barbary powers. The ability of the British navy to protect its merchant ships from the ravages of pirates far surpassed anything a small independent country could provide. This the colonies learned to their sorrow following the Revolution.

The value of such protection would be reflected in the rise in marine insurance rates for cargoes carried by American vessels after independence. Unfortunately, until research in process is completed, I do not have sufficient data to directly calculate the value of the protection of the British navy in this manner.

However, this benefit can be tentatively measured in an indirect manner. Insurance rates during the 1760s on the West Indies trade one way averaged about 3.5 percent of the value of the cargo. Rates to England were higher, averaging 7 percent. These rates on colonial cargoes existed while colonial vessels were protected by the British navy. During the French and Indian War, the risk of seizure increased the rates to the West Indies, which rose steadily until they reached 23 percent, while rates to England climbed as high as 28 percent, indicating the influence of risk upon marine insurance rates.

The colonists upon obtaining their independence lost the protection of the British fleet. Insurance rates, as a result, must have increased over the prerevolutionary levels. To estimate the approximate rise in insurance rates, we calculated the percentage decline in insurance rates for American merchant vessels following the launching in 1797 of three frigates which formed the foundation of the small, eighteenth-century American navy.

The percentage difference between the rates on an unprotected merchant marine and those charged on the merchant fleet safeguarded by our small navy was applied to the insurance rates prevailing before the Revolution. The weighted difference in rates between a barely protected merchant marine and a totally unprotected one was slightly over 50 percent.

Applying this percentage to existing prerevolutionary rates, it appears that the average cargo insurance rate, if the colonies had been independent, would have been at least 8.7 percent of the value of the cargo instead of 5.4 percent, a difference in rates of 2.7 percent. Figuring this increase in insurance charges on the value of colonial cargoes in 1770 gives a low estimate of the value derived from British naval protection of £103,000. Three ships were not the British navy and could not be expected to provide equal protection. Marine insurance thus probably increased more than 2.7 percent. An estimate that rates doubled does not seem unreasonable and would raise the annual value of naval protection to £206,000.

The estimate of the value of British protection for the American colonies is thus made up of the adjusted cost of the army in the colonies, £145,000, plus the estimated value of naval protection for the merchant marine of £206,000. The estimated total value of the protection afforded the colonies by their membership in the British Empire was thus calculated to be at least £351,000.

By way of a check upon this estimate, the government of the United States, during its first nine years under the Constitution, found it necessary to spend annually an average of $2,133,000, or £426,600, for national defense. This included the purchase of arms and stores, the fortification of forts and harbors, and the building and manning of a small navy. In addition, an independent America had to bear the expense of conducting an independent foreign policy. The support of ministers to foreign nations, the cost of negotiating and implementing treaties, the payment of tribute to the Barbary nations, all previously provided for by Great Britain, now had to be borne by the independent colonies. These expenses alone cost the United States, during the last decade of the eighteenth century, annually over £60,000.

After achieving independence, the United States found it necessary to spend annually about £487,000 to provide certain functions of government formerly provided by Great Britain. This suggests that our estimate of £351,000 for the value of British protection to the American colonists is too low. It is doubtful, in the light of history, whether the new nation was able to provide this type of government services of equal quality to those furnished by the British. If not, even the £487,000 a year understates the value of governmental services supplied by Great Britain to her American colonies. . . .

My findings with reference to the effect of the Navigation Acts upon the economy of the thirteen colonies indicate a net burden of £532,000, or $2,660,000, in 1770. The average burden for the decade 1763–1772, based upon official values, was somewhat lower—£451,000, or $2,255,000. These estimates are near the lowest estimates made by Harper and seem to strengthen his case that exploitation did exist.

Considering for a moment only the value of the losses on colonial exports and imports, the per capita annual cost to the colonist of being an Englishman instead of an American was $1.24 in 1770. The average

TABLE 1.  SUMMARY OF THE RESULTS

|  | 1763–1772 | 1770 |
| --- | --- | --- |
| *Burdens* | | |
| Burden on colonial foreign commerce | £ 451,000 | £ 532,000 |
|  | or | or |
|  | $2,255,000 | $2,660,000 |
| Burden per capita[a] | $1.20 | $1.24 |
| *Benefits* | | |
| Benefits of British protection | £ 351,000 | £ 351,000 |
|  | or | or |
|  | $1,775,000 | $1,775,000 |
| Benefit per capita | $.94 | $.82 |
| Balance[b] | | |
| Estimate 1 | $ −.26 | $ −.42 |

[a]Population for the decade average was figured to be 1,881,000, and for 1770 to be 2,148,000.
[b]The balance was obtained by subtracting the per capita benefits from the per capita burden.

per capita cost for the decade based upon official values was a somewhat lower $1.20. The benefits per capita in 1770 were figured to be 82 cents, and for the decade 94 cents. Subtracting the benefits from the burdens for 1770 shows a per capita loss of 42 cents. The estimate for the decade shows a smaller loss of 26 cents a person. It is unlikely, because of the nature of the estimating procedures employed, that these losses are too low. Conversely it is not at all improbable, and for the same reason, that the estimated losses are too high.

Suppose that these findings reflect the true magnitude of the cost of the Navigation Acts to the thirteen colonies. The relevant question becomes: How important were these losses? Albert Fishlow stated at last year's meetings that he believed that the average per capita income in the 1780s "could not have been much less than $100." George Rogers Taylor, in his presidential address, hazarded a guess that per capita income did not grow very rapidly, if at all, between 1775 and 1840. Therefore, assuming that average per capita income hovered about $100 between 1763 and 1772, what would it have been had the colonies been independent?

The answer is obvious from Table 1: it would not have been much different. The largest estimated loss on this basis is .54 of 1 percent of per capita income, or 54 cents on a hundred dollars. Suppose for a moment that my estimates are off by 100 percent; then, in that case the largest burden would be slightly more than 1 percent of national income. It is difficult to make a convincing case for exploitation out of these results.

# 4

# The American Revolution

## Revolutionary or Nonrevolutionary?

The American Revolution is, perhaps, the single most significant event in this country's history. Within twenty years—1763 to 1783—Americans declared their independence, waged a war of liberation, transformed colonies into states, and created a new nation. These changes occurred with such remarkable rapidity that their speed was truly revolutionary. But scholars disagree about using the term *revolutionary* to describe how new or different these developments were. Some historians argue that the Revolution was solely a colonial rebellion aimed at achieving only the limited goal of independence from Britain. Colonial society, they say, was a democratic society and there was a consensus among Americans about keeping things as they were once the break with Britain had been accomplished. Others claim that the Revolution was accompanied by a violent social upheaval—a class conflict—as the radical lower classes sought to gain a greater degree of democracy in what had been a basically undemocratic society in the colonial era. The question is, then, was the Revolution revolutionary, or was it not?

American historians for the most part did not probe very deeply into the revolutionary nature of the Revolution in the first century after the event. Throughout most of the nineteenth century, scholars reflected one of the underlying assumptions of that era—that the main theme of American history was the quest for liberty. Within this context, the Revolution was inevitably viewed in black and white terms as a struggle of liberty versus tyranny between America and Britain.

George Bancroft, one of the outstanding exponents of this point of view, set forth his thesis in his ten-volume *History of the United States* published between the 1830s and 1870s. To Bancroft the Revolution represented one phase of a master plan by God for the march of all mankind toward a golden age of greater human freedom. America, in his eyes, symbolized the forces of liberty and progress; Britain those of tyranny and reaction. The Revolution was "radical in its character," according to Bancroft, because it hastened the advance of mankind toward a millennium of "everlasting peace" and "universal brotherhood." He went on to add that the Revolution was achieved within the colonies in "benign tranquility" because the American people were united in their determination to fight for freedom.[1]

With the spirit of nationalism prevalent in nineteenth-century America, it is not too difficult to understand why Bancroft wrote as he did. There was an intense desire among the American people for a national historian who would tell the epic story of the Revolution in patriotic terms, and Bancroft fulfilled this longing. More important, Bancroft intuitively wrote the kind of history that could meet the needs of Americans in yet another way. Throughout much of the period between the 1830s and 1870s, the country was split; it was divided by the bitter political battles of the Jacksonian era and the brutal military conflict of the Civil War. Bancroft painted a picture of the Revolution as a great national struggle, reminding the Americans that they had once fought as a united people for many beliefs they held in common.[2]

Around the turn of the twentieth century, a reaction set in against Bancroft's ultrapatriotic interpretation. With the growing rapprochement between Britain and America after the signing of the Treaty of Washington in 1870, there was a tendency to view past relations between the two countries in a more favorable light. Developments on the domestic scene such as the Populist and Progressive movements also affected the outlook of some scholars. Influenced by these reform movements, which appeared to constitute a popular reaction against the concentration of power and wealth in the hands of a relatively small number of financial and business leaders in modern industrialized America, some historians began viewing the Revolution in a somewhat similar light as an uprising by the lower classes against the control of the upper classes. Finally, the rising class of professional academic historians who appeared on the scene about the 1880s also began to explore the Revolution from a different perspective than had Bancroft.

The scholars who revised Bancroft's interpretation between the 1890s and 1940s fell into two broad schools. One group—the imperial school of historians—believed that political and constitutional issues brought on the Revolution. The other—the Progressive historians—held that the

---

[1] George Bancroft, *History of the United States of America*, 10 vols. (Boston, 1852), 4:12–13.

[2] Wesley F. Craven, "The Revolutionary Era," in John Higham, ed., *The Reconstruction of American History* (New York, 1962), pp. 46–47.

primary causes were social and economic in nature. While these two groups of historians disagreed with Bancroft on the precise causes and nature of the Revolution, they were often in agreement with his conclusion that the movement was, indeed, a revolutionary one.

The imperial school of historians headed by George L. Beer, Charles M. Andrews, and Lawrence H. Gipson took the position that the Revolution was not to be viewed solely within the narrow confines of national history. To be properly understood, the Revolution had to be set in a broader context and considered as an integral part of the history of the British Empire as a whole. Hence they directed their attention to the empire, emphasizing in particular the political and constitutional relationship between the colonies and the mother country. Since Anglo-American relations were improving around the turn of the twentieth century, these scholars were inclined to be less harsh on the former mother country than Bancroft had been.

After examining the operations of the empire, the imperial historians concluded that Britain's colonial policies were not as unjust as Bancroft had declared. Beer wrote four monographs between the years 1893 and 1912 on Britain's commercial policies in the seventeenth and eighteenth centuries and claimed that the colonists prospered under a system that was both liberal and enlightened. Andrews, writing a four-volume work in the 1930s, saw benefits as well as burdens in Britain's Navigation Acts because of the protection provided for America's goods and ships. Gipson, who was a student of Andrews's, took an even more favorable view of imperial policies in his multivolume work, *The British Empire before the American Revolution*, published between the 1930s and 1960s. The British were justified in taxing the Americans and tightening the Navigation Acts after 1763, claimed Gipson, because it had been largely British blood and money that was expended in defending the North American colonies in the "Great War for Empire," 1754–1763.

All three historians believed that constitutional issues lay at the bottom of the dispute between the colonies and mother country. Andrews, for example, argued that the British Empire in North America from its beginnings down to the Revolution had been characterized by two movements working at cross purposes. The colonies kept moving steadily in the direction of greater self-government; the mother country toward greater control over the empire. By the eve of the Revolution, the colonists had arrived at a new concept of empire—colonies as self-governing units within an empire held together only by a common allegiance to the king. But the British, clinging to their traditional ideas of dependent colonies, considered this idea both radical and dangerous. "On the one side was the immutable, stereotyped system of the mother country, based on precedent and tradition and designed to keep things comfortably as they were," wrote Andrews, "on the other, a vital, dynamic organism, containing the seeds of a great nation, its forces untried, still to be proved."[3] The dispute, while constitutional in nature, was the very essence of revoultion for Andrews; it represented a deep-seated conflict between two incompatible societies.

The Progressive historians took quite a different point of view from the imperial school. They were firmly convinced that social and economic issues constituted the main causes of the Revolution. On the one hand, they tended to emphasize the growing economic split caused by the competition between the colonies and mother country. On the other, they placed great stress upon class conflict between the lower and upper classes in colonial America.

That the Progressive historians saw the Revolution in terms of an internal class conflict was hardly surprising. Many of these scholars were themselves committed to the reform movements of the early 1900s and tended to see their own era in terms of an unending struggle by the people to free themselves from the shackles of the large corporate monopolies and trusts that constituted the plutocracy of modern America. Consequently, they tended to read back into the Revolution the same conflict between the masses and the upper classes that seemed to be taking place before their eyes in the Progressive period from 1900 to 1920.

The emergence of Progressive historians such as Carl L. Becker, Charles A. Beard, Arthur M. Schlesinger, Sr., and J. Franklin Jameson during this period marked also a sharp shift toward an economic interpretation of history. Such scholars believed that materialistic forces—not ideological factors—were the major determinants in history. Some of these historians, therefore, were economic determinists who felt that man was motivated mainly by his economic self-interest. They insisted that any political or constitutional ideas that man might possess would be dictated by economic considerations. To their way of thinking, pocketbook interests, not ideas of patriotism, had motivated the leaders that Bancroft had pictured as heroes.

Carl L. Becker, one of the first and most effective of the Progressive historians, took the position that the American Revolution should be considered not as one revolution but two. The first was an external revolution—the colonial rebellion against Britain—caused by a clash of economic interests between tbe colonies and mother country. The second was an internal revolution—a conflict between America's social classes—to determine whether the upper or lower classes would rule once the British departed. In his first major study of the Revolution, *The History of Political Parties in the Province of New York, 1760–1776*, published in 1909, Becker summed up his thesis of a dual revolution in a striking

---

[3]Charles M. Andrews, "The American Revolution: An Interpretation," *American Historical Review* 31 (January 1926):231.

phrase. New York politics prior to the Revolution, he wrote, revolved around two questions—the "question of home rule" and the "question . . . of who should rule at home."[4]

Although Charles A. Beard's book, *An Economic Interpretation of the Constitution*, which was published in 1913, did not deal directly with the Revolution, it became a landmark for scholars writing about this era of American history. After an examination of the economic holdings of the framers of the Constitution, Beard advanced his now-famous hypothesis that the events leading to the convention of 1787 mirrored a split in American society—a conflict between the rich and the poor, farmers and merchants, debtors and creditors, and holders of real wealth and paper wealth. More than any other single work written in the Populist-Progressive era, Beard's book caused Progressive historians to view the period between the 1760s and the 1780s as one of continuous conflict between social classes in America over economic matters.

The conclusion that the Revolution might be seen in terms of a class struggle over economic issues was further spelled out in Arthur M. Schlesinger's work *The Colonial Merchants and the American Revolution*, published in 1918. Schlesinger studied the merchant class in all the colonies during the period 1763–1776 and noted that this usually conservative group played a leading role in bringing on the Revolution. Why had they done so? Disenchantment of the merchants with British rule, said Schlesinger, arose from the economic reverses they suffered as a result of the strict policy of imperial control enacted by the mother country after the French and Indian War. But resistance by the merchants against the mother country grew less intense after 1770, he noted, for fear of what might happen to their position and property if the more radical lower classes—"their natural enemies in society"—should gain the upper hand.

Schlesinger's book dealt mainly with the period prior to 1776, but the author went on to comment about the increasing dread of class conflict once independence was declared. The merchant class split and many men refused to participate enthusiastically in the struggle against the British lest the lower classes seize control and rule at home. Biding their time during the troubled years of the Confederation period, the merchants drew together again in the late 1780s to found a new government that would safeguard their class interests. Once united, the merchant class became, in Schlesinger's words, "a potent factor in the conservative counterrevolution that led to the establishment of the United States Constitution."[5] To Schlesinger, the Constitution was the antithesis of

[4]Carl L. Becker, *The History of Political Parties in the Province of New York, 1760–1776* (Madison, 1909), p. 22.

[5]Arthur M. Schlesinger, *The Colonial Merchants and the American Revolution, 1763–1776* (New York, 1918), p. 606.

the Revolution; the same classes and men who were pitted against one another in the 1770s continued to contend for control of the government in the 1780s.

J. Franklin Jameson, another historian writing within the Progressive tradition, likewise viewed the Revolution as a class conflict—a social movement by the lower classes to achieve a greater degree of democracy within American society. His book *The American Revolution Considered as a Social Movement*, published in 1926, described the sweeping social and economic reforms that took place during the war; reforms that reduced the power of the prewar aristocracy and improved the lot of the common man. Economic democracy advanced, Jameson claimed, as a result of the redistribution of landed property. Large Loyalist estates were confiscated and broken up into lots for sale to small farmers; vast domains controlled by the Crown and proprietors passed into the hands of state legislatures, which threw open these lands for settlement; and new state laws put an end to the old aristocratic practices of primogeniture and entail. Social democracy made similar strides as property qualifications for voting and officeholding were lowered, slavery and the slave trade were abolished in some states, and the Anglican church was disestablished in many parts of the country. Jameson's book summed up the point of view of the Progressive historians who exercised such a profound influence over the interpretation of the Revolution during the first part of the twentieth century. The Progressive approach to the Revolution was maintained by the late Merrill Jensen, a distinguished scholar, and by numerous other historians active from 1945 to the present.

Since World War II, however, a new group of scholars—the neoconservative school of historians—emerged to challenge the interpretation set forth by the Progressive historians. The fundamental disagreement between these two groups derived from the different way that each viewed the colonial period as a whole. To the Progressive historians, American society in the colonial era was undemocratic, giving rise to class conflicts throughout the entire period. The lower classes being poor, underprivileged, and deprived of the right to vote, kept up a constant class struggle to improve their lot in society. In the eyes of these historians, then, the Revolution represented the climax of a movement by the masses to advance their economic well-being and to wrest greater political rights from the upper classes.

The neoconservative historians, on the other hand, believed that American society was essentially a democratic society in the colonial period. Most colonists, rather than being poor, these scholars claimed, could qualify as members of the middle class by virtue of the property they owned. Political democracy was the order of the day because the majority of colonists were small farmers who possessed enough land to meet the necessary qualifications for voting. Colonial society was an open, not a closed society, and characterized by a high degree of social mobility. Thus, the common man in the colonial era was satisfied with his lot in society and felt no urge to participate in class conflict in order to achieve a greater degree of democracy.

As a corollary to this second point of view, neoconservative scholars argued that the Revolution was basically a conservative movement. Americans fought the Revolution, according to these historians, in order to preserve a social order that was already democratic in colonial days. When British reforms after 1763 threatened to upset the existing democratic social order in America, the colonists rose up in rebellion. In the struggle between the colonies and mother country, the Americans emerged as the "conservatives" because they were trying to keep matters as they were before 1763. It was the British who were the "radicals" because they kept insisting upon making changes and innovations in the colonial system after the French and Indian War.

Scholars of the neoconservative school rejected the idea of class struggle and stressed instead the concept of a general consensus among the American people in the Revolutionary War era. Most Americans held certain ideas in common, they argued, and these views united the colonists to the degree which made it possible for them to act in concert against Great Britain. One important element in this American consensus was the widespread belief among all social classes that the liberties of the people were based upon certain fundamental principles of self-government which could not be changed without their consent. Led by such scholars as Robert E. Brown and Daniel J. Boorstin, the neoconservative school saw consensus and continuity rather than class conflict and disunity as the main themes in this period of American history.

Robert E. Brown, in *Middle-Class Democracy and the Revolution in Massachusetts*, set out specifically to challenge the thesis of the Progressive school of historians that the Revolution was, in part, a class conflict over the question of who should rule at home. One of the starting assumptions of the Progressive scholars, Brown noted, was that the structure of American society in the colonial period was undemocratic because property qualifications for suffrage prevented many persons in the lower classes from voting. After studying the structure of society in prewar Massachusetts, Brown concluded that the vast majority of adult males in that colony were farmers whose real estate holdings were sufficient to meet the necessary property qualifications for voting. Middle-class democracy in Massachusetts before the war was an established fact, Brown maintained, and the purpose of the Revolution was to preserve the existing democratic social order on the local level—not to change it.

In a similar vein, Daniel J. Boorstin argued that the Revolution was a conservative movement on the imperial as well as the local level because Americans were fighting to retain traditional rights and liberties granted to them under the British constitution. The colonists rebelled against Great Britain to maintain the status quo, Boorstin insisted in *The Genius of American Politics,* not to initiate a new order. When the British introduced changes in the government of the empire after the French and Indian War, the Americans kept resisting these disturbing innovations on the grounds that they were contrary to the British constitution. In refusing to accept the principle of no taxation without representation, Boorstin wrote, the patriots were insisting upon an old liberty and not a new right.

The leaders of the Revolution, in Boorstin's view, were reluctant rebels. American patriots thought of themselves as Englishmen who were more true to the tenets of the British constitution than the British themselves. Resistance to imperial authority began when the Americans felt that they were being denied their rights as Englishmen by a misguided Parliament. After taking the drastic step of declaring their independence with considerable reluctance, Americans did not turn their backs upon their British heritage. Instead, they carried over into the new nation many of the traditional rights as Englishmen that they had prized so highly—trial by jury, due process of law, the concept of no taxation without representation, and the rights of free speech, free petition, and free assembly. Thus, in Boorstin's view, the American Revolution was regarded as an act of faith in favor of the British constitution. The patriots were defending the ancient British traditions and institutions when they waged the American Revolution. The first selection in this chapter is drawn from Boorstin's writings.

Edmund S. Morgan, the distinguished colonial historian, stressed two themes—the consensus among Americans on principles and the continuity of ideas—in his book *Birth of the Republic 1763–1789.* Certain principles and ideas unified most Americans from the time of the Stamp act in 1765 to the writing of the Constitution in 1787, according to Morgan. Throughout this period the majority of Americans consistently sought to realize three principles: the protection of property and liberty; the achievement of human equality; and—after the break from Britain—a form of American nationalism that would embrace the ideas of both liberty and equality. Morgan concluded that the Progressive historians had grossly exaggerated the divisions among the American people during the revolutionary era, and that the "most remarkable and exciting fact was union."[6]

In many respects, the neoconservative interpretation of the Revolution that arose after 1945 seemed to mirror the conservative climate of opinion that pervaded the United States after the end of World War II.

---

[6]Edmund S. Morgan, *The Birth of the Republic 1763–1789* (Chicago, 1956), p. 163. Even in the revised edition of this work, issued in 1977, Morgan barely mentioned the Loyalists.

In the area of foreign affairs, the Cold War era profoundly affected American thought. With the United States acting as the leader of the free world and facing the threat of Communist totalitarianism, Americans became increasingly preoccupied with the problem of national security. Historians reflected this concern, perhaps in an unconscious manner, by playing down the differences between the American people in the past in order to present an image of a nation that was strong and united throughout most of its history. Thus, the picture of the Revolution as a period of disorder and disunity gave way to one that emphasized a consensus among the American people and stressed the continuity between our colonial past and our beginnings as a nation.

Developments on the domestic scene during the 1940s and 1950s likewise caused historians to recast the Revolution along more conservative lines. Prosperity in the post–World War II period and the concomitant rise in affluence in American society coupled with an increase in social legislation aimed at improving the living conditions among lower-income groups tended to blur the lines of rigid class distinctions within the country. Living in an era in which class distinctions presumably played a less important role, neoconservative historians were less prone to see the element of class conflict in the Revolution. In short, the neoconservative school of historians seemed to be reflecting some of the dominant ideas of their own time in treating the Revolution as they did.

Although neoconservative historians continued to publish during the 1960s, they found their position subjected to attack from several quarters. One challenge came from the writings of certain intellectual historians who saw the Revolution as a radical rather than a conservative movement. Another came from a group of scholars who might be termed neo-Progressive historians who used different approaches or orientations in searching for the social and economic origins of the revolutionary movement. Yet a third challenge came from the revived interest in studies of the Loyalists—a group to whom the neoconservative historians had paid little or no attention.

The trend toward greater emphasis upon intellectual history resulted in part as a reaction against the Progressive scholars who had generally shown a profound distrust of ideas as determining forces in history. Strongly influenced by the thought of Freud and Marx, the Progressive historians looked upon ideas as mere rationalizations, designed to mask the deep-seated self-interests that motivated human behavior. They insisted that the upper classes in colonial America had manipulated ideas solely to suit the interests of their class. When members of the merchant class employed a slogan such as "No taxation without representation," their goal was basically to stir up support among the lower classes; they were not genuinely concerned about abstract principle. Colonial merchants turned the Stamp Act into a propaganda campaign over the issues of constitutionalism and natural rights, argued Progressive historians, in order to conceal their true class interests.

Rejecting this view of the role of ideas in history, certain historians writing since World War II emphasized the primacy of ideas in bringing on the Revolution. Some scholars who viewed the Revolution from the standpoint of intellectual history, including certain neoconservatives, came to the conclusion that conservative ideas had prevailed and that the movement was a conservative one. Other historians, however, came to exactly the opposite conclusion.

Bernard Bailyn was the foremost scholar to view the Revolution as a radical ideological movement. In his work *The Ideological Origins of the American Revolution*, Bailyn took the position that ideas themselves constituted the major determinants in history.[7] After analyzing the pamphlet literature written in the period just prior to the Revolution, Bailyn concluded that ideas had played a dual role in bringing about the break with Britain. First, he noted that the thought expressed in the pamphlets was *explanatory* in nature. The ideas taken up, in other words, not only revealed the position taken by the colonists but also gave the reasons *why* such a stand had been adopted. Second, the ideas themselves acted as determinants during the period by causing changes in the beliefs, attitudes, and assumptions of the colonists.

Bailyn argued that an elaborate theory of politics lay at the heart of the American revolutionary ideology—an ideology whose roots could be traced back to the antiauthoritarian tradition in England. This theory was based on an unflattering view of human nature—a belief in the innate selfishness of man. Man had a natural lust for power, this theory held, and power by its very nature was a corrupting force and could be attained only by depriving others of their liberty. To protect liberty against the corrupting force of power, all elements of the body politic had to be balanced off against one another in order to prevent one from gaining dominance over the others. The best solution, of course, was a balanced constitution; but the malignant influence of power was such that no system of government whatsoever could be safe or stable for very long.

Bailyn's thesis was that this theory of politics shaped the course of America's revolutionary thought from the 1730s through the "constitutional crisis" of the 1760s and 1770s. Viewed within the context of this theory, the arguments expressed in the pamphlets could be interpreted in a different light. The colonists, it seemed, were convinced that there was a sinister plot against liberty in both England and America. In England it was the king's ministers who were conspiring against liberty.

---

[7]Bernard Bailyn, *The Ideological Origins of the American Revolution* (Cambridge, 1967).

They usurped the prerogatives of the Crown, systematically encroached upon the independence of the Commons, and upset the balance of the British constitution in their corrupt drive for power. In America the king's ministers were assisted in their conspiratorial designs by royal officials who likewise aimed at destroying the balance of the constitution and seizing as much power and authority as possible. From the American point of view, then, the British measures after 1763 were nothing less than a widespread plot to rob all Englishmen of their liberties at home and abroad. Believing that the conspiracy had succeeded in England, the colonists came to feel that America represented the last bastion for the defense of English liberties and the freedom of all mankind. These ideas and this interpretation of British behavior, Bailyn believed, finally led the colonists in desperation to resort to armed rebellion.

Bailyn thus took issue with the Progressive historians who declared that the patriot leaders were indulging in mere rhetoric and propaganda when they employed such words as "conspiracy," "corruption," and "slavery." Bailyn concluded that the colonists meant what they said; that the fear of conspiracy against constitutional authority was built into the very structure of politics, and that these words represented "real fears, real anxieties, [and] a sense of real danger."[8] These assumptions, beliefs, and attitudes had fashioned the world view of the American Whigs and caused them to reinterpret British behavior in the manner that they did.

To Bailyn the Revolution represented, above all, an ideological revolution—a radical change in the way most Americans looked upon themselves and their institutions. The true revolution, he suggested, took place inside men's minds more than in the political or social sphere. This "ideological" revolution constituted a complete transformation in the image that the colonists had of themselves. Before the Revolution the Americans saw their divergences from the norms of European society as shortcomings; they felt a sense of inferiority because they lacked a titled aristocracy, cosmopolitan culture, stratified society, and established church along national lines. After the Revolution, on the other hand, they came to look upon these differences as good, not bad, as virtues, not vices, and as advantages rather than defects. This change in perspective, in Bailyn's eyes, was *the* American Revolution, and a section of his book is included as the second selection in this chapter.

The second trend in the 1960s and 1970s that contradicted the neoconservative view of the Revolution was contained in the writings of what might be called the neo-Progressive historians. These scholars resembled the older Progressive historians in several ways. They believed,

---

[8]*Ibid.,* p. ix.

for example, that the Revolution could be studied best from the perspective of the common people, the inarticulate masses, the disadvantaged, or the downtrodden. The chief sources of the revolutionary movement, they argued, were to be found in the profound economic and social dislocations within eighteenth-century America. In seeking the sources of social change, they pointed to the rapid rise in poverty during the period prior to the Revolution and to the resulting increase in social stratification. The tensions generated by such changes led to social unrest and protest on the part of the lower social orders during the Revolution. The neo-Progressive historians portrayed the Revolution as a democratic movement stimulated, in part, by these growing social inequalities. In their view the Revolution was a popular upsurge which aimed to broaden participation in American political life by breaking down the structures of authority by which local elites had ruled in the colonies.

The neo-Progressives were influenced in part by the writings of historians like Becker and Beard, but in large measure also by the social and political concerns of their own times. These scholars brought to the study of the Revolution a renewed awareness of the existence of minority and disadvantaged groups in American history. Protest movements of the 1960s and 1970s on behalf of the poor, blacks, and women made these scholars more sensitive to the claims of other social groups who had been oppressed in the past. The work of the neo-Progressives, then, reflected the passion for social justice so evident during the period when they wrote.

These concerns and attitudes were most obvious in the work of the so-called New Left historians—the most extreme of the neo-Progressives. One of the most aggressive spokesmen for this group was Jesse Lemisch. He was among the first of the New Left historians to argue that the history of the Revolution had too often been written "from the top down," that is, from the point of view of elites like Washington, Jefferson, and Adams. Such a historical perspective was by its nature blind to the concerns of the average man and inarticulate masses. History, according to Lemisch, should be written "from the bottom up." If viewed in this way, the Revolution might be shown to be more radical and characterized by greater conflict than the neoconservatives had suggested.

To make his point Lemisch in an article singled out the omission of any discussion of British impressment of American sailors in most works on the Revolution. Lowly American seamen, he argued, were deeply disturbed by this pernicious practice of the Royal Navy. Yet scholars all but ignored this issue because it was seldom voiced by members of the elite who were not personally involved. Lemisch concluded that other ordinary citizens, like these seamen, may have supported the Revolution for reasons historians had failed to investigate. In doing so he opened the possibility of viewing the Revolution as a radical movement undertaken by certain social groups to remedy specific oppressions they suffered under British rule. Lemisch went on to suggest that more research done from the perspective of the common people might reveal other instances of a similar nature, and this could result in the history of the Revolution being rewritten along different lines.[9]

One of the most important books written by the neo-Progressives to challenge the neoconservative historians was a collection of essays edited by Alfred F. Young entitled *The American Revolution: Explorations in the History of American Radicalism.* Many of the scholars writing in this volume likewise took issue with Bailyn's ideological interpretation of the Revolution. They rejected the idea that there was an ideological consensus among the American people or that the Revolution was mainly an ideological revolution. Some of them pictured the Revolution as a social movement—an internal struggle within the colonies—caused in part by class antagonisms. Other historians in the volume, however, held that one major source of conflict was ideological in nature. There were serious differences in ideology between the local leaders who shared a Whig view and the middle and lower orders of society who held different political beliefs.[10]

A third distinct challenge to the neoconservative interpretation came from a group of historians who studied the Loyalists. The neoconservatives had pictured the Revolution as a conservative movement aimed at preserving constitutional and political principles and undertaken to defend traditional American liberties. To the neoconservative historians the revolutionary era represented no break with the colonial past. They traced a line of continuity in political and constitutional principles from the late colonial period through the writing of the state constitutions to the federal Constitution in 1787. To them the Constitution was the culmination of the Revolution and not a conservative counterrevolution, as the older Progressive historians had maintained. Given the premise of a conservative Revolution, the neoconservatives could not fit the Loyalists comfortably within their interpretation. How could conservatives like the Loyalists oppose a conservative Revolution? For this reason the neoconservatives either failed to mention the Loyalists in their dis-

---

[9]Jesse Lemisch, "The American Revolution Seen from the Bottom Up," in *Towards a New Past: Dissenting Essays in American History,* ed. Barton J. Bernstein (New York, 1968), pp. 3–45.

[10]Alfred F. Young, ed., *The American Revolution: Explorations in The History of American Radicalism* (DeKalb, Illinois, 1976).

cussions of the Revolution, or made only superficial references to them.[11]

During the decades of the 1960s and 1970s, however, there was a great revival of interest in the Loyalists. The most important work to appear during the 1960s was William H. Nelson's *The American Tory.* Although Nelson's book was a form of intellectual history, it reflected two trends current among recent scholars: the tendency to concentrate more upon social history; and the inclination to resort to concepts drawn from other academic disciplines. Nelson presented a hypothesis that the Loyalists constituted a collection of isolated "cultural minorities"—certain social groups who were acutely conscious of the fact that they had never been assimilated into American society. These cultural enclaves, therefore, looked to Britain for protection against the threatening majorities surrounding them. Included among these social groups were the following: ethnic minorities such as the Scots, recent British immigrants, and Germans in the South; religious minorities—Anglicans in the North, Presbyterians in the South, along with Quakers and German pietists in the middle colonies; and certain racial minorities—numerous Indian tribes and many blacks. In defining these minorities by their sense of group consciousness and their feelings of alienation from the prevailing Whig majority, Nelson applied to history the negative reference group theory often employed by sociologists.[12]

The effort to analyze the social origins of the Loyalists was continued by Wallace Brown, who inquired into their socioeconomic and geographic backgrounds within each of the thirteen colonies. Contrary to the findings of many earlier historians, Brown argued that the Loyalists were not primarily members of the upper class; they came instead from the lower and middle classes in most colonies. Loyalism, moreover, was, "a distinctly urban and seaboard phenomenon"—except in New York and North Carolina, where there existed "major rural inland pockets." Despite John Adams's frequently misquoted estimate that the Loyalists constituted one-third of the population, Brown's statistics indicated that they composed only between 7.6 and 18 percent of the white population.[13]

---

[11]Daniel J. Boorstin in the *The Americans: The Colonial Experience* (New York, 1958), *The Americans: The National Experience* (New York, 1965), and "The American Revolution: Revolution Without Dogma," in *The Genius of American Politics* (Chicago, 1953), pp. 66–98, does not discuss the Loyalists. Louis Hartz, *The Liberal Tradition in America* (New York, 1955), p. 58; and Clinton Rossiter, *Seedtime of the Republic* (New York, 1953), pp. 3, 155, 319, 322, 340, 349, say very little. Edmund S. Morgan, in *The Birth of the Republic, 1763–1789* (Chicago, 1977), makes some mention, pp. 99, and 119–120, but Benjamin F. Wright, *Consensus and Continuity* (Boston, 1958), hardly accounts for the Loyalists at all.

[12]William H. Nelson, *The American Tory* (Oxford, 1961).

[13]Wallace Brown, *The King's Friends* (Providence, 1965), pp. v, 250, 257–58, 261–67. Two

Before and during the decade that the American Revolution Bicentennial was celebrated, at least three trends became increasingly noticeable in historical writings. One was the tendency among certain scholars to view the Revolution within a worldwide context rather than in a narrowly nationalistic framework. Instead of seeing the Revolution as a distinctly American event, they linked it to the long series of revolutions that rocked the Western world from the 1770s to the 1840s. By resorting to comparative history, scholars were able to gain new insights into the process of revolution itself.

The outstanding historian in this regard was Robert R. Palmer, who concluded that the period from the American Revolution in 1776 to the European revolutions of 1848 constituted one long uninterrupted epoch. In his two-volume work published in the late 1950s and early 1960s, Palmer called this period *The Age of Democratic Revolution*. Palmer's great work set the American Revolution within a broader context: that of the process of democratization taking place throughout the entire Western world at the time.[14]

Palmer specifically compared two revolutions—the American and French—that occurred within the Atlantic community in the late eighteenth century. He noted that even though the American Revolution had certain unique features, it resembled the French Revolution in many ways. In at least two respects—the number of émigrés who fled the two countries, and the amount of private property confiscated—the American Revolution appeared to be more radical than the French. But in other ways—in the institutions and traditions it tried to conserve—Palmer found the Revolution in the New World to be less revolutionary than that in the Old. He concluded, as a result, the American Revolution was ambivalent in character—it was both revolutionary and conservative at one and the same time.

A second trend occurred in the 1970s as scholars explored the nature of the Revolution in psychological terms. Historians resorted to classic psychoanalytical theories to come up with nonquantitative social science concepts that might prove useful. Several scholars, for example, made use of psychohistory—a subdiscipline that had recently come into prominence. They suggested that Americans might have been caught up in a serious identity crisis on the eve of the Revolution. This attitude, they said, might explain the colonists' rebellious behavior.

Viewed in psychoanalytical terms, America was said to be involved in an identity crisis—one that resulted in a love/hate relationship toward

---

important recent studies of the Loyalists were, Bernard Bailyn, *The Ordeal of Thomas Hutchinson* (Cambridge, 1974) and Robert Calhoon, *The Loyalists of Revolutionary America* (New York, 1973).

[14] Robert R. Palmer, *The Age of Democratic Revolution*, 2 vols. (Princeton, 1959 and 1964).

the mother country. Colonial society underwent a process of "Angliciza-
tion" in the eighteenth century, and, according to this hypothesis,
Americans became more self-consciously English as they copied British
ways. In becoming Anglicized, however, they turned their backs on
certain American styles, habits, and traditions that had developed during the seventeenth century. Hence, the colonists were torn. On the
one hand, they admired the mother country so much they aped British
customs. On the other, they resented the idea of emulating the British
because they were seeking to establish a separate sense of American
identity. Jack P. Greene, John M. Murrin, and Robert M. Weir, among
others, treated this theme in several essays.[15]

Other attempts at psychohistory explored the colonial relationship
within a Freudian framework. This hypothesis employed familiar symbols with sexual connotations—Great Britain as a mother country, the
English king as a father figure, and the colonists as rebellious
adolescents—and suggested they were all locked in an oedipal conflict.
That contemporaries had viewed the Revolution in such terms was obvious. John Adams exclaimed in 1765 that the colonists might be children, but "have not children a right to complain when their parents are
attempting to break their limbs... ?" Thomas Paine put it more
eloquently in 1777 when he wrote in his *American Crisis:* "To know
whether it be the interest of the continent to be independent, we need
only ask this easy, simple question, 'Is it the interest of a man to be a boy
all his life?'" Scholars like Winthrop D. Jordan, Edwin G. Burroughs,
Michael Wallace, and Bruce Mazlish probed the psychological dimensions of the Revolution along such lines.[16]

Psychobiography as well as psychohistory attracted scholars of the
Revolution. Some examined the lives of individuals, seeking to make a
connection between child-rearing practices and adult behavior. They

---

[15]Jack P. Greene, "Search for Identity: An Interpretation of the Meaning of Selected
Patterns of Social Response in Eighteenth-Century America," *Journal of Social History* 3
(1980):189–220; John M. Murrin, "The Legal Transformation: The Bench and Bar of
Eighteenth-Century Massachusetts," in *Essays in Politics and Social Development: Colonial
America,* ed. Stanley N. Katz (Boston, 1971 ed.); Jack P. Greene, "An Uneasy Connection:
An Analysis of the Pre-Conditions of the American Revolution," in *Essays on the American
Revolution,* ed. Stephen G. Kurtz and James H. Hutson (*Chapel Hill, 1973*); Rowland Berthoff
and John M. Murrin, "Feudalism, Communalism, and the Yeoman Freeholder: The Ameri-
can Revolution Considered as a Social Accident," *ibid.:* 256–88; and Robert M. Weir, "Who
shall Rule at Home: The American Revolution as a Crisis of Legitimacy for the Colonial
Elite," *Journal of Interdisciplinary History* 6 (1976):679–700.

[16]Winthrop D. Jordan, "Familial Politics: Thomas Paine and the Killing of the King,
1776," *Journal of American History* 60 (1973):294–308; Edwin C. Burroughs and Michael
Wallace, "The American Revolution: The Ideology and Psychology of National Liberation,"
*Perspectives in American History* 6 (1972):167–306; and Bruce Mazlish, "Leadership in the
American Revolution: The Psychological Dimension," in *Leadership in the American Revolution,*
Elizabeth H. Kagan, comp., (Washington, 1974).

were hoping to determine whether there were any patterns that might explain why persons from similar socioeconomic backgrounds became patriots, while others remained Loyalists. Other biographers, like Fawn M. Brodie, Kenneth Lynn, and William B. Willcox, relied upon theories of individual psychology to explain the actions of their subjects. One conclusion was inescapable in all these writings: The uses of psychological theories to explain the coming of the Revolution were bound to increase in the future.[17]

A third recent trend was the tendency to view the Revolution from a communitarian perspective. The term *community*, however, was defined in different ways. It sometimes meant the political community of the entire British Empire, and depicted the breakup that occurred as a result of the Revolution. At other times *community* was used to refer to a particular colony, and described its transformation as it moved from the status of province to state. Sometimes the term was applied to a single town or community—one that was examined as a kind of microcosm of the entire American society.

Earlier historians, as has been noted, argued that the policies of the imperial government had been wise, beneficent, and designed to serve the interests of the British Empire as a whole. But some recent scholars have analyzed the breakdown in understanding that took place within the British imperial community—a community celebrated in history for its so-called political genius. James Kirby Martin, in his *Men in Rebellion*, partially explained the reasons for the deterioration by describing the "status revolution" that occurred in the scramble for office in colonial America. Examining the public careers of almost five hundred governmental leaders who were intimately involved in the coming of the Revolution throughout the colonies, Martin concluded that the Revolution was the result of a structural crisis in power and political position. In the latter half of the eighteenth century, these leaders faced the phenomenon of political immobility within the governmental structure. There simply were not enough positions at the top level for all. No matter how wealthy, distinguished, or well educated a man might be, he could not hope to obtain one of the highest posts in the colonial bureaucracy if he lacked the right connections.

After the French and Indian War, the imperial government appointed either British officials or Americans who were British sympathizers to the best positions. With the top rungs of the political ladder occupied by such "higher" officials, "lesser" officials felt frustrated.

---

[17]Philip Greven, *The Protestant Temperament: Patterns of Child-Rearing, Religious Experience, and the Self in Early America* (New York, 1977); Kenneth S. Lynn, *A Divided People* (Westport, Conn., 1977); Fawn M. Brodie, *Thomas Jefferson* (New York, 1974); and William B. Willcox, *Portrait of a General* (New York, 1964).

Tensions arose between the two groups, as lesser officials sensed a relative loss of power and saw no prospects for upward political mobility. Many of these lesser politicians therefore organized political factions dedicated to embarrassing and harassing the favored few who held the highest provincial posts. The crisis was finally resolved when rebellious lesser officials overthrew British authority, and replaced the old political system with a new one which allowed for greater opportunities for men like themselves to advance on an open and competitive basis.[18]

Studies of various colonies were similarly directed toward the theme of a decline in the sense of community that led ultimately to the Revolution. Richard L. Bushman's *From Puritan to Yankee*, for example, described the changes taking place in Connecticut from 1690 to 1765. During that period, Connecticut was transformed from a homogeneous Puritan community held together by religious values to a secular society torn by conflict. Social changes and shifts within the social structure destroyed the previous sense of community, and the resulting unstable social order made Connecticut more vulnerable to the turbulent forces operating on the eve of the Revolution.[19]

Robert Gross, one of the "new social historians," made an intensive study of a single community—Concord, Massachusetts—to examine the impact of the Revolutionary War on the townspeople. Much of Gross's research was quantitative in nature, and he reconstructed life in Concord not from traditional literary sources but from church records, wills, deeds, petitions, tax lists, and minutes of town meetings. Rather than making sweeping statements about the Revolution as a social movement, Gross showed how the event directly affected the lives of individuals. His conclusion was that the townspeople had gone to war not to promote social change but to stop it. Concord's Minutemen were driven to rebellion by a desire to defend their traditional way of life from encroachment by the British and other outside forces. Ironically enough, according to Gross, the results of the Revolution opened the way to innovations which profoundly altered Concord's way of life.[20]

In summary, it should be noted that historians who have addressed themselves to the question of whether the Revolution was revolutionary or not must answer a number of related questions. Was American society democratic during the colonial period so that the Revolution became nothing more than a colonial rebellion? Or was American society undemocratic during the colonial era, thus resulting in a dual revolution: a

---

[18]James Kirby Martin, *Men in Rebellion* (New Brunswick, 1973).

[19]Richard L. Bushman, *From Puritan to Yankee* (New York, 1967).

[20]Robert Gross, *The Minutemen and Their World* (New York, 1976).

struggle to see who would rule at home, as well as a fight for home rule? Were the reforms that accompanied the Revolution the result of a gradual evolution, and carried out with the blessings of a basic consensus among the American people? Or were such reforms the product of a radical Revolution that resulted from class conflict between America's upper and lower classes? What was the true nature of the Revolution? Was there a radical ideological change in the ideas that most Americans had regarding their image of themselves and of their institutions? Or did most of the changes take place within political and social spheres rather than in the world of ideas? Were the Loyalists disloyal Americans in that they did not share the Whig consensus on constitutional and political principles? Or were they instead "cultural minorities" fearful of surrounding majorities they regarded as hostile? Was the Revolution a unique event, and therefore one to be examined within the context of American history and in terms of its own time? Or did it bear some relationship to revolutions that took place in other parts of the Western world at a later time? The answers to these questions, in the final analysis, will determine the answer to the broader question of whether the American Revolution was revolutionary or nonrevolutionary.

# Daniel J. Boorstin

DANIEL J. BOORSTIN (1914–     ), formerly professor of history at the University
of Chicago, currently is head of the Library of Congress. He has published
numerous books on various aspects of American history, including *The
Genius of American Politics* (1953) and *The Americans*, 3 vols. (1958–1973).

We are accustomed to think of the Revolution as the great age of American political thought. It may therefore be something of a shock to realize
that it did not produce in America a single important treatise on political
theory. Men like Franklin and Jefferson, universal in their interests,
active and spectacularly successful in developing institutions, were not
fertile as political philosophers. . . .

We have been slow to see some of the more obvious and more important peculiarities of our Revolution because influential scholars on the
subject have cast their story in the mold of the French Revolution of
1789. Some of our best historians have managed to empty our Revolution of much of its local flavor by exaggerating what it had in common
with that distinctively European struggle. This they have done in two
ways.

First, they have stressed the international character of the intellectual
movement of which the French Revolution was a classic expression—the
so-called Enlightenment. They speak of it as a "climate of opinion"
whose effects, like the barometric pressure, could no more be escaped in
American than in Europe. As Carl Becker put it in his *Heavenly City of the
Eighteenth-Century Philosophers:* "The Enlightenment . . . is not a peculiarly French but an international climate of opinion . . . and in the new
world Jefferson, whose sensitized mind picked up and transmitted
every novel vibration in the intellectual air, and Franklin of Philadelphia,
printer and friend of the human race—these also, whatever national or
individual characteristics they may have exhibited, were true children of
the Enlightenment. The philosophical empire was an international domain of which France was but the mother country and Paris the capital."

Second, they have treated ours as only a particular species of the

Daniel J. Boorstin, *The Genius of American Politics* (Chicago: University of Chicago Press,
1953), pp. 66–77, 81–87, 94–95, 98. Reprinted by permission of the author and the University of Chicago Press.

genus *Revolution*—of what should perhaps more properly be called *revolutio Europaensis*. Since the French Revolution has been made the model, from that European revolution historians have borrowed the vocabulary in which ours is discussed and the calendar by which it is clocked. "Thermidor," for example, is the name used in one of our best college textbooks to introduce its chapter on the federal Constitution.

It goes on:

> There comes a time in every revolutionary movement when the people become tired of agitation and long for peace and security. They then eliminate the radicals, trouble-makers and warmongers, and take measures to consolidate their government, hoping to secure what has already been gained through turmoil and suffering. *Thermidor* this time is called in leftist language, from the counter-revolution in France that overthrew Robespierre and ended the reign of terror. Thus, the establishment of Cromwell as Lord Protector was the Thermidor of the English Revolution in the seventeenth century; and the Stalin dictatorship and exile of Trotsky marks the Thermidor of the Russian Revolution. Every taking of the Bastille, it may be said, is inevitably followed by Thermidor, since human nature craves security, and the progress of a revolution must be stopped somewhere short of anarchy [Morison and Commager, *Growth of the American Republic*, 3d ed. (New York, 1942), 1:277].

The effect of all this has been to emphasize—or rather exaggerate—the similarity of ours to all other modern revolutions.

In so doing, historians have exaggerated the significance of what is supposed to have been the ideology of the Revolution. Such an emphasis has had the further attraction to some "liberal" historians of seeming to put us in the main current of European history. It has never been quite clear to me why historians would not have found our revolution significant enough merely as a victory of constitutionalism.

The most obvious peculiarity of our American Revolution is that, in the modern European sense of the word, it was hardly a revolution at all. The Daughters of the American Revolution, who have been understandably sensitive on this subject, have always insisted in their literature that the American Revolution was no revolution but merely a colonial rebellion. The more I have looked into the subject, the more convinced I have become of the wisdom of their naïveté. "The social condition and the Constitution of the Americans are democratic," De Tocqueville observed about a hundred years ago. "But they have not had a democratic revolution." This fact is surely one of the most important of our history.

A number of historians (J. Franklin Jameson and Merrill Jensen, for example) have pointed out the ways in which a social revolution, including a redistribution of property, accompanied the American Revolution. These are facts which no student of the period should neglect. Yet it seems to me that these historians have by no means succeeded in showing that such changes were so basic and so far-reaching as actually in themselves to have established our national republican institutions. When we speak of the Revolution, therefore, we are still fully justified in referring to something other than what Jameson's disciples mean by "the American Revolution as a social movement." If we consider the American Revolution in that sense, it would not be a great deal more notable than a number of other social movements in our history, such as Jacksonianism, populism, progressivism, and the New Deal. Moreover, in so far as the American Revolution was a social movement, it was not much to be distinguished from European revolutions; and the increasing emphasis on this aspect of our history is but another example of the attempt to assimilate our history to that of Europe.

The Revolution, as the birthday of our nation, must mean something very different from all this. It is the series of events by which we separated ourselves from the British Empire and acquired a national identity. Looking at our Revolution from this point of view, what are some features which distinguish it from the French Revolution of 1789 or the other revolutions to which western European nations trace their national identity? And, especially, what are those peculiarities which have affected the place of theory in our political life?

1. First, and most important, the United States was born in a *colonial* rebellion. Our national birth certificate is a Declaration of Independence and not a Declaration of the Rights of Man. The vast significance of this simple fact is too often forgotten. Compared even with other colonial rebellions, the American Revolution is notably lacking in cultural self-consciousness and in any passion for national unity. The more familiar type of colonial rebellion—like that which recently occurred in India—is one in which a subject people vindicates its local culture against foreign rulers. But the American Revolution had very little of this character. On the contrary, ours was one of the few conservative colonial rebellions of modern times.

We should recall several of the peculiar circumstances (most of them obvious) which had made this kind of revolution possible. At the time of the Revolution, the major part of the population of the American colonies was of British stock. Therefore, no plausible racial or national argument could be found for the superiority either of the inhabitants of the mother country or of the continental American colonies. Even when Jefferson, in his *Notes on Virginia*, went to some trouble to refute Buffon and the Abbé Raynal and others who had argued that all races, including man, deteriorated on the American continent, he did not go so far as to say that the American races were distinctly superior.

Since the climate and topography of substantial parts of the American colonies were similar to those of the mother country (and for a number of other reasons), there had been a pretty wholesale transplantation of British legal and political institutions to North America. Unlike the Spanish colonies in South America, which were to rebel, at least in part, because they had had so little home rule, the British colonies in North America were to rebel because, among other reasons, they had had so much. Finally, the North American continent was (except for sparse Indian settlements) empty of indigenous populations, hence barren of such local institutions and traditions as could have competed with what the colonists had brought with them.

All these facts were to make it easy, then, for the American Revolution to seem in the minds of most of its leaders an affirmation of the tradition of British institutions. The argument of the best theorists of the Revolution—perhaps we should call them lawyers rather than theorists—was not, on the whole, that Ameirca had institutions or a culture superior to that of the British. Rather their position, often misrepresented and sometimes simply forgotten, was that the British by their treatment of the American colonies were being untrue to the ancient spirit of their own institutions. The slogan "Taxation without Representation Is Tyranny" was clearly founded on a British assumption. As James Otis put it in his pamphlet *The Rights of the British Colonies* (1764), he believed "that this [British] constitution is the most free one, and by far the best, now existing on earth: that by this constitution, every man in the dominions is a free man: that no parts of His Majesty's dominions can be taxed without their consent: that every part has a right to be represented in the supreme or some subordinate legislature: that the refusal of this would seem to be a contradiction in practice to the theory of the constitution."

According to their own account, then, the Americans were to have forced on them the need to defend the ancient British tradition; to be truer to the spirit of that tradition than George III and Lord North and Townshend knew how to be. They were fighting not so much to establish new rights as to preserve old ones: "for the preservation of our liberties . . . in defense of the freedom that is our birthright, and which we ever enjoyed till the late violation of it" (Declaration of Causes of Taking up Arms, July 6, 1775). From the colonists' point of view, until 1776 it was Parliament that had been revolutionary, by exercising a power for which there was no warrant in English constitutional precedent. The ablest defender of the Revolution—in fact, the greatest political theorist of the American Revolution—was also the great theorist of British conservatism, Edmund Burke.

2. Second, the American Revolution was *not* the product of a nationalistic spirit. We had no Bismarck or Cavour or any nationalist

philosophy. We were singularly free from most of the philosophical baggage of modern nationalism.

Perhaps never was a new nation created with less enthusiasm. To read the history of our Revolution is to discover that the United States was a kind of *pis aller*. This fact explains many of the difficulties encountered in conducting the Revolution and in framing a federal constitution. The original creation of a United States was the work of doubly reluctant men: men reluctant, both because of their local loyalties—to Virginia, Massachusetts, Rhode Island, and New York—and because of their imperial loyalty. The story of the "critical period" of American history, of the Articles of Confederation and the Constitution, tells of the gradual overcoming of this reluctance. It was overcome not by any widespread conversion to a nationalist theory—even *The Federalist* papers are conspicuously lacking in such a theory—but by gradual realization of the need for effective union.

In the period of the American Revolution we do discover a number of enthusiasms: for the safety and prosperity of Virginia or New York, for the cause of justice, for the rights of Englishmen. What is missing is anything that might be called widespread enthusiasm for the birth of a new nation: the United States of America. Until well into the nineteenth century, Jefferson—and he was not alone in this—was using the phrase "my country" to refer to his native state of Virginia.

3. Our Revolution was successful at the first try. This is equally true whether we consider it as a revolt against British rule or as a movement for republican federalism. There was no long-drawn-out agitation, no intellectual war of attrition, of the sort which breeds dogmas and intransigence. Thomas Paine's *Common Sense*, which is generally considered "the first important republican tract to be issued in America . . . the first to present cogent arguments for independence," did not appear until January 10, 1776. Down to within six months of the break, few would have considered independence; and even then the colonists had only quite specific complaints. There had been no considerable tradition in America either of revolt against British institutions or of republican theorizing.

The political objective of the Revolution, independence from British rule, was achieved by one relatively short continuous effort. More commonly in modern history (take, for example, the European revolutions of the nineteenth century) any particular revolt has been only one in a long series. Each episode, then, ends on a note of suspense which comes from the feeling that the story is "to be continued." Under those circumstances, challenges to constituted authority follow one another, accumulating their ideological baggage.

In France, for example, 1789 was followed by 1830 and 1848 and 1870; a similar list could be made for Italy, Germany, and perhaps Russia.

Such repetition creates a distinctive revolutionary tradition, with continued agitation keeping alive certain doctrines. Repeated efforts provide the dogmatic raw material for a profusion of later political parties, each of which rallies under the banner of one or another of the defeated revolutions or of a revolution yet to be made. But, properly speaking, 1776 had no sequel, and needed none. The issue was separation, and separation was accomplished.

The student who comes for the first time to the literature of our Revolution is liable to be disappointed by the dull and legalistic flavor of what he has to read. Although the American Revolution occurred in an age which throughout Europe was laden with philosophic reflection and important treatises, our Revolution was neither particularly rich nor particularly original in its intellectual apparatus. The documents of that era, as Moses Coit Tyler described them, are "a vast morass of technical discussion, into which, perhaps, no living reader will ever follow the writer, from which, in fact, the writer himself never emerges alive."

Orators, textbook writers, and other tradition-makers have been hard put to it to find those ringing phrases, the battle cries and philosophical catchwords, which slip smoothly off the tongue, remain fixed in the memory, and uplift the soul. This helps explain why a few phrases and documents have been overworked and why even these have always been read only in part or out of context. The first two paragraphs of the Declaration of Independence have been worn thin; few bother to read the remaining thirty. People have grasped at "life, liberty, and the pursuit of happiness," forgetting that it was two-thirds borrowed and, altogether, only part of a preamble. We have repeated that "all men are created equal," without daring to discover what it meant and without realizing that probably to none of the men who spoke it did it mean what we would like it to mean. Or we have exploited passages in the "speeches" of Patrick Henry, which were actually composed less by Henry than by his biographers.

The proper slogan of the Revolution—if, indeed, there was a slogan—was "No Taxation without Representation." Such words are far too polysyllabic, far too legalistic, to warm the popular heart. But if we compare them with the "Liberty, Equality, Fraternity" of the French Revolution and the "Peace, Bread, and Land," of the Russian, we have a clue to the peculiar spirit of the American Revolution. It is my view that the major issue of the American Revolution was the true constitution of the British Empire, which is a pretty technical legal problem. This notion is supported by Professor Charles H. McIlwain, who, in his admirable little book on the American Revolution, comes closer than any other recent historian to the spirit of our revolutionary age.

In that age men were inclined to take their opponents at their word; the revolutionary debate seems to have been carried on in the belief that men meant what they said. But in this age of Marx and Freud we have begun to take it for granted that if people talk about one thing, they must be thinking about something else. Ideas are treated as the apparatus of an intellectual sleight of hand, by which the speaker diverts the audience's attention to an irrelevant subject while he does the real business unobserved. To study the revolutionary debate is then to try to see (in the phrase of one historian) how "the colonists modified their theory to suit their needs." From such a point of view, there is perhaps never much political or legal thought worth talking about; to be realistic we should focus our discussion on hormones and statistics.

But such an approach would bleach away the peculiar tone of our history and empty our Revolution of its unique significance. Therefore, even at the risk of seeming naïve, I should like to consider the outlandish possibility that men like Jefferson and Adams all along meant what they were saying, that is, that the Revolution had something to do with the British constitution. . . .

The feature to which I want to direct your attention might be called the conservatism of the Revolution. If we understand this characteristic, we will begin to see the Revolution as an illustration of the remarkable continuity of American history. And we will also see how the attitude of our revolutionary thinkers has engraved more deeply in our national consciousness a belief in the inevitability of our particular institutions, or, in a word, our sense of "givenness."

The character of our Revolution has nourished our assumption that whatever institutions we happened to have here (in this case the British constitution) had the self-evident validity of anything that is "normal." We have thus casually established the tradition that it is superfluous to the American condition to produce elaborate treatises on political philosophy or to be explicit about political values and the theory of community.

I shall confine myself to two topics. First, the manifesto of the Revolution, namely, the Declaration of Independence; and, second, the man who has been generally considered the most outspoken and systematic political philosopher of the Revolution, Thomas Jefferson. Of course, I will not try to give a full account of either of them. I will attempt only to call your attention to a few facts which may not have been sufficiently emphasized and which are especially significant for our present purpose. Obviously, no one could contend that there is either in the man or in the document nothing of the cosmopolitan spirit, nothing of the world climate of opinion. My suggestion is simply that we do find another spirit of at least equal, and perhaps overshadowing, importance and that this spirit may actually be more characteristic of our Revolution.

First, then, for the Declaration of Independence. Its technical, legalistic, and conservative character, which I wish to emphasize, will appear at once by contrast with the comparable document of the French Revolution. Ours was concerned with a specific event, namely, the separation of these colonies from the mother country. But the French produced a "Declaration of the Rights of *Man* and the Citizen." When De Tocqueville, in his *Ancien Régime* (Book I, chap. iii), sums up the spirit of the French Revolution, he is describing exactly what the American Revolution was not:

> The French Revolution acted, with regard to things of this world, precisely as religious revolutions have acted with regard to things of the other. It dealt with the citizen in the abstract, independent of particular social organizations, just as religions deal with mankind in general, independent of time and place. It inquired, not what were the particular rights of the French citizens, but what were the general rights and duties of mankind in reference to political concerns.
>
> It was by thus divesting itself of all that was peculiar to one race or time, and by reverting to natural principles of social order and government, that it became intelligible to all, and susceptible of simultaneous imitation in a hundred different places.
>
> By seeming to tend rather to the regeneration of the human race than to the reform of France alone, it roused passions such as the most violent political revolutions had been incapable of awakening. It inspired proselytism, and gave birth to propagandism; and hence assumed that quasi religious character which so terrified those who saw it, or, rather, became a sort of new religion, imperfect, it is true, without God, worship, or future life, but still able, like Islamism, to cover the earth with its soldiers, its apostles, and its martyrs [trans. John Bonner (New York, 1856), pp. 26f.].

In contrast to all this, our Declaration of Independence is essentially a list of specific historical instances. It is directed not to the regeneration but only to the "opinions" of mankind. It is closely tied to time and place; the special affection for "British brethren" is freely admitted; it is concerned with the duties of a particular king and certain of his subjects.

Even if we took only the first two paragraphs or preamble, which are the most general part of the document, and actually read them as a whole, we could make a good case for their being merely a succinct restatement of the Whig theory of the British revolution of 1688. Carl Becker himself could not overlook this fact. "In political theory and in political practice," he wrote parenthetically, "the American Revolution drew its inspiration from the parliamentary struggle of the seventeenth century. The philosophy of the Declaration was not taken from the French. It was not even new; but good old English doctrine newly formulated to meet a present emergency." To be understood, its words must be annotated by British history. This is among the facts which have led some historians (Guizot, for example) to go so far as to say that the English revolution succeeded twice, once in England and once in America.

The remaining three-quarters—the unread three-quarters—of the document is technical and legalistic. That is, of course, the main reason why it remains unread. For it is a bill of indictment against the king, written in the language of British constitutionalism. "The patient sufferance of these Colonies" is the point of departure. It deals with rights and franchises under British charters. It carefully recounts that the customary and traditional forms of protest, such as "repeated Petitions," have already been tried.

The more the Declaration is reread in context, the more plainly it appears a document of imperial legal relations rather than a piece of high-flown political philosophy. The desire to remain true to the principles of British constitutionalism up to the bitter end explains why, as has been often remarked, the document is directed against the king, despite the fact that the practical grievances were against Parliament; perhaps also why at this stage there is no longer an explicit appeal to the rights of Englishmen. Most of the document is a bald enumeration of George III's failures, excesses, and crimes in violation of the constitution and laws of Great Britain. One indictment after another makes sense only if one presupposes the framework of British constitutionalism. How else, for example, could one indict a king "for depriving us in many cases, of the benefits of Trial by Jury"?

We can learn a great deal about the context of our revolutionary thought by examining Jefferson's own thinking down to the period of the Revolution. We need not stretch a point or give Jefferson a charismatic role, to say that the flavor of his thought is especially important for our purposes. He has been widely considered the leading political philosopher of the Revolution. Among other things, he was, of course, the principal author of the Declaration of Independence itself; and the Declaration has been taken to be the climax of the abstract philosophizing of the revolutionaries. Because he is supposed to be the avant-garde of revolutionary thought, evidence of conservatism and legalism in Jefferson's thought as a whole is especially significant.

We now are beginning to have a definitive edition of Jefferson's papers (edited by Julian P. Boyd and published by the Princeton University Press), which is one of the richest treasures ever amassed for the historian of a particular period. This helps us use Jefferson's thought as a touchstone. Neither in the letters which Jefferson wrote nor in those he received do we discover that he and his close associates—at least down to the date of the Revolution—showed any conspicuous interest in political theory. We look in vain for general reflections on the nature of government or constitutions. The manners of the day did require that a cultivated gentleman be acquainted with certain classics of political thought; yet we lack evidence that such works were read with more than a perfunctory interest. To be sure, when Jefferson prepares a list of worthy books for a young friend in 1771, he includes references to Montesquieu, Sidney, and Bolingbroke; but such references are rare. Even when he exchanges letters with Edmund Pendleton on the more general problems of institutions, he remains on the level of legality and policy, hardly touching political theory. Jefferson's papers for the revolutionary period (read without the hindsight which has put the American and the French revolutions in the same era of world history) show little evidence that the American Revolution was a goad to higher levels of abstract thinking about society. We miss any such tendency in what Jefferson and his associates were reading or in what they were writing.

On the other hand, we find ample evidence that the locale of early Jeffersonian thought was distinctly *colonial*; we might even say *provincial*. And we begin to see some of the significance of that fact in marking the limits of political theorizing in America. By 1776, when the irreversible step of revolution was taken, the colonial period in the life of Jefferson and the other revolutionary thinkers was technically at an end; but by then their minds had been congealed, their formal education completed, their social habits and the cast of their political thinking determined. The Virginia society of the prerevolutionary years had been decidedly derivative, not only in its culture, its furniture, its clothes, and its books, but in many of its ideas and—what is more to our purpose—in perhaps most of its institutions.

It is an important and little-noted fact that for many American thinkers of the period (including Jefferson himself) the cosmopolitan period in their thought did not begin until several years *after* their Revolution. Then, as representatives of the new nation, some of them were to enter the labyrinth of European diplomacy. Much of what we read of their experiences abroad even in this later period would confirm our impression of their naïveté, their strangeness to the sophisicated Paris of Talleyrand, the world of the *philosophes*. In Jefferson's particular case, the cosmopolitan period of his thought probably did not begin much before his first trip abroad as emissary to France in 1784.

When John Adams had gone, also to France, a few years earlier on his first foreign mission, he thought himself fresh from an "American Wilderness." Still more dramatic is the unhappy career of John Marshall, who was an innocent abroad if there ever was one. The career of Franklin, who was at least two generations older than these revolutionary leaders, is something of an exception; but even in his case much of his charm for the salons of Paris consisted in his successful affectation of the character of a frontiersman.

The importance of this colonial framework in America, as I have already suggested, was to be enormous, not only from the point of view of revolutionary thought, but in its long-run effect on the role of political theory in American life. The legal institutions which Americans considered their own and which they felt bound to master were largely borrowed. Jefferson and John Adams, both lawyers by profession, like their English contemporaries, had extracted much of their legal knowledge out of the crabbed pages of Coke's *Institutes.* . . .

We begin to see how far we would be misled, were we to cast American events of this era in the mold of European history. The American Revolution was in a very special way conceived as both a vindication of the British past and an affirmation of an American future. The British past was contained in ancient and living institutions rather than in doctrines; and the American future was never to be contained in a theory. The Revolution was thus a prudential decision taken by men of principle rather than the affirmation of a theory. What British institutions meant did not need to be articulated; what America might mean was still to be discovered. This continuity of American history was to make a sense of "giveness" easier to develop; for it was this continuity which had made a new ideology of revolution seem unnecessary. . . .

The experience of our Revolution may suggest that the sparseness of American political theory, which has sometimes been described as a refusal of American statesmen to confront their basic philosophical problems, has been due less to a conscious refusal than to a simple lack of necessity. As the British colonists in America had forced on them the need to create a nation, so they had forced on them the need to be traditional and empirical in their institutions. The Revolution, because it was conceived as essentially affirming the British constitution, did not create the kind of theoretical vacuum made by some other revolutions. . . .

The Revolution itself, as we have seen, had been a kind of affirmation of faith in ancient British institutions. In the greater part of the institutional life of the community the Revolution thus required no basic change. If any of this helps to illustrate or explain our characteristic lack of interest in political philosophy, it also helps to account for the value which we still attach to our inheritance from the British constitution: trial by jury, due process of law, representation before taxation, habeas corpus, freedom from attainder, independence of the judiciary, and the rights of free speech, free petition, and free assembly, as well as our narrow definition of treason and our antipathy to standing armies in peacetime. It also explains our continuing—sometimes bizarre, but usually fortunate—readiness to think of these traditional rights of Englishmen as if they were indigenous to our continent. In the proceedings of the San Francisco Vigilance Committee of 1851, we hear crude adventurers on the western frontier describing the technicalities of habeas corpus as if they were fruits of the American environment, as natural as human equality.

# Bernard Bailyn

BERNARD BAILYN (1922–     ) is Adams University Professor of History at Harvard University. He has written numerous books in American colonial history, including *The New England Merchants in the Seventeenth Century* (1955), *Education in the Forming of American Society* (1960), *The Origins of American Politics* (1968), and *The Ordeal of Thomas Hutchinson* (1974).

What was essentially involved in the American Revolution was not the disruption of society, with all the fear, despair, and hatred that that entails, but the realization, the comprehension and fulfillment, of the inheritance of liberty and of what was taken to be America's destiny in the context of world history. The great social shocks that in the French and Russian revolutions sent the foundations of thousands of individual lives crashing into ruins had taken place in America in the course of the previous century, slowly, silently, almost imperceptibly, not as a sudden avalanche but as myriads of individual changes and adjustments which had gradually transformed the order of society. By 1763 the great landmarks of European life—the church and the idea of orthodoxy, the state and the idea of authority: much of the array of institutions and ideas that buttressed the society of the *ancien régime*—had faded in their exposure to the open, wilderness environment of America. But until the disturbances of the 1760s these changes had not been seized upon as grounds for reconsideration of society and politics. Often they had been condemned as deviations, as retrogressions back toward a more primitive condition of life. Then, after 1760—and especially in the decade after 1765—they were brought into open discussion as the colonists sought to apply advanced principles of society and politics to their own immediate problems.

The original issue of the Anglo-American conflict was, of course, the question of the extent of Parliament's jurisdiction in the colonies. But that could not be discussed in isolation. The debate involved eventually a wide range of social and political problems, and it ended by 1776 in what may be called the conceptualization of American life. By then Americans had come to think of themselves as in a special category, uniquely placed by history to capitalize on, to complete and fulfill, the promise of man's existence. The changes that had overtaken their provincial societies, they saw, had been good: elements not of deviance and retrogression but of betterment and progress; not a lapse into primitivism, but an elevation to a higher plane of political and social life than had ever been reached before. Their rustic blemishes had become the marks of a chosen people. "The liberties of mankind and the glory of human nature is in their keeping," John Adams wrote in the year of the Stamp Act. "America was designed by Providence for the theatre on which man was to make his true figure, on which science, virtue, liberty, happiness, and glory were to exist in peace."

The effort to comprehend, to communicate, and to fulfill this destiny was continuous through the entire revolutionary generation—it did not cease, in fact, until in the nineteenth century its creative achievements became dogma. But there were three phases of particular concentration: the period up to and including 1776, centering on the discussion of Anglo-American differences; the devising of the first state governments, mainly in the years from 1776 to 1780; and the reconsideration of the state constitutions and the reconstruction of the national government in the last half of the eighties and in the early nineties. In each of these phases important contributions were made not only to the skeletal structure of constitutional theory but to the surrounding areas of social thought as well. But in none was the creativity as great, the results as radical and as fundamental, as in the period before Independence. It was then that the premises were defined and the assumptions set. It was then that explorations were made in new territories of thought, the first comprehensive maps sketched, and routes marked out. Thereafter the psychological as well as intellectual barriers were down. It was the most creative period in the history of American political thought. Everything that followed assumed and built upon its results. . . .

It was an elevating, transforming vision: a new, fresh, vigorous, and above all morally regenerate people rising from obscurity to defend the battlements of liberty and then in triumph standing forth, heartening and sustaining the cause of freedom everywhere. In the light of such a conception everything about the colonies and their controversy with the mother country took on a new appearance. Provincialism was gone: Americans stood side by side with the heroes of historic battles for freedom and with the few remaining champions of liberty in the present. What were once felt to be defects—isolation, institutional simplicity, primitiveness of manners, multiplicity of religions, weakness in the authority of the state—could now be seen as virtues, not only by Americans themselves but by enlightened spokesmen of reform, renewal, and hope wherever they might be—in London coffeehouses, in Parisian *salons*, in the courts of German princes. The mere existence of the colonists suddenly became philosophy teaching by example. Their manners, their morals, their way of life, their physical, social, and political condition were seen to vindicate eternal truths and to demonstrate, as ideas and words never could, the virtues of the heavenly city of the eighteenth-century philosophers.

But the colonists' ideas and words counted too, and not merely because they repeated as ideology the familiar utopian phrases of the Enlightenment and of English libertarianism. What they were saying by 1776 was familiar in a general way to reformers and illuminati everywhere in the Western world; yet it was different. Words and concepts had been reshaped in the colonists' minds in the course of a decade of pounding controversy—strangely reshaped, turned in unfamilar directions, toward conclusions they could not themselves clearly perceive. They found a new world of political thought as they struggled to work out the implications of their beliefs in the years before independence. It was a world not easily possessed; often they withdrew in some confusion to more familiar ground. But they touched its boundaries, and, at certain points, probed its interior. Others, later—writing and revising the first state constitutions, drafting and ratifying the federal Constitution, and debating in detail, exhaustively, the merits of these efforts—would resume the search for resolutions of the problems the colonists had broached before 1776.

This critical probing of traditional concepts—part of the colonists' effort to express reality as they knew it and to shape it to ideal ends—became the basis for all further discussions of enlightened reform, in Europe as well as in America. The radicalism the Americans conveyed to the world in 1776 was a transformed as well as a transforming force. . . .

In no obvious sense was the American Revolution undertaken as a social revolution. No one, that is, deliberately worked for the destruction or even the substantial alteration of the order of society as it had been known. Yet it was transformed as a result of the Revolution, and not merely because Loyalist property was confiscated and redistributed, or because the resulting war destroyed the economic bases of some people's lives and created opportunities for others that would not otherwise have existed. Seizure of Loyalist property and displacements in the economy did in fact take place, and the latter if not the former does account for a spurt in social mobility that led earlier *arrivés* to remark, "When the pot boils, the scum will rise." Yet these were superficial changes; they affected a small part of the population only, and they did not alter the organization of society.

What did now affect the essentials of social organization—what in

time would help permanently to transform them—were changes in the
realm of belief and attitude. The views men held toward the relationships that bound them to each other—the discipline and pattern of
society—moved in a new direction in the decade before independence.

Americans of 1760 continued to assume, as had their predecessors
for generations before, that a healthy society was a hierarchical society,
in which it was natural for some to be rich and some poor, some honored and some obscure, some powerful and some weak. And it was
believed that superiority was unitary, that the attributes of the
favored—wealth, wisdom, power—had a natural affinity to each other,
and hence that political leadership would naturally rest in the hands of
the social leaders. Movement, of course, there would be: some would
fall and some would rise; but manifest, external differences among men,
reflecting the principle of hierarchical order, were necessary and proper,
and would remain; they were intrinsic to the nature of things.

Circumstances had pressed harshly against such assumptions. The
wilderness environment from the beginning had threatened the maintenance of elaborate social distinctions; many of them in the passage of
time had in fact been worn away. Puritanism, in addition, and the
epidemic evangelicalism of the mid-eighteenth century, had created
challenges to the traditional notions of social stratification by generating
the conviction that the ultimate quality of men was to be found elsewhere than in their external condition, and that a cosmic achievement
lay within each man's grasp. And the peculiar configuration of colonial
politics—a constant broil of petty factions struggling almost formlessly,
with little discipline or control, for the benefits of public authority—had
tended to erode the respect traditionally accorded the institutions and
officers of the state.

Yet nowhere, at any time in the colonial years, were the implications
of these circumstances articulated or justified. The assumption remained
that society, in its maturity if not in its confused infancy, would conform
to the pattern of the past; that authority would continue to exist without
challenge, and that those in superior positions would be responsible and
wise, and those beneath them respectful and content. These premises
and expectations were deeply lodged; they were not easily or quickly
displaced. But the Revolution brought with it arguments and attitudes
bred of arguments endlessly repeated, that undermined these premises
of the *ancien régime*.

For a decade or more defiance to the highest constituted powers
poured from the colonial presses and was hurled from half the pulpits of
the land. The right, the need, the absolute obligation to disobey legally
constituted authority had become the universal cry. Cautions and qualifications became ritualistic: formal exercises in ancient pieties. One
might preface one's charge to disobedience with homilies on the inevi-

table imperfections of all governments and the necessity to bear "some injuries" patiently and peaceably. But what needed and received demonstration and defense was not the caution, but the injunction: the argument that when injuries touched on "fundamental rights" (and who could say when they did not?) then nothing less than "duty to God and religion, to themselves, to the community, and to unborn posterity require such to assert and defend their rights by all lawful, most prudent, and effectual means in their power." Obedience as a principle was only too well known; disobedience as a doctrine was not. It was therefore asserted again and again that resistance to constituted authority was "a doctrine according to godliness—the doctrine of the English nation... by which our rights and constitution have often been defended and repeatedly rescued out of the hands of encroaching tyranny.... This is the doctrine and grand pillar of the ever memorable and glorious Revolution, and upon which our gracious sovereign George III holds the crown of the British empire." What better credentials could there be? How lame to add that obedience too "is an eminent part of Christian duty without which government must disband and dreadful anarchy and confusion (with all its horrors) take place and reign without control"—how lame, especially in view of the fact that one could easily mistake this "Christian obedience" for that "blind, enslaving obedience which is no part of the Christian institution but is highly injurious to religion, to every free government, and to the good of mankind, and is the stirrup of tyranny, and grand engine of slavery."

Defiance to constituted authority leaped like a spark from one flammable area to another, growing in heat as it went. Its greatest intensification took place in the explosive atmosphere of local religious dissent. Isaac Backus spoke only for certain of the Baptists and Congregational Separates and against the presumptive authority of ministers, when, in the course of an attack on the religious establishment in Massachusetts, he warned that

> we are not to obey and follow [ministers] in an implicit or customary way, but each one must consider and follow others no further than they see that the end of their conversation is Jesus Christ the same yesterday, and today, and forever more. ... . People are so far from being under obligation to follow teachers who don't lead in this way they incur guilt by such a following of them.

It took little imagination on the part of Backus's readers and listeners to find in this a general injunction against uncritical obedience to authority in any form. Others were even more explicit. The Baptist preacher who questioned not merely the authority of the local orthodox church but the very "etymology of the word [orthodoxy]" assured the world that the colonists have as just a right, before GOD and man, to oppose King, ministry, Lords, and Commons of England when they violate their rights as Americans as they have to oppose any foreign enemy; and that this is no more, according to the law of nature, to be deemed rebellion than it would be to oppose the King of France, supposing him now present invading the land.

But what to the Baptists was the establishment, to Anglicans was dissent. From the establishment in New England, ever fearful of ecclesiastical impositions from without, came a strong current of antiauthoritarianism as from the farthest left-wing sect. It was a pillar of the temple, a scion of the church, and an apologist for New England's standing order who sweepingly disclaimed "all human authority in matters of faith and worship. We regard neither pope nor prince as head of the church, nor acknowledge that any Parliaments have power to enact articles of doctrine or forms of discipline or modes of worship or terms of church communion," and, declaring that "we are accountable to none but *Christ*"—words that had struck at the heart of every establishment, civil and religious, since the fall of Rome—concluded with the apparent paradox that *"liberty* is the *fundamental* principle of our establishment."

In such declarations a political argument became a moral imperative. The principle of justifiable disobedience and the instinct to question public authority before accepting it acquired a new sanction and a new vigor. Originally, of course, the doctrine of resistance was applied to Parliament, a nonrepresentative assembly three thousand miles away. But the composition and location of the institution had not been as crucial in creating opposition as had the character of the actions Parliament had taken. Were provincial assemblies, simply because they were local and representative, exempt from scrutiny and resistance? Were they any less susceptible than Parliament to the rule that when their authority is extended beyond "the bounds of the law of God and the free constitution . . . 'their acts are, *ipso facto*, void, and cannot oblige any to obedience' "? There could be no doubt of the answer. Any legislature, wherever located or however composed, deserved only the obedience it could command by the justice and wisdom of its proceedings. Representative or not, local or not, any agency of the state could be defied. The freeholders of Augusta, Virginia, could not have been more explicit in applying to local government in 1776 the defiance learned in the struggle with Parliament. They wrote their delegates to Virginia's Provincial Congress that

> should the future conduct of our legislative body prove to you that our opinion of their wisdom and justice is ill-grounded, then tell them that your constitutents are neither guided nor will ever be influenced by that slavish maxim in politics, "that whatever is enacted by that body of men in whom the supreme power of the state is vested must in all cases be obeyed," and

that they firmly believe attempts to repeal an unjust law can be vindicated beyond a simple remonstrance addressed to the legislators.

But such threats as these were only the most obvious ways in which traditional notions of authority came into question. Others were more subtly subversive, silently sapping the traditional foundations of social orders and discipline.

"Rights" obviously lay at the heart of the Anglo-American controversy: the rights of Englishmen, the rights of mankind, chartered rights. But *"rights,"* wrote Richard Bland—that least egalitarian of revolutionary leaders—"imply *equality* in the instances to which they belong and must be treated without respect to the dignity of the persons concerned in them." This was by no means simply a worn cliché, for while "equality before the law" was a commonplace of the time "equality without respect to the dignity of the persons concerned" was not; its emphasis on social equivalence was significant, and though in its immediate context the remark was directed to the invidious distinctions believed to have been drawn between Englishmen and Americans its broader applicability was apparent. Others seized upon it, and developed it, especially in the fluid years of transition when new forms of government were being sought to replace those believed to have proved fatal to liberty. "An affectation of rank" and "the assumed distinction of 'men of consequence'" had been the blight of the Proprietary party, a Pennsylvania pamphleteer wrote in 1776. Riches in a new country like America signified nothing more than the accident of prior settlement. The accumulation of wealth had been "unavoidable to the descendants of the early settlers" since the land, originally cheap, had appreciated naturally with the growth of settlement.

> Perhaps it is owing to this accidental manner of becoming rich that wealth does not obtain the same degree of influence here which it does in old countries. Rank, at present, in America is derived more from qualification than property; a sound moral character, amiable manners, and firmness in principle constitute the first class, and will continue to do so till the origin of families be forgotten, and the proud follies of the old world overrun the simplicity of the new.

Therefore, under the new dispensation, "no reflection ought to be made on any man on account of birth, provided that his manners rises decently with his circumstances, and that he affects not to forget the level he came from."

The idea was, in its very nature, corrosive to the traditional authority of magistrates and of established institutions. And it activated other, similar thoughts whose potential threat to stability lay till then inert. There was no more familiar notion in eighteenth-century political thought—it was propounded in every tract on government and every

ministerial exhortation to the civil magistracy—than that those who
wield power were "servants of society" as well as "ministers of God,"
and as such had to be specially qualified: they must be acquainted with
the affairs of men; they must have wisdom, knowledge, prudence; and
they must be men of virtue and true religion. But how far should one go
with this idea? The doctrine that the qualifications for magistracy were
moral, spiritual, and intellectual could lead to conflict with the expectation that public leaders would be people of external dignity and social
superiority; it could be dangerous to the establishment in any settled
society. For the ancient notion that leadership must devolve on men
whose "personal authority and greatness," whose "eminence or nobility," were such that "every man subordinate is ready to yield a willing
submission without contempt or repining"—ordinary people not easily
conceding to an authority "conferred upon a mean man... no better
than selected out of their own rank"—this traditional notion had never
been repudiated, was still honored and repeated. But now, in the heated
atmosphere of incipient rebellion, the idea of leaders as servants of the
people was pushed to its logical extreme, and its subversive potentialities revealed. By 1774 it followed from the belief that "lawful rulers
are the servants of the people" that they were "exalted above their
brethren not for their own sakes, but for the benefit of the people; and
submission is yielded, not on account of their persons considered exclusively on the authority they are clothed with, but of those laws which in
the exercise of this authority are made by them comformably to the laws
of nature and equity." In the distribution of offices, it was said in 1770,
"merit only in the candidate" should count—not birth, or wealth, or
loyalty to the great; but merit only. Even a deliberately judicious statement of this theme rang with defiance to traditional forms of authority:
"It is not wealth—it is not family—it is not either of these alone, nor both
of them together, though I readily allow neither is to be disregarded,
that will qualify men for important seats in government, unless they are
rich and honorable in other and more important respects." Indeed, one
could make a complete inversion and claim that, properly, the external
affluence of magistrates should be the consequence of, not the prior
qualification for, the judicious exercise of public authority over others.

Where would it end? Two generations earlier, in the fertile seedtime
of what would become the revolutionary ideology, the ultimate subver-
siveness of the arguments advanced by "the men of the rights" had
already been glimpsed. "The sum of the matter betwixt Mr. Hoadly and
me," the Jacobite, High Church polemicist Charles Leslie had written in
1711, is this:

> I think it most natural that *authority* should *descend*, that is, be *derived* from a
> *superior* to an *inferior*, from God to *fathers* and *kings*, and from *kings* and

*fathers* to *sons* and *servants*. But Mr. Hoadly would have it *ascend* from *sons* to *fathers* and from *subjects* to *sovereigns,* nay to God himself, whose *kingship* the men of the *rights* say is *derived* to *Him* from the *people!* And the *argument* does naturally carry it all that *way*. For if *authority* does *ascend,* it must *ascend* to the *height.*

By 1774 it seemed undeniable to many, uninvolved in or hostile to the revolutionary effort, that declarations "before GOD . . . that it is no rebellion to oppose any king, ministry, or governor [who] destroys by any violence or authority whatever the rights of the people" threatened the most elemental principles of order and discipline in society. A group of writers, opposed not merely to the politics of resistance but to the effect it would have on the primary linkages of society—on that patterning of human relations that distinguishes a civilized community from a primitive mob—attempted to recall to the colonists the lessons of the past, the wisdom, as they thought of it, of the ages. Citing adages and principles that once had guided men's thoughts on the structure of society; equating all communities, and England's empire in particular with families; quoting generously from Filmer if not from Leslie; and explaining that anarchy results when social inferiors claim political authority, they argued, with increasing anxiety, that the essence of social stability was being threatened by the political agitation of the time. Their warnings, full of nostalgia for ancient certainties, were largely ignored. But in the very extremism of their reaction to the events of the time there lies a measure of the distance revolutionary thought had moved from an old to a very new world.

One of the earliest such warnings was written by a young Barbadian, Isaac Hunt, only recently graduated from the College of Philadelphia but already an expert in scurrilous pamphleteering. Opening his *Political Family,* an essay published in 1775 though written for a prize competition in 1766, with a discourse on the necessary reciprocity of parts in the body politic he developed as his central point the idea that "in the *body politic* all inferior jurisdictions should flow from *one superior fountain* . . . a due subordination of the less parts to the greater is . . . necessary to the *existence* of BOTH." Colonies were the children and inferiors of the mother country; let them show the gratitude and obedience due to parents, and so let the principle of order through subordination prevail in the greater as in the lesser spheres of life.

This, in the context of the widespread belief in equal rights and the compact theory of government, was anachronistic. But it expressed the fears of many as political opposition turned into revolutionary fervor. Arguments such as Hunt's were enlarged and progressively dramatized, gaining in vituperation with successive publications until by 1774 they were bitter, shrill, and full of despair. Three Anglican clergymen wrote wrathful epitaphs to this ancient, honorable, and moribund philosophy.

Samuel Seabury—Hamilton's anonymous opponent in the pamphlet wars and the future first bishop of the Episcopal church in America— wrote desperately of the larger, permanent dangers of civil disobedience. The legal, established authorities in New York—the courts of justice, above all—have been overthrown, he wrote, and in their places there were now "delegates, congresses, committees, riots, mobs, insurrections, associations." Who comprised the self-constituted Committee of Safety of New York that had the power to brand innocent people outlaws and deliver them over "to the vengeance of a lawless, outrageous mob, to be *tarred, feathered, hanged, drawn, quartered, and burnt*"? A parcel of upstarts "chosen by the weak, foolish, turbulent part of the country people"—"half a dozen fools in your neighborhood." Was the slavery imposed by their riotous wills to be preferred to the tyranny of a king? No: "If I must be devoured, let me be devoured by the jaws of a lion, and not *gnawed* to death by rats and vermin." If the upstart, pretentious committeemen triumph, order and peace will be at an end, and anarchy will result.

> Government was intended for the security of those who live under it—to protect the weak against the strong—the good against the bad—to preserve order and decency among men, preventing every one from injuring his neighbor. Every person, then, owes obedience to the laws of the government under which he lives, and is obliged in honor and duty to support them. Because if *one* has a right to disregard the laws of the society to which he belongs, *all* have the *same* right; and *then* government is at an end.

His colleague, the elegant, scholarly Thomas Bradbury Chandler, was at once cleverer, more thoughtful, and, for those who heeded arguments, more likely to have been convincing. Two of his pamphlets published in 1774 stated with peculiar force the traditional case for authority in the state, in society, and in the ultimate source and ancient archetype of all authority, the family. His *American Querist*, that extraordinary list of one hundred rhetorical questions, put the point obliquely. It asked:

> Whether some degree of respect be not always due from inferiors to superiors, and especially from children to parents; and whether the refusal of this on any occasion be not a violation of the general laws of society, to say nothing here of the obligations of religion and morality?

And is not Great Britain in the same relation to the colonies as a parent to children? If so, how can such "disrespectful and abusive treatment from children" be tolerated? God has given no dispensation to people under any government "to refuse *honor* or *custom* or *tribute* to whom they are *due*; to contract habits of thinking and *speaking evil of dignities*, and to weaken the natural principle of respect for those in authority."

God's command is clear: his will is that we *"submit to every ordinance of man for the Lord's sake;* and require[s] us on pain of *damnation* to be duly *subject to the higher powers,* and *not to resist* their lawful authority."

Chandler's *Friendly Address to All Reasonable Americans* was more direct. It touched the central theme of authority at the start, and immediately spelled out the implications of resistance. The effort "to disturb or threaten an established government by popular insurrections and tumults has always been considered and treated, in every age and nation of the world, as an unpardonable crime." Did not an apostle, "who had a due regard for the rights and liberties of mankind," order submission even to the cruelest of all despots, Nero? And properly so: "The bands of society would be dissolved, the harmony of the world confounded, and the order of nature subverted, if reverence, respect, and obedience might be refused to those whom the constitution has vested with the highest authority."

The insistence, the violence of language, increased in the heightening crisis. "Rebellion," Daniel Leonard wrote flatly in 1775, "is the most atrocious offense that can be perpetrated by man," except those committed directly against God. "It dissolves the social band, annihilates the security resulting from law and government; introduces fraud, violence, rapine, murder, sacrilege, and the long train of evils that riot uncontrolled in a state of nature." But the end was near. By the spring of 1775 such sentiments, fulminous and despairing, were being driven underground.

Jonathan Boucher's sermon "On Civil Liberty, Passive Obedience, and Nonresistance" had been written in 1775 "with a view to publication," and though it had been delivered publicly enough in Queen Anne's Parish, Maryland, it was promptly thereafter suppressed; "the press," Boucher later wrote, "was shut to every publication of the kind." Its publication twenty-two years afterward in a volume of Boucher's sermons entitled *A View of the Causes and Consequences of the American Revolution* was the result of the French Revolution's reawakening in the author, long since safely established in England, the fears of incipient anarchy and social incoherence that had agitated him two decades before. It was a fortunate result, for the sermon is a classic of its kind. It sums up, as no other essay of the period, the threat to the traditional ordering of human relations implicit in revolutionary thought.

Boucher sought, first and foremost, to establish the divine origins of the doctrine of obedience to constituted authority—a necessity, he felt, not merely in view of the arguments of the Reverend Jacob Duché whom he was ostensibly refuting, but, more important, in view of the gross misinterpretation rebellious Americans had for years been making of that suggestive verse of Galatians 5:1: "Stand fast, therefore, in the liberty wherewith Christ hath made us free." What had been meant by "liberty" in that passage, he said, was simply and unambiguously free-dom from sin, for "every sinner is, literally, a slave... the only true liberty is the liberty of being the servants of God." Yet the Gospel does speak to the question of public obligations, and its command could hardly be more unmistakable: its orders, always, "obedience to the laws of every country, in every kind or form of government." The rumor promoted in the infancy of Christianity "that the Gospel was designed to undermine kingdoms and commonwealths" had probably been the work of Judas, and patently mixed up the purpose of the First Coming with that of the Second. Submission to the higher powers is what the Gospel intends for man: "obedience to government is every man's duty because it is every man's interest; but it is particularly incumbent on Christians, because... it is enjoined by the positive commands of God."

So much was scriptural, and could be buttressed by such authorities as Edmund Burke, Bishop Butler, "the learned Mr. Selden," and Lan-celot Andrewes, whose biblical exegesis of 1650 was quoted to the effect that "princes receive their power only from God, and are by him consti-tuted and entrusted with government of others chiefly for his own glory and honor, as his deputies and vicegerents upon earth." More compli-cated was the application of this central thesis to the associated ques-tions of the origins and aims of government and of the equality of men. As for the former, the idea that the aim of government is "the common good of mankind" is in itself questionable; but even if it were correct, it would not follow that government should rest on consent, for common consent can only mean common feeling, and this a "vague and loose" thing not susceptible to proof. Mankind has never yet agreed on what the common good is, and so, there being no "common feeling" that can clearly designate the "common good," one can scarcely argue that gov-ernment is, or should be, instituted by "common consent."

Similarly popular, dangerous, and fallacious to Boucher was the no-tion "that the whole human race is born equal; and that no man is naturally inferior, or in any respect subjected to another, and that he can be made subject to another only by his own consent." This argument, he wrote, is "ill-founded and false both in its premises and conclusions." It is hard to see how it could conceivably be true in any sense. "Man differs from man in everything that can be supposed to lead to supremacy and subjection, *as one star differs from another star in glory.*" God intended man to be a social animal; but society requires government, and "without some relative inferiority and superiority" there can be no government.

A musical instrument composed of chords, keys, or pipes all perfectly equal in size and power might as well be expected to produce harmony as a society composed of members all perfectly equal to be productive of order and peace. . . . On the principle of equality, neither his parents nor even the vote of a majority of the society . . . can have . . . authority over any man. . . . Even an implicit consent can bind a man no longer than he chooses to be bound. The same principle of equality . . . clearly entitles him to recall and resume that consent whenever he sees fit, and he alone has a right to judge when and for what reasons it may be resumed.

A social and political system based on the principles of consent and equality would be "fantastic"; it would result in "the whole business of social life" being reduced to confusion and futility. People would first express and then withdraw their consent to an endless succession of schemes of government. "Governments, though always forming, would never be completely formed, for the majority today might be the minority tomorrow, and, of course, that which is now fixed might and would be soon unfixed."

Consent, equality—these were "particularly loose and dangerous" ideas, Boucher wrote; illogical, unrealistic, and lacking in scriptural sanction. There need be no mystery about the origins of government. Government was created by God. "As soon as there were some to be governed, there were also some to govern; and the first man, by virtue of that paternal claim on which all subsequent governments have been founded, was first invested with the power of government. . . . The first father was the first king: and . . . it was thus that all government originated; and monarchy is its most ancient form." From this origin it follows directly that resistance to constituted authority is a sin, and that mankind is "commanded to *be subject to the higher powers.*" True, "kings and princes . . . were doubtless created and appointed not so much for their own sakes as for the sake of the people committed to their charge: yet they are not, therefore, the creatures of the people. So far from deriving their authority from any supposed consent or suffrage of men, they receive their commission from Heaven; they receive it from God, the source and original of all power." The judgment of Jesus Christ is evident: the most essential duty of subjects with respect to government is simply "(in the phraseology of a prophet) *to be quiet, and to sit still.*"

How simple but yet how demanding an injunction, for men are ever "*prone* to be presumptuous and self-willed, always disposed and ready to despise *dominion,* and to *speak evil of dignities.*" And how necessary to be obeyed in the present circumstance. Sedition has already penetrated deeply; it tears at the vitals of social order. It threatens far more than "the persons invested with the supreme power either legislative or executive"; "the resistance which your political counselors urge you to practice [is exerted] clearly and literally against *authority* . . . you are encouraged to resist not only all authority over us as it now exists, but any and all that it is possible to constitute."

This was the ultimate concern. What Boucher, Leonard, Chandler, and other articulate defenders of the status quo saw as the final threat was not so much the replacement of one set of rulers by another as the triumph of ideas and attitudes incompatible with the stability of any standing order, any establishment—incompatible with society itself, as it had been traditionally known. Their fears were in a sense justified, for in the context of eighteenth-century social thought it was difficult to see how any harmonious, stable social order could be constructed from such materials. To argue that all men were equal would not make them so; it would only help justify and perpetuate that spirit of defiance, that refusal to concede to authority whose ultimate resolution could only be anarchy, demagoguery, and tyranny. If such ideas prevailed year after year, generation after generation, the "latent spark" in the breasts of even the most humble of men would be kindled again and again by entrepreneurs of discontent who would remind the people "of the elevated rank they hold in the universe, as men; that all men by nature are equal; that kings are but the ministers of the people; that their authority is delegated to them by the people for their good, and they have a right to resume it, and place it in other hands, or keep it themselves, whenever it is made use of to oppress them." Seeds of sedition would thus constantly be sown, and harvests of licentiousness reaped.

How else could it end? What reasonable social and political order could conceivably be built and maintained where authority was questioned before it was obeyed, where social differences were considered to be incidental rather than essential to community order, and where superiority, suspect in principle, was not allowed to concentrate in the hands of a few but was scattered broadly through the populace? No one could clearly say. But some, caught up in a vision of the future in which the peculiarities of American life became the marks of a chosen people, found in the defiance of traditional order the firmest of all grounds for their hope for a freer life. The details of this new world were not as yet clearly depicted; but faith ran high that a better world than any that had ever been known could be built where authority was distrusted and held in constant scrutiny; where the status of men flowed from their achievements and from their personal qualities, not from distinctions ascribed to them at birth; and where the use of power over the lives of men was jealously guarded and severely restricted. It was only where there was this defiance, this refusal to truckle, this distrust of all authority, political or social, that institutions would express human aspirations, not crush them.

# 5

# The Constitution

## Conflict or Consensus?

The Constitution remains one of the most controversial documents in all of American history. Generations of Supreme Court justices have reinterpreted the document according to their own predilections when handing down constitutional decisions bearing upon the problems of American society. Presidents and political parties in power traditionally have viewed the Constitution in the light of their own interests, pursuits, and philosophies of government. Historians, too, have presented conflicting interpretations of the Constitution in different periods of American history. But to a large degree such scholars have confined their controversies to the writing and ratification of the Constitution. They have usually disagreed about the intent of the founding fathers in framing parts of the Constitution and the motives of the men involved. The changing outlook of historians toward the Constitution has often tended to coincide with changes in the intellectual climate of opinion within America itself.

From the Convention of 1787 to the close of the Civil War, the Constitution was considered a controversial document by historians because of the questions it raised regarding the nature of the federal union. Politicians in both North and South were fond of citing the Constitution in support of their arguments concerning the relationship between the states and central government, and the respective rights of majorities and minorities under the federal form of government. Since the overwhelming preoccupation of American historians during this period was with politics, scholars tended to reflect this point of view in their writings about the Constitution. They usually interpreted the document in terms of two opposing doctrines—states' rights versus national sovereignty, or a strict versus a loose construction of the Constitution. The outcome of the Civil War seemed to settle the issue in favor of the national theory of the Constitution by force of arms.

In the century since the Civil War, however, five distinct groups of historians have arisen to offer differing interpretations of the Constitutional period. The first—the nationalist school—emerged in the

149

1870s and 1880s; its approach to the Constitution was conditioned by the intense nationalism that marked American society in the decades following the Civil War. Around the turn of the century, there appeared the Progressive school, which viewed the document and its framing in light of the Populist-Progressive reform movements of the 1890s and early 1900s. Charles A. Beard, the outstanding scholar in the Progressive school, saw the Constitution as a document that was intended to protect private property and one that reflected the interests of privileged groups in the American society of the 1780s. The Beardian interpretation remained the dominant view of the Constitution for more than four decades. Since World War II, three groups of historians—the neoconservatives, the "new" intellectual historians, and the so-called neo-Progressives—arose either to revise or to refine the Beardian interpretation.

The nationalist school, which developed in the decades after the Civil War, was best represented by George Bancroft and John Fiske. Both their histories were written in highly nationalistic terms. Within a broader context, both believed also in the racial superiority of white Anglo-Saxon Protestant peoples. They subscribed to the idea that the orderly progress of mankind in modern times toward greater personal liberty was due largely to the preeminent political ability of Anglo-Saxon peoples to build strong and stable national states. According to these two writers, America's democratic institutions could be traced all the way back to the ancient political practices of Teutonic tribes in the forests of Germany. TheConstitution, in their eyes, represented the high point in world history in man's efforts to civilize and govern himself. Thus, they dealt with it not only as a democratic document for America but also as a possible model instrument of government for the rest of mankind.

For Bancroft the Constitution symbolized the capstone of the American Revolution. In his two volumes on the Constitutional era published in the 1880s, he visualized the years 1782 to 1788 as a single period with the ratification of the Constitution coming as a climax of the Revolution itself.[1] The Articles of Confederation, ratified in 1781, in his opinion, represented a false start on the road to self-government. Faced with a need for a more coercive central government because of external threats from Britain and Spain and internal problems such as Shays's Rebellion, the American people demanded a new and better instrument of government. Since America was divinely ordained to create the first perfect republic on earth—according to Bancroft—the Constitution symbolized

---

[1]George Bancroft, *History of the Formation of the Constitution of the United States of America,* 2 vols. (New York, 1882).

the crowning success of the movement for a more popular government that had started with the Revolution.

Bancroft's work deified the Constitution and contributed to the growing reverence with which the document was viewed in the post–Civil War era. Indeed, the last paragraph in his *History* ended with a stirring preoration on the Constitution:

> In America a new people had risen up without king, or princes, or nobles, knowing nothing of tithes and little of landlords, the plough being for the most part in the hands of free holders of the soil. They were more sincerely religious, better educated, or serener minds, and of purer morals than the men of any former republic. By calm meditation and friendly councils they had prepared a constitution which . . . excelled every one known before; and which secured itself against violence and revolution by providing a peaceful method for every needed reform.[2]

Bancroft conveniently overlooked the bloody Civil War that had just been fought.

Fiske's work, *The Critical Period of American History, 1783–1789,* presented a dramatic story of the change in the state of the nation before and after the writing of the Constitution. In Fiske's view, the five-year period after the peace of 1783 represented "the most critical movement in all the history of the American people."[3] Under the Articles of Confederation, the nation was on the verge of collapse: the weak central government could not cope with the problems of diplomacy, quarrels between the states, the postwar economic depression, and the near anarchy of domestic disturbances like Shays's Rebellion. Once the Constitution was written, however, the situation changed dramatically. Most of these issues disappeared when they were dealt with by the new strong central government, and the country was saved from disaster.

Fiske's book, published one year after the centennial celebration of the Constitution, reflected the great awe in which the document was held. The British statesman Gladstone had called the Constitution "the most wonderful work ever struck off at a given time by the brain and purpose of man." Not to be outdone, Fiske called it "this wonderful work—this Iliad, or Parthenon, or Fifth Symphony, of statesmanship."[4]

---

[2]*Ibid.*, 2:366–67.

[3]John Fiske, *The Critical Period of American History,* 1783–1789 (New York, 1888), p. 55.

[4]*Ibid.*, p. 223. One exception to the almost universal chorus of praise showered on the Constitution was the multivolume work of the German-born historian Hermann von Holst in his *Constitutional History of the United States,* 8 vols. (Chicago, 1876–1892). Von Holst criticized American historians for viewing the document as a divine product of the unique wisdom of the founding fathers, but his was very much of a minority view among scholars of the period.

His glowing praise was typical of the generation of historians who sought to canonize the Constitution in the post–Civil War years.

The nationalist school of historians, then, was uncritical in its approach to the Constitution and viewed the document in terms of pious patriotism. In the eyes of these historians, the founding fathers were great men motivated mainly by the principles of right and justice and whose only concern was the welfare of the nation. The American people, they insisted, were united in their common devotion to these same principles of a democratic society, and the Constitution was the embodiment of the nation's dreams. Those opposed to the Constitution were dismissed lightly as men who lacked the faith and breadth of vision of the founding fathers.

Around the turn of the twentieth century, the rise of the Populist and Progressive reform movements brought about a marked change in attitude toward the Constitution. Progressive reformers, concerned with the problems that had arisen from the nation's increasing industrialization, became convinced that unless the imbalance in wealth and political power in American society could be redressed, democracy in the United States was doomed. Only by passing legislation which would regulate industry and improve the lot of the common people could democracy be saved. In response to such demands, state governments in the 1890s and early 1900s began extending their laws regulating various aspects of the economy under their jurisdiction. Congress at the same time was making serious efforts to regulate certain industries like the railroads and to break up business enterprises such as the trusts. Labor legislation was introduced to protect workers and to improve working conditions of both men and women. To check the growing maldistribution of wealth, income tax measures were passed by both the state and federal governments. When the Supreme Court declared much of this state and national legislation unconstitutional, however, many persons began to view the Constitution in a new light. To them the Constitution now seemed to be an undemocratic document whose express purpose was to protect the rich and powerful interests in society and to frustrate the fulfillment of the democratic aspirations of the American people.

The Progressive school of historians which arose at this time was greatly influenced by this growing disillusionment with the Constitution. These scholars proceeded, therefore, to read this hostile view of the Constitution of the early 1900s back into the motives of the men who framed the document in the 1780s. The Constitution, according to these scholars, was a reactionary rather than a democratic document. Just as the Constitution was being used in the Progressive period to protect the interests of the rich and powerful against the encroachments of the common man, they said, so the founding fathers in their day had written the document to defend their property rights and to protect themselves against the social reforms that were under way.

To Progressive historians, then, the Constitution represented a reactionary document—one written by the conservatives at the convention to thwart the radicals who held more liberal views and had visions of completely reforming American society. In support of their thesis, these scholars pointed to the undemocratic features of the Constitution—the system of checks and balances, the difficult procedure for adopting amendments, and the idea of judicial veto—which made majority rule all but impossible. Unlike the nationalist historians who had seen the Constitution as a forward step in the development of democracy, the Progressive historians considered the document a serious setback to the movement for popular government during the revolutionary era.

Besides being influenced by the general current of reform, Progressive scholars were affected also by certain developments within the historical profession itself. One of these was the emergence of what came to be known as the "new history." In the past, advocates of the "new history" claimed, history had been written by conservatives who used their findings to buttress the status quo. The "new historians" now wished to rewrite history along liberal lines and to use the lessons of the past as a means of bringing about progress and reform. Many of these scholars were personally involved in the reform movements of the Progressive era and wrote from a historical viewpoint in support of the idea of governmental intervention and regulation in the public interest. Thus, advocates of the "new history" such as Charles A. Beard looked at the Constitution in a completely different light from earlier conservative historians.

Many writers of the Progressive school reflected another major trend in historical circles at the time—the tendency toward an economic interpretation of history. Such scholars were convinced that man was motivated mainly by his economic self-interest and that economic factors were the major determinants in shaping the course of history. Man's political views and actions in particular, they charged, were determined primarily by economic considerations. Many Progressive historians, therefore, advanced the idea that the Constitution had been framed by men with certain economic interests in such a way as to protect their property rights.

The Progressive interpretation of the Constitution, then, was based upon class conflict along economic lines—a point of view that had grown out of the interpretation of the American Revolution as a dual revolution. They began with the premise of Carl L. Becker that the Revolution had been a twofold struggle—a question of home rule and a question of who should rule at home once the British departed. In the internal class struggle that took place, the lower classes—made up of small farmers in the interior and workingmen along the eastern seaboard towns—gained dominance over the upper classes—composed of merchants, financiers, and manufacturers. Once the lower classes were in control, the Progressive version continued, they proceeded to democratize American society by writing radical state constitutions and the Articles of Confederation. Being almost propertyless, the lower classes set up democratic governments which passed cheap paper money legislation, debtor laws, and measures that favored the small farmers whose interests lay in land and real estate.

Members of the upper classes who survived the war, according to the Progressive interpretation, became increasingly disenchanted with the political and economic state of affairs. Those whose economic stake was in personal property—holdings in money and public securities or investments in manufacturing, shipping, and commerce—became particularly alarmed because the democratic governments seemed to be discriminating against their kind of property and in favor of those who owned land and real estate. Failing to amend the Articles of Confederation in such a way as to protect their property interests, the conservative upper class carried out what was, in effect, a counterrevolution. They conspired to undermine the democratic Articles of Confederation and instituted instead the more conservative Constitution.

The Progressive point of view was most ably expressed in Charles A. Beard's book *An Economic Interpretation of the Constitution*, published in 1913. Although other scholars—historians like Richard Hildreth and John Marshall and political scientists like J. Allen Smith—had taken an economic approach to the Constitution, none had been able to demonstrate as convincingly as Beard that the document might be best interpreted in economic terms. The key to Beard's path-breaking study was a person-by-person examination of the economic holdings and status of the framers of the Constitution. Using the Treasury records, Beard was able to show that most of these men held public securities—a form of personal property which would obviously increase in value if a new Constitution were written to strengthen the government and improve the credit standing of the country. His research showed also that these men had heavy investments in three other kinds of personal property. Beard's findings led him to conclude, "The movement for the Constitution of the United States was originated and carried through principally by four groups of personalty interests which had been adversely affected under the Articles of Confederation: money, public securities, manufactures, and trade and shipping."[5] His implication was clear: the framers

[5]Charles A. Beard, *An Economic Interpretation of the Constitution of the United States*, rev. ed. (New York, 1935), p. 324.

had designed the Constitution to safeguard the kind of property in which they had a pocketbook interest.

If the lower classes represented a majority of the population, how could personal property holders who were a minority control the Constitutional Convention? Beard's answer to this question rested mainly upon his interpretation of the property qualifications for voting. Most small farmers and workingmen, according to him, were in debt or owned so little property that they could not qualify for voting rights. "A large propertyless mass was, under the prevailing suffrage qualifications, excluded at the outset from participation . . . in the work of framing the Constitution."[6] Thus Beard viewed the Constitution as an undemocratic document foisted upon the majority of the American people by a propertied minority.

When it came to ratifying the Constitution, the "propertyless masses," according to Beard, were excluded once again from political participation. Only one-fourth of adult white men in the nation voted on the question of ratification, because the rest were either disfranchised or disinterested. The total number voting in favor of the Constitution came to no more than one-sixth of the adult white males. Those who supported ratification on the state level, Beard wrote, had precisely the same economic interests as the framers of the document. In his eyes the voting on ratification, like the framing of the Constitution itself, gave clear evidence of a class conflict: the struggle pitted men with substantial personal property on the one hand against small farmers and debtors on the other.

Beard's book exercised a profound influence upon the historical profession. A whole generation of American historians became convinced that the Constitution could be understood only in terms of class conflict. Vernon L. Parrington's *Main Currents in American Thought,* published in 1927, and Louis M. Hacker's *Triumph of American Capitalism,* which appeared in 1940, expressed the Beardian point of view. Textbooks in history and political science repeated the Beard thesis in their pages verbatim. *An Economic Interpretation of the Constitution,* without doubt, was one of the most influential books on American history published in the twentieth century. Almost all interpretations of the Constitution written since its publication in 1913 have taken either a pro- or anti-Beard position. It is safe to say that down to World War II the dominant position taken by the historical profession on the Constitution was a pro-Beardian one.

Since World War II three groups of historians arose either to challenge or to extend the Beardian interpretation. Although these scholars

---

[6] *Ibid.*

often disagreed in their interpretations of the Constitution, they all agreed that Beard's study did not offer a satisfactory explanation of the document. These three groups may be identified in broad terms as the neoconservatives, the "new intellectual historians," and the neo-Progressives.

The neoconservative historians were the first to challenge the Beardian interpretation. Their tendency was to reject two at Beard's basic assumptions. First, they viewed the Constitution as evidence of a consensus rather than a class conflict among the American people. Second, they believed that the Revolution and Constitution periods represented a line of continuous growth; they dismissed Beard's idea of a period of radical revolution followed by one of conservative reaction.

These two themes were reflected in the suggestive title—*Consensus and Continuity, 1776–1787*—of a book written by Benjamin F. Wright in 1958. Wright, a political scientist, viewed the Constitution as a political, not an economic document. The most striking characteristic among the delegates at the Constitutional Convention, he claimed, was the broad area of agreement among them regarding what they considered to be the essentials of good government:

> The most fundamental political or constitutional issues were taken for granted without debate, or they were only briefly discussed. These include such basic issues as representative government, elections at fixed intervals, a written constitution which is a supreme law and which contains an amendment clause, separation of powers and checks and balances, a bicameral legislature, a single executive, and a separate court system. These principles could have been taken for granted in no other country in the eighteenth century, nor could they in combination have been accepted in any other country even after discussion and vote. The nature and extent of this basic agreement throws far more light upon the political and constitutional thought of Americans in 1787 than do the disputes over questions which were nearly always matters of detail, or which were based largely upon sectional disagreement, or upon the size of the several states.[7]

Thus, Wright viewed the writing of the Constitution as evidence of the basic consensus that existed among the American people.

Wright showed also an essential continuity between the Revolution and the Constitution periods so far as men and ideas were concerned. The very same men held responsible public offices in 1787 as had in 1776, he wrote. Other scholars who did research on this same point estimated that 89 percent of those who held office before the Revolution also occupied a public position under one of the new state governments. Wright noted, moreover, that the political ideas of the Revolution were expressed best in the state constitutions, which were, in many instances,

---

[7]Benjamin F. Wright, *Consensus and Continuity, 1776–1787* (Boston, 1958), p. 36.

framed by the very same men who had written and signed the Declaration of Independence. In view of this evidence, how could the constitutional period be considered a reaction to the Revolution? he asked. For Wright, as for most neoconservative historians, the Constitution was seen as the fulfillment of the Revolution. An excerpt from Wright's book is the first selection in this chapter.

A second line of attack on the Beardian thesis was taken by the neoconservative historian Robert E. Brown in his study *Charles Beard and the Constitution*, published in 1956. Brown challenged the evidence that Beard had used in making his case for an economic interpretation of the Constitution. He showed, first of all, that Beard had resorted to Treasury records dated several years after the Constitutional Convention in order to substantiate the point that the founding fathers had held public securities at the time they framed the document. After studying the property holdings of the signers, moreover, Brown came to the conclusion that the framers had more capital invested in land and real estate than in securities. This evidence dealt a blow to Beard's idea that the framers had written the document in order to protect their personal property in securities from those who held land and real estate.

Brown's study went one step further, however, and challenged one of Beard's underlying assumptions that the Constitution was an undemocratic document because the "propertyless masses" made up of small farmers and workingmen were unable to participate in the political process. American society in the 1780s, according to Brown, represented a "middle-class democracy." Most Americans were members of the middle class because they owned and operated their own small farms. American society was basically democratic, he claimed, because the majority of the population were small farmers who owned enough land to qualify for the right to vote. To Brown, then, the Constitution represented the wishes of a democratically-minded middle class rather than the wishes of an aristocratically-minded upper class. By viewing American society in terms of a broad middle class, Brown took a position completely opposite to that of the class-conflict interpretation of the Beardian school of historians.

The neoconservative school of writing resulted in a general reaction against the Beardian interpretation of the Constitution in the post–World War II period. There was an increasing emphasis placed upon the Constitution as a "consensus" document and less written about it as an undemocratic document. The attitude toward the framers of the Constitution was far more favorable than it had been a generation earlier, when many of them had been denounced by debunkers for taking political positions in order to protect their pocketbook interests. College textbooks stressed the areas of agreement between men at the Constitutional Convention and de-emphasized the areas of disagreement. Con-

stitutional historians such as Henry Steele Commager declared that the
Constitution was primarily a political document, focusing mainly on the
problem of federalism, and not an economic document. Many recent
historians praised the constitutional period as a constructive era rather
than describing it as a destructive age in which the majority of the
American people were robbed of their rights and liberties by a propertied minority.

In reevaluating the constitutional period in such laudatory terms,
many neoconservative historians in the 1950s were reflecting a response
to the challenges of communism abroad. In order to bolster America's
position as leader of the free world, many historians, whether consciously or unconsciously, felt compelled to show that the United States
had been a strong and united nation throughout most of its history.
Hence, they rewrote much of American history in terms of a basic consensus among the American people. Within this context, the consensus
thesis of the Constitution increasingly replaced the Beardian idea of the
Constitution as a document of dissent that emerged from a clash of
economic interests among various elements of American society.

The second challenge to the Beardian interpretation came from the
rise of a generation of "new intellectual historians" whose work first appeared in the mid-1950s. Their approach was to take the ideas of the
founding fathers seriously, and to accept their rhetoric as reflecting
more their view of reality. They rejected Beard's emphasis on economic
considerations and the Progressives' assumption that ideas were mere
rhetoric used to mask the desire for materialistic self-interests. Instead of
the Progressive materialistic view of history, they proposed an ideological interpretation. This renewed interest in ideas as an explanation of the
revolutionary era led scholars like Bernard Bailyn, Gordon Wood, Douglass Adair, and Cecelia Kenyon to view the confederation period and the
writing of the Constitution in a completely different light.

Many of these intellectual historians cast such ideas within a much
broader framework, and stressed America's intellectual inheritance from
Europe. Scholars like Caroline Robbins and Bernard Bailyn, writing in
the 1960s, demonstrated the importance of British antiauthoritarian
thought and how it influenced the formulation of America's republican
ideology. Hence, the coming of the Revolution and writing of the Constitution were placed within an Anglo-American framework. American
ideas regarding the role of representatives in government, the relationship of the rulers and ruled, the nature of human rights, the notion of a
written constitution, and the concept of divided sovereignty were traced
in many instances back to British traditions in seventeenth- and
eighteenth-century republicanism.

One major problem facing the founding fathers was how to erect a
republic whose representatives were elected by the people, and, at the
same time to prevent the formation of a majority faction which might

undermine the government. Republican governments in the past had inevitably succumbed to the tyranny of a majority faction. James Madison used an idea derived from his reading of David Hume, a Scottish philosopher, to propose a republican remedy. America's enormous size and the multiplicity of factions and interests arising from that size, Madison argued, would make it less likely that this country would suffer the fate of earlier republics. The existence of so many diverse interests would make it difficult, if not impossible, for factions to reconcile their differences and to come together to form a majority faction. In a large republic, as Hume had suggested, the clash among more competing factions would provide greater safety and stability for society. Douglass Adair, one of the "new intellectual historians," wrote an article pointing out that Madison's thoughts on the subject—contrary to Beard's presentist interpretation—could be traced back to Hume.[8]

Cecelia Kenyon took issue with Beard's view of the debate between the Federalists, who supported the Constitution and the Antifederalists, who opposed it. In an essay published in the mid-1950s, she examined the differences between the two groups in terms of their ideas. Beard had portrayed the Antifederalists as democrats and majority-minded men who opposed such antidemocratic devices in the Constitution as the separation of powers and checks and balances. The Federalists, Beard said, supported these same devices to protect their property interests from the threats posed by state legislatures dominated by democratic small farmers. Kenyon argued that the Antifederalists were as much antimajoritarians as the Federalists, and shared a common Whig mistrust of governmental power—legislative as well as executive. The Antifederalists believed, however, that a successful republic must be geographically small and composed of a homogeneous population. In support of their position the Antifederalists often cited the writings of Montesquieu, the French philosophical historian. What ultimately distinguished the Antifederalists from the Federalists, Kenyon concluded, was their lack of faith in the ability of Americans to create and sustain a republic continental in size.[9]

The single most important work representing the point of view of these intellectual historians was *The Creation of the American Republic, 1776–1787* by Gordon S. Wood, published in 1969. A student of Bailyn's, Wood agreed that the Revolution represented a radical intellectual transformation. Wood portrayed the American leaders at the beginning of the Revolution as idealists with dreams of creating a utopian commonwealth. They hoped to create a classical republic based upon a virtuous

[8]Douglass Adair, "'That Politics May be Reduced to a Science': David Hume, James Madison, and the Tenth *Federalist*," *Huntington Library Quarterly* 20 (1957):343–60.

[9]Cecelia M. Kenyon, "Men of Little Faith: The Antifederalists on the Nature of Representative Goverment," *William and Mary Quarterly*, 3d ser. 12 (1955):3–43.

people and rulers, a society which would set America apart from the materialism and monarchy of England. Republicanism was a radical ideology with moral implications according to Wood. Revolutionary leaders, believing there was a direct relationship between the type of government a nation had and the character of its people, hoped that a republican government would morally regenerate the American people and thereby enable them to sustain a republic that would rest ultimately upon the people's virtue.

Events of the late 1770s and early 1780s dashed these high hopes. The Revolution unleashed democratic forces that accelerated the breakdown of the existing organic hierarchical society. What emerged in the 1780s was a society characterized by excessive egalitarianism, a contempt for the law by state legislatures bent on abusing their supremacy, oppression of minorities by the majority, and an increasing love of luxury that undermined the people's virtue. The 1780s was a "critical period" in moral terms, Wood said, because it shattered the dreams American leaders had in 1776 of creating a republican government along traditional lines.

The writing of the Constitution, then, was an attempt to save the Revolution from possible failure by restraining some of its democratic excesses. To Wood the Constitution developed into a struggle between forward-looking Federalists and old-fashioned Antifederalists. The Federalists wrought a revolution by introducing an American science of politics based upon a new notion of sovereignty. Instead of the old idea of mixed government in which the Antifederalists believed, the Federalists proposed a new concept—that sovereignty resided in the people rather than in any single branch of government. Hence government should be divided into separate parts not because each part represented a different social constituency, as the Antifederalists supposed, but simply because it would serve as a check upon the other parts. Every branch of government, in effect, represented the people. The Federalists at the same time created a national republican government with other mechanical devices and institutional contrivances—mechanisms that were not dependent upon the virtue of the people and could contain the excesses of state legislatures. To Wood the conflict between the two groups was in the final analysis a dispute between the Federalists' conception of politics, which was democratic. The second selection in this chapter is from Wood's book.

Emerging from the writings of Wood and other recent intellectual historians was what one scholar called a "republican synthesis."[10] This

---

[10]Robert Shalhope, "Toward a Republican Synthesis: The Emergence of an Understanding of Republicanism in American Historiography," *William and Mary Quarterly*, 3d ser. 29 (1972):49–80. See also Lance Banning, *The Republican Persuasion* (Ithaca, 1978).

synthesis involved an increased appreciation of the role of eighteenth-century republican ideology upon the pattern of events. Scholars redis-covered the trans-Atlantic heritage of republican ideas from Britain. By stressing the importance of these ideas in America, scholars provided the background or context of the complex intellectual works in which the founding fathers were operating. The so-called republican synthesis singled out the concept of republicanism as the key to understanding American political culture for the entire era covering the Revolution, Constitution, and Federal periods. Embodied in this concept of repub-licanism was a constellation of ideas—the view of the inherent republi-can character of the American people, their desire for virtue and fear of tyranny and corruption, and their love of liberty and dread of power. The changing and developing views on these ideas, it was said, helped to instigate the Revolution, led to the writing of the Constitution, and influenced America's early national experience with political parties. The republican synthesis, whose outlines were still emerging, has pro-duced a reinterpretation of the writing of the Constitution in Wood and promises to offer a continuing debate on the subject in the future.[11]

The neo-Progressive scholars—the third group writing since World War II—presented an alternative point of view to the republican synthe-sis proposed by many "new intellectual historians." The aim of the neo-Progressives was to reinforce and refine the old Progressive interpreta-tion. This grouping was a loose one; it lumped together historians who often disagreed as much with one another as they did with some find-ings of the old Progressive school. It was characterized mainly by the fact that most of these scholars saw social and economic forces as crucial determinants in the stand that men took for or against the Constitution. Some neo-Progressive historians, moreover, agreed with Beard in view-ing American society in terms of polarized groups, while others pictured social divisions along more pluralistic lines.

The main heir of the Beardian tradition was the neo-Progressive historian Merrill Jensen. In two major works—*The Articles of Confedera-tion* (1940) and *The New Nation* (1950)—Jensen wrote the history of the period from 1774 to 1789 in terms of a socioeconomic division between two groups. The "nationalists" composed of conservative creditor and merchant interests favored the strengthening of the central government. On the other hand, those whom Jensen called the "federalists" were made up of radical agrarian democrats who controlled the state legisla-

---

[11]Biographical studies have shown that there were differing strands of republicanism during the period, and that republicanism meant different things to different men. See Gerald Stourzh, *Alexander Hamilton and the Idea of Republican Government* (Stanford, 1970); John R. Howe, Jr., *The Changing Political Thought of John Adams* (Princeton, 1966); and George Athan Billias, *Elbridge Gerry: Founding Father and Republican Statesman* (New York, 1976).

tures. They supported state sovereignty because their legislation favored rural and debtor interests. The struggle between these two groups was the major theme running throughout the entire revolutionary era, said Jensen. During the early 1770s, the radical agrarian democrats led the fight against both Britain and the entrenched colonial commercial aristocrats in order to achieve local self-government so they might pass legislation in keeping with their interests. While leading the Revolution, they created the Articles of Confederation, which embodied the idea of state sovereignty and enabled them to pass laws favoring agrarian democratic ideas. But in the 1780s, the agrarian democrats became apathetic and lost interest in keeping up the political organizations that had helped them to wage the Revolution. The commercial aristocrats, many of whom had withdrawn from politics, used this opportunity to move back into power. They mounted a conservative counterrevolution, overthrew the Articles of Confederation, and created a strong central government under the Constitution to protect their political and commercial interests.

Jensen's thesis was similar to Beard's in many ways. Like Beard, Jensen pictured American society as split into polarized groups throughout the period. Jensen was like Beard, too, in viewing the Constitution as a repudiation rather than a fulfillment of the Revolution. He argued that the Articles of Confederation was an expression of faith in the principles of the Declaration of Independence while the Constitution represented a determined political effort by the nationalists to overthrow the localist forces that had set up a decentralized form of government under the Articles. [12]

The leading neo-Progressive scholars in the 1960s and 1970s—Jackson Turner Main and E. James Ferguson—were Jensen's students. They carried on the tradition of their mentor, but made original contributions on their own. Main, in a number of books and articles, sketched out the broad outlines of the Progressive political dichotomy in the 1780s. He pictured the struggle over the Constitution as a fight within each state between two fairly cohesive "parties" divided along socioeconomic and geographical lines—"commercial cosmopolitans" versus "agrarian localists." In Main's view there existed a relationship between the degree to which individuals were tied into the commercial life of the region in which they lived and the stand they took for or against the Constitution. Ferguson reinforced the idea of social cleavages between mercantile capitalists and agrarians, but showed that they

---

[12]Jensen continued the neo-Progressive tradition in the documentary history of the ratification of the Constitution which he edited until his death. See Merrill Jensen, ed., *Documentary History of the Ratification of the Constitution*, 3 vols. to date (Madison, 1976–    ).

split over the issue of public finance. His book, *Power of the Purse*, explored the relationship between public finance and the movement for constitutional reform; he showed a connection between those individuals holding certain kinds of securities and paper money and their political stand on the Constitution.[13]

The neo-Progressive scholar who dealt most directly with Beard's thesis was Forrest McDonald. In two books McDonald tested Beard's major hypotheses regarding the origins and ratification of the Constitution by subjecting the economic interests of the delegates to the federal and state constitutional conventions to a close analysis. His conclusion was that Beard's use of polarized categories—lower classes versus upper classes, real property versus personalty, creditors versus debtors, and commercial interests versus agricultural ones—to explain the writing and ratification of the Constitution did not work. Such categories were too simplistic, and were more complicated than Beard had imagined. McDonald found pluralistic rather than polarized political and economic interests at work on local, state, and regional levels. Beard's explanation of a more uniform economic motivation was wrong, McDonald concluded, because there were many different kinds of property held by the Philadelphia delegates and the delegates at the state ratifying conventions.[14]

The most extreme wing of the neo-Progressives was a group of radical scholars called the New Left historians. Unlike most neo-Progressives, who were influenced by developments within the historical profession itself, the New Left scholars were affected more by events in the era in which they lived. They became disenchanted by the course of American history in the 1960s—the military intervention in Vietnam, the prevalence of poverty in many parts of the country, and the continuance of prejudice against blacks and other minorities. Consequently New Left scholars took a more jaundiced view of America's past and presented a radical critique of American society. When it came to the issue of the Constitution, they were exceedingly critical of the neoconservatives and "new intellectual historians" on the one hand, and disagreed with the conclusions of certain neo-Progressives on the other.

The greatest impetus to New Left historiography came from William Appleman Williams in his *Contours of American History* published in 1961. Although not a member of the New Left himself, Williams's book inspired the point of view adopted by this group of scholars. Williams

---

[13]Jackson Turner Main, *The Antifederalists* (Chapel Hill, 1961) and *Political Parties Before the Constitution* (Chapel Hill, 1973) among his many works. E. James Ferguson, *Power of the Purse* (Chapel Hill, 1961) and "The Nationalists of 1781–1783 and the Economic Interpretation of the Constitution," *Journal of American History* 56 (1969):241–61.

[14]Forrest McDonald, *We the People* (Chicago, 1958) and *E Pluribus Unum* (Boston, 1965).

insisted that the Revolution marked the triumph of the idea of mercantilism in America, and that the Constitution represented a mercantilist outlook. The Constitution provided the foundation for a national system of economics and politics that called for a constantly expanding American empire. This empire was destined to grow in the early nineteenth century at the expense of nearby European mercantilist empires and less powerful peoples on America's borders like the Indians or Mexicans, and in the late nineteenth and early twentieth centuries to spread throughout the world. Williams's radical thesis not only posed a provocative challenge to the more traditional explanations of the Constitution but spurred the New Left to formulate new hypotheses on the subject.

Staughton Lynd, a New Left scholar, went "beyond Beard" by changing the emphasis that Progressive scholars had placed upon the Constitution as an economic document. Beard had stressed that the Constitution represented an effort to protect certain kinds of property—the rights of holders of personalty such as securities and money at the expense of those who owned realty, or land. Lynd agreed there was a clash over economic issues, but he argued that the conflict was on different grounds—between those who owned property in slaves and those who did not. The economic struggle over slavery was not resolved with the Constitutional Convention, wrote Lynd: it took the "Second American Revolution"—the Civil War—to settle the issue by force of arms.[15]

This discussion of the three post–World War II approaches to the study of the Constitution by no means exhausts the historiography of this vast subject. During the postwar era, the controversy over the Constitution went off in a number of different directions. On the one hand, historians increasingly applied concepts of social science in their efforts to understand men's behavior during the period. Scholars like Oscar and Mary Handlin, Lee Benson, and Stanley Elkins and Eric McKitrick resorted to insights from sociology and psychology to revise the findings of the Progressive historians. Recent political scientists such as Martin Diamond continued the tradition of earlier scholars who had been interested primarily in political theory. At the same time, other political scientists in government departments carried on the old-fashioned interest in constitutional ideas—like federalism, sovereignty, separation of powers, and judical review—but often did not deal with these ideas as determinants of historical events.[16]

---

[15]Staughton Lynd, *Class Conflict, Slavery, and the United States Constitution* (Indianapolis, 1967).

[16]Oscar and Mary Handlin, "Radicals and Conservatives in Massachusetts after Independence," *New England Quarterly* 17 (1944): 343–55; Lee Benson, *Turner and Beard* (Glen-

History students coming to grips with the problem of evaluating the Constitution and developments in the confederation period come face to face with a series of complex questions. Was the Constitution a fulfill-ment or a rejection of the ideals of the Revolution as expressed in the Declaration of Independence? What was the nature of the Constitution, and in what ways did its framing reflect the developments in political thought during the 1780s? Were the differences that divided those who favored the Constitution ideological or materialistic in nature? Was the Constitution, as Beard and certain neo-Progressive historians argued, an undemocratic document—the work of a political and propertied minor-ity who drafted an instrument of government aimed at limiting the liberties of the American people? Or was the Constitution, as some neoconversative historians claimed, conclusive evidence of the consen-sus that existed among Americans of that day? Was the Constitution written within a pluralistic society characterized by intergroup conflict rather than a basic concensus, as some scholars contended? If there was a conflict, were the cleavages in society more social than economic in character? Would the impact of ideology as presented in the newfound republican synthesis change our fundamental understanding of the framing of the Constitution? Only by raising such questions can the student decide whether the Constitution was a document reflecting con-flict or consensus, and, in the case of a conflict interpretation, determine what the basis of the conflict was.

---

coe, 1960); Stanley Elkins and Eric McKitrick, "The Founding Fathers: Young Men of the Revolution," *Political Science Quarterly* 76 (1961): pp. 181–216; Martin Diamond, "Democ-racy and *The Federalist:* A Reconsideration of the Framers' Intent," *American Political Science Review* 53 (1959): 53–61. For the older tradition of scholars in government departments and law schools who were interested mainly in constitutional ideas in terms of political theory, see Andrew C.McLaughlin, *A Constitutional History of the United States* (New York, 1955); Charles G. Haines, *The American Doctrine of Judicial Supremacy* (Berkeley, 1932); and Edwin S. Corwin, "The Progress of Constitutional Theory Between the Declaration of Indepen-dence and the Meeting of the Philadelphia Convention," *American Historical Review* 30 (1925): 511–36.

# Benjamin F. Wright

BENJAMIN F. WRIGHT (1900–1976) was professor of government at Harvard University for many years and then president of Smith College. He was the author of numerous books and articles on American constitutional history and law, including *American Interpretations of Natural Law* (1931), *The Contract Clause of the Constitution* (1938), and *The Growth of American Constitutional Law* (1942).

The centennial of the Constitution was the occasion for an outburst of oratory and comparable writing in which the orators and authors sometimes seemed to have confused the work of the Convention of 1787 with the Tables handed down from Sinai, or at least with writings which had their origin on Olympus. As one reads some of these magniloquent statements he gets the impression that the authors of the Constitution were divinely inspired patriots of unsurpassed wisdom in whose work there is to be found no human flaw.

At about the same time we find the beginnings of a point of view, shortly to be widely accepted by twentieth century historians and political scientists, which is in almost complete contrast with the attitude of pious patriotism. According to this view the Constitution was the product of a reactionary movement engineered by the selfish rich; it is, therefore, an antidemocratic document, skillfully designed to secure the blessings of liberty only to the prosperous and the predatory.

Both of these views, though commonly in somewhat less extravagant form, are still to be found in writings and speeches. The first of them is interesting as a species of folklore or an example of zeal for popular favor, but those who express such views proceed "without fear and without research" and with scant attempt to document their conclusions. It is not a particularly profitable point of view to make the basis for scholarly analysis. The other and almost antithetical view is a much better point of departure for an examination of the nature of the American Constitution. . . .

Beard's *Economic Interpretation* was one of the most influential historical books published in this century. Beard's conclusions are extremely difficult to pin down, particularly in relation to the charge that the Con-

Benjamin F. Wright, *Consensus and Continuity, 1776–1787* (Boston: Boston University Press, 1958), pp. 40, 42–43, 53–60. Reprinted by permission of Boston University.

stitution was reactionary. The views attributed to Beard by Seagle and many others are more clearly expressed in another extremely influential book, Charles and Mary Beard's *The Rise of American Civilization*, which appeared in 1927. There we find these distinguished authors, when dealing with the federal convention, saying that "equally general was the conviction that the states should not be allowed to issue bills of credit or impair the obligation of contracts. Almost unanimous was the opinion that democracy was a dangerous thing, to be restrained, not encouraged, by the Constitution, to be given as little voice as possible in the new system, to be hampered by checks and balances...."

This general attitude continues to be widely accepted and reproduced. It necessarily involves the doctrine that the drafting and adoption of the federal Constitution meant a break in the continuity of the movement for popular government which was carried forward during the Revolution. For, according to this interpretation of our history, the Constitution was reactionary and therefore not in the line of continuous growth. The adoption of the Constitution meant a setback, a retrogression from which the development of democracy did not begin to recover until the victory of Jefferson in 1800. It is a view which is eminently worth careful examination, particularly so in a study attempting to place the essential elements of continuity in American constitutional history of the revolutionary and constitutional periods....

A considerable amount of the historical writing of the last half century or more has been based upon a curious pair of assumptions: the men who wrote and voted for the Declaration of Independence and for the state bills of rights and the first state constitutions were great patriots, whereas the men who wrote or voted for the Constitution of 1787 were selfish, economically determined plotters. The Declaration and the state bills of rights were liberating and democratic documents, whereas the later state constitutions, with their emphasis upon the separation of powers, and the federal Constitution were intended "to make the country safe from democracy." This dichotomy is evidence of an unhistorical rather than a historical interpretation of our past. It is founded not so much in the history of that time as in the history of a century or more later.

Of course the Founding Fathers sought stability, just as they sought personal security. They found stability and security in the institutional devices and guarantees of the state constitutions, particularly those of New York, Massachusetts and New Hampshire, and their work was in the central line of development, not only of the second half of the eighteenth century but also of the first half of the nineteenth century in this country.

Where were the breaks with the past? Certainly not in the principle of the rule of law or of constitutionalism. Not in the structure of government. Not in the system of elections, though the terms of office were longer than were to be found in most of the states. Not in the amending process, which was liberalized. Not even in the greater centralization of powers in the federal government, since there they were carrying on the tendency which goes back to 1776, if not to 1765. No, they were reflecting the same point of view, as many of them were the same men, of those amazing years of constitution-writing which began in 1776 with the Virginia Constitution.

I hestitate to use the word progressive, since it was not used in this sense at that time and has come to have dubious connotations in recent years, but the extent to which their ideas and institutional devices were foreshadowed by what went before and were continued by what came after might justify the use of that term. At least it is much more accurate than reactionary. For, with the rise of the common man in the first half of the nineteenth century, their work was applauded and continued, not repudiated and reversed. The only changes made in the form of government were matters of detail, such as the Twelfth Amendment, which straightened out the unanticipated problem of the same number of votes for president and vice-president. The Constitution of 1787 made but a shadowy and unclear provision for judicial review of congressional legislation and this section was not condemned by the Antifederalists. The institution of judicial review, which originated in the states, was strengthened in both state and national governments during the period of democratic expansion. Not even the provisions restricting the economic powers of the states were changed. Most of them were reinforced by state action. It is substantially correct to say that the provisions of the Constitution which have been characterized as undemocratic were, with the exception of the section on the slave trade, strengthened in the nineteenth century. Nearly all of the applicable ones were adopted in the popular constitutions of the states.

Since the framers included some of the most essential provisions customarily found in bills of rights at that time in the Constitution, they should, to be consistent, have included more. Apparently they believed additional guarantees to be unnecessary because the new government was one of the enumerated powers and because of the existence of the state bills of rights. It seems likely that they did not fully realize just what they had created in the way of a central government with the power to legislate for individual citizens. At times they understood the implications of the new system, at others they failed to see them clearly. This is not surprising in view of the fact that they had invented a new form of federalism. That they should have understood as fully as they did its nature and its meaning is as astonishing as it is unusual in the history of government.

Only as regards the relation of state governments to economic problems were they what can be called reactionary. They did react against some of the financial and economic legislation of the Revolution and the period of the confederation. They did take virtually all power over the currency from the states and they did forbid the states not only to pass bills of attainder, ex post facto laws, and to grant titles of nobility but also laws impairing the obligation of contracts, a measure copied from the Northwest Ordinance of 1787, a statute always regarded as one of the liberal achievements in our history. In the interests of a uniform currency they gave power to Congress to coin money and regulate its value; they refused to grant to Congress power to issue paper money or to make it legal tender. It is both interesting and significant that there was extremely little opposition to these economic provisions of the Constitution when it was before the state conventions, particularly when one compares the minute amount of opposition to some of these clauses to the great volume of criticism of the new government as being too strongly centralized.

Obviously, localism was the principal basis of Antifederalism. The Antifederalists were, as a scholar has recently put it, "men of little faith." They distrusted the new system because it would be remote and not so immediately subject to control. They did object to a number of provisions relating to structure, to selection, and to the powers of specific departments, just as they objected to the absence of a bill of rights, but what most of them seemed to want was a continuation of something like the Articles of Confederation, or at least of a much weaker central government than that provided in the proposed Constitution.

If the framers are not properly characterized as reactionary, it does not follow that they were seventeenth-century Levellers, or nineteenth-century reformers, nor were they Populists of the 1890s or Progressives, whether of the 1912, and 1924, or the 1948 vintage. Nor were they democrats in the sense that Tom Paine and a few, a very few, articulate though minor leaders of sentiment during the Revolution were democrats who wished to have the American constitutions embody the principles accepted two or three generations later: universal male suffrage, freedom for the slaves, together with the view advocated by Paine and others, but not generally accepted in the nineteenth century, simple majority rule rather than separation of powers and checks and balances.

To return to the comparisons suggested [earlier] ... why were the same men in responsible public offices in 1787 as in 1776? Why had the leaders of the Revolution not been ousted, hanged or exiled? Why were the leaders of the Revolution able to keep it to a moderate course, when revolutions as we know of them have usually run through a cycle involving a period of absolutism and frequently a restoration of the old order? And why, finally, were the men of 1776–1787 able to lay the foundations for successful self-government in both the states and the nation?

A full answer to those questions would involve more than has been or could be considered in these chapters. It would include such factors as the absence of feudalism, and the comparatively high degree of economic prosperity in this country. For although there were social and economic cleavages in America, and even enough contemporary awareness of them to speak of class consciousness, there was nothing comparable to the explosive situation which existed in France at the same time. Historians, especially those given to emphasizing economic factors, have made much of Shays's Rebellion as an example of class conflict. But that rebellion was no blindly violent uprising of long-oppressed peasants. It was a comparatively orderly protest of landowners temporarily embarrassed by postwar depression.

Another factor to be considered in explaining the success of the Revolution would be the absence of acute or profound religious conflict. To be sure, there was controversy, and considerable hard feeling in the areas where there had been an established church. But again, this conflict, when compared with the violent struggles between and against churches in other countries, is seen to be in a minor key.

These, and other factors not strictly political in their nature, are relevant. But essential to an understanding of the unique character of the American Revolution is the continuity of its political and constitutional aspects with the experience and institutions of the past. If we read only the Declaration of Independence and some of the speeches, pamphlets and journalistic letters of the fifteen years or so preceding 1776, we get the impression that Parliament or the Crown and Parliament denied Americans the elementary rights of self-government. This is far from the truth. The colonists continued to exercise extraordinary powers of self-government in all colonies, at least until 1774. In some of them, particularly Connecticut and Rhode Island, there was almost complete self-government. It was because the colonists had been virtually self-governing—and continued so—that the financial and administrative measures adopted by Britain after 1760 seemed harsh and reactionary. Edmund Burke understood this clearly when he advised Parliament to "Leave the Americans as they anciently stood. . . ."

This long experience in virtual self-government was essential to the success of independence and of self-government after independence. Because of it, both the people and the leaders whom they selected were politically sophisticated. They were well read in political theory; they quoted Locke, Montesquieu, Burlamaqui, Grotius, and others with ease. But they were generations ahead of these theorists in the practice of politics. They not only had definite ideas about the ends of government; but they also knew from experience something about the techniques of politics and politicians, and knowing these, they knew something of the difficulties involved in securing the kind of government they wanted.

Perhaps the most important product of this long experience in self-government was consensus. If I seem to belabor this concept, it is because we have so long taken it for granted, and because it has sometimes been obscured by the efforts of historians to trace the outlines of class conflict in this period of our past. But the consensus was there, and it was crucial. Moreover, it was not the consensus of ideology, or desperation, or crisis, or any other that may temporarily unite a people revolting against a specific evil. It was rather the consensus rooted in the common life, habits, institutions, and experience of generations. And furthermore, it was the consensus of contentment and success, not misery and oppression. It was therefore durable and flexible, associated with community self-confidence and conducive to moderation.

This consensus, together with long experience in practical politics gave the men of 1776–1787 a capacity for compromise rare in periods of revolutionary upheaval. As I have indicated, there was no necessity for the resolution of issues which were by their nature deeply divisive. On the great principles of liberty and justice, on the general ends and structure of representative government, there was almost universal agreement. As Madison wrote in *The Federalist,* the "genius" of America was republican. Yet on lesser—but not unimportant—questions there was conflict of opinion and interest which might have hardened into irreconcilable disputes. Such, of course, was the question of equal or proportionate representation of the states in the Congress, or the several issues relating to slavery which divided the North and the South. The Constitution, when it was finally signed, was not completely satisfactory to anyone. It embodied no individual's—and no group's—dream of perfection. The fact that both Franklin and Hamilton were willing to sign it reflects not only the degree to which it was a compromise—"a bundle of compromises" if you like—but also the extent of mutual confidence which made compromise possible and acceptable. This willingness to compromise was also a product of the experience of men long accustomed to the untidiness involved in both the procedures and the results of self-government. Our birth as a nation took place when we were already politically mature.

Compromise was not the only aspect of this maturity. Long experience, in local government and in colonial government, had equipped the men of this generation with sheer political "know-how". The leaders of the Revolution were not new to politics. The revolutionary assemblies were frequently the old colonial legislatures by another name, and minus their Tory membership. Colonial politicians already knew the uses and abuses of republican political techniques. They were, needless to say, skillful propagandists; they knew the dangers of demagogues. They were familiar with the caucus; they were on their guard against "cabals" and intrigues. They were aware of the possibilities of bribery and corruption; they knew something of the role of patronage in building up what we would call a political machine. Knowledge of this sort served as immunization against the kind of disillusionment suffered both by Paine and Hamilton after their initial enthusiasm of 1774–1776. They knew, too, the solid as distinguished from the possibly sordid aspects of political procedure. The easy and efficient use made of committees throughout the entire period is remarkable as a stage in the evolution of representative institutions. It is a technique absolutely essential to this form of government, for it combines the virtue of concentrated attention by a small group with responsibility to the whole. The men of the Revolution, when they used it in the deliberative sphere, used it with practiced skill. They were far less successful, of course, when they used it for executive purposes under the articles—a fact which they quickly recognized and remedied. This familiarity with and facility in the use of the ordinary procedures of self-government helped to make the transition from colonial to independent status smooth and easy.

Nowhere is their political maturity shown more clearly than in their innovations. Whether in adapting colonial frames of government to the needs of the independent states, or in fashioning a new species of federalism, they achieved much because they did not attempt the impossible. The adage "politics is the art of the possible" applies as well to the establishment of governments as to the carrying on of governments already established. In state and in nation the framers worked within the limits set by their inheritance and by the convictions of the people. Had they attempted more, had they sought a transformation of society into something altogether novel and strange to America—a degree of liberty and equality not dreamed of save by a handful of idealists—they might have wrought a miracle. More likely, they would have failed, either immediately or through encouragement of a reaction, compared with which the discontent with the articles and with economic legislation in the states would seem like placid satisfaction.

Their innovations are more accurately designated inventions. For, in the manner of the great inventors, the framers worked with what was available and usable; from existing experience and knowledge they devised new institutions which were also improved modifications of those then existing. In doing so they strengthened rather than severed the chain of continuity. These statesmen-inventors were not supermen or demigods. They had human failings—they were not without self-interest—and they did not create, nor did they long for, utopia. But when we judge them by relevant standards we necessarily conclude that the remarkable degree of their achievement entitles them to a place in the company of the legislators of myth and history who reshaped their country's laws to their country's good. They followed the ancient example of successful legislators in observing the principle of continuity. They departed from their example in that they worked by and with the consent of the governed.

# Gordon S. Wood

GORDON S. WOOD (1933–    ) is professor of history at Brown University. His
book, *The Creation of the American Republic, 1776-1787,* received the John H.
Dunning Prize of the American Historical Association in 1970.

The division over the Constitution in 1787–1788 is not easily analyzed. It
is difficult, as historians have recently demonstrated, to equate the supporters or opponents of the Constitution with particular economic
groupings. The Antifederalist politicians in the ratifying conventions
often possessed wealth, including public securities, equal to that of the
Federalists. While the relative youth of the Federalist leaders, compared
to the ages of the prominent Antifederalists, was important, especially
in accounting for the Federalists' ability to think freshly and creatively
about politics, it can hardly be used to explain the division throughout
the country. Moreover, the concern of the 1780s with America's moral
character was not confined to the proponents of the Constitution. That
rabid republican and Antifederalist, Benjamin Austin, was as convinced
as any Federalist that "the luxurious living of all ranks and degrees" was
"the principal cause of all the evils we now experience." Some leading
Antifederalist intellectuals expressed as much fear of "the injustice,
folly, and wickedness of the State Legislatures" and of "the usurpation
and tyranny of the majority" against the minority as did Madison. In the
Philadelphia Convention both Mason and Elbridge Gerry, later prominent Antifederalists, admitted "the danger of the levelling spirit" flowing from "the excess of democracy" in the American republic. There
were many diverse reasons in each state why men supported or opposed the Constitution that cut through any sort of class division. The
Constitution was a single issue in a complicated situation, and its acceptance or rejection in many states was often dictated by peculiar
circumstances—the prevalence of Indians, the desire for western lands,
the special interests of commerce—that defy generalization. Nevertheless, despite all of this confusion and complexity, the struggle over the

Gordon S. Wood, *The Creation of the American Republic,* 1776-1787 (Chapel Hill: University
of North Carolina Press, 1969) pp. 485–92, 494–99, 506–8, 513–18. Reprinted with omissions by permission of the University of North Carolina Press and the Institute of Early
American History and Culture.

Constitution, as the debate if nothing else makes clear, can best be understood as a social one. Whatever the particular constituency of the antagonists may have been, men in 1787–1788 talked as if they were representing distinct and opposing social elements. Both the proponents and opponents of the Constitution focused throughout the debates on an essential point of political sociology that ultimately must be used to distinguish a Federalist from an Antifederalist. The quarrel was fundamentally one between aristocracy and democracy. . . .

The disorganization and inertia of the Antifederalists, especially in contrast with the energy and effectiveness of the Federalists, has been repeatedly emphasized. The opponents of the Constitution lacked both coordination and unified leadership; "their principles," wrote Oliver Ellsworth, "are totally opposite to each other, and their objections discordant and irreconcilable." The Federalist victory, it appears, was actually more of an Antifederalist default. . . .

But the Antifederalists were not simply poorer politicians than the Federalists; they were actually different kinds of politicians. Too many of them were state-centered men with local interests and loyalties only, politicians without influence and connections, and ultimately politicians without social and intellectual confidence. In South Carolina the up-country opponents of the Constitution shied from debate and when they did occasionally rise to speak apologized effusively for their inability to say what they felt had to be said, thus leaving most of the opposition to the Constitution to be voiced by Rawlins Lowndes, a low-country planter who scarcely represented their interests and soon retired from the struggle. Elsewhere, in New Hampshire, Connecticut, Massachusetts, Pennsylvania, and North Carolina, the situation was similar: the Federalists had the bulk of talent and influence on their side "together with all the Speakers in the State great and small." In convention after convention the Antifederalists, as in Connecticut, tried to speak but "they were browbeaten by many of those Cicero'es as they think themselves and others of Superior rank." "The presses are in a great measure secured to *their* side," the Antifederalists complained with justice: out of a hundred or more newspapers printed in the late eighties only a dozen supported the Antifederalists, as editors, "afraid to offend the great men, or Merchants, who could work their ruin," closed their columns to the opposition. The Antifederalists were not so much beaten as overawed. . . .

[F]ear of a plot by men who "talk so finely and gloss over matters so smoothly" ran through the Antifederalist mind. Because the many "new men" of the 1780s, men like Melancthon Smith and Abraham Yates of New York or John Smilie and William Findley of Pennsylvania, had bypassed the social hierarchy in their rise to political leadership, they lacked those attributes of social distinction and dignity that went beyond mere wealth. Since these kinds of men were never assimilated to the gentlemanly cast of the Livingstons or the Morrises, they, like Americans earlier in confrontation with the British court, tended to view with suspicion and hostility the high-flying world of style and connections that they were barred by their language and tastes, if by nothing else, from sharing in. In the minds of these socially inferior politicians the movement for the strengthening of the central government could only be a "conspiracy" "planned and set to work" by a few aristocrats, who were at first, said Abraham Yates, no larger in number in any one state than the cabal which sought to undermine English liberty at the beginning of the eighteenth century. Since men like Yates could not quite comprehend what they were sure were the inner maneuverings of the elite, they were convinced that in the aristocrats' program, "what was their view in the beginning" or how "far it was Intended to be carried Must be Collected from facts that Afterwards have happened." Like American Whigs in the sixties and seventies forced to delve into the dark and complicated workings of English court politics, they could judge motives and plans "but by the Event." And they could only conclude that the events of the eighties, "the treasury, the Cincinnati, and other public creditors, with all their concomitants," were "somehow or other, . . . inseparably connected," were all parts of a grand design "concerted by a few *tyrants*" to undo the Revolution and to establish an aristocracy in order "to lord it over the rest of their fellow citizens, to trample the poorer part of the people under their feet, that they may be rendered their servants and slaves." In this climate all the major issues of the Confederation period—the impost, commutation, and the return of the Loyalists—possessed a political and social significance that transcended economic concerns. All seemed to be devices by which a ruling few, like the ministers of the English Crown, would attach a corps of pensioners and dependents to the government and spread their influence and connections throughout the states in order "to dissolve our present Happy and Benevolent Constitution and to erect on the Ruins, a proper Aristocracy."

Nothing was more characteristic of Antifederalist thinking than this obsession with aristocracy. Although to a European, American society may have appeared remarkably egalitarian, to many Americans, especially to those who aspired to places of consequence but were made to feel their inferiority in innumerable, often subtle, ways, American society was distinguished by its inequality. . . . In all communities, "even in those of the most democratic kind," wrote George Clinton (whose "family and connections" in the minds of those like Philip Schuyler did not "entitle him to so distinguished a predominance" as the governorship of New York), there were pressures—"superior talents, fortunes and public employments"—demarcating an aristocracy whose influence was difficult to resist.

Such influence was difficult to resist because, to the continual annoyance of the Antifederalists, the great body of the people willingly submitted to it. The "authority of names" and "the influence of the great" among ordinary people were too evident to be denied. "Will any one say that there does not exist in this country the pride of family, of wealth, of talents, and that they do not command influence and respect among the common people?" "The people are too apt to yield an implicit assent to the opinions of those characters whose abilities are held in the highest esteem, and to those in whose integrity and patriotism they can confide; not considering that the love of domination is generally in proportion to talents, abilities and superior requirements." Because of this habit of deference in the people, it was "in the power of the enlightened and aspiring few, if they should combine, at any time to destroy the best establishments, and even make the people the instruments of their own subjugation." Hence, the Antifederalist-minded declared, the people must be awakened to the consequences of their self-ensnarement; they must be warned over and over by the popular tribunes, by "those who are competent to the task of developing the principles of government," of the dangers involved in paying obeisance to those who they thought were their superiors. The people must "not be permitted to consider themselves as a grovelling, distinct species, uninterested in the general welfare."

Such constant admonitions to the people of the perils flowing from their too easy deference to the *"natural aristocracy"* were necessary because the Antifederalists were convinced that these "men that had been delicately bred, and who were in affluent circumstances," these "men of the most exalted rank in life," were by their very conspicuousness irreparably cut off from the great body of the people and hence could never share in its concerns nor look after its interests. It was not that these "certain men exalted above the rest" were necessarily "destitute of morality or virtue" or that they were inherently different from other men. "The same passions and prejudices govern all men." It was only that circumstances in their particular environment had made them different. There was "a charm in politicks"; men in high office become habituated with power, "grow fond of it, and are loath to resign it"; "they feel themselves flattered and elevated," enthralled by the attractions of high living, and thus they easily forget the interests of the common people, from which many of them once sprang. By dwelling so vividly on the allurements of prestige and power, by emphasizing again and again how the "human soul is affected by wealth, in all its faculties, . . . by its present interest, by its expectations, and by its fears," these ambitious Antifederalist politicians may have revealed as much about themselves as they did about the "aristocratic" elite they sought to displace. Yet at the same time by such language they contributed to a new appreciation of the nature of society.

In these repeated attacks on deference and the capacity of a conspicuous few to speak for the whole society—which was to become in time the distinguishing feature of American democratic politics—the Antifederalists struck at the roots of the traditional conception of political society. If the natural elite, whether its distinctions were ascribed or acquired, was not in any organic way connected to the "feelings, circumstances, and interests" of the people and was incapable of feeling "sympathetically the wants of the people," then it followed that only ordinary men, men not distinguished by the characteristics of aristocratic wealth and taste, men "in middling circumstances" untempted by the attractions of a cosmopolitan world and thus "more temperate, of better morals, and less ambitious, than the great," could be trusted to speak for the great body of the people, for those who were coming more and more to be referred to as "the middling and lower classes of people." The differentiating influence of the environment was such that men in various ranks and classes now seemed to be broken apart from one another, separated by their peculiar circumstances into distinct, unconnected, and often incompatible interests. With their indictment of aristocracy the Antifederalists were saying, whether they realized it or not, that the people of America even in their several states were not homogeneous entities each with a basic similarity of interest for which an empathic elite could speak. Society was not an organic hierarchy composed of ranks and degrees indissolubly linked one to another; rather it was a heterogeneous mixture of "many different classes or orders of people, Merchants, Farmers, Planter Mechanics and Gentry or wealthy Men." In such a society men from one class or group, however educated and respectable they may have been, could never be acquainted with the "*Situation* and Wants" of those of another class or group. Lawyers and planters could never be "adequate judges of tradesmens concerns." If men were truly to represent the people in government, it was not enough for them to be for the people; they had to be actually of the people. "Farmers, traders and mechanics... all ought to have a competent number of their best informed members in the legislature."

Thus the Antifederalists were not only directly challenging the conventional belief that only a gentlemanly few, even though now in America naturally and not artificially qualified, were best equipped through learning and experience to represent and to govern the society, but they were as well indirectly denying the assumption of organic social homogeneity on which republicanism rested. Without fully comprehending the consequences of their arguments the Antifederalists were destroying the great chain of being, thus undermining the social basis of republicanism and shattering that unity and harmony of social and political authority which the eighteenth century generally and indeed most revolutionary leaders had considered essential to the maintenance of order.

Confronted with such a fundamental challenge the Federalists initially backed away. They had no desire to argue the merits of the Constitution in terms of social implications and were understandably reluctant to open up the character of American society as the central issue of the debate. But in the end they could not resist defending those beliefs in elitism that lay at the heart of their conception of politics and of their constitutional program. All of the Federalists' desires to establish a strong and respectable nation in the world, all of their plans to create a flourishing commercial economy, in short, all of what the Federalists wanted out of the new central government seemed in the final analysis dependent upon the prerequisite maintenance of aristocratic politics. . . .

The course of the debates over the Constitution seemed to confirm what the Federalists had believed all along. Antifederalism represented the climax of a "war" that was, in the words of Theodore Sedgwick, being "levied on the virtue, property, and distinctions in the community." The opponents of the Constitution, despite some, "particularly in Virginia," who were operating "from the most honorable and patriotic motives," were essentially identical with those who were responsible for the evils the states were suffering from in the eighties—"narrowminded politicians . . . under the influence of local views." "Whilst many *ostensible* reasons are assigned" for the Antifederalists' opposition, charged Washington, "the real ones are concealed behind the Curtains, because they are not of a nature to appear in open day." "The real object of all their zeal in opposing the system," agreed Madison, was to maintain "the supremacy of the State Legislatures," with all that meant in the printing of money and the violation of contracts. The Antifederalists or those for whom the Antifederalists spoke, whether their spokesmen realized it or not, were "none but the horse-jockey, the mushroom merchant, the running and dishonest speculator," those "who owe the most and have the least to pay," those "whose dependence and expectations are upon changes in government, and distracted times," men of "desperate Circumstances," those "in Every State" who "have Debts to pay, Interests to support or Fortunes to make," those, in short, who "wish for scrambling Times." Apart from a few of their intellectual leaders the Antifederalists were thought to be an ill-bred lot: "Their education has been rather indifferent—they have been accustomed to think on the small scale." They were often blustering demagogues trying to push their way into office—"men of much self-importance and supposed skill in politics, who are not of sufficient consequence to obtain public employment." Hence they were considered to be jealous and mistrustful of "every one in the higher offices of society," unable to bear to see others possessing "that fancied blessing, to which, alas! they must themselves aspire in vain." In the Federalist mind therefore the struggle over the Constitution was not one between kinds of wealth or property, or one between commercial or noncommercial elements of the population, but rather represented a broad social division between those who believed in the right of a natural aristocracy to speak for the people and those who did not.

Against this threat from the licentious the Federalists pictured themselves as the defenders of the worthy, of those whom they called "the better sort of people," those, said John Jay, "who are orderly and industrious, who are content with their situations and not uneasy in their circumstances." Because the Federalists were fearful that republican equality was becoming "that *perfect equality* which deadens the motives of industry, and places Demerit on a Footing with Virtue," they were obsessed with the need to insure that the proper amount of inequality and natural distinctions be recognized.... Robert Morris, for example, was convinced there were social differences—even in Pennsylvania. "What!" he explained in scornful amazement at John Smilie's argument that a republic admitted of no social superiorities. "Is it insisted that there is no distinction of character?" Respectability, said Morris with conviction, was not confined to property. "Surely persons possessed of knowledge, judgment, information, integrity, and having extensive connections, are not to be classed with persons void of reputation or character."

In refuting the Antifederalists' contention "that all classes of citizens should have some of their own number in the representative body, in order that their feelings and interests may be the better understood and attended to," Hamilton in *The Federalist,* Number 35, put into words the Federalists' often unspoken and vaguely held assumption about the organic and the hierarchical nature of society. Such explicit class or occupational representation as the Antifederalists advocated, wrote Hamilton, was not only impractical but unnecessary, since the society was not as fragmented or heterogeneous as the Antifederalists implied. The various groups in the landed interest, for example, were "perfectly united, from the wealthiest landlord down to the poorest tenant," and this "common interest may always be reckoned upon as the surest bond of sympathy" linking the landed representative, however rich, to his constituents. In a like way, the members of the commercial community were "immediately connected" and most naturally represented by the merchants. "Mechanics and manufacturers will always be inclined, with few exceptions, to give their votes to merchants, in preference to persons of their own professions or trades.... They know that the merchant is their natural patron and friend; and... they are sensible that their habits in life have not been such as to give them those acquired endowments, without which in a deliberative assembly, the greatest natural abilities, are for the most part useless." However much many Federalists may have doubted the substance of Hamilton's analysis of American society, they could not doubt the truth of his conclusion. That the people were represented better by one of the natural aristocracy "whose situation leads to extensive inquiry and information" than by one "whose observation does not travel beyond the circle of his neighbors and acquaintances" was the defining element of the Federalist philosophy.

It was not simply the number of public securities, or credit outstanding, or the number of ships, or the amount of money possessed that made a man think of himself as one of the natural elite. It was much more subtle than the mere possession of wealth: it was a deeper social feeling, a sense of being socially established, of possessing attributes—family, education, and refinement—that others lacked, above all, of being accepted by and being able to move easily among those who considered themselves to be the respectable and cultivated. It is perhaps anachronistic to describe this social sense as a class interest, for it often transcended immediate political or economic concerns, and, as Hamilton's argument indicates, was designed to cut through narrow occupational categories. The Republicans of Philadelphia, for example, repeatedly denied that they represented an aristocracy with a united class interest. "We are of different occupations; of different sects of religion; and have different views of life. No factions or private system can comprehend us all." Yet with all their assertions of diversified interests the Republicans were not without a social consciousness in their quarrel with the supporters of the Pennsylvania Constitution. If there were any of us ambitious for power, their apology continued, then there would be no need to change the Constitution, for we surely could attain power under the present Constitution. "We have already seen how easy the task is for *any character* to rise into power and consequence under it. And there are some of us, who think not so meanly of ourselves, as to dread any rivalship from those who are now in office."

In 1787 this kind of elitist social consciousness was brought into play as perhaps never before in eighteenth-century America, as gentlemen up and down the continent submerged their sectional and economic differences in the face of what seemed to be a threat to the very foundations of society. Despite his earlier opposition to the Order of the Cincinnati, Theodore Sedgwick, like other frightened New Englanders, now welcomed the organization as a source of strength in the battle for the Constitution. The fear of social disruption that had run through much of the writing of the eighties was brought to a head to eclipse all other fears. Although state politics in the eighties remains to be analyzed, the evidence from Federalist correspondence indicates clearly a belief that never had there occurred "so great a change in the opinion of the best people" as was occurring in the last few years of the decade. The Federalists were astonished at the outpouring in 1787 of influential and respectable people who had earlier remained quiescent. Too many of "the better sort of people," it was repeatedly said, had withdrawn at the end of the war "from the theatre of public action, to scenes of retirement and ease," and thus "demagogues of desperate fortunes, mere adventurers in fraud, were left to act unopposed." After all, it was explained, "when the wicked rise, men hide themselves." Even the problems of Massachusetts in 1786, noted General Benjamin Lincoln, the repressor of the Shaysites, were not caused by the rebels, but by the laxity of "the good people of the state." But the lesson of this laxity was rapidly being learned. Everywhere, it seemed, men of virtue, good sense, and property, "almost the whole body of our enlighten'd and leading chracters in every state," were awakened in support of stronger government. "The scum which was thrown upon the surface by the fermentation of the war is daily sinking," Benjamin Rush told Richard Price in 1786, "while a pure spirit is occupying its place." "Men are brought into action who had consigned themselves to an eve of rest," Edward Carrington wrote to Jefferson in June 1787, "and the Convention, as a Beacon, is rousing the attention of the Empire." The Antifederalists could only stand amazed at this "weight of talents" being gathered in support of the Constitution. "What must the individual be who could thus oppose them united?"

Still, in the face of this preponderance of wealth and respectability in support of the Constitution, what remains extraordinary about 1787–1788 is not the weakness and disunity but the political strength of Antifederalism. That large numbers of Americans could actually reject a plan of government created by a body "composed of the first characters in the Continent" and backed by Washington and nearly the whole of the natural aristocracy of the country said more about the changing character of American politics and society in the eighties than did the Constitution's eventual acceptance. It was indeed a portent of what was to come. . . .

If the new national government was to promote the common good as forcefully as any state government, and if, as the Federalists believed, a major source of the vices of the eighties lay in the abuse of state power, then there was something apparently contradictory about the new federal Constitution, which after all represented not a weakening of the dangerous power of republican government but rather a strengthening of it. "The complaints against the separate governments, even by the friends of the new plan," remarked the Antifederalist James Winthrop, "are not that they have not power enough, but that they are disposed to make a bad use of what power they have." Surely, concluded Winthrop, the Federalists were reasoning badly "when they purpose to set up a government possess'd of much more extensive powers . . . and subject to much smaller checks" than the existing state governments possessed and were subject to. Madison for one was quite aware of the pointedness of this objection. "It may be asked," he said, "how private rights will be more secure under the Guardianship of the General Government than under the State Governments, since they are both founded in the republican principle which refers the ultimate decision to the will of the majority." What, in other words, was different about the new federal Constitution that would enable it to mitigate the effects of tyrannical majorities? What would keep the new federal government from succumbing to the same pressures that had beset the state governments? The answer the Federalists gave to these questions unmistakably reveals the social bias underlying both their fears of the unrestrained state legislatures and their expectations for their federal remedy. For all of their desires to avoid intricate examination of a delicate social structure, the Federalists' program itself demanded that the discussion of the Constitution would be in essentially social terms.

The Federalists were not as much opposed to the governmental power of the states as to the character of the people who were wielding it. The constitutions of most of the states were not really at fault. Massachusetts after all possessed a nearly perfect constitution. What actually bothered the Federalists was the sort of people who had been able to gain positions of authority in the state governments, particularly in the state legislatures. Much of the quarrel with the viciousness, instability, and injustice of the various state governments was at bottom social. "For," as John Dickinson emphasized, "*the government will partake of the qualities of those whose authority is prevalent.*" The political and social structures were intimately related. "People once respected their governors, their senators, their judges and their clergy; they reposed confidence in them; their laws were obeyed, and the states were happy in tranquility." But in the eighties the authority of government had drastically declined because "men of sense and property have lost much of their influence by the popular spirit of the war." "That exact order, and due subordination, that is essentially necessary in all well appointed governments, and which constitutes the real happiness and well being of society" had been deranged by "men of no genius or abilities" who had tried to run "the machine of government." Since "it cannot be expected that things will go well, when persons of vicious principles, and loose morals are in authority," it was the large number of obscure, ignorant, and unruly men occupying the state legislatures, and not the structure of the governments, that was the real cause of the evils so much complained of.

The Federalist image of the Constitution as a sort of "philosopher's stone" was indeed appropriate: it was a device intended to transmute base materials into gold and thereby prolong the life of the republic. Patrick Henry acutely perceived what the Federalists were driving at. "The Constitution," he said in the Virginia Convention, "reflects in the most degrading and mortifying manner on the virtue, integrity, and wisdom of the state legislatures; it presupposes that the chosen few who go to Congress will have more upright hearts, and more enlightened minds, than those who are members of the individual legislatures." The new Constitution was structurally no different from the constitutions of some of the states. Yet the powers of the new central government were not as threatening as the powers of the state governments precisely because the Federalists believed different kinds of persons would hold them. They anticipated that somehow the new government would be staffed largely by "the worthy," the natural social aristocracy of the country. "After all," said Pelatiah Webster, putting his finger on the crux of the Federalist argument, "the grand secret of forming a good government, is, to put good men into the administration: for wild, vicious, or idle men, will ever make a bad government, let its principles be ever so good. . . .

In short, through the artificial contrivance of the Constitution overlying an expanded society, the Federalists meant to restore and to prolong the traditional kind of elitist influence in politics that social developments, especially since the Revolution, were undermining. As the defenders if not always the perpetrators of these developments—the "disorder" of the 1780s—the Antifederalists could scarcely have missed the social implications of the Federalist program. The Constitution was intrinsically an aristocratic document designed to check the democratic tendencies of the period, and as such it dictated the character of the Antifederalist response. It was therefore inevitable that the Antifederalists should have charged that the new government was "dangerously adapted to the purposes of an immediate *aristocratic tyranny.*" In state after state the Antifederalists reduced the issue to those social terms predetermined by the Federalists themselves: the Constitution was a plan intended to "raise the fortunes and respectability of the *well-born few,* and oppress the plebians"; it was "a continental exertion of the *well-born* of America to obtain that darling domination, which they have not been able to accomplish in their respective states"; it "will lead to an aristocratical government, and establish tyranny over us." Whatever their own particular social standing, the Antifederalist spokesmen spread the warning that the new government either would be "in practice a *permanent* ARISTOCRACY" or would soon "degenerate to a compleat Aristocracy." . . .

Aristocratic principles were in fact "interwoven" in the very fabric of the proposed government. If a government was "so constituted as to admit but few to exercise the powers of it," then it would "according to the natural course of things" end up in the hands of "the natural aristocracy." It went almost without saying that the awesome president and the exalted Senate, "a compound of *monarchy* and *aristocracy*," would be dangerously far removed from the people. But even the House of Representatives, the very body that "should be a true picture of the people, possess a knowledge of their circumstances and their wants, sympathize in all their distresses, and disposed to seek their true interest," was without "a tincture of democracy." Since it could never collect "the interests, feelings, and opinions of three or four millions of people," it was better understood as "an Assistant Aristocratical Branch" to the Senate than as a real representation of the people. When the number of representatives was "so small, the office will be highly elevated and distinguished; the style in which the members live will probably be high; circumstances of this kind will render the place of a representative not a desirable one to sensible, substantial men, who have been used to walk in the plain and frugal paths of life." While the ordinary people in extensive electoral districts of thirty thousand inhabitants would remain "divided," those few extraordinary men with "conspicuous military, popular, civil or legal talents" could more easily form broader associations to dominate elections; they had family and other connections to "unite their interests." If only a half-dozen congressmen were to be selected to represent a large state, then rarely, argued the Antifederalists in terms that were essentially no different from those used by the Federalists in the Constitution's defense, would persons from "the great body of the people, the middle and lower classes," be elected to the House of Representatives. "The Station is too high and exalted to be filled but [by] the *first Men* in the State in point of Fortune and Influence. In fact no order or class of the people will be represented in the House of Representatives called the Democratic Branch but the rich and wealthy." The Antifederalists thus came to oppose the new national government for the same reason the Federalists favored it: because its very structure and detachment from the people would work to exclude any kind of actual and local interest representation and prevent those who were not rich, well born, or prominent from exercising political power. Both sides fully appreciated the central issue the Constitution posed and grappled with it throughout the debates: Whether a professedly popular government should actually be in the hands of, rather than simply derived from, common ordinary people.

Out of the division in 1787–1788 over this issue, an issue which was as conspicuously social as any in American history, the Antifederalists emerged as the spokesmen for the growing American antagonism to aristocracy and as the defenders of the most intimate participation in politics of the widest variety of people possible. It was not from lack of vision that the Antifederalists feared the new government. Although their viewpoint was intensely localist, it was grounded in as perceptive an understanding of the social basis of American politics as that of the Federalists. Most of the Antifederalists were majoritarians with respect to the state legislatures but not with respect to the national legislature, because they presumed as well as the Federalists did that different sorts of people from those who sat in the state assemblies would occupy the Congress. Whatever else may be said about the Antifederalists, their populism cannot be impugned. They were true champions of the most extreme kind of democratic and egalitarian politics expressed in the revolutionary era. Convinced that "it has been the principal care of free governments to guard against the encroachments of the great," the Antifederalists believed that popular government itself, as defined by the principles of 1776, was endangered by the new national government. If the Revolution had been a transfer of power from the few to the many, then the federal Constitution clearly represented an abnegation of the Revolution. For, as Richard Henry Lee wrote in his *Letters from the Federal Farmer*, "every man of reflection must see, that the change now proposed, is a transfer of power from the many to the few."

Although Lee's analysis contained the essential truth, the Federalist program was not quite so simply summed up. It was true that through the new Constitution the Federalists hoped to resist and eventually to avert what they saw to be the rapid decline of the influence and authority of the natural aristocracy in America. At the very time that the organic conception of society that made elite rule comprehensible was finally and avowedly dissolving, and the members of the elite were developing distinct professional, social, or economic interests, the Federalists found elite rule more imperative than ever before. To the Federalists the greatest dangers to republicanism were flowing not, as the old Whigs had thought, from the rulers or from any distinctive minority in the community, but from the widespread participation of the people in the government. It now seemed increasingly evident that if the public good not only of the United States as a whole but even of the separate states were to be truly perceived and promoted, the American people must abandon their revolutionary reliance on their representative state legislatures and place their confidence in the highmindedness of the natural leaders of the society, which ideally everyone had the opportunity of becoming. Since the Federalists presumed that only such a self-conscious elite could transcend the many narrow and contradictory interests inevitable in any society, however small, the measure of a good government became its capacity for insuring the predominance of these kinds of natural leaders who knew better than the people as a whole what was good for the society.

The result was an amazing display of confidence in constitutionalism, in the efficacy of institutional devices for solving social and political problems. Through the proper arrangement of new institutional structures the Federalists aimed to turn the political and social developments that were weakening the place of "the better sort of people" in government back upon themselves and to make these developments the very source of the perpetuation of the natural aristocracy's dominance of politics. Thus the Federalists did not directly reject democratic politics as it had manifested itself in the 1780s; rather they attempted to adjust to this politics in order to control and mitigate its effects. In short they offered the country an elitist theory of democracy. They did not see themselves as repudiating either the Revolution or popular government, but saw themselves as saving both from their excesses. If the Constitution were not established, they told themselves and the country over and over, then republicanism was doomed, the grand experiment was over, and a division of the confederacy, monarchy, or worse would result.

Despite all the examples of popular vice in the eighties, the Federalist confidence in the people remained strong. The letters of "Caesar," with their frank and violent denigration of the people, were anomalies in the Federalist literature. The Federalists had by no means lost faith in the people, at least in the people's ability to discern their true leaders. In fact many of the social elite who comprised the Federalist leadership were confident of popular election if the constituency could be made broad enough, and crass electioneering be curbed, so that the people's choice would be undisturbed by ambitious demagogues. "For if not blind to their own interest, they choose men of the first character for wisdom and integrity." Despite prodding by so-called designing and unprincipled men, the bulk of the people remained deferential to the established social leadership—for some aspiring politicans frustratingly so. Even if they had wanted to, the Federalists could not turn their backs on republicanism. For it was evident to even the most pessimistic "that no other form would be reconcilable with the genius of the people of America; with the fundamental principles of the Revolution; or with that honorable determination which animates every votary of freedom, to rest all our political experiments on the capacity of mankind for self-government." Whatever government the Federalists established had to be "strictly republican" and "deducible from the only source of just authority—the People."

# 6

# *The Federal Era*

## Hamiltonian or Jeffersonian?

The federal era—1789 to 1829—forms a distinct period in American history. It is preceded and followed by periods that are strikingly different: the period prior to the introduction of the federal Constitution in 1789 has a coherence all of its own; the years after 1829 mark the emergence of the Jacksonian movement. In the four decades after the framing of the new Constitution, Americans set up a functioning federal system, organized their first political parties, and laid the foundations of their foreign policy for years to come. The federal era thus represents one of the most important periods in our nation's history.

Historians have been so impressed by these formative influences that some of them in the first half of the twentieth century attributed to the federal era an even greater significance by viewing it as a microcosm for all of American history. To certain historians the political battle between Hamilton and Jefferson in the 1790s marked the beginning of an ideological and political split that shaped the entire future course of the country. These scholars tended to view the rest of American history in terms of a Hamiltonian-Jeffersonian dichotomy and went to the federal era to discover the origins of America's development as a nation.

To those who saw American history in this context, Hamilton and Jefferson symbolized a clash of conflicting principles at work in the country during this era. These historians interpreted the period as a struggle between aristocracy and democracy, industrialism versus agrarianism, and the supremacy of the national government as opposed to the idea of states' rights. In the area of foreign policy, they saw a similar polarity. There was general agreement among the parties and men of the period that America's foreign policy should result in a free and independent nation isolated in so far as possible from the affairs of Europe. The two protagonists were pictured as advocating different means of reaching the same ends—Hamilton being pro-British and Jefferson pro-French.

In this kind of interpretation, the Federalist party of Hamilton was presented as being the party of the aristocratic and conservative forces in

189

American society. Composed of the rich and well-born, it was headed by men of property who had no wish to yield political power to the lower classes. During the administrations of Washington and of John Adams, the Federalists set up a strong, centralized government which favored their own economic interests in commerce, finance, and industry and attempted to perpetuate a social and political system that was fundamentally undemocratic. The Federalists supposedly took a pro-British stand in foreign policy because they were in sympathy with Britain's ideas about class distinctions and her system of government. Although the Federalists were defeated in 1800, according to this interpretation, their influence continued well beyond this date. Federalist ideas were enacted into legislation by Jeffersonian Republican presidents who changed their point of view and endorsed programs for a protective tariff, a Bank of the United States, and American manufactures. Federalist doctrines were espoused in the Supreme Court by John Marshall, who presided over that body until the 1830s.

Conversely, the Jeffersonian Republican party was represented as being the party of the common people and of democracy. Made up of small farmers and led by Thomas Jefferson and James Madison, the party presumably was devoted to keeping America an agrarian paradise. Being suspicious of big government and big business, it stood for states' rights and the interests of the farming class. Since party members favored the idea of an egalitarian society, they were sympathetic to the French Revolution and generally pro-French in foreign policy. When the Federalists pressed their anti-democratic tendencies too far in the Alien and Sedition Acts of 1798, this interpretation continued, the small farmer class rose up in wrath and voted them out of office in what has been called the "Revolution of 1800."

Thus, this early twentieth-century interpretation viewed all American history as a continuous struggle between the democratic aspirations of the common people against the despotism of the upper classes. The Hamiltonian-Jeffersonian dichotomy was projected down through the rest of the nation's history. The Jeffersonian Republicans were looked upon as being the forebears of the democratic spirit—giving rise to the Jacksonian Democrats, Populists, Progressives and New Dealers of a later day. The Federalists, on the other hand, were considered to be the progenitors of the anti-democratic forces—making way for the Whig party of the pre-Civil War period and the Republican party of the post–Civil War era.

This interpretation of the federal era, however, has not always been accepted. Other interpretations were also advanced at various times as historians continued their never-ending evaluation of the course of American history. Generally speaking, historians have tended to view the federal era in terms of their own time and to reflect their personal beliefs when writing about the parties and personalities of the period. Despite their claims to the contrary, scholars have not always been impartial in their evaluations of the era; if they took a pro-Hamiltonian position, they were usually hostile to Jefferson; if, on the other hand, they favored a Jeffersonian stand, they characteristically were antagonistic to Hamilton.

Throughout most of the nineteenth century, the majority of American historians who wrote about the federal era did so within the context of a Hamiltonian-Jeffersonian split. Most of the historical writing in that century, indeed, was overwhelmingly political in tone. Scholars paid particular attention to national politics and political parties as a means of explaining the major trends in American life. It is safe to say that a far greater number of American historians took what might be described as a Federalist-Whig-Republican point of view toward the federal era than did those who took a Jeffersonian-Jacksonian-Democratic outlook.

The predominantly Federalist-Whig interpretation, for example, was readily evident in the work of Richard Hildreth—a Massachusetts Whig, historian, and journalist. In his six-volume *History of the United States,* published between 1849 and 1852, Hildreth dealt with American history down to the conclusion of the Missouri Compromise crisis in 1821. His work was friendly toward the Federalists, and he had high praise for Hamilton as the leader of the party and a man "possessed of practical talents of the highest orders."[1] Hamilton's wisdom, wrote Hildreth, resulted from his recognition that the greatest threat to the republic lay in the resistance of the state governments to federal power. Much of Hamilton's program, therefore, was directed toward strengthening the central government. Support for Hamilton's measures came from America's "natural aristocracy" comprised of judges, lawyers, clergymen, large landowners, merchants, and manufacturers. In the area of foreign affairs, as might be expected, Hildreth's sympathies lay with the Federalists and a pro-English policy.

Hildreth's history was anti-Jeffersonian in its outlook, but probably more for philosophical reasons than for narrowly partisan ones. A believer in the ideas of Jeremy Bentham—the English philosopher who propounded the concept of utilitarianism—Hildreth sought to apply such ideas in the writing of his history. Jefferson's predilection for theories did not fit into Hildreth's preconceived liberal utilitarian point of view and for this reason the historian was critical of him. As one recent scholar has observed, Hildreth's "temperamental preference for

---

[1] Richard Hildreth, *The History of the United States of America . . . 1788–1821,* 6 vols. (rev. ed.; New York, 1875), 4:296.

experience over theory," his New England background and training, and his utilitarianism, caused him to prefer Hamilton's practical achievements to Jefferson's theories.[2]

The coming of the Civil War simply reinforced the prevailing Hamiltonian point of view. Hamilton's place in history was made more secure by the outcome of events. To many historians the war appeared to vindicate Hamilton's position as an exemplar of national power. If Hamilton's plan for an even stronger central government had not been rejected in the federal Constitutional Convention of 1787, some scholars insisted, the Union might have been spared the bloody ordeal of civil strife in the 1860s. Jefferson's reputation, on the other hand, declined sharply because his advocacy of states' rights seemed to place him in the same camp as the defeated South. Moreover, the Democratic party was in disrepute in this period because of its close identification with the Southern cause; as one of the founders of that party, Jefferson's position to American history suffered accordingly.

Hamilton's reputation was raised still higher in the postwar period as the emerging Republican party proclaimed him one of its prophets. Devoted to the idea of building an industrial America, many Republicans maintained that Hamilton had anticipated the economic principles to which they were dedicated. Was it not Hamilton, they asked, who was the sole statesman of his time to prophesy the future destiny of America as a great industrial nation? Republicans advocating a sound money system and a high protective tariff as necessary attributes for industrial growth pointed to Hamilton's program as their model. From the end of the Civil War to the close of the nineteenth century, the Hamiltonian tradition supplied the rhetoric and arguments employed by the Republican party and the rising industrial order. Generally speaking, historians tended to reflect this same point of view in their writings.

Jefferson's reputation by way of contrast continued to decline during the post–Civil War period. The majority of American historians of the time took an anti-Jeffersonian stand when writing about the Federal era. Hermann E. von Holst, a foreign-born and German-trained scholar who came to America to write his multivolume *Constitutional and Political History of the United States*, published between 1876 and 1892, took a hostile view of Jefferson. John T. Morse, a Boston lawyer who wrote and edited a biographical series known as the American Statesmen series, showed a similar bias in his writing and choice of authors. His two-volume biography of Hamilton published in 1876 was highly critical of Jefferson and lauded Hamilton. In categorizing the American historians who dealt with Jefferson during the last quarter of the nineteenth cen-

---

[2]Arthur M. Schlesinger, Jr., "The Problem of Richard Hildreth, "*New England Quarterly* 13 (June 1940):233–45.

tury, one recent scholar has remarked: "The dominant theme of these historians was the *Union*. Most of them were New Englanders, many were influenced by Germans such as Holst, nearly all were Republicans. With marked exceptions such as Henry Adams and the lesser known James Schouler, whose seven-volume political history was nationalistic without enmity to Jefferson, their works were vehemently anti-Jeffersonian."[3]

The outstanding exception to this hostile trend in Jeffersonian historiography was the brilliant study of the great American historian Henry Adams. His nine-volume work, *The History of the United States during the Administrations of Jefferson and Madison*, published between 1889 and 1891, remains one of the masterpieces of American historical literature. What Adams did was to shift his focus from the period when the Federalist party was in power to a point in time—1800—when the Jeffersonians were in control. Since the Federalists were on the decline from that date on, Adams was able to pay less attention to the conflict between political parties and to concentrate instead upon other important developments. To Adams two main themes dominated the sixteen-year span when Jefferson and Madison were in office—the rise of nationalism and the development of American democracy.

Even Adams's *History*, however, did not make Jefferson a heroic figure. The work established beyond any doubt the crucial contribution of Jefferson and his administration in developing an American national consciousness and in fixing the direction that American democracy was to take. But at the same time, Adams made it clear that the course of events during the administration was not due to any philosophical design on the part of Jefferson. Time and again, Adams demonstrated, Jefferson was forced to deviate from his theories and to temper his doctrines when faced with the realities of governmental power. Adams delighted in showing the inconsistencies between Jefferson the theorist and Jefferson the pragmatist. In the final analysis, however, he failed to solve the enigma of Jefferson; scholars argue to this day whether Adams's *History* is pro- or anti-Jeffersonian.[4]

In many ways Adams was a transitional figure among the American historians who wrote about the federal era. Instead of approaching his subject in the traditional nineteenth-century manner of narrative history, Adams was impressed with the idea of a scientific philosophy of history and sought to apply concepts borrowed from physics and biology as the key to historical developments. Unlike many earlier writers who were amateur gentlemen-historians, he was a professional scholar

---

[3]Merrill D. Peterson, *The Jeffersonian Image in the American Mind* (New York, 1962), p. 279.

[4]*Ibid.*, pp. 281–91.

who taught medieval and American history at Harvard for a number of years. Contrary to the prevailing view among historians which favored the Federalists, Adams was openly hostile to that party; he considered the Federalist leaders to be conservative and decadent figures in an American society that was essentially dynamic and democratic.

The real turning point in the treatment of the federal era, however, came just after Adams had completed his magnum opus at the close of the nineteenth century. With the rise of the Populist and Progressive movements in the 1890s and early 1900s, the whole climate of opinion in America underwent a dramatic change. The currents of reform sweeping the country affected America's social and political thought and historians suddenly became more sympathetic to Jefferson's liberal ideas. Scholars increasingly began to pay more attention to the democratic tradition in American history and Jefferson came into his own. For the first time, the majority of historians began writing about the American past from a Jeffersonian-Jacksonian-Democratic rather than a Federalist-Whig-Republican point of view.

During the first three decades of the twentieth century, a trio of writers from the Progressive school of historians—Charles A. Beard, Claude G. Bowers, and Vernon L. Parrington—showed a keen interest in Jefferson and his place in American history. All three proceeded to rewrite the history of the federal era from the vantage point of Jeffersonian democracy. Viewed in broad terms, this triumvirate had certain distinguishing characteristics. They all hailed from the Middle West and believed in the Progressive ideas prevalent in that part of the country. Between them, they helped to break the hold of New Englanders over Jeffersonian historiography. They were influenced also by the new intellectual orientation sweeping scholarly circles called the "new history." Advocates of the "new history" were arguing that in the past history had been used by conservative elements in the United States to provide a rationale for maintaining the status quo. The Progressive scholars wanted to use history instead as an instrument of progress to recast the future of the country along more liberal lines. In short, the proponents of the "new history" wanted to employ history as a kind of intellectual weapon to bring about political changes and reforms. Finally, both Beard and Parrington were greatly influenced by the ideas of economic determinism that were becoming increasingly popular in the historical profession at this time.

Charles A. Beard's *Economic Origins of Jeffersonian Democracy*, the first work of these three men on the subject to appear, was published in 1915 and applied an economic interpretation of history to the federal era. Starting with his well-known hypothesis that the Constitution represented the work of a small group of capitalists who were intent upon establishing a strong central government to protect their property against the encroachments of the agrarian masses, Beard argued that the capitalist-agrarian split of the 1780s continued and was institutionalized by the formation of political parties in the 1790s. Those favoring the Constitution formed the agrarian base of the Republican party founded by Jefferson and other planter-aristocrats. Economic forces, in short, were the basis of party divisions in the period. Beard then went on to point out that, contrary to popular belief, the movement called Jeffersonian Democracy did not constitute an assault upon property or political privilege as such. It merely transferred political power from one socioeconomic group to another—the power shifted from the capitalist class to the agrarian masses. "Jeffersonian Democracy," wrote Beard, "simply meant the possession of the federal government by the agrarian masses led by an aristocracy of slave-owning planters, and the theoretical repudiation of the right to use the Government for the benefit of any capitalistic groups, fiscal, banking, or manufacturing."[5]

What were the consequences of this shift in political power, according to Beard? They were not as great, he claimed, as many Americans assumed. Beard, surprisingly enough, considered Jefferson something of a failure in this book. He noted that Jefferson as president made many concessions to the Federalists in his policies by perpetuating a number of aspects of the Hamiltonian economic system. Jefferson's mistrust of the "mobs of great cities" also resulted in a limitation of his democratic doctrine, Beard believed, because his plans failed to include the urban working classes. Moreover, Beard observed, Jefferson's ideas of political democracy did not differ greatly from those of the Federalists because he was just as anxious as they to guard against the "tyranny of majorities." Beard's book was actually something of a polemic addressed to his fellow Progressives and intended as a lesson in history from which they might draw a moral for their own day. He wanted to show them that Jefferson had not understood clearly the economic bases of politics and therefore had not gone far enough in supporting the forces of democracy against those of reaction and privilege. The first selection in this chapter is drawn from one of Beard's studies of the period.

Claude G. Bowers, whose work *Jefferson and Hamilton: The Struggle for Democracy in America* was published a decade after Beard's book, took a much more positive approach to Jeffersonian Democracy. To Bowers the conflict between Jefferson and Hamilton symbolized a clear-cut fight between the forces of democracy and aristocracy to determine nothing less than the future destiny of the nation. Viewing the protagonists in this light, Bowers portrayed the fierce struggle waged by the two men during the first crucial decade under the new Constitution. In Bowers's eyes, Jefferson was not a theoretician but a master politician who suc-

---

[5] Charles A. Beard, *Economic Origins of Jeffersonian Democracy* (New York, 1915), p. 467.

ceeded in marshaling the popular forces in America against the entrenched Federalist opposition. America, as the result of Jefferson's triumph, escaped the terrible fate that lay in store had the aristocratic forces under Hamilton maintained their power.

Bowers, a journalist for a Democratic newspaper at the time, wrote his biography in a popular style and from a present-minded point of view. From a literary perspective, the publication of his work was timely because it came on the eve of the centennial of Jefferson's death and the sesquicentennial of America's independence. But from a political viewpoint, his work was even more appropriate. The Democratic party was in the doldrums after the Wilsonian era and had split into warring factions. By reviving the image of Jefferson as the founder of the party and presenting a Democratic interpretation of the federal era, Bowers provided the politicians of his own day with a rallying point. In 1928 Bowers was named as keynote speaker of the Democratic National Convention and in eloquent phrases called upon his fellow Democrats to return to the principles of Jefferson. His writings and speeches on Jefferson helped to spark a revival of the Jeffersonian tradition in the popular imagination during the 1920s.

The climax in writing about Jefferson by the Progressive historians in the 1920s came with the publication of Vernon L. Parrington's three-volume work, *Main Currents in American Thought*. Parrington approached the nation's past in terms of intellectual history and looked upon American literature as the main form of expression employed by the nation's social and political thinkers. To Parrington the major current in American thought was the enduring dichotomy throughout the country's history between two rival political philosophies—the liberal and idealistic tradition of Jefferson and the conservative and materialistic one personified by Hamilton. Viewing all of American history in terms of a Jefferson-Hamilton dichotomy, Parrington proceeded to push his analogy backward into the colonial period and forward to the twentieth century. His overall view was that America's liberal tradition had been declining since Jefferson's day. But there was no question on which side his sympathies lay, for he admitted that his bias was "liberal rather than conservative, Jeffersonian rather than Federalistic."

Parrington believed that Jefferson symbolized a native American brand of liberalism that had arisen in the New World. American liberalism, as he saw it, was influenced by three separate strands of thought—French liberalism, English liberalism, and the democratizing influence of the frontier. French liberalism, or romantic and idealistic thought, resulted in egalitarianism; it rejected the Puritan idea of a degraded human nature and substituted instead the concept of man as a potentially perfectible being. English liberalism, or realistic and materialistic thought, looked upon human nature as being acquisitive; it called for a social and political philosophy to conform with capitalism rather than the rights of man. The American frontier, on the other hand, provided a free environment in which these often contradictory Old World philosophies could develop in a different way.

With the coming of the New Deal, the Jeffersonian tradition had an even greater appeal to the popular imagination. The Democratic party made a conscious effort during the Great Depression of the 1930s to revive Jeffersonian slogans and symbols to show that the proposed programs for the New Deal were in the American tradition. Among other things, the New Deal was pictured as a modern adaptation of long-standing Jeffersonian principles rather than any radical revision of the American system. Paradoxically, the opponents of the New Deal resorted to the same tradition for their arguments. They sought to show that Jeffersonianism in the past had defended liberty largely by abstaining from governmental restrictions and restraints.

The outbreak of World War II likewise proved a boon to the Jeffersonian tradition. In the struggle against totalitarianism there was a fight for men's minds, and democracy as a way of life became a faith to disseminate and defend. No other major American figure was better equipped to serve as a symbol of the democratic tradition than Jefferson, author of the Declaration of Independence. His ringing phrases were particularly relevant in the fight against totalitarianism being waged by the free world. Jefferson came into his own as never before as historians, journalists, and politicians sought to give renewed meaning to the liberal Jeffersonian tradition within an international as well as a national context.

In the post–World War II era the Jeffersonian tradition continued its popularity, but unlike earlier periods in American history the trend this time did not result in a decline of the Hamiltonian tradition. The Hamiltonian revival in the post–Civil War period had ground to a halt with the coming of the Progressive era. Although it was true that a small segment of Progressive historians praised Hamilton for his bold use of powers of the central government to achieve constructive national goals, the predominant view among scholars in the first three decades of the twentieth century favored the Jeffersonian tradition. Hamilton's reputation sank to its lowest point during the depression of the 1930s as the Republican party fell into disfavor. But from the late 1930s on, Hamilton's reputation was on the rise.

One of the first signs of the shift in Hamilton's favor was the publication of two perceptive articles on him by Rexford Guy Tugwell and Joseph Dorfman in the *Columbia University Quarterly* of 1937 and 1938. Tugwell, a member of Roosevelt's "brain trust" in the early days of the New Deal, was a vigorous advocate of government planning for bringing about reforms in the economic and social sphere. After leaving his government post, Tugwell coauthored two articles on Hamilton with Dorfman, a former colleague and professor of economics at Columbia University. In view of his recent experiences, Tugwell showed an increased appreciation of Hamilton's unprecedented use of strong national governmental powers to build up the new nation in its early years.

Developments during the decade of the 1940s continued the trend of a more favorable attitude toward Hamilton by historians. The booming American economy during the wartime and postwar period, no doubt, helped to enhance Hamilton's reputation. With the mounting affluence of American society, there was less tendency on the part of many historians to read an economic class conflict back into the American past, and Hamilton's economic program for shoring up the nation's economy in the 1790s and early 1800s came in for considerable praise in the post–World War II period.

At the same time, another side of Hamilton's career—his role as nation-maker—was being stressed anew. The decline of imperialism and the post–World War II settlement gave birth to a whole host of newly independent countries, and American historians came to view the problems involved in nation-building in a different perspective. There was a growing awareness of the great debt owed to Hamilton for helping to mold the foundations for a strong nation-state. Historians like Charles A. Beard, Louis M. Hacker, and Leonard D. White all touched upon Hamilton's contribution to statecraft in their writings in the 1940s.

The most important new tendency in the 1940s, however, was not the presentation of Hamilton in a more favorable light but rather the emergence of a more evenly balanced evaluation of the Hamiltonian-Jeffersonian dichotomy. This trend began with the approach taken by Richard Hofstadter in his book of essays, *The American Political Tradition and the Men Who Made It,* published in 1948. Hofstadter's essay on Jefferson de-emphasized the differences between the two men and stressed instead the continuance of Hamilton's system under Jefferson as president. The beliefs that Hamiltonians and Jeffersonians had in common, concluded Hofstadter, proved to be a more powerful bond in uniting them than the specific political issues that were dividing the two groups.

Hofstadter's thesis was that much of America's political past had to be viewed in terms of consensus rather than conflict. In studying the ideology of leading American statesmen such as Jefferson and Hamilton, he became convinced that there was a pressing need for reinterpreting our political traditions within a new framework—one that emphasized a common climate of opinion in America. The tendency of earlier historians to place political conflict in the foreground of American history, he claimed, had obscured the common areas of agreement among political leaders who were often pictured as antagonists. "However much at

odds on specific issues," Hofstadter wrote, "the major political traditions have shared a belief in the rights of property, the philosophy of
economic individualism, the value of competition; they have accepted
the economic virtues of capitalist culture as necessary qualities of man."[6]
The main theme of the federal era, according to Hofstadter, was the
essential agreement between Jefferson and Hamilton on these fundamental political traditions. This common area of agreement set the stage
for the assimilation of Jeffersonian Democracy into Hamiltonian
capitalism that took place after the election of 1800.

The consensus thesis characterized much of the writing on the federal era in the 1950s and 1960s. Louis Hartz, during the mid-1950s, for
example, identified the liberal tradition as being the one tradition forming the common climate of opinion in America.[7] The clash of principles
attributed to Hamilton and Jefferson represented nothing more than a
sham battle, Hartz said, because such controversy took place within the
confines of a liberal society whose values were already agreed upon.
There was no deep ideological split between the two men, and the
differences between them occurred within the Lockean liberal tradition
which all Americans accepted.

Although a conscious "school" of consensus historians writing about
the federal era cannot be identified as such, there was a noticeable trend
toward a more balanced assessment of the Hamiltonian-Jeffersonian
dichotomy among scholars in the post–World War II period. This tendency was evident in many general studies on the era. Marcus Cunliffe,
covering the years 1789–1837, warned readers not to view the period
solely in terms of a struggle between Hamiltonianism and Jeffersonianism and stressed instead a number of other forces in conflict—
urban versus rural areas, nationalism versus sectionalism, and conservatism versus experimentalism. A second general study, by John C.
Miller, dealing only with the period when the Federalist party was in
power—1789–1801—argued that out of the two extreme positions held
by Hamiltonians and Jeffersonians there had emerged a middle-of-the-
road approach that served the nation well in future years.[8]

This more balanced view was apparent also in many of the biographies written since World War II. Dumas Malone's multivolume work
on Jefferson, begun in the late 1940s, presented him in a more impartial
light than earlier works and stressed the consistency of his thought.

---

[6]Richard Hofstadter, *The American Political Tradition and the Men Who Made It* (New
York, 1948), p. viii.

[7]Louis Hartz, *The Liberal Tradition in America* (New York, 1955).

[8]Marcus F. Cunliffe, *The Nation Takes Shape, 1789–1837* (Chicago, 1959); John C. Miller,
*The Federalist Era, 1789–1801* (New York, 1960).

John Dos Passos and Nathan Schachner, who wrote studies and sketches of Jefferson in the 1950s, likewise avoided the pitfalls of violent partisanship in their writings.[9] Such portrayals led one Jeffersonian scholar, Merrill Peterson, to remark in the early 1960s that "Jefferson . . . appears less radical and more conservative, less theoretical and more practical, less universal and more national."[10] The one-volume biography of Hamilton by John C. Miller written in the late 1950s showed the same influence. Miller maintained that Hamilton's political thought was a curious blend of contradictions that made him more moderate than he was usually pictured.[11]

College textbooks published in the post–World War II period reflected this same shift in emphasis. Some saw a line of continuity from Federalists to Jeffersonian presidents—there was no "Revolution of 1800" and the election represented a change of men, not measures. Other texts treated the federal era in terms of intellectual history, claiming that the ideas of Hamilton, Jefferson, Adams, and Madison were all derived from the same source—the Enlightenment. Hence these founding fathers were pictured as sharing almost the same political philosophy and differing only in particulars. Still others de-emphasized the Hamilton-Jefferson split by arguing that the clash of political extremes in the 1790s quickly gave way to a more moderate and middle-of-the-road approach. At any rate the trend was unmistakingly moving away from the Hamiltonian-Jeffersonian dichotomy as an explanation of all American history.

There were many reasons for this de-emphasis by American historians of political conflict during the Federal era. In the Cold War era of the late 1940s and 1950s the need for strong national unity in the face of external threats from Communist countries abroad placed a greater premium on conformity and consensus among the American people. Some scholars responded to the felt needs of their own generation, either consciously or subconsciously, by stressing the consensus thesis in order to present the image of a strong and united America. Thus they read their own predilections back into the past and concluded that there was relatively little class strife in the federal era. Moreover, the trend toward intellectual history brought about a de-emphasis on class conflict. The editorial projects that brought forth definitive editions of the papers of Thomas Jefferson, Alexander Hamilton, John Adams, and James Madison in the 1950s and 1960s provided more primary sources

---

[9]Dumas Malone, *Jefferson and His Time*, 5 vols. to date (Boston, 1948–     ); John Dos Passos, *The Men Who Made the Nation* (New York, 1957); Nathan Schachner, *Thomas Jefferson: A Biography*, 2 vols. (New York, 1951).

[10]Peterson, *Jeffersonian Image in the American Mind*, p. 450.

[11]John C. Miller, *Alexander Hamilton: Portrait in Paradox* (New York, 1959).

on the founding fathers than ever before, and shed new light on the ideas current during the early national years. To many historians, the papers proved that these men were closer to one another in terms of political thought than they or their contemporaries believed, and that despite their differences there were broad areas of agreement among them. One conclusion was clear in this post–World War II development: never in American history did scholars seem to be closer to declaring a truce in the war that has raged between Hamiltonians and Jeffersonians over the past 175 years.

In the 1960s and 1970s, however, the general fragmentation of American history was reflected in the writing about political parties—a topic of increasing concern to recent scholars. These historians challenged the assumptions and conclusions of the Progressives and neoconservatives on many fronts by raising different questions and resorting to new strategies and techniques. One major challenge came from a group of scholars identified with the "new social history," the so-called "new political historians," who focused their attention on the social origins of political conflict and the bases of political parties. Another challenge came from the "new intellectual historians" who examined the ideas of the entire political culture of the new republic. Still other scholars used the comparative history approach to place the creation of the American party system within a broader context by comparing it with political parties developing in other cultures and periods. These new approaches to the study of politics during the early years of the republic tended to turn away from the Hamiltonian-Jeffersonian polarity that had characterized much of the earlier writing on this subject. They sometimes challenged also the consensus interpretation of the neoconservatives which stressed the continuities in the transition from Hamiltonianism to Jeffersonian Democracy.

The older Progressive interpretation, it will be recalled, tended to picture the origins and development of political parties in polarized terms.Parties were characterized by intense conflict which pitted antithetical forces in society against one another. Within this oversimplified dichotomous view the following forces were seen as arrayed against one another: upper versus lower classes; fluid capital versus agrarian interests; urban versus rural groups; creditors versus debtors; aristocrats versus democrats; and westerners versus easterners. Charles Beard, for example, had pictured the struggle of the 1790s as being between two interest groups—fluid capital and agrarian interests. These two groups, according to Beard, had clashed in the Constitutional Convention in the 1780s and continued to struggle in the party battles in the decade that followed. The overall tendency of the new approaches used in the 1960s and 1970s was to demonstrate that American political parties did not represent such polarities; they reflected instead pluralistic interests of a broad cross-section of society. Older generalizations based upon the presumed class, sectional, and ideological differences were shown to be inaccurate in numerous revisionist studies.

The most important challenge to the older interpretations came from the so-called "new political historians"—a group within the larger category of scholars called the "new social historians." Like many contemporary scholars, the "new political historians" resorted to concepts and models drawn from the other social sciences or relied upon newer methodological techniques such as quantification. Certain "new political historians" made an intensive effort to formulate more precise definitions of such terms as *political party* and *party system*. In general their work tended to be more empirical in nature, and they often utilized case studies to examine in detail the workings of a political party within a state, county, or community. The perspective of these scholars reflected in large part the influence of the behavioral approach to politics—an approach that had gained wider acceptance among political scientists after Charles Merriam and others wrote pioneering studies during the 1930s and 1940s.

To achieve a greater precision in their findings, some of these historians resorted to new quantitative techniques. Noble Cunningham used roll-call analyses, for example, to pinpoint the time when political parties first appeared within the Congress. Two articles—one by H. James Henderson and the other by Mary P. Ryan—employed even more sophisticated quantitative methods to identify voting blocs in the first Congresses. They concluded that it was probably in the third Congress that sectional voting blocs were transformed into a two-bloc system covering a broad spectrum of issues. Rudolph M. Bell made great use of computers to write the most comprehensive study of voting patterns within the Congresses of the 1790s.[12]

The "new political historians," for the most part, rejected the consensus interpretation of the neoconservatives and held that the early national period was characterized by conflict. At the same time, however, they disagreed with the older Progressive interpretation over the bases of that conflict. They took issue with the Beardian view that the politics of the era was a clear-cut struggle between agrarian Antifederalists, who had opposed the Constitution and a coalition of merchants, planters, and security-holders, who had favored the document. In their search for

---

[12]Noble E. Cunningham, Jr., *The Jeffersonian Republicans: The Formation of Party Organization, 1789–1801* (Chapel Hill, 1957) and *The Jeffersonians in Power, 1801–1809* (Chapel Hill, 1963). H. James Henderson, "Quantitative Approaches to Party Formation in the United States Congress," *William and Mary Quarterly*, 3d ser. 30 (1973):307–24; Mary P. Ryan, "Party Formation in the United States Congress 1789 to 1796: A Quantitative Analysis," *ibid.*, 28 (1971)523–42, and Rudolph M. Bell, *Party Faction in American Politics* (Westport, Conn., 1973).

the causes of conflict, the "new political historians" examined numerous economic and political groups on the local level and concluded that existing differences were based not on narrow economic grounds but rather upon broad symbolic social issues. They de-emphasized sectional and economic sources of conflict and stressed instead ethnocultural considerations—racial, ethnic, and religious ties—as well as ideological commitments and localized concerns.

The "new political historians" held that many conflicts arose from underlying antagonisms between social groups. Ethnic groups were aligned against each other, members of one religion were opposed to those of a different faith, and even groups with differing cultural traditions—in terms of their attitudes toward the Sabbath, drinking, and marriage customs—were pitted against one another. Such hatreds and feuds persisted over time, aroused group consciousness, and often determined the way people voted. Lee Benson, one of the early advocates of the behavioral approach to political history, for example, reexamined some of Beard's conclusions in such terms. He analyzed voting patterns in New York to determine the ethnic, religious and geographic sources of political conflict during the constitutional period. His conclusions suggested that ethnocultural considerations were probably more important than the economic forces Beard had stressed. Generally speaking, the most important conclusion of the "new political historians" was that conflict in the early national period reflected a complex set of issues that precluded Beard's simplistic polarities.[13]

One major question addressed by these scholars concerned the origin and development of political parties. Beard's *Economic Origins of Jeffersonian Democracy* had set the stage for such a debate; he claimed that the battle between Federalists and Republicans in the 1800 election was nothing more than a continuation of the alignment of Federalist and Antifederalist forces that had appeared during the struggle over the Constitution in 1787. Joseph Charles, in a book published in the 1950s, challenged the idea of party continuity. He concluded that parties had not originated in the fight over Hamilton's financial program, as many Beardian scholars had supported, but in differences over foreign policy such as the Jay treaty of 1795. Other historians, such as Noble Cunningham and Paul-Goodman, however, claimed that there was break in continuity because political groups were realigned in the 1790s as new issues arose.[14]

---

[13]Lee Benson, *Turner and Beard: American Historical Writing Reconsidered* (Glencoe, Illinois, 1960). For a sweeping interpretation of American political history from an ethnocultural perspective which touches upon this period, see Robert Kelley, "Ideology and Political Culture from Jefferson to Nixon," *American Historical Review* 82 (1977):531–82.

[14]Beard, *Economic Origins of Jeffersonian Democracy*; Joseph Charles, *Origins of the American Party System* (Williamsburg, 1956). Alfred Young, *Democratic Republicans of New York*

Another question these scholars argued was whether political parties had been formed from the bottom up or the top down. Noble Cunningham advanced the hypothesis that factions—a more primitive form of political organization—had developed into parties within the Congress and inside Washington's cabinet. Then, like a stone thrown into a pool, these parties radiated outward in waves from the capital into the states in 1794–1795. Leaders in the nation's capital, through the use of party organization and machinery, were able to link up with local elites and to create parties that became truly national in scope.[15]

Even as Cunningham's interpretation was being accepted in many quarters, two case studies appeared that showed localism was a very powerful political determinant in Massachusetts and New York. Both studies underscored the fact that parties had arisen in response to local conditions and concerns. Implicit in these works was the assumption that the parties in these states had been formed from the bottom up rather than the top down.[16]

The two case studies—written by Paul Goodman and Alfred Young on the Democratic Republicans of Massachusetts and New York respectively—inquired also into the social backgrounds of party members. Goodman took issue with the polarized Progressive view of parties and concluded that "the social sources of parties were far more complex and less homogeneous than Beard suggested."[17] Massachusetts Republicans, he found, represented a heterogenous coalition of far-flung interests which cut across the more conventional lines of sectional, economic, and occupational groupings. Included among the Republicans were rich and poor, land speculators and squatters, professional persons and artisans, and Deists and Calvinists. The one bond that united these diverse groups was the widespread belief that persons long entrenched in positions of authority were blocking the advance of more capable people who were out of power. Thus, the Massachusetts Republicans tended to

---

(Chapel Hill, 1967) and Norman K. Risjord, "The Evolution of Political Parties in Virginia, 1782–1800," *Journal of American History* 60 (1974):961–84 agree with Beard that there was continuity in the groups who lined up for and against the Constitution and those who became Federalists and Jeffersonians. Noble Cunningham, in his *Jeffersonian Republicans: The Formation of Party Organization, 1789–1801*, and Paul Goodman, *Democratic-Republicans of Massachusetts* (Cambridge, 1964) argue that there was a break in continuity because political groups realigned themselves in the 1790s as new sets of issues appeared on the scene. The discussion of party development which follows draws heavily on the article by Ronald P. Formisano, "Deferential-Participant Politics: The Early Republic's Political Culture, 1789–1840," *American Political Science Review* 68 (1974):473–87.

[15]Cunningham, *The Jeffersonian Republicans: The Formation of Party Organization, 1789–1801*. See also, Manning Dauer, *The Adams Federalists*, 2d ed., 1953 (Baltimore, 1953).

[16]Goodman, *Democratic-Republicans of Massachusetts;* Young, *Democratic Republicans of New York.*

[17]Goodman, *Democratic-Republicans of Massachusetts*, p. xi.

attract newcomers, men on-the-make, and outsiders. An excerpt from Goodman's book is the second selection in this chapter.

Young's book inquired into the social sources of the Republican party in New York and also discovered complex pluralistic forces at work. Young agreed with Beard on one crucial point: there was considerable continuity between the New York Antifederalists and those who subsequently became Republicans in the 1790s, and that both reflected mainly the agrarian interests. But Young proved also there was an important urban wing to the Republican party located in New York City— one based primarily upon mechanics, or skilled workers. He went on to show that the Republicans succeeded precisely because they were the first to recognize the power of the common people and to take steps to mobilize that segment of the electorate.

Another "new political historian," David Hackett Fischer, challenged the Beardian interpretation of politics in the early national period from a different perspective. Fischer produced the most important book on the Federalists during this era. Focusing on the Federalists in the years 1800 to 1816, he concluded that the country had undergone a "revolution of American conservatism." Conservative Federalist leaders experienced a revolution in attitudes and beliefs before and after the election of 1800. Before 1800 Federalist leaders were members of the "Old School"— those who had led the movement for American independence, subscribed firmly to the idea of deference, and insisted upon "standing" for office. After the defeat of 1800, these leaders were replaced by "young Federalists" who revolutionized the party. The younger Federalists proved to be more flexible in their political principles. They were willing to suppress their preference for a deferential society, to "run" for office, and to borrow the political tactics of their Jeffersonian opponents to organize and seek votes from the masses. Fischer's study, like those of Goodman and Young, sought also to identify the social sources that affected the composition of the political parties in the new nation.[18]

A second challenge to the older interpretations of politics in the early national period came from the "new intellectual historians." These scholars concentrated on the ideas influencing the development of political parties and the American party system. They focused primarily upon the thinking of American leaders concerning political parties and the concept of a loyal opposition. One theme that intrigued scholars was the seeming paradox between the thought and practice of the founding fathers regarding the rise of political parties. On the one hand, Federalists and Jeffersonians took a public stance in the crisis-ridden 1790s that opposed the formation of any parties since they seemed to

---

[18]David Hackett Fischer, *The Revolution of American Conservatism* (New York, 1965).

pose a threat to the body politic. On the other, politicians went to work furiously to establish party organizations almost as soon as the new national government was founded.

Richard Hofstadter, in *The Idea of a Party System*, dealt with the shift in attitude toward political parties by both Federalist and Jeffersonian leaders. Although strong antiparty feelings prevailed during the time of the Constitution, many men who had previously resisted the idea of parties participated in the formation of America's first party system. In Hofstadter's words, these men became "antiparty party builders." After the election of 1800, the American party system presented the world with a shining example of the peaceful transfer of governmental power from one popularly elected party to another. Even after the election, however, the concept of a legitimate political opposition failed to take hold in the United States. General acceptance of the idea of a legitimate loyal opposition, Hofstadter argued, did not occur until much later, in the period of Andrew Jackson. [19]

Other "new intellectual historians" tackled the problem from a different vantage point by seeking to show how public opinion and attitudes influenced the shaping of the first party system. Richard Buel, in *Securing the Revolution*, demonstrated that ideological differences in accounting for public opinion while formulating government policy was a basic issue that separated the Federalists from Republicans. He argued, moreover, that the success of the Republicans during this period was rooted in their acceptance of the role of public opinion in the decision-making process. [20]

Certain of these scholars focused on the ideology of only a single party. Federalist ideology was analyzed in a state study by James M. Banner, Jr., who traced the sources of Massachusetts Federalist thought back to the late eighteenth century. Banner concluded that this ideology arose in the Bay State after the Revolution in response to new disruptive forces set loose by that cataclysmic event. Massachusetts Federalists continued to share these same concerns down to the Hartford Convention of 1814. Frustrated by a series of setbacks—the declining influence of New England, the Embargo Acts which ruined commerce, the political success of the Jeffersonians, and the badly managed War of 1812—the Federalists called the Hartford Convention. Fortunately the more moderate elements of the party in the state dominated the convention, thereby preventing the more extremist wing from following a course

---

[19]Richard Hofstadter, *The Idea of a Party System: The Rise of Legitimate Opposition in the United States, 1780–1840* (Berkeley, 1969).

[20]Richard Buel, Jr., *Securing the Revolution: Ideology in American Politics, 1789–1815* (Ithaca, 1972).

of secession. Banner argued that ideological concerns linked the Revolution to subsequent developments in party politics in Massachusetts.[21]

Lance Banning did for Jeffersonian ideology within the country at large what Banner had done for the Massachusetts Federalists. Banning's book, however, traced the antecedents or what he called "the Jeffersonian persuasion" back to British roots. Jeffersonian thought, Banning argued, was an American version of the ideology developed by British opposition politicians in the eighteenth century. This ideology encompassed a theory of mixed government whose balance was designed to preserve both liberty and authority. Involved in this creed were certain significant ideas—the separation of powers, the balancing of social interests, and the principle of a stake-in-society to qualify persons for voting and office-holding—which Jeffersonians transformed to fit the needs of the new republic. Within the American scheme of things, this ideology called for a strict construction of the Constitution, and thereby helped to keep party conflict within reasonable bounds. At the same time, the Jeffersonian persuasion warned that liberty and the fruits of the Revolution were under constant danger from schemes to undermine the Constitution and the social structure upon which liberty was based. Within this context, Republicans viewed many Federalist policies as part of a conspiracy to destroy liberty. After the Republicans came to power in 1800, this ideology of opposition continued to play an important role in shaping their policies.[22]

A third challenge to older interpretations of the early national period came from the comparative history approach employed by some scholars to place the development of the American party system within an international perspective. The studies of Seymour M. Lipset and William N. Chambers, for example, compared the political experiences of the infant American republic in the late eighteenth century with those of the newly emerging nations in Africa and Asia during the mid-twentieth century. Lipset, a political sociologist using a multidisciplinary approach, pointed out certain important parallel developments. He compared the turbulent 1790s when the Federalist party was in office and seeking to legitimize the new national system of authority through the charismatic power of George Washington with the turmoil experienced by the newly independent African country of Ghana in the 1950s. Like the United States, Ghana sought to achieve some semblance of legitimacy for the new regime through the person of a charismatic leader—Kwame Nkrumah.[23]

---

[21]James Banner, *To the Hartford Convention* (New York, 1970).

[22]Lance Banning, *The Jeffersonian Persuasion* (Ithaca, 1978).

[23]Seymour M. Lipset, *The First New Nation* (New York, 1963).

Scholars such as Chambers dealt with the issue of political party development within a comparative perspective by introducing a new concept—the idea of a "party system." This concept presupposed the existence of a competitive two-party system in America and assumed that political developments arose from the pattern of rivalry between competing groups. It was, in short, the symbiotic relationship between the two parties rather than the parties themselves which determined political events. The concept of a party system was developed best in *Political Parties in a New Nation,* and Chambers concluded that America had invented the first modern political parties in world history. He went on to suggest that this American "invention" of the late eighteenth century provided a useful model for the new nations that had come into being in Africa and Asia during the 1960s. This book, besides its important thesis, was significant for its methodology which resorted to a social science approach and employed concepts used by political scientists.[24]

Robert R. Palmer, on the other hand, set the process of America's party development in a worldwide context—within an "age of democratic revolution" that affected much of Western civilization at the close of the eighteenth century. Americans, it should be remembered, had created their republic at a time when nearly all countries in Europe were ruled by monarchs. When the French, following the American example, overthrew their king and established a republic, everyone in the United States rejoiced. But for many Americans that joy was short-lived when the French Revolution entered upon a reign of terror where persons were killed and property confiscated. America was soon divided into two camps—those who favored the French Revolution because France represented a sister republic, and those who opposed it for fear that foreign terrorism might spread to the United States. When France and England went to war in 1793, the cleavage within the United States widened. The Federalists in power sympathized with England, and their Jeffersonian opponents sided with France. Party lines became even sharper after Washington signed Jay's Treaty—a move that was viewed as being pro-British. Palmer's work assessed the impact of the French Revolution on American politics, evaluated its effect on party development, and viewed the process of democratization from a comparative perspective that covered both sides of the Atlantic.[25]

All three major challenges to the older interpretations were revisionist. Some were characterized by the increased use of social science concepts such as intergroup conflict, status anxiety, reference group theory, the part played by the subconscious, social mobility, the roles of

---

[24]William N. Chambers, *Political Parties in a New Nation* (New York, 1963).

[25]Robert R. Palmer, *The Age of Democratic Revolution,* 2 vols. (Princeton, 1959 and 1964).

leaders and followers in the political process, microanalysis and mac-roanalysis. Others resorted to quantitative techniques to measure in a more precise manner the group behavior of various elements in society. In the questions they raised and the conclusions they reached, recent scholars were moving away from the Hamiltonian-Jeffersonian polarity that had dominated the field for so long.

A host of new questions have been raised about the four decades between 1789 and 1829. To what degree was the older polarized Pro-gressive view of the period correct? To what degree were the neoconser-vative historians right in their assumption that the Federalists and Jeffer-sonians were close to agreement on fundamental issues? What were the social origins of political conflict during the period? Were the "new social historians" too intent upon stressing social conflict as the major explana-tion for political change? Were the "new political historians" on the right track in focusing upon the development political parties and the rise of the first party system? These are only a few of the questions which must be answered before one can decide whether the period can be under-stood more fully than in terms of a symbolic conflict between Hamil-tonianism and Jeffersonianism.

# Charles A. Beard

CHARLES A. BEARD (1874–1948) was one of the most influential American historians of the first half of the twentieth century. He taught at Columbia University until 1917, and then left teaching for research and writing. Beard wrote more than a dozen books, including (with his wife Mary R. Beard) *The Rise of American Civilization* (1927).

It is customary to separate American political history into three periods, using changes in party names as the basis of the division. According to this scheme, there have been three great party alignments since the formation of the Constitution: Federalists against Republicans (1789–1816), Whigs against Democrats (1830–1856), and Republicans against Democrats (1856 to the present time). Although the dates are merely approximate, they furnish useful chronological clues.

But this division is arbitrary and only for convenience. In fact, there has been no sharp break in the sources of party strength, in policy, or in opinion. On the contrary, these three alignments have been merely phases of one unbroken conflict originating in the age of George Washington and continuing without interruption to our own time.

## Federalist Measures

The first of these alignments—Federalists against Republicans—was connected more or less directly with the contest over the framing and adoption of the federal Constitution.

Authorities are generally agreed that the main support for the Constitution came from merchants, manufacturers, government bond holders, and other people of substantial property interests "along the line of the seaboard towns and populous regions." They are likewise agreed that the opposition came mainly from the inland farmers, debtors, and less prosperous sections of the country.

The feelings aroused by the contest over the Constitution had not disappeared when the first administration was organized in 1789 with Washington as president and friends of the new system installed in all branches of the government—executive, legislative, and judicial. With Alexander Hamilton, first Secretary of the Treasury, in the lead, the advocates of the new order, soon to be known as Federalists, carried through a series of economic measures which in time divided the country into two powerful parties. In summary form, these measures were as follows:

1. The funding of the national debt. All the old bonds, certificates, and other evidences of indebtedness issued by the Continental Congress during the Revolution were called in and new bonds for face value given to the holders.
2. The assumption of the revolutionary debts of the states. The federal government also called in the revolutionary debts of the states and issued new federal bonds instead; that is, the federal government assumed the obligations of the states and added them to the general debt of the nation.

    These two operations, funding and assumption, deeply affected the purses of classes and masses. Before Hamilton began his work, the old bonds and notes issued during the Revolution had been selling at from ten to twenty cents on the dollar, because the national government and several states had failed to meet their obligations. During the dark days of uncertainty, a large part of this paper had been bought by speculators from the original holders at low prices with a view to profit taking. In the end, funding and assumption increased the value of the depreciated securities to the amount of approximately $40 million—a huge sum for those days. To raise the money to pay the interest on the debt, the federal government had to lay heavy taxes on the people, most of whom were farmers, not bondholders.
3. Protective tariff. The third measure on the Federalist program was the protection of American industries by the imposition of customs duties on imports coming into competition with American products. Hamilton openly favored an elaborate system of protection. Although his plans were not adopted in full, the first revenue bill passed in 1789 was mildly protective and, in time, other protective features were added.
4. The United States Bank. Under Hamilton's leadership, Congress chartered a banking corporation, authorized it to raise a large capital composed, three-fourths, of new federal bonds, and empowered it to issue currency and do a general banking business.
5. A sound national currency. Under the new Constitution, the states had to stop issuing paper money. The gold and silver coin of the United States now provided by law became the money of the country, with the notes of the United States Bank circulating on a parity.
6. Discrimination in favor of American shipping. To encourage the construction of an American merchant marine, Congress provided that the tonnage duties on foreign-built and foreign-owned ships should be five times as high as the duties on American ships. In line with this, other concessions were made to native shipping, especially that engaged in the China trade.
7. National defense. In creating a navy and a standing army, Congress had

more in mind than the mere defense of the country against foreign foes. The navy was useful in protecting commerce on the high seas and the army in suppressing uprisings such as had occurred in Massachusetts in 1786. In other words, economic factors as well as patriotism were involved in the process.

8. Foreign affairs. When the wars of the French Revolution broke out in Europe, the Washington administration, largely inspired by Hamilton, frankly sympathized with England as against France and looked on the contest in the Old World as a conflict between property and order on the one side and democracy and anarchy on the other—akin in fact to the political dispute at home.

## The Rise of Opposition

Now these measures were not excursions in theory. They were acts of power involving the pocketbooks of groups, affecting the distribution of wealth and the weight of classes in politics. Certainly the first six of them bore directly upon the economic interests of the citizens.

Under these laws, large sums of money were paid to the holders of government bonds who had been receiving little or nothing; people who were moderately well off one day found themselves rich the next. Under these laws, stockholders in the United States Bank earned handsome profits on their investment; protected manufacturers entered upon a period of prosperity; and merchants and moneylenders were enabled, by the sound currency system and adequate judicial assistance, to carry on their operations safely in all parts of the country. Under these laws, heavy taxes were collected to pay the interest on the bonds and to maintain the new government.

Were these things done for beneficiaries at the expense of other classes, notably the farmers, or did the increased production caused by the operations more than cover the cost? On this point economists disagree and the historian cannot answer the question mathematically.

At all events, however, a considerable portion of the American people came to the conclusion that the Federalist measures and policies above enumerated in fact transferred money to investors, merchants, manufacturers, and the capitalistic interests in general, at the expense of the masses—a majority of whom were farmers and planters. "This plan of a National Bank is calculated to benefit a small part of the United States, the mercantile interest only; the farmers, the yeomanry, will derive no advantage from it," complained a member of Congress from Georgia. The protective tariff on steel will operate "as an oppressive, though indirect, tax upon agriculture," lamented a congressman from Virginia. "The funding system was intended to effect what the Bank was contrived to accelerate: 1. Accumulation of great wealth in a few hands. 2. A political moneyed engine," protested another Virginia statesman.

In time, the citizens who took this view of the Hamiltonian program were marshaled, first as Antifederalists and later as Republicans, under the leadership of Thomas Jefferson, who was by occupation and opinion well fitted for his mission. A planter, Jefferson was acquainted with the interests of agriculture. Moreover, he believed and said openly that "cultivators of the earth are the most valuable citizens. They are the most vigorous, the most independent, the most virtuous, and they are tied to their country and wedded to its liberty and interests by the most lasting bonds." In logical relation, he had a low opinion of commerce and industry, which created urban masses. "The mobs of great cities," he asserted, "add just so much to the support of pure government as sores do to the strength of the human body."

Holding such opinions, Jefferson set out to enlist a large following in his struggle against the capitalistic measures of Hamilton. He made his strongest appeal directly to the agriculturalists of the country. And when his party was fully organized he took pride in saying that "the whole landed interest is republican," that is, lined up on his side of the contest.

Speaking of the Federalists arrayed against him on the other side, Jefferson said that they included all the federal office holders, "all who want to be officers, all timid men who prefer the calm of despotism to the boisterous sea of liberty, British merchants and Americans trading on British capitals, speculators and holders in the banks and public funds, a contrivance invented for the purposes of corruption."

Appealing to the farmers and the masses in general against the larger capitalistic interests, Jefferson's party inevitably took a popular, that is, a democratic turn. This was in keeping with his theories, for he thought that kings, clergy, nobles, and other ruling classes of Europe had filled their countries with poverty and misery and kept the world in turmoil with useless wars. The common people, he reasoned, if given liberty and let alone, would be happier under their own government than under any ruling class.

To their economic arguments, the Jeffersonians added a constitutional theory. They declared that the Constitution did not give Congress the power to charter a bank, provide protection for manufacturers, and pass certain other measures sponsored by the Federalists. This was a "strict contruction" of the Constitution; that is, the powers of Congress were to be interpreted narrowly and the rights of the states liberally. Although the Federalists included in their ranks most of the leading men who had made the Constitution, they were thus accused of violating the very fundamental law which they had conceived and adopted. In this way, arose the wordy battle over the "true meaning" of the Constitution and the "rights of states" which occupies such a large place in the history of American political loquacity.

To the disputes over domestic questions were added differences of opinion about foreign policies. In the very spring in which Washington was inaugurated with such acclaim, the Estates General met at Versailles and opened the first scene in the great drama of the French Revolution; in 1791 a new constitution was put into effect and the power of the king was practically destroyed; the next year the first French republic was established; in 1793 Louis XVI was executed, and war was declared on England. These events were watched with deep interest by American citizens.

The more radical elements of the population, fresh from their own triumph over George III, remembered with satisfaction the execution of Charles I by their ancestors, and took advantage of the occasion to rejoice in the death of another ruler—the French monarch. A climax came in 1793, when France called on the United States to fulfill the terms of the treaty of 1778, in return for the assistance which had been given to the Americans in their struggle with England. The radicals wanted to aid France, either openly or secretly, in her war on England, but Washington and his conservative supporters refused to be drawn into the European controversy. So the Americans were divided into contending groups over foreign policy, and the division ran in the main along the line already cut by the Federalist-Republican contest over domestic questions.

## The Federalist-Republican Battle

As the critics of the administration, known at first as Antifederalists, slowly changed from a mere opposition group into a regular party and took on the name Republican, the friends of the administration with Hamilton, John Jay, and John Adams in the lead, began to organize for political warfare under the banner of federalism. In the third presidential election, the party alignment was complete. Jefferson, the leader of the Republicans, was roundly denounced as an atheist and leveler; while Adams, the Federalist candidate, was condemned by his opponents as "the monarchist." So sharply drawn was the contest that Adams was chosen by the narrow margin of three electoral votes.

During Adams's administration, the Federalist party was thoroughly discredited. The Republican newspapers heaped indiscriminate abuse upon the head of the president and the Federalists generally. As a result Congress pushed through the Alien and Sedition acts—the first authorizing the president to expel certain aliens deemed dangerous to the safety and peace of the country, and the second making the publication of attacks on any branch of the federal government a crime.

Under the Sedition Act, many Republicans were severely punished for trivial criticisms of the administration. For example, Callender, a friend of Jefferson's, was convicted for saying, among other things: "Mr. Adams has only completed the scene of ignominy which Mr. Washington began." In letter and spirit the act seemed contrary to the amendment to the federal Constitution guaranteeing freedom of press and speech against federal interference. At all events, the two laws called forth the famous Kentucky and Virginia Resolutions, and convinced even those moderately inclined toward democracy that federalism meant the establishment of political tyranny. The death knell of the Federalist party was rung. Jefferson was elected in 1800 by a substantial majority over the Federalist candidate.

It has been the fashion to ascribe to the Federalists a political philosophy born of innate ill-will for the people. "Your people, sir," Hamilton is supposed to have said, "is a great beast"—as if in a burst of petulance.

Now this imputation is not entirely just. No doubt some of the emotions to which Federalists gave free vent were the feelings common to persons of large property—feelings of superiority and virtue. But there were practical grounds for distrusting "the people." Throughout the Revolution "the lower orders" had given trouble to the right wing of patriotism, threatening to upset the new ship of state before it was launched. Indeed, some blood had been shed in conflicts among the patriots themselves before independence was won.

To the Tories who remained in America and rallied to the Federalist cause, the masses were, of course, contemptible in opinion and conduct. In the eyes of the patriots of the right, the new democracy was responsible for the failure to pay the interest on the national and state debts between 1783 and 1789, for the refusal to grant aid and protection to American industry, for the uprising against the "rich and well-born" in Massachusetts in 1786, and for sundry other disturbances in the body politic. When, therefore, Federalists cursed the people—as they did in gross and in detail—they were not merely expressing a conservative temper. Rather were they reasoning, so they thought, from experience, bitter realistic experience at that.

# Paul Goodman

PAUL GOODMAN (1934–     ) is professor of history at the University of California at Davis. He has edited several books and written a number of articles and *The Democratic-Republicans of Massachusetts* (1964).

Although political parties have come to play a vital role in the conduct of American democracy, providing an orderly means of managing public affairs and offering the citizenry alternative programs and leadership sensitive to the varied interests of a diverse electorate, they are not as old as the Republic. The revolutionary generation did not inherit these formalized institutions for decision making, nor did they create them overnight upon gaining independence. Rather they evolved slowly and hesitatingly from experiences in the young Republic which led Americans to seek new modes of governance better suited to the needs of postrevolutionary society than those with which they were familiar.

Historians have not always thought so. Over half a century ago, Charles A. Beard propounded an influential interpretation of American history which located the origins of political parties in continuing conflicts between the poor and the rich, farmers and merchants, debtors and creditors, owners of real wealth and paper wealth. The sources of these rivalries, he argued, went back into the colonial past, accounted for divisions in the revolutionary era, persisted into the national period, and formed the binding thread that ran all through the fabric of American experience.

The Federalist and Democratic-Republican parties that emerged in the 1790s were thus not new formations but essentially the "conservative" and "radical" elements in American society that had split over independence and then continued to struggle for control of the new state and national authorities. The conservatives, comprising the wealthy, aristocratic elements, united to resist the humbler citizenry, who saw the Revolution as an opportunity to realize ambitions long thwarted during generations of British rule. Not always able to resist democratic pressures during the Revolution that weakened their grip on local government, conservatives favored creation of a powerful central government to protect the interests of birth and wealth. While the Confederation disappointed their expectations, it did not dampen their nationalism. For over a decade they labored tirelessly to strengthen national authority and curb state power. Success finally came in 1789.

The adoption of the Constitution, Beard argued, was a triumph for conservative personalty interests over the radical, agrarian groups that had opposed ratification as a threat to democratic rule. The victory of the proconstitutionalists made control of the new national government a central political issue during the next decade as those who had fought ratification became Republicans and their opponents Federalists. For a decade Federalists prevailed, governing in the interests of merchants and security holders, bankers and manufacturers, and those hostile to the claims of the democratic yeomanry. After a decade of Federalist rule, an aggrieved husbandry, organized within the Republican party and skillfully marshaled by Jefferson and Madison, recaptured the Republic from the "paper aristocracy." The "Revolution of 1800" transferred power from one social group to another, for the triumph of Jeffersonian Democracy, Beard explained in *Economic Origins of Jeffersonian Democracy*, "meant the possession of the federal government by the agrarian masses led by an aristocracy of slaveowning planters, and the theoretical repudiation of the right to use the Government for the benefit of any capitalistic groups, fiscal, banking, or manufacturing."

The present study challenges the validity of Beard's thesis for Massachusetts and questions the assumptions upon which it rests. The social sources of party were far more complex and less homogenous than Beard suggested." Bay State Republicans did not seek to oust capitalist classes in favor of agrarian masses but rather united a diverse coalition of urban and rural folk, merchants and farmers, artisans and professionals, speculators and squatters, deists and Calvinists. These groups made common cause against entrenched interests, usually Federalists, who thwarted the desires of newcomers and outsiders, rising merchants and ambitious office seekers, religious dissenters and landless yeomen eager to share access to authority and to broaden social opportunities.

Moreover, the evolution of Massachusetts Republicanism was neither the outgrowth of earlier conflicts in colony and Commonwealth, nor part of a fixed partisan alignment that Beard thought punctuated the entire course of American history. Yet while the parties were genuine innovations of the 1790s, responsive to the pressures and tensions of that decade, they were not full-scale models of the modern party system. Although they did look forward to the political institutions of a later age, they still retained links with experiences in the colonial past.

By focusing primarily on national politics and on the great events and personalities at the center of the Union, and by assuming fixed continuities in political history, historians have often read the present into the past. The first parties were loose and unstable collections of local forces. Innovative and unique, they lacked deep roots in tradition and experienced great difficulty overcoming the parochialism and fluidity of American society, which retarded the permanent polarization of the electorate into stable, competitive groupings. Differing from earlier and later political formations, the precise nature of the first parties was shaped by the postrevolutionary society in which they evolved. . . .

Party growth was painfully slow. The emergence of two rival groups at the national captial did not suddenly divide the rest of the country. Gradually, competitive parties evolved and by 1800 were spreading across the commonwealth, penetrating sparsely settled areas in Maine, bustling commercial towns along the coast, and quiet rural hamlets in the interior. The Democratic-Republican formation was a heterogeneous coalition of interests which cut across regional, economic, occupational, and religious lines. The party attracted persons alienated from established authority, convinced that those long entrenched in positions of influence blocked the advancement of worthy and ambitious though less favored citizens.

The party builders were not primarily national statesmen directing affairs from Philadelphia or professional politicians operating from Boston. Unlike later professional party leaders, they were generally ambitious merchants, tradesmen, capitalists, speculators, ministers, and office seekers who formed an interest and mobilized relatives, friends, acquaintances, and dependents to oppose those in power. As they fought for influence, they tried to swell the party showing at the polls by mustering wide support in the community. By linking together a varied collection of leaders and championing a broad spectrum of dissatisfied elements, the Republican party in Massachusetts formed a powerful alliance whose importance steadily mounted after 1800.

The common bond that united Republican Berkshire farmers with Salem merchants and rural Calvinists with urban rationalists was an interpretation of postrevolutionary experience. More than any other event, the French Revolution defined the content and style of politics. More than any other act, the Jay Treaty influenced the development of party. A strange and unreal debate developed in the 1790s which pictured two hostile groups, each dedicated to undermining the established order. Both linked their vision to the future and their understanding of the present with events abroad.

The general sympathy for France did not last much past 1793. As the Revolution turned radical and as war in Europe clouded the prospects of American neutrality, disillusionment spread. But many Americans did not lose faith. Those who became Republicans identified the cause of

France with the cause of popular government everywhere. Britain's assault on Franco-American trade and her attempts to suppress enlightenment in Europe roused latent but highly nationalistic, anti-English emotions. If the French were defeated, Republicans believed, England would tyrannize the oceans and undermine American independence. The Jay Treaty confirmed fears that some groups at home, hostile to republican institutions, were anxious to tie the United States to the Tory kingdom. The treaty was "pregnant with Evil," Governor Adams said, not simply because it sacrificed commercial interests, but because "it may restore to Great Britain such an influence over the Government and People of this Country, as may not be consistent with the general welfare." To Republicans the treaty meant abandoning neutrality, jeopardizing friendly relations with France, and becoming utterly dependent on Britain. Rejecting economic imperatives which drove many to accept the treaty, Republicans depicted their opponents as aristocrats bent on subverting the Republic. To defend the cause of republicanism at home and abroad, citizens formed societies in Boston, Portland, and throughout the nation.

The appearance of these organizations aroused deep suspicion because they resembled the feared Jacobin clubs of France, which had seized control and engulfed the nation in a blood bath. The Republican societies might be the vanguard of a movement to subvert established authority and remake America in the image of France, where the mob ruled and distinctions of rank and wealth vanished.

A harsh and divisive dialogue pervaded the political atmosphere. Men argued not over means but over ultimate ends. Republicans pictured their antagonists as aristocrats, British agents, former Tories, and refugees; Federalists characterized their adversaries as levelers, Jacobins, and anarchists dedicated to upsetting the settlement of 1789. Each condemned the other for placing enthusiasm for a foreign power over loyalty to the Union. Both images were unreal, bearing but a faint connection with the inclinations of either group. Yet they rested on a semblance of truth, because extremists on both sides lent substance at times to the parties' images of the other.

More important, however, the dominant elements in both parties were loyal to the arrangement of 1789. Republicans praised the French Revolution but would never accept political theory or practice that violated traditional notions of constitutionalism. Jeffersonians did not relish the violence of revolutionary change abroad and had no plans to alter the distribution of wealth or to remodel the social structure at home. Most Federalists were similarly devoted to preserving the settled order. They became hostile to the Revolution because they believed the French had rejected the politics of balance and overturned established authority without stabilizing a new one. Except for some highly placed extremists, however, few Federalists had serious intentions of recasting America in the image of Britain. The party had its share of old patriots who regarded England primarily as the major bulwark against the spread of Gallic influence and the key to the nation's economic health.

Paradoxically, while both parties were committed to the existing polity, disagreement appeared more fundamental, the political dialogue more intemperate, and the possibilities of compromise seemingly fewer than in almost any other period of American history. The roots of this conflict are to be found in the unstable and dynamic character of post-revolutionary American society.

*The Republican Leadership.* Eighteenth century Massachusetts was neither a pure democracy where the people ruled directly nor a closed preserve dominated by a hereditary elite. From the earliest days, political power dispersed and fell into the hands of clusters of local groups. Ambitious and rising newcomers were able to gain access to office and enter the local gentry, becoming the judges, justices of the peace, tax assessors, sheriffs, ministers, lawyers, doctors, and traders who constituted the ruling elite. Though farmers and artisans were usually content to let men of substance guide the community, many could vote, demand justice, turn out an old representative, and attach themselves to factions eager to challenge long-entrenched interests. But generally officials expected and enjoyed popular acquiescence.

The Revolution did not tear apart the social fabric. In many towns the county leaders were patriots, and little displacement occurred, while in other communities Tories fled or retired from public life and old-line families made way for the new. The war opened numerous opportunities for men in the lower ranks of the gentry to gain prominence and improve their positions through military service, politics, and trade. Thus continuity and change were both part of the revolutionary experience. While the war did not cause the wholesale displacement of one group by another, it did alter the social structure, creating opportunities for many who lacked the wealth, family, or experience that characterized the older elites. As untrained and inexperienced men appeared on the scene competing for recognition, it was no longer as clear as it once had been who was entitled to lead. Moreover, even as the governing groups settled down and became better defined, they faced unprecedented problems: wartime economic dislocation, constitutional changes, and the formation of a viable union in place of the Confederation.

Two great crises followed the Revolution—Shays's Rebellion and the debate over ratification. Twice citizens challenged traditional leadership, but the threats to the social order proved brief and not entirely successful. By 1790 Massachusetts and the nation had moved fast and far toward mastering discontent and pacifying the unruly. Confronting armed hostility, the judges and militia leaders, doctors and lawyers, merchants and capitalists, newcomers and oldtimers, stood united against disorder. The conflict over the Constitution, however, was less clear-cut, though most of the gentry finally favored ratification.

But the unity of the 1780s did not last, because the social order was unstable. While the Revolution created new opportunities, it also weakened the traditional lines of authority. Groups who themselves had but recently arrived lacked the force of tradition and custom to buttress their position. Moreover social mobility—the openness of professions, the varied chances in trade, the creation of new communities requiring leadership, and the rise in older communities of newcomers aspiring to prominence—left persistent sources of tension. In this social context, two rival groups in the 1790s competed to guide the commonwealth's future.

Men's positions in the social structure shaped their responses to the events of the decade. Those most securely established in local office, trade, and finance, those controlling the seats of authority in church and state, came to view the French Revolution with horror. Fearing that involvement would undermine prosperity, they also believed that the spread of French doctrine threatened the social order. They recoiled from Jacobinism, clung to the protection of a British alliance, and attempted to uproot subversion at home. Well-placed individuals such as the judges, justices, probate officers, county treasurers, sheriffs, the complex array of entrenched officials together with the older county families and their professional and mercantile allies, led the Federalist party.

The sources of Republican leadership were different. The party attracted persons either outside the elite or enjoying a recently acquired and insecure position in local society. They were often new men who came from rising families that had been excluded from the highest levels of influence and standing. Frequently men of substance in their own communities, they desired but lacked countywide influence, and unlike some of the newly arrived had not gained a firm position in the social order. Rising from obscurity or modest circumstances, they identified revolution and republicanism at home and abroad with opportunity. The French had uprooted privilege, destroyed ecclesiastical and monarchic establishments, and had given power to those who had been excluded for centuries. Americans who condemned change and feared and distrusted popular rule cast doubt on the validity of republicanism.

Federalism, according to Republicans, threatened the future of the newcomer, the ambitious man, the outsider. To a few, the Hamiltonian financial system spelled the creation of a monied aristocracy that would rule the land and widen the distinctions between various levels of society. Federalist partiality for Britain appeared to mark that corrupt kingdom as a model for American imitation. Federalist foreign policy moved the nation closer to war with France, bringing with it heavy taxes and the persecution of dissent. Federalist commercial policy doomed newly developed and profitable ties with France and the Continent. Within Massachusetts itself, Federalists hoarded power and privilege, narrowing rather than widening opportunity. The party stood for monopoly of local office, charter privileges, the natural resources of Maine, and the religious, institutional, and professional life of the community.

The nation was misruled, Republicans announced, because government did not truly reflect the interests of the people. Voters were often deceived and lacked direct representation. For generations they had submitted to a system of indirect rule whereby the lawyer, not the merchant, the local judge, not the farmer, sat in the General Court. But indirect government did not always work. It suffered anarchic breakdown in the 1780s and now a decade later once again was under heavy attack. Republicans repeatedly demanded direct representation. Communities should select men whose interests closely reflected those of the voters. Merchants, not lawyers, should sit for the trading towns; farmers, not judges, should represent the inland communities. Only then would an identity exist between voters and officials.

The Republican appeal was essentially an attack on traditional sources of leadership, not a call for social upheaval but a demand for enlarged opportunities for the excluded. Finding difficulty in meeting the argument, Federalists rehearsed the notion of a harmony of interest and denounced their critics as "ignorant rich men" eager for power. The Republican polemic proved to be more than shrewd propaganda: it worked. Merchants such as Orchard Cook and Jacob Crowninshield, farmers such as Joseph B. Varnum, and mechanics such as Thompson Skinner replaced many of the Federalist attorneys who sat in Congress. By questioning the assumption by which Federalists ruled, Republicans hoped to gain influence. The obstacles to opportunity must be weakened and above all the nation must avoid war with France and entanglement with Britain. The channels of trade with the Continent and the Far East must remain open; expansive measures must replace repressive political and economic ones; access to corporate privilege must become available to everyone; and the professional and communal life of the state must comprehend groups that had been excluded previously. These were the general objectives of the Republican interest; their precise formulation varied. Eastern merchants were concerned with foreign trade and sharing in grants of corporate charters, while their inland allies were moved by other problems. But everywhere Jeffersonians joined to remove the barriers to advancement.

After two decades of struggle, the party enjoyed considerable success. In many communities Republicans became the dominant group, replacing the older leadership or at least sharing influence. In time they merged into the social order and eventually distinctions blurred and became almost imperceptible. Party labels lost their meaning as the older differences narrowed and eventually disappeared, yet the experience of rivalry in the early Republic left a discernible trace. Amid the bitterness of political warfare, fine distinctions of position were maintained. Striving to achieve a coherent and secure place in New England life, Republicans constituted a social group united by ties of kinship and marriage. The Austins, Townsends, and Gerrys intermarried, as did the Harrises and Devenses of Charlestown; out in the Connecticut Valley marriage cemented ties between the families of William Lyman and Samuel Fowler. Eastern Republicans such as William Eustis and James Swan formed connections with the Langdons, New Hampshire's leading Jeffersonian family. The formation of Republican social connections was only one aspect of the process by which aspiring elements united to further their interests. The party's development did not follow precisely the same course everywhere, but an examination of the sources of the Republican interest will indicate the character of the movement.

*The Republicanism of Inland Massachusetts.* Throughout the rural communities of Massachusetts, from Middlesex to Hampshire County, from the eastern District of Maine to the western Berkshires, Republican groups challenged the reigning authorities. They did not enjoy equal success everywhere; in some areas outstanding leadership failed to compete with entrenched elements and circumstances were unfavorable to dissent. Out in the Berkshires, however, one of the earliest successful Republican organizations developed in the 1790s. . . .

*Republicanism and the Churches.* Religious problems aroused men because they were local and personal, and because they stimulated disputation by many of the most articulate members of the community. The growing controversy over the establishment was important not only because of the substantive issues involved, but also because it gave parties a cause which cut across sectional, economic, and class lines. Advocacy of the separation of church and state gave Republicans a popular issue which appealed to large groups dissatisfied with the standing order and opened fresh possibilities of forging new links between the party and the people. . . .

On this basis, Bay State Republicanism could unite rural Calvinists and urban rationalists, inland dissenters from the religious order and urban critics of the social order. It was through such processes that a diverse coalition of far-flung interests became a political party. Political change in the eastern maritime communities and the District of Maine further enlarged, broadened, and strengthened the Republican formation.

# 7

# Jacksonian Democracy

## Fact or Fiction?

To many historians the election of Andrew Jackson as president in 1828 represents a pivotal turning point in American history. Prior to Jackson's election, the men who occupied the presidency had come from either Virginia or Massachusetts; they were closely identified with an aristocratic elite which seemed far removed from the great mass of Americans. Andrew Jackson, on the other hand, seemed to symbolize the common man rather than the aristocrat. Being a self-made man and military hero—characteristics which made him a somewhat charismatic figure—Jackson's election was viewed by many as representing the ultimate triumph of democracy in American society.

Although historians for many years accepted the relationship between Jackson and political democracy, they disagreed sharply over the precise nature of what came to be known as Jacksonian Democracy. Indeed, the period from 1828 to 1840 became one of the most controversial eras in American history insofar as scholars were concerned. This was hardly surprising. Americans traditionally had attempted to define the unique characteristics that separated them from the rest of the world—a quest that inevitably led to an extended discussion of democracy and its meaning. Historians were no exception to this rule and much of their writing revolved around a historical examination of the nature and development of democracy in America. Because Andrew Jackson and democratic politics seemed so closely related, both topics became the subject of innumerable books and articles.[1]

Like that of Jefferson before him and other political leaders after him, Jackson's historical reputation has changed markedly from time to time. The earliest evaluations of his presidential career tended to be highly critical and hostile in tone. James Parton, Jackson's first serious biographer, freely admitted that Old Hickory was indeed the idol of the American people. Yet his portrait of Jackson was anything but flattering.

---

[1] For a significant analysis of the historiography of Jacksonian Democracy see Charles G. Sellers, Jr., "Andrew Jackson versus the Historians," *Mississippi Valley Historical Review* 44 (March 1958):615–34.

Recognizing the complex nature of his subject, Parton concluded that "his elevation to power was a mistake on the part of the people of the United States. The good which he effected has not continued; while the evil which he began [the spoils system] remains, has grown more formidable, has now attained such dimensions that the prevailing feeling of the country, with regard to the corruptions and inefficiency of the government, is despair."[2]

Parton's criticisms were echoed even more strongly by other nineteenth-century writers, including Hermann E. von Holst, William Graham Sumner, and James Schouler. These writers agreed that Jackson was illiterate, uneducated, uninformed, emotional, and that his actions were motivated by a desire to dominate merely for the sake of power. In short, his election as president in 1828 was considered to be a mortal blow to cherished American ideals. "His ignorance," wrote Parton, "was as a wall around him—high, impenetrable. He was imprisoned in his ignorance, and sometimes raged round his little, dim enclosure like a tiger in his den."[3]

The hostility of these historians toward Jackson, oddly enough, did not arise from the fact that their own political ideology and preferences differed sharply from those held by Old Hickory. Indeed, most of these scbolars were all nineteenth-century economic liberals who staunchly championed laissez-faire principles, condemned governmental intervention in the economy, and supported a sound currency. In this respect they were in general agreement with many of Jackson's policies, including his attack on the Second Bank of the United States and his hard-money views. Moreover, they approved of his forceful and assertive nationalism—particularly his bold stand during the South Carolina nullification controversy.

What these nineteenth-century scholars found most deplorable about Jackson's presidency, however, was the fact that the democratization of American politics had resulted in the exclusion from high public office of those individuals and groups that had been traditionally accustomed to hold the reins of power. The older political leaders were being replaced by the wrong sort of men—men who pandered to the desires and wishes of the mob and acted according to the dictates of political expediency rather than to the principles of right and justice. "The undeniable and sadly plain fact," wrote von Holst, "is, that since that time the people have begun to exchange the leadership of a small number of statesmen and politicians of a higher order for the rule of an ever increasing crowd of politicians of high and low degree, down even to the

---

[2]James Parton, *Life of Andrew Jackson*, 3 vols, (New York, 1861), 3:694.
[3]*Ibid.*, p. 699.

pot-house politician and the common thief, in the protecting mantle of demagogism ... politics became a profession in which mediocrity—on an ever descending scale—dominated, and moral laxity became the rule, if not a requisite."[4] Von Holst's words were echoed by other writers. Since Jackson, Parton charged, "the public affairs of the United States have been conducted with a stupidity which has excited the wonder of mankind."[5]

The antipathy of these nineteenth-century scholars toward Jackson is not difficult to understand. Most of them had come from eastern, middle class, patrician families that had enjoyed social and political leadership for well over a century. Viewing themselves as an aristocratic elite that held a monopoly of the ability to govern wisely and effectively, they were especially resentful of the democratization and seeming debasement of American politics. In their eyes Jacksonian democracy was the movement that had resulted in their own loss of status and power. Believing that the affairs of state should be conducted by the "right" sort of people, they condemned Jackson for supposedly beginning the process of corrupting an ideal state of affairs. The masses of people, these patrician aristocrats believed, were incapable of self-government; their interests could best be looked after by an uncorruptible aristocracy truly devoted to the welfare of the nation. Their historical writings, then, represented a Federalist-Whig-Republican point of view. Consequently, they were in most respects highly critical of and hostile toward Jackson.

By the beginning of the twentieth century, the study of history in the United States had begun to undergo a profound transformation. No longer did eastern patricians dominate historical writing. Instead, their places were taken by younger scholars, many of whom came from different parts of the country and who did not hold aristocratic elitist views. These younger historians saw in their discipline both a means of illuminating contemporary problems and providing guidelines for future action. Staunch believers in democracy and progress, they tended to favor those leaders and movements that had contributed the most to the growing democratization of the American people and their institutions. Unlike the patricians, they did not write about American history in terms of decline from some supposed earlier golden age. On the contrary, they wrote American history in terms of a protracted conflict between the people and the special interests, between the forces of democracy as against aristocracy, so that each epoch brought their country closer and closer to what they felt was its true democratic destiny. These historians, most of whom were part of the Progressive school of

---

[4]Hermann E. von Holst, *The Constitutional and Political History of the United States*, 8 vols. (Chicago, 1876–1892), 2:77.

[5]Parton, *Life of Andrew Jackson*, 3:700.

American historiography, began to break with the views of the older patrician school. In doing so, they set the stage for a radical reevaluation of Jackson and his role in American history.

The changing attitude toward Andrew Jackson first became evident in the writings of Frederick Jackson Turner, one of the earliest of the great Progressive historians. Just as Parton and other patrician historians leaned toward aristocracy, so Turner leaned toward democracy. Indeed, his famous paper on the significance of the frontier in American history in 1893 was an effort to differentiate Americans from Europeans by emphasizing the democratizing influence of a frontier environment. According to Turner, Andrew Jackson was in some ways the logical culmination of the triumph of democratic values in the United States. "On the whole," Turner wrote, "it must be said that Jackson's Presidency was more representative of the America of his time than would have been that of any of his rivals. The instincts of the American people in supporting him conformed to the general drift of the tendencies of this New World democracy—a democracy which preferred persons to property, an active share by the people in government to the greater system and efficiency of a scientific administration by experts or by an established elite who dealt with the people from above."[6] The first selection in this chapter is drawn from Turner's book.

From the turn of the century until the end of World War II, the Progressive school interpretation of Jacksonian Democracy remained dominant among American historians. In numerous books and articles, scholars contributed to the growing identification between the triumph of political democracy and the accession of Jackson to the presidency. Even the supposed introduction of the spoils system—a development that patrician historians had regarded as an unmitigated disaster—began to be studied in a new light. The spoils system, Progressive historians emphasized, was both a reflection and a result of democracy. Prior to Jackson, public office had been monopolized by a small social and economic elite who had regarded government as their own private preserve. But the introduction of universal manhood suffrage and the emergence of a broad-based two-party system destroyed the monopoly of this elite and threw open governmental office to all persons regardless of their class or background. The spoils system, then, was the democratic alternative to an elitist monopoly. Far from abhorring the spoils system, Progressive historians saw it as the logical consequence of democracy even though they recognized that it was, under certain conditions, susceptible to abuses.

The culmination of the Progressive interpretation of Jacksonian De-

---

[6]Frederick Jackson Turner, *The United States 1830–1850: The Nation and Its Sections* (New York, 1935), p. 28.

mocracy came in 1945 when Arthur M. Schlesinger, Jr., published his Pulitzer Prize–winning study *The Age of Jackson*. This book immediately became the starting point for historiographical controversy and scholars, generally speaking, fell into either the pro- or anti-Schlesinger camp. Indeed, so great was the impact of this book that much of the current debate over Jacksonian democracy may be dated from the publication of *The Age of Jackson*.

What Schlesinger succeeded in doing was to sharpen and elucidate in a brilliant and provocative manner the Progressive school interpretation of the Jacksonian era. While his Progressive predecessors had regarded Jackson and democracy as related subjects, they had never clearly spelled out the nature of the relationship in other than general and vague terms. Earlier Progressive historians, for example, had assumed that throughout most of American history economic opportunity had prevented a potential plutocracy from consolidating its rule. Although concerned over the growing disparities between rich and poor in twentieth-century America, they believed that periodic renewals of the democratic faith would modify or ameliorate the overt class struggles that wracked European society. Like most middle-class Americans, they disliked open class conflict; in their historical writings, therefore, they played down open class strife and stressed instead a sectional conflict between the democratic West, the capitalist Northeast, and the aristocratic slave-owning South.

Schlesinger, on the other hand, minimized sectional conflict as the key to an understanding of American politics during the 1830s. "It seems clear now," he argued, "that more can be understood about Jacksonian democracy if it is regarded as a problem not of sections but of classes."[7] In his eyes the impetus behind Jackson came from noncapitalists, farmers, and workingmen, who were reacting to the economic hardships of the period as well as to the domination of business interests seeking to extend their control over the economy. Where Turner and other sectional historians had emphasized the support that Jackson drew from the West, Schlesinger argued that it was the Eastern urban working class that had played the more important role.

Schlesinger's interpretation of Jacksonian Democracy in terms of class conflict was set within a broader framework of his understanding of American history as a whole. The Jacksonian era, Schlesinger maintained, was simply one phase in the continual conflict between liberalism and conservatism in America. American democracy, he wrote, had always accepted the idea of an enduring struggle among competing groups for control of the state. Such a struggle was one of the

---

[7]Arthur M. Schlesinger, Jr., *The Age of Jackson* (Boston, 1945), p. 263.

guarantees of liberty, for it prevented the domination of the government by any single group. "The business community," Schlesinger forcefully remarked, "has been ordinarily the most powerful of these groups, and liberalism in America has been ordinarily the movement on the part of the other sections of society to restrain the power of the business community. This was the tradition of Jefferson and Jackson, and it has been the basic meaning of American liberalism."[8]

Within this framework, Schlesinger's approach to Jackson and his followers was highly favorable. Jackson's attack on the Second Bank of the United States was justified, for the bank, although performing public functions, was completely independent of popular control. Indeed, the bank symbolized the alliance between the federal government and the business community. Although Schlesinger clearly pointed out that antipathy toward Nicholas Biddle and the bank came from diverse, even opposing forces, his point was that the bank war represented a phase in the struggle to restrain and curtail the power of the business community. In this sense Jackson and Jacksonian Democracy could only be understood and interpreted within the liberal reformist tradition.

Schlesinger's interpretation of Jacksonian Democracy, however, did not long go unchallenged. Indeed, within two years after the publication of *The Age of Jackson* a number of scholars expressed their dissent in no uncertain terms. While few of these critics could agree on an alternative hypothesis, they concurred that Schlesinger's democratic and class conflict hypothesis was not substantiated by the facts. The result was an extended debate among American historians over the problem of explaining the nature and significance of Jacksonian Democracy.

Generally speaking, Schlesinger's critics fell into two general schools. The first, known as the entrepreneurial school, maintained that Jackson did not represent the great masses of people who were attempting to curb the power and authority of the business community. On the contrary, the Jacksonians themselves were middle-class entrepreneurs and businessmen seeking to free themselves from the restraining hand of government and who sought to embark on ventures that would bring them immediate wealth regardless of the human and social costs involved. The second tradition in American historiography that emerged after 1945 went even further and denied the existence of a movement known as Jacksonian Democracy. The political struggles of the 1830s, argued some of these historians, revolved around local issues and a desire for public office; no ideological divisions whatsoever were involved.

The first criticisms from the entrepreneurial school came shortly after

---

[8]*Ibid.*, p. 505.

Schlesinger had published *The Age of Jackson*. In a series of articles and then in a Pulitzer Prize-winning book, Bray Hammond, a scholarly official of the Federal Reserve Board, took to task Schlesinger's interpretation of the Second Bank of the United States. Hammond denied Schlesinger's contention that the bank was "the keystone in the alliance between the government and the business community."[9] He argued instead that this institution performed the role of a central bank; that is, it was a responsible regulatory agency that had as its function the prevention of disastrous, periodic economic crises by pursuing sound monetary and fiscal policies. However, within the Democratic party, Hammond wrote, there existed a rising group of entrepreneurs who resented the obstacles that prevented them from embarking on speculative ventures that would bring them quick wealth. They resented particularly the Second Bank of the United States, in part because its sound monetary policy hampered speculative enterprises, and in part because the bank was controlled by Philadelphia interests. These entrepreneurs—centered in New York State and particularly New York City (and Wall Street)—wanted to destroy the national power of the Bank in order to further their own economic interests.

In Andrew Jackson, according to Hammond, these rising entrepreneurs found their champion. For Jackson seemed to epitomize the rising tide of democracy in the United States. The appeal of the Jacksonians was extraordinarily broad, for it was phrased in traditional agrarian, democratic, and individualistic terms. Jackson, who never clearly comprehended the issues involved, was persuaded that the bank, by virtue of its privileged position, was destroying economic opportunity. Hence, he destroyed the bank. But the result was more than the end of a single financial institution; the power of the federal government to regulate the economy through fiscal and economic policy was thereby greatly diminished. Consequently, American society throughout the nineteenth century was subjected to the extreme ups and downs of the business cycle, with all of the human suffering and other undesirable effects that attended periodic depressions. Indeed, by the beginning of the twentieth century the federal government was forced, once again, to reassert the type of financial control required in any modern complex industrial nation. The price of industrialization during the nineteenth century, Hammond concluded, was much greater than it might have been had the bank been able to continue its regulatory activities.[10]

---

[9] *Ibid.*, p. 76.

[10] Hammond's most extended discussion of Jacksonian Democracy appeared in his book *Banks and Politics in America: From the Revolution to the Civil War* (Princeton, 1957), pp. 286 ff.

Hammond's thesis, of course, was in some respects diametrically opposed to that of Schlesinger, who had seen Jackson as the champion of the masses. Hammond, on the other hand, saw Jackson and his followers as middle-class entrepreneurs committed to a laissez-faire policy solely to benefit their own narrow ends. In this sense Jacksonian Democracy was not strictly a democratic movement; it was a movement by expectant capitalists seeking only to free themsleves from government restraint.

Oddly enough, the entrepreneurial school's interpretation of Jackson and that of Schlesinger had a great deal in common. Both Schlesinger and his entrepreneurial critics viewed Jacksonian Democracy in terms of classes; both rejected an exclusively agrarian approach to the Jacksonians; and both emphasized the urban sources of the movement. Despite these seeming similarities, the two came to sharply differing conclusions. By emphasizing the middle-class sources of Jacksonian Democracy, the entrepreneurial historians were, in effect, denying that the movement was in the American liberal tradition as Schlesinger had claimed. Instead of championing the cause of the people, Jackson was upholding the cause of liberal capitalism. Thus the political struggles of the 1830s, these scholars emphasized, could not be viewed within a class framework that pitted the people against business and other special interests; some other hypothesis would have to be found in order to make some sense out of the politics and personalities of that era.

Hammond's entrepreneurial approach was echoed in one form or another by other historians, notably Richard Hofstadter and Joseph Dorfman, both of whom saw in Jackson a president who was fundamentally probusiness in his outlook. In his book *The American Political Tradition and the Men Who Made It,* Hofstadter entitled one of his chapters "Andrew Jackson and the Rise of Liberal Capitalism." The Jacksonian movement, he emphasized, was "a phase in the expansion of liberated capitalism" and "was closely linked to the ambitions of the small capitalist." To Hofstadter the popular hatred of privilege and the dominant laissez-faire ideology—both of which came together in Jacksonian Democracy—made an unhappy combination. Their convergence in a single political movement created a mythology that defined democracy in terms of a weak central government, thereby permitting powerful economic interests a disproportionate share of influence in questions involving national policy. [11]

The reaction against the Progressive school interpretation of Jacksonian Democracy by entrepreneurial historians was also reinforced after

---

[11]Richard Hofstadter, *The American Political Tradition and the Men Who Made It* (New York, 1948), pp. 55–63.

1945 by neoconservative historians, who rejected a class analysis of history and emphasized instead a basic consensus that supposedly united all Americans. In the United States, these historians argued, politics never revolved around ideological and class conflicts precisely because Americans shared a common outlook founded on Lockean middle-class liberalism. Reacting to the external threat posed to American institutions by the Soviet Union in particular and Marxism in general, the work of these historians reflected the emphasis on national unity so characteristic of the postwar era. The rejection of a clear class interpretation of Jacksonian politics was further reinforced by the work of historians who were influenced by the quantitative studies undertaken in other social science disciplines, especially political science, and who attempted to analyze party struggles by gathering and analyzing aggregate voting behavior of large numbers of individuals. Their statistical findings raised some serious questions about the validity of an interpretation that relied on a simple class division and the platforms and statements of parties and leaders.

Although neoconservative and quantitative-minded historians rejected a class conflict analysis of Jacksonian Democracy, they were set apart from the entrepreneurial school, which viewed the period in terms of a struggle between competing economic groups. The entrepreneurial school, it will be recalled, viewed Jackson as a symbol of the rising middle class in American civilization. The basic struggle in the 1830s, they suggested, was not between the haves and the have-nots, but between two sets of capitalists—between newer entrepreneurs seeking to free themselves of the shackles imposed by the government regulation that was exercised through the Second Bank of the United States, and the older and more conservative entrepreneurs seeking to guide economic development through a neomercantilist policy that gave the central government an important role in economic affairs.

These newer historians, however, went far beyond the approach of the entrepreneurial school in rejecting a class-conflict approach altogether. Although they conceded that the entrepreneurial historians had made a significant contribution in emphasizing the middle-class rather than the lower-class nature of the Jacksonian movement, these scholars believed that the movement had to be interpreted within a different framework. Consequently, they began to advance their own explanation of the nature of Jacksonian Democracy, its sources, its development, and its significance in American history.

Some historians, to cite one example, began to deal with the Jacksonian era within a psychological framework. Influenced by work done in the social and behavioral sciences, they sought to apply certain concepts from these disciplines in such a way as to arrive at new insights in the study of history. The idea of reform was particularly susceptible to a psychological analysis, for historians had long been interested in understanding the motivation and behavior of various types of reformers.

In the hands of this psychologically-oriented school of historians, the Jacksonians could only be understood in terms of status insecurity. The participation of the Jacksonians in various reform efforts, including their attack on the Second Bank of the United States, resulted not from their ideology but rather from their feelings of anxiety regarding their status in society. Reform served as a compensation for this insecurity and gave them an alternative outlet for self-expression. What these scholars were implying was that the Jacksonians resorted to reform activities because of their inability to adjust to the changing ways of American society. Reform, in effect, served largely as a therapeutic function to calm their fears regarding their own status insecurity. Within such a framework, the psychological school reduced all issues to psychological terms.

The most sophisticated example of the psychological interpretation of Jacksonian Democracy was Marvin Meyer's prize-winning book *The Jacksonian Persuasion*. Meyer argued that the Jacksonians wanted to preserve the virtues of a simple agrarian republic without having to sacrifice the rewards and conveniences of modern capitalism. By the 1830s, Meyer suggested, the United States was already on the road toward industrialization. The Jacksonians, together with many of their supporters, were unprepared for all of the changes taking place in their society—changes that were undermining traditional values and giving rise to unfamiliar and unwelcome institutions. Their response was a crusade to try and restore the virtues of the simple agrarian republic that had supposedly existed about the time of the American Revolution. The enemy, according to Jackson and his followers, was best personified in the Second Bank of the United States, for this institution did not create true wealth, but merely represented a *"paper* money power, the *corporate* money power—i.e., concentrations of wealth arising suddenly from financial manipulation and special privilege, ill-gotten gains." Because the bank was corrupting the plain republican order that they held so dear, the Jacksonians decided to cut out this source of corruption in the body politic. Herein, Meyers concluded, lay a paradox. The Jacksonians believed that in attacking the bank they were destroying an institution that menaced their idealized agrarian republic; in reality, they were destroying a regulatory institution, thereby paving the way for the triumph of laissez-faire capitalism.[12]

Historians of the psychological school, of course, were considerably indebted to their predecessors. Meyers, for example, had accepted Schlesinger's description of Jacksonian political rhetoric as well as

---

[12]Marvin Meyers, *The Jacksonian Persuasion: Politics and Belief* (Stanford, 1957).

Hammond's argument that Jacksonian Democracy implied laissez-faire capitalism. Nevertheless, his synthesis simply reduced the Jacksonian movement to a set of psychological adjustments; one could not understand Jackson and his followers as part of a long and viable reform tradition. Nor were class conflicts determining factors in the movement. The ferment during the Jacksonian era was the result of competition for status and position by certain groups within society rather than competition between classes.

The psychological interpretation of Jacksonian Democracy was only one approach taken by post-1945 historians. Within the last two decades, another group of scholars has gone farther; they have denied that Jacksonian Democracy, as an organized movement or even a concept, ever existed. They argued instead that American historians who had utilized the concept had been influenced by their commitment to a democratic ideology. Such a commitment had led these historians to read their own values back into the past, thereby making Andrew Jackson a symbolic champion of the people in what they saw as a perennial struggle against the business class and other special interests. An examination of the sources, these historians emphasized, would completely discredit the Progressive school interpretation of Jacksonian Democracy.

But if Andrew Jackson was neither the champion of the people nor even the representative of the emerging laissez-faire capitalism, then how could the politics of the 1830s be interpreted? In answering this question, these historians tended to borrow heavily from the behavioral sciences and to use quantitative techniques in order to demonstrate that the American people were not divided along class and ideological lines. In this respect their work paralleled the suffrage studies of Robert E. Brown and other colonial historians who had argued that seventeenth- and eighteenth-century America was already a middle-class democratic society. If American society was obviously democratic by the 1820s, Jackson could hardly be considered within a democratic reformist tradition.

Thus Richard P. McCormick, in several studies of voting behavior during the Jacksonian era, challenged the thesis that an unprecedented upsurge in voting had been responsible for Jackson's victories in 1828 and 1832. Indeed, McCormick argued, the real upsurge in voter participation came after Jackson was out of office in 1840. The growth of what he called the second American party system (to distinguish it from the Federalist and Jeffersonian party system) was not precipitated by ideological or class issues. It originated rather in the successive presidential contests between 1824 and 1840. "It did not emerge," McCormick wrote, "from cleavages within Congress, nor from any polarization of attitudes on specific public issues, nor did it represent merely the revival in new form of pre-existing party alignments. The second party system did not spring into existence at any one time. Rather, new party alignments appeared at different times from region to region. The most influential factor determining when alignments appeared within a particular region was the regional identifications of the presidential candidates. As changes occurred in the personnel involved in the contest for the presidency, corresponding changes took place in regional party alignments. New England, for example, was politically monolithic in support of John Quincy Adams, but when Clay was substituted for Adams, a two-party situation resulted. The South was monolithic behind Jackson, but when he was replaced by Van Buren, the South divided into two parties."[13] The implication of McCormick's interpretation was obvious; Jacksonian Democracy, in terms of a distinct ideological party structure, never existed.

In a similar vein Edward Pessen also insisted that the age of Jackson was simply too heterogeneous and defied simple labeling. In a study of the distribution of wealth during this era, reprinted as the second selection in this chapter, he emphasized the theme of inequality rather than equality. Wealth, rather than being widely distributed, was becoming ever more concentrated, and the nation's social structure more rigid and less fluid. Those who succeeded were generally born into affluent families. If society was becoming more unequal, Pessen asked, how can historians continue to equate the age of Jackson with egalitarianism? Indeed, in an earlier work he noted that there was something to be said for calling the Jacksonian period "an age of materialism and opportunism, reckless speculation and erratic growth, unabashed vulgarity, and a politic, *seeming* deference to the common man by the uncommon men who actually ran things."[14]

In an equally significant work, Lee Benson shifted the focus from political parties to the electorate. Rejecting a socioeconomic approach, Benson was among the earliest historians to emphasize the role of national origins and religion as among the most important determinants of voting behavior. Influenced by both behavioral theory developed in the social science disciplines and quantification, he attempted to demonstrate that voting behavior was due in large measure to basic differences

---

[13]Richard P. McCormick, *The Second American Party System: Party Formation in the Jacksonian Era* (Chapel Hill, 1966), p. 13. See also McCormick's two articles, "New Perspectives on Jacksonian Politics," *American Historical Review* 65 (January 1960):288–301; and "Suffrage Classes and Party Alignments: A Study in Voter Behavior," *Mississippi Valley Historical Review* 46 (December 1959):397–410.

[14]Edward Pessen, *Jacksonian America: Society, Personality and Politics* (Homewood, Ill., 1969), pp. 350–51. Surprisingly enough, New Left scholars have all but ignored the Jacksonian era. One exception is Michael A. Lebowitz, "The Jacksonians: Paradox Lost?", in *Towards a New Past: Dissenting Essays in American History*, ed. Barton J. Bernstein (New York, 1968), pp. 65–89.

in religious values and world views. Ethnic and cultural differences, he insisted, helped to shape the voters' perceptions of issues and thus to determine party affiliation. Drawing upon the work of the sociologist Robert K. Merton, Benson also argued that homogeneous groups often affiliated with one party because the other party already claimed the allegiance of groups with differing ethnic and religious characteristics and holding dissimilar views on moral and cultural issues. Jacksonian Democracy, he concluded, was a fiction created by American historians, and in *The Concept of Jacksonian Democracy: New York as a Test Case* he attempted to prove the validity of the proposition that since the 1820s "ethnic and religious differences have tended to be *relatively* the most important sources of political differences." During the past decade and a half a number of scholars have followed Benson's lead in developing an ethnocultural interpretation of American politics, thus vitiating the very reality of Jacksonian Democracy as a conceptual construct. [15]

Benson, moreover, categorically denied the very existence of an organized and cohesive reform movement centered around Andrew Jackson and his followers. Indeed, he insisted that the program of the Jacksonian party—which included states' rights, a strong executive leadership, freedom of conscience, and the idea of representative government—could hardly be equated with democracy. Such a program, he even suggested, was the negation of the democratic, egalitarian, and humanitarian movements that emerged during the nineteenth century. As an alternative hypothesis, Benson suggested that the era be named the "Age of Egalitarianism." Ideological changes, a phenomenal growth of the nation, and a high rate of physical mobility all combined to increase sharply the opportunities available to Americans and hence produced a more egalitarian society by 1860.

In recent years historians have increasingly rejected simple dualisms and explanations. As Ronald P. Formisano noted in a recent review of the literature, Whigs and Democrats *did* diverge in their conception of the individual, society, and relationship between government and the economy, but the patterns of divergence were complex rather than simple. "It is unlikely, however," he noted, "that parties in this period will be fitted to a liberal-conservative schema or that Jackson and his opponents will be divided again into radical democrats and aristocrats. No

---

[15]Lee Benson, *The Concept of Jacksonian Democracy: New York as a Test Case* (Princeton, 1961). For a more recent discussion by Benson of the Jacksonian period see his essay "Middle Period Historiography: What Is to Be Done," in *American History: Retrospect and Prospect*, ed. George A. Billias and Gerald N. Grob (New York, 1971), pp. 154–90. For a perceptive discussion of the ethnocultural approach to nineteenth-century American political history see Richard L. McCormick, "Ethno-Cultural Interpretations of Nineteenth-Century American Voting Behavior," *Political Science Quarterly* 89 (June 1974): pp. 351–77.

single ideological scheme will do to order the political, social, and cultural conflicts of that world, and certainly none exists which would allow scholars to vote comfortably for either of those parties."[16]

In a similar vein, some scholars have insisted that the consequences of actions by such political leaders as Andrew Jackson have been exaggerated. In an important and seminal study of the Jacksonian economy and the cycle of inflation, crisis, and deflation, Peter Temin maintained that the role of Jackson was far less than contemporaries believed; historians also erred in making Jackson a prime mover on the economic scene. "His policies," Temin concluded, "did not help the economy to adjust to the harsh requirements of external forces, but they were of little importance beside these far stronger influences."[17]

Despite the recent criticisms of the very concept of Jacksonian Democracy, the conviction that there were significant ideological and programmatic differences between parties has persisted (even though the Democratic party was no longer necessarily regarded as the champion of liberal reform). In a study of the legislative behavior of Whigs and Democrats in six selected states, Herbert Ershkowitz and William G. Shade came to the conclusion that there were key differences between the parties, at least at the state level. Although both parties shared a commitment to a democratized version of the liberal republicanism fashioned in the revolutionary struggle, they disagreed over the role of government. The Whigs were willing to use governmental authority to foster economic and social development; they also desired to legislate morality and to use public authority to set moral standards. The Democrats, on the other hand, feared concentrations of power and hence emphasized limited government and individual freedom and choice; they opposed humanitarian reform because it diminished individual liberty by making the government the arbiter of American society. Suggesting that differences at the state level reflected comparable differences at the national level, Ershkowitz and Shade concluded that the two major parties in the Jacksonian era represented somewhat differing beliefs and ideologies and fought over more than the spoils of office. Interestingly enough, their work represented a partial repudiation of the Progressive thesis that the Democratic party represented liberalism and the Whigs conservatism.[18]

Nor have more traditional explanations of Jackson's presidency dis-

---

[16]Ronald P. Formisano, "Toward a Reorientation of Jacksonian Politics: A Review of the Literature, 1959–1975," *Journal of American History* 63 (June 1976): 64.

[17]Peter Temin, *The Jacksonian Economy* (New York, 1969), p. 176.

[18]Herbert Ershkowitz and William G. Shade, "Consensus or Conflict? Political Behavior in the State Legislatures During the Jacksonian Era," *Journal of American History*, 58 (December 1971): 591–621.

appeared from view. In a recent study, for example, Richard B. Latner emphasized that the election of 1828 represented the rise of the West as an integral partner of the second American party system. Conceding his debt to Frederick Jackson Turner, Latner nevertheless rejected any simple generalizations about the role of sections or the importance of frontier democracy. Instead he found in Andrew Jackson the prototype of the modern president; the "Kitchen Cabinet" was the counterpart of the modern presidential bureaucracy that emerged during the twentieth century. Jackson's agenda, moreover, was directed toward the restoration of Jeffersonian principles to government. In effect, Latner synthesized Turner's emphasis on the importance of the West with Schlesinger's interpretation of Jackson as a part of America's liberal tradition.[19]

Considering the ways in which historians have approached the Jacksonian era, is it possible to offer any judgment about their relative worth? Was the Progressive school right in arguing that Jackson and his followers represented the people in their struggle against privilege and vested interests, and that the movement was one phase in the continuing conflict for political, social, and economic democracy? Or were the entrepreneurial historians correct in stressing the identification of the Jacksonians with laissez-faire capitalism? Were both wrong, as some recent historians have insisted? Was national politics simply a struggle between competing electoral machines? Did voter preferences reflect ethnic and cultural rather than class differences? Above all, is Jacksonian Democracy an appropriate designation for this important era of American history?[20]

These are indeed difficult questions to answer; perhaps no historian can provide any definitive or binding conclusions. Undoubtedly this historical controversy reflects the perennial—and valuable—effort to define with precision the nature and significance of the American experience. If so, perhaps the quest itself is of value, apart from any other possible benefits.

---

[19]Richard B. Latner, *The Presidency of Andrew Jackson: White House Politics, 1829–1837* (Athens, Ga., 1979).

[20]For a periodization of nineteenth-century political history that all but ignores the Jacksonian era as a distinct entity, see Richard L. McCormick, "The Party Period and Public Policy: An Exploratory Hypothesis," *Journal of American History* 66 (September 1979): 279–98.

# Frederick Jackson Turner

FREDERICK JACKSON TURNER (1861–1932) was professor of history at Harvard University before retiring in 1924. His essay on the significance of the frontier in American history was of seminal importance. His books included *Rise of the New West* (1906), *The Frontier in American History* (1920), and *The Significance of Sections in American History* (1932).

In order to understand the means by which this leader, trained on the frontier, expressing its militant quality and its democracy, won the presidency, we must draw a distinction between the Jackson men and the Jacksonian Democrats in 1828. The "Jackson men" included, not only the trans-Allegheny followers of the "Old Hero," and the kindred people of Pennsylvania, but also the New York democracy and the tidewater aristocracy of the southern seaboard. Nevertheless, Jacksonian Democracy was based primarily upon the characteristics of the back country. Jackson was himself a product of the frontier West—that West which was born of the southern upland in the days when a sharp contrast existed between the interior farmers and the tidewater planters.

Although he grew up in this frontier society, he had become a man of property, a cotton planter, a leader who used his leadership to protect the interests of himself and conservative friends in days when all men on the frontier, in the midst of abundant opportunities, strove to build up their fortunes. He had even found himself, in Tennessee, in opposition to political groups whose policies were later to become his own. Among his earlier friends were men to whom the stigma of "Federalists" was attached. "Opportunist" in his politics, as he has been described, he was none the less the national leader to whom frontier democracy turned, who bore in his own personal experiences and qualities many of the frontiersmen's fundamental characteristics. This by no means prevented, in his own state of Tennessee, bitter factional rivalries, and resentments when he gave to statesmen from other sections his confi-

---

Frederick Jackson Turner, *The United States 1830–1850: The Nation and Its Sections* (New York: Henry Holt and Company, 1935). Reprinted by permission of Jackson Turner Main.

dence and his political rewards. He sometimes purchased national leadership at the cost of losing his own state.

The widening of the suffrage in the older states, by statute and by constitutional change, had been in active progress, and the newer states had, almost from their birth, reposed political power in the hands of the people, either by white manhood suffrage or by so low a tax qualification as to amount to the same thing. By 1830 there were few states that, in practice, had not come to this. The western states had also based representation, in both houses of their legislatures, on numbers rather than on a combination of property and population. This marked a revolt, characteristic of the period, against the idea that property was entitled to a special representation, against the planter conviction, voiced by John Randolph, that the mere majority, "King Numbers," was tyrannous.

But Randolph's doctrine was ascendant in the tidewater counties of the South Atlantic States, and the terms of the Declaration of Independence which were inconsistent with the alleged primary purpose of government to protect the property-holding class, were repudiated. When, in previous years, the flood of Scotch-Irish, Germans, and other newcomers had passed into the backcountry from the North and had cut across the old lines of slow expansion from the eastern shores, the small counties of the tidewater refused to subdivide the large interior counties as the increased population entered them. They refused to reapportion legislative representation and to make adequate changes in the franchise to meet the changed conditions. Fearing that their historic social structure, and their political control, would be endangered and that the poor and rude but ambitious democracy of the nonslaveholding farmers of the interior would exploit the coast by taxing its property for the building of their roads, the development of their schools, and like expenditures, the tidewater planters determined that the coastal minority must retain its power. They even feared the antislavery sentiment of the western counties and their responsiveness to national, rather than to state, leadership. Gradual abolition had many friends in these counties.

Property's defense of its special privileges, by means of legislative apportionments and the limitation of the franchise, had been exhibited in the constitutional conventions of New York and Massachusetts in 1820. In Massachusetts, however, where the small towns in the interior of the state had a long established advantage in representation proportionate to population, it was the rapidly increasing urban population which sought to secure political power in proportion to its numbers. In New York the argument had been made that an enlargement of the franchise would increase the actual power of the master of industry by his control over the votes of his workmen. Thus, while the contest in the South Atlantic section was that of a western democracy seeking adequate political recognition, in these northern states the struggle was made by the growing coastal cities, seeking more adequate representation. In both cases there resulted regional struggles within the state.

To many Americans, Jackson's election seemed a humiliating catastrophe. John Quincy Adams refused to attend the ceremonies when Harvard bestowed the degree of doctor of laws upon his successor, explaining that he would not be present to witness her disgrace in conferring her highest literary honors upon a barbarian who could not write a sentence of grammar and hardly could spell his own name. Jackson's penmanship was not clerkly, his spelling was at times modern in the directness with which he reached the desired result, and the grammarian can often find flaws in his sentences. But Adams's description does injustice to the manuscripts of Jackson. The political judgment and foresight which were imperfectly clothed in orthographic garments soon make one forget these aspects.

"General Jackson's manners," said Webster in 1824, "are more presidential than those of any of the candidates. He is grave, mild, and reserved." Harriet Martineau, who visited him in the early thirties and who was sufficiently familiar with the highest English official society to be a good judge, said that he did the honors of his house with gentleness and politeness. He seemed to her "a man made to impress a very distinct idea of himself on all minds." She noted that his countenance commonly bore an expression of melancholy gravity, but from his eyes, when aroused, the fires of passion flashed and his whole person then looked formidable enough. We have a pen portrait from Thomas Hamilton, another English traveler of the time:

> Tall and thin, with an erect, military bearing, and a head set with considerable *fierté* upon his shoulders. A stranger would at once pronounce upon his expression, on his frame and features, voice and action, on a natural and most peculiar warlikeness. He has, not to speak disrespectfully, a *game cock* all over him. His face is unlike any other. Its prevailing expression is energy; but there is, so to speak, a lofty honorableness in its worn lines; his eye is of a dangerous fixedness, deep set and overhung by bushy gray eyebrows; his features long with strong, ridgy lines running through his cheeks, his forehead a good deal seamed and his white hair stiff and wirey, brushed obstinately back.

Here we perceive a man of prejudice, passion, and will, born to fight, and carrying a commission from the populace.

His triumph constituted an epoch in American history. To the late historian, Professor von Holst, it appeared the beginning of a downward path for the body politic, the rejection of the rule of the better classes, of the intelligent and well-to-do, and the substitution of the feelings and will of the masses for the organized and disciplined direction of the more efficient.

But the "reign of Andrew Jackson" is a test of men's attitude toward the problem of government. On the whole, it must be said that Jackson's presidency was more representative of the America of his time than would have been that of any of his rivals. The instincts of the American people in supporting him conformed to the general drift of the tendencies of this New World democracy—a democracy which preferred persons to property, an active share by the people in government to the greater system and efficiency of a scientific administration by experts or by an established élite who dealt with the people from above.

In the presidential election of 1828, Jackson's victory was decisive. Calhoun, who had withdrawn as a candidate for the presidency in the election of 1824, had then been accepted by both Adams and Jackson for the vice-presidency and was elected to that office, which he won again in 1828, although he had expressed apprehension as to the course of some of the adherents of Jackson with regard to the tariff of that year and had urged his South Carolina followers to support Old Hickory as a southerner and slaveholder and as a preferable alternative to Adams. Jackson secured 178 electoral votes against 83 for Adams, and a popular vote of 647,000 against Adams's 508,000. In Jackson's vote, moreover, there is no record for South Carolina, where the electors were chosen for him by the legislature without significant opposition. In Delaware, where likewise the legislature chose the electors, the parties were fairly evenly divided.

Adams carried all the counties of New England except a few in Maine and New Hampshire, as well as those counties of New York in which the people of New England origin were powerful, and the similar counties of the Western Reserve along the shore of Lake Erie in Ohio. These regions, with the connecting triangle of northwestern Pennsylvania, constituted the zone of Greater New England. Adams also won counties in the coastal extension of the old Federalist area in New Jersey and Delaware, counties interested in internal improvements along the Potomac River, and parts of the Ohio Valley, as well as the strongholds of Clay in Kentucky. Taken as a whole, the traditionally Democratic portions of New York, practically all of Pennsylvania, the South Atlantic and South Central states (except Kentucky), and the almost unbroken area of Indiana, Illinois, and Missouri, gained the victory for Jackson over Greater New England and the groups of counties which had followed the leadership of Henry Clay, in Kentucky, Ohio, and Virginia.

The election of Andrew Jackson was significant in American history for many reasons. It meant that, in the expansion of the American people, the rural society which had first occupied Pennsylvania, then spread beyond the tidewater country of the South Atlantic States, and, finally, passed into the Ohio Valley and the Gulf Basin, had now achieved such power that it was able to persuade the politicians to nominate a president who proved to represent its own ideals, as against the candidate whose strength lay in the zone of New England expansion.

As the outcome showed, it meant that an agricultural society, strongest in the regions of rural isolation rather than in the areas of greater density of population and of greater wealth, had triumphed, for the time, over the conservative, industrial, commercial, and manufacturing society of the New England type. It meant that a new, aggressive, expansive democracy, emphasizing human rights and individualism, as against the old established order which emphasized vested rights and corporate action, had come into control.

Superficially, this was not so clear. To one distinguished historian, using the geographical classifications of our own time, it has seemed that a "solid South" had united upon a "Southern" slaveholder and cotton planter and, aided by the Democracy of Pennsylvania and New York, had brought him to the presidency. But these classifications of today do not fit the facts of 1828.

It is obvious that, if one conceives of the "West" of that time as limited to Ohio, Indiana, and Illinois, with their twenty-four electoral votes, the West could not have elected Jackson. But what was the West of the period? And was there a solid South? By 1820 the states beyond the Alleghenies had come to number nine, and their population had grown so rapidly that it was about one-fourth of the total for the Union. A decade later, this region had nearly 30 percent of the nation's population. The election, however, was held under the census of 1820, and these newer states thus suffered by an apportionment which took no account of eight years of astonishing growth in population. Even so, the trans-Allegheny states had one-fourth of the electoral college. By the apportionment under the census of 1830, the proportion rose to nearly 30 percent. In these reckonings, no account is taken of the kindred society in the western counties of the old states.

What is common to most of this great interior area, is that its society was extemporized in a single generation of pioneering. Even the old French life of Louisiana and parts of Missouri had been engulfed and subjected by the tide of newcomers. By 1828, with the exception of parts · of Ohio, the settled portions of the Mississippi Valley were colonized largely by the people of the *interior* of the South Atlantic States, and their children. The upland area of this section must be sharply distinguished, in the sources of its population, its economic and social life, and its political ideals, from the lowland. There was no solid South in 1828. The Mississippi Valley's psychology and politics were shaped by its pioneering experience to such an extent that it had a sectional attitude of its own. It would be impossible to understand the events of Jackson's administration if we regarded that portion of the Mississippi Valley which lies south of the Ohio River, reinforced by the slaveholding state of Missouri, as a part of a solid South, dominated by slaveholding cotton planters in 1828.

Fundamentally, the whole interior—the land of the "Western Waters"—was still a distinct section, even if a changing and unstable one. Through the entire region from Pittsburgh to New Orleans, the Mississippi River and its affluents (the Ohio, the Tennessee, and the Missouri) constituted the great artery of trade and intercourse. Flatboats, rafts, and steamboats carried the agricultural surplus to New Orleans.

The westerners made a creed of innovation, and emphasized the right of the individual man to equal opportunity, unfettered by custom and as little checked by government as possible. The frontier's rough-and-ready impatience with technicality, and its preference for directness and vigor of action, as well as its ideals of democracy and simplicity and its distrust of government by a trained and established class, all combined to unite the support of the Mississippi Valley upon Jackson, its hero. He was not so much a cotton planter and slaveholder as a personification of western wishes and western will.

The men of the time still thought of this region as the West, though already the designation "Southwest" was gradually coming into use for the southern half of the Mississippi Valley. For example, Clay's correspondence of this period shows that "Harry of the West" thought of Kentucky as in the West, as did J. D. Breckenridge (a member of Congress from that state), who spoke in 1823 of the "nine Western States and Territories." Similarly, in 1825, Thomas Ritchie, the editor of the *Richmond Enquirer*, wrote of "8 western states" which might be expected to vote for Jackson in the House of Representatives. Illinois being conceded to Adams, in that election, this implies that the southwestern as well as northwestern states were included in the list. In his first cabinet, Jackson refused the advice of the South Carolina delegation and, while he included some members friendly to Calhoun, the representation from the southern sections was chiefly selected on the recommendations of J. H. Eaton, of Tennessee. Van Buren, who was chosen secretary of state, complained: "The best known and most influential politicians . . . in Virginia and in South Carolina," who had supported Jackson, were dissatisfied with the cabinet choices. In 1831, on the breakup of this first cabinet, Calhoun lamented that his "old, talented and virtuous section" would have "but one member in the Cabinet, . . . while the west will have the President [Jackson, of Tennessee], the Secretary of State [Edward Livingston, of Louisiana], the Secretary of war [he thought that Hugh Lawson White, of Tennessee, was slated] and the Post Master General [W. T. Barry, of Kentucky]." Jackson himself, in his message vetoing the United States Bank in 1832, uses the expression "the nine Western States."

So late as 1850, the census classified Kentucky and Missouri with the Northwest; and Alabama, Mississippi, Louisiana, Texas, Arkansas, and Tennessee constituted the Southwest. A gradual change was in progress, and it is no more important to dwell upon the western aspect of the election of 1828 than it is to realize that, before long, the Mississippi Valley became conscious that its unity was yielding to the influence of rival interests which tended to draw its upper half toward a connection with the North Atlantic States and its lower half toward a connection with the South Atlantic section. . . .

Viewing the growing power of the South Central section, and willing to avail themselves of one of its favorite sons in order to defeat the combined forces of Adams, of New England, and Clay, of the Ohio Valley, the leaders of the tidewater planters in 1828 threw their forces to Jackson, whom they expected to use as their instrument to destroy the nationalistic, loose-construction policy of Clay as embodied in the "American System" of protective tariff and internal improvements. The Virginia and South Carolina state-rights leaders, fearing for the safety of slavery under this system, thought they saw in Jackson a better alternative than Adams.

But their apprehensions, as well as their hopes,were clearly in evidence. Governor Floyd, of Virginia, made it clear that this group had expected Jackson to rely upon a cabinet including orthodox Virginia state-rights politicians and such South Carolinians as Langdon Cheves, James Hamilton, Jr., and Robert Y. Hayne. In consultation with Vice-President Calhoun ("the one on which we placed the highest value") they were expected to dominate the policy of the administration. John Tyler, of Virginia, one of the strictest of the sect of state-rights men, flattered himself that Jackson would "come in on the shoulders of the South, aided and assisted by New York and Pennsylvania," and that he must "in the nature of things . . . surround himself by a cabinet composed of men advocating, to a great extent, the doctrines so dear to us," and that, in the strong opposition which he would encounter, he would require the active support of the Virginia group. But he added: "Should he abuse Virginia, by setting at naught her political sentiments, he will find her at the head of the opposition."

The mistaken ideas, followed by rude disillusionment, of the planting interest of the coast are probably expressed by Governor Floyd, who wrote in his "Diary" in 1832:

> At this juncture the Southern Party brought out[?] Jackson who was thought to be a States Rights politician. . . . When he was elected, to our utter consternation, we found him without principle and of very feeble intellect. He gave himself up to the opposite party, was willing to take any course which would keep him in a majority . . . I did act for the best but we failed to

effectuate the good desired because our instrument was vicious though this we did not know when we embraced his cause.

Jackson's age and health were such that, even if he survived four years, he was not expected to seek a second term, and Calhoun was regarded by the state-rights men as his natural successor. How deeply the Virginia and South Carolina statesmen, who thought they saw in Jackson a convenient instrument of their policy, were deceived, events were soon to show. They were deceived, also, by failing to recognize the western self-consciousness and its determination to carry its own ideals into the conduct of the government. These ideals were, in reality, in conflict with those of the seaboard southern states. It was to take many years before the policy of the South Atlantic prevailed in the South Central section, and the change will form one of the important topics of this volume.

While they hoped, the seaboard planters considered, also, the possibility of disappointment. In 1827 Van Buren had been in correspondence with Thomas Ritchie concerning plans for an alliance between "the planters of the South and the plain Republicans of the North," based on party principles instead of personal and sectional preferences. Otherwise, Van Buren said, "geographical divisions founded on local interests, or what is more, prejudices between free and slaveholding states will inevitably take their place." He saw in nonsectional adjustment of party an antidote for sectional prejudices. In discussing the propriety of selecting a newspaper organ in Washington, Van Buren, and L. W. Tazewell of Virginia, agreed that Ritchie would be the desirable editor. But Tazewell, in his correspondence with Ritchie, looked forward beyond the inauguration of a Democratic President in 1829. He apprehended that an overwhelming success in the election would involve the danger of party dissensions and felt "solicitous that a Southern Editor should have acquired and established the reputation of the proposed Journal before that day" arrived. Evidently the South Atlantic section regarded the alliance as experimental and of doubtful strength.

This not only shows a foresight which was interesting, but it aids in understanding the distrustful attitude of the seaboard southern men who entered into combination with the Middle Atlantic States and the West. The importance of a national journal, to give the keynote to the party organs of the various sections, was recognized by the friends of both Adams and Jackson and is an indication of the new forces of public opinion which had arisen in the nation. Later events, as we shall see, emphasized the significance of contests for the control over the party organ at the seat of government.

The election of 1828 could not, of course, be decided by any one section, for no section controlled a majority of the electoral college. It was determined by a combination of the West, the South Atlantic States, and the Middle Atlantic section, agreeing upon little more than common opposition to John Quincy Adams of New England. It was not the work of the solid South, conceived of as the slaveholding states, for no such solid South existed. The South Atlantic and the South Central states were at this time separate sections, and upcountry and tidewater South Atlantic were far from "solid." Moreover, Delaware gave its vote to Adams, and Maryland was divided.

In the free states as a whole, Jackson had a larger popular vote than Adams, and lacked but one electoral vote of equality with him. Of the slaveholding states, Missouri and Kentucky, at least, thought of themselves as western and normally joined the Ohio Valley states north of the river in the important congressional issues, such as land legislation, internal improvements, and tariff. Missouri's slaves constituted less than one-fifth of her population, and Kentucky's, less than one-fourth (located in the counties of the Blue Grass Basin, which normally followed the leadership of Henry Clay). If these two states be removed from the so-called southern group, Jackson's electoral vote, as well as his popular vote, outside of the slaveholding states, was decisively greater than that of Adams. Moreover, it is a striking fact that, in the slaveholding states of the South Central section, the strength of the vote for Adams, rather than for Jackson, lay, generally, in the counties which possessed the larger proportion of slaves and raised the larger amount of cotton. Only slowly, and toward the close of the period, were they won to the Democratic party.

Nor was Jackson's election achieved by "overrepresentation of the South," on the assumption that only the free white population should have been considered in the apportionment of power in the electoral college. Among the various arbitrary compromises which had made the Constitution possible, was the provision for representation of three-fifths of the slaves in the states which held such property. But had this provision not existed, Jackson would have won without it, for the number of votes so secured could not have turned the scale.

On the other hand, the Constitution included other artificial arrangements inconsistent with the idea that representation in the electoral college ought to be according to free population. The more populous states were placed at a disadvantage by the provision assigning two electors to each state as a state, regardless of population. New England, with its numerous small states, gained by this provision. Had it not existed, Jackson would have won the electoral vote decisively in the region that had no slaves at all.

Jackson would have been victorious in the free-state area, with no help from the slaveholding states, had the electoral college been based on the actual population. If it is true that the nine states called western by the men of the time could not alone have elected Jackson, it is also true that the states which raised nine-tenths of the cotton of the United States could not have elected him.

If we consider the influence of particular groups of states, the Middle Atlantic, and especially Pennsylvania, had a position of pivotal importance. It was the opinion of Van Buren, an excellent judge, that the influence of Pennsylvania in bringing forward Jackson for the presidency controlled the result. The outcome in this state could not be attributed to "unjustifiable methods by his partisans," as has been alleged, for Pennsylvania gave a two-to-one vote for Jackson. Henry Clay believed that, if the three great states of Virginia, Pennsylvania, and New York should unite on any one candidate, opposition to that candidate would be unavailing, in all probability.

But the real question, whether a man of "southern," western, or Middle Atlantic States affiliations had been chosen, would be answered by the history of his administration. It depended upon the psychology and actions of Andrew Jackson himself, as shown by his earlier career and as exhibited in his choice of men and policies after his election. Here, as we shall see, there can be little doubt. In joining with the West and Pennsylvania in preferring Jackson, the South Atlantic section had deceived itself. It had aided in placing in the White House a man of the frontier, and as a result the West took the reins of authority.

Political power, which had earlier reposed in the South Atlantic section, was in the process of transfer to the trans-Allegheny states, and particularly to Tennessee, whose children had already spread into the northern portions of the Gulf Basin, into the southern counties of Illinois, and across the Mississippi into Missouri and Arkansas, carrying with them political and social ideals of the type of the parent state and thus constituting a great Tennessee area, from which came the western following of Jackson, Hugh Lawson White, and, later, James K. Polk and John Bell. The rival state of Kentucky, likewise, was still spreading its people into the counties north of the Ohio River—the political domain of Henry Clay and, later, of William Henry Harrison. . . .

A change in American social and political ideals likewise took place between 1830 and 1850. Slavery was far from being the only leading issue of ideals in those years. Jacksonian Democracy implied a fuller trust in the common people and in their right and capacity to rule. A stronger note of optimism, as well as of innovation, came into American life with the confident new forces that formed in the rural communities and especially in the West. Organized labor in the eastern cities also awoke to self-conscious activity and found in Jacksonian doctrines a support for its desire to reshape society in accordance with the gospel of "equal rights," in opposition to "special privilege," "vested interests," and monopolies. Social theorists, mingling with Locofoco leaders and land reformers like George H. Evans and Horace Greeley, introduced the new humanitarian and radical movements which characterized the forties and found clear expression in the new state constitutional conventions at the close of the period. Greeley's *New York Tribune* carried the gospel from East to West. These were the years when the public-school system was revolutionized, foreign and domestic missionary movements flourished, and temperance agitation, nativism, Fourierism, woman's rights, relief of the debtor class, an elective judiciary, homestead exemption, mechanic's-lien laws, reforms in penology, and many similar movements for ameliorating the conditions of life in America, were active. . . . Looking at the country and the era as a whole, whether we consider politics, inventions, industrial processes, social changes, journalism, or even literature and religion, the outstanding fact is that, in these years, the common man grew in power and confidence, the peculiarly American conditions and ideals gained strength and recognition. An optimistic and creative nation was forming and dealing with democracy and with things, in vast new spaces, in an original, practical, and determined way and on a grand scale. Not even in the South, where the slaveholding planter doubted the doctrines of the Declaration of Independence and looked with fear upon the tendencies of democracy, nor in the industrial centers, where class struggles between capital and labor began to emerge, could these forces be overlooked or defeated.

# Edward Pessen

EDWARD PESSEN (1920-    ) is Distinguished Professor of History at Baruch College and the City University of New York Graduate Center. He has published a number of books and articles on the Jacksonian era, including *Most Uncommon Jacksonians* (1967), *Jacksonian America* (revised edition, 1978), and *Riches, Class and Power Before the Civil War* (1973).

According to the egalitarian thesis the United States was a society dominated by the great mass of the people who composed the middling orders. Unfortunate minorities aside, few men here were either very poor or very rich. For that matter the rich here were rich only by American standards, their wealth not comparing in magnitude to the great fortunes accumulated by wealthy European families. What rich men there were in America were typically self-made, born to poor or humble families. Nor did they long hold on to their wealth. Flux ruled this dynamic society; riches and poverty were ephemeral states in this kaleidoscopic milieu. The limited extent and the precariousness of wealth helped explain the dwindling influence of its possessors. At a time when the most liberal of European states was grudgingly permitting some wealthy bourgeois to share the suffrage with great landholders, America was brushing aside all important restrictions on voting. Deference gave way to the strident rule of the masses, as the beleaguered rich turned their backs on a politics permeated by vulgarity, opportunism, and other loveless expressions of popular power. Social and economic democracy followed on the heels of, as they were in part caused by, political democracy. In a society that exalted work over status, class barriers loosened and diminished in significance. And a near if not a perfect equality of condition resulted from the unparalleled equality of opportunity that in Tocqueville's time complemented the abundant natural resources, the technological advances, and the human energy that had been present in America since its settlement. . . .

I have gathered much evidence—or what nowadays is called quan-

Edward Pessen, "The Egalitarian Myth and the American Social Reality: Wealth, Mobility, and Equality in the 'Era of the Common Man'," *American Historical Review* 76 (October 1971): 989–1034. Reprinted with deletions and without footnotes by permission of Edward Pessen.

titative data—from major cities of the Northeast in order to subject the thesis of antebellum egalitarianism to the kind of detailed check it has hitherto been largely spared. What follows is a report on how well several fundamental axioms of the egalitarian theory stand up to the test of empirical verification. . . .

Nor have many attempts been made by scholars to date to fix the wealth of the great accumulators. In effect the supply of authoritative information is slim, while what is authoritive is unavoidably inexact. If precise scholarly appraisals are lacking, there exists interesting contemporary published evidence that in effect takes up the question: were there very few or no Americans who had substantial fortunes during the era? . . .

In the absence of other reliable data the manuscript tax assessment records of the nation's wealthiest cities were consulted, therefore, in order to determine who were the rich and how great were their fortunes.

Urban residents were taxed not on incomes but on the total wealth, real and personal, they owned within the city. During the era Boston printed annual records of all persons who paid taxes on twenty-five dollars or more. New York City, unfortunately, did not. Lists of New York City's taxpayers for 1828 and 1845 were thus created out of the unindexed assessment data: over 100,000 separate items, which in their raw form simply listed, street by street, location by location, the assessed value of each property or estate owned in the city, and alongside it the name of its owner, agent, trustee, administrator, or executor. A John Jacob Astor, who owned hundreds of separate properties, appeared hundreds of times in the original records. Similar lists were drawn up for the then separate—and wealthy—city of Brooklyn. (Philadelphia's tax records did not permit such treatment, since assessors there did not distinguish between owners and users of real property.)

Such lists, if not requiring "a lifetime of research," were indeed time consuming to prepare. Their redeeming value is that they make possible not only the creation of reliable lists of comparative wealth, but answers to a number of important questions raised by the egalitarian thesis.

The assessments have a number of weaknesses, the chief one being their undervaluation of the estates, particularly the personal estates of wealthy men. Tax officials bemoaned the practice of great merchants, men known to be owners of vast real estate holdings and substantial shareholders in banks and insurance companies, coolly to swear that they possessed no personal wealth whatever. Who could say them nay in view of the incorporeality and the impossibility of tracking down this form of wealth? Boston's property owners may have been unusual in disclosing to assessors much personal wealth, yet officials even in that highly moral city were rightly convinced that property there was assessed substantially below its market value. The consoling feature of the sums disclosed by the tax records is that they are solid bedrock. Charles Hoyt in 1841 was worth at least the $242,226 Brooklyn's assessors of his real property said he was; Hezekiah B. Pierrepont was worth at least the $629,000 that his many lots were assessed for—although if the poor chap could be believed he had not a penny in liquid assets.

Even when the assessed valuations are taken at face value. New York City at the time of Tocqueville's visit had about one hundred persons worth $100,000 or more, while Boston had seventy-five worth at least the sum. A decade later, shortly after the second volume of *Democracy in America* appeared, New York's tax data disclosed that John Jacob Astor and Peter G. Stuyvesant were millionaires, while three hundred other persons were worth $100,000 or more. Boston by then had 150 individuals worth the later sum, in addition to Peter Chardon Brooks, the millionaire. Brooklyn, by 1841 the nation's seventh city, had twenty-six individuals assessed for $100,000 or more, if none at one million. While Philadelphia's assessments, in not distinguishing between owners and users of real property, do not indicate the total assessed wealth owned by citizens within the city, there is evidence that the Wealthy Citizens listing for that city, like the similar lists for Boston and Brooklyn, was reliable in important respects. Its publisher claimed that Philadelphia had eleven millionaires and another 350 persons each worth $100,000 or more. In any case, the death in 1831 of Stephen Girard, that city's great banker, revealed that he was worth more than $6,000,000, or almost precisely what he was listed for.

The $100,000 figure that many hundreds of northeasterners were assessed at may not appear to be an impressive sum. Yet even if one makes the most unrealistic assumption that the assessment figures accurately recorded the extent of an individual's wealth, the sums in question were hardly paltry. According to John Jacob Astor's grandson—and he was in a good position to know—a member of the "exclusives" could in 1850 have devoted himself entirely to the good life, including leisurely travel in Europe, on ten thousand a year, in "dollars not pounds," as he hastened to add.

The dollar of the 1830s was capable of wondrous things. William E. Dodge was able to rent a two-story house on Bleecker Street in New York City for an annual rental of $300, while one or two hundred dollars more could pay for an elegant place on "aristocratic Park Place among the Motts, Hones, Costers, Haggertys, Austins, Beekmans, and Hosacks," the *créme de la créme* of New York City society. Room and board at the new Astor House cost $1.50 in 1836, that sum paying for four meals consisting of "all the delicacies of the season . . . served in a most ample manner." Philip Hone, who was sufficiently demanding a gourmet to have found the famed Delmonico's Restaurant wanting, though the fare at the Astor House capital; he had never seen "a table better set out, better provided, or a dinner better cooked." A wealthy Philadelphian of midcentury held that fifty dollars "constituted the millionarism of money aristocracy of those days," since this sum enabled a man to keep a carriage. According to Sidney George Fisher of Philadelphia, his annual income of less than $3,000 gave him "a comfortable house—servants, a good table—wine—a horse—books—'country quarters,'—a plentiful wardrobe—the ability to exercise hospitality," while an additional one thousand would have enabled him to live like a truly rich man. In view of the prices of other representative goods and services, one understands better why at late as 1852 an informant could advise Carl Schurz that in New York City $150,000 was considered a fortune. There is good reason to believe that men assessed at $100,000 were typically worth many times that sum.

In the absence of income taxes, as well as the presence of a local tax that characteristically took less than 1 percent of what a man claimed to be worth, assessed wealth of $100,000 made him a functional millionaire several times over, in terms of modern costs and prices. His real estate was undervalued conservatively by half. Personal estate, regarded by tax authorities and insiders as typically equal in value to real, was almost totally masked. Possessions and investments outside the city were treated by assessors as nonexistent. Not one penny was yielded up to a federal tax bureau that in our own era appropriates a substantial portion of a rich man's wealth. In view of the fact, finally, that the dollar of 1840 appeared to be worth roughly between five and six and one-half dollars of 1970, wealth that 130 years ago was assessed at $100,000 is the equivalent of about forty times that gross amount in our own day....

"In America," wrote Tocqueville, "most of the rich men were formerly poor." The idea that, in the words of Henry Clay, the wealthy and successful were "self-made men," came close to being an article of faith, so widely was it subscribed to by Americans during the era. The common man was constantly reminded that "the most exalted positions" or great wealth were accessible to men of humble origin, since in this country "merit and industry" rather than "exclusive privileges of birth" determined the course of one's career. The merchant prince, William E. Dodge, offered the estimate that 75 percent of the era's wealthy men "had risen from comparatively small beginnings to their present position." If few modern historians would commit themselves to a precise ratio, many have nevertheless agreed that a remarkable movement up the social and economic ladder characterized the second quarter of the nineteenth century. We have evidently convinced our colleagues in sociology, including some of the leading students of social mobility and stratification, that for the Jacksonian period the facts are in: intergenerational economic and occupational mobility were the rule. Actually it is not the facts that are in but rather a continuing series of firmly stated generalizations that essentially do nothing more than assume that the facts would bear them out.

That Tocqueville in some instances was ready to spin his marvelous social theorems by reference more to logic than to pedestrian data is well known. What is fascinating is the extent to which scholars, ordinarily skeptical of unverified observation, have relied on it in discussing the origins of the rich in the "age of the common man."

The social origins and parental status of wealthy citizens of Boston, Philadelphia, New York City, and Brooklyn have been investigated in order to test the belief that typically they were born poor. Information has been gathered on the several hundred wealthiest citizens in each of these great cities. The evidence indicates that some of the best known among the wealthy citizens did in fact have the kind of background ascribed to them by the egalitarian thesis.... The most interesting feature of such evidence, however, is its uncommonness....

During the age of alleged social fluidity, the overwhelming majority of wealthy persons appears to have been descended of parents and families who combined affluence with high social status. The small number of these families that had been less than rich had typically been well to do. Only about 2 percent of the Jacksonian era's urban economic elite appear to have actually been born poor, with no more than about 6 percent of middling social and economic status. Included in the middle are the families of Peter Cooper, William E. Dodge, Gerard Hallock, Joseph Sampson, Cornelius Vanderbilt, Moses Yale Beach, Peter Chardon Brooks, Amos and Abbot Lawrence, Thomas H. Perkins, George C. Shattuck, George Hall, Thomas Everitt, Jr., Samuel R. Johnson, Cyrus P. Smith, and Samuel Smith, all of whom appeared to have been both better off and of higher status occupations than the mechanics, cartmen, milkmen, and laborers who predominated in the cities. The middle category was composed of ministers, petty officials, professionals other than successful lawyers and doctors, shopkeepers, skilled artisans who doubled as small tradesmen, and independent or moderately prosperous farmers. The evidence for these generalizations, inevitably imperfect, requires explanation.

It was of course impossible to obtain reliable information on the family status of all persons, but fortunately abundant evidence exists on the backgrounds of most of the wealthiest persons in the great cities. Data were secured on 90 percent of the more than one hundred New Yorkers who in 1828 were assessed for $100,000 and upward, and in 1845 at $250,000 or more; on 85 percent of the more than one hundred Bostonians worth $100,000 or better in 1833, and $200,000 or more in 1848; and on about 90 percent of the seventy-five Brooklynites who in 1841 were evaluated at $60,000 or more. For Philadelphia as was indicated earlier, the nature of the tax records does not permit them to be used to disclose the assessed total wealth of individuals. One can differentiate the "super rich" of that city from other rich or well-to-do persons only by accepting at face value the sums attributed in the anonymous *Memoirs and Auto-Biography of Some of the Wealthy Citizens of Philadelphia.* (Information was obtained on 70 percent of the 365 persons each claimed by the *Memoirs* to be worth $100,000 or more.) The pattern of the social backgrounds of the urban rich was strikingly similar for all the northeastern cities. About 95 percent of New York City's one hundred wealthiest persons were born into families of wealth or high status and occupation; 3 percent came of "middling" background; only 2 percent were born poor. As small a portion of Boston's one hundred wealthiest citizens started humble, with perhaps 6 percent originating from middling families. Philadelphia's statistics differ from Boston's only in that 4 percent of the former city's 365 richest citizens were born into families of middling status; 2 percent of her wealthiest citizens started poor. Cornelius Heeney and John Dikeman were the only wealthy Brooklynites of truly humble origins, with 16 percent born into middling status, and the remaining 81 percent of wealthy or high-status families.

Evidence was not as freely available for the "lesser rich" of the great cities. Data were obtained on about 70 percent of the more than 450 New Yorkers assessed at between $25,000 and $100,000 in 1828, and for 63 percent of the 950 New Yorkers who in 1845 were worth between $45,000 and $250,000; on close to 65 percent of the 260 Bostonians evaluated at between $50,000 and $200,000, in 1833, and on the same percentage of the four hundred Bostonians similarly assessed in 1848; and 63 percent of the one hundred Brooklynites assessed in 1841 at $30,000 to $60,000. It is of course possible that the backgrounds of the "missing persons" were unlike those of the much larger number of persons for whom information was obtained. It could be argued that the omissions concern less eminent persons, whose families probably were not as wealthy or of as high status as the families whose careers and records are better publicized. Yet a significant feature of the evidence is its disclosure that there appeared to be no difference in the patterns of social origin among the "lesser wealthy" as against the "super rich"; or in the patterns of family background of the relatively little known or unknown rich for whom information was obtained as against the eminent rich.

Many of the era's richest men, while born into relative affluence, managed to carve out fortunes that far surpassed their original inheritances. Such persons were self-made only in a special sense, their careers hardly illustrating what publicists of the era meant by that term. That the children of high-status parents, living in an age of dynamic growth, convert their original advantages into fortunes of unprecedented scope is—as Jackson Turner Main has noted in another context—hardly a sign of social mobility. A family whose adult heads for four or five generations were among the economic elite of their city or community cannot be said to have experienced upward social movement because their always inordinate wealth kept increasing. . . .

A related belief holds that the second quarter of the nineteenth century was "a highly speculative age in which fortunes were made and lost overnight, in which men rose and fell . . . with dexterous agility." Tocqueville believed that fortunes here were both scanty and "insecure," wealth ostensibly circulating with "inconceivable rapidity." Contemporary American merchants insisted that theirs was the most precarious of callings, incapable of attaining the "security which accompanied the more pedestrian occupations." True, the eminent Philip Hone had noted the resiliency of businessmen: "Throw down our merchants ever so flat [and] they roll over once and spring to their feet again"; but this optimistic judgment was confided to his private diary. The prevailing view was that the preindustrial decades were characterized by great intragenerational economic mobility. It has recently been shown, however, that antebellum Philadelphia witnessed slight movement up and down the occupational ladder or to and from residential districts of clearly differentiated wealth and status. Another recent study examines the changing economic circumstances of thousands of Bostonians and New York City residents of different wealth levels over the course of a generation. Some generalizations, drawn from its detailed findings, follow.

The richest Bostonians of the early Jacksonian era were invariably among the very richest Bostonians late in the period. Very few persons of the upper-middle wealth level—only 7 percent of that group—moved upward into the wealthy category whose members were each assessed for $50,000 or more. The extent of an individual's early wealth was the major factor determining whether he would be among the rich later. Absolute increases in wealth of any sort followed the rule: the greater an individual's initial wealth, the greater the amount by which it was augmented. A companion rule was that the greater one's original riches, the more likely was he to enjoy an increase. Since the population by midcentury had increased substantially in two decades the ranks of the later rich necessarily had to be filled by many persons who earlier were not among the wealthy. More often than not these newly rich taxpayers were younger members of old families, since fewer than 10 percent of the later group of Boston's rich were new men. Not one member of the $100,000 group of midcentury who had paid taxes earlier had paid them on less than the $20,000 owned by the wealthiest 2 percent of the Boston population. Since many contemporaries claimed that the careers of suc-

cessful merchants followed an erratic course in this kaleidoscopic economy, changes over short-run periods were also investigated to determine whether persons who started and ended the race strong may have
lagged in between. They did not. In Boston "few new great families
sprang up while fewer still fell away" during the era.

New York City's statistics for the period were not an exact replica of
the Boston evidence. Since New York was richer all categories of wealth
from the upper middle on up experienced greater gains in absolute
wealth than did their counterparts in Boston. For the rest the general
pattern was remarkably similar for the two great cities. Between the
period of Andrew Jackson's first election to the presidency and his death
not quite two decades later only one of New York City's fifty richest
persons fell from the class of the rich, and even he barely failed to
qualify. As in Boston the few New Yorkers who rose from the upper-
middle wealth level to the rich during the course of the era "were more
often than not from families of great wealth." The "newcomers" were
younger members of the great Hendricks, Jones, Lenox, Lorillard,
Barclay, Cruger, Grinnell, Bronson, Grosvenor, Hone, Lawrence, Post,
Murray, Storm, Ward, Remsen, Schieffelin, and Van Rensselaer families
or of "others of like distinction." About 75 percent of the New York City
families constituting the plutocracy of the so-called industrial era of the
mid-1850s were families that comprised the elite of the merchant-
capitalist era of a generation earlier.

Brooklyn assessment data exist for 1810 and 1841. If the earlier date
falls before what even the most flexible classifications would consider
the Jacksonian era, that fact hardly detracts from its value. If anything
the earlier starting point permits those so inclined to draw conclusions
about economic fluidity between the Jeffersonian and Jacksonian
periods. Brooklyn's wealthiest families of the early nineteenth century
remained among the wealthiest families of the 1840s. Only one of the
truly rich of 1810 fell by the wayside, and not because of poverty but
because of death. In Brooklyn, as in its mighty neighbor, riches achieved
by early in the nineteenth century appeared to be the surest guarantee to
the possession of wealth a generation later. The many wealthy persons
of 1841 who were relative newcomers to the city had achieved their
success almost without exception "as a result of a great boost given them
at birth by wealthy or comfortably situated parents or relatives. . . ."

The pursuit of wealth in Jacksonian America was marked not by
fluidity but by stability if not rigidity. Great fortunes earlier accumulated
held their own through all manner of vicissitudes. . . .

The final question to be considered in this discussion concerns the
distribution of wealth in the age of equality. Did the rich command an
inordinate share and did it increase or dwindle during the period?

A keystone of the egalitarian intellectual structure is the belief that, in

Tocqueville's words, a "general equality of condition" prevailed here. A perfect equality was of course out of the question. Pariah ethnic groups and hordes of unwashed new immigrants obviously were not in on the feast. But that the cornucopia was almost equally available to most others, like other elements in the egalitarian canon, remains a living belief. Even a modern scholar who dissents from the consensus, finding that in New York State "heavy immigration and industrialization" after 1830 widened the gulf between the classes, concedes that earlier "there did not appear to be any contradiction between the notion of equality of opportunity and a general equality of condition." By this version, the prefactory age, or what economic historians have called the age of merchant capitalism, was indeed an age of equality. The comprehensive evidence I have gathered on what almost every urbanite was worth early and late in the era makes possible an empirical test of this thesis. The fact that other scholars have performed similar quantitative studies of the distribution of wealth for earlier periods and that useful evidence exists for the Civil War years and later permits us to compare the degree of equality in the "age of egalitarianism" with that of other periods in American history.

During the colonial era wealth had become more unequally distributed with the passing years. This at least is the burden of the modern studies of scattered towns and villages. In Chester County, Pennsylvania, the richest ten per cent of the population owned slightly less than one-quarter of the wealth in 1693. Over the course of the next century their share increased to slightly under two-fifths, from 23.8 per cent to 38.3 per cent of the total, at the same time as the proportion owned by the poorest three-fifths of the population declined from 38.5 percent to 17.6 percent. Wealth was distributed less equally in commercial or seaport towns, and the tempo of increasing maldistribution was swifter in such communities. Where the wealthiest 5 percent of property owners in Salem owned about one-fifth of its wealth during the quarter century before 1660, by 1681 their portion had risen to about one-half of the prospering Massachusetts town's total. In colonial Boston the wealthiest 1 percent of the population owned about one-tenth, the richest 5 percent about one-quarter, and the upper 15 percent about one-half of the city's real and personal estate in 1687. By 1771 the wealthiest 3 per cent of Boston's population held slightly over one-third of the city's wealth, while the upper 10 percent owned about 55 percent of the property of a Boston community that had become "more stratified and unequal." Precisely the same share was owned by Philadelphia's upper tenth of "potential wealthholders" in 1774. On the eve of the Revolution, the richest 10 percent of northerners owned about 45 percent of the wealth, a figure slightly greater than the amount of net worth controlled by the richest tenth of the middle colonies for 1774. A less detailed comparison of New

York City between 1789 and 1815 notes that the wealthiest 30 percent of the city's fourth ward increased slightly their share, from 71 to 76 percent of the community's wealth during that quarter of a century.

Was the inegalitarian trend reversed in the nineteenth century? During the age of equality wealth in Boston became more unequally distributed than ever before. On the eve of the Revolution Boston's richest tenth had held slightly more than one-half of the city's wealth. Very little change evidently occurred over the course of the next half century, according to a local census report, whose table of Boston's tax payments for 1820 indicated that the upper 1 percent controlled about one-sixth of the city's wealth, while the richest tenth continued to own the slightly more than one-half they had held in 1771. Significant changes occurred over the following decade, since by 1833 the pattern of distribution had been sharply altered. The inegalitarian trend accelerated during the next fifteen years. (See tables 1 and 2.)

Actually the richest Bostonians owned a larger share of their city's wealth than tables 1 and 2 indicate. In Boston as elsewhere a small number of rich men appeared to own most of the capital of their city's great financial institutions. A careful check reveals that Boston's wealthiest merchants and businessmen were the officers and directors, and therefore the major shareholders, of the city's fifty largest banks and insurance companies. The disparity between the actual proportion of Boston's entire wealth owned by the elite and the share indicated in the tables 1 and 2 (based on the assessments) is not as great, it will be shown, as were the disparities for New York City and Brooklyn. Boston banks and insurance companies were assessed only on their real estate, a relatively small component of the city's wealth. Private individuals who owned corporate wealth were evidently assessed for their holdings; in sharp contrast to New York City and Brooklyn, therefore, taxpayers in Boston were assessed for personal property almost equal in value to their real estate. The fact, however, that in Boston as elsewhere the undervaluation of all property favored the rich above all, since they had the most to hide, is the chief assurance that actual wealth was more unequally distributed than was assessed wealth. . . .

TABLE 1.  DISTRIBUTION OF WEALTH IN BOSTON IN 1833

| LEVEL OF WEALTH | PERCENTAGE OF POPULATION | APPROXIMATE TOTAL WEALTH OWNED[a] | PERCENTAGE NON-CORPORATE WEALTH |
|---|---|---|---|
| $75,000 or more | 1% | $19,439,000 | 33% |
| $30,000 to $75,000 | 3% | $15,000,000 | 26% |
| $ 5,000 to $30,000 | 10% | $16,047,400 | 27% |
| Under $5,000 | 86% | $ 8,331,000 | 14% |

[a]In 1833 Boston wealth was listed at one-half its assessed value. In this table, therefore, the sums are doubled.

TABLE 2.  DISTRIBUTION OF WEALTH IN BOSTON IN 1848

| LEVEL OF WEALTH | PERCENTAGE OF POPULATION | APPROXIMATE TOTAL WEALTH OWNED | PERCENTAGE NON-CORPORATE WEALTH |
|---|---|---|---|
| $90,000 or more | 1% | $47,778,500 | 37% |
| $35,000 to $90,000 | 3% | $34,781,800 | 27% |
| $ 4,000 to $35,000 | 15% | $40,636,400 | 32% |
| Under $4,000 | 81% | $ 6,000,000 | 4% |

In the year of Andrew Jackson's election to the presidency the wealthiest 4 percent of the population of New York City, in owning almost half the wealth, controlled a larger proportion of the city's wealth than the richest 10 percent had evidently owned in the urban Northeast as a whole a half century earlier. By 1845 the disparities had sharply increased.

To judge from the New York City evidence, the rate by which the rich got proportionately richer became much more rapid during the nineteenth century than it had been during the seventeenth or eighteenth. As for the city's inequality in 1828 and 1845, its full extent is not disclosed in the assessment figures for these years. . . .

The trend toward increasingly unequal distribution of wealth in the antebellum era was not confined to the great cities of the Northeast. While the pattern of distribution in rural communities and small towns was not as skewed as it was in large urban centers, inequality in the former milieus was dramatic and worsening. In Hamilton, Ontario, "a small commercial lakeport almost entirely lacking in factory industry, with a population just over 14,000" shortly after midcentury, the poorest four-fifths of the population owned less than 4 percent of the town's property, in contrast to the richest tenth, who owned almost ninety per cent. As small Massachusetts communities, such as Worcester, became increasingly urbanized, the rich became relatively richer, the numbers of propertyless citizens increased drastically, and "patterns of ownership" became "sharply skewed."

Recent research indicates that on the eve of the Civil War the pattern of maldistribution in Philadelphia and in a number of Southern and Western cities was quite similar to the inequality that prevailed in New York City, Brooklyn, and Boston in the 1840s. By 1860 the wealthiest one per cent of Philadelphia's population evidently owned one-half, while the lower 80 percent held only 3 percent of the city's wealth. In Baltimore, New Orleans, and St. Louis the richest 1 percent of the population owned about two-fifths, the richest 5 percent better than two-thirds, and the upper 10 percent more than four-fifths of the wealth. An impressionistic recent account of Galveston at midcentury finds that the affluent social and economic elite were one hundred times wealthier than their fellow citizens, the wealth of the former group contrasting "strikingly with that of their nearest neighbors." The division of property was not as unequal in rural counties, southern or western, although even in such areas the distribution has been found to have been skewed to a surprising extent. In cotton counties the wealthiest 5 percent of landholders held more than two-fifths of the wealth, while the upper 10 percent owned almost three-fifths. (According to Gavin Wright, a close student of rural wealth distribution, the actual degree of inequality was greater than the census data indicate.) While wealth was more equally distributed on the northeastern frontier, even there the upper tenth by 1860 held close to two-fifths of taxable wealth. In the words of two modern students, property holding on the Michigan frontier became "more concentrated" with the passage of time, while the distribution of wealth "scarcely supports the typical American image of the frontier as the land of promise for the poor, ambitious young man."

During the age of egalitarianism wealth became more unequally distributed with each passing season. Shared less equally, even at the era's beginnings, than it had been a generation or two earlier, in the aftermath of the Revolution, wealth became concentrated in the hands of an ever smaller percentage of the population. The trend persisted through the 1850s, resulting in wider disparities than ever by the time of the Civil War. Far from being an age of equality, the antebellum decades were featured by an inequality that surpasses anything experienced by the United States in the twentieth century.

According to Gerhard Lenski, the central question in studying social stratification is: "Who gets what and why?" For the era of Tocqueville the answer to the first part of this question is clear enough. The few at the top got a share of society's material things that was disproportionate at the start and became more so at the era's end. Why they did is of course more difficult to explain.

It may be, as Lenski has argued, that in a free market system "small inequalities tend to generate greater inequalities and great inequalities still greater ones." Even if Lenski's comment is true, it is more descriptive than analytical, while leaving unanswered the question: Why? The explanation, popular since Karl Marx's time, that it was industrialization that pauperized the masses, in the process transforming a relatively egalitarian social order, appears wanting. Vast disparities between urban rich and poor antedated industrialism. Commercial wealth, as surely as industrial, enabled its fortunate inheritors to command a disproportionate share of society's good things and the children of the fortunate to hold a still greater share. A massive internal migration, above all of younger, marginal persons of little standing, into and out of the nation's cities increased both the power and the share of wealth commanded by more substantial and therefore more stable elements. It is hard to disagree with Robert Gallman's generalization that "there were forces at work in the American economy during the nineteenth century that tended to produce greater inequality in the distribution of wealth over time." A not insignificant task of future scholarship will be to ascertain as precisely as possible the nature of these "forces." I would venture the judgment that the transportation revolution and the de facto single national market it helped create made possible and indeed decisively fostered great increases in profitmaking opportunities even before the victory of industrialism, while the system of inheritance and the minimal influence of the nonproperty-owning classes enabled private accumulators to command a larger share of society's product than they would be able to in a later era of vastly greater absolute productivity and profits. Amid all the hulabaloo about the "common man" during the era, he in fact got what was left over.

It has long been argued that equality of opportunity if not of condition prevailed in antebellum America, the era's numerous success stories testifying to the rule of the former principle. In David Potter's language, in America equality did not mean the possession of uniform wealth so much as "parity in competition." The evidence, however, indicates that if dramatic upward climbs were more fanciful than real in Jacksonian America, competition was also marked by anything but parity. The absence of legal disabilities did not mean that poor men started the race for success on equal terms with their more favored contemporaries.

According to Charles Astor Bristed, the young man who hoped to gain entry into New York's upper one thousand was one who, possessed of "fair natural abilities, adds to these the advantages of inherited wealth, a liberal education and foreign travel." It need hardly be pointed out that the travel and liberal education mentioned by Bristed were not available to most Americans. Rather, they were accessible to men such as Abram C. Dayton, son of "an opulent merchant" of New York City, who had "all the accomplishments that education, travel and wealth could give." They were available to Andrew Gordon Hamersley, who inherited from his father a fortune, which, by "judicious management," he succeeded in substantially enlarging. Like other of his golden contemporaries he never went into business, owing his success rather to his name, his original possessions, and his "entertaining conversation and courtly manner." They were available to John Collins Warren, Valentine Mott, David Hosack, and Philip Syng Physick, brilliant physicians all, who from childhood had moved in the most rarified circles, attending the greatest universities and studying with the most learned masters at home and abroad, accumulating much wealth largely because they had much to begin with. Means rather than need gave one access to the services of these eminences.

It is of course possible that innate ability or a fortunate genetic inheritance accounted for the success achieved by most of the era's socioeconomic elite. Such traits no doubt played a significant part in some cases. The biographical data indicate, however, that a material inheritance was the great initial advantage that enabled most of those fortunate enough to have it to become worldly successes. Robert A. Dahl has contended that the era was marked by a "cumulative inequality: when one individual was much better off than another in one resource, such as wealth, he was usually better off in almost every other resource," including political influence. It is clear that almost all of the era's successful and wealthy urbanites had initially been much better off than their fellows in possessing the "resource" of wealth.

The race was indeed to the swift, but unfortunately the requisite swiftness was beyond the power of ordinary men to attain. For this swiftness was of a special sort. Unlike the speed of thoroughbred horses, which is a rare but a natural if inbred gift, the ability to cover great ground in the race for human material success appeared to depend less on the possession of innate abilities than on the inheritance of the artificial gifts of wealth and standing. During the "age of the common man" opportunity was hardly more equal than was material condition.

The evidence presented here has been drawn primarily from four large Northeastern cities, communities that were hardly typical of the nation as a whole. Yet, as has been indicated, earlier detailed if not quantitative studies of antebellum Natchez, Detroit, Cincinnati, and other Southern and Western cities revealed patterns of increasing inequality and social rigidity along the "urban frontier." Recent quantitative studies have disclosed that wealth was distributed most unequally in agricultural areas, in small towns, and in Baltimore. New Orleans, and St. Louis, even if the precise patterns of maldistribution were not quite as skewed as for the great cities of the Northeast. The data on the origins, the immensity, the durability, and the distribution of wealth in the United States during the second quarter of the nineteenth century therefore suggest that egalitarianism, in accord with Webster's definition of a myth, may have existed more in the imagination of men than in the lives they led.

The limitation of such evidence lies precisely in its inability to penetrate the imagination of the thinking and feeling of men, in Freudian terms, their conscious and unconscious. A significant component of what I have called the "egalitarian myth," in being immaterial or metaphysical, is resistant to the quantitative method. There appear to be important questions that quantitative studies have not answered and may be unable to answer. Who would aspire to a comprehensive grasp of the age of egalitarianism must consider such questions. What has been attempted in this article has been the measurement of the measurable—or, to be more precise, the measurement of some of the measurable. The behavior and influence of the rich, phenomena that are measurable if difficult to gauge, remain to be evaluated. It may be, as one scholar has recently written, that the latter kind of information is "more crucial for history than the social origins" of the elite. The purpose of this investigation has not been the grandiose one of answering the most crucial questions—whatever they may be—about Jacksonian society. I have chosen, rather, to discuss important questions, the answers to which may be crucial to an understanding of that society. The evidence on the backgrounds and the wealth of the rich indicates that the second quarter of the nineteenth century was something other than an age of egalitarianism. Since ancient historical rubrics confirmed by long usage are powerfully resistant to scholarly attempts to discard them, historians might spend their time more fruitfully by rethinking their estimates of the period in the light of the new evidence than by trying to replace old labels with new. Truer captions will follow on the heels of truer explanations of the nature of the era.

# 8

# Mid-Nineteenth-Century Reform

## Creative or Futile?

"In the history of the world the doctrine of Reform had never such scope as at the present hour," confided Ralph Waldo Emerson in his journal in 1840. In the past, he noted, many institutions had been accorded respect. "But now all these & all else hear the trumpet & are rushing to judgment. Christianity must quickly take a niche that waits for it in the Pantheon of the past, and figure as Mythology henceforward and not a kingdom, town, statute, rite, calling, man, woman, or child, but is threatened by the new spirit."[1] Such was the bewildering array of reform movements that nothing and no one escaped their influence.

The reform movements that swept across America during the first half of the nineteenth century took a variety of forms. The most famous was the antislavery crusade. Less known ones, but equally important, were the movements to improve the condition of such groups as the blind, the inebriate, the deaf, the insane, the convict, and other unfortunate members of society. Some of these reform movements were intended to help individuals and groups powerless to change their condition; others had broader social and humanitarian goals, including the abolition of war, the remaking of society by establishing model utopian communities, the establishment of greater equality between the sexes, and the founding of a free system of universal education. Thus reform was characterized by heterogeneity in form as well as in function.

It is equally difficult to categorize the ideologies of those involved in reform movements. Some saw social evils arising out of improvident and immoral behavior on the part of the individual. Others believed that an imperfect environment was at fault and that a meaningful solution to

---

[1] *The Journals and Miscellaneous Notebooks of Ralph Waldo Emerson*, 14 vols. to date (Cambridge, 1960–1978), 7:403. This quote was later incorporated into Emerson's essay entitled "Man the Reformer."

the problem at hand involved structural changes in American society. A few viewed reform as being conservative in nature in that it would diminish class rivalries and antagonisms, thereby preserving a fundamentally good and moral social order; others saw reform in more radical terms and urged fundamental changes in the fabric and structure of society. Similarly, there was little agreement about the use of the state to effect reform, for some regarded state intervention as an absolute necessity while others felt that reform efforts should be confined to private endeavors.

Although reform movements were heterogeneous in nature, there were a few themes common to them all. In the first place, all reformers by definition were optimists. In their eyes no problem was so difficult that it could not be solved; no evil was so extreme as to be ineradicable; no person was so sinful as to be unredeemable; no situation was so far gone as to be beyond control; and no illness was so severe as to be incurable. Second, an extraordinarily large number of them held strong religious convictions. Although disinterested in and even hostile to the fine points of doctrinal dispute, most were motivated by a firm sense of obligation and stewardship. All individuals, they argued, were under a moral law that gave them a responsibility for the welfare of their fellow man. No individual could ignore this obligation. Third, most reformers believed that science and reason complemented rather than contradicted religious faith. Indeed, reason and science provided the means of fulfilling the moral and religious obligations that bound all individuals. Finally, most reformers recognized the complexity and interdependency of society. Consequently, they were catholic in their concerns and shared one other characteristic; they were frequently involved in more than one type of reform. Horace Mann, for example, first came to national attention as a crusader on behalf of the mentally ill. But he turned later to educational reform partly out of his conviction that the evils and diseases that manifested themselves in later life could be minimized or prevented by proper education and training during youth when the individual's character was unformed and pliable rather than fixed. Mann's broad interests were fairly typical, for he—like most activists— recognized that a multifaceted attack on existing evils was indispensable for social betterment.

Many of the intended beneficiaries of reform, it should be noted, were either from the lower classes or else included a disproportionately high percentage of poor. Responsibility for the welfare of such lower-class groups was generally entrusted to those individuals in more fortunate straits—if only because of the inability of these dependent groups to change significantly the conditions under which they lived. Slaves, for example, were in no position to help bring about their own liberation. Nor could mentally-ill persons, orphans, drunkards, or convicts agitate for the establishment or improvement of institutions that would benefit them. Moreover, reformers had to have both leisure time and a sufficient income to permit them to pursue their careers as social activists. Reform movements, therefore, drew much of their inspiration and personnel from the ranks of the middle class and the well-to-do.

Though few middle-class reformers embarked on their activistic careers with a clear and cohesive ideology, their experiences with evils often led to sophisticated social analyses. An analytical approach, however, often had a self-extending mechanism in that it was difficult to deal with an individual problem without bringing under scrutiny broader institutional arrangements and structures. The result was a searching analysis that frequently involved judgments about the basic morality or immorality of American society, a judgment that was certain to engender conflict and controversy. Those active in the woman's rights movement, to offer one illustration, found it difficult to discuss that issue without becoming involved in an examination of the larger society in which they lived. Aside from goals, reformers also had to face the question of means. What tactics were appropriate to the problem? What should be done if slaveowners refused to countenance the idea of abolishing slavery, or inebriates to discontinue the use of liquor?

It is clear that most mid-nineteenth-century reformers found it difficult, if not impossible, to avoid making judgments about their country. And such judgments inevitably either confirmed or repudiated time-honored values concerning the legitimacy or illegitimacy of institutional relationships within American society. Whatever the case, it is clear that the searching analysis of the fabric of society that was under way during the first half of the nineteenth century did not occur solely within a framework of reason and rationality. Few individuals and groups, after all, possessed the confidence and self-restraint that enabled them to discuss the issues with which they were concerned without become emotionally involved. Reformers often experienced an intense internal conflict, if only because their vision concerning what American society was and what it should be were often so wide apart. Abolitionists, for example, saw slavery not only in terms of immorality per se, but as an institution that ultimately corrupted most of Southern society and tainted even those who remained neutral. Southerners, on the other hand, saw abolitionists as a collection of fanatics who did not understand either the slave or the South and who were intent on forcing all others to conform to their own unique definitions of morality and justice.

Just as Americans between 1800 and 1860 argued and fought over various visions of what constituted a just and moral society, so historians have argued over the nature, sources, and intentions of reformers. Indeed, those historians undertaking a study of individuals and groups seeking changes in American society sooner or later became involved in judgments about these reformers, including their means, goals, and even reasons for becoming social activists. The result has been a bewildering multiplicity of interpretations of the many reform movements that developed during the first half of the nineteenth century, interpretations that more often than not reflected the personal values of the historians writing about the problem.

The writing of American history in the twentieth century was dominated by scholars who held a liberal ideology and who tended to interpret the past in terms of a struggle between the mass of people on the one hand and narrow, selfish, and grasping special interests on the other. It was not surprising, therefore, that reformers and reform movements were generally held in high esteem. "In that time, if ever in American history," wrote Alice F. Tyler in her comprehensive study of antebellum reform, "the spirit of man seemed free and the individual could assert his independence of choice in matters of faith and theory. The militant democracy of the period was a declaration of faith in man and in the perfectibility of his institutions. The idea of progress so inherent in the American way of life and so much a part of the philosophy of the age was at the same time a challenge to traditional beliefs and institutions and an impetus to experimentation with new theories and humanitarian reforms."[2] The origins of reform, she argued, were to be found in the interaction of Enlightenment rationalism, religious revivalism, transcendentalism, and the democratization of society that resulted from the impress of the frontier.

Scholars within the Progressive school tradition held diverse views about the nature and origin of early nineteenth century reform. Arthur E. Bestor, Jr., for example, insisted that the communitarian movement of this era reflected a unique social context. Unlike Tyler, he did not trace the origins of the communitarian experiments to a frontier experience, nor did he perceive of a shared tradition that bound together reformers in different eras of American history. A majority of these novel communities did not arise on the frontier, nor was communitarian thinking a product of the westward movement. Communitarianism rather reflected a faith that the establishment and success of small modern communities would ultimately lead to a vast social reorganization that would transform American society. Most Americans believed in the plasticity of institutions, and the West seemed to provide living proof that social forms were neither rigid nor fixed. Thus the formation of model communities would act as a demonstration project in a society that was not yet fixed and rigid. In this sense, concluded Bestor, early-nineteenth-

---

[2]Alice Felt Tyler, *Freedom's Ferment: Phases of American Social History from the Colonial Period to the Outbreak of the Civil War* (Minneapolis, 1944), p. 1.

century reformers faced fundamentally different problems than did their late-nineteenth-century successors who had to confront the task of altering institutions already firmly established. Bestor's article is included as the first selection in this chapter.

Although most accounts seemed generally favorable toward antebellum reform, more often than not they were critical of specific movements. Not all reform movements, argued some historians, were necessarily for the good. The temperance crusade, after all, was led by narrow-minded and bigoted individuals seeking to impose their own moral code upon the rest of the people. Indeed, Tyler in her generally sympathetic survey of reform noted that in back of the temperance crusade "lay the danger, ever present in a democracy, of the infringement by a majority of the rights of a minority and the further dangers inherent in the use of force to settle a moral issue."[3] Equally distasteful to historians was the strong current of nativism—a movement that took a marked anti-Catholic turn during and after the 1830s and which entered politics in the form of the Know-Nothing or Native American party during the 1850s. Most scholars found it difficult to deal with this movement and its accompanying intolerance, which seemed to set it apart from the general current of reform.[4] Much the same pattern was true of abolitionism. Virtually no scholar defended slavery, yet a large number were extraordinarily critical of the abolitionist movement because of its fanaticism and intolerance.

Indeed, abolitionism offers a dramatic illustration of the way in which historians have interpreted the past in terms of their own values and the concerns of the present. To Northerners writing in the 1870s and 1880s the abolitionists were courageous men and women who were so convinced that slavery was immoral that they were willing to dedicate their lives to its elimination in spite of being ostracized and even endangered by the hostility of their outraged countrymen. Many of these early writers, of course, had themselves been participants in the Civil War; their works in part represented both an explanation and a justification for their actions. Southerners, on the other hand, flatly laid the blame for the Civil War at the doorstep of the abolitionists. Some even charged that the intolerance and fanaticism of the abolitionists had aborted a moderate and sensible emancipation movement that had been under way in the South. Such was the position of Robert E. Lee, who told a reporter in 1866 that he had always favored emancipation, and that in Virginia "the feeling had been strongly inclined in the same

---

[3]*Ibid.*, p. 350.

[4]Ray A. Billington, *The Protestant Crusade 1800–1860: A Study of the Origins of American Nativism* (New York, 1938).

direction, till the ill-judged enthusiasms (amounting to rancour) of the abolitionists in the North had turned the Southern tide of feeling in the other direction."[5]

The Southern view of abolitionism by the early part of the twentieth century had become the dominant tradition in American historiography. One reason for this in part was that a significant number of scholars came from the South and shared the outlook and loyalties of that section. Since they placed the blame for the coming of the Civil War on the North, they tended to treat the abolitionists as an irresponsible group who had stirred up sectional animosities to the point where an armed confrontation was all but inevitable. Thus in his discussion of the causes of the Civil War, Frank L. Owsley (in his presidential address before the Southern Historical Association in 1940) condemned the abolitionists in harsh and unequivocal terms. "One has to seek in the unrestrained and furious invective of the present totalitarians," he stated, "to find a near parallel to the language that the abolitionists and their political fellow travelers used in denouncing the South and its way of life. Indeed, as far as I have been able to ascertain, neither Dr. Goebbels nor Virginio Gayda nor Stalin's propaganda agents have as yet been able to plumb the depths of vulgarity and obscenity reached and maintained by George Bourne, Stephen Foster, Wendell Phillips, Charles Sumner, and other abolitionists of note. . . . Neither time nor good taste permits any real analysis of this torrent of coarse abuse; but let it be said again that nothing equal to it has been encountered in the language of insult used between the nations today—even those at war with one another."[6]

But not all the hostility of historians toward the abolitionists can be attributed to sectional partisanship alone, since many of these scholars came from other regions of the country. The dislike of these individuals arose not out of sympathy with the institution of slavery, but rather out of a distaste of the fanaticism of the abolitionists and their incessant quarrels over tactics and programs. Moreover, historians reflected some of the general apathy—even hostility—toward the plight of black Americans that was characteristic of the first three or so decades of the twentieth century, a fact that made it all the more difficult to attribute wisdom or sincerity to the abolitionist movement. A few scholars also noted that not all abolitionists were committed to the proposition that blacks and whites were equal. Consequently, the allegation that abolitionists were

---

[5]Robert E. Lee, *Recollections and Letters of General Robert E. Lee* (New York, 1924), p. 231, cited in Fawn M. Brodie, "Who Defends the Abolitionists?" in *The Antislavery Vanguard: New Essays on the Abolitionists*, ed. Martin Duberman (Princeton, 1965), p. 58.

[6]Frank L. Owsley, "The Fundamental Cause of the Civil War: Egocentric Sectionalism," *Journal of Southern History* 7 (February 1941): 16–17.

"insincere" and "hypocritical" seemed to have some substance. The result was a constant and subtle denigration of the abolitionst movement in historical literature.

In one highly influential study published in 1933, for example, Gilbert H. Barnes argued that abolitionism was an outgrowth of the evangelical religious revivals of the 1820s and 1830s that could be linked to such preachers as the Reverend Charles Grandison Finney. Associated with these revivals was a spirit of reform that led some individuals to regard their own moral regeneration as evidence of the need to redeem sinners elsewhere. The concern of the abolitionists, noted Barnes, "was not the abolition of slavery; it was 'the duty of rebuke which every inhabitant of the Free States owes to every slaveholder.' Denunciation of the evil came first; reform of the evil was incidental to that primary obligation."[7] The portrait that Barnes drew of some of the abolitionists was scarcely flattering.

Another reason for the denigration of the abolitionists was the use by scholars of insights and concepts borrowed from the social and behavioral sciences to inquire into the motives of reformers. It was not difficult to interpret fanaticism in psychiatric terms and thus reduce abolitionism to a form of social or psychological pathology. Hazel Wolf, for example, described the behavior of individual abolitionists as obsessive and paranoic in nature. All of them, she wrote, were "eagerly bidding for a martyr's crown."[8] David Donald, in an essay that has become a classic since its publication in 1956, resorted to social psychology to explain the behavior of the abolitionists as a reform group:

> Descended from old and socially dominant Northeastern families, reared in a faith of aggressive piety and moral endeavor, educated for conservative leadership, these young men and women who reached maturity in the 1830s faced a strange and hostile world. Social and economic leadership was being tranferred from the country to the city, from the farmer to the manufacturer, from the preacher to the corporation attorney. Too distinguished a family, too gentle an education, too nice a morality were handicaps in a bustling world of business. Expecting to lead, these young people found no followers. They were an elite without function, a displaced class in American society.
>
> Some—like Daniel Webster—made their terms with the new order and lent their talents and their family names to the greater glorification of the god of trade. But many of the young men were unable to overcome their traditional disdain for the new money-grubbing class that was beginning to

---

[7]Gilbert H. Barnes, *The Antislavery Impulse 1830–1844* (New York, 1933), p. 25.

[8]Hazel C. Wolf, *On Freedom's Altar: The Martyr Complex in the Abolition Movement* (Madison, 1952), p. 4.

rule. In these plebeian days they could not be successful in politics; family tradition and education prohibited idleness; and agitation allowed the only chance for personal and social self-fulfillment. . . .

They did not support radical economic reforms because fundamentally these young men and women had no serious quarrel with the capitalistic system of private ownership and control of property. What they did question, and what they did rue, was the transfer of leadership to the wrong groups in society, and their appeal for reform was a strident call for their own class to re-exert its former social dominance. Some fought for prison reform; some for women's rights; some for world peace; but ultimately most came to make that natural identification between moneyed aristocracy, textile-manufacturing, and Southern slave-grown cotton. An attack on slavery was their best, if quite unconscious, attack upon the new industrial system.[9]

While the majority of historians were unfriendly in their treatment of the abolitionists, the older and more favorable views held by Northern writers in the 1860s and 1870s did not completely disappear. Indeed, by the late 1930s—especially when it began to be increasingly apparent that the problem of black-white relationships was becoming more and more tense as a result of a growing militancy within the black community and the general discrediting of racist theory—the beginnings of a change in the existing unfavorable portrait of abolitionism began to be evident. Dwight L. Dumond, for example, showed considerable sympathy for the abolitionists in his study of the origins of the Civil War in 1939.[10] The broadening of the civil rights movement and the struggle for equality in the 1950s and 1960s further shifted the framework of the debate, for it was difficult, if not impossible, for historians to avoid dealing with the tragedy of black-white relationships in America. Indeed, by the 1960s a significant number of historians clearly sympathized with the abolitionists, and their approach now seemed to be dominant. In a major study on antislavery in 1961 Dumond began by stating his own viewpoint in clear and straightforward language:

> The course of the men and women who dedicated their lives to arresting the spread of slavery was marvelously direct and straightforward. They denounced it as a sin which could only be remedied by unconditional repentance and retributive justice. They denounced it as antithetical to the foundation principles of the nation, contrary to both natural law and moral law. . . .
>
> These people were neither fanatics nor incendiaries. They appealed to the

---

[9]David Donald, *Lincoln Reconsidered: Essays on the Civil War Era* (New York, 1956), pp. 33–34. For a critique of Donald's thesis see Robert A. Skotheim, "A Note on Historical Method: David Donald's 'Toward a Reconsideration of Abolitionists,'" *Journal of Southern History* 25 (August 1959): 356–65.

[10]Dwight L. Dumond, *Antislavery Origins of the Civil War in the United States* (Ann Arbor, 1939).

minds and consciences of men. They precipitated an intellectual and moral crusade for social reform, for the rescue of a noble people, for the redemption of democracy.[11]

Dumond was not alone in rehabilitating the abolitionists. Aside from the publication of numerous favorable biographies, there was a clear tendency to write about the movement in friendly, even glowing, terms. One book of essays by various authorities in 1965 explicitly rejected earlier views of abolitionism as a movement of maladjusted and evil fanatics. Indeed, in the concluding essay Howard Zinn argued that abolitionist radicalism was highly constructive when compared with the extreme inhumanity of slavery.[12] Similarly, Donald G. Mathews, who analyzed the arguments and rhetoric of the abolitionists, concluded that they were neither irrational nor fanatic. The abolitionists as agitators were not attempting to change the values of Americans—rather they were trying to extend them to human beings who were generally considered to be outside of society. Nor were the men and women who spent much of their lives fighting against slavery guilty of oversimplification, according to Mathews. They freely admitted that many slaveholders were good people, that not all were sinners, and that slavery was a complex institution. Nevertheless, slavery involved the exercise of arbitrary and absolute power. Such power enabled good Southerners to live with an immoral and evil institution. The absolute power of whites over blacks, moreover, corrupted not only individuals, but the South as a section as well as the entire nation. The abolitionists ultimately rejected the idea that proper social agitation was ameliorative. They opted instead for an ideology that sought to change society so that there would be no oppression of one human being by another. Mathews's interpretation reflected the more sympathetic views of abolitionism characteristic of historical literature during the last few decades.[13]

Historians, however, have not treated all reform movements in the same manner as they have abolitionists. Indeed, during the 1950s and 1960s, when fissures and flaws in American society began to appear more pronounced, scholars began to view the reform movements of the mid-nineteenth century as harbingers of many of the unsolved dilemmas and problems of the present day. The theme of social control, to cite one example, tended to loom larger even in the writings of scholars who were in no way identified with the hostile critique of American history

---

[11]Dwight L. Dumond, *Antislavery: The Crusade for Freedom in America* (Ann Arbor, 1961), p.v.

[12]Martin Duberman, ed., *The Antislavery Vanguard: New Essays on the Abolitionists* (Princeton, 1965), pp. 417–51.

[13]Donald G. Mathews, "The Abolitionists on Slavery: The Critique Behind the Social Movement," *Journal of Southern History* 23 (May 1967): 163–82.

associated with the New Left school of historiography. Historians began to suggest that the motivation behind the actions of many reformers, either consciously or unconsciously, was to impose some form of social control over those whom they were ostensibly trying to help.

Religious benevolence—clearly a major theme in mid-nineteenth-century America—underwent a sharp reevaluation. For example, Clifford S. Griffin, noting the phenomenal increase in the number of national societies established for such benevolent purposes as education, conversion, temperance, peace, antislavery, moral reform, and the dissemination of the Bible, saw in them more than merely the disinterested exercise of charitable impulses. As more and more people confronted political and social upheavals, and the homogeneity of American society splintered before their very eyes, many turned to religion—especially Protestantism—as the only social force capable of restoring "stability and order, sobriety and safety." A theocratic state where moral legislation buttressed and embodied a religious code was clearly impossible to institute within the United States. Both clergymen and laymen, therefore, turned to new national societies they founded for theocratic purposes. Such societies, organized to promote religious benevolence and charity, embodied also a belief on the part of their trustees that God wished all men to obey His laws, and that these societies were the proper and legitimate interpreters of God's laws. Most of the leaders of these societies were relatively well-to-do, and viewed religious benevolence as a means of social control. "Religion and morality, as dispensed by the benevolent societies throughout the seemingly chaotic nation," argued Griffin, "became a means of establishing secular order." That this version of morality strengthened the status quo and ensured the retention of power in the hands of affluent groups was hardly surprising.[14]

In a similar vein Michael Katz was critical of those historians who had interpreted the educational reform movement as merely an outgrowth of mid-nineteenth-century humanitarian zeal and the extension of political democracy. "Very simply," he wrote, "the extension and reform of education in the mid-nineteenth century were not a potpourri of democracy, rationalism, and humanitarianism. They were the attempt of a coalition of the social leaders, status-anxious parents, and status-hungry educators to impose educational innovation, each for their own reasons, upon a reluctant community."[15] Those community leaders promoting

---

[14]Clifford S. Griffin, *Their Brothers' Keepers: Moral Stewardship in the United States, 1800–1855* (New Brunswick, N.J., 1960), pp. x–xiii. In recent years some historians have sharply modified the social control interpretation of recent benevolence by emphasizing that the effort to establish a general standard of right conduct is characteristic of many groups. See Paul Boyer, *Urban Masses and Moral Order in America 1820–1920* (Cambridge, 1978).

[15]Michael B. Katz, *The Irony of Early School Reform: Educational Innovation in Mid-Nineteenth-Century Massachusetts* (Cambridge, 1968), p. 218.

education sought a school system that would simultaneously harmonize America's economic growth with a business-oriented value system that would prevent the violent consequences that had accompanied the rise of industrialism in countries such as England. Educational reform moreover, was not a consequence of a broad and diverse coalition of various social and economic groups; rather it was imposed on a society by leaders who identified education with their own interests and values. Consequently, education did not gain the allegiance of working- and lower-class groups, who reacted adversely precisely because the schools obviously did not serve their particular needs. After analyzing a number of local case studies in Massachusetts, Katz concluded that urban school reformers failed to achieve their goals.

> The schools failed to reach their ends, first, because those ends were impossible to fulfill. They failed, second, because of the style of educational development. Educational reform and innovation represented the imposition by social leaders of schooling upon a reluctant, uncomprehending, skeptical, and sometimes ... hostile citizenry. Social and cultural antagonisms that delayed and made difficult the achievement of innovation could not be simply erased after new schools had been built. From on high the school committees, representing the social and financial leadership of towns and cities, excoriated the working-class parents. They founded schools with a sense of superiority, not compassion. They forced education, and they forced it fast and hard; no time was allowed for the community to accustom itself to novel institutions or ideas about the length of school life. School committees hoped to serve their own ends and the ends of the status-seeking parents that supported them; one of those ends involved the unification of urban society. Ironically, their ideology and style could not have been better designed to alienate the very people whom they strove to accommodate in a more closely knit social order. In making the urban school, educational promoters of the mid-nineteenth century fostered an estrangement between the school and the working-class community that has persisted to become one of the greatest challenges to reformers of our own times.[16]

The themes of social control and imposition of reform have by no means been confined to religious benevolence or education. Joseph R. Gusfield, a sociologist by profession, analyzed the temperance movement in much the same manner as Donald, Griffin, and Katz viewed their reform movements. To Gusfield temperance was a "symbolic crusade" in that it had unconscious roots far removed from the outward form that it took. Issues of moral reform, in his eyes, represented the manner in which a cultural group acts to preserve, defend, and enhance the dominance and prestige of its own style of living within a total society. During the federal era temperance attracted a declining social elite bent on retaining its power and leadership. This elite "sought to make Americans

---

[16]*Ibid.*, p. 112.

into a clean, sober, godly, and decorous people"—a people that reflected the values of New England Federalists themselves. By the 1840s temperance had become a reflection of the tensions between native Americans and immigrants or between Protestants and Catholics. Those who favored temperance, in short, saw the curtailment of the use of liquor as a means "of solving the problems presented by an immigrant, urban poor whose culture clashed with American Protestantism." Similarly, David J. Rothman insisted that fear of social disorder in the early nineteenth century led elite groups to espouse institutional solutions in the hope of controlling deviant behavior by predominantly lower-class groups. Prisons, mental hospitals, and almshouses, he observed, were not the fruits of benevolent reform; they reflected rather a desire to control and to change behavior through the application of institutional solutions. Precisely because of their emphasis on discipline, order, and obedience, these institutions quickly became custodial in nature; they were the places to which society relegated a large number of socially undesirable persons and groups.[17]

In the second selection in this chapter Michael B. Katz attempts to explain the early-nineteenth-century origins of the "Institutional State." In relating social context, social position, ideology, and policy, he employs the concept of *deviance* in a retrospective manner. Deviancy, Katz argues, is at least a political or social category. In the early nineteenth century its meaning was altered at precisely the same time that the mercantile-peasant economy was being superseded by a commercial capitalist economy. As capitalism (which is distinct from industrialism) spread, social relations changed and a new dependent population was created. Traditional means of caring for dependent groups declined and were replaced by institutions devoted to the care of the casualties of the new social order. Reflecting their social origins, these institutions sought to reshape character along certain lines. The ideal components of character in a capitalist society, Katz notes, were sensual restraint, dependability, a willingness to work, and acceptance of the social order and one's position within it. Those who could not function within capitalism were swept into custodial institutions; by the single standard of capitalism they were unworthy and unproductive. The dismal legacy of the institutional activists of the early nineteenth century, Katz concludes, is still with us.

Much of the literature pertaining to reform, therefore, has been as much a commentary on the values held by the individual historian as it

---

[17]Joseph R. Gusfield, *Symbolic Crusade: Status Politics and the American Temperance Movement* (Urbana, 1963), pp. 5–6; David J. Rothman, *The Discovery of the Asylum: Social Order and Disorder in the New Republic* (Boston, 1971). For a somewhat different interpretation from Rothman's, see Gerald N. Grob, *Mental Institutions in America: Social Policy to 1875* (New York, 1973).

has been the creation of a supposedly objective past. Those historians who shared the ideals, values, vision, and tactics of a particular reform movement have generally written about it in a favorable and approving manner. Those who disagreed tended to find unconscious or semiconscious forces at work that made reform an instrument of social control, often by well-to-do groups seeking to retain or extend their power and authority. Within this framework the historian, in effect, had taken on the role of social critic.

Nevertheless, some historians found such an approach too limiting or circumscribed to serve as a satisfactory means of explaining reform movements. To classify some reforms as good (i.e., abolitionism) and others as less than good (i.e., temperance, religious benevolence, and education) posed some difficulties. One such difficulty arose out of the fact that reformers tended to be eclectic rather than narrow in their concerns. More often than not, an individual active in one reform movement was likely to be active in several others, though perhaps not with the same degree of intensity or involvement. Horace Mann and Samuel Gridley Howe, to cite only two cases, were active in educational reform, in movements to establish facilities for the mentally ill and deaf, dumb, and blind, as well as abolitionism. To characterize one of these movements as "bad" and another as "good" raised serious intellectual problems.

A "good-bad" dichotomy also tended to obscure for some historians a more general issue; namely, what was responsible for the pervasiveness of reform during the first half of the nineteenth century? Had there been only a few reform movements, each could have been explained in terms of a particular and specific situation. Abolitionism, for example, could be viewed simply as a response to the existence of slavery. But the fact of the matter was that considerably more than a dozen reform movements were operating during the first five decades of the nineteenth century. Was it not plausible to argue that something within American society that transcended a particular evil or void was responsible for this state of affairs?

To Merle Curti, a scholar writing within the Progressive tradition of American history in the early 1940s, the roots of reform were to be found in a complex combination of Enlightenment beliefs—faith in reason, natural law, and the idea of progress—and a liberal humanitarian religion that assumed the goodness of man and the perfectibility of the individual. Two other intellectuals trends also played a role in stimulating reform: romanticism, with its enthusiasm of man as a human being without reference to a person's status in terms of inheritance and education; and utilitarianism, which insisted that all institutions be judged by standards of social utility rather than tradition or custom. Social and economic tensions—especially those brought on by the recurring swings in the business cycle, likewise stimulated individual reform movements. Labor leaders, to cite but one example, fought against exploitation by employers (including slaveowners), and added their voices to the movement for free public education because education clearly served the needs of their constituents. All these considerations gave rise to a current of reform that drew strength and sustenance from all strata of American society.[18]

Many scholars, however, were less confident about Curti's conclusions regarding reformers and reform. Not all reform movements, they noted, necessarily resulted in a good outcome. It was true that certain institutions—notably slavery—were abolished. Yet those who had fought to do away with slavery failed to eradicate the roots of racial prejudice that gave rise to a crisis of massive proportions in the United States in the mid-twentieth century. In his seminal work on slavery, published in 1959, Stanley M. Elkins provided a major reinterpretation of the abolitionists in particular and reformers in general. To Elkins the most distinctive feature of American society in the early nineteenth century was the general breakdown of a number of key social institutions. The older establishments that had stood for order and stability— the church, the bar, the Federalist party, the eastern merchant aristocracy—had been stripped of their power by the 1830s and replaced by an almost mystical faith in the individual. With formal institutions losing their influence, a new kind of reformer emerged who did not rely upon such agencies to bring about social change. The pressures on such an individual were not the concrete demands of an institution or organization; there was no necessity to consider the needs of a clientele and there was no urge to spell out a program that was sound both tactically and strategically. On the contrary, reformers tended to be so free that their thinking was "erratic, emotional, compulsive, and abstract." Above all, they became preoccupied with a sense of self-guilt regarding society's problems. The result was an emotional demand for a total solution. When abolitionists sought to abolish slavery, for example, they did not feel impelled to discuss institutional arrangements in their proposed solutions to the problem. They treated slavery not as a concrete social issue, but as a moral abstraction. Protest, therefore, occurred in an institutional vacuum, and reformers were never called upon to test their ideas in concrete situations or offer programmatic solutions. Out of Elkins' interpretation emerged a more generalized description of the abstract and moral nature of American reform and its failure to come to grips with concrete and specific problems.[19]

---

[18]Merle Curti, *The Growth of American Thought* (3rd ed., New York, 1964), esp. Chap. 15. The first edition of this book appeared in 1943.

[19]Stanley M. Elkins, *Slavery: A Problem in American Institutional and Intellectual Life*

In an influential article published in 1965 John L. Thomas attempted to synthesize many of the diverse and even conflicting interpretations of antebellum reform. Beginning originally as a romantic faith in perfectibility and confined to religious institutions, wrote Thomas, reform quickly overflowed its barriers and spread across society and politics. Curiously enough, the religious impulse that gave birth to reform was conservative in both political and social terms. Arising out of a reaction to democratic politics, egalitarianism, and demands for church disestablishment, religious leaders began to organize benevolent societies to strengthen what they viewed as America's essentially Christian character and to save the nation from infidelity and ruin. By the time Jackson entered the White House, such associations formed a vast network of conservative reform enterprises that were supported and staffed by clergy and wealthy laymen who served as self-appointed guardians of America's morals. What was not anticipated, however, was a reorientation of theology that released the forces of romantic perfectionism that assumed all men could be saved and that man's improvement was a matter of immediate consequence. Defining social sin as the sum total of individual sin, reformers worked to regenerate and to educate individuals. Moral regeneration of the individual, then, would lead ultimately to the disappearance of social problems. Reform, therefore, involved a broad moral crusade, but with a strong anti-institutional bias, since it was based on the concept of the free and regenerate individual. In an important sense, Thomas was echoing Elkins's argument about the nature of mid-nineteenth-century reform. Even the communitarian experiments, Thomas noted, were anti-institutional institutions, for they involved an abandonment of political and religious institutions in favor of an ideal society giving full rein to the free individual. It was not until after the Civil War that a counterrevolution took place. In the course of the war both a revival of institutions and a renewal of the organic theory of the state occurred. The romantic perfectionist individualism characteristic of the first part of the nineteenth century declined sharply as a result.[20]

Thomas's view of reform was echoed a decade later in the historiography of abolitionism. Recent students of abolitionism have tended to

---

(Chicago, 1959), pp. 140–222. Several historians, on the other hand, have argued that reformers and abolitionists were more realistic than most of their countrymen. See in particular Aileen S. Kraditor, *Means and Ends in American Abolitionism: Garrison and His Critics on Strategy and Tactics, 1834–1850* (New York, 1969) and James M. McPherson, *The Struggle for Equality: Abolitionists and the Negro in the Civil War and Reconstruction* (Princeton, 1964).

[20]John L. Thomas, "Romantic Reform in America, 1815–1865," *American Quarterly* 17 (Winter 1965): 656–81. For a recent work that explores the social and cultural conditions that permitted reformers to perceive reality as they did, see Ronald G. Walters, *American Reformers 1815–1860* (New York, 1978).

emphasize the social and cultural context of the movement and the concern of individual abolitionists with the realization of self. In 1976, for example, Ronald G. Walters published a study of antislavery after 1830 that emphasized the interplay between individuals and culture. Three years later Lewis Perry and Michael Fellman brought out a collection of essays by different historians representative of this trend. This work, together with several others, dealt with the desire of abolitionists to create an atomistic universe of free and autonomous individuals, each able to realize his own destiny and free from social constraints. In pointing to the relationship between abolitionism and mid-nineteenth-century religious, civic, and moral culture, recent scholars have also drawn a parallel between antislavery and the developing capitalist order; autonomous individuals seeking self-realization prepared the way for the primacy of the marketplace as the guiding element in American society.[21]

Fascination with reformers and reform movements remained as strong as ever in the 1960s and 1970s, if only because of the seeming relevance to present day concerns. It was by no means unexpected, therefore, that social and ideological currents of these decades subtly began to alter perceptions of America's reform tradition. Just as the civil rights movement helped to develop a more sympathetic portrait of the abolitionists, so the women's movement helped to transform the ways in which historians interpreted earlier efforts to further social change.

No longer concerned—as were their predecessors in the nineteenth and early twentieth century—with the legal right to vote, many women in the 1960s and 1970s began to demand equality in the full meaning of that term. In so doing they questioned traditional institutional arrangements that made the home and the family the primary responsibility of females. The general concern with patterns of discrimination and unanswered questions about the status of women, past and present, left an especially strong mark on many of the nation's colleges and universities as well as on a number of academic disciplines. Out of this concern came a new field of research, namely, women's history. The growing importance of social history merely reinforced interest in the history of a group that in the past had been neglected by scholars concerned with political and diplomatic themes.

Although the new emphasis on women focused attention on the history of sex roles and the family in particular, it also created some

---

[21]Ronald G. Walters, *The Antislavery Appeal: American Abolitionism After 1830* (Baltimore, 1976); Lewis Perry and Michael Fellman, eds., *Antislavery Reconsidered: New Perspectives on the Abolitionists* (Baton Rouge, 1979); Peter F. Walker, *Moral Choices: Memory, Desire, and Imagination in Nineteenth-Century American Abolition* (Baton Rouge, 1978); Lewis Perry, *Childhood, Marriage, and Reform: Henry Clarke Wright 1797–1870* (Chicago, 1980).

novel ways of interpreting familiar data. It had long been known, for example, that women played important roles in philanthropic and charitable organizations. Few historians, however, paid attention to the women who took active parts in these organizations. Given the heightened interest in women, it was not surprising that some historians would begin to follow new paths and raise novel questions. Slowly but surely the focus shifted from the philanthropic agencies to the women themselves. Women, some younger historians began to argue, were implicitly protesting against their own subordinate status when they joined organizations dedicated to a variety of socially desirable goals. Moreover, the movement of women into the mainstream of American society coincided with changes in the structure of the family. As institutions like the school took over functions heretofore reserved to the family, the role of women began to change; middle-class women in particular were less inclined to accept the status of their mothers.

Indicative of the newer trends was Carroll Smith Rosenberg's study of the early history of the New York Female Moral Reform Society, which was founded in 1834. The society's goal, she noted, was as simple as it was bold; its members hoped to convert the city's prostitutes to evangelical Protestantism and to close permanently the numerous brothels. Within a short period of time, however, the society developed a rationale that rejected a male-dominated society and laid out new roles for women. As Rosenberg attempted to demonstrate, the women who joined this organization were not simply protesting against prostitution; they simultaneously developed an ideology based upon female autonomy that rejected male dominance and insisted upon the right of women to change male behavior. When men behaved in immoral and illegal ways, women had the right and the duty to leave the confines of their homes and to work to purify the male-dominated society. Although the members of the New York Female Moral Reform Society did not openly support the women's rights movement with its emphasis on the suffrage, the two groups were not fundamentally dissimilar; both wished to change the world in which they lived in order to give new meaning to their lives.[22]

In surveying this large body of scholarship dealing with antebellum reform, one is struck by its ambivalent nature. On the one hand, the idea of reform has always appealed to historians, most of whom have been sympathetic to a liberal, reformist, secular ideology. On the other

---

[22]Carroll Smith Rosenberg, "Beauty, the Beast and the Militant Woman: A Case Study in Sex Roles and Social Stress in Jacksonian America," *American Quarterly* 23 (October 1971): 562–84. See also Kathryn K. Sklar, *Catherine Beecher: A Study in American Domesticity* (New Haven, 1973), and Nancy Cott, *The Bonds of Womanhood: "Woman's Sphere" in New England, 1780–1835* (New Haven, 1977).

hand, the same historians could not help but note that mid-nineteenth-century reform movements had failed in the sense that later generations of Americans (including their own) were confronting many of the same problems. The approach to reform inevitably implied an implicit judgment of failure.

The theme that reform had failed tended to vary in intensity; the greater the perception of unresolved problems in their own society, the more likely were historians prone to see earlier reform movements in terms of their shortcomings. Consequently—with some exceptions—scholars since the 1950s have tended to emphasize the failures of reform rather than its achievements. Yet these same scholars have often been vague about the standards which they were employing in judging the past. The result has been to complicate further the task of evaluating antebellum reform; hard and fast criteria seemed lacking, and most scholars appeared to be employing a personal and often implicit subjective standard in their evaluations.

As long as Americans continue to disagree over what constitutes the proper framework and structure of their society, the nature of antebellum reform will continue to be a controversial subject among historians. In examining activists who sought to change society in the past, historians will probably ask the same questions as their predecessors and contemporaries. What was the nature of mid-nineteenth-century reform? Were the goals of reformers conservative or radical? Were reformers responding to objective social evils? Or did their activities embody psychological and group frustration? Did these reformers really achieve their objectives? If not, who or what was responsible for their failures? Were the tactics of reformers appropriate to the goals and objectives they were seeking? Were the American people prepared to organize their society in such a way that justice would be granted in an equitable manner? These are only a few of the issues that scholars have faced and probably would continue to face when dealing with the problem of antebellum reform.

# Arthur E. Bestor, Jr.

ARTHUR E. BESTOR, JR. (1908–    ) is emeritus professor of history at the University of Washington. His book *Backwoods Utopia* (1950) received the Beveridge Prize of the American Historical Association; he has also written several critical analyses of American education.

In the mechanical realm, nineteenth-century American inventiveness left as its most characteristic record not a written description or a drawing but a working model, such as the Patent Office then required. In somewhat similar fashion, the societal inventiveness of the first half of the nineteenth century embodied itself in a hundred or so cooperative colonies, where various types of improved social machinery were hopefully demonstrated. Patent-office models of the good society we may call them.

To build a working model is not the same thing as to draw a picture. Hence it is necessary, at the outset, to distinguish between communitarianism, or the impulse which constructed these hundred model communities, and utopianism, or the impulse to picture in literary form the characteristics of an ideal but imaginary society. The distinction is more than verbal. A piece of utopian writing pictures a social order superior to the present, and it does so, of course, in the hope of inspiring men to alter their institutions accordingly. But a utopian work (unless it happens also to be a communitarian one) does *not* suggest that the proper way of going about such a reform is to construct a small-scale model of the desired society. Edward Bellamy's *Looking Backward,* for example, was a utopian novel, but definitely *not* a piece of communitarian propaganda, because the social transformation that Bellamy was talking about could not possibly be inaugurated by a small-scale experiment; it could come about only through a great collective effort by all the citizens of the state.

The communitarian, on the other hand, was by definition the apostle of small-scale social experiment. He believed that the indispensable first step in reform was the construction of what the twentieth century

---

Arthur E. Bestor, Jr., "Patent-Office Models of the Good Society: Some Relationships Between Social Reform and Westward Expansion," *American Historical Review* 58 (April 1953): 505–26. Reprinted by permission of Arthur E. Bestor, Jr.

would call a pilot plant. The communitarian was not necessarily a uto-pian; few of the religious communities, for example, attempted to visualize an ideal future society this side of heaven. When the com-munitarian did indulge in utopian visions, the characteristic fact about them was that they always pictured the future as something to be realized through a small-scale experiment indefinitely reduplicated. The communitarian conceived of his experimental community not as a mere blueprint of the future but as an actual, complete, functioning unit of the new social order. As the American communitarian Albert Brisbane wrote:

> The whole question of effecting a Social Reform may be reduced to the establishment of one Association, which will serve as a model for, and in-duce the rapid establishment of others. . . . Now if we can, with a knowledge of true architectural principles, build one house rightly, conveniently and elegantly, we can, by taking it for a model and building others like it, make a perfect and beautiful city: in the same manner, if we can, with a knowledge of true social principles, organize one township rightly, we can, by organiz-ing others like it, and by spreading and rendering them universal, establish a true Social and Political Order.

This is a fair summary of the communitarian program.

Historically speaking, the idea of undertaking social reform in this particular way—by constructing a patent-office model or a pilot plant—is not a common idea but a distinctly uncommon one. No other period comes close to matching the record of the first half of the nineteenth century, which saw a hundred communitarian experiments attempted in the United States alone. The vogue of communitarianism can be de-limited even more sharply than this. During a period of precisely fifty years, beginning in 1805, when the first communitarian colony was planted in the Old Northwest, at least ninety-nine different experiments were actually commenced in the United States. Nearly half of these—forty-five to be exact—were located in the Old Northwest, strictly de-fined. Another twenty-eight were in areas which belonged to the same general cultural region—that is, western New York, the parts of the Ohio River valley outside the Old Northwest, and certain adjoining areas on the other side of the upper Mississippi. A total of seventy-three communities—roughly three quarters of the total—thus belonged to what can be described, without undue geographical laxness, as the Middle West.

Such a clear-cut localization of communitarian ideas in time and place can hardly be fortuitous. It is the kind of fact that cries aloud for explanation in terms of historical relationships. What, then, were the unique elements in the historical situation of the Old Northwest that help to explain why communitarianism should have reached its peak there during the first half of the nineteenth century?

Twenty years ago an answer would have been forthcoming at once, and would probably have gone unchallenged: *the frontier*. If, however, the frontier is given anything like a satisfactorily limited definition—if, in other words, the term is taken to signify primarily that "outer margin of the 'settled area'" which figured in Frederick Jackson Turner's original essay—then a close relationship between the frontier and communitarianism is hard to find.

In the first place, communitarian ideas cannot be said to have arisen spontaneously among any groups living in actual frontier zones. The leading communitarian philosophies, in point of fact, were elaborated in Europe—not only those of Robert Owen, Charles Fourier, and Etienne Cabet but also those of most of the religious sects. The Moravians in the eighteenth century found their "general economy" well adapted to new settlements, but its principles were ones the sect had worked out and partially practiced before they came to America. The Shakers faced frontier conditions when they first arrived in America, but they worked out their communistic polity later. It was, in fact, their way of settling down after the frontier stage had passed. The nonreligious communitarianism of the nineteenth century drew its ideas from sources even more obviously unconnected with the frontier. Robert Owen's plan was a response to conditions which the factory system had created in Britain, and it made no significant impression in American until Owen himself brought it to this country. Americans did take the initiative in importing certain communitarian theories, but here again frontier motivation was absent. Albert Brisbane, though the son of a pioneer settler of western New York, became aware of social problems gradually, first in New York City, then in the ancient but impoverished realms of eastern Europe. He finally brought back from the Continent the most sophisticated social theory of the period, Fourierism, and made it the leading American communitarian system of the 1840s, by dint of propaganda directed largely from New York and Boston.

If the ideas of the communitarians did not arise on the frontier, neither did the impulse to put them in practice. The handful of communities that were actually located in or near true frontier zones were all planted there by groups from farther east or from Europe. They were not established there with the hope or expectation of gaining recruits from among the frontiersmen; on the contrary, communitarian leaders were often warned against accepting local settlers. Finally, communitarians were misled if they expected greater toleration of their social nonconformity in the West than in the East. The mobs who attacked the Shakers in Ohio, at any rate, were indistinguishable from those who attacked them in Massachusetts.

Nothing created by the frontier contributed positively to the growth of communitarianism. Only as a passive force—as an area of relatively cheap land or relatively few restrictions—could the frontier be said to have had anything to do with the communitarian movement. These passive advantages of the frontier were, as a matter of fact, almost wholly delusive. The Shakers afforded an excellent test case, for their villages were to be found in regions of various types. The most successful were in long-settled areas, reasonably close to cities. The one Shaker settlement on the actual frontier—at Busro on the Wabash River above Vincennes—had a dismal history of discontent, hostility, and failure, from the time of its founding in 1810, through its evacuation at the time of the War of 1812, until its abandonment in 1827. The withdrawal of the Rappites from their westernmost outpost—in the very same region and at the very same time—may be taken as evidence that they too felt the frontier to be basically unfavorable to communitarianism. Thomas Hunt, a British Owenite who led a colony to Wisconsin in the 1840s, had to admit that whatever physical advantages the frontier might offer could "be secured, not only by bodies of men, but by private individuals." This fact was quickly discovered by members of cooperative communities which moved to the frontier. "On their arrival here," Hunt observed, "they . . . find many opportunities of employing their labour *out of the society they are connected with.*" Though Hunt saw advantages for communitarianism in the cheaper lands of the frontier, he saw none in the state of mind which the frontier engendered. Among the factors prejudicial to success, he listed, with emphasizing italics, "the *influence which the circumstances of this country may exert over their minds, in drawing them again into the vortex of competition.*"

Hunt was probably wrong in regarding even the cheap lands of the frontier as a real economic boon to communitarianism. They proved to be the exact opposite, according to the shrewdest of all the nineteenth-century historians of the movement. This was John Humphrey Noyes, himself founder of the successful Oneida Community (located, incidentally, far from the frontier), who reached the following conclusions after carefully analyzing the history—particularly the record of landholdings—of communitarian ventures contemporaneous with his own:

> Farming is . . . the kind of labor in which there is . . . the largest chance for disputes and discords in such complex bodies as Associations. Moreover the lust for land leads off into the wilderness, "out west," or into by-places, far away from railroads and markets; whereas Socialism, if it is really ahead of civilization, ought to keep near the centers of business, and at the front of the general march of improvement. . . . Almost any kind of a factory would be better than a farm for a Community nursery. . . . Considering how much they must have run in debt for land, and how little profit they got from it, we may say of them almost literally, that they were "wrecked by running aground."

The frontier, then, did not generate communitarianism. It did not inspire its inhabitants to join communitarian ventures. It did not show itself particularly hospitable to communitarian ideas. It did not even offer conditions that could contribute substantially to communitarian success. Communitarianism, in other words, cannot be explained as an outgrowth of the conditions of frontier life.

In point of fact, communitarianism developed in a fairly normal environment of settled agricultural and commercial life. The foreign-language sectarian communities, it is true, were not indigenous to the localities in which they were established. The Rappites, for example, were conducted as a body from Germany to Harmonie, Pennsylvania, then to Harmonie, Indiana, and finally back to Economy, Pennsylvania. None of the original members had any previous connection with these places, and the number of members recruited in the neighborhood was negligible. The same could be said of communities like Zoar, Ebenezer, and Amana. In the history of the communitarian movement as a whole, however, this pattern was the exception rather than the rule. The Shakers illustrated a more typical development. Each village of theirs was "gathered" (the phrase was a favorite one with them) from among the converts in a given locality, and was established upon a farm owned by one of the group or purchased with their combined resources. When communitarianism assumed a secular character, beginning in the 1820s, this local pattern became even more characteristic of the movement.

Of the thirty-six Owenite and Fourierist communities established in the United States during the half century under consideration, only one—Hunt's colony in Wisconsin—represented an immigrant group comparable to the Rappites or Zoarites. Only ten others involved any substantial migration of members, and in many of these the recruits from the immediate vicinity clearly outnumbered those drawn from a distance. At least two-thirds of the Owenite and Fourierist communities were experiments indigenous to the neighborhood in which they were located. Sometimes groups in a small village or on adjoining farms threw their lands together or traded them for a larger tract nearby. Sometimes groups in a larger town moved to a domain which they acquired a few miles out in the country. It is difficult to distinguish between the two processes, and unnecessary. In neither case did the moving about of men and women constitute anything like a true migration to a new environment. Clearly enough, communitarianism as a secular doctrine of social reform made its impact in already settled areas and it inspired its adherents to act in their own neighborhoods far more frequently than it led them to seek the frontier.

Yet the fact remains that the great outburst of communitarian activity occurred during the period when the frontier of agricultural settlement was pushing ahead most rapidly, and it tended to concentrate in the area lying in the wake of that forward thrust. Some connection obviously existed between the idea and the situation. The true nature of that relationship must be explored.

In his original statement of the so-called frontier thesis, Frederick

Jackson Turner enumerated certain ideas and habits of mind that he deemed characteristically American. "These," he exclaimed, "are traits of the frontier, or traits called out elsewhere because of the existence of the frontier."[1] The latter half of the sentence has a rather off-hand air about it, suggesting that Turner did not fully recognize how radically different were the two types of causation he was bracketing together.[2] Indeed, if the implications of the second part of the statement had been followed out fully and carefully by Turner and his disciples, the frontier thesis itself might have been saved from much of the one-sidedness that present-day critics discover in it.[3] Be that as it may, the second part of the quoted sentence does describe the kind of relationship that existed

---

[1]Frederick Jackson Turner, "The Significance of the Frontier in American History" (1893), as reprinted in his *The Frontier in American History* (New York, 1920), p. 37. Turner's most explicit discussion of communitarianism and its relation to the frontier is in his "Contributions of the West to American Democracy" (1903), *ibid.*, pp. 261-63.

[2]Turner's actual illustrations were such traits as the "practical, inventive turn of mind," the "masterful grasp of material things," and the "restless, nervous energy," which he believed were engendered by conditions of life on the actual frontier. If these traits were, as he believed, transmitted directly to other areas and to later generations, and if they constituted the dominant features of American thought as a whole, then no one could deny his thesis "that to the frontier the American intellect owes its striking characteristics." But then there would be no need for the saving clause, "traits called out elsewhere because of the existence of the frontier." This afterthought constitutes, in effect, a confession of weakness so far as the central thesis is concerned, for it introduces a totally different causal explanation. The traits that induced men to go to the frontier become, in this way of thinking, valid examples of frontier influence. To argue that the frontier was a creative force in such circumstances is a little like saying that the cheese created the mouse because it lured him into the trap.

[3]By failing to take seriously the ideas "called out elsewhere"—that is, by failing to reckon with these ideas as potent historical facts in their own right—the frontier school was trapped into its most notorious blunder: the acceptance of the "safety-valve" doctrine as an objective fact of economic history. The exposure of this error by recent scholarship has dealt a more serious blow to the frontier thesis than is sometimes realized. Turner shared very largely the nineteenth-century positivistic aim of explaining ideas as the products of external physical and material conditions of life. The frontier thesis must be understood partly in this light. By implication it denied (or at least played down) the importance not merely of ideas imported from Europe but of ideas generally, as creative, causative factors in history. The safety-valve doctrine served as a crucial test-case of the adequacy of this positivistic approach. If the frontier actually operated as a safety valve drawing off discontent from settled areas, then here was a clear-cut example of materialistic events or forces generating ideas directly and at a distance. But it turns out that the safety-valve doctrine was a preconception about the frontier, not a generalization from actual occurrences there. It was so powerful a preconception, moreover, that it actually generated action (in the form of homestead legislation, etc.) which directly affected the current of events in the West itself. By destroying the historicity of the safety-valve doctrine, scholarship did more than correct a mere detail of the frontier interpretation; it stood the whole theory on its head. Today the intellectual historian who would deal with "frontier" ideas is forced to take as a starting-point, not the conditions of life at the edge of settlement and the traits supposedly born out of that life, but rather the body of preexisting ideas concerning the West and the significance therof for mankind. One may even argue that the frontier thesis itself was less an induction from historical data than a restatement, with historical illustrations, of a time-honored set of intellectual assumptions concerning American westward expansion.

between westward expansion and the vogue of such an idea as communitarianism. The latter was one of the "traits called out elsewhere because of the existence of the frontier."

This paper purposes to explore the process through which communitarianism—and, by extension, a variety of other social ideas—were "called out" by the mere existence of the frontier. The statement we are using is, in part, a figurative one. For the sake of precision it ought to be restated at the outset in completely literal terms. Three points require brief preliminary discussion. In the first place, ideas are not produced by the mere existence of something. They result from reflection upon that something, reflection induced either by direct observation or by knowledge derived at second hand. We are, by definition, interested in the reflections of men and women who did not participate in, and did not directly observe, the frontier process. In the second place, ideas rarely, if ever, spring into existence fresh and new. Reflection upon a new occurrence does not produce a set of new ideas. It exercises a selective influence upon old ones. It represses some of these. It encourages others. It promotes new combinations. And it may infuse the whole with deeper emotional feeling. The resulting complex of ideas and attitudes may be new, but the newness lies in the pattern, not in the separate elements. Finally, though we have adopted Turner's phrase, and with it his use of the word "frontier," we will find that it was really the westward movement as a whole, and not the events at its frontier fringe, that the men and women "elsewhere" were meditating upon.[4]

With these three considerations in mind, we are ready to restate the subject of our inquiry in distinct, if prosaic, terms. The rephrasing will be clearer if cast in the form of a series of questions, although these will not have to be taken up in order or answered separately in the discussion that follows. How, then, did the expansion of population into unsettled areas, and the planting of civilized institutions there, strike the imaginations of those who took no direct part in the process? What ideas of theirs about the nature of social institutions were confirmed and

---

[4]Turner's central theme, likewise, was really not the frontier, but something larger: the westward movement, the West which it created, and the influence of both on American life. With something of the instinct of a poet, Turner seized upon one special aspect, the frontier, to serve as a symbol of the whole. But in the end, it seems to me, he was led astray by his own symbolism. The frontier was a picturesque part, but only a part, of the larger theme he was exploring. Instead of dropping the symbol, however, when it became obviously inapplicable to the other matters under discussion, he struck to the word "frontier" until gradually its value as a denotative term was destroyed. Worst of all, vices of language are apt to become vices of thought. Having grown accustomed to speak of the influence or the significance of the frontier, rather than of the westward movement, Turner and his disciples tended to look for crucial factors solely among the events and ideas that occurred along the very margins of settlement, and then to assume that the intellectual life of the entire West (and, through it, the entire nation) derived from this pioneer thinking.

amplified by their reflections upon this continuing event? Which of their hopes were encouraged, which desires rendered more certain of fulfillment, by what they conceived to be taking place? And how did this new pattern of ideas and aspirations correspond to the pattern embodied in a doctrine of social reform like communitarianism?

Now, communitarianism involved, as we have seen, certain very definite convictions about the way social institutions are actually created. It assumed the possibility of shaping the whole society of the future by deliberately laying the appropriate foundations in the present. And it called upon men to take advantage of this possibility by starting at once to construct the first units of a new and better world.

In this set of beliefs can we not immediately detect certain of the ideas that took shape in the minds of men as they contemplated—from near or far—the upbuilding of a new society in the American West?

First among these ideas, certainly, was the sense of rapid growth and vast potentiality. No theme was so trite in American oratory and American writing; quotations of a general sort are not needed to prove the point. But one particular aspect of this belief in the future greatness of the United States requires special notice. The point in question was enshrined in a couplet which was composed in New England in 1791 and which quickly became one of the most hackneyed in the whole of American verse:

> Large streams from little fountains flow;
> Tall oaks from little acorns grow.

American civilization, to spell out the interpretation which hearers instinctively gave to these lines, was destined for greatness, but this greatness was growing, and would grow, out of beginnings that were small indeed.

The converse of this idea formed a second important element in the reflections which the westward movement induced. The habit of tracing greatness back to its tiny source, led easily to the conception that every beginning, however casual and small, held within it the germ of something vastly greater. In a stable society, small happenings might have no consequences. But to men who pondered the expansion going on in the West, there came a sense that no event was so insignificant that it might not affect the future character of an entire region—perhaps for evil (if men lacked vigilance), but more probably for good.

A third idea, closely linked to these others, provided the most distinctive element in the entire pattern. Human choice could play its part in determining the character of the small beginnings from which great institutions would in future infallibly grow. But—and this is the uniquely important point—an organized effort to shape them would be effective only during the limited period of time that institutions remained in embryo. This concept is not, of course, the obvious and quite unremarkable idea that what one does today will affect what happens tomorrow. On the contrary, it assumed that there was something extraordinary about the moment then present, that the opportunity of influencing the future which it proffered was a unique opportunity, never to be repeated so fully again.

The corollary to all this—the fourth element in the complex of ideas—was a moral imperative. Men and women were duty-bound to seize, while it still existed, the chance of building their highest ideals into the very structure of the future world. When men spoke of "the mission of America," it was this particular idea, more than any other, that imparted to their words a sense of urgency. This moral imperative applied to the transplanting of old institutions as well as the establishment of new. The link between reformer and conservative was their common belief that institutions required positively to be planted in the new areas. Naturally the *best* institutions were the ones that should be so planted. For most men and women this meant the most familiar institutions, or at least the most respected among the familiar ones. Consequently the greater part of the effort which this concept inspired went into reproducing old institutions in the new West. A few men and women, however, always sought these best institutions not among those that already existed but among those that might exist. Hence the concept gave scope for reform as well as conservation.

Even when it assumed a reformist character, however, this concept must not be equated with reform in general. That it is to say, it was not identical with the sense of duty that urges men to remedy social injustices and to remake faulty institutions wherever they find them. The present concept was much narrower. Without necessarily overlooking abuses hoary with age, those who thought in this particular way concentrated their attention upon institutions at the rudimentary stage, believing that the proper shaping of these offered the greatest promise of ultimate social reformation.

The group of four concepts we have been considering formed an altruistic counterpart to the idea of the West as a land of opportunity for the individual. The dreams of wealth, of higher social station, and of greater freedom were doubtless the most influential ideas which the West generated in the minds of those who reflected upon its growth. The action which such dreams inspired was participation in the westward movement. But all men who thought about the West did not move to it. There were also dreams which men who remained in the East might share, and there were actions appropriate to such dreams. Throughout the world, as men reflected upon the westward movement, they grew more confident that success would crown every well-intended effort to create a freer and better society for themselves and their fellows. And many of them felt that the proper way to create it was to copy the process of expansion itself, by planting the tiny seeds of new institutions in the wilderness.

What men thought about the West might or might not conform to reality. But in the fourfold concept we have analyzed, there was much that did correspond with developments actually taking place in America. At the beginning of the nineteenth century the vast area beyond the Appalachians was in process of active settlement, yet its future social pattern was still far from irrevocably determined. Different ways of living existed within its borders: aboriginal, French, English, Spanish, Southern, Yankee, the ways of the fur trader and the ways of the settled farmer. The pressures from outside that were reinforcing one or another of these patterns of life were vastly unequal in strength, and this fact portended ultimate victory to some tendencies and defeat to others. But the victory of no one of the contending social systems had yet been decisively won. And the modifications which any system would inevitably undergo as it spread across the region and encountered new conditions were beyond anyone's predicting. Half a century later this indeterminateness was no longer characteristic of the West. Many of the fundamental features of its society had been determined with such definiteness as to diminish drastically the range of future possibilities. Just as the surveyors had already laid down the township and section lines which fixed certain patterns irrevocably upon the land, so the men and women of the region, in subtler but no less certain fashion, had by the middle of the nineteenth century traced and fixed for the future many of the principal lines in the fundamental ground plan of their emergent society.

The consciousness that they were doing this was stronger in the minds of Americans during the first fifty years of the nineteenth century than ever before or since. The idea had found expression earlier, of course, but never had it been validated by so vast a process of institutional construction as was taking place in the Mississippi Valley. The idea might linger on after the middle of the nineteenth century, but every year it corresponded less with the realities of the American scene, where social institutions were being elaborated or painfully reconstructed rather than created fresh and new. The first half of the nineteenth century was the period when it was most natural for Americans to assert and to act upon the belief that the new society of the West could and should be shaped in embryo by the deliberate, self-conscious efforts of individuals and groups.

This conviction received clearest expression in the pulpit and in the publications devoted to missions. An eastern clergyman, addressing the American Home Missionary Society in 1829, called upon the imagination of his hearers, asking that they place themselves "on the top of the

Alleghany, survey the immense valley beyond it, and consider that the character of its eighty or one hundred million inhabitants, a century hence, will depend on the direction and impulse given it now, in its forming state." "The ruler of this country," he warned, "is growing up in the great valley: leave him without the gospel, and he will be a ruffian giant, who will regard neither the decencies of civilization, nor the charities of religion."

The tone of urgency increased rather than diminished as the great valley filled up and men sensed the approaching end of the time during which its institutions might be expected to remain pliant. "The next census," wrote the editor of *The Home Missionary* in 1843, "may show, that the majority of votes in our national legislature will belong to the West." The myriads there, in other words, "are soon to give laws to us all." The conclusion was obvious: *"Now is the time when the West can be saved; soon it will be too late!"*

> Friends of our Country—followers of the Saviour—[the editor continued] ... surely the TIME HAS COME ... when the evangelical churches must occupy the West, or the enemy will. ... The way is open—society in the West is in a plastic state, worldly enterprise is held in check, the people are ready to receive the Gospel. ...
>
> When the present generation of American Christians have it in their power, instrumentally, to determine not only their own destiny and that of their children, but also to direct the future course of their country's history, and her influence on all mankind, they *must* not be—we hope they *will not be*—false to their trust!

If one is tempted to regard this as the attitude only of easterners seeking to influence western society from outside, listen for a moment to a sermon preached before the legislature of Wisconsin Territory in 1843:

> It will not answer for you to fold your hands in indolence and say "Let the East take care of the West. ... " The West must take care of itself—the West *must* and *will* form its own character—it must and will originate or perpetuate its own institutions, whatever be their nature. ... Much as our brethren in the East have done, or can do for us, the principal part of the task of enlightening and evangelizing this land is *ours;* if good institutions and virtuous principles prevail, it must be mainly through our own instrumentality. ... In the Providence of God, you have been sent to spy out and to take possession of this goodly land. To *you* God has committed the solemn responsibility of impressing upon it your own image: the likeness of your own moral character—a likeness which ... it will, in all probability, bear through all succeeding time. Am I not right then in saying that you ... occupy a position, both in time and place, of an exceedingly important nature?

The same evangelical fervor began to infuse the writings of educational reformers in the second quarter of the nineteenth century, and the same arguments appeared. When Horace Mann bade his "official

Farewell" to the school system of Massachusetts, he too spoke in terms of "a futurity rapidly hastening upon us." For the moment this was "a futurity, now fluid,—ready, as clay in the hands of the potter, to be moulded into every form of beauty and excellence." But, he reminded his fellow citizens, "so soon as it receives the impress of our plastic touch, whether this touch be for good or for evil, it is to be struck into . . . adamant." "Into whose form and likeness," he asked, "shall we fashion this flowing futurity?" The West was explicitly in his mind. In settlements already planted, the lack of educational provision posed problems of peculiar exigency, for "a different mental and moral culture must come speedily, or it will come too late." Nor was this all.

> Beyond our western frontier [he continued], another and a wider realm spreads out, as yet unorganized into governments, and uninhabited by civilized man. . . . Yet soon will every rood of its surface be explored. . . . Shall this new empire . . . be reclaimed to humanity, to a Christian life, and a Christian history; or shall it be a receptacle where the avarice . . . of a corrupt civilization shall . . . breed its monsters? If it is ever to be saved from such a perdition, the Mother States of this Union,—those States where the institutions of learning and religion are now honored and cherished, must send out their hallowing influences to redeem it. And if . . . the tree of Paradise is ever to be planted and to flourish in this new realm; . . . will not the heart of every true son of Massachusetts palpitate with desire . . . that her name may be engraved upon its youthful trunk, there to deepen and expand with its immortal growth?

Religious and educational ideals were not the only ones which Americans cherished and whose future they were unwilling to leave to chance. In establishing their political institutions, they were weighed down with thoughts of posterity, and of a posterity that would occupy lands as yet almost unexplored. At the Constitutional Convention James Wilson of Pennsylvania spoke to the following effect: "When he considered the amazing extent of country—the immense population which is to fill it, the influence which the Govt. we are to form will have, not only on the present generation of our people & their multiplied posterity, but on the whole Globe, he was lost in the magnitude of the object."

Such ideas as these found embodiment in the great series of documents which provided for the extension of government into the American West. Usually the purpose was so self-evident as to require no explicit statement. The Northwest Ordinance of 1787, for example, was without a preamble. It proceeded directly to the task of providing frames of government for the Northwest Territory, through all the stages up to statehood, and it concluded by setting forth certain "articles of compact" which were to "forever remain unalterable" and whose manifest purpose was to determine irrevocably for the future certain institutional patterns of the region. The framers of this and similar constitutional documents were proclaiming, by actions rather than words, their adherence to the set of beliefs under discussion here, namely, that the shape of western society was being determined in their own day, and that they possessed both the opportunity and the responsibility of helping to direct the process. "I am truly Sensible of the Importance of the Trust," said General Arthur St. Clair in 1788 when he accepted the first governorship of the Northwest Territory. He was aware, he continued, of "how much depends upon the due Execution of it—to you Gentlemen, over whom it is to be immediately exercised—to your Posterity! perhaps to the whole Community of America!"

Economic and social patterns, Americans believed, could also be determined for all future time during a few crucial years at the outset. Nothing was of greater concern to most inhabitants of the United States than the pattern of landownership which was likely to arise as a consequence of the disposal of the public domain. In this as in other matters, the present interests of the persons involved were naturally more compelling than the prospective interests of unborn generations. Nevertheless, concern for the latter was never pushed very far into the background. "Vote yourself a farm" was doubtless the most influential slogan of the land reformers. But not far behind in persuasiveness were arguments that dwelt upon the kind of future society which a particular present policy would inevitably produce. The argument was often put in negative form; propagandists warned of the evils that would inescapably follow from a wrong choice made during the crucial formative period.

> The evil of permitting speculators to monopolize the public lands [said a report of the land reformers in 1844], is already severely felt in the new states. . . . But what is this evil compared with the distress and misery that is in store for our children should we permit the evil of land monopoly to take firm root in this Republic? . . .
>
> Time rolls on—and in the lapse of a few ages all those boundless fields which now invite us to their bosom, become a settled property of individuals. Our descendants wish to raise themselves from the condition of hirelings, but they wish it in vain . . . and each succeeding age their condition becomes more and more hopeless. They read the history of their country; they learn that there was a time when their fathers could have preserved those domains, and transmitted them, free and unincumbered, to their children.

If once lost, the opportunity could never be regained. But if seized upon "by one bold step," the report continued, "our descendants will be in possession of an independence that cannot fail so long as God hangs his bow in the clouds."

Certain aspects even of the slavery controversy grow clearer when examined in the light of this characteristic American belief. One central paradox, at least, becomes much more understandable. "The whole controversy over the Territories," so a contemporary put it, "related to an imaginary negro in an impossible place." This was a large measure true. Even the admission of new slave states or of new free ones—and such admissions were occurring regularly—aroused no such controversy as raged about the exclusion of slavery from, or its extension to, unsettled areas where no one could predict the possible economic utility of the institution or its ability to survive. The violence of this controversy becomes explicable only if one grasps how important in the climate of opinion of the day was the belief that the society of the future was being uniquely determined by the small-scale institutional beginnings of the present.

From the Missouri crisis of 1819–1821 onwards, practically every major battle in the long-continued contest was fought over the question of whether slavery should go into, or be excluded from, territories whose social institutions had not yet crystallized. So long as both sides could rest assured that the existence or nonexistence of slavery was settled for every inch of territory in the United States, then the slavery controversy in politics merely smoldered. Such a salutary situation resulted from the Missouri Compromise, which drew a geographical dividing line across the territories. But when the Mexican War opened the prospect of new territorial acquisitions, the controversy burst into flame again with the Wilmot Proviso, which aimed to nip in the bud the possibility that slavery might ever become an institution in the new areas. The Compromise of 1850 composed the dispute with less definitiveness than had been achieved thirty years before, for the question of slavery in New Mexico and Utah was left open until those territories should be ripe for statehood. Though the Compromise was, for this reason, intrinsically less stable than the earlier one, the uncertainties that it left were in areas which settlement was hardly likely to reach in the near future. Comparative calm thus ensued until the Kansas-Nebraska Act of 1854. By opening to slavery the territories north of the old Missouri Compromise line, this measure threw back into uncertainty the character of the future social order of an area now on the verge of rapid settlement. Bleeding Kansas resulted from the effort to settle by force what could no longer be settled by law, namely, the kind of social institutions that should be allowed to take root in the new territory and thus determine its future for untold ages to come.

Abraham Lincoln in his speech at Peoria on October 16, 1854, made perfectly clear his reasons for opposing the doctrine of popular sovereignty embodied in the new act:

> Another important objection to this application of the right of self-government, is that it enables the first FEW, to deprive the succeeding

MANY, of a free exercise of the right of self-government. The first few may get slavery IN, and the subsequent many cannot easily get it OUT. How common is the remark now in the slave States—"If we were only clear of our slaves, how much better it would be for us." They are actually deprived of the privilege of governing themselves as they would, by the action of a very few, in the beginning.

Four years later Lincoln restated the argument in a letter to an old-time Whig associate in Illinois. His point of departure was a statement of Henry Clay's. "If a state of nature existed, and we were about to lay the foundations of society, no man would be more strongly opposed than I should to incorporate the institution of slavery among it's elements," Clay was quoted as saying. "Exactly so," was Lincoln's comment.

> In our new free ter[r]itories, a state of nature *does* exist. In them Congress lays the foundations of society; and, in laying those foundations, I say, with Mr. Clay, it is desireable that the declaration of the equality of all men shall be kept in view, as a great fundamental principle; and that Congress, which lays the foundations of society, should, like Mr. Clay, be strongly opposed to the incorporation of slavery among it's [sic] elements.

These statements come as close as any to explaining the true nature of the issue which neither side was willing to compromise in 1860–1861. In the midst of the crisis, it will be remembered, Congress passed and transmitted to the states for ratification a proposed constitutional amendment forever prohibiting any alteration of the Constitution that would permit Congress to interfere with slavery in the states. This provision was acceptable to Lincoln and the Republicans even though they were refusing to concede a single inch to slavery in the territories. On the other hand, the complete guarantee of slavery where it actually existed was insufficient to satisfy the Southern leaders, so long as permission to extend slavery into new areas was withheld. For both sides the issue was drawn over potentialities. But this does not mean that it involved unrealities. In the mid-nineteenth-century climate of opinion, potentialities were among the most real of all things. The issue of slavery in the territories was an emotionally potent one because it involved a postulate concerning the creation and development of social institutions, and a corresponding ethical imperative, both of which were woven into the very texture of American thought.

How communitarianism fitted into this tradition should now be clear. The communitarian point of view, in simplest terms, was the idea of commencing a wholesale social reorganization by first establishing and demonstrating its principles completely on a small scale in an experimental community. Such an approach to social reform could command widespread support only if it seemed natural and plausible. And it was plausible only if one made certain definite assumptions about the nature of society and of social change. These assumptions turn out to be precisely the ones whose pervasive influence on American thought this paper has been examining.

A belief in the plasticity of social institutions was prerequisite, for communitarians never thought in terms of a revolutionary assult upon a stiffly defended established order. To men and women elsewhere, the West seemed living proof that institutions were indeed flexible. If they failed to find them so at home, their hopes turned westward. As Fourierism declined in the later 1840s, its leaders talked more and more of a "model phalanx" in the West. George Ripley, founder of Brook Farm in Massachusetts, defended this shift, though it belied his earlier hopes for success in the East:

> There is so much more pliability in habits and customs in a new country, than in one long settled, that an impression could far more easily be produced and a new direction far more easily given in the one than in the other. An Association which would create but little sensation in the East, might produce an immense effect in the West.

But it was more than pliancy which communitarians had to believe in. Their doctrine assumed that institutions of worldwide scope might grow from tiny seeds deliberately planted. Such an assumption would be hard to make in most periods of history. The great organism of society must usually be taken for granted—a growth of untold centuries, from origins wrapped in obscurity. Rarely does experience suggest that the little projects of the present day are likely to develop into the controlling institutions of the morrow. Rarely has society been so open and free as to make plausible a belief that new institutions might be planted, might mature, and might reproduce themselves without being cramped and strangled by old ones. In America in the early nineteenth century, however, men and women believed that they could observe new institutions in the making, and they were confident that these would develop without check and almost without limit. Large numbers of Americans could be attracted to communitarianism because so many of its postulates were things they already believed.

Large numbers of Americans *were* attracted to communitarianism. If the experimental communities of the Middle West had been exclusively colonies of immigrants, attracted to vacant lands, then communitarianism would have had little significance for American intellectual history. But for the most part, as we have seen, communitarian colonies were made up of residents of the region. Though such experiments did not arise spontaneously on the frontier itself, they did arise with great frequency and spontaneity in the settled areas behind it. There men possessed a powerful sense of the plasticity of American institutions but were at the same time in contact with the social ideas circulating throughout the North Atlantic world. One strain of thought, fertilized the other. In a typical communitarian experiment of the Middle

West, men might pay lip service to Owen or Fourier, but their central idea was the conviction that a better society could grow out of the patent-office model they were intent on building.

On the whole, the fact that communitarianism stood in such a well-defined relationship to a central concept in American thought is perhaps the most important thing which the intellectual historian can seize upon in attempting to assess the significance of the communitarian movement. This movement has been looked at from many different points of view: as part of the history of socialism or communism, as a phase of religious history, as one manifestation of a somewhat vaguely defined "ferment" of democratic ideas. Communitarianism was relevant to these different categories, of course, but its true nature is hardly made clear by considering it within the limits of any one of these classifications. The only context broad enough to reveal the true significance of the communitarian point of view was the context provided by the early-nineteenth-century American way of thinking about social change.

This way of thinking was summed up and applied in the manifesto with which Victor Considerant launched his ambitious but ill-fated colony of French Fourierites in Texas in 1854:

> If the nucleus of the new society be implanted upon these soils, to-day a wilderness, and which to-morrow will be flooded with population, thousands of analogous organizations will rapidly arise without obstacle and as if by enchantment around the first specimens. . . .
>
> It is not the desertion of society that is proposed to you, but the solution of the great social problem on which depends the actual salvation of the world.

The last sentence stated an essential part of the true communitarian faith. A remaking of society, not an escape from its problems, was the aim of communitarian social reform during the period when it exerted a real influence upon American social thought. The dwindling of the ideal into mere escapism was the surest symptom of its decline. Such decline was unmistakable in the latter half of the nineteenth century. By 1875 a genuinely sympathetic observer could sum up in the following modest terms of the role which he believed communitarian colonies might usefully play in American life:

> That communistic societies will rapidly increase in this or any other country, I do not believe. . . . But that men and women can, if they *will*, live pleasantly and prosperously in a communal society is, I think proved beyond a doubt; and thus we have a right to count this another way by which the dissatisfied laborer may, if he chooses, better his condition.

In the late nineteenth century, it is true, numerous communitarian experiments were talked about and even commenced, and their prospectuses echoed the brave old words about planting seeds of a future universal social order. But such promises had ceased to be credible to any large number of Americans. Industrialism had passed beyond the stage at which a community of twenty-five hundred persons could maintain, as Owen believed they could, a full-scale manufacturing establishment at current levels of technological complexity and efficiency. Before the end of the nineteenth century, even communitarian sects like the Rappites and Shakers were in visible decline. The impulse to reform had not grown less, but it had found what it believed were more promising methods of achieving its ends. Men and women who were seriously interested in reform now thought in terms of legislation, or collective bargaining, or organized effort for particular goals, or even revolutionary seizure of power. Rarely did they consider, as so many in the first half of the century instinctively did, the scheme of embodying their complete ideal in a small-scale experimental model. When they did so, it was almost always a temporary move, a way of carrying on in the face of some setback, or a way of organizing forces for a future effort of a quite different sort. Such revivals of the communitarian program were apt to be sternly denounced as escapism by the majority of up-to-date socialists. In America, as in the world at large, communitarianism had become a minor eddy in the stream of socialism, whose main channel had once been defined by the communitarian writings of Robert Owen, William Thompson, Charles Fourier, Albert Brisbane, Victor Considerant, and Etienne Cabet.

The decline of communitarian confidence and influence paralleled the decline of the cluster of beliefs or postulates which this paper has been exploring. These intellectual assumptions faded out, not because the so-called free land was exhausted nor because the frontier line had disappeared from maps of population density but simply because social patterns had become so well defined over the whole area of the United States that the possibility no longer existed of affecting the character of the social order merely by planting the seeds of new institutions in the wilderness.

How quickly and completely the old set of beliefs vanished from the American mind was revealed by certain observations of James Bryce in 1888. In a speech to a western legislature Bryce reminded his hearers of "the fact that they were the founders of new commonwealths, and responsible to posterity for the foundations they laid." To his immense surprise, he discovered that this point of view—"trite and obvious to a European visitor," so he believed—had not entered the minds of these American legislators. In this instance it was not Bryce but his hearers who showed the greater perception. The idea he expressed had once been held in tenacity. In the end, however, it had grown not trite but anachronistic. No longer did it state a profound reality, as it might have done half a century before. By the 1880s there was no point in talking about laying the foundations of new commonwealths within the United States. The reforms in American life which Bryce thought necessary were not to be achieved that way. Serious social reformers in the later nineteenth century were faced with the task of altering institutions already firmly established. Henry George and Edward Bellamy recognized this in their writings; Grangers and trade unionists in their organizations; opponents of monopoly in the legislative approach they adopted. For most American reformers in an industrialized age, communitarianism was a tool that had lost its edge, probably forever.

# Michael B. Katz

MICHAEL B. KATZ (1939–      ) is professor of education and history at the University of Pennsylvania. His books include *The Irony of Early School Reform* (1968), *Class, Bureaucracy and Schools* (1971), and *The People of Hamilton, Canada West* (1975).

We live in an institutional state. Our lives spin outwards from the hospitals where we are born, to the school systems that dominate our youth, through the bureaucracies for which we work, and back again to the hospitals in which we die. If we stray, falter, or lose our grip, we are led or coerced towards the institutions of mental health, justice, or public welfare. Specialists in obstetrics, pediatrics, education, crime, mental illness, unemployment, recreation, to name only some of the most obvious, wait in the yellow pages to offer their expertise in the service of our well-being. Characteristically, we respond to a widespread problem through the creation of an institution, the training of specialists, and the certification of their monopoly over a part of our lives.

We accept institutions and experts as inevitable, almost eternal. That, after all, is the way the world works. It is hard—almost impossible—for us to recall that they are a modern invention.

In North America prior to the nineteenth century few experts or specialized institutions existed. The sick, the insane, and the poor mixed indiscriminately within relatively undifferentiated almshouses. Criminals of all ages and varieties remained in prison for fairly short periods awaiting trial. If guilty they were punished, not by long incarceration but by fine, whipping, or execution. Dependent or troublesome strangers did not receive much charity; they were simply warned out of town. Children learned to read in a variety of ways and attended schools irregularly. In short, families and communities coped with social and personal problems traditionally and informally.

Everything changed within fifty to seventy-five years. By the last quarter of the nineteenth century, specialized institutions were dealing with crime, poverty, disease, mental illness, juvenile delinquency, the blind, the deaf and dumb, and the ignorant. Institutions proliferated so

Michael B. Katz, "Origins of the Institutional State," *Marxist Perspectives* 1 (Winter, 1978): 6–22. Reprinted by permission of *Marxist Perspectives* and Michael B. Katz.

rapidly that by the 1860s some states began to create Boards of State Charities to coordinate and rationalize public welfare.

The treatment of crime, poverty, ignorance, and disease repeated the same story with different details. Institutions suddenly came to dominate public life in a radical departure in social policy. Aside from their sudden creation, most new public institutions experienced a similar cycle of development during their early histories: a shift from reform to custody. Mental hospitals, school systems, reformatories, and penitentiaries began optimistically with assumptions about the tractability of problems and the malleability of human nature. Early promoters expected them to transform society through their effect upon individual personalities. In some instances, as in the case of early mental hospitals or the first reformatory for young women, the optimism appeared justified for a few years. However, institutions, as even their supporters soon came to admit, could not work miracles. Rates of recovery remained low, recidivism high; school systems did not eliminate poverty and vice; ungrateful inmates even, on occasion, set their institutions on fire.

The public had invested heavily in new institutions that a reasonable person might conclude were failures. Nonetheless, the newly created institutional managers did not intend either to admit failure or to abandon the intricate hierarchical professional worlds they had created. Instead, they altered their justification: Mental illness and crime frequently arose from heredity and were incurable; lower-class children were incorrigible; paupers genetically unable and unwilling to work. Institutions existed to keep deviants off the streets; to prevent a glut on the labor market; to contain, not cure, the ills of society. This shift from reform to custody characterized the history of reformatories, mental hospitals, prisons, and school systems within the first two or three decades of their existence.

Social historians disagree about the impulse underlying institutional development. Why did the institutional State emerge at the time and in the manner it did? The question is straightforward, the answer complex and elusive. Actually, two sets of events must be explained: the origins and founding of institutions and the shift from reform to custody. Here, I shall consider only the former and attempt to show a connection between the origins of institutions and the early history of capitalism in North America.

First, consider the pattern and timing of institutional development. The new institutions of the early nineteenth century divide into various groups. Those on which historians have focused most sharply treated deviance: mental hospitals, poorhouses, reformatories, penitentiaries. The first mental hospital, the private McLean's opened in 1818, followed by the first state hospital in Worcester, Massachusetts in 1835. The first reformatory, also a private corporation, the New York House of Refuge, opened in 1825; the first state reform school incarcerated its first boys in 1848. Both Massachusetts and New York established a network of poorhouses in the 1820s as a result of the famous Quincy and Yates reports which urged the virtual abolition of outdoor relief. In Ontario the provincial penitentiary opened in 1835 and the lunatic asylum in 1850.

New institutions were not solely residential nor did they serve only those whom we today label deviant. The most notable of the nonresidential institutions designed to service a clearly defined sector of more ordinary people was the public school. Nineteenth-century educational promoters equated ignorance with deviance and both with poverty, but they intended public schools to serve a broader portion of the population than the children of the slums. And public schooling became especially popular among the middle classes. Tax-supported schools of sorts certainly had existed for centuries. The novelty during the nineteenth century rested in the creation of systems of public education—age-graded, finely articulated, nominally universal institutions presided over by specially trained experts and administrators. In New York City the system of public schools began with the organization of the Free School Society in 1805. The first state board of education was established in Massachusetts in 1837 and the Superintendency of Public Instruction in the Provinces of Canada in 1841. By 1880 elaborate, hierarchical educational systems existed in most urban centers.

New or novel institutions served other groups as well. Private boarding schools for the children of the rich developed in the antebellum period in the United States. The most influential of them, according to their historian, was St. Paul's, started in Concord, New Hampshire, in 1855. Indeed, it is fascinating to observe the parallels between private academies and other institutions. In their educational philosophy, organizational ideal, and theory of human nature, early reform schools resembled nothing so much as academies for the poor.

Within New York City, as Alan Horlick has shown, merchants developed a series of institutions to control and socialize the incoming hordes of young, aggressive, and undeferential clerks. This effort gave rise during the early nineteenth century to the YMCA, the Mercantile Library Association, and similar organizations.

The first general hospitals opened in 1752 in Philadelphia, in 1792 in New York City, and in 1821 in Boston. Construed primarily as charities, early hospitals were supposed to cure both the physical and moral afflictions of the poor who composed their patient populations. As with schools, prisons, or reformatories, the purposes of early hospitals included the reformation of character, and, like the sponsors of other institutions, hospital supporters compounded poverty, crime, ignorance, and disease into a single amalgam. Hospitals proved no more able than schools, prisons, or reformatories to uplift social character, and by the 1870s their purpose narrowed to the treatment of specific diseases. At the same time the internal development of hospitals traced a path similar to that followed in other institutions: a growth in size and complexity accompanied by an emphasis upon professional management increasingly divorced from lay influence.

At the most intimate level even the family reflected the thrust of institutional development in more public spheres. Decreasingly the place of both work and residence, with boundaries more tightly drawn between itself and the community, and decreasingly the custodian of the deviant and deficient, the family—the working-class as well as the middle-class family—became a sharply delimited haven, a specialized agency for the nurture of the young. Within families sex roles became more clearly defined, and by the mid-nineteenth century Catherine Beecher, among others, was attempting to certify the institutionalization of the home through the conversion of domesticity into a science.

In sum, the institutional explosion did not issue directly or solely from state sponsorship, nor were institutions directed only towards deviance or solely asylums. More accurately, institutional development during the early and middle nineteenth century should be described as the creation of formal organizations with specialized clienteles and a reformist, or characterbuilding, purpose.

Institutions were not in themselves novel. Poorhouses had existed in colonial New England. Indeed, Foucault labels the seventeenth century the age of the great confinement. Nonetheless, the use of institutions as deliberate agencies of social policy, their specialization, and their emphasis upon the formation or reformation of character represented a new departure in modern history.

Most major social institutions originated in a two-stage process. They commenced as private corporations to serve public purposes but within a few decades were imitated, superseded, augmented, or expanded by the State. The transition from voluntarism to the State did not represent a simple evolution. Certainly, the magnitude of the problems undertaken by early voluntary corporations—the alleviation of poverty, mental illness, delinquency, ignorance—strained private resources. Financially, voluntary corporations, however, did not rely solely, or, in many cases, at all, upon private contributions. Rather, they commonly received public funds. The assumption of primary responsibility for the operation as well as the funding of institutions, consequently, represented a shift in generally acceptable models for public organization. Elsewhere, I have called this shift the transition from paternalistic and corporate voluntarism to incipient bureaucracy. Voluntarism upheld an ideal of organizations controlled by self-perpetuating corporations of wealthy, enlightened, a public-spirited citizens, essentially limited in size, staffed by talented generalists. The shift to the State reflected a belief that public funding required public control, a commitment to expansion of scale, and an emphasis upon the importance of specialized, expert administration.

The shift from voluntarism to the State appears in the New York House of Refuge, the McLean Hospital, the New York Free School Society, and another interesting variant, the Boston Primary School Committee. When these voluntary corporations went public they often altered their purpose as well as their form. In the case of mental hospitals, the entrance of the State meant the extension of service from the well-to-do served by McLean's to the poor treated at Worcester; in the case of public schools the opposite occurred, as school promoters sought to incorporate the children of the affluent into the free schools, which in their early years had suffered from their association with pauperism and charity. Both the mental hospitals and the public schools illustrate an attempt to broaden the social composition of public institutions.

The early history of hospitals formed an instructive, if partial, exception to the shift away from corporate voluntarism. The great early hospitals in Philadelphia, New York, and Boston, to name three, remained under the control of private, nonprofit corporations. When public representatives wanted hospitals to expand their size, role, or scope, they could not bring them under State control. Rather, they sometimes had to establish parallel institutions. In Boston in the 1860s the board and staff of the Massachusetts General Hospital fought against the creation of Boston City Hospital, which they explicitly viewed as an institution more "democratic" and more accessible to public influence in such important ways as admission procedures and internal routines like visiting hours. The social group that wanted Boston City was not the very poor served by Massachusetts General but the skilled workers, petty proprietors, and clerks who were less welcome at the older hospital yet unable to afford easily the cost of medical care at home. The reason that hospitals remained under private control probably rests in their relation to the medical profession. Often, physicians instigated the founding of hospitals and played the principal roles not only in a strictly professional capacity but also in institutional design and administration. Hospitals differed from other major social institutions in that a prestigious, prosperous, and generally cohesive corps of professionals preceded their establishment. By contrast, mental hospitals and schools, to take two examples, created two new professions. The founding of mental hospitals and school systems, therefore, much more than of general hospitals, depended upon lay support, and they consequently remained much more susceptible to public influence during their early years.

Although private hospitals did not go public, they still reflected one process that characterized other institutions: the shift in the social origins of their clientele. For years hospital supporters had tried to broaden the social composition of the patient population, but, as in the case of early public education, the aura of charity clung to hospitals. In sharp contrast to public schools, however, hospitals were unable to shed that aura until a series of demographic changes and medical advances coalesced during the late nineteenth and early twentieth centuries. The transition from home to hospital care by the affluent was symbolized dramatically by the construction of the expensive and luxurious Phillips House as a branch of the Massachusetts General in 1817.

The supersession of corporate voluntarism reflected the increasingly sharp distinction between public and private, which formed part of a larger theme in social development: the drawing of sharp boundaries between the elements of social organization; the separation of family and community; the division of community into discrete and specialized functions.

The connection that exists between the emergence of modern society and the expansive specialization of both public and private institutions remains open to interpretation. How are we to account, in this case, for the origins of public institutions? What, precisely, did they signify?

Historians currently offer two principal, competing interpretations, which, put crudely, can be called the fear of social disorder versus the humanitarian impulse. The most notable exponent of the former is David Rothman, of the latter, Gerald Grob. Here I must risk some violence to their complex and subtle work in order to highlight the central point in contention and the problems left unresolved. Although Grob has attacked Rothman, the two share much common ground, as Rothman points out in a review of Grob's most recent book. Both tell a similar story and even stress many of the same factors, but they differ in the interpretation they give to events and, ultimately, in the meaning they assign to American history in the formative years between the Revolution and the Civil War.

Rothman argues that the fear of disorder arising from the breakdown of traditional communal controls spurred the discovery of the asylum. He writes, "The response in the Jacksonian period to the deviant and the dependent was first and foremost a vigorous attempt to promote the stability of the society at a moment when traditional ideas and practices appeared outmoded, constricted, and ineffective . . . all represented an effort to insure the cohesion of the community in new and changing circumstances." Elsewhere he asserts, "under the influence of demographic, economic and intellectual developments, they [Americans] perceived that the traditional mechanisms of social control were obsolete."

Grob emphasizes the individualist philosophy and humanitarian impulses that arose from the Second Awakening. Although he cannot deny the pervasive fear of social disorder or the manifest influence of class in the social origins of reformers, he argues:

> Since the absence of broad theoretical models relating to public policy made it difficult to gather or to use empirical data in a meaningful way, policy often reflected external factors such as unconscious class interests or similar social assumptions that were never questioned. This is not to imply that mid-nineteenth century legislators and administrators were deficient in intelligence or malevolent in character. It is only to say that lack of theory and methodology often led to the adoption of policies that in the long run had results which were quite at variance with the intentions of those involved in their formulation.

Grob's arresting and partly true statement rests on the assumption that knowledge—hard data—scientific in character and free from bias does in fact exist and awaits discovery by students of deviance and dependence. It assumes further that the acquisition of scientific knowledge automatically leads to rational, humanitarian solutions framed in the best interests of the people to which they were directed. The history of social and behavioral science should make us skeptical.

Five problems, which appear in varying degrees in different accounts, underlie most formulations of both the social disorder and humanitarian interpretations, the very problems that appear in most attempts to explain early-nineteenth-century social reforms and institutional creation.

First, most interpretations do not provide a link between institutions created for deviants and the other institutional developments of the time. An adequate interpretation must encompass not only the asylum, not only prisons, mental hospitals, and poorhouses, but also public schools, academies, the YMCA, and, ultimately, the family. Striking parallels exist between the timing, theory, and shape of those developments which affect deviants, dependents, children, adolescents, and families. An understanding of any of them depends upon an exploration of their interconnection.

Second, definitions of disorder usually remain loose. Scholars invoke industrialization and urbanization, but these broad concepts mask as much as they reveal. What was it, exactly, about the development of cities that created social disorder? What type of mechanisms broke down, when, and why? The arrival of hundreds of thousands of impoverished immigrants might explain a heightened concern with poverty or account for some of the nervousness on the part of genteel natives, but it assists little in an attempt to comprehend the origins of academies or even the special attention paid to the mentally ill.

Third, the way in which historical context intersects with the perception of people differentially situated in the social order usually remains unclear. The exact relation between the periodization of socioeconomic and institutional development rarely is made explicit, and the identity of institutional sponsors and opponents—and opposition did exist—remains unclear in most accounts. We are left with David Rothman's "Americans," surely a category within which significant differences of opinion existed. But which Americans wanted the asylum? How did their perceptions influence public policy?

There are, however, few, if any, historical subjects more treacherous than human motivation—thus, the fourth problem with existing interpretations. They simplistically use models of individual behavior. They confuse, that is, the analysis of individual motivation with the analysis of class. Class analysis does not deny that individuals believe they do good works. It regards individual sincerity as irrelevant. Class analysis concerns the actions of groups and the relation between activity and class position. It does not deny the role of religion or tradition in the formulation and expression of class action. The theory of class is neither crudely reductionist nor contradicted by the existence of deeply felt humanitarian conviction. To argue that institutional promoters believed they were acting in the best interests of the poor, the criminal, the mentally ill, or the ignorant, and to leave the argument there, is not to refute a class analysis but merely to finesse it.

The reluctance to probe the interconnections between social context, social position, ideology, and policy underlies the fifth problem. Most accounts of institutional development and social reform uncritically accept the interpretation of problems offered by institutional promoters and social reformers. They fail to question the description of crime, poverty, mental illness, or illiteracy offered in official sources. Thus, Grob simply accepts the proposition that immigrants were more prone than others to insanity and does not probe the social characteristics shaping definitions of mental illness. Other historians similarly accept the proposition that crime increased disproportionately in early-nineteenth-century cities, that industrialization eroded the stability of the lower-class family, or that, as Oscar Handlin has written, the Irish were degraded.

The acceptance of official descriptions of reality ignores important considerations. First, deviance is at least partly a social or political category and cannot be defined as a universal. It is the product of prevailing laws, customs, and views. Second, institutional promoters sometimes gauged popular sentiments inaccurately. The poor occasionally used new institutions in ways that violated the purposes and perceptions of their sponsors. For example, parents themselves provided the largest source of commitments to reform schools. The working-class family, however, was not breaking down. Rather, poor parents turned to reform schools, which had not yet acquired their present stigma, precisely as other and more affluent parents turned to academies as places that would remove their refractory children from trouble and educate them at the same time. Other poor parents used reform schools in difficult periods as places in which children could stay safely during episodes of family crisis. The people at whom institutions were directed were not inert or passive. The image of degradation and helplessness that emerges from institutional promoters must be treated, always, with skepticism. Indeed, wherever historians have looked with care—and the recent historiography of slavery has been especially rich in this regard—severe disjunctions emerge between official perception of client populations and their actual behavior.

Thus, a new interpretation of the origin of the institutional State should be set within a revised framework of North American social development between the late eighteenth and the middle nineteenth century. In particular, it should rest on a substitution of a three-stage for the more familiar two-stage paradigm that underlies much of North American history. The focus of the revised framework should be the spread of wage labor and the values associated with capitalism rather than urbanization and industrialization.

Most North American history rests on a simple two-stage paradigm—a shift from a preindustrial to an industrial society or from rural to urban life—which obscures the relationship between institutions and social change. For, though the transformation of economic structures and the creation of institutions did take place at roughly the same period, attempts to construct causal models or to develop tight and coherent explanations usually appear mechanistic or vague.

When a three-stage paradigm replaces the two-stage one, the connection between social change and institutional creation becomes tighter. In the three-stage paradigm North America shifted from a peculiar variety of a mercantile-peasant economy to an economy dominated by commercial capital to industrial capitalism. Though the pace of change varied from region to region and stages overlapped each other, the most important aspect of the late eighteenth and early nineteenth centuries was not industrialization or urbanization but, rather, the spread of capitalism defined, in Maurice Dobb's words, as "not simply a system of production for the market... but a system under which labour-power had itself become a commodity and was bought and sold on the market like any other object of exchange." Capitalism was the necessary, though conceptually distinct, antecedent of industrialization.

Consider the following as reflections of the spread of capitalist relations prior to industrialization. Between 1796 and 1855, prior to industrialization, the most striking change in New York City's occupational structure, according to Carl Kaestle's figures, was the increase in the proportion of men who listed themselves simply as laborers—an increase from 5.5 percent to 27.4 percent. Moreover, apprenticeship, whose emphasis on bound labor is incompatible with capitalism, had ceased to function with anything like its traditional character well before industrialization. In both Buffalo, New York, and Hamilton, Ontario, prior to their industrialization, there were about eleven skilled wage workers and several semiskilled and unskilled ones for every independent master or manufacturer. From a different point of view one historian recently has pointed to an unmistakable increase in the wandering of the poor from place to place in late-eighteenth-century Massachusetts. The expansion of commerce in this period has been documented extensively, and it was in this era that state governments exhanged their essentially mercantilist policies for reliance upon competition and private initiative to regulate the economy.

The problem, thus, becomes one of formulating the connection between the development of capitalism and the spread of institutions. The drive towards institutional development preceded the industrial takeoff in the Northeast. Any interpretation based upon industrialization must fall simply upon considerations of time. A much better temporal connection exists between institutional origins and the spread of capitalist relations of production.

The most profound statement of the relation between capitalism and the institutional State occurs in the remarkable book by the late Harry Braverman, *Labor and Monopoly Capital*. It is worth considering in detail:

> The ebbing of family facilities, and of family, community, and neighborly feelings upon which the performance of many social functions formerly depended, leaves a void. As the family members, more of them now at work away from home, become less and less able to care for each other in time of need, and as the ties of neighborhood, community and friendship are reinterpreted on a narrower scale to exclude onerous responsibilities, the care of humans for each other becomes increasingly institutionalized. At the same time, the human detritus of the urban civilization increases, not just because of the aged population, its life prolonged by the progress of medicine grows ever larger; those who need care include children—not only those who cannot "function" smoothly but even the "normal" ones whose only defect is their tender age. Whole new strata of the helpless and dependent are created, or familiar old ones enlarged enormously: the proportion of "mentally ill" or "deficient," the "criminals," the pauperized layers at the bottom of society, all representing varieties of crumbling under the pressures of capitalist urbanism and the conditions of capitalist employment or unemployment. In addition, the pressures of urban life grow more intense and it becomes harder to care for any who need care in the conditions of the jungle of the cities. Since no care is forthcoming from an atomized community, and since the family cannot bear all such encumbrances if it is to strip for action in order to survive and "succeed" in the market society, the care of all these layers becomes institutionalized, often in the most barbarous and oppressive forms. Thus understood, the massive growth of institutions stretching all the

way from schools and hospitals on the one side to prisons and madhouses on the other represents not just the progress of medicine, education, or crime prevention, but the clearing of the marketplace of all but the "economically active" and "functioning" members of society. . . .

Note that Braverman isolates three processes that link capitalism and institutions: (1) the absolute growth of a dependent population through underemployment, accidents, and other means; (2) the end of traditional ways of caring for dependents; (3) the creation of new types of dependents—not just the sick, poor, or criminal, but all who are economically unproductive and, as a consequence, put out of the way and out of sight. In fact, all three processes can be shown clearly at work in late-eighteenth- and early-nineteenth-century North America. Take some examples:

First, the rise in transiency. By the early nineteenth century a highly mobile class of wage laborers, cut off from close ties with any communities, drifted about and between cities. Living for the most part in nuclear families, with no personal or communal resources for the periods of recurrent poverty or frequent disaster that disfigured their lives, they swelled the dependent class.

The recognition that transiency had become a widespread way of life impelled the reform of the poor laws called for by the Quincy and Yates reports in Massachusetts and New York during the second decade of the nineteenth century. Previously, counties had retained legal responsibility for their own poor almost wherever they wandered. Poor strangers were warned out of town or shipped back to the communities from which they came. But after a point who could claim that any particular community could be considered home for the poor who wandered through it? The upsurge in population movement made obsolete the concept of a community of origin, and the very size of the problem meant that the customary practice would produce an endless stream of poor people shipped back and forth between counties. The sensible solution appeared to be to end the traditional practice and to require each county to support the poor within its boundaries, whatever their place of origin, in a new network of poorhouses strung out across the state.

The problem of the poor illustrates both the growth of dependency and breakdown of traditional ways of coping with poverty. Other developments underscore another process—the creation of new categories of dependency. One of these categories was youth. In earlier times the life cycle of young people had followed a clear and well-defined sequence. At no point in their lives were they uncertain how they should spend their time or in what setting they should live. But the erosion of apprenticeship and, contrary to popular belief, the lack of wage work for

young men in the early phase of capitalist development, occurred before
the creation of any set of institutions to contain or instruct them. In
consequence, young people in the nineteenth-century city faced a crisis
that cut across class lines. In the 1820s, for instance, a group of Boston
merchants gathered at the home of William Ellery Channing to discuss
their anxieties about their sons, no longer needed in the countinghouse
or on shipboard at the age of fourteen. The result of that meeting was
Boston English High School. In Hamilton, Ontario, the rapid creation of
a public school system with special provisions for adolescent students
followed the period in which the crisis of idle youth became most acute.
Similarly, the disruption of traditional career patterns and living arrangements for young men in New York City provoked worried merchants to create new institutions to guide their behavior and refine their
manners.

The nineteenth century's institutionalized population represented
the casualities of a new social order: landless workers exposed without
buffers to poverty and job-related accidents; men broken by the strain of
achievement in a competitive, insecure world; women driven to desperation by the enforced repression inherent in contemporary ideals of
domesticity; or even children—casualties on account of their age. But
how did institutions assume the shape they did? Why did the response
to problems take the form not simply of institutions but of ones
specialized in organization and reformist in intent?

Peter Dobkin Hall offers an answer applicable to the early, voluntarist
stage of institutional development. After the Revolution, he argues, merchants sought to expand the scope of their activities. To do so, they had
to increase specialization, pool risks, create joint-stock corporations, and
accumulate capital outside of family firms:

> The disengagement of capital from family firms was achieved through two
> fundamental innovations in the means of wealth transmission: the testamen-
> tary trust and the charitable endowment. Under testamentary trusts it be-
> came possible for testators to entirely avoid the partible division of their
> estates. . . . The charitable endowment was also a kind of trust. Through it
> moneys could be left in perpetuity to trustees or to a corporate body for the
> accomplishment of a variety of social welfare purposes—most of which had,
> in Massachusetts, been traditionally carried out through families. Once the
> merchants began to search for means of disengaging capital from familial
> concerns, they quickly recognized the usefulness of charitable endowments
> both for the accumulation of capital and for relieving their families from the
> burdens of welfare activity.

The specialization in mercantile life between institutions for credit,
insurance, wholesaling, retailing, warehousing, and other activities reflected the division of labor that characterizes capitalist development.
That division, as Marx observed, takes opposite forms in social life and

in industry. Within manufacturing the division of labor results from the combination of previously distinct operations into one process. By contrast, the social division of labor requires the decomposition of tasks—all originally performed by the family—into separate organizations. "In one case," wrote Marx, "it is the making dependent what was before independent; in the other case the making independent what was before dependent." Equally, with cotton mills, foundries, or shoe factories, new social institutions—schools, penitentiaries, mental hospitals, reformatories—exemplified in their own way the division of labor as the dynamic organizational principle of their age.

The spread of what Christopher Lasch called the "single standard of honor" accompanied the early history of capitalism in North America. By that standard the unproductive became more than a nuisance; they became unworthy. In an attempt to raise their usefulness, the unproductive were swept into massive brick structures that looked distressingly like factories and there taught those lessons in social and economic behavior which, it was hoped, would facilitate their reentry into real workplaces. The depressing sameness about the look of schools, prisons, mental hospitals, and factories belied the sentimentality of the age. The romantic proclamation of the child's innocence, purity, and potential masked the disdain and exasperation that designed urban schools or reformatories. As in the case of children, a transmutation of disdain into purity justified the confinement of women in the institution called home. Indeed, the unwillingness to acknowledge confinement as nasty proved a remarkable feature of early nineteenth-century institutional promotion. But promoters protested too much: Their love for, or at least neutrality towards, those they would incarcerate sounds hollow when echoing through the halls of a nineteenth-century mental hospital, prison, or school. We do no better today, though our particular specialty is perhaps the aged. We construct ghettos for the aged, ostensibly because they want them. In fact, we want to have them out of the way. The single standard of honor remains our legacy and our trademark.

Early capitalist development was experienced by the immediate heirs of the Enlightenment and the Revolution—by people swept simultaneously by optimistic theories of human nature and evangelical religion. Their intellectual and religious heritage composed complex lenses through which people filtered their perceptions of social and economic change. The refraction undoubtedly contributed to their interpretation of crime, poverty, mental illness, ignorance, and youth as conditions of character. Imbued with a belief in progress and committed to either a secular or spiritual millenium, institutional promoters approached their work optimistically, defining their task as the shaping of souls. Nonetheless, characters were to be shaped to a standard with clear components: sensual restraint, dependability, willingness to work, acquiescence in the legitimacy of the social order, and acceptance of one's place within it—all serviceable traits in early capitalist America.

One example sums up the problem of character, its relation to social institutions, to cultural definitions of deviance, and to the personal strain exacted by early capitalism: the trouble with the first patient admitted to the New York State Lunatic Asylum when it opened on January 14, 1843. He thought he was Tom Paine.

# 9

# American Slavery

## Benign or Malignant?

Although Americans of the mid-nineteenth century were prone to glorify their nation and its institutions, they were also aware that millions of blacks remained enslaved and possessed none of the legal rights and privileges promised to citizens by the Declaration of Independence. Paradoxically, a people who prided themselves on having created one of the freest societies in the world also sanctioned slavery—an institution that many other nations less free had long since abolished.

The existence of the "peculiar institution," of course, played a crucial role in American history. In the Constitutional Convention of 1787, the founding fathers were forced to deal with its presence. Despite subsequent efforts at suppression, the slavery controversy would not remain quiescent. The presumed compromise settlements of 1820 and 1850 proved transitory. Ultimately it took a long and bloody civil war to end the legal existence of the "peculiar institution." Even after that war the problems posed by the presence of a black minority in a predominantly white society continued to plague generations of Americans from the Civil War to the present.

Just as Northerners and Southerners debated the morality and legitimacy of slavery in antebellum decades, so too have later historians disagreed over the nature of the "peculiar institution." Controversy rather than consensus characterizes the debates among historians. Scholars cannot agree on the origins of slavery; they debate why it was that only blacks were enslaved, and Indians and indentured servants were not. They disagree whether racism preceded slavery, or if racial prejudice developed as a rationalization of an already established institution.[1] Similarly, historians continue to debate the nature of slavery and its immediate and enduring impact upon black Americans.

---

[1]Cf. Oscar and Mary F. Handlin, "Origins of the Southern Labor System," *William and Mary Quarterly*, 3d ser. 7 (1950): 199–222; Winthrop D. Jordan, *White Over Black: American Attitudes Toward the Negro, 1550–1812* (Chapel Hill, 1968); and Edmund S. Morgan, *American Slavery, American Freedom: The Ordeal of Colonial Virginia* (New York, 1975).

The framework for the historical debate over slavery was first established by the participants in the controversy in the decades preceding the Civil War. Northerners bent on making a strong case against slavery were prone to seek out those facts that buttressed their positions. Southerners, on the other hand, were equally determined to show the beneficence of their "peculiar institution." Similarly, the large number of eyewitness accounts of travelers in the South tended to reflect personal views regarding the morality or immorality of slavery. From the very beginning, therefore, questions about the nature of slavery tended to be discussed within a predominantly moral framework.

The first serious scholarly effort to delineate the nature of slavery came from a group of historians who came to the fore in the 1880s and 1890s. Being a generation removed from the Civil War, they were less involved emotionally in the issue. These scholars tended to view the end of slavery as a blessing to both North and South. The Civil War, once and for all, had sealed the bonds of unity in blood, and had created a single nation rather than a collection of sovereign states. Nationalistic in their orientation, these historians developed an interpretation of slavery similar in many respects to the one held by some prewar antislavery partisans.

James Ford Rhodes, a businessman turned historian who published a major multivolume history of the United States covering the period from 1850 to 1877, was perhaps typical of this nationalist school of scholars. His first volume began with an unequivocal statement of his position: slavery was an immoral institution. Rhodes's treatment of slavery was little more than a restatement of Henry Clay's famous dictum that "slavery is a curse to the master and a wrong to the slave." He cited evidence that blacks were often overworked and underfed. The institution was brutalizing; the slave and slave family lacked any legal rights to afford a measure of protection against the arbitrary and often cruel behavior by white masters. Pointing to the sexual exploitation of black women, Rhodes insisted that slavery had debased the entire nation.[2] His study established the pattern for much of the subsequent treatment of American slavery by historians.

Surprisingly enough, Rhodes's work gained general acceptance not only among Northern historians but among Southern scholars as well. Southerners were willing to condemn slavery as a reactionary institution that inhibited the economic development of their section. They now welcomed its abolition, and looked forward to a new era of prosperity in which the South would share in the nation's industrial progress. Rhodes's hostility toward the Radical Reconstruction program after 1865

---

[2]James Ford Rhodes, *History of the United States from the Compromise of 1850 to the Final Restoration of Home Rule in the South in 1877*, 7 vols. (New York, 1893–1906), 1.

and his willingness to acquiecse in the right of Southern whites to deal with the race question as they saw fit made his views acceptable in that part of the country.

For nearly a quarter of a century, the historical view of slavery followed the pattern set forth by Rhodes and other nationalist scholars. In 1918, however, Ulrich Bonnell Phillips—undoubtedly the most important historian of the ante-bellum South—published his *American Negro Slavery*. From that moment, the debate over slavery assumed a somewhat different form. Subsequent historians, whatever their views, had to take Phillips's work into account. Indeed, it may not be too much to claim that the vitality of the historiographical debate over slavery was due in large measure to Phillips's pioneering contributions.

Born in Georgia in 1877, Phillips attended the state university and then went on to receive his doctorate at Columbia University. Rather than returning to the South, he accepted an offer from the University of Wisconsin, then a center of American Progressivism. Phillips adopted many of the tenets of Progressivism; as a scholar he attempted to break with the emphasis on political and legal events and to study the underlying social and economic factors responsible for shaping the nation's history. Aside from his commitment to much of the ideology of Progressivism, Phillips was an indefatigable researcher; his work was marked by deep and intensive study of original sources drawn from plantation records.

Phillips's view of slavery grew out of his general interpretation of antebellum Southern society. Focusing on the plantation system, he sought to demonstrate that it was much more than a system of landholding or of racial exploitation. The plantation was rather a complete social system in which paternalism and capitalism went hand in hand. Indeed, his commentaries on the new postwar South tended to be highly critical because he believed that industrial capitalism without any redeeming humane and paternalistic features was cruel and harsh. His sympathetic portrayal of the Old South, as Eugene Genovese remarked, was "an appeal for the incorporation of the more humane and rational values of pre-bourgeois culture into modern industrial life."

Slavery, according to Phillips, was above all a system of education. Sharing the racial views held by many Southerners and Northerners (particularly those who believed in the Progressive ideology), Phillips viewed blacks as a docile, childlike people who required the care and guidance of paternalistic whites. In this sense, he rejected another stereotype held by many of his contemporaries who feared and hated blacks. Bringing together massive evidence from original sources, Phillips painted a subtle and complex portrait of slavery that repudiated the older allegations that the system was inhumane and cruel. Indeed, he emphasized over and over again the profound human relationships that existed between paternal white masters and faithful and childlike black slaves. Yet Phillips, despite the sharp differences in interpretation, owed a significant debt to earlier scholars like Rhodes, for his categories in studying slavery—labor, food, clothing, shelter, care, and the profitability of the system—were precisely the same as those of his predecessor. *American Negro Slavery*, then, was both a sympathetic portrait of the past and a commentary on a harsh and impersonal present.[3] For nearly a generation, Phillips's view of slavery remained the dominant one. Scholars who followed in his footsteps made a few revisions, but none altered the general picture he had so skillfully sketched. One of the few exceptions was Herbert Aptheker's study of slave revolts in 1943. Aptheker challenged Phillips's portrait of docile slaves and insisted that "discontent and rebelliousness" was more characteristic.[4]

At the same time that Phillips's interpretation of slavery was becoming dominant, a reaction began setting in against the prevailing theories of race. The work of figures like Franz Boas and others had begun to undermine racial interpretations of culture; an emphasis on environment slowly began to replace the earlier belief in the primacy of race. The experiences of the 1930s and 1940s further discredited racist theories, particularly after the ramifications of this doctrine were revealed by events in Nazi Germany. The political ideologies of these decades, moreover, involved a rejection of race theory on both scientific and philosphical grounds. In view of these developments, it was not surprising that the interpretation espoused by Phillips began to be challenged by critics who did not share his historical, racial, or political ideas.

The attack on Phillips and the efforts to discredit *American Negro Slavery*, oddly enough, did not alter the framework within which the debate over slavery took place. Indeed, critics accepted the same categories of analysis employed by Phillips and his predecessors. Their differences with him were largely moral in character. Where Phillips painted a portrait of a harmonious, interdependent, and humane system, his detractors emphasized the cruel and arbitrary nature of slavery, its economic and sexual exploitation, and the degree to which blacks resisted the abominations practiced by their masters. Moreover, Phillips's research methodology came under careful scrutiny. Richard Hofstadter, in an article published in 1944, argued that *American Negro Slavery* was flawed because its thesis rested on a faulty sampling of plantation rec-

---

[3]For sympathetic evaluations of Phillips's achievements see Eugene D. Genovese, "Race and Class in Southern History: An Appraisal of the Work of Ulrich Bonnell Phillips," *Agricultural History* 41 (October 1967): 345–58, and Daniel J. Singal, "Ulrich Bonnell Phillips: The Old South as the New," *Journal of American History* 63 (March 1977): 871–91.

[4]Herbert Aptheker, *American Negro Slave Revolts* (New York, 1943).

ords. Most slaves lived on smaller plantations or farms, Hofstadter noted, whereas Phillips used records of large plantations.[5]

The attack on Phillips culminated in 1956 when Kenneth M. Stampp published *The Peculiar Institution*. Stampp, some years earlier, had become convinced that the time was ripe for a complete reappraisal of the subject. Besides the problems of a biased sample of plantation records and a reluctance to use unfavorable contemporary travel accounts, Stampp charged, Phillips had accepted without question assumptions about the supposed inferiority of blacks.[6] *The Peculiar Institution*, then, was written specifically to revise *American Negro Slavery*. In place of a harmonious antebellum South, Stampp pictured a system of labor that rested upon the simple element of force. In a chapter entitled "To Make Them Stand in Fear," he argued that, without the power to punish, the system of bondage could not have been sustained.

Yet Stampp was unable to break out of the mold within which the debate over slavery had taken place; his analytical categories were virtually identical to those of Rhodes and Phillips. The difference—which was by no means insignificant—was that Stampp's view of slavery was quite similar to that held by Northern abolitionists.

*The Peculiar Institution* summed up nearly a century of historical controversy. Its author, as a matter of fact, was forced by his own evidence to qualify any sweeping generalization about slavery. He conceded that the "only generalization that can be made with relative confidence is that some masters were harsh and frugal, others were mild and generous, and the rest ran the whole gamut in between." Moreover, Stampp's egalitarian commitment led him to see slavery not through the eyes of slaves (an admittedly difficult task) but through the eyes of whites. "Negroes," he wrote in his introduction, "*are*, after all, only white men with black skins, nothing more, nothing less."[7]

Shortly after Stampp published his book, the debate over slavery took a new shape. There were a number of reasons for this transformation. No doubt the diminishing returns within the traditional conceptual framework played a role. More important, historians and social scientists were beginning to raise certain kinds of issues about the nature of the black experience in America that resulted in some radical rethinking about slavery. Computer technology also made it possible for the first time to use data in ways that were previously impracticable. But perhaps

---

[5]Richard Hofstadter, "U. B. Phillips and the Plantation Legend," *Journal of Negro History* 29 (April 1944): 109–24. The criticisms of Phillips can be followed in the pages of the *Journal of Negro History*.

[6]Kenneth M. Stampp, "The Historian and Southern Negro Slavery," *American Historical Review* 57 (April 1952): 613–24.

[7]Kenneth M. Stampp, *The Peculiar Institution: Slavery in the Ante-Bellum South* (New York, 1956), pp. vii, 616.

the most significant factor was the changes in the intellectual milieu of the late 1950s and the period thereafter. During the civil rights movement, blacks and whites alike challenged the prevailing patterns of social and economic relations between the races. The ensuing reorientation of social and political thought quickly influenced the writing of American history. Slavery became one of the most vital and controversial subjects in American history, and the evidence is strong that the subject will continue to be of great interest to future scholars.

The first major challenge to traditional historiography came in 1959 when Stanley Elkins published a brief study entitled *Slavery: A Problem in American Institutional and Intellectual Life.* Elkins's book was not based on new data. Indeed, when compared with Stampp's *The Peculiar Institution*, it was evident that *Slavery* was written without significant research in existing primary sources. What Elkins did—and herein lay the significance of his work—was to pose a series of questions that moved the debate over the nature of slavery to a totally new plane.

Elkins began his study by noting that the abolition of slavery in Latin America had not left the severe race problem faced by the United States. Intrigued by this observation, Elkins concluded that it was the absence of countervailing institutions in the United States such as a strong national church that permitted slavery to develop without any obstructions that might mitigate its power. Secondly, Elkins stressed the harshness of American slavery and argued that it had a devastating impact on the black personality. He insisted that the Black Sambo stereotype—the shuffling, happy-go-lucky, not very intelligent black—had a basis in fact. Elkins used the analogy of the Nazi concentration camps to demonstrate that total, or totalitarian, institutions could reduce their inmates to perpetual childlike dependency. Hence, the all-encompassing institution of slavery had given rise to the Sambo personality type. Implicit in Elkins's work was the belief that slavery victimized blacks by stripping them of their African heritage, making them dependent on whites, and preventing them from forming any cohesive family structure. The first selection in this chapter is a section from Elkins's book.

Elkins's thesis seemed acceptable to historians and other Americans, at first, partly because it undermined still further a racial ideology that had assumed the innate inferiority of blacks. By stressing that blacks were victims of slavery, Elkins repudiated the more benign view of that institution and even made Stampp's unflattering description far less potent. Morever, Elkins appeared to provide intellectual support for compensatory social and economic programs in the 1960s designed to help blacks overcome a residual effects of slavery. Elkins implicitly placed the responsibility for the nation's racial dilemmas squarely upon whites by picturing blacks as unwilling victims of white transgressions.

Elkins's book had (and still has) a profound influence. First, it raised questions heretofore neglected, such as the relationship between slavery and subsequent racial conflict. Second, it inspired a group of scholars to undertake studies of comparative slave systems in order to answer some questions posed by Elkins. Third, it placed the slavery debate within a new conceptual framework, for Elkins had focused less on slavery as an institution and more upon blacks themselves. Finally, Elkins—more than his colleagues—had linked history with other social science disciplines.[8]

Yet, within a few years after the appearance of his book, Elkins found himself under attack from both within and outside his discipline. Some historians were concerned about the book's facile use of hypotheses taken from the other social sciences and its relative neglect of data from primary sources. Others felt that Elkins had made too much of the Sambo stereotype; evidence of slave resistance seemed to disprove the thesis that blacks had been reduced to childlike dependency. Still others, though not explicitly contradicting Elkins, produced studies that demonstrated that slavery was a far more complex institution that Elkins implied. Richard C. Wade's study of urban slavery, for example, showed that there were behavioral differences between urban black slaves and those who labored on plantations and farms. Conceding that urban slavery was in a state of decline before the Civil War because of the difficulties in maintaining social control, Wade's portrait of urban slaves was not always in agreement with Elkins's Sambo stereotype.[9]

The major assault on Elkins, however, came from outside the ranks of historians. By the mid-1960s a number of ideologies had emerged within the black community. Although integration was still the dominant goal for most blacks, a significant number of them turned inward and articulated black nationalist or other separatist points of view. Bitter at continued white resistance to black demands for full equality, they rejected the goal of integration and assimilation as inappropriate and unattainable. To such spokesmen Elkins's Sambo stereotype undermined the search for a usable past that emphasized instead black achievement and black pride in the face of unremitting white oppression. Moreover, some blacks (and whites) did not care for a thesis that emphasized deprivation. They felt it was simply a sophisticated re-

[8]See Ann J. Lane, ed., *The Debate Over Slavery: Stanley Elkins and His Critics* (Urbana, 1971), and Kenneth M. Stampp, "Rebels and Sambos: The Search for the Negro's Personality in Slavery," *Journal of Southern History* 27 (August 1971): 367–92. For examples of the recent concern with comparative slave systems see Herbert S. Klein, *Slavery in the Americas: A Comparative Study of Cuba and Virginia* (Chicago, 1967); Carl N. Degler, *Neither Black nor White: Slavery and Race Relations in Brazil and the United States* (New York, 1971); and David Brion Davis, *The Problem of Slavery in Western Culture* (Ithaca, 1966) and *The Problem of Slavery in the Age of Revolution* (Ithaca, 1975).

[9]Richard C. Wade, *Slavery in the Cities: The South 1820–1860* (New York, 1964).

statement of racism because it placed part of the responsibility or blame upon the deprived group. Finally, some radicals were hostile to the Sambo image. They posited the idea of perpetual conflict between the oppressors and oppressed, and acceptance of the concept of a docile and nonresisting slave would contradict their own ideological position.

Disagreement with Elkins's view of slave personality and his emphasis on the absence of resistance to white pressure soon led some scholars to study anew the actual life of slaves on plantations. Previous scholarship dealing with slavery, of course, was largely dependent on predominantly *white* sources, including plantation records, newspapers, manuscripts, court records, and travel accounts. The newer scholarship, however, was based on hitherto neglected sources, including a significant number of slave narratives published both before and after the Civil War. During the Depression of the 1930s, moreover, the Federal Writers' Project of the Works Projects Administration had subsidized an oral history project in which more than two thousand ex-slaves who were still alive were interviewed. Using these and other sources, historians began to raise some new questions. If, for example, the control of whites was so complete, why did some slaves run away and other engage in all kinds of covert resistance? What kind of institutional structures developed within the slave community? To what degree were these black institutions partly or fully autonomous? Influenced by the "new social history," scholars began to study slave society not as one created by whites but as one that represented to some degree the hopes, aspirations, and thoughts of blacks.

Indicative of the newer approach was the publication in 1972 of two works. The first—*From Sundown to Sunup: The Making of the Black Community*—was based upon the interviews with ex-slaves during the 1930s. Its author, George P. Rawick, also edited eighteen additional volumes printing the text of the interviews. Rawick emphasized that slaves were not passive; he insisted that plantation life showed considerable interaction between whites and blacks. Forcibly removed from Africa, blacks created a way of life that fused their African heritage with the "social forms and behavior patterns" of Southern society. the slave personality, Rawick emphasized, was ambivalent. On the one hand, slaves were submissive and accepted the belief that one deserved to be a slave. On the other hand, they demonstrated the kind of anger that served as a protection against infantilization and dependency. Blacks, concluded Rawick, "developed an independent community and culture which molded the slave personality" and permitted a measure of autonomy. [10]

---

[10]George P. Rawick, *From Sundown to Sunup: The Making of the Black Community* (Westport, 1972), and *The American Slave: A Composite Autobiography*, 18 vols. (Westport, 1972).

In a similar vein, John Blassingame's book *The Slave Community: Plantation Life in the Ante-Bellum South* described a social setting in which slaves employed a variety of means to circumscribe and inhibit white authority. Family ties among slaves persisted, thus creating a partial protective shield. Blacks also developed and retained religious and mythological beliefs that enabled them to maintain a high degree of autonomy. Slowly but surely the focus of the debate over slavery began a shift of emphasis away from white slaveowners and toward the slaves themselves.[11]

The works of Rawick and Blassingame were received without fanfare or extended debate. Although some criticisms were raised, their contributions were relatively noncontroversial. The same was not true of a book by Robert Fogel and Stanley L. Engerman, *Time on the Cross: The Economics of American Negro Slavery*, which appeared in 1974. Based on quantified data, computer-based analysis, and modern economic theory, Fogel and Engerman presented an interpretation of slavery that set off a fierce and heated debate. Purportedly rejecting virtually every previous work on slavery, the two "new economic historians" presented what seemed to be a series of novel findings about the institution.

Slavery, the two authors emphasized, was not an economically backward system kept in existence by plantation owners unaware of their true interests. On the contrary, Southern slave agriculture was highly efficient on the eve of the Civil War. "Economies of large-scale operation, effective management, and intensive utilization of labor and capital made southern slave agriculture 35 percent more efficient than the northern system of family farming." Nor were slaves Sambolike caricatures; they were hardworking individuals who within the limitations of bondage were able to pursue their own self-interest precisely because they internalized the capitalist values of their masters. Slaveowners encouraged stable black families, rejected the idea of indiscriminate force, did not sexually abuse black women, and provided—by the standards of that era—adequate food, clothing, and shelter. Slavery, therefore, was a model of capitalist efficiency. Within its framework blacks learned and accepted the tenets of the "Protestant ethic" of work. They received, in return, incentives in the form of material rewards, opportunities for upward mobility within the plantation hierarchy, and a chance to create their own stable families. Although Fogel and Engerman in no way diminished the moral evil of slavery, they claimed their goal was "to strike down the view that black Americans were without culture, without achievement, and without development for their first two hundred and fifty years on American soil." A major corollary to their view of slavery was their conclusion that in the century following

[11]John W. Blassingame, *The Slave Community: Plantation Life in the Ante-Bellum South* (New York, 1972).

its abolition white Americans systematically attacked and degraded black citizens. Whites drove freed blacks out of skilled occupations, paid them minimal wages, limited their access to education, and imposed a rigid system of segregation that deprived them of many of the opportunities available to whites.[12]

*Time on the Cross* immediately became the object of an acrimonious debate. Some condemned the hypothesis that slaves willingly accepted white-imposed values. Others attacked the way in which the two authors used historical data to reach flawed conclusions. Still others were unwilling to accept many of the underlying assumptions of the two authors. Indeed, within a short period of time the literature criticizing *Time on the Cross* was enormous.[13]

At precisely the same time that *Time on the Cross* appeared, Eugene D. Genovese published *Roll, Jordan, Roll: The World the Slaves Made.* Genovese, who had already written some distinguished works on the antebellum South, denied in his book that slavery was to be understood within the context of modern capitalism. The key to an understanding of the peculiar institution, he insisted, was to be found in the crucial concept of *paternalism*. The destinies of masters and slaves were linked by a set of mutual duties and responsibilities comparable in many ways to the arrangements between lords and serfs under the feudal system. Whites exploited and controlled the labor of socially inferior blacks and, in return, provided them with the basic necessities of life. To blacks slavery meant a recognition of their basic humanity, and this gave them a claim upon their masters. This claim could be manipulated by slaves who accepted the concessions offered to them by their masters and molded them to suit themselves. Within the limitations of the legal system of bondage, therefore, blacks were able to create their own culture. Genovese particularly emphasized slave religion because its affirmation of life served as a weapon for "personal and community survival." The price the blacks paid for this partial autonomy was the development of a nonrevolutionary and prepolitical consciousness. The second selection in this chapter comprises excerpts from *Roll, Jordan, Roll.*[14]

In keeping with the newer focus upon the autonomy of slave society as contrasted with the earlier emphasis on dependency, Herbert G. Gutman in 1976 published his study of the black family. Gutman had

[12]Robert W. Fogel and Stanley L. Engerman, *Time on the Cross: The Economics of American Slavery,* 2 vols. (Boston, 1974). The second volume was subtitled *Evidence and Methods.*

[13]See Herbert G. Gutman, *Slavery and the Numbers Game: A Critique of Time on the Cross* (Urbana, 1975), and Paul A. David *et al., Reckoning With Slavery: A Critical Study in the Quantitative History of American Negro Slavery* (New York, 1976).

[14]Genovese's previous works included *The Political Economy of Slavery: Studies in the Economy & Society of the Slave South* (New York, 1965); and *The World the Slaveholders Made: Two Essays in Interpretation* (New York, 1969).

been one of the most severe critics of *Time on the Cross*, and he wrote a book-length critique which attacked Fogel and Engerman precisely because of their claims of "black achievement under adversity." In *The Black Family in Slavery and Freedom, 1750–1925*, Gutman offered his own views, which—surprisingly enough—were not at all at variance with Fogel and Engerman or, for that matter, with Rawick, Blassingame, or Genovese.

Like many recent "new social historians," Gutman stressed the ability of blacks to adapt themselves to oppression in their own unique ways. In this respect, he rejected the claims of Elkins and others about the debilitating impact of slavery upon its unwilling victims. Yet Gutman at the same time denied that plantation capitalism (Fogel and Engerman) and paternalism (Genovese) were necessary components in the process of adaptation. Slaves were able to create their own society not by reacting to white offers of rewards or by molding the concessions granted them by their masters, but rather by developing a sophisticated family and kinship network that transmitted the Afro-American heritage from generation to generation. The black family, in effect, served to cushion the shock of being uprooted from Africa. If parents were separated from their children by being sold, other relatives became surrogate parents to the remaining children. The stability of the black family rested upon a closely knit nuclear arrangement. Adultery after wedlock, for example, was infrequent. These family values were not imposed by white masters, according to Gutman, for they were rooted in the African cultural inheritance. Blacks were more loyal to each other than were whites, moreover, because the community was the basic means of survival.[15]

The newer emphasis on slave society and culture has had several curious results. One has been the subtle transformation of slavery from an ugly and malignant system to an institution that is somewhat more benign in its character. This is not to imply that scholars like Fogel, Engerman, Genovese, and Gutman are in any way sympathetic to slavery, for all of them concede without reservation its immorality. But by focusing on the ability of black slaves to create a partially autonomous culture and society, they implicitly diminish the authority of dominant white masters whose control was less than complete. Ironically, the emphasis on an indigenous black culture moved contemporary scholarship closer to Ulrich Bonnell Phillips, who had emphasized the contentment of blacks under slavery. Recent scholars, of course, take a quite different approach, but there is a distinct implication in their work that whites did not control many major elements in the lives of their slaves, who exercised considerable authority in determining their per-

---

[15]Herbert G. Gutman, *The Black Family in Slavery and Freedom, 1750–1925* (New York, 1976).

sonal and familial relations. Compared with the Stampp and Elkins interpretation of slavery, these more recent works diminish, in part, the tragic view of slavery as an institution.

There is little doubt also that the parameters of the lively debate over the nature of slavery has been defined by a strong intellectual current that emphasizes the autonomy rather than the dependence of the American black experience. White scholars have been extremely sensitive to charges (particularly by blacks) that they have made the history of blacks a mere appendage of white actions and behavior. Consequently, the emphasis on a unique and separate black identity and culture has had the effect of diminishing the importance of the white man's oppression as a major determinant in black history. By way of contrast, the Stampp-Elkins approach emphasized white responsibility for black problems.[16]

Virtually all of the interpretations of slavery since the 1950's tended to treat the "peculiar institution" as a single unit; with only an occasional exception hisotrians did not distinguish between time and place. In 1980, however, Ira Berlin threw down an explicit challenge to his colleagues. In a significant article in the *American Historical Review*, he noted that "time and space"—the "traditional boundaries of historical inquiry"—had been largely ignored by American historians, most of whom had produced a "static vision of slave culture." In a detailed examination of seventeenth- and eighteenth-century slavery, Berlin went on to identify three distinct slave systems: a Northern nonplantation system; and two Southern plantation systems, one in the Chesapeake Bay region and the other in the Carolina and Georgia low country. In each of these areas slavery developed in a unique manner; the differences had important consequences for black culture and society.

In the North, according to Berlin, acculturation incorporated blacks into American society while at the same time making them acutely conscious of their African past. Whites, who outnumbered blacks by a wide margin, allowed their slaves considerable autonomy. In the Southern low country, on the other hand, blacks were deeply divided; urban blacks pressed for incorporation into white society while plantation blacks remained physically separated and estranged from the Anglo-American world and closer to their African roots. In the Chesapeake region, a single unified Afro-American culture emerged. Because of the

---

[16]For some recent discussions of this point see Stanley M. Elkins, *Slavery: A Problem in American Institutional and Intellectual Life* (3rd ed.: Chicago, 1976), pp. 223–302, and George M. Fredrickson, "The Gutman Report," *New York Review of Books* 23 (September 30, 1976): 18–23. For a different attempt to recreate black culture using folklore see Lawrence W. Levine's *Black Culture and Black Consciousness: Afro-American Folk Thought from Slavery to Freedom* (New York, 1977).

impress of white paternalism, Afro-American culture paralleled Anglo-American culture; the African heritage was submerged. Berlin's analysis constituted an explicit and clear challenge to the parameters of the debate over slavery from the 1950s through the 1970s. "If slave society during the colonial era can be comprehended only through a careful delineation of temporal and spatial differences among Northern, Chesapeake, and low-country colonies," Berlin observed, "a similar division will be necessary for a full understanding of black life in nineteenth-century America. The actions of black people during the American Revolution, the Civil War, and the long years of bondage between these two cataclysmic events cannot be understood merely as a function of the dynamics of slavery or the possibilities of liberty, but must be viewed within the specific social circumstances and cultural traditions of black people. These varied from time to time and from place to place. Thus no matter how complete recent studies of black life appear, they are limited to the extent that they provide a static and singular vision of a dynamic and complex society."[17]

In evaluating the competing interpretations of American slavery, it is important to understand that more than historical considerations are involved. Any judgment upon the nature of slavery implicitly offers a judgment of the present and a prescription for the future. To emphasize the harshness of slavery and the dependence of its victims is to maximize the white man's responsibility. On the other hand, to downplay the effectiveness of white authority is to move toward a position that concedes black autonomy and hence accepts the view that responsibility for post–Civil War developments rests in part with blacks.

Which of the various viewpoints of slavery are correct? Were slaves contented or discontented under slavery? In what ways were they successful in resisting the efforts of their masters to make them totally dependent human beings? To what degree did an autonomous black culture and social order develop during slavery? Was slavery a pre-bourgeois feudal system or a modern version of rational capitalism? What was the nature of the master-slave relationship? Is it possible to generalize about the lives of several millions of individuals under slavery? Must historians begin to distinguish between the common and the unique elements of the institution of slavery in terms of time and space? The answers to these questions undoubtedly will rest upon the continued analysis of surviving sources. But to a considerable degree, they will rest also upon the attitudes and values of historians, whose own personal commitments play a role in shaping their perceptions of the past and their view of the present and future.

---

[17]Ira Berlin, "Time, Space, and the Evolution of Afro-American Society on British Mainland North America," *American Historical Review* 85 (February 1980): 44–78.

# Stanley Elkins

STANLEY ELKINS (1925–    ) is professor of history at Smith College. In addition to his influential book on slavery, he has published a number of articles and edited with Eric McKitrick *The Hofstadter Aegis: A Memorial* (1974).

It will be assumed that there were elements in the very structure of the plantation system—its "closed" character—that could sustain infantilism as a normal feature of behavior. These elements, having less to do with "cruelty" per se than simply with the sanctions of authority, were effective and pervasive enough to require that such infantilism be characterized as something much more basic than mere "accommodation." It will be assumed that the sanctions of the system were in themselves sufficient to produce a recognizable personality type.

It should be understood that to identify a social type in this sense is still to generalize on a fairly crude level—and to insist for a limited purpose on the legitimacy of such generalizing is by no means to deny that, on more refined levels, a great profusion of individual types might have been observed in slave society. Nor need it be claimed that the "Sambo" type, even in the relatively crude sense employed here, was a universal type. It was, however, a plantation type, and a plantation existence embraced well over half the slave population. Two kinds of material will be used in the effort to picture the mechanisms whereby this adjustment to absolute power—an adjustment whose end product included infantile features of behavior—may have been effected. One is drawn from the theoretical knowledge presently available in social psychology, and the other, in the form of an analogy, is derived from some of the data that have come out of the German concentration camps. It is recognized in most theory that social behavior is regulated in some general way by adjustment to symbols of authority—however diversely "authority" may be defined either in theory or in culture itself—and that such adjustment is closely related to the very formation of personality. A corollary would be, of course, that the more diverse those symbols of authority may be, the greater is the permissible variety of adjustment to

Stanley Elkins, *Slavery: A Problem in American Institutional and Intellectual Life* (Chicago, 1959), pp. 86–89, 115–39. Reprinted by permission of the author and the University of Chicago Press.

them—and the wider the margin of individuality, consequently, in the development of the self. The question here has to do with the wideness or narrowness of that margin on the antebellum plantation.

The other body of material, involving an experience undergone by several million men and women in the concentration camps of our own time, contains certain items of relevance to the problem here being considered. The experience was analogous to that of slavery and was one in which wide-scale instances of infantilization were observed. The material is sufficiently detailed, and sufficiently documented by men who not only took part in the experience itself but who were versed in the use of psychological theory for analyzing it, that the advantages of drawing upon such data for purposes of analogy seem to outweigh the possible risks.

The introduction of this second body of material must to a certain extent govern the theoretical strategy itself. It has been recognized both implicitly and explicitly that the psychic impact and effects of the concentration-camp experience were not anticipated in existing theory and that consequently such theory would require some major supplementation. It might be added, parenthetically, that almost any published discussion of this modern Inferno, no matter how learned, demonstrates how "theory," operating at such a level of shared human experience, tends to shed much of its technical trappings and to take on an almost literary quality. The experience showed, in any event, that infantile personality features could be induced in a relatively short time among large numbers of adult human beings coming from very diverse backgrounds. The particular strain which was thus placed upon prior theory consisted in the need to make room not only for the cultural and environmental sanctions that sustain personality (which in a sense Freudian theory already had) but also for a virtually unanticipated problem: actual change in the personality of masses of adults. It forced a reappraisal and new appreciation of how completely and effectively prior cultural sanctions for behavior and personality could be detached to make way for new and different sanctions, and of how adjustments could be made by individuals to a species of authority vastly different from any previously known. The revelation for theory was the process of detachment.

These cues, accordingly, will guide the argument on Negro slavery. Several million people were detached with a peculiar effectiveness from a great variety of cultural backgrounds in Africa—a detachment operating with infinitely more effectiveness upon those brought to North America than upon those who came to Latin America. It was achieved partly by the shock experience inherent in the very mode of procurement but more specifically by the type of authority system to which they were introduced and to which they had to adjust for physical and psychic survival. The new adjustment, to absolute power in a closed system, involved infantilization, and the detachment was so complete that little trace of prior (and thus alternative) cultural sanctions for behavior and personality remained for the descendants of the first generation. For them, adjustment to clear and omnipresent authority could be more or less automatic—as much so, or as little, as it is for anyone whose adjustment to a social system begins at birth and to whom that system represents normality. We do not know how generally a full adjustment was made by the first generation of fresh slaves from Africa. But we do know—from a modern experience—that such an adjustment is possible, not only within the same generation but within two or three years. This proved possible for people in a full state of complex civilization, for men and women who were not black and not savages. . . . The immense revelation for psychology in the concentration-camp literature has been the discovery of how elements of dramatic personality change could be brought about in masses of individuals. And yet it is not proper that the crude fact of "change" alone should dominate the conceptual image with which one emerges from this problem "Change" per se, change that does not go beyond itself, is productive of nothing; it leaves only destruction, shock, and howling bedlam behind it unless some future basis of stability and order lies waiting to guarantee it and give it reality. So it is with the human psyche, which is apparently capable of making terms with a state other than liberty as we know it. The very dramatic features of the process just described may upset the nicety of this point. There is the related danger, moreover, of unduly stressing the individual psychology of the problem at the expense of its social psychology.

These hazards might be minimized by maintaining a conceptual distinction between two phases of the group experience. The process of detachment from prior standards of behavior and value is one of them, and is doubtless the more striking, but there must be another one. That such detachment can, by extension, involve the whole scope of an individual's culture is an implication for which the vocabulary of individual psychology was caught somewhat unawares. Fluctuations in the state of the individual psyche could formerly be dealt with, or so it seemed, while taking for granted the more or less static nature of social organization, and with a minimum of reference to its features. That such organization might itself become an important variable was therefore a possibility not highly developed in theory, focused as theory was upon individual case histories to the invariable minimization of social and cultural setting. The other phase of the experience should be considered as the "stability" side of the problem, that phase which stabilized what the "shock" phase only opened the way for. This was essentially a process of adjustment to a standard of social normality, though in this case a drastic *re*adjustment and compressed within a very short time—a process which under typical conditions of individual and group existence is supposed to begin at birth and last a lifetime and be transmitted in many and diffuse ways from generation to generation. The adjustment is assumed to be slow and organic, and it normally is. Its numerous aspects extend much beyond psychology; those aspects have in the past been treated at great leisure within the rich provinces not only of psychology but of history, sociology, and literature as well. What rearrangement and compression of those provinces may be needed to accommodate a mass experience that not only involved profound individual shock but also required rapid assimilation to a drastically different form of social organization, can hardly be known. But perhaps the most conservative beginning may be made with existing psychological theory.

The theoretical system whose terminology was orthodox for most of the Europeans who have written about the camps was that of Freud. It was necessary for them to do a certain amount of improvising, since the scheme's existing framework provided only the narrowest leeway for dealing with such radical concepts as out-and-out change in personality. This was due to two kinds of limitations which the Freudian vocabulary places upon the notion of the "self." One is that the superego—that part of the self involved in social relationships, social values, expectations of others, and so on—is conceived as only a small and highly refined part of the "total" self. The other is the assumption that the content and character of the superego is laid down in childhood and undergoes relatively little basic alteration thereafter. Yet a Freudian diagnosis of the concentration-camp inmate—whose social self, or superego, did appear to change and who seemed basically changed thereby, is, given these limitations, still possible. Elie Cohen, whose analysis is the most thorough of these, specifically states that "the superego acquired new values in a concentration camp." The old values, according to Dr. Cohen, were first silenced by the shocks which produced "acute depersonalization" (the subject-object split: "It is not the real 'me' who is undergoing this"), and by the powerful drives of hunger and survival. Old values, thus set aside, could be replaced by new ones. It was a process made possible by "infantile regression"—regression to a previous condition of childlike dependency in which parental prohibitions once more became all-powerful and in which parental judgments might once more be internalized. In this way a new "father-image," personified in the SS guard, came into being. That the prisoner's identification with the SS could be so positive is explained by still another mechanism: the principle of "identification with the aggressor." "A child," as Anna Freud writes, "interjects some characteristic of an anxiety-object and so assimilates an anxiety-experience which he has just undergone. . . . By impersonating the aggressor, assuming his attributes or imitating his aggression, the child transforms himself from the person threatened into the person who makes the threat." In short, the child's only "defense" in the presence of a cruel, all-powerful father is the psychic defense of identification.

Now one could, still retaining the Freudian language, represent all this in somewhat less cumbersome terms by a slight modification of the metaphor. It could simply be said that under great stress the superego, like a bucket, is violently emptied of content and acquires, in a radically changed setting, new content. It would thus not be necessary to postulate a literal "regression" to childhood in order for this to occur. Something of the sort is suggested by Leo Alexander. "The psychiatrist stands in amazement," he writes, "before the thoroughness and completeness with which this perversion of essential superego values was accomplished in adults... [and] it may be that the decisive importance of childhood and youth in the formation of [these] values may have been overrated by psychiatrists in a society in which allegiance to these values in normal adult life was taken too much for granted because of the stability, religiousness, legality, and security of the 19th Century and early 20th Century society."

A second theoretical scheme is better prepared for crisis and more closely geared to social environment than the Freudian adaptation indicated above, and it may consequently be more suitable for accommodating not only the concentration-camp experience but also the more general problem of plantation slave personality. This is the "interpersonal theory" developed by the late Harry Stack Sullivan. One may view this body of work as the response to a peculiarly American set of needs. The system of Freud, so aptly designed for a European society the stability of whose institutional and status relationships could always to a large extent be taken for granted, turns out to be less clearly adapted to the culture of the United States. The American psychiatrist has had to deal with individuals in a culture where the diffuse, shifting, and often uncertain quality of such relationships has always been more pronounced than in Europe. He has come to appreciate the extent to which these relationships actually support the individual's psychic balance—the full extent, that is, to which the self is "social" in its nature. Thus a psychology whose terms are flexible enough to permit altering social relationships to make actual differences in character structure would be a psychology especially promising for dealing with the present problem.

Sullivan's great contribution was to offer a concept whereby the really critical determinants of personality might be isolated for purposes of observation. Out of the hopelessly immense totality of "influences" which in one way or another go to make up the personality, or "self," Sullivan designated one—the estimations and expectations of others—as the one promising to unlock the most secrets. He then made a second elimination: the *majority* of "others" in one's existence may for theoretical purposes be neglected; what counts is who the *significant* others are. Here, "significant others" may be understood very crudely to mean those individuals who hold, or seem to hold, the keys to security in one's own personal situation, whatever its nature. Now as to the psychic processes whereby these "significant others" become an actual part of the personality, it may be said that the very sense of "self" first emerges in connection with anxiety about the attitudes of the most important persons in one's life (initially, the mother, father, and their surrogates— persons of more or less absolute authority), and automatic attempts are set in motion to adjust to these attitudes. In this way their approval, their disapproval, their estimates and appraisals, and indeed a whole range of their expectations become as it were internalized, and are reflected in one's very character. Of course as one "grows up," one acquires more and more significant others whose attitudes are diffuse and may indeed compete, and thus "significance," in Sullivan's sense, becomes subtler and less easy to define. The personality exfoliates; it takes on traits of distinction and, as we say, "individuality." The impact of particular significant others is less dramatic than in early life. But the pattern is a continuing one; new significant others do still appear, and theoretically it is conceivable that even in mature life the personality might be visibly affected by the arrival of such a one—supposing that this new significant other were vested with sufficient authority and power. In any event there are possibilities for fluidity and actual change inherent in this concept which earlier schemes have lacked.

The purest form of the process is to be observed in the development of children, not so much because of their "immaturity" as such (though their plasticity is great and the imprint of early experience goes deep), but rather because for them there are fewer significant others. For this reason—because the pattern is simpler and more easily controlled— much of Sullivan's attention was devoted to what happens in childhood. In any case let us say that unlike the adult, the child, being drastically limited in the selection of significant others, must operate in a "closed system."

Such are the elements which make for order and balance in the normal self: "significant others" plus "anxiety" in a special sense— conceived with not simply disruptive but also guiding, warning functions. The structure of "interpersonal" theory thus has considerable room in it for conceptions of guided change—change for either beneficent or malevolent ends. One technique for managing such change would of course be the orthodox one of psychoanalysis; another, the actual changing of significant others. Patrick Mullahy, a leading exponent of Sullivan, believes that in group therapy much is possible along these lines. A demonic test of the whole hypothesis is available in the concentration camp.

Consider the camp prisoner—not the one who fell by the wayside but the one who was eventually to survive; consider the ways in which he was forced to adjust to the one significant other which he now had— the SS guard, who held absolute dominion over every aspect of his life. The very shock of his introduction was perfectly designed to dramatize this fact; he was brutally maltreated ("as by a cruel father"); the shadow of resistance would bring instant death. Daily life in the camp, with its fear and tensions, taught over and over the lesson of absolute power. It prepared the personality for a drastic shift in standards. It crushed whatever anxieties might have been drawn from prior standards; such standards had become meaningless. It focused the prisoner's attention constantly on the moods, attitudes, and standards of the only man who mattered. A truly childlike situation was thus created: utter and abject dependency on one, or on a rigidly limited few, significant others. All the conditions which in normal life would give the individual leeway— which allowed him to defend himself against a new and hostile signifi- cant other, no matter how powerful—were absent in the camp. No competition of significant others was possible; the prisoner's comrades for practical purposes were helpless to assist him. He had no degree of independence, no lines to the outside, in any matter. Everything, every vital concern, focused on the SS: food, warmth, security, freedom from pain, all depended on the omnipotent significant other, all had to be worked out within the closed system. Nowhere was there a shred of privacy; everything one did was subject to SS supervision. The pressure was never absent. It is thus no wonder that the prisoners should become "as children." It is no wonder that their obedience became unquestion- ing, that they did not revolt, that they could not "hate" their masters. Their masters' attitudes had become *internalized* as a part of their very selves; those attitudes and standards now dominated all others that they had. They had, indeed, been "changed."

There still exists a third conceptual framework within which these phenomena may be considered. It is to be found in the growing field of "role psychology." This psychology is not at all incompatible with inter- personal theory; the two might easily be fitted into the same system. But it might be stategically desirable, for several reasons, to segregate them for purposes of discussion. One such reason is the extraordinary degree to which role psychology shifts the focus of attention upon the individu- al's cultural and institutional environment rather than upon his "self." At the same time it gives us a manageable concept—that of "role"—for mediating between the two. As a mechanism, the role enables us to isolate the unique contribution of culture and institutions toward main- taining the psychic balance of the individual. In it, we see formalized for the individual a range of choices in models of behavior and expression, each with its particular style, quality, and attributes. The relationship between the "role" and the "self," though not yet clear, is intimate; it is at least possible at certain levels of inquiry to look upon the individual as the variable and upon the roles extended him as the stable factor. We thus have a potentially durable link between individual psychology and the study of culture. It might even be said, inasmuch as its key term is directly borrowed from the theater, the role psychology offers in workable form the long-awaited connection—apparently missed by Ernest Jones in his *Hamlet* study—between the insights of the classical dramatists and those of the contemporary social theorist. But be that as it may, for our present problem, the concentration camp, it suggests the most flexible account of how the ex-prisoners may have succeeded in resuming their places in normal life.

Let us note certain of the leading terms. A "social role" is definable in its simplest sense as the behavior expected of persons specifically located in specific social groups. A distinction is kept between "expectations" and "behavior"; the expectations of a role (embodied in the "script") theoretically exist in advance and are defined by the organization, the institution, or by society at large. Behavior (the "performance") refers to the manner in which the role is played. Another distinction involves the roles which are "pervasive" and those which are "limited." A pervasive role is extensive in scope ("female citizen") and not only influences but also sets bounds upon the other sorts of roles available to the individual ("mother," "nurse," but not "husband," "soldier"); a limited role ("purchaser," "patient") is transitory and intermittent. A further concept is that of "role clarity." Some roles are more specifically defined than others; their impact upon performance (and, indeed, upon the personality of the performer) depends on the clarity of their definition. Finally, it is asserted that those roles which carry with them the clearest and most automatic rewards and punishments are those which will be (as it were) most "artistically" played.

What sorts of things might this explain? It might illuminate the process whereby the child develops his personality in terms not only of the roles which his parents offer him but of those which he "picks up" elsewhere and tries on. It could show how society, in its coercive character, lays down patterns of behavior with which it expects the individual to comply. It suggests the way in which society, now turning its benevolent face to the individual, tenders him alternatives and defines for him the style appropriate to their fulfilment. It provides us with a further term for the definition of personality itself: there appears an extent to which we can say that personality is actually made up of the roles which the individual plays. And here, once more assuming "change" to be possible, we have in certain ways the least cumbersome terms for plotting its course.

The application of the model to the concentration camp should be simple and obvious. What was expected of the man entering the role of camp prisoner was laid down for him upon arrival:

> Here you are not in a penitentiary or prison but in a place of instruction. Order and discipline are here the highest law. If you ever want to see freedom again, you must submit to a severe training. . . . But woe to those who do not obey our iron discipline. Our methods are thorough! Here there is no compromise and no mercy. The slightest resistance will be ruthlessly suppressed. Here we sweep with an iron broom!

Expectation and performance must coincide exactly; the lines were to be read literally; the missing of a single cue meant extinction. The role was pervasive; it vetoed any other role and smashed all prior ones. "Role clarity"—the clarity here was blinding; its defintion was burned into the prisoner by every detail of his existence.

> In normal life the adult enjoys a certain measure of independence; within the limits set by society he had a considerable measure of liberty. Nobody orders him when and what to eat, where to take up his residence or what to wear, neither to take his rest on Sunday nor when to have his bath, nor when to go to bed. He is not beaten during his work, he need not ask permission to go to the W.C., he is not continually kept on the run, he does not feel that the work he is doing is silly or childish, he is not confined behind barbed wire, he is not counted twice a day or more, he is not left unprotected against the actions of his fellow citizens, he looks after his family and the education of his children.
>
> How altogether different was the life of the concentration-camp prisoner! What to do during each part of the day was arranged for him, the decisions were made about him from which there was no appeal. He was impotent and suffered from bedwetting, and because of his chronic diarrhea he soiled his underwear. . . . The dependence of the prisoner on the SS . . . may be compared to the dependence of children on their parents. . . .

The impact of this role, coinciding as it does in a hundred ways with that of the child, has already been observed. Its rewards were brutally simple—life rather than death; its punishments were automatic. By the survivors it was—it had to be—a role *well played*.

Nor was it simple, upon liberation, to shed the role. Many of the inmates, to be sure, did have prior roles which they could resume, former significant others to whom they might reorient themselves, a repressed superego which might once more be resurrected. To this extent they were not "lost souls." but to the extent that their entire personalities, their total selves, had been involved in this experience, to the extent that old arrangements had been disrupted, that society itself had been overturned while they had been away, a "return" was fraught with innumerable obstacles.

It is hoped that the very hideousness of a special example of slavery has not disqualified it as a test for certain features of a far milder and more benevolent form of slavery. But it should still be possible to say, with regard to the individuals who lived as slaves within the respective systems, that just as on one level there is every difference between a wretched childhood and a carefree one, there are, for other purposes, limited features which the one may be said to have shared with the other.

Both were closed systems from which all standards based on prior connections had been effectively detached. A working adjustment to either system required a childlike conformity, a limited choice of "significant others." Cruelty per se cannot be considered the primary key to this; of far greater importance was the simple "closedness" of the system, in which all lines of authority descended from the master and in which alternative social bases that might have supported alternative standards were systematically suppressed. The individual, consequently, for his very psychic security, had to picture his master in some way as the "good father," even when, as in the concentration camp, it made no sense at all. But why should it not have made sense for many a simple plantation Negro whose master did exhibit, in all the ways that could be expected, the features of the good father who was really "good"? If the concentration camp could produce in two or three years the results that it did, one wonders how much more pervasive must have been those attitudes, expectations, and values which had, certainly, their benevolent side and which were accepted and transmitted over generations.

For the Negro child, in particular, the plantation offered no really satisfactory father-image other than the master. The "real" father was virtually without authority over his child, since discipline, parental responsibility, and control of rewards and punishments all rested in other hands; the slave father could not even protect the mother of his children except by appealing directly to the master. Indeed, the mother's own role loomed far larger for the slave child than did that of the father. She controlled those few activities—household care, preparation of food, and rearing of children—that were left to the slave family. For that matter, the very etiquette of plantation life removed even the honorific attributes of fatherhood from the Negro male, who was addressed as "boy"—until, when the vigorous years of his prime were past, he was allowed to assume the title of "uncle."

From the master's viewpoint, slaves had been defined in law as property, and the master's power over his property must be absolute. But then this property was still human property. These slaves might never be quite as human as *he* was, but still there were certain standards that could be laid down for their behavior: obedience, fidelity, humility, docility, cheerfulness, and so on. Industry and diligence would of course be demanded, but a final element in the master's situation would undoubtedly qualify that expectation. Absolute power for him meant absolute dependency for the slave—the dependency not of the developing child but of the perpetual child. For the master, the role most aptly fitting such a relationship would naturally be that of the father. As a father he could be either harsh or kind, as he chose, but as a *wise* father he would have, we may suspect, a sense of the limits of his situation. He must be ready to cope with *all* the qualities of the child, exasperating as well as ingratiating. He might conceivably have to expect in this child—besides his loyalty, docility, humility, cheerfulness, and (under supervision) his diligence—such additional qualities as irresponsibility, playfulness, silliness, laziness, and (quite possibly) tendencies to lying and stealing. Should the entire prediction prove accurate, the result would be something resembling "Sambo."

The social and psychological sanctions of role-playing may in the last analysis prove to be the most satisfactory of the several approaches to Sambo, for, without doubt, of all the roles in American life that of Sambo was by far the most pervasive. The outlines of the role might be sketched in by crude necessity, but what of the finer shades? The sanctions against overstepping it were bleak enough, but the rewards—the sweet applause, as it were, for performing it with sincerity and feeling—were something to be appreciated on quite another level. The law, untuned to the deeper harmonies, could command the player to be present for the occasion, and the whip might even warn against his missing the grosser cues,but could those things really insure the performance that melted all hearts? Yet there was many and many a performance, and the audiences (whose standards were high) appear to have been for the most part well pleased. They were actually viewing their own masterpiece. Much labor had been lavished upon this chef d'oeuvre, the most genial resources of Southern society had been available for the work; touch after touch had been applied throughout the years, and the result—embodied not in the unfeeling law but in the richest layers of Southern lore—had been the product of an exquisitely rounded collective creativity. And indeed, in a sense that somehow transcended the merely ironic, it was a labor of love. "I love the simple and unadulterated slave, with his geniality, his mirth, his swagger, and his nonsense," wrote Edward Pollard. "I love to look upon his countenance shining with content and grease; I love to study his affectionate heart; I love to mark that peculiarity in him, which beneath all his buffoonery exhibits him as a creature of the tenderest sensibilities, mingling his joys and his sorrows with those of his master's home." Love, even on those terms, was surely no inconsequential reward.

But what were the terms? The Negro was to be a child forever. "The Negro . . . in his true nature, is always a boy, let him be ever so old. . . . " "He is . . . a dependent upon the white race; dependent for guidance and direction even to the procurement of his most indispensable neces-saries. Apart from this protection he has the helplessness of a child—without foresight, without faculty of contrivance, without thrift of any kind." Not only was he a child; he was a happy child. Few Southern writers failed to describe with obvious fondness the bubbling gaiety of a plantation holiday or the perpetual good humor that seemed to mark the Negro character, the good humor of an everlasting childhood.

The role, of course, must have been rather harder for the earliest generations of slaves to learn. "Accommodation," according to John Dollard, "involves the renunciation of protest or aggression against un-desirable conditions of life and the organization of the character so that protest does not appear, but acceptance does. It may come to pass in the end that the unwelcome force is idealized, that one identifies with it and takes it into the personality; it sometimes even happens that what is at first resented and feared is finally loved."

Might the process, on the other hand, be reversed? It is hard to imagine its being reversed overnight. The same role might still be played in the years after slavery—we are told that it was—and yet it was played to more vulgar audiences with cruder standards, who paid much less for what they saw. The lines might be repeated more and more mechani-cally, with less and less conviction; the incentives to perfection could become hazy and blurred, and the excellent old piece could degenerate over time into low farce. There could come a point, conceivably, with the old zest gone, that it was no longer worth the candle. The day might come at last when it dawned on a man's full waking consciousness that he had really grown up, that he was, after all, only playing a part.

One might say a great deal more than has been said here about mass behavior and mass manifestations of personality, and the picture would still amount to little more than a grotesque cartoon of humanity were not some recognition given to the ineffable difference made in any social system by men and women possessing what is recognized, anywhere and at any time, simply as character. With that, one arrives at something too qualitatively fine to come very much within the crude categories of the present discussion; but although it is impossible to generalize with any proper justice about the incidence of "character" in its moral irreduci-ble, individual sense, it may still be possible to conclude with a note or two on the social conditions, the breadth or narrowness of their com-pass, within which character can find expression.

Why should it be, turning once more to Latin America, that there one finds no Sambo, no social tradition, that is, in which slaves were defined by virtually complete consensus as children incapable of being trusted with the full privileges of freedom and adulthood? There, the system surely had its brutalities. The slaves arriving there from Africa had also undergone the capture, the sale, the Middle Passage. They too had been uprooted from a prior culture, from a life very different from the one in which they now found themselves. There, however, the system was not closed.

Here again the concentration camp, paradoxically enough, can be instructive. There were in the camps a very small minority of the survivors who had undergone an experience different in crucial ways from that of the others, an experience which protected them from the full impact of the closed system. These people, mainly by virtue of wretched little jobs in the camp administration which offered them a minute measure of privilege, were able to carry on "underground" activities. In a practical sense the actual operations of such "undergrounds" as were possible may seem to us unheroic and limited: stealing blankets; "organizing" a few bandages, a little medicine, from the camp hospital; black market arrangements with a guard for a bit of extra food and protection for oneself and one's comrades; the circulation of news; and other such apparently trifling activities. But for the psychological balance of those involved, such activities were vital; they made possible a fundamentally different adjustment to the camp. To a prisoner so engaged, there were others who mattered, who gave real point to his existence—the SS was no longer the "only" one. Conversely, the role of the child was not the only one he played. He could take initiative; he could give as well as receive protection; he did things which had meaning in adult terms. He had, in short, alternative roles; this was a fact which made such a prisoner's transition from his old life to that of the camp less agonizing and destructive; those very prisoners, moreover, appear to have been the ones who could, upon liberation, resume normal lives most easily. It is, in fact, these people—not those of the ranks—who have described the camps to us.

It was just such a difference—indeed, a much greater one—that separated the typical slave in Latin America from the typical slave in the United States. Though he too had experienced the Middle Passage, he was entering a society where alternatives were significantly more diverse than those awaiting his kinsman in North America. Concerned in some sense with his status were distinct and at certain points competing institutions. This involved multiple and often competing "significant others." His master was, of course, clearly the chief one—but not the only one. There could, in fact, be a considerable number: the friar who boarded his ship to examine his conscience, the confessor; the priest who made the rounds and who might report irregularities in treatment to the *procurador*; the zealous Jesuit quick to resent a master's intrusion upon such sacred matters as marriage and worship (a resentment of no small consequence to the master); the local magistrate, with his eye on the king's official protector of slaves, who would find himself in trouble were the laws too widely evaded; the king's informer who received one-third of the fines. For the slave the result was a certain latitude; the lines did not all converge on one man; the slave's personality, accordingly, did not have to focus on a single role. He was, true enough, primarily a slave. Yet he might in fact perform multiple roles. He could be a husband and a father (for the American slave these roles had virtually no meaning); open to him also were such activities as artisan, peddler, petty merchant, truck gardener (the law reserved to him the necessary time and a share of the proceeds, but such arrangements were against the law for Sambo); he could be a communicant in the church, a member of a religious fraternity (roles guaranteed by the most powerful institution in Latin America—comparable privileges in the American South depended on a master's pleasure). These roles were all legitimized and protected *outside* the plantation; they offered a diversity of channels for the development of personality. Not only did the individual have multiple roles open to him as a slave, but the very nature of these roles made possible a certain range of aspirations should he some day become free. He could have a fantasy life not limited to catfish and watermelons; it was within his conception to become a priest, an independent farmer, a successful merchant, a military officer. The slave could actually—to an extent quite unthinkable in the United States—conceive of himself *as a rebel*. Bloody slave revolts, actual wars, took place in Latin America; nothing on this order occurred in the United States. But even without a rebellion, society here had a network of customary arrangements, rooted in antiquity, which made possible at many points a smooth transition of status from slave to free and which provided much social space for the exfoliation of individual character.

To the typical slave on the antebellum plantation in the United States, society of course offered no such alternatives. But that is hardly to say that something of an "underground"—something rather more, indeed, than an underground—could not exist in Southern slave society. And there were those in it who hardly fitted the picture of "Sambo."

The American slave system, compared with that of Latin America, was closed and circumscribed, but, like all social systems, its arrangements were less perfect in practice than they appeared to be in theory. It was possible for significant numbers of slaves, in varying degrees, to escape the full impact of the system and its coercions upon personality. The house servant, the urban mechanic, the slave who arranged his own employment and paid his master a stipulated sum each week, were all figuratively members of the "underground." Even among those working on large plantations, the skilled craftsman or the responsible slave foreman had a measure of independence not shared by his simpler brethren. Even the single slave family owned by a small farmer had a status much closer to that of house servants than to that of a plantation labor gang. For all such people there was a margin of space denied to the majority;

the system's authority-structure claimed their bodies but not quite their souls.

Out of such groups an individual as complex and as highly developed as William Johnson, the Natchez barber, might emerge. Johnson's diary reveals a personality that one recognizes instantly as a type—but a type whose values came from a sector of society very different from that which formed Sambo. Johnson is the young man on the make, the ambitious free-enterpriser of American legend. He began life as a slave, was manumitted at the age of eleven, and rose from a poor apprentice barber to become one of the wealthiest and most influential Negroes in antebellum Mississippi. He was respected by white and black alike, and counted among his friends some of the leading public men of the state.

It is of great interest to note that although the danger of slave revolts (like Communist conspiracies in our own day) was much overrated by touchy Southerners; the revolts that actually did occur were in no instance planned by plantation laborers but rather by Negroes whose qualities of leadership were developed well outside the full coercions of the plantation authority-system. Gabriel, who led the revolt of 1800, was a blacksmith who lived a few miles outside Richmond; Denmark Vesey, leading spirit of the 1822 plot at Charleston, was a freed Negro artisan who had been born in Africa and served several years aboard a slave-trading vessel; and Nat Turner, the Virginia slave who fomented the massacre of 1831, was a literate preacher of recognized intelligence. Of the plots that have been convincingly substantiated (whether they came to anything or not), the majority originated in urban centers.

For a time during Reconstruction, a Negro elite of sorts did emerge in the South. Many of its members were Northern Negroes, but the Southern ex-slaves who also comprised it seem in general to have emerged from the categories just indicated. Vernon Wharton, writing of Mississippi, says:

> A large portion of the minor Negro leaders were preachers, lawyers, or teachers from the free states or from Canada. Their education and their independent attitude gained for them immediate favor and leadership. Of the natives who became their rivals, the majority had been urban slaves, blacksmiths, carpenters, clerks, or waiters in hotels and boarding houses; a few of them had been favored body-servants of affluent whites.

The William Johnsons and Denmark Veseys have been accorded, though belatedly, their due honor. They are, indeed, all too easily identified, thanks to the system that enabled them as individuals to be so conspicuous and so exceptional and, as members of a group, so few.

# Eugene D. Genovese

EUGENE D. GENOVESE (1930-     ) is professor of history at the University of
Rochester. His books include *The Political Economy of Slavery* (1965), *The World
the Slaveholders Made* (1969), and *Roll, Jordan, Roll: The World the Slaves Made*
(1974).

Cruel, unjust, exploitative, oppressive, slavery bound two peoples together in bitter antagonism while creating an organic relationship so
complex and ambivalent that neither could express the simplest human
feelings without reference to the other. Slavery rested on the principle of
property in man—of one man's appropriation of another's person as
well as the fruits of his labor. By definition and in essence it was a
system of class rule, in which some people lived off the labor of others.
American slavery subordinated one race to another and thereby rendered its fundamental class relationships more complex and ambiguous;
but they remained class relationships. The racism that developed from
racial subordination influenced every aspect of American life and remains powerful. But slavery as a system of class rule predated racism
and racial subordination in world history and once existed without
them. Racial subordination, as postbellum American developments and
the history of modern colonialism demonstrate, need not rest on slavery. Wherever racial subordination exists, racism exists; therefore,
Southern slave society and its racist ideology had much in common with
other systems and societies. But Southern slave society was not merely
one more manifestation of some abstraction called racist society. Its history was essentially determined by particular relationships of class
power in racial form.

The Old South, black and white, created a historically unique kind of
paternalist society. To insist upon the centrality of class relations as
manifested in paternalism is not to slight the inherent racism or to deny
the intolerable contradictions at the heart of paternalism itself. Imamu
Amiri Baraka captures the tragic irony of paternalist social relations
when he writes that slavery "was, most of all, a paternal institution" and

347

yet refers to "the filthy paternalism and cruelty of slavery." Southern paternalism, like every other paternalism, had little to do with Ole Massa's ostensible benevolence, kindness, and good cheer. It grew out of the necessity to discipline and morally justify a system of exploitation. It did encourage kindness and affection, but it simultaneously encouraged cruelty and hatred. The racial distinction between master and slave heightened the tension inherent in an unjust social order.

Southern slave society grew out of the same general historical conditions that produced the other slave regimes of the modern world. The rise of a world market—the development of new tastes and of manufactures dependent upon non-European sources of raw materials—encouraged the rationalization of colonial agriculture under the ferocious domination of a few Europeans. African labor provided the human power to fuel the new system of production in all the New World slave societies, which, however, had roots in different European experiences and emerged in different geographical, economic, and cultural conditions. They had much in common, but each was unique.

Theoretically, modern slavery rested, as had ancient slavery, on the idea of a slave as *instrumentum vocale*—a chattel, a possession, a thing, a mere extension of his master's will. But the vacuousness of such pretensions had been exposed long before the growth of New World slave societies. The closing of the ancient slave trade, the political crisis of ancient civilization, and the subtle moral pressure of an ascendant Christianity had converged in the early centuries of the new era to shape a seigneurial world in which lords and serfs (not slaves) faced each other with reciprocal demands and expectations. This land-oriented world of medieval Europe slowly forged the traditional paternalist ideology to which the southern slaveholders fell heir.

The slaveholders of the South, unlike those of the Caribbean, increasingly resided on their plantations and by the end of the eighteenth century had become an entrenched regional ruling class. The paternalism encouraged by the close living of masters and slaves was enormously reinforced by the closing of the African slave trade, which compelled masters to pay greater attention to the reproduction of their labor force. Of all the slave societies in the New World, that the Old South alone maintained a slave force that reproduced itself. Less than 400,000 imported Africans had, by 1860, become an American black population of more than 4 million.

A paternalism accepted by both masters and slaves—but with radically different interpretations—afforded a fragile bridge across the intolerable contradictions inherent in a society based on racism, slavery, and class exploitation that had to depend on the willing reproduction and productivity of its victims. For the slaveholders paternalism represented an attempt to overcome the fundamental contradiction in slavery: the impossibility of the slaves' ever becoming the things they were suppose to be. Paternalism defined the involuntary labor of the slaves as a legitimate return to their masters for protection and direction. But, the masters' need to see their slaves as acquiescent human beings constituted a moral victory for the slaves themselves. Paternalism's insistence upon mutual obligations—duties, responsibilities, and ultimately even rights—implicitly recognized the slaves' humanity.

Wherever paternalism exists, it undermines solidarity among the oppressed by linking them as individuals to their oppressors. A lord (master, *padrone, patron, padrón, patrào*) functions as a direct provider and protector to each individual or family, as well as to the community as a whole. The slaves of the Old South displayed impressive solidarity and collective resistance to their masters, but in a web of paternalistic relationships their action tended to become defensive and to aim at protecting the individuals against aggression and abuse; it could not readily pass into an effective weapon for liberation. Black leaders, especially the preachers, won loyalty and respect and fought heroically to defend their people. But despite their will and considerable ability, they could not lead their people over to the attack against the paternalist ideology itself.

In the Old South the tendencies inherent in all paternalistic class systems intersected with and acquired enormous reinforcement from the tendencies inherent in an analytically distinct system of racial subordination. The two appeared to be a single system. Paternalism created a tendency for the slaves to identify with a particular community through identification with its master; it reduced the possibilities for their identification with each other as a class. Racism undermined the slaves' sense of worth as black people and reinforced their dependence on white masters. But these were tendencies, not absolute laws, and the slaves forged weapons of defense, the most important of which was a religion that taught them to love and value each other, to take a critical view of their masters, and to reject the ideological rationales for their own enslavement.

The slaveholders had to establish a stable regime with which their slaves could live. Slaves remained slaves. They could be bought and sold like any other property and were subject to despotic personal power. And blacks remained rigidly subordinated to whites. But masters and slaves, whites and blacks, lived as well as worked together. The existence of the community required that all find some measure of self-interest and self-respect. Southern paternalism developed as a way of mediating irreconcilable class and racial conflicts; it was an anomaly even at the moment of its greatest apparent strength. But, for about a century, it protected both masters and slaves from the worst tendencies inherent in their respective conditions. It mediated, however unfairly and even cruelly, between masters and slaves, and it disguised, however imperfectly the appropriation of one man's labor power by another. Paternalism in any historical setting defines relations of superordination and subordination. Its strength as a prevailing ethos increases as the members of the community accept—or feel compelled to accept—these relations as legitimate. Brutality lies inherent in this acceptance of patronage and dependence, no matter how organic the paternalistic order. But Southern paternalism necessarily recognized the slaves' humanity—not only their free will but the very talent and ability without which their acceptance of a doctrine of reciprocal obligations would have made no sense. Thus, the slaves found an opportunity to translate paternalism itself into a doctrine different from that understood by their masters and to forge it into a weapon of resistance to assertions that slavery was a natural condition for blacks, that blacks were racially inferior, and that black slaves had no rights or legitimate claims of their own.

Thus, the slaves, by accepting a paternalistic ethos and legitimizing class rule, developed their most powerful defense against the dehumanization implicit in slavery. Southern paternalism may have reinforced racism as well as class exploitation, but it also unwittingly invited its victims to fashion their own interpretation of the social order it was intended to justify. And the slaves, drawing on a religion that was supposed to assure their compliance and docility, rejected the essence of slavery by projecting their own rights and value as human beings. . . .

When Mao Tse-tung told his revolutionary army, "Political power grows out of the barrel of a gun," he stated the obvious, for as Max Weber long before had observed as a matter of scientific detachment, "The decisive means of politics is violence." This viewpoint does not deny an ethical dimension to state power; it asserts that state power, the conquest of which constitutes the object of all serious political struggle, represents an attempt to monopolize and therefore both discipline and legitimize the weapons of violence.

One of the primary functions of the law concerns the means by which command of the gun becomes ethically sanctioned. But if we left it at that, we could never account for the dignity and élan of a legal profession in, say, England, that has itself become a social force; much less could we account for the undeniable influence of the law in shaping the class relations of which it is an instrument of domination. Thus, the fashionable relegation of law to the rank of a superstructural and derivative phenomenon obscures the degree of autonomy it creates for itself. In modern societies, at least, the theoretical and moral foundations of the legal order and the actual, specific history of its ideas and institutions influence, step by step, the wider social order and system of class rule, for no class in the modern Western world could rule for long without

some ability to present itself as the guardian of the interests and sentiments of those being ruled.

The idea of "hegemony," which since Gramsci has become central to
Western Marxism, implies class antagonisms; but it also implies, for a
given historical epoch, the ability of a particular class to contain those
antagonisms on a terrain in which its legitimacy is not dangerously
questioned. As regards the law specifically, note should be taken of the
unhappy fate of natural-law doctrines and assorted other excursions
into "revolutionary" legal theory. The revolutionary bourgeoisie, during
its rise to power in Europe, counterposed natural-law doctrines to feudal
theory but once in power rushed to embrace a positive theory of law,
even while assimilating natural-law doctrines to a new defense of property. Nor did the experience of the Communist movement in Russia
differ after its conquest of power. However much sentimentalists and
utopians may rail at the monotonous recurrence of a positive theory of
law whenever revolutionaries settle down to rebuild the world they
have shattered, any other course would be doomed to failure. Ruling
classes differ, and each must rule differently. But all modern ruling
classes have much in common in their attitude toward the law, for each
must confront the problem of coercion in such a way as to minimize the
necessity for its use, and each must diguise the extent to which state
power does not so much rest on force as represent its actuality. Even
Marxian theory, therefore, must end with the assertion of a positive
theory of law and judge natural-law and "higher-law" doctrines to be
tactical devices in the extralegal struggle.

In Southern slave society, as in other societies, the law, even narrowly defined as a system of institutionalized jurisprudence, constituted
a principal vehicle for the hegemony of the ruling class. Since the
slaveholders, like other ruling classes, arose and grew in dialectical response to the other classes of society—since they were molded by white
yeomen and black slaves as much as they molded them—the law cannot
be viewed as something passive and reflective, but must be viewed as an
active, partially autonomous force, which mediated among the several
classes and compelled the rulers to bend to the demands of the ruled.
The slaveholders faced an unusually complex problem since their regional power was embedded in a national system in which they had to
share power with an antagonistic northern bourgeoisie. A full evaluation of the significance of the law of slavery will have to await an
adequate history of the Southern legal system in relation to the national;
until then a preliminary analysis that risks too much abstraction must
serve.

The slaveholders as a socioeconomic class shaped the legal system to
their interests. But within that socioeconomic class—the class as a
whole—there were elements competing for power. Within it, a political

center arose, consolidated itself, and assumed a commanding position during the 1850s. The most advanced fraction of the slaveholders—those who most clearly perceived the interests and needs of the class as a whole—steadily worked to make their class more conscious of its nature, spirit, and destiny. In the process it created a world-view appropriate to a slaveholders' regime.

For any such political center, the class as a whole must be brought to a higher understanding of itself—transformed from a class-in-itself reacting to pressures on its objective position, into a class-for-itself, consciously striving to shape the world in its own image. Only possession of public power can discipline a class as a whole, and through it, the other classes of society. The juridical system may become, then, not merely an expression of class interest, nor even merely an expression of the willingness of the rulers to mediate with the ruled; it may become an instrument by which the advanced section of the ruling class imposes its viewpoint upon the class as a whole and the wider society. The law must discipline the ruling class and guide and educate the masses. To accomplish these tasks it must manifest a degree of evenhandedness sufficient to compel social conformity; it must, that is, validate itself ethically in the eyes of the several classes, not just the ruling class. Both criminal and civil law set standards of behavior and sanction norms that extend well beyond the strictly legal matters. The death penalty for murder, for example, need not arise from a pragmatic concern with deterrence, and its defenders could justifiably resist psychological arguments. It may arise from the demand for implementation of a certain idea of justice and from the educational requirement to set a firm standard of right and wrong. "The Law," as Gramsci says, "is the repressive and negative aspect of the entire positive civilising activity undertaken by the State."

The law acts hegemonically to assure people that their particular consciences can be subordinated—indeed, morally must be subordinated—to the collective judgment of society. It may compel conformity by granting each individual his right of private judgment, but it must deny him the right to take action based on that judgment when in conflict with the general will. Those who would act on their own judgment as against the collective judgment embodied in the law find themselves pressed from the moral question implicit in any particular law to the moral question of obedience to constituted authority. It appears mere egotism and antisocial behavior to attempt to go outside the law unless one is prepared to attack the entire legal system and therefore the consensual framework of the body politic.

The white South shaped its attitude toward its slaves in this context. With high, malicious humor, William Styron has his fictional T. R. Gray explain to Nat Turner how he, a mere chattel, can be tried for the very human acts of murder and insurrection:

' ... The point is that *you* are *animate* chattel and animate chattel is capable of craft and connivery and wily stealth. You ain't a wagon, Reverend, but chattel that possesses moral choice and spiritual violition. Remember that well. Because that's how come the law provides that animate chattel like you can be tried for a felony, and that's how come you're goin' to be tried next Sattidy."

He paused, then said softly without emotion: "And hung by the neck until dead."

Styron may well have meant to satirize Judge Green of the Tennessee Supreme Court, who declared in 1846, "A slave is not in the condition of a horse." The slave [Green continued] is made in the image of the Creator: "He has mental capacities, and an immortal principle in his nature that constitute him equal to his owner, but for the accidental position in which fortune has placed him. ... The laws ... cannot extinguish his high born nature, nor deprive him of many rights which are inherent in man." The idea that chattels, as the states usually defined slaves, could have a highborn nature, complete with rights inherent in man, went down hard with those who thought that even the law should obey the rules of logic. Four years before Judge Green's humane observations, Judge Turley of the same court unwittingly presented the dilemma. "The right to obedience ... " he declared in *Jacob (a Slave) v. State*, "in all lawful things ... is perfect in the master; and the power to inflict any punishment, not affecting life or limb ... is secured to him by law." The slave, being neither a wagon nor a horse, had to be dealt with as a man, but the law dared not address itself direct to the point. Had the law declared the slave a person in a specific class relationship to another person, two unpleasant consequences would have followed. First, the demand that such elementary rights as those of the family be respected would have become irresistible in a commercialized society that required the opposite in order to guarantee an adequate mobility of capital and labor. Second, the slaveholders would have had to surrender in principle, much as they often had to do in practice, their insistence that a slave was morally obligated to function as an extension of his master's will. However much the law generally seeks to adjust conflicting principles in society, in this case it risked undermining the one principle the slaveholders viewed as a *sine qua non*.

Yet, as Styron correctly emphasizes in the words he gives to T. R. Gray, the courts had to recognize the humanity—and therefore the free will—of the slave or be unable to hold him accountable for antisocial acts. Judge Bunning of Georgia plainly said, "It is not true that slaves are only chattels ... and therefore, it is not true that it is not possible for them to be prisoners. ... " He did not tell us how a chattel (a thing) could also be nonchattel in any sense other than an agreed-upon fiction, nor did he wish to explore the question why a fiction should have become necessary. Since much of the law concerns agreed-upon fictions, the judges, as judges, did not have to become nervous about their diverse legal opinions, but as slaveholders, they could not avoid the prospect of disarray being introduced into their social philosophy. Repeatedly, the courts struggled with and tripped over the slave's humanity. Judge Hall of North Carolina, contrary to reason, nature, and the opinion of his fellow judges, could blurt out, *en passant*, "Being slaves, they had no will of their own. . . . " If so, then what of the opinion expressed by the State Supreme Court of Missouri: "The power of the master being limited, his responsibility is proportioned accordingly"?

The high court of South Carolina wrestled with the conflicting principles of slave society and came up with an assortment of mutually exclusive answers. Judge Waites, in *State v. Cynthia Simmons and Lawrence Kitchen* (1794): "Negroes are under the protection of the laws, and have personal rights, and cannot be considered on a footing only with domestic animals. They have wills of their own—capacities to commit crimes; and are responsible for offences against society." The court in *Fairchild v. Bell* (1807): "The slave lives for his master's service. His time, his labor, his comforts, are all at the master's disposal." Judge John Belton O'Neall in *Tennent v. Dendy* (1837): "Slaves are our most valuable property. . . . Too many guards cannot be interposed between it and violent unprincipled men. . . . The slave ought to be fully aware that his master is to him . . . a perfect security from injury. When this is the case, the relation of master and servant becomes little short of that of parent and child." But in Kentucky, the high court had pronounced in 1828: "However deeply it may be regretted, and whether it be politic or impolitic, a slave by our code is not treated as a person, but (*negotium*) a thing, as he stood in the civil code of the Roman Empire." But one year later we hear: "A slave has volition, and has feelings which cannot be entirely disregarded." And again in 1836: "But, although the law of this state considers slaves as property, yet it recognizes their personal existence, and, to a qualified extent, their natural rights."

The South had discovered, as had every previous slave society, that it could not deny the slave's humanity, however many preposterous legal fictions it invented. That discovery ought to have told the slaveholders much more. Had they reflected on the implications of a wagon's inability to raise an insurrection, they might have understood that the slaves as well as the masters were creating the law. The slaves' action proceeded within narrow limits, but it realized one vital objective: it exposed the deception on which the slave society rested—the notion that in fact, not merely in one's fantasy life, some human beings could become mere extensions of the will of another. The slaves grasped the significance of their victory with deeper insight than they have usually been given credit for. They saw that they had few rights at law and that those could easily be violated by the whites. But even one right, imperfectly defended, was enough to tell them that the pretensions of the master class could be resisted. Before long, law or no law, they were adding a great many "customary rights" of their own and learning how to get them respected.

The slaves understood that the law offered them little or no protection, and in self-defense they turned to two alternatives: to their master, if he was decent, or his neighbors, if he was not; and to their own resources. Their commitment to a paternalistic system deepened accordingly, but in such a way as to allow them to define rights for themselves. For reasons of their own the slaveholders relied heavily on local custom and tradition; so did the slaves, who turned this reliance into a weapon. If the law said they had no right to property, for example, but local custom accorded them private garden plots, then woe to the master or overseer who summarily withdrew the "privilege." To those slaves the privilege had become a right, and the withdrawal an act of aggression not to be borne. The slaveholders, understanding this attitude, rationalized their willingness to compromise. The slaves forced themselves upon the law, for the courts repeatedly sustained such ostensibly extralegal arrangements as having the force of law because sanctioned by time-honored practice. It was a small victory so far as everyday protection was concerned, but not so small psychologically; it gave the slaves some sense of having rights of their own and also made them more aware of those rights withheld. W. W. Hazard of Georgia ran the risk of telling his slaves about their legal rights and of stressing the legal limits of his own power over them. He made it clear that he had an obligation to take care of them in their old age, whereas free white workers had no such protection, and argued deftly that their being whipped for insubordination represented a humane alternative to the practice of shooting soldiers and sailors for insubordination. His was an unusual act, but perhaps not so risky after all. He may have scored a few points while not revealing much they did not already know. . . .

Those slaves whose disaffection turned into violence and hatred—those who resisted the regime physically—included slaves who made stealing almost a way of life, killed their overseers and masters, fought back against patrollers, burned down plantation buildings, and ran away either to freedom or to the woods for a short while in order to effect some specific end, as well as those who took the ultimate measures and rose in revolt. Class oppression, whether or not reinforced and modified by racism, induces servility and feelings of inferiority in the oppressed. Force alone usually has not sufficed to keep the lower classes in subjugation. Slavishness constitutes the extreme form of the psychology of the oppressed, although we may doubt that it ever appears in pure form. It longs for acceptance by the other, perceived as the epitome of such superior qualities as beauty, goodness, virtue, and above all, power. But the inevitable inability of the lower classes, especially but not uniquely slave classes, to attain that acceptance generates disaffection, hatred, and violence.

The slaves' response to paternalism and their imaginative creation of a partially autonomous religion provided a record of simultaneous accommodation and resistance to slavery. Accommodation itself breathed a critical spirit and disguised subversive actions and often embraced its apparent opposite—resistance. In fact, accommodation might best be understood as a way of accepting what could not be helped without falling prey to the pressures for dehumanization, emasculation, and self-hatred. In particular, the slaves' accommodation to paternalism enabled them to assert rights, which by their very nature not only set limits to their surrender of self but actually constituted an implicit rejection of slavery.

Stark physical resistance did not represent a sharp break with the process of accommodation except in its most extreme forms—running away to freedom and insurrection. Strictly speaking, only insurrection represented political action, which some choose to define as the only genuine resistance since it alone directly challenged the power of the regime. From that point of view, those activities which others call "day-to-day resistance to slavery"—stealing, lying, dissembling, shirking, murder, infanticide, suicide, arson—qualify at best as prepolitical and at worst as apolitical.

These distinctions have only a limited usefulness and quickly lose their force. Such apparently innocuous and apolitical measures as a preacher's sermon on love and dignity or the mutual support offered by husbands and wives played—under the specific conditions of slave life—an indispensable part in providing the groundwork for the most obviously political action, for they contributed to the cohesion and strength of a social class threatened by disintegration and demoralization. But "day-to-day resistance to slavery" generally implied accommodation and made no sense except on the assumption of an accepted status quo the norms of which, as perceived or defined by the slaves, had been violated.

The definition of resistance as political response nonetheless draws attention to a break—a qualitative leap—in the continuum of resistance in accommodation and accommodation in resistance. The slaves who unambiguously chose to fight for or fly to freedom represented a new quality. They remained a small portion of the total, but their significance far transcended their numbers. The maturation of that new quality, so vital to the health and future of the black community, depended upon those less dramatic efforts in the quarters which produced a collective spiritual life. . . .

Accommodation and resistance developed as two forms of a single process by which the slaves accepted what could not be avoided and simultaneously fought individually and as a people for moral as well as physical survival. The hegemony of the slaveholders—their domination of society through command of the culture rather than solely through command of the gun—has no meaning except on the assumption of deep class antagonisms and on the further assumption that command of the culture could not readily have been established without command of the gun. The slaveholders' hegemony, as reflected in their relationship to nonslaveholding whites, for example, did not eliminate the chasm between the classes of white society. Antebellum political struggles often became sharp and reflected class antagonisms, which appear to have been sharpening during the 1850s. To speak of the slaveholders' hegemony is to speak of their ability to confine the attendant struggles to terrain acceptable to the ruling class—to prevent the emergence of an effective challenge to the basis of society in slave property.

The slaveholders established their hegemony over the slaves primarily through the development of an elaborate web of paternalistic relationships, but the slaves' place in that hegemonic system reflected deep contradictions, manifested in the dialectic of accommodation and resistance. The slaves' insistence on defining paternalism in their own way represented a rejection of the moral pretensions of the slaveholders, for it refused that psychological surrender of will which constituted the ideological foundation of such pretensions. By developing a sense of moral worth and by asserting rights, the slaves transformed their acquiescence in paternalism into a rejection of slavery itself, although their masters assumed acquiescence in the one to demonstrate acquiescence in the other.

The slaves' world-view emerged primarily in their actions. But at each point at which this implicit world-view conflicted with that of the masters and provoked a crisis within the web of paternalistic relations, the slaves moved, as peoples generally do at such moments, toward articulating their position. Some slaves always reflected on the theoretical implications of their position. But even the preachers, drivers, and mechanics could not decisively organize their people politically and, therefore, could not move them toward the formulation of a protonational consciousness, expressed primarily through a religious sensibility, that enabled a mass of oppressed individuals to cohere as a people.

The rise of a religious community among the slaves, with that looseness of organization inevitable in a slaveholding society and with its specific theological tendencies, ordered the life of the collective. Ralph Ellison's comment on the problems of black people in the twentieth-century South applies with added force to the slave period:

> The pre-individualistic black community discourages individuality out of self-defense. Having learned through experience that the whole group is punished for the actions of a single member, it has worked out efficient techniques of behavior control. For in many Southern communities everyone knows everyone else and is vulnerable to his opinions.

No people can respond in this way unless it has achieved considerable moral coherence. For the slaves such moral coherence was the more important since they could not provide the institutional coherence achieved by the postbellum black churches.

The slaves' religion developed into the organizing center of their resistance within accommodation; it reflected the hegemony of the master class but also set firm limits to that hegemony. Not often or generally did it challenge the regime frontally. It rendered unto Caesar that which was Caesar's, but it also narrowed down considerably that which in fact was Caesar's. Black religion, understood as a critical world-view in the process of becoming—as something unfinished, often inconsistent, and in some respects even incoherent—emerged as the slaves' most formidable weapon for resisting slavery's moral and psychological aggression. Without it or its moral equivalent, "day-to-day resistance to slavery" might have been condemned to the level of a pathetic nihilism, incapable of bridging the gap between individual action against an oppressor and the needs of the collective for self-discipline, community élan, and a sense of worth as a people rather than merely as a collection of individuals. With it, the slaves were able to assert manhood and womanhood in their everyday lives and were able to struggle, by no means always successfully, for collective forms of resistance in place of individual outbursts.

However much the slaves, as Christians, felt the weight of sin, they resisted those perversions of doctrine which would have made them feel unworthy as a people before God. Their Christianity strengthened their ties to their "white folks" but also strengthened their love for each other and their pride in being black people. And it gave them a firm yardstick with which to measure the behavior of their masters, to judge them and to find them wanting. The slaves transformed the promise of personal redemption, prefigured in the sign of Jonas, into a promise of deliverance as a people in this world as well as the next. Through tests of flood and fire they laid the moral and spiritual foundations for the struggle of subsequent generations of black Americans to fulfill that prophecy they have made their own:

> But that which ye have already hold
>     fast till I come.
> And he that overcometh, and keepeth
>     my works unto the end, to him will I
>     give power over the nations. . . .
> I am the root and the offspring of
> David, and the bright and morning star.

—Revelation, 2:25–26; 22:16

# 10

# *The Civil War*

## Repressible or Irrepressible?

Few events in American history have been studied more than the Civil War. Scarcely a year passes that does not see the publication of a wave of books and articles dealing with the war as well as the events leading up to it. So widespread has been interest in the origins and consequences of the conflict that many organizations as well as journals have been founded expressly for the purpose of furthering additional research and stimulating popular and professional interest in this subject. Indeed, to refer to the "cult" of the Civil War enthusiasts is not to exaggerate the intense interest that this topic has generated.

One of the reasons for the enduring interest in the Civil War era undoubtedly lies in the fact that this conflict pitted Americans against Americans. Under such circumstances responsibility for the coming of the war could not easily be placed on an external foe or upon factors beyond the control of Americans. The symbolic influence of the conflict as a major dividing line in American history also helps to explain the continued fascination with this problem. To American historians the Civil War bears the same relationship to the American people as the French Revolution to Frenchmen, the English Civil War to Englishmen, and the Russian Revolution to Russians. Questions involving vital national issues seemed to be at stake: the problem of nationalism versus states' rights and sectionalism; the role the war played in promoting industrialization and urbanization; and the status blacks were to have in American society.

Despite the vast body of published material dealing with the Civil War, however, historians have been unable to come to any agreement as to why the war occurred in the first place. "Historians, whatever their predispositions," noted a famous scholar more than thirty years ago, "assign to the Civil War causes ranging from one simple force or phenomenon to patterns so complex and manifold that they include, intricately interwoven, all the important movements, thoughts, and actions of the decades before 1861."[1] This comment is as true today as it was

---

[1]Howard K. Beale, "What Historians Have Said About the Causes of the Civil War," in

when it was first written. Disagreements among historians over the problem of Civil War causation seem to be as sharp today as they were when the conflict began over a century ago.

The disagreement over the coming of the conflict was hardly surprising; Americans have traditionally engaged in a debate over all of the wars in which they participated. Historians still argue over the desirability or wisdom of America's participation in World Wars I and II; they discuss the War of 1812, the Mexican War, and the Spanish-American War in terms of American aggression—thereby questioning the desirability and morality of these conflicts; and they debate the question of whether or not the Korean War was due to the ineptitude of America's foreign policies. The Civil War, however, has undoubtedly been the most controversial of all of these conflicts insofar as scholars were concerned. Unlike the American Revolution—whose good and beneficent results few ever questioned—American historians have, by and large, never been fully convinced that the war was necessary or that its results were worthwhile. Consequently, they have continued to seek to fix responsibility for its causes upon specific groups or institutions.

In the three decades following the end of fighting in 1865, many authors published their own evaluations of the causes of the war. Most of these early writers themselves had participated in one way or another in the war; their books represented an attempt to justify their own actions or those of their respective sections. When they looked at the war, therefore, they viewed it in terms of a conspiracy. Northern writers portrayed Southern secessionists as men dedicated to the advance of the cause of slavery, regardless of the harm to the rest of the nation. The slave power, wrote Henry Wilson in a famous book published in the 1870s, "after aggressive warfare of more than two generations upon the vital and animating spirit of republican institutions, upon the cherished and hallowed sentiments of a Christian people, upon the enduring interests and lasting renown of the Republic organized treasonable conspiracies, raised the standard of revolution, and plunged the nation into a bloody contest for the preservation of its threatened life."[2] To most Northern writers, the war resulted from a conspiracy of slaveowners committed to an immoral institution; the North was defending the Union and the Constitution against the unprovoked and immoral aggression of the South.

Southern writers, on the other hand, depicted an aggressive North determined to destroy the South and its institutions. The war, they insisted, was not a moral conflict over the issue of slavery; slavery was

---

*Theory and Practice in Historical Study: A Report of the Committee on Historiography,* Social Science Research Council, *Bulletin* 54 (1946):55.

[2]Henry Wilson, *History of the Rise and Fall of the Slave Power in America,* 3 vols. (Boston, 1872–1877), 1: vi–vii.

the occasion of the conflict, not its cause. The basic cause of the war was the unconstitutional and aggressive acts of the North, which used its power for political and economic gain. Although Southerns denied that the war had stemmed from differences over slavery, they did argue that both sections had differing and imcompatible ways of life. One of the basic factors leading to hostilities, therefore, was the North's domineering attitude toward the South. Thus Abraham Lincoln and the Republican party deliberately provoked the conflict by their aggressive and unwarranted actions in 1860 and 1861, thereby forcing the South to defend the Constitution as well as its rights. For this reason Southerns refused to accept the term "Civil War" or the "War of the Great Rebellion"; both implied that the South was wrong. Instead they used the designation "War Between the States," which seemed to justify the Southern emphasis on states' rights and local automony.

While Northern and Southern partisans were attacking each other, a third school of writers was developing the concept of a "needless' or "avoidable" conflict. The origins of this approach to the problem of Civil War interpretation arose first among those individuals who had been critical of the activities of both Northern and Southern statesmen between 1860 and 1865. President James Buchanan, for example, argued in 1865 that the cause of the Civil War was to be found in "the long, active, and persistent hostility of the Northern Abolitionists, both in and out of Congress, against Southern slavery, until the final triumph of President Lincoln; and on the other hand, the corresponding antagonism and violence with which the advocates of slavery resisted these efforts, and vindicated its preservation and extension up till the period of secession."[3] Implied in Buchanan's statement was the assumption that the war need not have taken place had it not been for Northern fanatics and, to a lesser extent, Southern extremists. To put it another way, there was no substantive issue important enough in 1861 to necessitate a resort to arms; the war had been brought on by extremists on both sides.

These three contemporary views of the causes of the Civil War set the stage for the historical debate that began at the end of the nineteenth century and continues right down to the present. Despite massive research into the sources, both published and unpublished, historians continued to divide into competing and antagonistic schools. It was not that scholars disagreed over what constituted the "facts" in each case; indeed, their data, whatever school they belonged to, were remarkably similar. What divided them was the different way in which they read and interpreted the data.

The first serious attempts to explain the coming of the Civil War in a way that was free from the bitterness of contemporary accounts came

---

[3]James Buchanan, *The Administration of the Eve of the Rebellion: A History of Four Years Before the War* (London, 1865), p. iv.

from the writings of the postwar generation of historians who came to maturity in the 1890s. To them the Civil War was "history" rather than a part of current events. Most of them had been very young when the war began; their memories of the war years were not as personally and emotionally involved as were their parents. The writings of this later generation reflected a decline in the heated partisanship characteristic of earlier accounts.

These scholars were influenced also by the rising tide of American nationalism during the 1890s and early part of the twentieth century. By that time, both North and South had come to the conclusion that the outcome of the Civil War had been a blessing in disguise. Not only had the slavery issue disappeared, but the intense sectional strife that had inhibited the growth of the nation at large had been laid to rest. After the war to stage was set for the phenomenal industrial growth of the United States, a development that made the nation a world power by the turn of the century. Even more significant, the war had tested the mettle and fiber of all Americans; they had not been found wanting. While the nationalist school did not gloss over the war, they began to present a more balanced and less partisan picture of an event that had cemented for all time the bonds of American nationality.

One of the first—and in some respects the most influential—works in the nationalist tradition was written by James Ford Rhodes whose multivolume history of the United States from 1850 to 1877 became a classic. Like many of his Northern predecessors, Rhodes accepted the idea that slavery was the basic cause of the war. He rejected the claim by Southerners that they had been persecuted; instead, he argued that the South had fought the war to extend slavery. In his eyes, however, slavery was an immoral institution. The Civil War, Rhodes concluded, involved an "irrepressible conflict" between North and South, and the South had been clearly in the wrong.

Despite his obvious Northern sympathies, Rhodes modified considerably his own partisan approach in his discussion of the South and its peculiar institution. Slavery had prospered, he wrote, because of technological progress; the cotton gin had prevented the peaceful abolition of slavery. Moreover, both England and New England had played an important role in the preservation of slavery; their citizens had purchased slave-grown cotton without any moral compunctions. Rhodes also distinguished between the institution of slavery and individual slaveowners; he absolved the latter of any crime and insisted that they were deserving of sympathy rather than of censure. Indeed, Rhodes's discussion of the South was by no means hostile; he found much to praise in his descriptions of Southern life. To Rhodes the Civil War came about through the collision of impersonal forces, not individuals; out of the conflict, he concluded, had emerged a modern united America.

Rhodes's general approach was followed by other nationalist historians, many of whom were native Southerners. To the nationalist school the causes of war were less important than its results. Southern scholars, for example, emphasized nationalism, sectional reconciliation, and the integration of the South into national life so that their section was able to share in the blessings of industrialization and prosperity. These writers were not critical of the South—they unabashedly loved their region—but they were critical of slavery and secession. Their condemnation of slavery, however, did not rest on a moral foundation that accepted blacks as the equals of whites. Instead, they condemned the peculiar institution because it had prevented the South from making progress in industrial, economic, social and cultural matters. Woodrow Wilson, for example (who prior to entering public life had achieved a national reputation as a historian), emphasized the development of American nationalism in many of his works. Unfortunately, he concluded, the South remained outside the rising spirit of nationalism precisely because of slavery; consequently, it developed differently from the rest of the country. The result, according to Wilson, was the Civil War—a conflict that came about because differences between North and South "were removable in no other way."

Generally speaking, nationalist historians often wrote about the Civil War in terms of an "irrepressible conflict." The sectional approach to history that developed in the early part of the twentieth century tended to reinforce this concept. The conflict between North and South, some historians argued, was basically one that grew out of sectional differences on issues of national policy—of which slavery was but one issue. "By the middle of the [nineteenth] century," wrote Edward Channing, one of America's most distinguished historians, "two distinct social organizations had developed within the United States, the one in the South and the other in the North. Southern society was based on the production of staple agricultural crops by slave labor. Northern society was bottomed on varied employments—agricultural, mechanical, and commercial—all carried on under the wage system. Two such divergent forms of society could not continue indefinitely to live side by side within the walls of one government. . . . One or the other of these societies must perish, or both must secure complete equality . . . or the two societies must perish, or both must secure complete equality . . . or the two societies must separate absolutely and live each by itself under its own government."[4]

Those historians who wrote within the nationalist tradition obviously

[4]Edward Channing, A History of the United States, 6 vols. (New York, 1905–1925), 6:3–4; James Ford Rhodes, History of the United States from the Compromise of 1850 to the Final Restoration of Home Rule in the South in 1877, 7 vols. (New York, 1893–1906).

approved of the outcome of the Civil War. Most of them felt that the growth of industry—a development that dated from the Civil War—was good. Few of these scholars were interested in social reform nor were they antibusiness in their ideological views. Rhodes had been a businessman before taking up the study of history, and he shared the conservative outlook of many late nineteenth-century businessmen. Wilson in the 1890s was a conservative Democrat of the Cleveland stripe; his conversion to Progressivism did not occur until later. Even Channing was not noted for being antibusiness. All of these nationalist historians, therefore, were pleased with developments after 1865. The climate of opinion around the turn of the century was such that few took occasion to protest the fact that blacks had not yet achieved a measure of equality with whites. Like most white Americans, many of these scholars—though by no means all—believed blacks to be inferior beings. Such a belief seemed to them to be buttressed by contemporary scientific findings. They therefore accepted the subordinate role of blacks in American society as a natural development.

By the early twentieth century, the dominance of the nationalist school of Civil War historiography began to face a formidable challenge from the rising Progressive school. As we have already seen, the Progressive school had developed during the period of domestic reform around the turn of the century. Concerned with contemporary social problems, particularly those involving injustices in society arising out of a maldistribution of wealth and power, Progressive historians attempted to provide answers to these problems by showing how they had developed in the past. Thus they began to restudy American history in terms of a conflict between democracy and aristocracy, between the have-nots and the haves in American society. Led by men like Charles A. Beard and others, these scholars emphasized not the development of a beneficent nationalism, but the emergence of democracy, particularly economic democracy. Consequently, they divided America's past into alternating periods of reform and reaction—a cycle that was generated by class and social conflict in each instance.

In the writings of these historians, the Civil War began to be studied within a new framework. Perhaps the most lucid and influential Progressive interpretation of the Civil War came from the pen of Charles and Mary Beard, who published in 1927 their famous Progressive synthesis of American history, *The Rise of American Civilization*. To the Beards, the resort to arms in 1861 precipitated by secession was merely a facade for a much more deeply rooted conflict. Stripped of all nonessentials, they emphasized, the Civil War "was a social war, ending in the unquestioned establishment of a new power in the government, making vast changes in the arrangement of classes, in the accumulation and distribution of wealth, in the course of industrial development, and in the Constitution inherited from the Fathers. . . . In any event neither accident nor rhetoric should be allowed to obscure the intrinsic character of that struggle. If the operations by which the middle classes of England broke the power of the king and the aristocracy are to be known collectively as the Puritan Revolution, if the series of acts by which the bourgeois and peasants of France overthrew the king, nobility, and clergy is to be called the French Revolution, then accuracy compels us to characterize by the same term the social cataclysm in which the capitalists, laborers, and farmers of the North and West drove from power in the national government the planting aristocracy of the South."[5]

Unlike the nationalist interpretation, a Progressive synthesis such as that of the Beards condemned the results of the Civil War in no uncertain terms. Between 1865 and 1900 the American economy came to be dominated by ruthless and immoral capitalists who thought of nothing but their own aggrandizement. To Matthew Josephson, a writer in the Progressive tradition, the postwar era saw the rise to power of the great "Robber Barons." "Under their hands the renovation of our economic life proceeded relentlessly; large-scale production replaced the scattered, decentralized mode of production; industrial enterprises became more concentrated, more "efficient" technically, and essentially 'cooperative,' where they had been purely individualistic and lamentably wasteful. But all this revolutionizing effort is branded with the motive of private gain on the part of the new captains of industry. To organize and exploit the resources of a nation upon a gigantic scale, to regiment its farmers and workers into harmonious corps of producers, and to do this only in the name of an uncontrolled appetite for private profit—here surely is the great inherent contradiction whence so much disaster, outrage and misery has flowed."[6] Such an approach to the Civil War and the postwar era seemed to be written to provide the rationale from some democratic reforms lest America become the private preserve of a small group of capitalists.

While the Beardian economic interpretation of the Civil War was growing in importance during the depression decade of the 1930s, a small group of Marxian historians were going far beyond the Beards in stressing the importance of economic factors. These scholars were convinced that the end of the capitalistic system was fast approaching. They therefore periodized American history within a Marxian framework; each successive stage brought the nation closer and closer to the inevitable and final proletarian revolution. The place of the Civil War within

---

[5]Charles A. and Mary R. Beard, *The Rise of American Civilization*, 2 vols. (New York, 1927), 2: 53–54.

[6]Matthew Josephson, *The Robber Barons: The Great American Capitalists 1861–1901* (New York, 1934), p. viii.

this framework was clear; the Civil War was indeed—as the Beards claimed—a "Second American Revolution." Unlike the Beards, however, Marxist historians were not critical of the results of war. The war, they emphasized, had destroyed the slave power and prepared the ground for the triumph of capitalism—a necessary concomitant to the inevitable triumph of the proletariat. "The sectional nature of the conflict and the geographical division of the contending classes," one Marxian scholar wrote, "have obscured the essential revolutionary nature of the Civil War. But this conflict was basically a revolution of a bourgeois democratic character, in which the bourgeoisie was fighting for power against the landed aristocracy.... The destruction of the slave power was the basis for real national unity and the further development of capitalism, which would produce conditions most favorable for the growth of the labor movement.... The stage was being cleared of outworn and hackneyed properties to make way for a new and contemporary drama in which the chief protagonists would be the bourgeoisie and the proletariat."[7]

While the economic interpretation was flowering during the depression of the 1930s, two other schools of historical scholarship arose to make their own evaluations of the Civil War. The first of these schools came out of the resurgence of interest of native Southerners in their own section. The reawakened interest in the South, which took the form of a loosely defined and generally romantic movement, had a variety of sources. Taken as a whole, however, the movement attempted to portray the Southern way of life as being far better than the urbanized and industrialized way of life that seemed characteristic of twentieth-century America. Symbolic of the resurgence of Southern nationalism was the publication of 1930 of *I'll Take My Stand*—a symposium written by twelve Southern intellectuals seeking to show the superiority of the agrarian South over the industrial North. Southerners, in addition, were increasingly sensitive to the vast body of literature critical of their section which had originated in other regions of the nation. Consequently, some Southerners began to undertake a reappraisal of the relations between the South and the rest of the country in order to vindicate their section.

The rise of Southern nationalism in the 1930s was sharply mirrored in the historical treatment of the South by its native historians. Such scholars as Ulrich B. Phillips, Charles W. Ramsdell, and Frank L. Owsley set out to portray the South in a far more sympathetic light than any of their predecessors. When they wrote about the Civil War, therefore, they exonerated the South and blamed the North. In some ways their writings resembled the contemporary Confederate accounts writ-

---

[7]James S. Allen, *Reconstruction: The Battle for Democracy 1865–1876* (New York, 1937), pp. 18, 26–28. The quotations are taken from the 1955 edition of this work.

ten in the 1860s and 1870s; these twentieth-century scholars tended to idealize the South and its institutions while at the same time portraying the North in hostile, even savage, terms.

In an article published in 1941, for example, Owsley argued that the basic cause of the Civil War was the "egocentric sectionalism" of the North. The North, he charged, considered itself the nation; it destroyed the sectional balance of power by insisting on its own dominance; and it failed to recognize "the dignity and self-respect of the people in other sections." Owsley was particularly critical of the abolitionists, who aroused the entire population of the North by their savage lies. He denied that slavery was the cause of the war.[8] Actually his position combined the Beardian interpretation of the Civil War as a conflict between an agrarian South and an industrial North with the older claims of Southerners in the 1860s that the North was seeking the destruction of the South and its beneficent institutions and superior way of life.

The second school of Civil War historiography that flourished in the 1930s and 1940s was the revisionist school. Unlike the followers of Beard or those historians seeking to vindicate the South, revisionist scholars approached the problem within a quite different framework. Their basic assumption was that wars in general and the Civil War in particular were evil. Even more significant was their underlying belief that the war had been avoidable and that there had been genuine alternatives facing the political leaders in both sections.

It is not difficult to understand why some scholars held such views during these years. The United States, after all, had gone to war in 1917 supposedly to make the world safe for democracy and to achieve other laudatory and moral objectives. Instead of finding a brave new world, however, the postwar generation saw their idealistic hopes dashed by a supposedly unjust and unfair Versailles peace treaty that caused the rise of totalitarian and dictatorial regimes throughout the world. Americans during the 1930s were deeply disillusioned with the results of World War I; they were even more concerned about staying out of future conflicts that seemed to be in the offing. Hence, revisionist historians examined the causes of the Civil War at a time when war as a means of solving problems was not considered to be a sound solution.

Some revisionists came to the conclusion that the Civil War had been an "avoidable" or "repressible" conflict. The belief that the conflict could have been averted was already evident in some scholarly works

---

[8]Frank L. Owsley, "The Fundamental Cause of the Civil War: Egocentric Sectionalism," *Journal of Southern History* 7 (February 1941): 3–18. Owsley had also argued in 1930 that slavery was primarily a racial rather than an ethical issue. The blacks of the South, he had written, were "cannibals and barbarians"; slavery was simply a system of racial discipline. See Owsley, "The Irrepressible Conflict," in Twelve Southerners, *I'll Take My Stand* (New York, 1930), pp. 77–78.

published during the 1920s which had begun the task of rehabilitating the reputations of those moderates in 1860 and 1861 who had struggled so valiantly to find a peaceable way out of the impasse. The biographers of James Buchanan and Stephen A. Douglas, for example, had argued that a peaceable solution could have been found had Americans heeded the advice and example of these two leading statesmen. Conversely, the extremists on both sides—particularly Northern abolitionists—were condemned for their role in bringing on the war and all that followed.[9]

The most mature formulation of the revisionist hypothesis, however, came from the pens of Avery Craven and James G. Randall in the years just before Pearl Harbor. Both of these distinguished scholars hated war in general; both were convinced that the results of war never approximated the supposedly noble objectives for which such conflicts were fought; both regarded war as abnormal and peace as normal; and both equated war with pathological emotionalism and irrationalism. Given these assumptions, it was understandable that these two historians should have rejected many other interpretations that had been offered about the causes of the Civil War. For both Craven and Randall were convinced that the Civil War was a "repressible conflict"; they therefore explained the coming of the war in terms of a failure on the part of the generation of the 1850s and 1860s.

Craven, for example, argued that sectional differences—economic, social, political—could not explain the causes of the war; many countries had pronounced sectional dissimilarities without having had civil strife. Nor was slavery the cause of the war. "If it had not become a symbol first of sectional differences and then of southern depravity, or superiority, according to the point of view—it might have been faced as a national question and dealt with as successfully as the South American countries dealt with the same problem."[10] The war, Craven maintained, occurred because normal sectional differences—which were not serious and could have been resolved through political means—were magnified and emotionalized until they could no longer be dealt with in rational terms. "Stripped of false assumptions, the tragedy of the nation in bloody strife from 1861 to 1865 must, in large part, be charged to a generation of well-meaning Americans, who, busy with the task of getting ahead, permitted their shortsighted politicians, their overzealous editors, and their pious reformers to emotionalize real and potential differences and to conjure up distorted impressions of those who dwelt

---

[9]For typical examples see the following works: Philip G. Auchampaugh, *James Buchanan and His Cabinet on the Eve of Secession* (Lancaster, 1926); George Fort Milton, *The Eve of Conflict: Stephen A. Douglas and the Needless War* (New York, 1934); Gilbert H. Barnes, *The Antislavery Impulse, 1830–1844* (New York, 1933).

[10]Avery Craven, *The Repressible Conflict 1830–1861* (Baton Rouge, 1939), p. 64.

in other parts of the nation. For more than two decades, these molders of public opinion steadily created the fiction of two distinct peoples contending for the right to preserve and expand their sacred cultures. . . . They awakened new fears and led men to hate. In time a people came to believe that social security, constitutional government and the freedom of all men were at stake in their sectional differences; that the issues were between right and wrong; good and evil. Opponents became devils in human form. Good men had no choice but to kill and to be killed."[11]

Like Craven, Randall also rejected an approach that romanticized war. Realists, he suggested, would not use the term *war*, but rather *organized murder* or *human slaughterhouse.* The war was indeed a "needless one," for the Union could have been continued and slavery abolished without the conflict. Its causes, according to Randall, could only be understood within a pathological framework; it was a proper subject for social psychiatry. Without abnormality, bogus leadership, or inordinate ambition, war would not have occurred; no issues were so vital as to require a violent resolution. Responsibility for the Civil War, concluded Randall, must be placed at the feet of a "blundering generation."[12]

Although the revisionist "needless war" approach remained popular throughout the 1940s and even afterward,[13] some historians began to attack its basic premises in sharp terms. While wars could never be good in themselves, these scholars argued, not to go to war in certain cases was even a far greater evil. Pointing to the Second World War, Samuel Eliot Morison—one of America's most distinguished historians—argued in his presidential address before the American Historical Association that "war does accomplish something, that war is better than servitude, that war has been an inescapable aspect of the human story."[14] Influenced by the rise of totalitarian regimes, Morison and other scholars insisted that war could indeed involve fundamental moral and ethical issues that could not be compromised. Moreover, some of these historians were influenced by the writings of Reinhold Niebuhr and other theologians and philosophers who had insisted that evil was a reality within the framework of human experience and had to be taken into account in any adequate explanation of past events. Armed confrontations were occasionally

---

[11]Avery Craven, *The Coming of the Civil War* (New York, 1942), p. 2.

[12]J. G. Randall, "The Blundering Generation," *Mississippi Valley Historical Review,* 27 (June 1940): 4–16.

[13]Two outstanding revisionist works published after the end of the Second World War include Roy F. Nichols, *The Disruption of American Democracy* (New York, 1948), and Kenneth M. Stampp, *And the War Came: The North and the Secession Crisis 1860–1861* (Baton Rouge, 1950).

[14]Samuel Eliot Morison, "Faith of a Historian," *American Historical Review,* 56 (January 1951): 267.

necessary precisely because of man's egotistical and sinful nature. Finally, the growing demands since the 1940s that blacks be given the same rights as white Americans also contributed to the reevaluation of the problem of the coming of the Civil War.

The criticisms of antiwar historians were most cogently put in an influential article by Arthur M. Schlesinger, Jr. Schlesinger was particularly hostile to the revisionist thesis, especially as presented by Craven and Randall. To rebut their hypothesis, he asked one specific question: If the war could have been avoided, what course should American leaders have followed? Noting that none of the revisionists had ever spelled out the proper policies that contemporary figures should have adopted, Schlesinger listed three possible alternatives: that the South might have abolished slavery by itself it left alone; that slavery would have died because it was economically unsound; or that the North might have offered some form of emancipated compensation. Finding that all three of these possibilities were either inadequate or unattainable, Schlesinger charged that revisionism "is connected with the modern tendency to seek in optimistic sentimentalism an escape from the severe demands of moral decision; that it is the offspring of our modern sentimentality which at once evades the essential moral problems in the name of a superficial objectivity and asserts their unimportance in the name of an invincible progress." The South was indeed becoming a closed society by the time of the Civil War; its citizens, in defending their evil institution, had posed moral differences too profound to be solved by political compromise. In effect, Schlesinger insisted that the revisionists glossed over slavery because of their own belief that war could never involve real issues. Human conflict, he concluded, is a perennial concomitant of human behavior; to write as though it never existed is to rule out one of the moral dimensions of humanity.[15]

At about the same time that Schlesinger was attacking the revisionists, Allan Nevins's magisterial history of the United States from the 1840s through the 1860s was beginning to appear. In the *Ordeal of the Union* Nevins combined elements from both the nationalist and revisionist traditions (although the former was clearly more dominant). Conceding that economic factors were involved in the coming of war, he nevertheless rejected an economic interpretation. The Civil War, wrote Nevins, "should have been avoidable," but "the problem of slavery *with its complementary problem of race-adjustment*" involved basic differences between North and South. Given the refusal of the South to take some step in the direction of ending slavery, the Civil War then followed. The first selection in this chapter is from Nevins's fourth volume.

---

[15]Arthur M. Schlesinger, Jr., "The Causes of the Civil War: A Note on Historical Sentimentalism," *Partisan Review* 16 (October 1949): 969–81.

During the 1960s the debate over the Civil War began to change. Given the strong antiwar protest movements and criticisms of American society of that decade, it was hardly surprising that some younger historians, especially those who associated themselves with the New Left and sought to rewrite American history from a radical perspective, would begin to reject the views of their predecessors. Growing to maturity at a time when many had become disillusioned with war, these scholars began to reappraise America's war from a hostile point of view. Indeed, some of them related war with domestic developments; they argued that American internationalism was a facade for an imperialistic foreign policy that had as its basic objective economic domination of the world.

In a challenging article written in 1969, John S. Rosenberg—a young historian writing from a radical perspective—sketched out a somewhat new thesis about the causes of the Civil War. Critical of earlier antiwar revisionists as well as historians like Schlesinger who defended the Civil War on moral grounds, Rosenberg argued in favor of an approach that was frankly presentist in orientation. The results of the war from Reconstruction to the present hardly justified the six hudnred thousand lives taken during that conflict. As a matter of fact, black militants "argue quite effectively that it would have been much better for all concerned if the slaves had seized their freedom rather than received it in bits and pieces as a result of quarrels among their oppressors." Rejecting also the assertion that America's moral superiority made imperative its preservation as a nation, Rosenberg in effect condemned the Civil War because of the subsequent failure to realize any of the ideals for which it was fought. In effect, he saw that conflict through the eyes of a disillusioned contemporary radical. Yet, oddly enough, Rosenberg was far closer to Randall and other historians who saw the Civil War as a "needless" and "avoidable" conflict, though for far different reasons.[16]

Although the debate over the causes of the Civil War remained embedded within a somewhat static conceptual framework,[17] developments within the historical profession during the 1960s slowly began to

---

[16]John S. Rosenberg, "Toward a New Civil War Revisionism," *American Scholar* 38 (Spring, 1969): 250–72. Rosenberg's effort to link the present and past did not go unchallenged. In a rejoinder Phillip S. Paludan insisted that Rosenberg was pursuing a poorly executed presentism that ignored advances made by blacks after the abolition of slavery. The persistence of inequality, noted Paludan, was no reason for ignoring the benefits of freedom. The debate appeared in Paludan's "The American Civil War: Triumph Through Tragedy," *Civil War History* 20 (September 1974): 239–50; Rosenberg, "The American Civil War and the Problem of 'Presentism': A Reply to Phillip S. Paludan," *ibid.*, 21 (Septemeber 1975): 242–53; and Paludan, "Taking the Benefits of the Civil War Seriously: A Rejoinder to John S. Rosenberg," *ibid.* 21 (September 1975): 254–60.

[17]Indeed, David Donald wrote in 1960 that historians were no longer concerned with the causes of the Civil War. See David Donald, "American Historians and the Causes of the Civil War," *South Atlantic Quarterly* 59 (Summer, 1960): 351–55.

undermine traditional approaches and questions. The rise of what can be termed the "new political history" (an approach that emphasized the social basis of politics and employed quantification) led some historians to move away from focusing on the issue of slavery in isolation from the totality of American society. In addition to slavery, these scholars began to study behavior as more than merely a reaction to the challenge posed by slavery. Some emphasized the role of religion and culture in determining political ideology and voting behavior; others examined the war within the framework of a modernizing society. Slowly but surely the Civil War was brought back and integrated again into the wider events of American historical developments of the nineteenth century. The problem of slavery in the territories lost its central position as historians began to study social cleavages, voting behavior, mass voter participation, the rise of new types of agitators in both the North and South and their impact upon political structures, and the transformation of the nation's political system. Although the outlines of a new synthesis are as yet vague, there is little doubt that interest in the causes of the Civil War is entering a new stage.[18]

Illustrative of some of the more recent trends was Michael F. Holt's analysis of political developments during the 1850s. Combining a behavioral and an ideological approach, Holt conceded that the sectional conflict over slavery was crucial. Nevertheless, he de-emphasized the conflict over the institution of slavery. Most Americans, Holt insisted, were preoccupied with their republican ideology and alleged threats to its survival. Fearful that republican society might be undermined by corruption, white Americans were determined to pursue self-government, liberty, and equality. During the 1850s, however, the second party system collapsed, and

> a sense of crisis developed that government was beyond control of the people, that it had become a threatening power dominated by some gigantic conspiracy, and hence that republican institutions were under attack. Politicians in the North and South responded to this sense of crisis by making an enemy in the other section the chief menace to republicanism who would enslave the residents of their own section. As a result, sectional antagonism became much more inflamed in the 1850s than it had ever been. Along with Know Nothingism, this strategy restored a sense of political efficacy in most of the nation, because antirepublicanism devils were associated with rival parties that could be stopped simply by voting against them. In the Deep South, however, no internal enemy was identified who could be defeated through the normal political process. Men there thought that more drastic

---

[18]For a perceptive analysis of recent trends see Eric Foner, "The Causes of the American Civil War: Recent Interpretations and New Directions," *Civil War History* 20 (September 1974): 194–214.

action was necessary to escape slavery. The consequence was secession and a tragic Civil War.[19]

The second selection in this chapter, by Eric Foner, illustrates at least some of the newer trends in Civil War historiography. In the half century following the adoption of the federal Constitution, argues Foner, the political system functioned "as mechanism for relieving social tensions, ordering group conflict, and integrating the society." By the 1830s and 1840s a new element had entered the national scene, namely, the creation of distinct party structures that channeled voter participation in politics. Although Jacksonian politics were for the most part nonideological, they did help to create a link between the people and their government. But this very link had serious implications for underlying sectional antagonisms, for it made possible the emergence of sectional agitators in both the North and the South who hoped to force public opinion—and hence government—to confront the issue of slavery. The result was a polarization of American politics along ideological lines and an inability on the part of the political system to resolve basic differences between the sections. In both the North and the South an ideological coalition emerged that was completely antithetical to the idea of national unity and national integration on other than its own terms. The Civil War, concludes Foner, accomplished the goal originally envisaged by the founding fathers when they wrote the Constitution and established a unique political system—the creation of a single nation. Although aware of the paramount importance of the slavery issue, Foner's interpretation rests upon his conviction that the causes of the Civil War cannot be isolated from the nature of the American political system and the social and economic values that became the foundation of competing ideologies.

By the 1980s the problem of Civil War causation seemed as confusing as ever. Given all of the conflicting schools of thought, how can the student select and choose in order to arrive at a more "objective" view of the war? The answer to this question is difficult indeed; sooner or later students will have to cope with the same problems that confronted historians for nearly a century. Was the North, for example, fighting the war solely on moral grounds? Were Southern leaders determined to have their own way in 1861, even if it meant destroying the Union? Was the North trampling on the South and ignoring the Constitution? What role did social and economic differences play in the coming of the war? Is it appropriate even to ask the question as to whether the war was a repressible or irrepressible conflict? Did American leaders fail because of their inability to deal with the issues in a statesmanlike and rational

---

[19]Michael F. Holt, *The Political Crisis of the 1850s* (New York, 1978), pp. 258–59.

framework? How did other variables—religion, ethnicity, culture—influence ideology and national political structures?

More than two decades ago one historian surveying the many ways that his colleagues had approached the problem of the Civil War, noted with concern that "the further the Civil War receded into the past, the greater the strength of the emotions with which these divergent viewpoints were upheld." The reason for this anomalous situation, he suggested, was that American historians still found the issues of the 1850s and 1860s of contemporary concern; as long as historians wrote about the role of blacks in American society, debated the wisdom of fighting in wars, and studied majority rule and minority rights, the causes of the Civil War would remain a matter of dispute.[20] In a certain sense his analysis was correct. Yet recent contributions to Civil War historiography suggest that contemporary scholars are in the process of creating a new synthesis that relates the moral controversy over slavery to a variety of other social, political, and economic structures that were slowly giving the nation its basic configuration. In so doing they have transferred the issue of Civil War causation from a largely moral domain to a domain that seeks understanding and explanations rather than condemnation. Only the future will tell whether this newer approach will bring us closer to a better answer to this vexing historical problem.

---

[20]Thomas J. Pressly, *Americans Interpret Their Civil War* (Princeton, 1954), pp. 321–23.

# Allan Nevins

ALLAN NEVINS (1890–1971) was professor of history at Columbia University. He was one of the most prolific American historians of the twentieth century. In addition to his multivolume study of the Civil War era, he also wrote biographies of John D. Rockefeller and Henry Ford, among many other books.

Great and complex events have great and complex causes. Burke, in his *Reflections on the Revolution in France*, wrote that "a state without the means of some change is without the means of its conservation," and that a constant reconciliation of "the two principles of conservation and correction" is indispensable to healthy national growth. It is safe to say that every such revolutionary era as that on which the United States entered in 1860 finds its genesis in an inadequate adjustment of these two forces. It is also safe to say that when a tragic national failure occurs, it is largely a failure of leadership. "Brains are of three orders," wrote Machiavelli, "those that understand of themselves, those that understand when another shows them, and those that understand neither by themselves nor by the showing of others." Ferment and change must steadily be controlled; the real must, as Bryce said, be kept resting on the ideal; and if disaster is to be avoided, wise leaders must help thoughtless men to understand, and direct the action of invincibly ignorant men. Necessary reforms may be obstructed in various ways; by sheer inertia, by tyranny and class selfishness, or by the application of compromise to basic principles—this last being in Lowell's view the main cause of the Civil War. Ordinarily the obstruction arises from a combination of all these elements. To explain the failure of American leadership in 1846–1861, and the revolution that ensued, is a baffling complicated problem.

Looking backward from the verge of war in March, 1861, Americans could survey a series of ill-fated decisions by their chosen agents. One unfortunate decision was embodied in Douglas's Kansas-Nebraska Act of 1854. Had an overwhelming majority of Americans been ready to accept the squatter sovereignty principle, this law might have proved a statesmanlike stroke; but it was so certain that powerful elements North and South would resist it to the last that it accentuated the strife and confusion. Another disastrous decision was made by Taney and his associates in the Dred Scott pronouncement of 1857. Still another was made by Buchanan when he weakly accepted the Lecompton Constitution and tried to force that fraudulent document through Congress. The Northern legislatures which passed Personal Liberty Acts made an unhappy decision. Most irresponsible, wanton, and disastrous of all was the decision of those Southern leaders who in 1858–1860 turned to the provocative demand for Congressional protection of slavery in all the Territories of the republic. Still other errors might be named. Obviously, however, it is the forces behind these decisions which demand our study; the waters pouring down the gorge, not the rocks which threw their spray into the air.

At this point we meet a confused clamor of voices as various students attempt an explanation of the tragic denouement of 1861. Some writers are as content with a simple explanation as Lord Clarendon was when he attributed the English Civil War to the desire of Parliament for an egregious domination of the government. The bloody conflict, declared James Ford Rhodes, had "a single cause, slavery." He was but echoing what Henry Wilson and other early historians had written, that the aggressions of the Slave Power offered the central explanation. That opinion had been challenged as early as 1861 by the London *Saturday Review*, which remarked that "slavery is but a surface question in American politics," and by such Southern propagandists as Yancey, who tried to popularize a commercial theory of the war, emphasizing a supposed Southern revolt against the tariff and other Yankee exactions. A later school of writers was to find the key to the tragedy in an inexorable conflict between the business-minded North and the agrarian-minded South, a thrusting industrialism colliding with a rather static agricultural society. Still another group of writers has accepted the theory that the war resulted from psychological causes. They declare that agitators, propagandists, and alarmists on both sides, exaggerating the real differences of interest, created a state of mind, a hysterical excitement, which made armed conflict inevitable.

At the very outset of the war Senator Mason of Virginia, writing to his daughter, asserted that two systems of society were in conflict; systems, he implied, as different as those of Carthage and Rome, Protestant Holland and Catholic Spain. That view, too, was later to be elaborated by a considerable school of writers. Two separate nations, they declared, had arisen within the United States in 1861, much as two separate nations had emerged within the first British Empire by 1776. Contrasting ways of life, rival group consciousness, divergent hopes and fears made a movement for separation logical; and the minority people, believing its peculiar civilization in danger of suppression, began a war for independence. We are told, indeed, that two types of nationalism came into conflict: a Northern nationalism which wished to preserve the unity of the whole republic, and a Southern nationalism intent on creating an entirely new republic.

It is evident that some of these explanations deal with merely superficial phenomena, and that others, when taken separately, represent but subsidiary elements in the play of forces. Slavery was a great fact; the demands of Northern industrialism constituted a great fact; sectional hysteria was a great fact. But do they not perhaps relate themselves to some profounder underlying cause? This question has inspired one student to suggest that "the confusion of a growing state" may offer the fundamental explanation of the drift to war; an unsatisfactory hypothesis, for westward growth, railroad growth, business growth, and cultural growth, however much attended with "confusion," were unifying factors, and it was not the new-made West but old-settled South Carolina which led in the schism.

One fact needs emphatic statement: of all the monistic explanations for the drift to war, that posited upon supposed economic causes is the flimsiest. This theory was sharply rejected at the time by so astute an observer as Alexander H. Stephens. South Carolina, he wrote his brother on New Year's Day, 1861, was seceding from a tariff "which is just what her own Senators and members in Congress made it." As for the charges of consolidation and despotism made by some Carolinians, he thought they arose from peevishness rather than a calm analysis of facts. "The truth is, the South, almost in mass, has voted, I think, for every measure of general legislation that has passed both houses and become law for the last ten years." The South, far from groaning under tyranny, had controlled the government almost from its beginning, and Stephens believed that its only real grievance lay in the Northern refusal to return fugitive slaves and to stop the antislavery agitation. "All other complaints are founded on threatened dangers which may never come, and which I feel very sure would be averted if the South would pursue a judicious and wise course." Stephens was right. It was true that the whole tendency of federal legislation 1842–1860 was toward free trade; true that the tariff in force when secession began was largely Southern-made; true that it was the lowest tariff the country had known since 1816; true that it cost a nation of 30 million people but $60 million in indirect revenue; true that without secession no new tariff law, obnoxious to the Democratic party, could have passed before 1863—if then.

In the official explanations which one Southern state after another published for its secession, economic grievances are either omitted entirely or given minor position. There were few such supposed grievances which the agricultural states of Illinois, Iowa, Indiana, Wisconsin, and Minnesota did not share with the South—and they never threatened to secede. Charles A. Beard finds the taproot of the war in the resistance of the planter interest to Northern demands enlarging the old Hamilton-Webster policy. The South was adamant in standing for "no high protective tariffs, no ship subsidies, no national banking and currency system; in short, none of the measures which business enterprise deemed essential to its progress." But the Republican platform in 1856 was silent on the tariff; in 1860 it carried a milk-and-water statement on the subject which western Republicans took, mild as it was, with a wry face; the incoming president was little interested in the tariff; and any harsh legislation was impossible. Ship subsidies were not an issue in the campaign of 1860. Neither were a national banking system and a national currency system. They were not mentioned in the Republican platform nor discussed by party debaters. The Pacific Railroad was advocated both by the Douglas Democrats and the Republicans; and it is noteworthy that Seward and Douglas were for building both a Northern and a Southern line. In short, the divisive economic issues are easily exaggerated. At the same time, the unifying economic factors were both numerous and powerful. North and South had economies which were largely complementary. It was no misfortune to the South that Massachusetts cotton mills wanted its staple, and that New York ironmasters like Hewitt were eager to sell rails dirt-cheap to Southern railway builders; and sober businessmen on both sides, merchants, bankers, and manufacturers, were the men most anxious to keep the peace and hold the Union together.

We must seek further for an explanation; and in so doing, we must give special weight to the observations of penetrating leaders of the time, who knew at firsthand the spirit of the people. Henry J. Raymond, moderate editor of the *New York Times*, a sagacious man who disliked Northern abolitionists and Southern radicals, wrote in January 1860 an analysis of the impending conflict which attributed it to a competition for power.

> In every country there must be a just and equal balance of powers in the government, an equal distribution of the national forces. Each section and each interest must exercise its due share of influence and control. It is always more or less difficult to preserve their just equipoise, and the larger the country, and the more varied its great interests, the more difficult does the task become, and the greater the shock and disturbance caused by an attempt to adjust it when once disturbed. I believe I state only what is generally conceded to be a fact, when I say that the growth of the Northern States in population, in wealth, in all the elements of political influence and control, has been out of proportion to their political influence in the Federal Councils. While the Southern States have less than a third of the aggregate population of the Union, their interests have influenced the policy of the government far

more than the interests of the Northern States. . . . Now the North has made rapid advances within the last five years, and it naturally claims a proportionate share of influence and power in the affairs of the Confederacy.

It is inevitable that this claim should be put forward, and it is also inevitable that it should be conceded. No party can long resist it; it overrides all parties, and makes them the mere instruments of its will. It is quite as strong today in the heart of the Democratic party of the North as in the Republican ranks and any party which ignores it will lose its hold on the public mind.

Why does the South resist this claim? Not because it is unjust in itself, but because it has become involved with the question of slavery, and has drawn so much of its vigor and vitality from that quarter, that it is almost merged in that issue. The North bases its demand for increased power, in a very great degree, on the action of the government in regard to slavery—and the just and rightful ascendency of theNorth in the Federal councils comes thus to be regarded as an element of danger to the institutions of the Southern States.

In brief, Raymond, who held that slavery was a moral wrong, that its economic and social tendencies were vicious, and that the time had come to halt its growth with a view to its final eradication, believed that the contest was primarily one for power, and for the application of that power to the slave system. With this opinion Alexander H. Stephens agreed. The Georgian said he believed slavery both morally and politically right. In his letter to Lincoln on December 30, 1860, he declared that the South did not fear that the new Republican Administration would interfere directly and immediately with slavery in the states. What Southerners did fear was the ultimate result of the shift of power which had just occurred—in its application to slavery:

Now this subject, which is confessedly on all sides outside of the constitutional action of the Government, so far as the States are concerned, is made the 'central idea' in the platform of principles announced by the triumphant party. The leading object seems to be simply, and wantonly, if you please, to put the institutions of nearly half the States under the ban of public opinion and national condemnation. This, upon general principles, is quite enough of itself to arouse a spirit not only of general indignation, but of revolt on the part of the proscribed. Let me illustrate. It is generally conceded by the Republicans even, that Congress cannot interfere with slavery in the States. It is equally conceded that Congress cannot establish any form of religious worship. Now suppose that any one of the present Christian churches or sects prevailed in all the Southern States, but had no existence in any one of the Northern States,—under such circumstances suppose the people of the Northern States should organize a political party, not upon a foreign or domestic policy, but with one leading idea of condemnation of the doctrines and tenets of that particular church, and with an avowed object of preventing its extension into the common Territories, even after the highest judicial tribunal of the land had decided they had no such constitutional power. And

suppose that a party so organized should carry a Presidential election. Is it
not apparent that a general feeling of resistance to the success, aims, and
objects of such a party would necessarily and rightfully ensue?

Raymond and Stephens agreed that the two sections were competing
for power; that a momentous transfer of power had just occurred; and
that it held fateful consequences because it was involved with the issue
of slavery, taking authority from a section which believed slavery moral
and healthy, and giving it to a section which held slavery immoral and
pernicious. To Stephens this transfer was ground for resuming the ultimate sovereignty of the states. Here we find a somewhat more complex
statement of James Ford Rhodes's thesis that the central cause of the
Civil War lay in slavery. Here, too, we revert to the assertions of Yancey
and Lincoln that the vital conflict was between those who thought slavery right and those who thought it wrong. But this definition we can
accept only if we probe a little deeper for a concept which both modifies
and enlarges the basic source of perplexity and quarrel.

The main root of the conflict (and there were minor roots) was the
problem of slavery *with its complementary problem of race adjustment;* the
main source of the tragedy was the refusal of either section to face these
conjoined problems squarely and pay the heavy costs of a peaceful settlement. Had it not been for the difference in race, the slavery issue
would have presented no great difficulties. But as the racial gulf existed,
the South inarticulately but clearly perceived that elimination of this
issue would still leave it the terrible problem of the Negro. Those historians who write that if slavery had simply been left alone it would soon
have withered overlook this heavy impediment. The South as a whole in
1846–1861 was not moving toward emancipation, but away from it. It
was not relaxing the laws which guarded the system, but reinforcing
them. It was not ameliorating slavery, but making it harsher and more
implacable. The South was further from a just solution of the slavery problem in 1830 than it had been in 1789. It was further from a tenable solution
in 1860 than it had been in 1830. Why was it going from bad to worse?
Because Southern leaders refused to nerve their people to pay the heavy
price of race adjustment. These leaders never made up their mind to
deal with the problem as the progressive temper of civilization demanded. They would not adopt the new outlook which the upward
march of mankind required because they saw that the gradual abolition
of slavery would bring a measure of political privilege; that political
privilege would usher in a measure of economic equality; that on the
heels of economic equality would come a rising social status for the
Negro. Southern leadership dared not ask the people to pay this price.

A heavy responsibility for the failure of America in this period rests
with this Southern leadership, which lacked imagination, ability, and

courage. But the North was by no means without its full share, for the North equally refused to give a constructive examination to the central question of slavery as linked with race adjustment. This was because of two principal reasons. Most abolitionists and many other sentimental-minded Northerners simply denied that the problem existed. Regarding all Negroes as white men with dark skins, whom a few years of schooling would bring abreast of the dominant race, they thought that no difficult adjustment was required. A much more numerous body of Northerners would have granted that a great and terrible task of race adjustment existed—but they were reluctant to help shoulder any part of it. Take a million or two million Negroes into the Northern States? Indiana, Illinois, and even Kansas were unwilling to take a single additional person of color. Pay tens of millions to help educate and elevate the colored population? Take even a first step by offering to pay the Southern slaveholders some recompense for a gradual liberation of their human property? No Northern politician dared ask his constituents to make so unpopular a sacrifice. The North, like the South, found it easier to drift blindly toward disaster.

The hope of solving the slavery problem without a civil war rested upon several interrelated factors, of which one merits special emphasis. We have said that the South as a whole was laboring to bolster and stiffen slavery—which was much to its discredit. But it is nevertheless true that slavery was dying all around the edges of its domain; it was steadily decaying in Delaware, Maryland, western Virginia, parts of Kentucky, and Missouri. Much of the harshness of Southern legislation in the period sprang from a sense that slavery was in danger from *internal* weaknesses. In no great time Delaware, Maryland, and Missouri were likely to enter the column of free states; and if they did, reducing the roster to twelve, the doom of the institution would be clearly written. Allied with this factor was the rapid comparative increase of Northern strength, and the steady knitting of economic, social, and moral ties between the North and West, leaving the South in a position of manifest inferiority. A Southern Confederacy had a fair fighting chance in 1861; by 1880 it would have had very little. If secession could have been postponed by two decades, natural forces might well have placed a solution full in sight. Then, too, the growing pressure of world sentiment must in time have produced its effect. But to point out these considerations is not to suggest that in 1861 a policy of procrastination and appeasement would have done anything but harm. All hope of bringing Southern majority sentiment to a better attitude would have been lost if Lincoln and his party had flinched on the basic issue of the restriction of slavery; for by the seventh decade of nineteenth-century history, the time had come when that demand had to be maintained.

While in indicting leadership we obviously indict the public behind the leaders, we must also lay some blame upon a political environment which gave leadership a poor chance. American parties, under the pressure of sectional feeling, worked badly. The government suffered greatly, moreover, from the lack of any adequate planning agency. Congress was not a truly deliberative body, and its committees had not yet learned to do long-range planning. The president might have formulated plans, but he never did. For one reason, no president between Polk and Lincoln had either the ability or the prestige required; for another reason, Fillmore, Pierce, and Buchanan all held that their duty was merely to execute the laws, not to initiate legislation. Had the country possessed a ministerial form of government, the Cabinet in leading the legislature would have been compelled to lay down a program of real scope concerning slavery. As it was, leadership in Washington was supplied only spasmodically by men like Clay, Douglas, and Crittenden.

And as we have noted, the rigidity of the American system was at this time a grave handicap. Twice, in the fall of 1854 and of 1858, the elections gave a stunning rebuke to the Administration. Under a ministerial system, the old government would probably have gone out and a new one have come in. In 1854, however, Pierce continued to carry on the old policies, and in 1858 Buchanan remained the drearily inept helmsman of the republic. Never in our history were bold, quick planning and a flexible administration of policy more needed; never was the failure to supply them more complete.

Still another element in the tragic chronicle of the time must be mentioned. Much that happens in human affairs is accidental. When a country is guided by true statesmen the role of accident is minimized; when it is not, unforeseen occurrences are numerous and dangerous. In the summer and fall of 1858, as we have seen, the revival of a conservative opposition party in the upper South, devoted to the Union, furnished a real gleam of hope. If this opposition had been given unity and determined leadership, if moderate Southerners had stood firm against the plot of Yancey and others to disrupt the Democratic Party, if Floyd had been vigilant enough to read the warning letter about John Brown and act on it, the situation might even then have been saved. Instead, John Brown's mad raid fell on public opinion like a thunderstroke, exasperating men everywhere and dividing North and South more tragically than ever. The last chance of persuading the South to submit to an essential step, the containment of slavery, was gone.

The war, when it came, was not primarily a conflict over state rights, although that issue had become involved in it. It was not primarily a war born of economic grievances, although many Southerners had been led to think that they were suffering, or would soon suffer, economic wrongs. It was not a war created by politicians and publicists who fomented hysteric excitement; for while hysteria was important, we have always to ask what basic reasons made possible the propaganda which aroused it. It was not primarily a war about slavery alone, although that institution seemed to many the grand cause. It was a war over slavery *and* the future position of the Negro race in North America. Was the Negro to be allowed, as a result of the shift of power signalized by Lincoln's election, to take the first step toward an ultimate position of general economic, political, and social equality with the white man? Or was he to be held immobile in a degraded, servile position, unchanging for the next hundred years as it had remained essentially unchanged for the hundred years past? These questions were implicit in Lincoln's demand that slavery be placed in a position where the public mind could rest assured of its ultimate extinction.

Evasion by the South, evasion by the North, were no longer possible. The alternatives faced were an unpopular but curative adjustment of the situation by the opposed parties, or a war that would force an adjustment upon the loser. For Americans in 1861, as for many other peoples throughout history, war was easier than wisdom and courage.

# Eric Foner

ERIC FONER (1943–    ) is professor of history at the City College of the City University of New York. His published works include *Free Soil, Free Labor, Free Men: The Ideology of the Republican Party Before The Civil War* (1970) and *Tom Paine and Revolutionary America* (1976).

It has long been an axiom of political science that political parties help to hold together diverse, heterogeneous societies like our own. Since most major parties in American history have tried, in Seymour Lipset's phrase, to "appear as plausible representatives of the whole society," they have been broad coalitions cutting across lines of class, race, religion, and section. And although party competition requires that there be differences between the major parties, these differences usually have not been along sharp ideological lines. In fact, the very diversity of American society has inhibited the formation of ideological parties, for such parties assume the existence of a single line of social division along which a majority of the electorate can be mobilized. In a large, heterogeneous society, such a line rarely exists. There are, therefore, strong reasons why, in a two-party system, a major party—or a party aspiring to become "major"—eschew ideology, for the statement of a coherent ideology will set limits to the groups in the electorate the party can hope to mobilize. Under most circumstances, in other words, the party's role as a carrier of a coherent ideology will conflict with its role as an electoral machine bent on winning the widest possible number of votes.

For much of the seventy years preceding the Civil War, the American political system functioned as a mechanism for relieving social tensions, ordering group conflict, and integrating the society. The existence of national political parties, increasingly focused on the contest for the presidency, necessitated alliances between political elites in various sections of the country. A recent study of early American politics notes that "political nationalization was far ahead of economic, cultural, and social

Eric Foner, "Politics, Ideology, and the Origins of the American Civil War," in *A Nation Divided: Problems and Issues of the Civil War and Reconstruction*, ed. George M. Fredrickson (Minneapolis, 1975), pp. 15–34. Reprinted with the permission of Burgess Publishing Company.

nationalization"—that is, that the national political system was itself a major bond of union in a diverse, growing society. But as North and South increasingly took different paths of economic and social development and as, from the 1830s onwards, antagonistic value systems and ideologies grounded in the question of slavery emerged in these sections, the political system inevitably came under severe disruptive pressures. Because they brought into play basic values and moral judgments, the competing sectional ideologies could not be defused by the normal processes of political compromise, nor could they be contained within the existing intersectional political system. Once parties began to reorient themselves on sectional lines, a fundamental necessity of democratic politics—that each party look upon the other as a legitimate alternative government—was destroyed.

When we consider the causes of the sectional conflict, we must ask ourselves not only why civil war came when it did, but why it did not come sooner. How did a divided nation manage to hold itself together for as long as it did? In part, the answer lies in the unifying effects of intersectional political parties. On the level of politics, the coming of the Civil War is the story of the intrusion of sectional ideology into the political system, despite the efforts of political leaders of both parties to keep it out. Once this happened, political competition worked to exacerbrate, rather than to solve, social and sectional conflicts. For as Frank Sorauf has explained:

The party of extensive ideology develops in and reflects the society in which little consensus prevails on basic social values and institutions. It betokens deep social disagreements and conflicts. Indeed, the party of ideology that is also a major, competitive party accompanies a politics of almost total concern. Since its ideology defines political issues as including almost every facet of life, it brings to the political system almost every division, every difference, every conflict of any importance in society.

"Parties in this country," wrote a conservative northern Whig in 1855, "heretofore have helped, not delayed, the slow and difficult growth of a consummated nationality." Rufus Choate was lamenting the passing of a bygone era, a time when 'our allies were everywhere . . . there were no Alleghenies nor Mississippi rivers in our politics." Party organization and the nature of political conflict had taken on new and unprecedented forms in the 1850s. It is no accident that the break up of the last major intersectional party preceded by less than a year the break up of the Union or that the final crisis was precipitated not by any "overt act," but by a presidential election.

From the beginning of national government, of course, differences of opinion over slavery constituted an important obstacle to the formation of a national community. "The great danger to our general government," as Madison remarked at the Constitutional Convention, "is the great southern and northern interests of the continent, being opposed to each other." "The institution of slavery and its consequences," according to him, was the main "line of discrimination" in convention disputes. As far as slavery was concerned, the Constitution amply fulfilled Lord Acton's dictum that it was an effort to avoid settling basic questions. Aside from the Atlantic slave trade, Congress was given no power to regulate slavery in any way—the framers' main intention seem to have been to place slavery completely outside the national political arena. The only basis on which a national politics could exist—the avoidance of sectional issues—was thus defined at the outset.

Although the slavery question was never completely excluded from political debate in the 1790s, and there was considerable Federalist grumbling about the three-fifths clause of the Constitution after 1800, the first full demonstration of the political possibilities inherent in a sectional attack on slavery occurred in the Missouri controversy of 1819–1821. These debates established a number of precedents which forecast the future course of the slavery extension issue in Congress. Most important was the fact that the issue was able for a time to completely obliterate party lines. In the first votes on slavery in Missouri, virtually every northerner, regardless of party, voted against expansion. It was not surprising, of course, that northern Federalists would try to make political capital out of the issue. What was unexpected was that northern Republicans, many of whom were aggrieved by Virginia's long dominance of the presidency and by the Monroe administration's tariff and internal improvement policies, would unite with the Federalists. As John Quincy Adams observed, the debate "disclosed a secret: it revealed the basis for a new organization of parties. . . . Here was a new party really formed . . . terrible to the whole Union, but portentously terrible to the South." But the final compromise set another important precedent: enough northern Republicans became convinced that the Federalists were making political gains from the debates and that the Union was seriously endangered to break with the sectional block and support a compromise which a majority of northern Congressmen—Republicans and Federalists—opposed. As for the Monroe administration, its semiofficial spokesman, the *National Intelligencer,* pleaded for a return to the policy of avoiding sectional issues, even to the extent of refusing to publish letters which dealt in any way with the subject of slavery.

The Missouri controversy and the election of 1824, in which four candidates contested the presidency, largely drawing support from their home sections, revealed that in the absence of two-party competition, sectional loyalties would constitute the lines of political division. No one recognized this more clearly than the architect of the second-party system, Martin Van Buren. In his well-known letter to Thomas Ritchie of

Virginia, Van Buren explained the need for a revival of national two-party politics on precisely this ground: "Party attachment in former times furnished a complete antidote for sectional prejudices by producing counteracting feelings. It was not until that defense had been broken down that the clamor against Southern Influence and African Slavery could be made effectual in the North." Van Buren and many of his generation of politicians had been genuinely frightened by the threats of disunion which echoed through Congress in 1820; they saw national two-party competition as the alternative to sectional conflict and eventual disunion. Ironically, as Richard McCormick has made clear, the creation of the second party system owed as much to sectionalism as to national loyalties. The South, for example, only developed an organized, competitive Whig party in 1835 and 1836 when it became apparent that Jackson, the southern President, had chosen Van Buren, a northerner, as his successor. Once party divisions had emerged, however, they stuck, and by 1840, for one of the very few times in American history, two truly intersectional parties, each united behind a single candidate, competed for the presidency.

The 1830s witnessed a vast expansion of political loyalties and awareness and the creation of party mechanisms to channel voter participation in politics. But the new mass sense of identification with politics had ominous implications for the sectional antagonisms which the party system sought to suppress. The historian of the Missouri Compromise has observed the "if there had been a civil war in 1819–1821 it would have been between the members of Congress, with the rest of the country looking on in amazement." This is only one example of the intellectual and political isolation of Washington from the general populace which James Young has described in *The Washington Community*. The mass, nonideological politics of the Jackson era created the desperately needed link between governors and governed. But this very link made possible the emergence of two kinds of sectional agitators: the abolitionists, who stood outside of politics and hoped to force public opinion—and through it, politicians—to confront the slavery issue, and political agitators, who used politics as a way of heightening sectional self-consciousness and antagonism in the populace at large.

Because of the rise of mass politics and the emergence of these sectional agitators, the 1830s was the decade in which long-standing, latent sectional divisions were suddenly activated, and previously unrelated patterns of derogatory sectional sectional imagery began to emerge into full-blown sectional ideology. Many of the antislavery arguments which gained wide currency in the 1830s had roots stretching back into the eighteenth century. The idea that slavery degraded white labor and retarded economic development, for example, had been voiced by Benjamin Franklin. After 1800, the Federalists, increasingly localized in New

England, had developed a fairly coherent critique, not only of the social
and economic effects of slavery, but of what Harrison Gray Otis called
the divergence of "manners, habits, customs, principles, and ways of
thinking" which separated northerners and southerners. And, during
the Missouri debates, almost every economic, political, and moral argument against slavery that would be used in the later sectional debate was
voiced. In fact, one recurring argument was not picked up later—the
warning of northern Congressmen that the South faced the danger of
slave rebellion if steps were not taken toward abolition. (As far as I
know, only Thaddeus Stevens of Republican spokesmen in the 1850s
would explicitly use this line of argument.)

The similarity between Federalist attacks on the South and later
abolitionist and Republican arguments, coupled with the fact that many
abolitionists—including Garrison, Phillips, the Tappans, and others—
came from Federalist backgrounds, has led James Banner to describe
abolitionism as "the Massachusetts Federalist ideology come back to
life." Yet there was a long road to be travelled from Harrison Gray Otis
to William H. Seward, just as there was from Thomas Jefferson to
George Fitzhugh. For one thing, the Federalist distrust of democracy,
social competition, the Jeffersonian cry of "equal rights," their commitment to social inequality, hierarchy, tradition, and order prevented
them from pushing their antislavery views to their logical conclusion.
And New England Federalists were inhibited by the requirements of
national party organization and competition from voicing antislavery
views. In the 1790s, they maintained close ties with southern
Federalists, and after 1800 hope of reviving their strength in the South
never completely died. Only a party which embraced social mobility and
competitive individualism, rejected the permanent subordination of any
"rank" in society, and was unburdened by a southern wing could develop a fully coherent antislavery ideology.

An equally important reason why the Federalists did not develop a
consistent sectional ideology was that the South in the early part of the
nineteenth century shared many of the Federalists' reservations about
slavery. The growth of an antislavery ideology, in other words, depended in large measure on the growth of proslavery thought, and, by
the same token, it was the abolitionist assault which brought into being
the coherent defense of slavery. The opening years of the 1830s, of
course, were ones of crisis for the South. The emergence of militant
abolitionism, Nat Turner's rebellion, the Virginia debates on slavery,
and the nullification crisis suddenly presented assaults to the institution
of slavery from within and outside the South. The reaction was the
closing of southern society in defense of slavery, "the most thoroughgoing repression of free thought, free speech, and a free press ever witnessed in an American community." At the same time, southerners increas-

ingly abandoned their previous, highly qualified defenses of slavery and embarked on the formulation of the proslavery argument. By 1837, as is well known, John C. Calhoun could thank the abolitionists on precisely this ground:

> This agitation has produced one happy effect at least; it has compelled us at the South to look into the nature and character of this great institution, and to correct many false impressions that even we had entertained in relation to it. Many in the South once believed that it was a moral and political evil; that folly and delusion are gone; we see it now in its true light, and regard it as the most safe and stable basis for free institutions in the world.

The South, of course, was hardly as united as Calhoun asserted. But the progressive rejection of the Jeffersonian tradition, the suppression of civil liberties, and the increasing stridency of the defense of slavery all pushed the South further and further out of the intersectional mainstream, setting it increasingly apart from the rest of the country. Coupled with the Gag Rule and the mobs which broke up abolitionist presses and meetings, the growth of proslavery thought was vital to a new antislavery formulation which emerged in the late 1830s and which had been absent from both the Federalist attacks on slavery and the Missouri debates—the idea of the slave power. The slave power replaced the three-fifths clause as the symbol of southern power, and it was a far more sophisticated and complex formulation. Abolitionists could argue that slavery was not only morally repugnant, it was imcompatible with the basic democratic values and liberties of white Americans. As one abolitionist declared, "We commenced the present struggle to obtain the freedom of the slave; we are compelled to continue it to preserve our own." In other words, a process of ideological expansion had begun, fed in large measure by the sequence of response and counterresponse between the competing sectional outlooks. Once this process had begun, it had an internal dynamic which made it extremely difficult to stop. This was especially true because of the emergence of agitators whose avowed purpose was to sharpen sectional conflict, polarize public opinion, and develop sectional ideologies to their logical extremes.

As the 1840s opened, most political leaders still clung to the traditional basis of politics, but the sectional, ideological political agitators formed growing minorities in each section. In the South, there was a small group of outright secessionists and a larger group, led by Calhoun, who were firmly committed to the Union but who viewed sectional organization and self-defense, not the traditional reliance on intersectional political parties, as the surest means of protecting southern interest within the Union. In the North, a small radical group gathered in Congress around John Quincy Adams and Congressmen like Joshua

Giddings, William Slade, and Seth Gates—men who represented areas of the most intense abolitionist agitation and whose presence confirmed Garrison's belief that, once public opinion was aroused on the slavery issue, politicians would have to follow step. These radicals were determined to force slavery into every Congressional debate. They were continually frustrated but never suppressed, and the reelection of Giddings in 1842 after his censure and resignation from the House proved that in some districts party discipline was no longer able to control the slavery issue.

The northern political agitators, both Congressmen and Liberty party leaders, also performed the function of developing and popularizing a political rhetoric, especially focused fear of the slave power, which could be seized upon by traditional politicians and large masses of voters if slavery ever entered the center of political conflict.

In the 1840s, this is precisely what happened. As one politician later recalled, "Slavery upon which by common consent no party issue had been made was then obtruded upon the field of party action." It is significant that John Tyler and John C. Calhoun, the two men most responsible for this intrusion, were political outsiders, men without places in the national party structure. Both of their careers were blocked by the major parties but might be advanced if tied to the slavery question in the form of Texas annexation. Once introduced into politics, slavery was there to stay. The Wilmot Proviso, introduced in 1846, had precisely the same effect as the proposal two decades earlier to restrict slavery in Missouri—it completely fractured the major parties along sectional lines. As in 1820, opposition to the expansion of slavery became the way in which a diverse group of northerners expressed their various resentments against a southern-dominated administration. And, as in 1821, a small group of northern Democrats eventually broke with their section, reaffirmed their primary loyalty to the party, and joined with the South to kill the proviso in 1847. In the same year, enough southerners rejected Calhoun's call for united sectional action to doom his personal and sectional ambitions.

But the slavery extension debates of the 1840s had far greater effects on the political system than the Missouri controversy had had. Within each party, they created a significant group of sectional politicians—men whose careers were linked to the slavery question and who would therefore resist its exclusion from future politics. And in the North, the 1840s witnessed the expansion of sectional political rhetoric—as more and more northerners became familiar with the "aggressions" of the slave power and the need to resist them. At the same time, as antislavery ideas expanded, unpopular and divisive elements were weeded out, especially the old alliance of antislavery with demands for the rights of free blacks. Opposition to slavery was already coming to focus on its lowest common denominators—free soil, opposition to the slave power, and union.

The political system reacted to the intrusion of the slavery question in the traditional ways. At first, it tried to suppress it. This is the meaning of the famous letters opposing the immediate annexation of Texas issued by Clay and Van Buren on the same spring day in 1844, probably after consultation on the subject. It was an agreement that slavery was too explosive a question for either party to try to take partisan advantage of it. The agreement, of course, was torpedoed by the defeat of Van Buren for the Democratic nomination, a defeat caused in part by the willingness of his Democratic opponents to use the Texas and slavery questions to discredit Van Buren—thereby violating the previously established rules of political conduct. In the North from 1844 onwards, both parties, particularly the Whigs, tried to defuse the slavery issue and minimize defection to the Liberty party by adopting antisouthern rhetoric. This tended to prevent defections to third parties, but it had the effect of nurturing and legitimating antisouthern sentiment within the ranks of the major parties themselves. After the 1848 election in which northern Whigs and Democrats vied for title of "free soil" to minimize the impact of the Free Soil party, William H. Seward commented, "Antislavery is at length a respectable element in politics."

Both parties also attempted to devise formulas for compromising the divisive issue. For the Whigs, it was "no territory"—an end to expansion would end the question of the spread of slavery. The Democratic answer, first announced by Vice-President Dallas in 1847 and picked up by Lewis Cass, was popular sovereignty or nonintervention: giving to the people of each territory the right to decide on slavery. As has often been pointed out, popular sovereignty was an exceedingly vague and ambiguous doctrine. It was never precisely clear what the power of a territorial legislature were to be or at what point the question of slavery was to be decided. But politically such ambiguity was essential (and intentional) if popular sovereignty were to serve as a means of setting the slavery issue on the traditional basis—by removing it from national politics and transferring the battleground from Congress to the territories. Popular sovereignty formed one basis of the compromise of 1850, the last attempt of the political system to expel the disease of sectional ideology by finally settling all the points at which slavery and national politics intersected.

That compromise was possible in 1850 was testimony to the resiliency of the political system and the continuing ability of party loyalty to compete with sectional commitments. But the very method of passage revealed how deeply sectional divisions were embedded in party politics. Because only a small group of Congressmen—mostly northwestern Democrats and southern Whigs—were committed to compromise on every issue, the "omnibus" compromise measure could not pass. The compromise had to be enacted serially with the small compromise bloc, led by Stephen A. Douglas of Illinois, aligned with first one sectional bloc then the other, to pass the individual measures.

His role in the passage of the compromise announced the emergence of Douglas as the last of the great Unionists, compromising politicians, the heir of Clay, Webster, and other spokesmen for the center. And his career, like Webster's, showed that it was no longer possible to win the confidence of both sections with a combination of extreme nationalism and the calculated suppression of the slavery issue in national politics. Like his predecessors, Douglas called for a policy of "entire silence on the slavery question," and throughout the 1850s, as Robert Johannsen has written, his aim was to restore "order and stability to American politics through the agency of a national, conservative Democratic party." Ultimately, Douglas failed—a traditional career for the Union was simply not possible in the 1850s—but it is equally true that in 1860 he was the only presidential candidate to draw significant support in all parts of the country.

It is, of course, highly ironic that it was Douglas's attempt to extend the principle of popular sovereignty to territory already guaranteed to free labor by the Missouri Compromise which finally shattered the second party system. We can date almost exactly the final collapse of that system—February 15, 1854—the day a caucus of southern Whig Congressmen and Senators decided to support Douglas's Nebraska bill, despite the fact that they could have united with northern Whigs in opposition both to the repeal of the Missouri Compromise and the revival of sectional agitation. But in spite of the sectionalization of politics which occurred after 1854, Douglas continued his attempt to maintain a national basis of party competition. In fact, from one angle of vision, whether politics was to be national or sectional was the basic issue of the Lincoln-Douglas debates of 1858. The Little Giant presented local autonomy—popular sovereignty for states and territories—as the only "national" solution to the slavery question, while Lincoln attempted to destroy this middle ground and force a single, sectional solution on the entire Union. There is a common critique of Douglas's politics, expressed perhaps most persuasively by Allan Nevins, which argues that, as a man with no moral feelings about slavery, Douglas was incapable of recognizing that this moral issue affected millions of northern voters. This, in my opinion, is a serious misunderstanding of Douglas's politics. What he insisted was not that there was no moral question involved in slavery but that it was not the function of the politician to deal in moral judgments. To Lincoln's prediction that the nation could not exist half slave and half free, Douglas replied that it had so existed for seventy years and could continue to do so if northerners stopped trying to impose their own brand of morality upon the South.

Douglas's insistence on the separation of politics and morality was expressed in his oft-quoted statement that—in his role as a politician—he did not care if the people of a territory voted slavery "up or down." As he explained in his Chicago speech of July 1858, just before the opening of the great debates:

> I deny the right of Congress to force a slave-holding state upon an unwilling people. I deny their right to force a free state upon an unwilling people. I deny their right to force a good thing upon a people who are unwilling to receive it. . . . It is no answer to this argument to say that slavery is an evil and hence should not be tolerated. You must allow the people to decide for themselves whether it is a good or an evil.

When Lincoln, therefore, said the real purpose of popular sovereignty was "to educate and mould public opinion, at least northern public opinion, to not care whether slavery is voted down or up," he was, of course, right. For Douglas recognized that moral categories, being essentially uncompromisable, are unassimilable in politics. The only solution to the slavery issue was local autonomy. Whatever a majority of a state or territory wished to do about slavery was right—or at least should not be tampered with by politicians from other areas. To this, Lincoln's only possible reply was the one formulated in the debates—the will of the majority must be tempered by considerations of morality. Slavery was not, he declared, an *"ordinary* matter of domestic concern in the states and territories." Because of its essential immorality, it tainted the entire nation, and its disposition in the territories, and eventually in the entire nation, was a matter of national concern to be decided by a national, not a local, majority. As the debates continued, Lincoln increasingly moved to this moral level of the slavery argument: "Everything that emanates from [Douglas] or his coadjutors, carefully excludes the thought that there is anything wrong with slavery. All their arguments, if you will consider them, will be seen to exclude the thought. . . . If you do admit that it is wrong, Judge Douglas can't logically say that he don't care whether a wrong is voted up or down."

In order to press home the moral argument, moreover, Lincoln had to insist throughout the debates on the basic humanity of the blacks; while Douglas, by the same token, logically had to define blacks as subhuman, or at least, as the Dred Scott decision had insisted, not part of the American "people" included in the Declaration of Independence and the Constitution. Douglas's view of the black, Lincoln declared, conveyed "no vivid impression that the Negro is a human, and consequently has no idea that there can be any moral question in legislating about him." Of course, the standard of morality which Lincoln felt the nation should adopt regarding slavery and the black was the sectional morality of the Republican party.

By 1860, Douglas's local majoritarianism was no more acceptable to southern political leaders than Lincoln's national and moral majoritarianism. The principle of state rights and minority self-determination had always been the first line of defense of slavery from northern interference, but southerners now coupled it with the demand that Congress intervene to establish and guarantee slavery in the territories. The Lecompton fight had clearly demonstrated that southerners would no longer be satisfied with what Douglas hoped the territories would become—free, Democratic states. And the refusal of the Douglas Democrats to accede to southern demands was the culmination of a long history of resentment on the part of northern Democrats, stretching back into the 1840s, at the impossible political dilemma of being caught between increasingly antisouthern constituency pressure and loyalty to an increasingly prosouthern national party. For their part, southern Democrats viewed their northern allies as too weak at home and too tainted with antisouthernism after the Lecompton battle to be relied on to protect southern interests any longer.

As for the Republicans, by the late 1850s they had succeeded in developing a coherent ideology which, despite internal ambiguities and contradictions, incorporated the fundamental values, hopes, and fears of a majority of northerners. As I have argued elsewhere, it rested on a commitment to the northern social order, founded on the dignity and opportunities of free labor, and to social mobility, enterprise, and "progress." It gloried in the same qualities of northern life—materialism, social fluidity, and the dominance of the self-made man—which twenty years earlier had been the source of widespread anxiety and fear in Jacksonian America. And it defined the South as a backward, stagnant, aristocratic society, totally alien in values and social order to the middle-class capitalism of the North.

Some elements of the Republican ideology had roots stretching back into the eighteenth century. Others, especially the Republican emphasis on the threat of the slave power, were relatively new. Northern politics and thought were permeated by the slave power idea in the 1850s. The effect can perhaps be gauged by a brief look at the career of the leading Republican spokesman of the 1850s, William H. Seward. As a political child of upstate New York's burned-over district and anti-masonic crusade, Seward had long believed that the Whig party's main political liability was its image as the spokesman of the wealthy and aristocratic. Firmly committed to egalitarian democracy, Seward had attempted to reorient the New York State Whigs into a reformist, egalitarian party, friendly to immigrants and embracing political and economic democracy, but he was always defeated by the party's downstate conservative wing. In the 1840s, he became convinced that the only way for the party to counteract the Democrats' monopoly of the rhetoric of democracy and equality was for the Whigs to embrace antislavery as a party platform.

The slave power idea gave the Republicans to antiaristocratic appeal with which men like Seward had long wished to be associated politically. By fusing older antislavery arguments with the idea that slavery posed a threat to northern free labor and democratic values, it enabled the Republicans to tap the egalitarian outlook which lay at the heart of northern society. At the same time, it enabled Republicans to present antislavery as an essentially conservative reform, an attempt to reestablish the antislavery principles of the founding fathers and rescue the federal government from southern usurpation. And, of course, the slave power idea had a far greater appeal to northern self-interest than arguments based on the plight of black slaves in the South. As the black abolitionist Frederick Douglass noted, "The cry of Free Men was raised, not for the extension of liberty to the black man, but for the protection of the liberty of the white."

By the late 1850s, it had become a standard part of Republican rhetoric to accuse the slave power of a long series of transgressions against northern rights and liberties and to predict that, unless halted by effective political action, the ultimate aim of the conspiracy—the complete subordination of the national government to slavery and the suppression of northern liberties—would be accomplished. Like other conspiracy theories, the slave power idea was a way of ordering and interpreting history, assigning clear causes to otherwise inexplicable events, from the Gag Rule to Bleeding Kansas and the Dred Scott decision. It also provided a convenient symbol through which a host of anxieties about the future could be expressed. At the same time, the notion of a black Republican conspiracy to overthrow slavery and southern society had taken hold in the South. These competing conspiratorial outlooks were reflections, not merely of sectional "paranoia," but of the fact that the nation was every day growing apart and into two societies whose ultimate interests were diametrically opposed. The South's fear of black Republicans, despite its exaggerated rhetoric, was based on the realistic assessment that at the heart of Republican aspirations for the nation's future was the restriction and eventual eradication of slavery. And the slave power expressed northerners' conviction, not only that slavery was incompatible with basic democratic values, but that to protect slavery, southerners were determined to control the federal government and use it to foster the expansion of slavery. In summary, the slave power idea was the ideological glue of the Republican party—it enabled them to elect in 1860 a man conservative enough to sweep to victory in every northern state, yet radical enough to trigger the secession crisis.

Did the election of Lincoln pose any real danger to the institution of slavery? In my view, it is only possible to argue that it did not if one takes a completely static—and therefore ahistorical—view of the slavery issue. The expansion of slavery was not simply an issue; it was a fact. By 1860, over half the slaves lived in areas outside the original slave states. At the same time, however, the South had become a permanent and shrinking minority within the nation. And in the majority section, antislavery sentiment had expanded at a phenomenal rate. Within one generation, it had moved from the commitment of a small minority of northerners to the motive force behind a victorious party. That sentiment now demanded the exclusion of slavery from the territories. Who could tell what its demands would be in ten or twenty years? The incoming President had often declared his commitment to the "ultimate extinction" of slavery. In Alton, Illinois, in the heart of the most proslavery area of the North, he had condemned Douglas because "he looks to no end of the institution of slavery." A Lincoln adminstration seemed likely to be only the beginning of a prolonged period of Republican hegemony. And the succession of generally weak, one-term presidents between 1836 and 1860 did not obscure the great expansion in the potential power of the presidency which had taken place during the administration of Andrew Jackson. Old Hickory had clearly shown that a strong-willed president, backed by a united political party, had tremendous power to shape the affairs of government and to transform into policy his version of majority will.

What was at stake in 1860, as in the entire sectional conflict, was the character of the nation's future. This was one reason Republicans had placed so much stress on the question of the expansion of slavery. Not only was this the most available issue concerning slavery constitutionally open to them, but it involved the nation's future in the most direct way. In the West, the future was *tabula rasa*, and the future course of western development would gravely affect the direction of the entire nation. Now that the territorial issue was settled by Lincoln's election, it seemed likely that the slavery controversy would be transferred back into the southern states themselves. Secessionists, as William Freehling has argued, feared that slavery was weak and vulnerable in the border states, even in Virginia. They feared Republican efforts to encourage the formation of Republican organizations in these areas and the renewal of the long-suppressed internal debate on slavery in the South itself. And, lurking behind these anxieties, may have been fear of antislavery debate reaching the slave quarters, of an undermining of the masters' authority, and, ultimately, of slave rebellion itself. The slaveholders knew, despite the great economic strength of King Cotton, that the existence of slavery as a local institution in a larger free economy demanded an intersectional community consensus, real or enforced. It was this consensus which

Lincoln's election seemed to undermine, which is why the secession convention of South Carolina declared, "Experience has proved that slaveholding states cannot be safe in subjection to non-slaveholding states."

More than seventy years before the secession crisis, James Madison had laid down the principles by which a central government and individual and minority liberties could coexist in a large and heterogeneous Union. The very diversity of interests in the nation, he argued in *The Federalist* papers, was the security for the rights of minorities, for it ensured that no one interest would ever gain control of the government. In the 1830s, John C. Calhoun recognized the danger which abolitionism posed to the South—it threatened to rally the North in the way Madison had said would not happen—in terms of one commitment hostile to the interests of the minority South. Moreover, Calhoun recognized, when a majority interest is organized into an effective political party, it can seize control of all the branches of government, overturning the system of constitutional checks and balances which supposedly protected minority rights. Only the principle of the concurrent majority—a veto which each major interest could exercise over policies directly affecting it—could reestablish this constitutional balance.

At the outset of the abolitionist crusade, Calhoun had been convinced that, while emancipation must be "resisted at all costs," the South should avoid hasty action until it was "certain that it is the real object, not by a few, but by a very large portion of the non-slaveholding states." By 1850, Calhoun was convinced that "Every portion of the North entertains views more or less hostile to slavery." And by 1860, the election returns demonstrated that this antislavery sentiment, contrary to Madison's expectations, had united in an interest capable of electing a president, despite the fact that it had not the slightest support from the sectional minority. The character of Lincoln's election, in other words, completely overturned the ground rules which were supposed to govern American politics. The South Carolina secession convention expressed secessionists' reaction when it declared that once the sectional Republican party, founded on hostility to southern values and interests, took over control of the federal government, "the guarantees of the Constitution will then no longer exist."

Thus the South came face to face with a conflict between its loyalty to the nation and loyalty to the South—that is, to slavery, which, more than anything else, made the South distinct. David Potter has pointed out that the principle of majority rule implies the existence of a coherent, closely recognizable body of which more than half may be legitimately considered as a majority of the whole. For the South to accept majority rule in 1860, in other words, would have been an affirmation of a common nationality with the North. Certainly, it is true that in terms of ethnicity, language, religion—many of the usual components of nationality—Americans, North and South, were still quite close. On the other hand, one important element, community of interest, was not present. And perhaps most important, the preceding decades had witnessed an escalation of distrust—an erosion of the reciprocal currents of good will so essential for national harmony. "We are not one people," declared the *New York Tribune* in 1855. "We are two peoples. We are a people for Freedom and a people for Slavery. Between the two, conflict is inevitable." We can paraphrase John Adams's famous comment on the American Revolution and apply it to the coming of the Civil War— the separation was complete, in the minds of the people, before the war began. In a sense, the Constitution and national political system had failed in the difficult task of creating a nation—only the Civil War itself would accomplish it.

# 11

# The Reconstruction Era

## Constructive or Destructive?

To students of American history, the Civil War years stand in sharp contrast to those of the Reconstruction era. The war years represented a period of heroism and idealism; out of the travail of conflict there emerged a new American nationality that replaced the older sectional and state loyalties. Although the cost in lives and money was frightful, the divisions that had plagued Americans for over half a century were eliminated in the ordeal of fire. Henceforth, America would stand as a united country, destined to take its rightful place as one of the leading nations in the world.

The Reconstruction era, on the other hand, conjures up a quite different picture. Just as the war years were dominated by heroism, the postwar period was characterized as being dominated by evil, power-seeking scoundrels intent upon pursuing their narrow self-interest regardless of the cost to either the South or the nation. The result was a tragedy for all Americans—Northerners, Southerners, whites and blacks alike. Nothing short of a revolution, it seemed, could displace the forces of evil from power and restore the South and the nation to its rightful rulers.

Between 1890 and 1930 few historians would have disagreed with this contrast of the two periods. If anything, most scholars during these years characterized Reconstruction in even harsher terms. Led by Professor William A. Dunning of Columbia University—who literally founded the school of Reconstruction historiography that still bears his name—the historical profession set out to prove that the years following the Civil War were marked by tragedy and pathos because men of good will were momentarily thrust out of power by the forces of evil. This period, in the words of one historian, "were years of revolutionary turmoil.... The prevailing note was one of tragedy.... Never have American public men in responsible positions, directing the destiny of the Nation, been so brutal, hypocritical, and corrupt.... The Southern people literally were put to the torture."[1]

---

[1]Claude G. Bowers, *The Tragic Era: The Revolution After Lincoln* (Cambridge, 1929), pp. v–vi.

Underlying the interpretation of the Dunning school were two important assumptions. The first was that the South should have been restored to the Union quickly and without being exposed to Northern vengeance. Most Southerners, it was argued, had accepted their military defeat gracefully and were prepared to pledge their good faith and loyalty to the Union. Secondly, responsibility for the freedmen should have been entrusted to white Southerners. Blacks, these historians believed, could never be integrated into American society on an equal plane with whites because of their former slave status and inferior racial characteristics.

Working within the framework of these two assumptions, historians in the Dunning school tradition proceeded to study Reconstruction in terms of a struggle between elements of good and evil. On one side stood the forces of good—Northern and Southern Democrats and Republicans of the Andrew Johnson variety. These men, recognizing the necessity for compassion and leniency, were willing to forget the agonies of war and to forgive the South. On the opposing side were the forces of evil—scalawags, carpetbaggers, and above all, a group of radical and vindictive Republicans intent upon punishing the South by depriving the native aristocracy of their power and status, thereby ensuring the dominance of the Republican party in that section. Caught in the middle of this struggle were the helpless, impotent, and ignorant blacks, whose votes were sought for sinister purposes by Radical Republicans who had little or not real concern for the welfare of the freedman once he had left the ballot box.

The result of such a political alignment in the South, according to the Dunning school, was disastrous. The Radical carpetbag state governments that came into power proved to be totally incompetent—in part because they included illiterate blacks who were unprepared for the responsibilities of self-government. Still worse, these governments were extraordinarily expensive because they were corrupt. Most of them, indeed, left nothing but a legacy of huge debts. "Saddled with an irresponsible officialdom," one Dunning school historian concluded, "the South was now plunged into debauchery, corruption, and private plundering unbelievable—suggesting that government had been transformed into an engine of destruction."[2]

The decent whites in the South, the Dunning argument continued, united out of sheer desperation to force the carpetbaggers, scalawags, and blacks from power. In one state after another Radical rule was eventually overthrown and good government restored. By the time of the presidential campaign of 1876 only three states remained under Radical

---

[2]E. Merton Coulter, *The South During Reconstruction 1865–1877* (Baton Rouge, 1947), p. 148.

control. When the dispute over the contested election was resolved, Hayes withdrew the remaining federal troops from the South, and the three last Radical regimes fell from power. Thus the tragic era of Reconstruction came to an end.

For nearly three decades after the turn of the century the Dunning point of view was dominant among most American historians. Many monographs on the history of individual Southern states were published, but most of them simply filled in pertinent details and left the larger picture virtually unchanged. All of these studies, despite their individual differences, agreed that the Reconstruction period had been an abject and dismal failure. Not only had Reconstruction destroyed the two-party system in the South; it had left behind an enduring legacy of bitterness and hatred between the races.

The first selection by Albert B. Moore is a good example of a historian writing about Reconstruction within the Dunning tradition. The events between 1865 and 1877, Moore argues, had the effect of converting the South into a colonial appendage of the North. To put it another way, the Reconstruction period was simply one phase of the process whereby the North attempted to remake the South in its own image; it was an attempt by a victor to punish the vanquished. Rejecting completely the assertion that the North was lenient, Moore emphasizes property confiscations, mental torture, and vindictive military rule. The political enfranchisement of blacks, which laid the basis for carpetbag government, is to Moore perhaps the most incredible event of an incredible era. The result was the continued exacerbation of Southern economic, political, and social problems. The South, he concludes, was still paying for the dark legacy of Reconstruction in the twentieth century.

In the late 1920s, however, historians began to look at the events between 1865 and 1877 from a new and different perspective. These revisionists—a term that distinguishes them from followers of the Dunning school—were much less certain that Reconstruction was as bad as had been commonly supposed. Influenced by the Progressive school of American historiography—which emphasized underlying economic factors in historical development—the revisionists began to restudy the entire Reconstruction period. As a result, they posed a sharp challenge to the Dunning school by changing the interpretive framework of the Reconstruction era.

Generally speaking, the revisionists accepted most, if not all, of the findings of the Dunning school. The disagreement between the two groups, therefore, arose from their different starting assumptions and the consequent interpretation of data rather than over disputed empirical data as such. Unlike the Dunningites, the revisionists could not view events between 1865 and 1877 in terms of a morality play that depicted Reconstruction as a struggle between good and evil, white and black,

and Democrats and Radical Republicans. Nor were the revisionists willing to accept the view that responsibility for the freedmen should have
been entrusted to native white Southerners. Given these differences, it
was understandable that the revisionist interpretation should differ
sharply from that of the Dunning school.

In 1939 Francis B. Simkins, a distinguished Southern historian who
published with Robert Woody in 1932 one of the first revisionist studies,
summed up some of the findings of the revisionist school. Pointing out
that the overwhelming majority of Southerners lived quietly and peace-
fully during these years, he emphasized many of the constructive
achievements of this era. Simkins, as a matter of fact, denied that the
Radical program was radical within the accepted meaning of the word;
indeed, the Radicals failed because they did not provide freedmen with
a secure economic base. Past historians, he concluded, had given a distorted picture of Reconstruction because they had assumed that blacks
were racially inferior. The result was a provincial approach to Reconstruction that was based on ignorance and priggishness. Only by abandoning their biases could historians contribute to a more accurate understanding of the past, thereby making possible rational discussion of one
of the nation's most critical dilemmas.[3]

While the revisionists often disagreed as much among themselves as
they did with the Dunning school, there were common areas of agreement that gave their writings a certain unity. Most revisionists viewed
the problems of American society during these years in a broader context
and concluded that they were national rather than sectional in scope.
Corruption, to cite but one example, was not confined to the South. It
was a national phenomenon in the postwar era and involved all sections, classes, and political parties alike. To single out the South in this
regard was patently unfair and ahistorical.[4]

Revisionist historians attempted also to refute many of the familiar
assertions of the Dunning school. In the first place, they denied that the
Radical governments in the South were always dishonest, incompetent,
and inefficient. On the contrary, they claimed, such governments accomplished much of enduring value. The new constitutions written during Reconstruction represented a vast improvement over the older ones
and often survived the overthrow of the men who had written them.
Radical governments brought about many long-needed social reforms,
including state-supported school systems for both blacks and whites, a

---

[3]Francis B. Simkins, "New Viewpoints of Southern Reconstruction," *Journal of Southern History* 5 (February 1939): 49–61.

[4]For a revisionist synthesis see J. G. Randall and David Donald, *The Civil War and Reconstruction* (2d ed.: Boston, 1961). The first edition, written by Randall in 1937, was in the Dunning school tradition.

revision of the judicial system, and improvements in local administration. Above all, these governments operated—at least in theory—on the premise that all men, white and black alike, were entitled to equal political and civil liberties.

Second, the revisionists drew a sharply different portrait of blacks during Reconstruction. They denied that developments in the postwar South resulted from black participation in government or that the freedmen were illiterate, naive, and inexperienced. In no Southern state, they pointed out, did blacks control both houses of the legislature. Moreover, there were no black governors and only one black state supreme court justice. Only two blacks were elected to the United States Senate and fifteen to the House of Representatives. Such statistics hardly supported the charge that the supposed excesses of Reconstruction were due to political activities of black Americans.

Indeed, the revisionists maintained that blacks, as a group, were quite capable of understanding where their own interests lay without disregarding the legitimate interests of others. The freedmen were able to participate at least as intelligently as other groups in the American political process. As Vernon L. Wharton concluded in his pioneering revisionist study of the Negro in Mississippi after the Civil War, there was "little difference... in the administration of... counties [having blacks on boards of supervisors] and that of counties under Democratic control.... Altogether, as governments go, that supplied by the Negro and white Republicans in Mississippi between 1870 and 1876 was not a bad government.... With their white Republican colleagues, they gave to the state a government of greatly expanded functions at a cost that was low in comparison with that of almost any other state."[5]

If black Americans were not the dominant group in most Radical governments, where did these governments get their support? In attempting to answer this question, revisionists again endeavored to refute the Dunning school contention that these governments were controlled by evil, power-hungry, profit-seeking carpetbaggers and renegade scalawags who used black votes to maintain themselves in power. The stereotype of the carpetbagger and scalawag, according to revisionists, was highly inaccurate and far too simplistic. Carpetbaggers, to take one group, migrated to the South for a variety of reasons—including the lure of wider and legitimate economic opportunities as well as a desire to serve the former slaves in some humanitarian capacity. The scalawags were an equally diverse group. Within their ranks

---

[5]Vernon L. Wharton, *The Negro In Mississippi 1865-1890* (Chapel Hill, 1947), pp. 172, 179-180. See also Willie Lee Rose, *Rehearsal for Reconstruction: The Port Royal Experiment* (New York, 1964), and Joel Williamson, *After Slavery: The Negro in South Carolina During Reconstruction 1861.-1877* (Chapel Hill, 1965).

one could find former Southern unionists and Whigs, lower-class whites who sought to use the Republican party as the vehicle for confiscating the property of the planter aristocrats, and businessmen attracted by the promise of industrialization. The Radical governments, then, had a wide base of indigenous support in most Southern states.[6]

Finally, the revisionists rejected the charge that the Radical governments were extraordinarily expensive and corrupt, or that they had saddled the South with a large public debt. It was true that state expenditures went up sharply after the war. This situation was due, however, to understandable circumstances and not to inefficiency or theft. As in most postwar periods, the partial destruction of certain cities and areas required an infusion of public funds. Deferring regular appropriations during the war years also meant that a backlog of legitimate projects had accumulated. Most important of all, the South for the first time had to provide certain public facilities and social services for its black citizens. Southern states and communities had to build schools and provide other facilities and services for blacks which did not exist before the 1860s and for which public funds had never been expended prior to this time. It is little wonder, then, that there was a rise in spending in the Reconstruction era.

In examining the financial structure of Southern governments between 1865 and 1877, the revisionists also found that the rise in state debts, in some instances, was more apparent than real. Grants to railroads promoters, which in certain states accounted for a large proportion of the increase in the debt, were secured by a mortgage on the railroad property. Thus, the rise in the debt was backed by sound collateral. The amount of the debt chargeable to theft, the revisionists maintained, was negligible. Indeed, the restoration governments, which were dominated by supposedly honest Southerners, proved to be far more corrupt than those governments controlled by the Radicals.

Although revisionists agreed that the Dunning interpretation of Reconstruction was inadequate—if not misleading—they had considerable difficulty themselves in synthesizing their own findings. If there was one idea on which the revisionists were united, it was their conviction that economic forces, which were related to the growth of an urban and industrialized nation, somehow played a major role during this period. Beneath the political and racial antagonisms of this era, some revisionists argued, lay opposing economic rivalries. Anxious to gain an advantage over their competitors, many business interests used politics as the vehicle to further their economic ambitions—especially since the

---

[6]See Otto H. Olsen, "Reconsidering the Scalawags," *Civil War History* 12 (December 1966): 304–20, and Allen W. Trelease, "Who Were the Scalawags?," *Journal of Southern History* 29 (November 1963): 445–68.

South, like the North and West, was ardently courting businessmen. The result was that economic rivalries were translated into political struggles.

Revisionists also emphasized the crucial issue of race. During Reconstruction many former Whigs joined the Republican party because of its probusiness economic policies. These well-to-do- conservatives, at first, were willing to promise blacks civil and political rights in return for their support at the polls. Within the Democratic party, however, lower-class whites, fearful of possible encroachments by blacks upon their social status and economic position, raised the banner of race. Conservatives found their affiliation with the Republican party increasingly uncomfortable, and they slowly began to drift back into the Democratic party. The fact that both parties were under the control of conservatives made it easier for former Republicans to shift their political allegiance. One result of the political alignment was that it left Southern blacks politically isolated and without allies among the whites. When the move to eliminate them from political life in the South got started, blacks could find little support among Southern whites. This political move came at a time when Northerners were disillusioned by the failure of the Radicals to achieve many of their idealistic aims for the freedmen. Tired of conflict and turmoil, Northerners became reconciled to the idea of letting the South work out its own destiny—even if it meant sacrificing the black people. Northern businessmen likewise became convinced that only Southern conservatives could restore order and stability and thus create a favorable environment for investment.

The result was both a polarization of Southern politics along racial rather than economic lines and the emergence of the Democratic party as the white man's party. For whites of lower-class background, the primary goal was to maintain the South as a white man's country. Upper-class whites were also contented with the existing one-party political structure because they were permitted the dominant role in determining the future economic development of their section.

The end of Reconstruction, according to the revisionists, was closely related to the triumph of business values and industrial capitalism. When the contested presidential election of 1876 resulted in an apparent deadlock between Rutherford B. Hayes, the Republican candidate, and Samuel J. Tilden, his Democratic opponent, some prominent Republicans saw an opportunity to rebuild their party in the South upon a new basis. Instead of basing their party upon propertyless, former slaves, they hoped to attract well-to-do former Whigs who had been forced into the Democratic party as a result of events during the Reconstruction. To accomplish this goal, a group of powerful Republican leaders began to work secretly to bring about a political realignment. If Southern Democratic congressmen would not stand in the way of Hayes's election and also provide enough votes to permit the Republicans to organize the House of Representatives, these leaders were willing to promise the South federal subsidies—primarily for railroads—and also to name a Southerner as postmaster general.

The "Compromise of 1877," as this political deal was called, was not fully carried out, but its larger implications survived unscathed. As C. Vann Woodward, the revisionist historian who propounded the thesis of such a political bargain, concluded, the compromise "did not restore the old order in the South, nor did it restore the South to parity with other sections. It did assure the dominant whites political autonomy and nonintervention in matters of race policy and promised them a share in the blessings of the new economic order. In return the South became, in effect, a satellite of the dominant region. So long as the Conservative Redeemers held control they scotched any tendency of the South to combine forces with the internal enemies of the new economy— laborites, Western agrarians, reformers. Under the regime of the Redeemers the South became a bulwark instead of a menace to the new order."[7]

After the early 1950s, a new school of Reconstruction historiography called the neorevisionists emerged. These historians emphasized the moral rather than the economic basis of Reconstruction. The differences between the revisionists and neorevisionists were often minimal since the latter frequently relied upon the findings of the former to reach their conclusions, and it is difficult, if not impossible, to categorize certain historians as belonging to one group or another. Generally speaking, while the neorevisionists accepted many findings of the revisionists, they rejected the idea of interpreting Reconstruction in strictly economic terms. The Republican party, the neorevisionists maintained, was not united on a probusiness economic program; it included individuals and groups holding quite different social and economic views.[8]

In interpreting Reconstruction, the neorevisionists stressed the critical factor of race as a moral issue. One of the unresolved dilemmas after the Civil War, they claimed, was the exact role that blacks were to play in American society. Within the Republican party, a number of factions each offered their own solution to this question. Andrew Johnson, who had been nominated as Lincoln's running mate in 1864 on a Union party ticket despite his Democratic party affiliations, spoke for one segment of the party. To Johnson blacks were incapable of self-government. Con-

---

[7]C. Vann Woodward, *Reunion and Reaction: The Compromise of 1877 and the End of Reconstruction* (Boston, 1951), p. 246.

[8]Robert Sharkey, *Money, Class, and Party: An Economic Study Study of the Civil War and Reconstruction* (Baltimore, 1959), and Irwin Ungar, *The Greenback Era: A Social and Political History of American Finance, 1865–1879* (Princeton, 1964).

sequently, he favored the state governments in the South that came back into the Union shortly after the end of the war under his own plan of reconstruction and went along with the Black Codes that denied black Americans many of their civil rights.

Although Johnson was president as well as titular head of the Republican party, there was a great deal of opposition to his policies by a group known as the Radicals. Who were the Radical Republicans and what did they stand for? To the Dunning school the Radicals were a group of vindictive politicians who were utterly amoral in their quest after power; they were merely interested in the black man for his vote. To revisionists the Radicals represented, at least in part, the interests of the industrial Northeast—men who wanted to use black votes to prevent the formation of a coalition of Western and Southern agrarian interests against the industrial capitalism of the Northeast.[9]

To the neorevisionists, on the other hand, the Radicals were a much more complex group. Many of the Radicals, they claimed, joined the Republican party in the 1850s for moral and idealistic reasons—their antislavery zeal—rather than for economic motives. These men, seeking to eradicate all vestiges of slavery, were consistent in their demands before and after the war that blacks be given the same rights as white Americans. Their beliefs, of course, brought them to a face-to-face confrontation with President Johnson in the postwar period. In the ensuing struggle, the President, because of his political ineptness, soon found himself isolated. Taking advantage of the situation, the Radicals first won the support of conservative Republicans and then set out to remake Southern society by transferring political power from the planter class to the freedmen. The program of the Radicals, therefore, was motivated in large measure by idealism and a sincere humanitarian concern.[10]

In 1965 Kenneth M. Stampp published an important synthesis that emphasized the moral dimension of the Reconstruction years. Stampp rejected the traditional stereotype of the average Radical as a figure motivated by vindictive considerations. He argued that the issues of the 1860s were not artificial ones as the Dunning school had claimed. The central question of the postwar period was the place of the freedmen in American society. President Johnson and his followers believed in the innate racial inferiority of blacks; therefore they rejected any program based upon egalitarian assumptions. The Radicals, on the other hand, took seriously the ideals of equality, natural rights, and democracy.

[9]This point of view was best expressed by Howard K. Beale, one of the fathers of the revisionist school, in *The Critical Year: A Study of Andrew Johnson and Reconstruction* (New York, 1930).

[10]See James H. McPherson, *The Struggle for Equality: Abolitionists and the Negro in the Civil War and Reconstruction* (Princeton, 1964), and Hans L. Trefousse, *The Radical Republicans: Lincoln's Vanguard for Social Justice* (New York, 1969).

Indeed, most of these men had been closely associated with the antebellum abolitionist crusade. Stampp did not deny that the Radicals had other motives as well, for he admitted that they saw black Americans as valuable additions to the Republican party. But most politicians, he insisted, identify the welfare of the nation with the welfare of their party. To argue that the Radicals had invidious and selfish motives, Stampp concluded, does them a severe injustice and results in a distorted picture of the Reconstruction era.

The Radicals, according to the neorevisionists, ultimately failed in their objectives. Most Americans, harboring conscious and unconscious racial antipathies, were not willing to accept blacks as equals. By the 1870s the North was prepared to abandon blacks to the white South for three reasons: a wish to return to the amicable prewar relations between the sections; a desire to promote industrial investment in the South; and a growing conviction that the cause of black Americans was no longer worth further strife. The tragedy of Reconstruction, the neorevisionists maintained, was not that it occurred, but that it had ended short of achieving the major goal sought by the Radicals.

The struggle over Reconstruction, nevertheless, had not been in vain. In addition to the many achievements of the Radical governments, the Radicals had succeeded in securing the adoption of the Fourteenth and Fifteenth amendments. These amendments, in Stampp's words, "which could have been adopted only under the conditions of radical reconstruction, make the blunders of that era, tragic though they were, dwindle into insignificance. For if it was worth four years of civil war to save the Union, it was worth a few years of radical reconstruction to give the American Negro the ultimate promise of equal civil and political rights."[11]

In the second selection in this chapter, Allen W. Trelease sums up the neorevisionist interpretation of Reconstruction. Given a commitment to racism that by 1865 was deeply embedded in the minds of a majority of white Americans, Trelease argues that Southerners could hardly be expected to abandon their antipathies toward blacks after emancipation. Although blacks were simply seeking the same rights enjoyed by whites, the latter were unable to accept the former as equals. Seeing the race question as crucial, Trelease insists that Radical Reconstruction failed because the seed of biracial democracy was planted on barren ground in the South. Moreover, the federal government failed to nurture the seeds of democracy. Despite significant achievements in the years following the end of slavery, most Radical state governments were quickly overthrown by a society committed to inequality.

[11]Kenneth M. Stampp, *The Era of Reconstruction* (New York, 1965), p. 215.

The heroic (though tragic) interpretation of Reconstruction offered by Stampp and, to a lesser extent, by Trelease did not remain unchallenged. Given the internal strife engendered by the continued existence of economic, political, and legal inequality, and the seeming resurgence of a radical critique of American institutions and society in the 1960s, it was not surprising that historians associated with the New Left would slowly begin to reevaluate the events of the postwar years in a way that took sharp issue with scholars such as Stampp. Staughton Lynd, for example, argued that it was pointless to debate endlessly the issue whether Northern policy was too hard or too soft following the end of the Civil War. Historians should focus instead on the discussion of strategies of planned social change that might have succeeded in avoiding the tragedies that followed. Conceding that Reconstruction failed and that American society during the succeeding century would reflect this failure, Lynd concluded "that the fundamental error in Reconstruction policy was that it did not give the freedman land of his own. Whether by confiscation of the property of leading rebels, by a vigorous Southern homestead policy, or by some combination of the two, Congress should have given the ex-slaves the economic independence to resist political intimidation."[12]

Nor were the New Left scholars alone in rejecting the revisionist or neorevisionist views of Reconstruction. Although not sufficiently in agreement to constitute a specific school, some individual historians began to place specific events during Reconstruction within a somewhat different structural setting. In his study of the presidential election of 1876, for example, Keith I. Polakoff came to conclusions that were partly at variance with those expressed by C. Vann Woodward some twenty-five years before. Woodward assumed that national political parties were centralized organizations under the control of their leaders. Polakoff, on the other hand, was influenced by the work of more recent social and political historians. Where Woodward saw centralized authority, Polakoff saw structural weakness; he insisted that American political parties at this time were decentralized.

> Not only was factionalism practically the central characteristic of both parties, but the precise balance existing between the various factions remained remarkably stable; and no wonder: each faction had its own little constituency on which it could always depend. The diffuseness of power in the Republican and Democratic parties was merely a reflection of the remarkable diversity of the American electorate. If there was one thing nineteenth-century parties did well, it was to represent their constituents. In the process rational

---

[12]Staughton Lynd, ed., *Reconstruction* (New York, 1967), p. 8. See also Lynd's article, "Rethinking Slavery and Reconstruction," *Journal of Negro History* 50 (July 1965): 198–209. For reasons that are not clear, New Left historians tended to ignore Reconstruction.

programs of government action were trampled underfoot. . . . The resulting irrelevance of much of the political process was actually one of its principal sources of strength. Because the stakes involved were more symbolic than substantial, much like the outcome of the Army-Navy football game a century later, politicking served as a means of transcending the dull routine of everyday life, a means of identifying with the distinctive democratic greatness of the United States while socializing with like-minded men. [13]

During the 1970s there was no indication that interest in the Reconstruction period was diminishing. On the contrary, neorevisionist scholars continued to debate the same issues and problems as their predecessors. To what degree were Americans committed to an equal-rights ideology? Why were black Americans left in a defenseless position? What was the nature of such political events as the impeachment of Andrew Johnson? Why did Reconstruction come to an end far short of achieving its goals?[14]

To these and other questions historians gave varied answers that demonstrated that few differences had been conclusively resolved. Michael Les Benedict, for example, argued that Andrew Johnson was impeached because he seemed to be violating the principle of separation of powers and because he failed to carry out some key provisions in legislation pertaining to Reconstruction.[15] Hans Trefousse emphasized the degree to which Johnson thwarted radical policies and strengthened conservative forces, thereby facilitating their eventual triumph in the 1870s. Michael Perman insisted that in the context of the political tensions that prevailed in the immediate postwar era, the very moderation and conciliation that marked presidential and congressional Reconstruction was doomed to fail; only a coercive policy could have succeeded. Of three recent studies of Andrew Johnson, two (by Patrick W. Riddleberger and James E. Sefton) emphasized his commitment to sometimes incompatible principles which rendered him impotent, and one (by Albert Castel) accentuated the degree to which his inordinate ambition and desire for power helped to destroy him.[16] In a broad study of national

---

[13]Keith I. Polakoff, *The Politics of Inertia: The Election of 1876 and the End of Reconstruction* (Baton Rouge, 1973), pp. 320–22. See also Allan Peskin, "Was There a Compromise of 1877?," *Journal of American History* 40 (June 1973): 63–75; C. Vann Woodward, "Yes, There was a Compromise of 1877," *ibid.* 40 (September 1973): 215–23; and M. Les Benedict, "Southern Democrats in the Crisis of 1876–1877: A Reconsideration of *Reunion and Reaction*," *Journal of Southern History* 46 (November 1980): 489–524.

[14]For a descriptive analysis of black Americans after slavery that does not deal with Reconstruction as a political event, see Leon F. Litwack's important *Been in the Storm So Long: The Aftermath of Slavery* (New York, 1979).

[15]Michael Les Benedict, *The Impeachment and Trial of Andrew Johnson* (New York, 1973). See also Benedict's *A Compromise of Principle: Congressional Republicans and Reconstruction, 1863–1869* (New York, 1974) and *The Fruits of Victory: Alternatives in Restoring the Union, 1865–1877* (Philadelphia, 1975).

[16]Hans L. Trefousse, *Impeachment of a President: Andrew Johnson, the Blacks, and Reconstuction* (Knoxville, 1975); Michael Perman, *Reunion Without Compromise: The South and*

politics, William Gillette noted that Reconstruction was so easily reversed because it had always been "fragmentary and fragile."

> From the very beginning, reconstruction had no more than tenuous support and had been wracked by chronic crises, marred by profound uncertainties, unsettled because of inner tensions, riddled through with unsolved ambiguities involving race relations and public policy, and blighted by the latent contradictions in the Republicans' attitudes and actions. Moreover, all these problems had been compounded by necessary compromises and incessant change, both of which are inherent in the democratic process itself. Clearly, the American people, their presidents, and their government had not been persevering or resourceful enough to see reconstruction through; and since the Republican governments in the South, with their numerous and supreme crises, had been unable or would not govern, their regimes were inevitably and inexorably replaced by those of Democrats, who did govern, but in accordance with their own rules.
>
> Thus reconstruction—which had been neglected, discredited, and deserted by many of its friends—fell an easy prey to its enemies.[17]

At the same time that interest in national politics remained high, historians also continued to write monographic studies dealing with individual states. Here too the traditional dichotomy appeared; some emphasized the degree to which Reconstruction succeeded while others pointed to its failures.[18] In a somewhat novel study of black political leadership in South Carolina that utilized quantitative techniques, Thomas Holt provided a somewhat novel thesis. Holt emphasized the continued persistence of class and caste, but argued that the Afro-American population of South Carolina was not an unvariegated classless mass. Black leaders were divided among themselves; their divisions contributed to the fall of the Republican party in the state. On the other hand, his profile of black leadership demonstrated that most owned property and were literate, and 10 percent were professionally or college trained.[19]

To a considerable extent, the differences between the various schools of Reconstruction historiography grew out of the milieu in which each had grown to maturity. The Dunning point of view, for example, originated in the late nineteenth century and flowered in the early part of the twentieth. During these years the vast majority of white Americans

---

*Reconstruction, 1865–1868* (New York, 1973); Patrick W. Riddleberger, *1866: The Critical Year Revisited* (Carbondale, 1979); James E. Sefton, *Andrew Johnson and the Uses of Constitutional Power* (Boston, 1980), and Albert Castel, *The Presidency of Andrew Johnson* (Lawrence, 1979).

[17]William Gillette, *Retreat from Reconstruction 1869–1879* (Baton Rouge, 1979), p. 380.

[18]Jerrell H. Shofner, *Nor Is It over Yet: Florida in the Era of Reconstruction, 1863–1877* (Gainesville, 1974); Joe Gray Taylor, *Louisiana Reconstructed, 1863–1877* (Baton Rouge, 1974); William C. Harris, *The Day of the Carpetbagger: Republican Reconstruction in Mississippi* (Baton Rouge, 1979).

[19]Thomas Holt, *Black over White: Negro Political Leadership in South Carolina during Reconstruction* (Urbana, 1977).

assumed that blacks constituted an inferior race, one that was incapable of being fully assimilated into their society. Most Southerners had come to this conclusion well before the Civil War; many Northerners arrived at the same conclusion after the debacle of Reconstruction seemingly vindicated this belief. Racism in America was buttressed further by the findings of the biological and social sciences in the late nineteenth century. Influenced by evolutionary concepts of Darwinism, some scientists argued that blacks had followed a unique evolutionary course which resulted in the creation of an inferior race. The racial prejudices of many Americans thus received what they believed to be scientific justification.

Given these beliefs, it is not difficult to understand why the Dunning school interpretation gained rapid acceptance. The attempt by the Radicals to give equal rights to a supposedly inferior race did not appear to be sensible; state governments that included black officials and held power in part through black votes were bound to be inefficient, incompetent, and corrupt. Moreover, the Southern claim that responsibility for black people had to be entrusted to whites seemed entirely justifiable. The findings of the Dunning school that Reconstruction was a tragic blunder doomed to failure from its very beginning came as no surprise to early-twentieth-century Americans, most of whom were prepared to believe the worst about black Americans.

The revisionist school, on the other hand, originated in a somewhat different climate of opinion. By the 1920s American historiography had came under the influence of the Progressive, or New History, school. This school, growing out of the dissatisfaction with the older scientific school of historians that emphasized the collection of impartial empirical data and eschewed "subjective" interpretations, borrowed heavily from the new social sciences. The New History sought to explain historical change by isolating underlying economic and social forces that transformed institutions and social structures. In place of tradition and stability it emphasized change and conflict. Progressive and democratic in their orientation, Progressive historians attempted to explain the present in terms of the dynamic and impersonal forces that had transformed American society.

The revisionists, then, rejected the moralistic tone of the Dunning school. They sought instead to identify the historical forces responsible for many of the developments following the Civil War. Economic and social factors, they maintained, were basic to this era. The real conflict was not between North and South, white and black; it was between industrial capitalism and agrarianism, with the former ultimately emerging victorious. Thus, the question of the status of black people in American society was simply a facade for the more basic conflicts that lay hidden beneath the surface. Reconstruction, they concluded, was the first phase in the emergence of the United States as a leading industrial and capitalist nation.

The neorevisionist school, although owing much to the revisionists, was influenced by the egalitarian emphasis of the 1940s and the period following the Second World War. Indicative of changing attitudes toward blacks was the publication in 1944 of the monumental study by Gunnar Myrdal and his associates, *An American Dilemma: The Negro Problem and Modern Democracy.* Myrdal, a distinguished Swedish sociologist, was commissioned by the Carnegie Foundation in the late 1930s to undertake a comprehensive study of black people in the United States. Although emphasizing that a variety of complex factors were responsible for the depressed condition of American blacks, Myrdal argued that the problem was basically a moral one. Americans, he wrote, held a political creed that stressed the equality of all men. This ideal, however, was constantly confronted with the inescapable reality that in the United States white citizens refused to accept blacks as their equals. Thus many Americans were caught in a dilemma between theory and practice, causing them to suffer an internal moral conflict. Myrdal's work anticipated, in part, the thinking behind the civil rights movement of the 1950s.

In evaluating events between 1865 and 1877, neorevisionist historians began to shift the focus of previous schools. The issue of equal rights for blacks, neorevisionists maintained, was not a false one, even though it was complicated by economic and other factors. In a real sense, the fundamental problem of Reconstruction was whether or not white Americans were prepared to accept the freedmen as equal partners. Even though the Radicals ultimately failed in achieving their egalitarian goals, they left an enduring legacy in the form of the Fourteenth and Fifteenth amendments. These amendments gave black people citizenship, promised them equal protection under the laws, and gave them the right to vote. That America did not honor these promises in the decades after Reconstruction in no way detracted from the idealism of those responsible for these amendments. Indeed, the importance of these amendments took on a new meaning as they gave legal sanction to civil rights after the Second World War.

Historians of the New Left, on the other hand, saw Reconstruction as a failure because Americans had not faced up to the problems arising from the end of slavery. Reflecting their own disillusionment and dissatisfaction with contemporary America, they condemned the post–Civil War generation for its failure to restructure society and thereby give blacks (and other poor groups as well) an equitable share of America's wealth. Reconstruction, they argued, represented but another unhappy chapter of American history; the past as well as the present merely revealed the widespread hypocrisy and corruption of ruling groups in the United States.

Although it is possible to demonstrate that particular interpretations grew out of and reflected their own milieu, historians must still face the larger and more important problem of determining the accuracy or inaccuracy of each interpretation.[20] Was Reconstruction, as the Dunning school argues, a tragedy for all Americans? Were the revisionists correct in stressing the achievements as well as the partial failures of this period, and emphasizing the fundamental economic factors? Were the neorevisionists justified in insisting that the major issue during Reconstruction was indeed a moral one? Or were New Left historians correct in their assessment of the general failure of Reconstruction and American society? Did the particular structural form of state and national politics preclude effective governmental action in dealing with the problems growing out of emancipation?

To answer these questions, historians must deal also with a number subsidiary issues. Should the North have forgotten that it had taken four years of bloody and expensive conflict to keep America united and welcomed the South back into the Union in 1865 with open arms? Or was it proper for Northern Republicans to lay down certain conditions to ensure that slavery, legal or implied, would never again exist within the United States? What should have been the proper policy for both the federal and state governments to follow with regard to black Americans, and how were the voices of blacks to be heard during policy formation and implementation? Were Southerners justified in their belief that blacks were incapable of caring for themselves and that their future should be left in the hands of white men? Or were the Radicals correct in insisting that blacks had to be given the same legal and political rights that all Americans enjoyed?

The answers to some of these questions will, in large measure, determine the broader interpretive framework of the Reconstruction era. Although that period is a century away from our own, some of the basic conflicts common to both remain unresolved and are as pressing as ever. Time and circumstance may have changed; new leaders may have emerged; yet the fundamental dilemma of what role black people should play in American civilization remains a controversial and crucial one.

------

[20]For a discussion and an implicit condemnation of most schools of Reconstruction historiography see Gerald N. Grob, "Reconstruction: An American Morality Play," in *American History: Retrospect and Prospect*, ed. George A. Billias and Gerald N. Grob (New York, 1971), pp. 191–231. See also Richard O. Curry, "The Civil War and Reconstruction, 1861–1877: A Critical Overview of Recent Trends and Interpretations," *Civil War History* 20 (September 1974): 215–38, and Michael Les Benedict, "Equality and Expediency in the Reconstruction Era: A Review Essay," *ibid.* 23 (December 1977): 322–35.

# Albert B. Moore

ALBERT B. MOORE (1887–1967), taught at the University of Alabama from 1923 to
1958, where he also served as Dean of the graduate school and chairman of
the Department of History. He was the author of several books on the history of the South. The selection reprinted here was his presidential address
before the Southern Historical Association in 1942.

The South has long been, and to some extent still is, in the throes of
being reconstructed by forces operating from outside the region. Ramifications of this reconstruction process account in large degree for certain
conditions in the South today and for its place in the nation. They
explain how the South has acquired a colonial status, not only in the
economic system but also in the psychology, sentiment, culture, and
politics of the nation.

While this address is concerned primarily with the reconstruction of
the South after the Civil War, it takes cognizance of the fact that the
reconstruction of the South by the North has been going on more than
one hundred years. Prior to the Civil War it took the form of a savage
attack upon slavery and Southern society, though it had other connotations. The Northeast with its western extensions, possessed of what one
writer has called "egocentric sectionalism"—that is, the conviction that
it was not a section but the whole United States and that, therefore, its
pattern of life must prevail throughout the country—undertook after
1830 to reconstruct the South into conformity and into a subordinate
position. With furious denunciations and menacing gestures and actions
it drove the South into secession and war, destroyed its power, and
reconstructed it with a vengeance and violence remarkable in the history
of human conflict. This is not to give the South a clear bill of health; but
whatever the rights and wrongs of the controversy, the Civil War,
broadly speaking, was the tragic drama of a movement to reconstruct
the South.

We have formed the habit of examining the phenomena of the reconstruction of the South after the Civil War—that is, the period 1865–
1877—in a very objective, almost casual, way and with little regard to

"One Hundred Years of Reconstruction of the South," *Journal of Southern History* 9 (May
1943): 153–65. Copyright 1943 by the Southern Historical Association. Reprinted without
footnotes by permission of the managing editor.

their essence and their significance in Southern and national history. While avoiding the emotional approach one should not forget that it was, after all, a settlement imposed by the victors in war, and should be studied in all its effects, immediate and far reaching, on its victims. An investigation of the effects on the victors themselves would also be an interesting adventure. It is a chapter in the history of the punishment of the defeated in war. The observations of a competent historian from another country, coming upon the subject for the first time, taking nothing for granted and making a critical analysis of its severity compared with the punishment of losers in wars in general, would make interesting reading.

The war set the stage for a complete reconstruction of the South. Furious hatred, politics, economic considerations, and a curious conviction that God had joined a righteous North to use it as an instrument for the purging of the wicked South gave a keen edge to the old reconstruction urge. The victories of bullets and bayonets were followed by the equally victorious attack of tongues and pens. Ministers mounted their pulpits on Easter Sunday, the day following President Lincoln's tragic death, and assured their sad auditors that God's will had been done, that the President had been removed because his heart was too merciful to punish the South as God required. An eminent New York divine assured his audience that the vice-regent of Christ, the new president, Andrew Johnson, was mandated from on high "to hew the rebels in pieces before the Lord." "So let us say," with becoming piety and sweet submissiveness he enjoined, "God's will be done." Whether the ministers thought, after they discovered that Johnson was opposed to a reign of terror, that the Lord had made a mistake is not a matter of record. As Professor Paul H. Buck has said, "It was in the churches that one found the utmost intolerance, bitterness, and unforgiveness during the sad months that followed Appomattox." Henry Ward Beecher, one of the more moderate Northern preachers, thought the South was "rotten." "No timber," said he, "grown in this cursed soil is fit for the ribs of our ship of state or for our household homes." The newspapers spread abroad the preachers' gospel of righteous vindictiveness and expounded further the idea that drastic punishment of the South was essential for the security of the Union.

Many unfriendly writers invaded the South, found what they wanted, and wrote books, articles, and editorials that strengthened the conviction that the South must be torn to pieces and made anew. Books, journals, and newspapers stimulated the impulse to be vigilant and stern, to repress and purge. A juggernaut of propaganda, stemming from the various sources of public instruction, prepared the way for the crucifixion of the South. The South of slavery and treason, of continuous outrages against the Negroes and Northerners, of haughty spirit and stubborn conviction, and of superiority complex, must be humbled and made respectable or be annihilated, so that it could never become again a strong factor in national politics.

The South did little or nothing to neutralize Radical Northern propaganda. To be sure, a few journalists, like A. T. Bledsoe, complained about "the cunningly devised fables, and the vile calumnies, with which a partisan press and a Puritanical pulpit have flooded the North," but their vituperative responses to vituperative attacks did more harm than good. There was, in the very nature of things, little that the South could do to disabuse the Radical Northern mind that was disposed to believe evil of it. There was simply no escape for Southerners from an awful scourge. Even more courage and fortitude than they had displayed on the battlefield would be required to endure what was in store for them.

As much as Reconstruction has been studied in this country it should not at this late hour be necessary to point out its severity, its permanent effects upon the South, and its influence upon various aspects of our national history. Yet few have examined critically the harshness of it and its persistent and manifold effects. While crucifying the South, the dominant Radical group of the North, thanks to the blindness of hatred, believed it was being lenient. Because no lives were taken—but there are some things more agonizing than death—for the "crimes of treason and rebellion," the North has prided itself on its magnanimity; and its historians have been strangely oblivious of property confiscations and mental tortures. It seemed to the late James Ford Rhodes "the mildest punishment ever inflicted after an unsuccessful Civil War." But this was no ordinary civil war, if indeed, it should be classed as a civil war. The thesis of leniency has oddly persisted. When the Germans protested to high heaven against the severity of the Versailles Treaty they had sympathizers in this country who compared the generosity of the North in its treatment of the South with the harshness of the Versailles Treaty. But the late Professor Carl Russell Fish of the University of Wisconsin, in his article on "The German Indemnity and the South," discredited the theory of generosity on the part of the North. He showed that the South was punished more than Germany, though he touched upon only a few phases of the South's burdens.

Professor Buck in his delightful and highly informative book, *The Road to Reunion*, recognized Reconstruction as "disorder worse than war and oppression unequalled in American annals," but made a serious error when he stated that "virtually no property" was confiscated. He overlooked the confiscation of large quantities of cotton—estimated in the minority report of the Ku Klux Klan Committee at two million bales—then selling for a very high price and most of which belonged to private citizens. The abolition of slavery wiped out about two billion dollars of capital and reduced the value of real estate by at least that amount. This was confiscation of property, and the repudiation of Confederate currency, the Confederate bonded debt, and the war debts of the states, all amounting to no less than $3 billion, was confiscation of property rights. As inevitable as much of this was, it represented a frightful confiscation of property.

The freeing of the slaves not only cost the South $2 billion but it also forced upon that section an economic and social revolution. It subverted a mode of life almost as old as the South itself. The repudiation of its debts impoverished the South and destroyed its financial relationships. While the South lost its debts, it had to pay its full share of the Northern debts which amounted to about four-fifths of the total Northern war expenses. The money for this debt was spent in the North for its upbuilding. It paid also its share of the $20 million returned by the federal treasury to the Northern states for direct taxes collected from them during the war, and of extravagant pensions to Union soldiers. Professor James Sellers estimates that the South paid in these ways an indemnity of at least a billion dollars to the North.

The South accepted the results of the war—the doom of slavery and the doctrine of secession—as inevitable and its leaders sought to restore their respective states as speedily as possible to their normal position in the Union. But despite its acceptance in good faith of the declared aims of the North, the South was forced through the gauntlet of two plans of Reconstruction. The people conformed in good faith to the requirements of President Johnson's plan, but Congress repudiated this plan and forced the South to begin *de novo* the process of Reconstruction. Pending its restoration, it was put under the heel of military authority, though there was no problem that exceeded the power of civil authority to handle. Objectively viewed, it is a singular fact that it took three years to restore the South to the Union. It is little short of amazing that for a dozen years after the war federal troops were stationed in the South among an orderly people who had played a leading role in the building and guidance of the nation since colonial times, and who now sought nothing so much as peace and surcease from strife. For much of the period government was a hodgepodge of activities by the civil authorities, the army, and the Freedmen's Bureau, with the president of the United States working through any or all of these agencies. Most of the serious problems of government were precipitated by outside influences and conspiracies.

The political enfranchisement of four million Negroes, from whose necks the yoke of slavery had just been lifted, is the most startling fact about Reconstruction, and a fact of tremendous impact in Southern history. There is nothing in the history of democracy comparable to it. To give the Negroes the ballot and office—ranging from constable to governor—and the right to sit in state legislatures and in Congress, while depriving their former masters of their political rights and the South of its trained leadership, is one of the most astounding facts in the history of reconstruction after war. It was a stroke of fanatical vengeance and design. The basic purpose of this sort of political reconstruction was to vouchsafe for the North—while chastising the South—the future control of the nation through the Republican party. The South was never again to be allowed to regain the economic and political position which it had occupied in the nation prior to 1860.

Negro voting laid the basis for the carpetbag regime. For eight years Radical Northern leaders, backed by the Washington authorities and the army and aided by some native whites, pillaged and plundered and finished wrecking the South. Northern teachers who invaded the South to reconstruct its educational and social system, and Northern preachers who came down to restore the unity of the churches by a reconstruction formula that required Southerners to bend the knee and confess their sins helped the politicians, the Freedmen's Bureau, and the Loyal League to undermine the Negroes' confidence in their white neighbors. The reconstruction policy of the churches did its part in stirring up both racial and sectional enmities. The *Nation* remarked, in 1879, the "Churches are doing their full share in causing permanent division." Reconstruction affected the religious life of the country for fifty years and more after the Radicals were overthrown. The character of the carpetbag-scalawag-Negro governments was well stated by the *New York Herald* which said the South is "to be governed by blacks spurred on by worse than blacks. . . . This is the most abominable phase barbarism has assumed since the dawn of civilization. . . . It is not right to make slaves of white men even though they have been former masters of blacks. This is but a change in a system of bondage that is rendered the more odious and intolerable because it has been inaugurated in an enlightened instead of a dark and uncivilized age."

It would be safe to say that the people of the North never understood how the South suffered during the Radical regime. The Radicals who controlled most of the organs of public opinion were in no attitude of mind to listen to Southern complaints, and most people were too busy with the pursuit of alluring business opportunities that unfolded before them to think much of what was going on down South. In some respects conditions in the South at the end of the Radical regime remind one of the plight of the Germans at the end of the Thirty Years' War.

The South staggered out of the Reconstruction, which ended *officially* in 1877, embittered, impoverished, encumbered with debt, and discredited by Radical propaganda. It had won after many frightful years the right to govern itself again, but there were still white men who could not vote and for many years there was danger of the federal regulation of elections and a resurgence of Negro power in politics.

The tax load had been devastating. The lands of thousands upon thousands had been sold for taxes. Huge state and local debts, much of which was fraudulent, had been piled up. So many bonds, legal and illegal, had been sold that public credit was destroyed. The people stood, like the servant of Holy Writ, ten thousand talents in debt with not one farthing to pay. They had to solve the paradoxical problem of scaling down public debts—a bewildering compound of legal and illegal and far too large to be borne—while restoring public credit. Northern hands had imposed the debts and Northern hands held the repudiated bonds. Repudiation became another source of misunderstanding between the sections and another basis for charges of "Southern outrages."

Reconstruction profoundly and permanently affected the political life of the South. It gave the South the one-party system. The white people rallied around the Democratic party standards to overthrow the Radical regime, and their continued cooperation was necessary to prevent the Negroes from acquiring again the balance of power in politics. The terrible record of the Republican party during the Radical regime was an insuperable obstacle to its future success in the South. Hostility toward this party promoted devotion to the Democratic party. The complete domination of the latter party not only invested Southern politics with the disadvantages of the one-party system, but proved to be costly to the South in national politics. The Democratic party has been out of power most of the time in national politics and the Republican party naturally has not felt under obligation to do much for the South when it has had control of the national government. Even when the Democratic party has been in power the South has not had its share of patronage and appropriations, or of consideration in the formulation of national policies. The inequitable distribution of federal relief funds between the states since 1930 is an illustration in point. Political expediency has been the controlling consideration and not gratitude for party loyalty, which calls to mind an old Virginian's definition of political gratitude. Political gratitude, he said, is a lively appreciation of favors yet to be received.

Radical Reconstruction corrupted Southern politics, and the prejudice aroused against Negro participation in politics led ultimately to the disfranchisement of most of the Negroes. Political habits formed in counteracting carpetbag machinations and the presence of Negro voters continued to influence politics. Fraudulent methods were employed to control the Negro votes and when factions appeared among the whites they employed against each other the chicanery and frauds which they had used against the Radicals.

Reconstruction contributed to the proscription of the South in national politics and to provincialism in Southern politics. Southerners so feared a recrudescence of Reconstruction in some form or other that for a generation they generally shrank from active participation in national affairs. Their attitude, generally speaking, was that if the North would leave them alone it could direct national affairs. This begat provincialism and made the continued proscription of the South easier. Such a situation was not good for either the South or the North.

Race friction and prejudice were engendered by Reconstruction, which was an unfortunate thing for both races and especially for the Negroes. It caused greater discriminations against the Negroes in politics and education, and in other ways. The Negroes had been so pampered and led as to arouse false notions and hopes among them and to make them for many years lame factors in the rebuilding of the South. The Negro after Reconstruction, and in large degree because of it, continued and continues to be a source of division between the North and South. The North either could not or would not understand the necessity of race segregation, and the idea that the Negro must have a definite place in the scheme of life was obnoxious. Disfranchisement of the Negro, occasional race riots, and the sporadic mobbing of Negroes accused of heinous crimes gave rise to continued charges of "Southern outrages." Criticisms from the North, generally based upon a lack of understanding of the problem, seemed more a matter of censure than of true interest in the Negro. Thus, those who expected to see sectional strife over the status of the Negro disappear with the emancipation of the slaves were disillusioned.

The Negro has been the cause of more misunderstanding and conflict between the sections than all things else. The North freed the Negro from slavery but by repressing and exploiting the South it has contributed much to conditions that have deprived him of some of the opportunities that a free man should have. If Southern whites have suffered the pangs and restraints of poverty, the lot of the Negro has inevitably been worse. The shackles upon the Negro's economic and cultural advancement have been formidable and deadening in their effects. Their inescapable lack of educational opportunities has been epitomized by the saying that the South has had the impossible task of educating two races out of the poverty of one.

In some respects the South has not pursued an enlightened policy toward the Negro. In ways it has exploited him. In the struggle for existence the Negro too often has been overlooked. Prejudice, too, resulting to a large extent from Reconstruction experiences, has done its part. Southerners, determined that the political control of Negroes back in the old Reconstruction days shall not be repeated, and probably too apprehensive about the breaking down of social barriers between the two races, have been conservative and slow to see adjustments that need to be made and can be made for the good of both races. Northerners with little information, but sure of their superior understanding, have scolded and denounced after the fashion of the old abolitionists.

They have protested and cast sweeping aspersions without making constructive suggestions or troubling themselves to procure information upon which such suggestions could be based. Occasional violence against Negroes by ignorant mobs and discriminations against the Negroes in the enforcement of laws have evoked brutal and indiscriminating attacks from the Northern press that remind one of journalism in the old Reconstruction days. Needless to say, such criticisms have contributed nothing to the Southern Negro's welfare or to national unity.

The growing political power of the Negro in the North is adding to the Negro problem in the South. Many Northern politicians to gain the political support of the Northern Negroes—and, eventually, those of the South—are now supporting radical Negro leaders in their demand for a sweeping change in the status of the Negro in the South. But efforts to subvert the social system of the South will lead to more friction between the North and South and to bitter racial antagonisms.

The impoverishment of the people by Reconstruction and the heavy debt load imposed by it were most serious impediments to progress. They hindered economic advancement and educational achievement. Vast hordes of children grew to maturity unable even to read and write. It is impossible to measure the cost to the South of illiteracy alone resulting from the war and Reconstruction. Conditions brought about by Reconstruction also caused a tremendous loss of manpower. They caused a large exodus of the white people of the South to diverse parts, and made the Negroes unfit to apply their productive powers. The loss of whites is well illustrated by Professor Walter L. Fleming's statement that Alabama lost more manpower in Recontruction than it lost in the war.

The poverty attending Reconstruction laid the basis for the crop lien system and promoted sharecropping, and these more than all things else have hindered rural progress. Hundreds of thousands of both the landless and the landed had nothing with which to start life over and the only source of credit was cotton. Merchants, with the assistance of eastern creditors, advanced supplies to farmers upon condition that they would produce cotton in sufficient quantity to cover the advances made to them. The merchant charged whatever prices he chose to and protected himself by taking a lien upon the cotton produced. Under the system the great mass of farmers became essentially serfs. To throw off the shackles required more resources than most of them possessed.

Even at present a majority of Southern tenant farmers depend for credit on their landlords, or on the "furnish merchants" for their supplies. The landlord, moreover, who stakes all on cotton or tobacco, is a bad credit risk. For this reason he pays interest rates as high as 20 percent, and naturally his tenants pay more. It has been estimated that those who depend on the merchant for supplies pay as much as 30 percent interest even on food and feed supplies. Credit unions and the

Farm Security and Farm Credit Administrations have helped many of the farmers, but farm credit facilities are still sadly lacking in the South. Louis XIV's remark that "Credit supports agriculture, as the rope supports the hanged" has been abundantly verified in the South.

Thus, Reconstruction made a large contribution to the development of a slumfolk class in the rural South. The sharecropper-crop-lien farm economy of the South has produced a human erosion system more costly than soil erosion. In fact the two have gone hand in hand. These things always come to mind when in this day of national championships the South is referred to as the nation's "Economic Problem No. 1."

Reconstruction and its aftermath prevented the flow of population and money into the South. The 37 million increase in population between 1870 and 1900 was largely in the North. The South's increase, except in Florida and Texas, was principally native and, as has been observed, it lost part of this increment. Northerners who moved and the millions of Europeans who came in either flocked to the industrial centers of the North or settled down on expansive fertile lands between Ohio and Kansas, made available by the Homestead Act. Most of the nation's capital and credit resources were put into railroad building and industrial and business pursuits north of the Mason and Dixon line. By 1890 the railroad pattern was laid and most of the roads had been built to feed the North. In every phase of economic activity the South was a bad risk compared with the North. Not the least of the things that kept men and money out of the South were its debt load and the stigma of debt repudiation. Northern newspapers and journals lambasted the South for the sin of repudiation and warned investors and emigrants to shun the South. In addition to other risks, they would find, the *Nation* said, that in the South the "Sense of good faith is benumbed, if not dead," and if they had anything to do with the South they would make themselves a part "of a community of swindlers." Even Henry Clews, who had conspired with the carpetbag racketeers to sell shoddy Reconstruction bonds to gullible buyers in the North and Europe, railed out against the spectacle of "Southern robbery." The notion of Southern depravity was long-lived.

Between 1865 and 1900 a new republic of tremendous wealth and productive power was forged and concurrently there was a great educational development and a general advance in culture throughout the North. The South was a mere appendage to the new nation advancing through these epochal transformations; Reconstruction had assigned it a colonial status in all its relations with the North. J. M. Cross of New York City, for example, wrote to John Letcher of Virginia on March 8, 1867, that "Northern civilization must go all the way over the South, which is only a question of time." Some of those who had wanted to make the Northern way of life the national way lived to see their wish a *fait accompli.* The patterns of national life were forming and henceforth were to be formed in the North and national unity was to be achieved by the conformity of the South to these patterns. Northerners have made little or no distinction between the North and the nation. The idea has become deeply imbedded throughout the country. For example, Professor Buck unconsciously expresses this attitude when he says, "The small farm worked in countless ways to bring Southern life into closer harmony with the major trends in national life"—that is, Northern life. The same idea is carried in one of the chapter titles—"Nationalization of the South"—in Professor William B. Hesseltine's recent *History of the South.* When the South has failed to conform it has been stigmatized as backward, provincial, and sectional.

By 1900 the Old South was largely a thing of memory. Yearning for some of the good things of life, impulsive young men rejected antebellum traditions as inadequate to the needs of the New South which must be built. They sneered at "mummies," "mossbacks," and "Bourbons" who cherished the Old South. Others, just as avid about the future of business and industry, hoped to bring over into the New South of their dreams the best of the old and thus merge "two distinct civilizations" into a compound that some good day would surpass anything the North could show. They would leaven the lump of crass materialism with the leaven of graceful living. But to the older generation it seemed that those who were breaking loose from old moorings were bending "the knee to expediency" with little or no regard for principle.

# Allen W. Trelease

ALLEN W. TRELEASE (1928–      ) is professor of history at the University of North
Carolina, Greensboro. He is the author of several books, including *Indian
Affairs in Colonial New York: The Seventeenth Century* (1960), *Reconstruction: The
Great Experiment* (1971), and *White Terror: The Ku Klux Klan Conspiracy and
Southern Reconstruction* (1971).

After promoting for a generation and more the idea of innate Negro
inferiority in order to justify slavery, Southerners could hardly be expected suddenly to abandon it with the coming of emancipation, especially in the wake of military defeat. The newly freed slave, regarded as
occupying an intermediate stage between humanity and the lower orders of animal life, fell into a niche already prepared for him—that of the
antebellum free Negro. As such, he was not a citizen and had no civil or
political rights except those which the white community deemed proper
to confer. "He still served, we still ruled," as Cable pointed out a few
years later; "all need of holding him in private bondage was dis-
proved. . . . Emancipation had destroyed private, but it had not disturbed public, subjugation. The ex-slave was not a free man; he was
only a free Negro." In effect Negroes were now the slaves of every white
man. As subordination and discipline had been enforced by the lash
before, it continued to be so now, but without the restraining influence
of the slaveholder's self-interest. "The pecuniary value which the individual negro formerly represented having disappeared," Carl Schurz
reported in 1865, "the maiming and killing of colored men seems to be
looked upon by many as one of those venial offenses which must be
forgiven to the outraged feelings of a wronged and robbed people."
Most whites, he said, appeared to believe that Negroes existed for the
special purpose of providing for their needs. If Schurz exaggerated, the
history of the Ku Klux Klan will show that he did not do so very much.
Certainly whipping and corporal punishment were regarded as the white
man's right and duty, emancipation or no emancipation; organized reg-

ulators or vigilantes took up this task with the advent of emancipation, and the Klan further institutionalized the practice.

Negroes often suffered by their liberation.

> As a slave [a Mississippi official pointed out in 1871], the negro was protected on account of his value; humanity went hand in hand with the interest of the owner to secure his protection, to prevent his being overworked, underfed, insufficiently clothed, or abused, or neglected when sick. But as a free man, he was deprived of all the protection which had been given to him by his value as property; he was reduced to something like the condition of a stray dog.

For all the talk of white suffering during the Reconstruction era, it was the black man who experienced the greatest deprivation and mistreatment, first and last. But it was a rare freedman who regretted emancipation; stories to the contrary could almost invariably be traced to white men's rationalizations of slavery.

Negroes wanted the same freedom that white men enjoyed, with equal prerogatives and opportunities. The educated black minority emphasized civil and political rights more than the masses, who called most of all for land and schools. In an agrarian society, the only kind most of them knew, landownership was associated with freedom, respectability, and the good life. It was almost universally desired by Southern blacks, as it was by landless peasants the world over. Give us our land and we can take care of ourselves, said a group of South Carolina Negroes to a Northern journalist in 1865; without land the old masters can hire us or starve us as they please. A major failure of Reconstruction was that, except for a favored few, they never got it. Not only did they lack money or credit, but the government made no substantial effort to help them obtain it. Whites in many areas refused to sell, or even rent land to Negroes when they did not have the means to buy, and often actively conspired to keep them from acquiring it. Negro landownership would have enhanced the economic and social well-being of the entire section, but it smacked too much of equality and independence. Some Negroes who did acquire farms of their own were driven off by mobs or the Ku Klux Klan. A Negro state senator in Florida believed that there was a general understanding among whites to deprive blacks of a great part of the income and property they had rightfully acquired. In many places this was correct.

The desire for education was reflected in the avidity with which blacks of all ages took advantage of the limited schooling made available to them immediately after the war. Knowledge and literacy too were associated with freedom. Some of this enthusiasm was transitory, particularly among the elders, but parents continued to send their children to schools, where they existed, and to cry for their establishment where they did not.

Although a minority of Negroes moved to town—occasionally driven there by white terrorism—the overwhelming majority stayed on the land as wage laborers and sharecroppers. There was little motivation to work harder than they had under slavery. Many whites repeated the stock attitudes regarding Negro character: they were lazy, irresponsible, wasteful, and careless of property; they procrastinated, lacked forethought or perseverance, and derived no satisfaction from a job well done; they engaged in petty thievery and had no sense whatever of right and wrong or truth and falsehood. These characterizations were valid in varying measure—the natural defense mechanisms generated by a life of slavery. One well-disposed Northerner trying to cope with a Georgia cotton plantation reiterated nearly all of these traits from experience with his own laborers, but pointed out that the one thing which seemed to overcome Negro heedlessness was the desire to own their own land. Native Southerners admitted, however, that Negroes were performing far better than they had had any reason to expect at emancipation. A few proclaimed Negro labor the best in the world. The truth seems to be that, after a brief exultation with the idea of freedom, Negroes realized that their position was hardly changed; they continued to live and work much as they had before.

But white men generally agreed on the Negroes' good behavior after the war, and it was for many a matter of pleasant surprise; they had assumed that slavery alone could keep the blacks in good order. Most freedmen were as submissive and deferential to white men as before the war. The great majority were totally dependent upon white favor for a livelihood, and self-interest dictated subservience as a matter of second nature. If some aggressive souls—usually a minority of younger Negroes and other free spirits—talked back or refused to give up the sidewalk, this "insolence" was rare. Seldom were Negroes willing to stand up to a white man and resist or defy him to his face; those who did automatically incurred the wrath of the white community, and risked their lives. Concerted resistance was almost never successful and was apt to prove fatal. Whites were more numerous in most areas, and better armed. More important, they were used to commanding and the blacks to obeying. Next to poverty and economic dependence, this was the freedman's greatest handicap in asserting real freedom during the Reconstruction era.

When Negroes did strike back or defy the master race it was more often the product of impetuosity and extreme aggravation than forethought and planning. Whites commonly ascribed Negro violence, whether directed against them or (more often) among the blacks themselves, as the product of a congenitally passionate nature. The blacks were like children, it was said, who flared up without thought of consequences and then almost as quickly subsided. Negroes seemingly committed fewer murders than whites in proportion to their number, and most of these were crimes of passion in which other Negroes were the victims. Certainly black men were more often the victims than the perpetrators of interracial violence.

A partial exception to the rule of Negro passivity was the crime of arson. The fires almost invariably occurred at night, with barns, gin houses, and other outbuildings the chief targets, and the culprits were seldom discovered. This was, in fact, one of the few relatively safe ways Negroes had of evening the score with white terrorism, although the fire victims were not always those guilty of the terror. Whites frequently imagined incendiary plots when there were none, just as they had long imagined servile insurrections.

But the chief crime complained of was petty thievery. Most thefts occurred after dark, with no witnesses, and it was almost impossible to discover the culprits. Cotton and corn were stolen from the fields, hams were abducted from smokehouses, tools and equipment disappeared from sheds and barns. Occasionally cows, sheep, and hogs were stolen and slaughtered. Some planters who had raised their own meat supplies before the war now gave up trying to keep livestock. Negro larceny, too, was a legacy of slavery: a poverty-stricken people, systematically denied the fruits of their labors and having no property of their own to consider sacred, appropriated what they needed to make life more livable. . . .

Whites of every class united in opposition to what they called social equality—a completely integrated society—as leading inevitably to intermarriage and degeneration of the white race. In that event, a South Carolinian declared, "we shall become a race of mulattoes . . . another Mexico; we shall be ruled out from the family of white nations. . . . It is a matter of life and death with the Southern people to keep their blood pure." A Republican of Georgia pointed out, "If you talk about equality, they at once conclude that you must take the negro into your parlor or into your bed—everywhere that you would take your wife. They seem to be diseased upon that subject. They do not seem to consider that he is merely to be equal before the law, but take it, I suppose designedly, to mean equality in the broadest sense; and hence they stir themselves up and lash themselves into a fury about it."

Emancipation increased the Southern white rape complex because freedom presumably stimulated the Negro's innate passion for white women and removed external restraints. This was the supreme taboo, which evoked white supremacy in its most virulent form. Whether or

not Negro rape of white women actually increased during Reconstruction, it certainly was not widespread; more important was the fact that
whites *thought* it was on the increase. The only penalty sufficient to
deter the tendency was violent and speedy death—lynching without the
delay and dignity of formal trial. The *Fayetteville* (Tennessee) *Observer*
echoed widespread opinion when it condoned the lynching of an alleged
Negro rapist in 1868: "The community said amen to the act—it was just
and right. We know not who did it, whether Ku Klux or the immediate
neighbors, but we feel that they were only the instruments of Divine
vengeance in carrying out His holy and immutable decrees." Here too
the Ku Klux Klan helped to institutionalize a practice which preceded
and long outlived it.

The physical and psychological necessities of keeping Negroes in
subordination led to the wildest inconsistencies of attitude and expression. On the one hand the black man was best fitted by nature and
temperament for a life of servility and happiest in his carefree dependence on white protectors. On the other hand he was only a degree
removed from the wild beasts of the jungle, and the most constant
surveillance was needed to keep him from bursting the bonds of discipline and turning upon his friends and protectors in a bloody insurrection. The first theory was necessary to rationalize slavery and the ensuing peonage, but as it never fully squared with the facts, the second
argument served to justify necessary repressive measures. Both reinforced Negro subordinance. . . .

Northern Reconstruction policy evolved against this background of
myths and realities. Again, the race question was crucial. The North
began fighting the Civil War to defeat secession and ended by abolishing
slavery as well. Emancipation brought the unavoidable problem of defining the freedmen's status. Northern Democrats generally shared the
racial views of the white South and sanctioned the most minimal adjustments required by the ending of legal servitude. This was also the
tendency of Abraham Lincoln and of Andrew Johnson afterward. Most
Republicans fell between this conservatism and the Radicals' advocacy
of full legal and political equality at war's end, but they were gradually
driven toward egalitarianism by the course of events between 1865 and
1867. And as theirs was the majority party in the North, that drift determined federal government policy.

Lincoln had assumed the right to reorganize the South and guide her
back into the Union, largely on his own authority as commander in
chief. During the war, therefore, he sponsored new Loyal, or Unionist,
state governments in Virginia, Tennessee, Louisiana, and Arkansas.
Following Appomattox and Lincoln's death, Andrew Johnson took
advantage of a congressional recess to organize the remaining seven

states of the late Confederacy. Seemingly all that remained was for Congress to seat the senators and representatives chosen under these governments. But Congress delayed and ultimately refused to do so.

While the Lincoln and Johnson regimes were dominated in the South by men who had taken a back seat in the secession movement, or opposed it altogether, and who accepted the end of slavery as a price of military defeat, they subscribed as a matter of course to the view that white men must continue to rule in the South. To this end they enacted a series of Black Codes in 1865 and 1866 which clearly and deliberately relegated the Negro to a second-class citizenship. No state extended the right to vote to black men, even to the few who might be educated or well-to-do. Nor was any hope extended for equality someday in the future.

When new horizons did open up for the Negro, as they soon did, it was because of the Republican majority in Congress. Just as the war closed, Congress created a Bureau of Refugees, Freedmen, and Abandoned Lands, attached to the Army, primarily to care for the newly freed black population. The Freedmen's Bureau, as it was called, always suffered from inadequate funds and personnel to perform the tasks assigned it, but the services it did provide were indispensable. Under the direction of General O. O. Howard it distributed food and clothing to those of both races who needed them, protected Negroes against the most blatant forms of exploitation and mistreatment, arranged labor contracts with employers, and attempted with some success to enforce these contracts against infractions on either side. It established hospitals, schools, and colleges for its black charges with the cooperation of Northern charitable agencies.

The bureau represented an unprecedented extension of federal authority, regulating the economic, social, and legal affairs of individual persons within the respective states. Intended as an emergency device to cope with wartime and immediate postwar conditions, it was due to expire a year after the war ended. But the needs it was created to meet showed no sign of disappearing. Negroes were continually subjected to exploitation, discrimination, and outright violence, which they were powerless to combat alone. The new state governments not only failed to protect them or to assume the educational and other responsibilities of the Freedmen's Bureau, but their Black Codes actually perpetuated many of the hallmarks of slavery. So far as the Northern war effort had become a crusade to free the slaves, the victory seemed in danger of becoming undone. Thus the Republicans pushed through Congress in July 1866, over President Johnson's veto, a law continuing the bureau for two years more.

In the same spirit were the Civil Rights Act and its sequel, the Fourteenth Amendment, which the Republican majority enacted over the

President's objections in April and June of 1866. The former measure defined United States citizenship to include Negroes and extended to them the basic civil rights to sue and to testify in the courts, to hold and convey property, and most importantly, to enjoy equal benefit of the laws with white people. The Fourteenth Amendment, which was ratified and went into effect in 1868, incorporated the provisions of the Civil Rights Act into the Constitution; it also set forth a program for Southern Reconstruction which represented a compromise between the quick restoration favored by the white South and President Johnson and the stricter requirements (such as Negro suffrage) advocated by Radical Republicans. . . .

A basic assumption behind the Reconstruction acts was that the Negro freedmen would support congressional Reconstruction and would vote for the party which had freed them and granted them civil rights and the ballot. The assumption proved sound, for Negroes backed the Republican party overwhelmingly as long as they had the chance to do so. In fact they provided the bulk of the Republican electorate; in most states white supporters were more important for their leadership than for their numbers. No matter how dependent the freedmen were upon their former masters, or how much they continued to trust and confide in them as individuals, only a tiny minority of Uncle Toms willingly cast their ballots for the party of white supremacy.

Negroes were elected to office in every state, leading Conservatives in moments of bitter abandon to characterize the whole policy as one of "Negro rule," an accusation made partly for political effect but also arising from the common conviction that racial sovereignty was indivisible. If whites did not rule blacks, it must therefore be the other way around. The charge of Negro rule was absurd, for blacks never held office in proportion to their total number and they rarely held the most prominent posts. This situation resulted in part from the race prejudice which white Republicans shared, or which they sought to appease in nominating attractive party slates. But equally important was the plain fact that slavery was a poor training ground for the responsibilities of public office. The quality of those Negro officeholders high and low who did pass the barrier was not notably better or worse than that of white men who held comparable posts at that time, before, or later. Some, especially in the lower levels, were illiterate, but so were some of their white counterparts of both parties. Incompetent and illiterate officials did not begin or end with Reconstruction, nor were they typical of that period.

The so-called carpetbaggers—Northerners who settled in the South during and after the war and affiliated with the Republican party—were only a tiny minority numerically. They had great influence, however, particularly in the deep South where the Negro population was heavy and there was no significant native white Republican element to provide leadership. The term *carpetbagger* was another canard. These men supposedly descended on the South like a swarm of locusts, bringing no more than they could carry in a carpetbag; their purpose was to prey on the defenseless region through political manipulation of the gullible freedmen. Actually most of these persons moved South by 1866, well before Radical Reconstruction was conceived or the Republican party was even organized in most of the South. Some were stationed there by the Army or Freedmen's Bureau, but most moved South for the same reasons of economic betterment that led greater numbers to go West. When the Republican party was organized and new governments were in process of formation these men filled a need for educated and occasionally experienced leadership. In fact, they usually raised the caliber of Radical government rather than lowering it. Of course, their motives, abilities, and accomplishments ran the usual human scale; along with the incompetent or corrupt there were honest and highly able men whom posterity would have celebrated under other circumstances. Active Republicans required a tough skin and often great physical courage to withstand the social ostracism, economic boycott, verbal abuse, character assassination, and physical violence to which they were commonly subjected by Southern whites. In a few cases at least, this courage was inspired by a high degree of dedication. "That I should have taken a political office seems almost inexplicable," wrote General Adelbert Ames a quarter-century after he had been forced out of the governorship of Mississippi:

> My explanation may seem ludicrous now, but then, it seemed to me that I had a Mission with a large M. Because of my [earlier] course as Military Governor, the colored men of the State had confidence in me and I was convinced that I could help to guide them successfully, keep men of doubtful integrity from control, and the more certainly accomplish what was every patriots' [*sic*] wish, the enfranchisement of the colored men and the pacification of the country.

Men of Northern origin were to be found in local and subordinate offices here and there, and they served conspicuously in Congress, as governors, and in other high offices.

The native white Republicans—scalawags to their enemies—were drawn from every walk of Southern life. Some had been Democrats and others were Whigs before the war. A few had served the Confederacy in conspicuous fashion, but most were wartime Unionists; the more uncompromising their Unionism had been, the more apt they were to embrace the Republican party afterward. Although they could be found at least as isolated examples, throughout the South, most white Republican voters were concentrated in the hilly and mountainous regions where slavery had gained little foothold. The Appalachian highlands from western Virginia to northern Alabama and the Ozark Mountains of Arkansas were the major strongholds of white Republicanism during Reconstruction and for generations afterward. The term *scalawag* was of course another form of political abuse; the personal character of Southern Republicans did not suffer by comparison with their accusers. Many joined the Republican party because it was the Unionist party and it opposed the planter interest as they themselves had done for years. Most of them shared in some measure the racial views common to the white South, and this helped make the Republican coalition unstable, but for the most part they lived in regions where the Negro was hardly more of a factor locally than in the North. In such places they commonly filled all of the political offices and supplied nearly all of the Republican votes. At the state level, particularly in the upper South, they filled many of the higher offices as well. A few members of the antebellum ruling class, usually ex-Whigs who had not been enthusiastic secessionists, also joined the Republican party, hoping to hold it to a moderate course and exercise a paternalistic rein on the Negroes while profiting by their strength at the polls. Such men carried great prestige and were given some of the highest offices in an effort to make the party more appealing to the white population generally, but the number of these converts was small. Governor James L. Alcorn of Mississippi belonged to this class, as did former governors Lewis E. Parsons of Alabama and James L. Orr of South Carolina.

In terms of ideology, Republicans were clearly the democratic party of the Reconstruction South. Unquestionably there was an element of political expediency involved in the raising of Negroes to civil equality with white men, but a great many believed in it as a matter of principle. The *Charleston Daily Republican*, a voice of moderation and a critic of corruption and ineptitude within the party in South Carolina, attacked Democratic predictions that white men must at some near day control the state again.

> Such talk is as wickedly idle as for colored men to say that their race shall have complete control. It is not to be a matter of race at all. It is to be a matter of citizenship, in which colored and white are to have their rights and their due share of power; not because they are white, not because they are colored, but because they are American citizens. By-and-by we shall stop talking of the color of a man in relation to citizenship and power, and shall look at his wealth of mind and soul.

Radicalism was also aimed less spectacularly at raising the status of poorer whites. Within limits the Republican party was a poor man's party which sought to obliterate racial lines as much as popular prejudice made it politically safe to do. Democrats defeated the effort, as they later did when the Populists tried it, by crying "nigger"; most Southern whites placed white supremacy above all other issues.

Many public offices which had been appointive were now made elective, sometimes at the cost of efficiency. In some states, but not all, more home rule was extended, making local government more responsive to local wishes and less subject to central control. Property qualifications for officeholding, where they still existed in 1867, were removed. Legislatures were reapportioned to provide more equal representation, although Negro counties in some states were slighted. By far the most important democratic extension was the granting of Negro suffrage. This had been required by the Reconstruction acts, and it was incorporated in all the new constitutions.

The only exception to universal manhood suffrage lay in the partial and temporary disfranchisement of ex-Confederates. This provision had been written into the Reconstruction acts to help ensure further that the new state governments would be organized by Unionists, but state law governed the matter thereafter. Where disfranchisement survived as a significant factor—in Tennessee and Arkansas—Republicans felt themselves outnumbered and regarded it as a continuing necessity to keep the former rebels and the Democratic party from taking control. However dubious this policy may have been in those states, a free and unfettered majority rule permitted Republican victories in most states, and disfranchisement was abandoned either at once or very soon. Much the same was true of eligibility for public office, which was more nearly determined by federal law. By 1872 Congress had removed the disqualifications of all but a relative handful of ex-Confederate leaders. The Radical governments made no effort to outlaw the Conservative opposition or create a dictatorship. On the contrary, they were too lenient in enforcing law and order against those who used force to overthrow them.

There was corruption, electoral as well as financial, in nearly every state during the period of Republican control. Conservatives at the time succeeded in pinning on the Radical regimes a blanket charge of dishonesty which has never worn off, but the actual picture was not so simple. Corruption was rampant throughout the country after the war, and Democrats North and South were about as guilty as Republicans. The Tweed Ring in New York City supposedly stole more than all Southern politicians combined, if only because New York had more to steal. Within the South corruption varied widely from state to state. It flourished most in South Carolina, where it had been comparatively unknown, and in Louisiana, where it was endemic. In South Carolina the Republicans at least partially cleaned their own house under Governor Chamberlain after 1874. In Louisiana both parties were corrupt and remained so for generations. In Mississippi an honest Republican administration gave way to less honest Democratic regimes after 1875. During the period of Republican control, moreover, minority Democratic officials were sometimes as venal as their Republican counterparts, and Democratic businessmen sometimes offered the bribes that Republicans accepted. In the matter of electoral, as opposed to fiscal, corruption generalization is easier. Republicans were occasionally guilty of manipulating election returns, but these practices paled in comparison with the massive campaigns of fraud and intimidation, symbolized by the Ku Klux Klan, with which Democrats sought to return to power in nearly every state. It was largely owing to these methods that they did assume power in one state after another during the 1870s. . . .

Radical egalitarianism for the Negro was primarily political and legal, but it also extended to economic and social matters. Republican governments repealed nearly all of the earlier laws requiring racial discrimination, and in some states it was specifically forbidden. A few states enacted laws to prevent racial segregation in railroad cars, theaters, restaurants, and hotels, but compliance was never complete and actual practice varied widely. It is mistaken to say that segregation did not begin until well after Reconstruction, although positive laws requiring it certainly were hostile to Republican policy. Both constitutional and legal enactments guaranteed racial equality before the law.

The greatest and most enduring achievement of the Radical governments was the establishment of a functioning public school system for the first time in Southern history. As in politics, the greatest change lay in the fact that Negroes were included in the new dispensation. Building on the work of the Freedmen's Bureau and various charitable agencies before 1868, they created school systems which could not compare with most of those in the North, but which represented a great accomplishment in the light of Southern traditions and resources. Straitened finances and the difficulty of securing qualified teachers plagued the new school systems in every state. Economy was hampered further by the fact that almost everywhere separate schools were established for the two races—Negroes seldom demanded integrated facilities, which were opposed even by most white Republicans. Often churches or other buildings were converted to school purposes, and many schools were erected by groups of individuals on their own initiative, sometimes, in the case of Negro schools, with financial aid from interested whites. Local whites served as teachers of both white and Negro schools; literate Negroes also taught in Negro schools, as did white men and women from the North. Most who taught in Negro schools did so at the price of social ostracism and sometimes physical danger; they required a high degree of dedication and a high resistance to poverty, given the pay scales. The new state governments provided support for higher education for both races. In some cases this meant the creation of Negro colleges and universities, and in others it entailed efforts, largely unsuccessful, to desegregate existing institutions.

New hospitals, orphanages, insane asylums, poorhouses, and other institutions were created, and older facilities enlarged. Jails and penitentiaries were built on a larger scale than before. Negro emancipation had rendered all of this necessary, for as slaves they had been under the wardship of their masters and rarely used public facilities. Moreover, the Radicals were somewhat readier than their predecessors to assume public responsibility for the welfare of citizens of both races, in many respects adopting attitudes and precedents which had been gaining headway in the North for a generation or more but which had lagged in the South.

The Radical regimes generally shared the old Whig-Republican willingness to use government power to stimulate business activity and economic growth, especially in the field of transportation. As elsewhere in the country, the major beneficiaries of public aid were railroads, although a good deal of money was spent on roads, bridges, levees, and other public works. These projects were expensive, taken collectively, and some states assumed greater debts than the returns justified. Everywhere, North and South, politics and personal profiteering motivated some of these expenditures. For the most part, however, they were relatively sound, and in the South they decidedly enhanced the region's economic growth and prosperity. Some of the projects were essential to repair wartime deterioration and destruction.

Radical governments did comparatively little to alter the conditions of labor or raise the incomes of citizens of either race; no governments did in nineteenth-century America. The Freedmen's Bureau continued most of its operations through 1868 and then gradually closed down because of congressional nonsupport, suspending altogether in 1872. This was a misfortune, especially for the Negroes, as the state governments lacked the funds, personnel, and legal power to advise and protect them as effectively in relations with the white community. Even in Republican-controlled localities, the scales of justice were weighted against the impoverished freedmen. A number of states did enact laws, however, to protect persons against foreclosures of all their property for debt. These homestead exemptions were designed to appeal to both races, and some Democrats found them to be embarrassingly popular with poorer whites.

One of the most cogent criticisms of Radical Reconstruction is that it failed to distribute land to the freedmen while it was giving them the ballot. Continuing economic dependence on the whites endangered every other right the Negro received. Some halting steps were taken by the federal government and the state of South Carolina to provide land to Negroes on easy terms, but they came to almost nothing, requiring as they did a social concern and an expenditure of tax money which most people in that generation did not have or were unwilling to make. At the same time, Southern whites were suspicious of Negro landownership and continued to discourage it, sometimes by outright violence. This was another service rendered by the Ku Klux Klan.

The Radical governments spent more money and levied higher taxes than Southerners had been used to, as it was. But public needs were also unprecedented. Even the Johnson governments had raised taxes and expenditures to repair war damage, but left much yet to be done. The necessary new social services, and especially the schools, were extremely costly by previous governmental standards. When the aid extended to railroads is also added in, it is no wonder that both taxes and public debt rose unprecedentedly at every level of government. States, counties, and municipalities all raised what money they could and then mortgaged the future to meet immediate needs and finance improvements which required time to repay themselves. If debts occasionally climbed beyond a prudent level this was by no means universal; Democrats sometimes raised them further when they returned to power in the 1870s.

Even with these increases the Southern tax level remained considerably below that which prevailed in the North. The average tax rate in the eleven ex-Confederate states in 1870, including all state, county, town, and city taxes, was 1.57 percent of assessed valuation; the comparable figure in all the remaining states was 2.03 percent. The Southern states were much poorer than the Northern, and less able to afford improvements and services; but this poverty was usually reflected in lower assessed valuations and hence a lower tax return at the same rate. Taxes levied by the Radical governments were extravagant only by comparison with the section's previous parsimonious standards.

Equally controversial as the level of taxes and debts was the matter of who paid the taxes and who derived the benefits. Landowners, who had previously governed the South in their own interest, now found themselves bearing the major tax burden while the benefits went in large measure to businessmen and Negroes. Republican fiscal policies thus further infuriated the old ruling class and convinced them that civilization had given way to barbarism.

Republicans were often accused of partiality in law enforcement, winking at black criminality. Law enforcement was always difficult in the sparsely settled South, and lawlessness increased with the unsettled conditions that prevailed during and after the war. Negro criminality, chiefly petty theft, may well have grown temporarily, but it was always comparatively easy to convict Negro criminals when they were known. Republican officials (including Negroes) usually leaned over backward to demonstrate their impartiality in this respect. Republican governors were also accused of pardoning Negro criminals indiscriminately. This charge too was exaggerated if not wholly false. Whatever substance it may have had probably derived from the fact that some pardons were granted (after proper investigation) to redress the manifest injustices of many Southern courts against Negroes in interracial cases. White Conservatives often recommended such pardons in individual cases, but collectively it was easy to accuse the Radicals of yet another outrage against white civilization.

Actually it was white men who committed most of the violence, and much of it was racially and politically inspired. When these overtones were not present, it was punished about as effectively, or ineffectively, in areas of Republican control as Democratic, and as was true in earlier and later periods of Southern history. A great deal of violence was deliberate and organized, however, committed by mobs and by armed bands in and out of disguise. A disproportionate share was directed at Negroes and white Unionists, partly to avenge real or imaginary injuries arising from the war, partly to keep the Negro "in his place" economically and socially, and partly to overthrow the Republican party by intimidating, exiling, or assassinating its members. The Ku Klux Klan exemplified this kind of violence in the most spectacular way, but it extended far beyond the Klan. The greatest short-run deficiency of the Republican regimes—it would soon prove fatal—was their physical weakness. In the face of implacable white resistance they proved unable to preserve law and order, or their own existence, against attempts at violent overthrow. In certain parts of the South the authorities were almost paralyzed by organized lawlessness.

When conspiracies to obstruct justice assumed this dimension the only solution was armed force. Republican officials repeatedly called on the Army for help in suppressing combinations which they could not handle by the usual means, but the results were usually discouraging. In the first place, too many troops were mustered out of service too quickly amid the euphoric celebration of victory in 1865. Only 20,000 troops remained on duty in the South by the fall of 1867, and this number gradually fell to 6,000 by the fall of 1876; moreover, one-quarter to half of these were stationed in Texas, chiefly on frontier duty. A much larger occupation force would have had trouble in maintaining order throughout the South. Furthermore, the traditional constitutional and legal safeguards against military power now sharply restricted the Army's peacekeeping potential. Its political and legal jurisdiction disappeared as soon as the new state governments were recognized by Congress. The military were limited thereafter to intervention only on application from, and in subordination to, the civil authorities. Where the latter did not act effectively, through incapacity, fear, or sympathy with the outlaws, the soldiers had little more than symbolic value.

For this reason most of the states organized militias, the traditional standby in times of emergency. But this weapon too was of doubtful value under the peculiar circumstances of Reconstruction. A militia composed in large part of the very white men who were engaged in lawlessness, or were sympathetic with it, seemed worse than useless. The only safe recruits were white Unionists and Negroes, but mobilizing these was equivalent to arming one political party against the other. The arming of Negroes in particular inflamed Conservatives and added fuel to the fire it was intended to quench. It summoned up the old fear of Negro insurrection and portended a race war which no Southern official was prepared to be responsible for. In the Deep South, where white Republicans were few and far between, militia were seldom mobilized and they played a negligible peacekeeping role. Governors in the upper South organized white Unionist recruits, for the most part, to stamp out Democratic terrorism, a tactic that was relatively effective but highly dangerous politically, for it fed Conservative charges of military despotism.

In the last analysis, Radical Reconstruction failed because the seed of biracial democracy which it planted fell on barren ground in the South, and the artificial nurture it received from the federal government was soon discontinued. Democracy has always required a high degree of popular homogeneity and consensus, a precondition which was altogether lacking in the South. Conservative opposition to Reconstruction was about as deeply felt as political opposition ever gets. As South Carolina whites expressed it in a protest to Congress in 1868:

> Intelligence, virtue, and patriotism are to give place, in all elections, to ignorance, stupidity and vice. The superior race is to be made subservient to the inferior.... They who own no property are to levy taxes and make all appropriations.... The consequences will be, in effect, confiscation. The appropriations to support free schools for the education of the negro children, for the support of old negroes in the poor-houses, and the vicious in jails and penitentiary, together with a standing army of negro soldiers [the militia], will be crushing and utterly ruinous to the State. Every man's property will have to be sold to pay his taxes.... The white people of our State will never quietly submit to negro rule.... By moral agencies, by political organization, by every peaceful means left us, we will keep up this contest until we have regained the heritage of political control handed down to us by honored ancestry. That is a duty we owe to the land that is ours, to the graves that it contains, and to the race of which you and we are alike members—the proud Caucasian race, whose sovereignty on earth God has ordained....

Such views contrasted sharply with the vision of a biracial democracy quoted already from the *Charleston Daily Republican*.

Conservatives mercilessly pilloried the Negroes, carpetbaggers, and scalawags who staffed and supported the Republican regimes. The

Democratic newspaper press—which far outstripped the Southern Republican press in numbers and circulation—played a vital role in stimulating and disseminating hatred of all things Radical. The wildest allegations and *ad hominem* arguments were at least half believed and unblushingly broadcast because they fit preconceived notions. Moreover, character assassination and slander were resorted to even when editors did not believe them, because they "served a good end" in discrediting the enemy. The *Little Rock Daily Arkansas Gazette,* for example, characterized the state constitutional convention of 1868 as "the most graceless and unconscionable gathering of abandoned, disreputable characters that has even assembled in this state, outside of the penitentiary walls . . . a foul gathering whose putridity stinks in the nostrils of all decency." Altogether the whole tone of Southern government had been debased, Conservatives felt, and they proceeded to debase the tone of political discourse correspondingly. "So far as our State governments is [*sic*] concerned, we are in the hands of camp-followers, horse-holders, cooks, bottle-washers, and thieves," declared General James H. Clanton of Alabama. "We have passed out from the hands of the brave soldiers who overcame us, and are turned over the tender mercies of squaws for torture. . . ." Negroes were characterized as unfit to vote, much less hold office, and Democrats excoriated the federal and state enactments which had brought these things to pass. Few Southern Democrats in public life had any constructive proposal to make in behalf of the freedman. The whole thrust of their policy was to "put him back in his place" economically, socially, and politically. Some Conservatives disapproved in principle of universal manhood suffrage, even among whites, regarding it as a denial of character and intelligence in government and a threat to property; Negro suffrage was simply the ultimate outrage. An increasing number of so-called New Departure Democrats, like Benjamin H. Hill of Georgia, reluctantly accepted Negro suffrage as a *fait accompli* and hoped to control the black vote as they controlled black labor, but a majority rejected the idea out of hand and pledged themselves to repeal or nullify it at the earliest opportunity.

To Conservatives, Republican affiliation was itself a sign of moral turpitude which only the flimsiest additional evidence sufficed to confirm. The laws of libel had no practical existence in that day, and such evidence was commonly embroidered or manufactured to suit the occasion. Those Republicans who mingled socially with Negroes were morally depraved; those who refused to do so were hypocrites who betrayed their own political teachings. Those who came from the North were outlanders having no ties of knowledge or sympathy with the land and people they despoiled; those who were native to the South were traitors to their race and section and therefore equally unworthy of trust or confidence. Those who had owned slaves were now discovered to have treated them cruelly; those who had not owned them were the dregs of society who would never have risen to the surface in decent times. The greatest opprobrium was always heaped on those who associated most with the freedmen or who had substantial Negro followings. Eric Hoffer has remarked that hatred requires a vivid and tangible devil. Conservative Southern whites conjured them up by the hundreds.

But although Radical policies were condemned as a matter of course, Democrats in fact supported some of them unobtrusively. This was true of the exemption of homesteads from foreclosure, and also a great proportion of the railway expenditures. Opinion was divided on the subject of public schooling, especially for Negroes, but most Democrats accepted the policy and continued it when they later assumed power. Opposition was strongest in Mississippi, as noted earlier, but schools were unpopular with many rural people everywhere. The major complaints arose from the unprecedented cost of establishing and maintaining them and from the fact that Republicans sponsored the policy. Many persons objected less to Negro schools per se than to the Negro and Yankee teachers who staffed them. Most of these were advocates of racial equality, and some were quite militant about it. Hence Southerners resented them as they did the political carpetbaggers—outside agitators whose main purpose and effect was to alienate Negroes from the white population and make them less docile. H. C. Luce, a Northerner living in western North Carolina who had never engaged in politics at all, wrote of threats he received after establishing a school for local Negro children: "It is one of the perils of a Northern man residing in such a community that, however unexceptionable his conduct may be, if he is kind to the negroes and tries to help them, a report will very soon be put in circulation that he is inciting the negroes to revenge, and the chances are against him if he does not promptly and publicly convince his neighbors of their mistake in believing the report." Like countless teachers or sponsors of Negro schools across the South, Luce became a target of the Ku Klux Klan.

In general, Conservatives advocated retrenchment and economy at the expense of many social services favored by the Radicals. Apart from white supremacy, their most popular and effective cry was for economy in government and lower taxes—a cry that often came from the heart as they compared present and past tax bills. The position of most Democrats on most issues was plainly reactionary. They appealed largely to a rural, agrarian, racist past which had become increasingly hostile to new ideas, and except for the most minimal accommodations required by the war's outcome they proposed to return to it. Later, after the Radicals had been swept aside, they were to become more enamored of the vision of an industrialized New South.

The bitterest opposition was always reserved for those Radical policies that portended racial equality. This was the supreme Radical sin. Laws enacted for that purpose "have no binding force or moral sanction," the *New Orleans Times* declared in July 1868, "and will be disregarded and declared null and void as soon as the inalienable rights of the people are again recognized. . . . No privilege can be secured to the negro to which his white neighbors do not consent, and if he attempts to enforce privileges on the strength of carpetbag authority he will simply destroy his claims of future peace, and heap up wrath against the day of wrath." Political and legal equality for the Negro was rendered all the more noxious by the common assumption that it would lead inevitably to social mixing. "[If] I sit side by side in the Senate, House, or on the judicial bench, with a coloured man," one gentleman inquired indignantly, "how can I refuse to sit with him at the table? . . . If we have social equality we shall have intermarriage, and if we have intermarriage we shall degenerate; we shall become a race of mulattoes; . . . we shall be ruled out from the family of white nations."

The Radical revolution, as some contemporaries on both sides regarded it, was only a halfway revolution. Within the South, Radical Reconstruction was clearly revolutionary in its overthrow of the old ruling class and above all in its establishment of political and legal equality for Negroes; hence the bitterness of the Conservative reaction. But economically and socially there was far less change, and most blacks remained a landless peasantry subject to manifold discrimination. In the larger national context, Radical Reconstruction reflected a revival of the old nationalistic constitutional doctrine of Hamilton and Marshall submerged by the state rights creed of Jefferson, Jackson, and their successors before 1860. The Radicals were not revolutionary by traditional American standards; if they appeared to be so it was chiefly because of the archaic social and political structure of the South. Nor did most of them regard themselves as revolutionaries. Southern Republicans, in trying to broaden their base of support at home, denied the charge and sought repeatedly to identify themselves with established political traditions. They claimed to stand for state rights within the higher national context and for the liberation doctrines expressed in the Declaration of Independence. The Fourteenth and Fifteenth Amendments, the Reconstruction acts, the civil rights legislation, and other related laws attempted to guarantee Negro rights and a loyal South within the accepted federal framework set forth in the Constitution. National authority and military rule were applied only partially and temporarily after 1865, and often reluctantly at that. The chief reliance in day-to-day government rested on the existing civil authorities. When the new state governments were formed after 1867, national and military control were withdrawn and the new regimes had to rely for their survival on customary legal institutions.

The experiment failed, and these regimes were overthrown in a few years because the ideas underlying them had become alien to the South during a generation or more of defending slavery, and because the Radicals' adherence to traditional forms weakened their resistance to attack. Radical regard for the civil liberties of ex-Confederates enabled the latter to sabotage the Reconstruction program almost from the start. Democrats had full access to the polls almost everywhere after 1868 and controlled hundreds of county and local governments throughout the period; they exercised the right to express themselves freely on every occasion, and they controlled the great majority of the section's newspapers. When they were charged with illegal activity and violence they had full access to the courts—in fact often dominated them. In such cases it was often impossible to get grand juries to indict, prosecutors to prosecute, or petit juries to convict, even if sheriffs were willing to arrest or judges to try them. This was even true in Republican-controlled localities. All of the safeguards for the accused in the Anglo-Saxon system of justice were mobilized to enforce the higher law of white supremacy. The Republicans themselves insisted upon certain limits to federal authority, and this was another source of weakness. Conservative violence against Negroes and Radicals involved crimes which had always fallen within state rather than federal jurisdiction, and as a result the federal government refused to intervene soon enough or strongly enough to check the error effectively. Thus the Radicals were defeated within a few years by their very conservatism and unwillingness to employ more than halfway measures.

# Index